GERMANY ASCENDANT

OSPREY
PUBLISHING

DEDICATION

To Amit, a tireless if sometimes baffled helper.

GERMANY ASCENDANT

THE EASTERN FRONT 1915

PRIT BUTTAR

First published in Great Britain in 2015 by Osprey Publishing,
PO Box 883, Oxford, OX1 9PL, UK
PO Box 3985, New York, NY 10185-3985, USA
E-mail: info@ospreypublishing.com

Osprey Publishing, part of Bloomsbury Publishing Plc

A CIP catalogue record for this book is available from the British Library

Prit Buttar has asserted his right under the Copyright, Designs and Patents Act, 1988, to be identified as
the Author of this Work.

ISBN: 978 1 4728 0795 3
ePub ISBN: 978 1 4728 1580 4
PDF ISBN: 978 1 4728 1581 1

Index by Zoe Ross
Typeset in Adobe Garamond Pro & Trajan Pro
Originated by PDQ Media, Bungay, UK
Printed in China through Worldprint Ltd.

15 16 17 18 19   10 9 8 7 6 5 4 3 2 1

Front cover: German soldiers with machine guns are pictured here in their lines at Johannisburg in the
winter of 1914 (Topfoto)

Osprey Publishing is supporting the Woodland Trust, the UK's leading woodland conservation charity, by
funding the dedication of trees.

www.ospreypublishing.com

CONTENTS

LIST OF ILLUSTRATIONS

Poles fleeing the fighting, summer 1915.
Artist's impression of Russian trenches in southern Galicia, 1915.
Troops of the *k.u.k.* Army in a trench in eastern Galicia, 1915.
German machine-gun company during the Second Battle of the Masurian Lakes.
Austro-Hungarian telegraph station in the Alps, 1915.

LIST OF MAPS

AUTHOR'S NOTE

As usual, many people contributed to this work. It's unfair to single out individuals, but Amit Sumal was hugely helpful in obtaining documents for me. As ever, my thanks to my family for their forbearance.

DRAMATIS PERSONAE

AUSTRIA-HUNGARY

Arz, Arthur – commander of VI Corps

Berchtold, Leopold von – foreign minister

Böhm-Ermolli, Eduard Freiherr von – commander of Third Army

Boroević, Svetozar – commander of Third Army, replaced by Puhallo, later commander of Fifth Army

Burián von Rajecz, Stephan – foreign minister

Conrad von Hötzendorf, Franz Xaver Josef – chief of general staff

Dankl, Viktor – commander of First Army, replaced by Kirchbach, commander of *k.u.k.* forces in Tyrol May 1915

Frederick, Archduke – commander-in-chief *k.u.k.* Army

Joseph Ferdinand, Archduke – commander of Fourth Army

Kirchbach, Karl Freiherr von – commander of I Corps, briefly commander of First Army, May 1915

Kövesz, Hermann von – commander of Third Army September 1915

Krautwald, Josef – commander of X Corps April 1915, replaced by Martiny

Křitek, Karl – commander of XVII Corps

Kusmanek, Hermann von – garrison commander, Przemyśl

Martiny, Hugo – commander of X Corps May 1915

Meixner, Hugo – commander of X Corps, replaced by Krautwald

Pflanzer-Baltin, Karl von – commander of eponymous army group, later upgraded to Seventh Army

Puhallo, Paul – commander of Third Army May 1915, then commander of First Army

Roth, Josef – commander of XIV Corps

Tersztyánszky, Karl – commander of eponymous army group, later Third Army, replaced by Kövesz

Trollmann, Ignaz – commander of XIX Corps

BULGARIA

Boyadzhiev, Kliment – commander of First Army
Ferdinand – tsar of Bulgaria
Radoslavov, Vasil – prime minister
Todorov, Georgi – commander of Second Army

GERMANY

Below, Otto von – commander of Eighth Army, later commander of Army of the Niemen
Behr, Karl von – commander 119th Infantry Division, commander of eponymous corps June 1915
Beseler, Hans von – commander of siege artillery, Novogeorgievsk
Bethmann-Hollweg, Theobald von – German chancellor
Bothmer, Felix Graf von – commander of eponymous corps, later commander of South Army
Cramon, August von – liaison officer at *AOK*
Eichhorn, Hermann von – commander of Tenth Army
Emmich, Otto von – commander of X Corps
Fabarius, Friedrich – commander of 82nd Reserve Infantry Division
Falk, Adalbert von – commander of 2nd Infantry Division
Falkenhayn, Erich von – chief of the general staff
Falkenhayn, Eugen von – commander of XXII Reserve Corps
Gallwitz, Max von – commander of Twelfth Army, later commander of Eleventh Army in Serbia
Haeften, Hans von – adjutant to Moltke the Younger and press officer at *Ober Ost*
Hell, Emil – chief of staff, Tenth Army
Hindenburg, Paul Ludwig Hans Anton von Beneckendorff und von – commander of *Ober Ost*
Hoffmann, Max – staff officer at *Ober Ost*
Kosch, Robert – commander of X Reserve Corps
Lauenstein, Otto von – commander of XXXIX Reserve Corps, commander of

eponymous army group April 1915

Leopold, Prince of Bavaria – commander of Ninth Army April 1915

Linsingen, Alexander von – commander of South Army, replaced by Bothmer, later commander of Army of the Bug

Litzmann, Karl – commander of XL Reserve Corps

Ludendorff, Erich – chief of staff, *Ober Ost*

Mackensen, August von – commander of Ninth Army, replaced by Prince Leopold; commander of Eleventh Army April 1915

Marwitz, Georg von der – commander of XXXVIII Reserve Corps, commander of *Beskidenkorps* March 1915

Morgen, Curt von – commander of I Reserve Corps

Plettenberg, Karl von – commander of Guards Corps

Scholtz, Friedrich ('Fritz') von – commander of XX Corps, later also commander of Eighth Army

Seeckt, Hans von – chief of staff, Eleventh Army

Woyrsch, Remus von – commander of eponymous army

Ziethen, Alfred – artillery commander, Eleventh Army

RUSSIA

Alexeyev, Mikhail Vasiliyevich – chief of staff, Southwest Front, later commander of Northwest Front

Balanin, Dmitri Vasiliyevich – commander of XXVII Corps

Bezobrazov, Vladimir Miklailovich – commander of Guards Corps, replaced by Olukhov

Bonch-Bruyevich, Mikhail Dmitriyevich – commander of 176th Infantry Regiment, 44th Infantry Division

Bobrinsky, Georgi Alexandrovich – second governor of Lemberg

Bobyr, Nikolai Pavlovich – commander of Novogeorgievsk garrison

Brinsen, Aleksandr Fridrikhovich – commander of XXII Corps

Brusilov, Alexei Alexeyevich – commander of Eighth Army

Bulgakov, Pavel Ilyich – commander of XX Corps

Churin, Alexei Evgravovich – commander of Twelfth Army June 1915

Danilov, Yuri Nikiforovich – quartermaster-general

Delvig, Sergei Nikolayevich – artillery commander of IX Corps, commandant of Przemyśl garrison

Dimitriev, Radko – commander of Third Army, replaced by Lesh

Dragomirov, Vladimir Mikhailovich – commander of VIII Corps, later chief of staff, Southwest Front, replaced by Savich

Epanchin, Nikolai – commander of III Corps, replaced by Zegelov

Evert, Alexei – commander of Fourth Army, later commander of Western Front

Gerngross, Alexander Alexeyevich – commander of XXVI Corps

Gorbatovsky, Vladimir Nikolayevich – commander of XIX Corps, later commander of Thirteenth Army

Grigoriev, Vladimir Nikolayevich – commander of Kovno garrison

Gulevich, Arseny – chief of staff, Northwest Front

Gurko, Vasily Iosifovich – commander of VI Corps

Ivanov, Nikolai Iudevich – commander of Southwest Front

Kaledin, Alexei Maximovich – commander of XII Corps

Lechitsky, Platon – commander of Ninth Army

Lesh, Leonid Vilgelmovich – commander of XII Corps, later commander of Third Army

Litvinov, Alexander Ivanovich – commander of First Army

Lomnovsky, Piotr – chief of staff, Eighth Army

Myasoyedov, Sergei Nikolayevich – intelligence officer Northwest Front, ally of Sukhomlinov

Nikolai Nikolayevich, Grand Duke – commander-in-chief

Nostitz, Grigory Ivanovich – chief of staff, Guards Corps

Olukhov, Vladimir Apollonovich – commander of XXIII Corps, later commander of Guards Corps

Plehve, Pavel Adamovich – commander of Fifth Army

Polivanov, Alexei Andreyevich – minister for war June 1915

Protopopov, Nikolai Ivanovich – commander of X Corps

Radkevich, Evgeny Alexandrovich – commander of III Siberian Corps, later commander of Tenth Army

Ruzsky, Nikolai Vladimirovich – commander of Northwest Front, replaced by Alexeyev

Savich, Sergei Sergeyevich – chief of staff Southwest Front May 1915

Sazonov, Sergei – foreign minister

Selivanov, Andrei – commander of siege forces at Przemyśl

Shcherbachev, Dmitri Gregorovich – commander of IX Corps, later commander of Eleventh Army

Shchkinsky, Jakov Feodorovich – commander of XXI Corps

Sievers, Thadeus von – commander of Tenth Army, replaced by Radkevich

Skalon, Yestafy Nikolayevich – city governor of Lemberg

Smirnov, Vladimir Vasiliyevich – commander of Second Army
Stelnitsky, Sergei Fedorovich – commander of XXXIX Corps
Sukhomlinov, Vladimir Alexandrovich – minister for war, replaced by Polivanov
Trofimov, Vladimir Onufreyevich – commander of III Siberian Corps
Tsurikov, Afanasy Andreyevich – commander of XXIV Corps
Yanushkevich, Nikolai Nikolayevich – chief of the general staff
Zayontchovsky, Andrei Medardovich – commander of XXX Corps
Zegelov, Alexander Alexandrovich – commander of III Corps

SERBIA

Jurišić Šturm, Pavle – commander of Third Army
Mišić, Živojin – commander of First Army
Pašić, Nikola – prime minister
Putnik, Radomir – chief of the general staff
Stepanović, Stepa – commander of Second Army
Živković, Mihajlo – commander of the Belgrade garrison

INTRODUCTION

The war that engulfed Europe in 1914 was meant to be over by Christmas. All the combatants had expected a swift outcome, built on their ability to put huge armies into the field of battle, where sweeping offensive operations would crush their enemies. But the opening offensives that the Great Powers launched ultimately failed to deliver the expected outcomes, leaving all of the nations caught up in the war with a new set of problems, ranging from purely tactical and operational military issues, through logistic and training matters, to the industrial support that a prolonged war would need.

A great deal has been written about the failure of the Schlieffen Plan in the west, which left the armies of Germany, France, Britain and Belgium facing each other across a line of trenches running from the English Channel to the Swiss border.[1] The plan itself has been scrutinised in great detail, with varying theories about whether it was ever intended as an operational plan; when he wrote the plan, Schlieffen made no secret that he believed the German Army was not powerful enough to execute such a sweeping offensive.[2] Regardless of whether it was the plan itself or the execution of the plan that was flawed, the outcome was a bloody stalemate that would prove impossible for either side to overcome for many years. By contrast, events on the Eastern Front were far more fluid, though here, too, neither side was able to find a way to land a lethal blow. The reasons for this were very different from those in the west.

The nations involved in the war in the east had very different expectations of what they might achieve. The Russian Army was perhaps the only one that expected to win a decisive victory by Christmas; once the fabled Russian steamroller was ready, it was widely believed, the forces of the Central Powers would be crushed – or if they were to be saved, it would be by a major diversion of troops from the Western Front, which would open the door to a French triumph over Germany. Although the tsar's armies won decisive victories over the Austro-Hungarian forces in Galicia, the initial invasion of East Prussia ended in disaster, with Samsonov's Second Army being destroyed at Tannenberg and

Rennenkampf's First Army driven back with heavy losses in the First Battle of the Masurian Lakes in September 1914. Eventually, Grand Duke Nikolai, the commander of the Russian Army, managed to assemble a formidable force along the middle Vistula and, after beating off a German attack towards Warsaw from the southwest, launched his troops towards the German frontier. This great advance, which met little serious resistance, proved as illusory as the German attack towards Warsaw, and ground to a halt largely through supply problems exacerbated by the devastation of Poland's infrastructure by the retreating Germans. As winter arrived, a German counterattack at Łódź nearly ended in disaster, but the ultimate escape of the attacking German forces firmly established their military supremacy over the Russians in the minds of officers on both sides of the front line. Any lingering thoughts of a swift Russian victory vanished when the armies of the Austro-Hungarian Empire, assisted by German reinforcements, drove the Russians back from the approaches to Krakow in the Battle of Limanowa-Łapanów in December 1914.

The Russians had singularly failed to deliver the crushing blow against Germany that had been anticipated by many observers. It is difficult to measure the degree to which this caused disappointment in the tsar's court; for years, senior officials had been abundantly aware of the tendency of officers at all levels to tell their superiors what they thought their superiors wanted to hear, and as a consequence they had become accustomed to learning at a later date that matters were not as rosy as they had been initially told. On the evening of the first day of serious fighting, at Stallupönen in August 1914, Yuri Danilov, the Russian quartermaster-general, commented:

> Thus we saw on the first day of fighting, the reopening of the old wound that had long poisoned the wellbeing of our army, a tendency to dissimulate facts. During the course of the war, this malady, never eliminated, repeatedly prevented us from seeing the situation clearly and correcting such errors in a timely manner, as they were detected.[3]

Like all armies of the era, the *k.u.k.* ('*Kaiserlich und Königlich*' or 'Imperial and Royal') Army of the Austro-Hungarian Empire was strongly imbued with the cult of offensive operations.[4] The strongest proponent of mounting offensives at all costs was Franz Conrad von Hötzendorf, the Austro-Hungarian chief of general staff, whose long involvement in training within the army ensured that a large proportion of the officer corps was also inclined to disregard the importance of defence. As was the case elsewhere in Europe, this obsession with attacking in all circumstances – and launching immediate counterattacks with whatever forces were available – resulted in catastrophic casualties, with nearly a million Austro-Hungarian soldiers killed, wounded, taken prisoner, or succumbing to sickness in the fighting against Russia.[5] The problem was exacerbated by Conrad's belief that the purpose of attacking was to destroy the enemy's army rather than to take strategic geographical objectives. On the occasions that gaps were discovered or created in Russian lines, the doctrine of the *k.u.k.* Army was to use these to attack the exposed flanks of the enemy battle line, rather than to make any attempt to exploit into the rear areas. As a consequence, most battles – even those where the Austro-Hungarian forces achieved an advantage – degenerated into bloody face-to-face slugging matches, as it was usually possible for the Russians to reinforce their exposed flanks quickly enough to prevent the attackers from making much of their temporary advantage. Outflanking operations would only have succeeded if attacking troops had been permitted to penetrate deeply enough to evade any defensive realignment, but the formations of the *k.u.k.* Army lacked both the speed and the doctrine to achieve this. While Conrad appreciated the importance of locating and exploiting weaknesses and exposed flanks, he also insisted that the troops assigned to face the main Russian positions should attack constantly in order to try to pin down the enemy; in the context of 1914, such attacks achieved little other than greatly increasing the number of soldiers killed or wounded. There was no attempt to use the repeatedly demonstrated advantages of defensive firepower to allow stronger forces to be gathered elsewhere for decisive attacks – indeed, all the armies of Europe were slow to learn this lesson, even though more visionary observers had predicted such developments after analysing earlier conflicts, such as the Anglo-Boer War and the Russo-Japanese War.[6]

Whilst Conrad and his generals had not really expected to win the war against Russia on their own, they had hoped that the Germans would join them in mounting a major offensive against the Russians in Poland at the outset of the war. But given that the German plan had always been for victory over France before turning east in strength, this was little more than wishful thinking, and the reality of the situation was that Conrad's armies were always likely to suffer major losses while they diverted as much of Russia's strength towards them and away from the Germans, allowing Germany to concentrate its main strength in the west. Nevertheless, Conrad complained repeatedly that he felt let down by his allies, both in their failure to achieve a quick victory over France and their refusal to join him in early attacks on the Russians. Such criticism ignored the fact that Conrad was wishing for mutually exclusive things – any early German attack in the east would have weakened the German presence on the Western Front and ensured no victory over France, while concentrating even more troops in the west to try to overwhelm France would necessarily have left the Eastern Front even weaker.

The highest levels of command in the Austro-Hungarian Empire continued to be dominated by Conrad. After the disasters in Galicia, the Germans proposed unifying command on the Eastern Front under a single figure, but whatever the views of Emperor Franz Joseph, Conrad refused to consider such a suggestion, aware that the role of the *k.u.k.* Army – and therefore of himself – would be subordinated to German control. From his headquarters in Teschen (now Cieszyn), he continued to insist on attacks against the Russians, refusing to accept any contrary suggestion. Like Hitler in a future war, he treated divisions and corps as if they were still at full strength, and took no account of the fact that many could barely muster half the men that their establishment specified. Similarly, he dismissed arguments from corps and army commanders about the weakness of Austro-Hungarian artillery. Neglected for years before the war, the artillery had declined even further after the losses of the opening months, both in terms of guns and trained personnel. Whilst a few weapons might have been regarded as world-class – particularly heavy howitzers – these were present in too few numbers to make a decisive impact. Austro-Hungarian mountain artillery, which was highly regarded, might be adequate in the mountains of Serbia, but against the Russians in the Carpathians, the mountain howitzers were too light, and too few.

If Austro-Hungarian expectations against Russia were limited, the same was not true of the Serbian front. Here, in the mountainous Balkans, the *k.u.k.* Army expected to overcome its weak opponent quickly, achieving revenge for the murder in Sarajevo that had started the landslide to war. To the surprise of most of the world though, the Serbian forces beat off the first Austro-Hungarian invasion in August, and followed this with an even more remarkable victory in December, when the Austro-Hungarian armies under Oskar Potiorek were driven back across the frontier in disarray, leaving behind 274,000 casualties. Whilst it was beyond the power of the Serbs to follow this up with an offensive of their own – the entire nation was exhausted by its remarkable achievement – the Serbian Army had achieved all that could be expected of it, and continued to hope for a Russian victory that would bring the war to a satisfactory conclusion.

Despite the great advances and retreats, the Eastern Front therefore remained as insoluble a military problem as the Western Front. Although the greater space allowed all armies to manoeuvre with a degree of freedom that rapidly disappeared in the west, the constraints of logistics ensured that it was difficult for either side to achieve a major, sustainable advance in 1914. It was only in Galicia that a significant amount of territory changed hands, and even here, although the Russian forces reached the Carpathian Mountains and threatened to push through the passes to the Hungarian Plain beyond, there seemed little prospect of a decisive outcome. For all the Great Powers, the problem was that the very space that allowed them greater freedom of manoeuvre also ensured that significant objectives were further apart.

At a tactical level, too, there appeared to be few answers to the stalemate, but local, limited successes by all sides in the last months of 1914 left officers continuing to believe in victory through offensive action. Of the three main armies, the Germans had the greatest grounds for such confidence. Late in the year, their troops had launched a series of frontal assaults on Russian positions in central Poland, resulting in heavy losses for almost no gain, but in almost all their other operations, they showed great skill in probing for weaknesses and exploiting the relatively slow movement and reactions of their Russian foes. The Russian infantry showed considerable resilience in defensive fighting, but officers at all levels lacked the ability demonstrated by the Germans to react quickly to events on the battlefield. The Germans were greatly impressed by the accuracy of Russian artillery, but even after the first few months of the war, losses of well-trained artillery officers began to take a toll on the performance of Russian guns. An even greater constraint upon the Russian artillery was a crippling shortage of ammunition, caused by no provision for anything other than a short war.

Casualties on all sides had been far heavier than even the most pessimistic pre-war forecasts. As was the case all across Europe, the Austro-Hungarian officer corps had suffered proportionally heavier losses than lower ranks, with particularly serious consequences. Whilst all armies lamented the loss of so many highly trained officers, the impact in the multi-lingual armies of the Austro-Hungarian Empire was severe. Many replacement officers did not speak the language of their men, and few showed any inclination to learn. In such circumstances, alienation between the nationalities of Emperor Franz Joseph's fragile empire could only grow worse.

The almost universal expectation that the war would be over within months led to many miscalculations. By the end of 1914, the armies of all nations were reporting alarming shortages of artillery ammunition. The Russians had gone to war with the lowest stocks of ammunition, and discovered too late that foreign companies were unable to produce sufficient shells to replenish the rapidly emptying ammunition parks, not least because those companies were busy producing war *matériel* for their own governments. Russia's own industry was simply not geared up to produce sufficient shells; in September, a French estimate suggested that Russian factories could produce perhaps 35,000 shells a month, at a time when *daily* consumption was close to 45,000 rounds.[7] Desperate to relieve pressure on their own depleted armies, the French constantly urged their Russian ally to maintain pressure on the Central Powers, even suggesting that if artillery ammunition was a limiting factor, attacks might nevertheless be made in the Carpathians, where the terrain was less favourable for artillery.[8] Such advice ignored the fact that, regardless of terrain, attacks made without artillery support were almost certain to fail.

Shell shortages in the *k.u.k.* Army were also critical by the winter, and despite Conrad's insistence on offensive operations at every opportunity, gun batteries were repeatedly told to reserve ammunition for use in the event of a Russian attack, rather than in support of Austro-Hungarian attacks. Attempts were made to divert production away from small arms ammunition to produce rounds for the artillery, but such changes would take time to bear fruit. In combination with the losses of guns during the 1914 campaigns, the ammunition shortage ensured that the *k.u.k.* Army's artillery reached its nadir in terms of efficacy during the first winter of the war.[9]

Ammunition shortages were not the only problem. The Russians struggled to produce sufficient rifles for the hundreds of thousands of men now serving in the front, a problem exacerbated by weapons being abandoned on the battlefield. Austro-Hungarian quartermasters faced similar difficulties, and although weapons being produced by the great Steyr armaments factory for Romania and Mexico were appropriated, this resulted in some units being equipped with rifles that fired different cartridges, making supply problems even worse. By early 1915, the Steyr arsenal had increased its production from 2,000 rifles per month in September 1914 to 32,000, but it would take time for this additional output to reach the front line.[10] Machine-guns, regarded by many traditionally minded officers before the war as little more than overly complex toys, were now widely regarded as critically important, and all armies tried to increase the number of such guns per battalion. At first, though, even replacing weapons lost in the opening months proved to be difficult.

Uniforms and boots, too, were in short supply. During the marches across Galicia in the opening weeks of the war, many Austro-Hungarian and Russian soldiers abandoned their heavy coats, and as the weather turned colder, shortages of appropriate winter clothing – as will be seen, particularly in the Carpathians – greatly exacerbated casualty rates. Even the supply of ordinary uniforms was problematic; some Austro-Hungarian reservists were deployed in civilian clothing, with only a single black armband to indicate their status as combatants.

Inevitably, the unexpected casualties of the first few months of the war had a major impact on the morale of the combatants. On the Eastern Front, the German armies were perhaps least disheartened; although their losses – particularly in Ludendorff's futile assaults in central Poland in December – had been high, the Germans had repeatedly beaten off Russian attempts to penetrate into German territory, and only a small part of southeast Prussia was left in Russian hands. It is difficult to gauge the impact of the war on the Russian armies, as they contained large numbers of illiterate soldiers, and the stoical endurance of the Russian soldier was such a large part of popular culture that few raised their voices to protest at the heavy losses, which were greatly exacerbated by command and logistic failings. War-weariness was perhaps most pronounced in the *k.u.k.* Army, where the multi-national nature of Franz Joseph's empire created unique problems. Compared with their German and even their Russian equivalents, many of those serving in the Austro-Hungarian armies had a relatively weak sense of nationalist loyalty. Ethnic Romanian and Slav populations in particular began to show signs of strain early in the war, with Czech units apparently surrendering to the Russians en masse on more than one occasion. In the Czech homelands, Austro-Hungarian officials noted with alarm that proclamations that the Russians were coming as liberators were widely circulated, resulting in the first convictions and even executions for treason.[11] By the end of 1914, some of the Czech troops who had surrendered to the Russians had been organised into Czech Legions, though as yet there was no suggestion that they would be used as combatants. Nevertheless, their existence had a powerful propaganda effect on the restive population of the Austro-Hungarian Empire. Many regiments had been raised from the Polish and Ruthenian populations of Galicia, an area now under Russian occupation, and the Russians made repeated calls for these men to desert, promising them a swift return to their families. To the relief of *Armee-Oberkommando* (*AOK*, the Austro-Hungarian Army High Command), few heeded the call. But whilst the generals expressed growing concern at the effect of civilian unrest on the reliability of the troops, the politicians shied away from harsher measures, fearful that a widespread crackdown would only make the problems of the empire worse. Only a decisive victory on the battlefield could reverse the growing centrifugal tensions in the empire, and during the first winter of the war, such a victory seemed increasingly remote.

By the end of 1914, the industries of all nations were struggling to catch up with events. The British naval blockade of Germany ensured that it was almost impossible for the Central Powers to obtain large supplies of materials such as nitrates, which were essential for the manufacture of explosives as well as fertiliser, but in this respect at least, Germany's scientists had already provided their nation with alternative sources. Shortly after the turn of the century, Friedrich Ostwald, who was born in a Baltic German family in Estonia before moving to East Prussia, patented an eponymous process by which ammonia could be used to manufacture nitric acid, though this was at first little more than a chemical novelty due to the relative difficulty in obtaining large amounts of ammonia. A few years later, Fritz Haber devised a process by which atmospheric nitrogen could be used to manufacture ammonia on a large scale. The combination of these two processes by German industry resulted in the ability to produce nitrates in quantities that ensured Germany a sufficient supply of explosives, and also of fertiliser for agricultural use. Nevertheless, the conversion of these explosives into war munitions still required German industry to reorganise on a huge scale. A key man in this task was Walther Rathenau, an industrialist whose father was the founder of the German industrial giant, AEG, and his tireless energy contributed hugely to the rapid transformation of German industry to a war footing. The main obstacles that he faced were the reluctance of privately owned companies to cooperate, and personal antipathy – Rathenau was a Jew, in an era when anti-Semitism was widespread.[12]

Throughout Europe, the public rallied to support their nations. In Russia, anti-government strikes and protests on the eve of the war were replaced by demonstrations against Germany and in support of Serbia. Everywhere, mass mobilisation had taken no account of which personnel might be better left in their civilian jobs – with the expectation of a short war, it was anticipated that large numbers of men would be demobilised before Christmas, allowing the disruption of industry and agriculture to be kept to a minimum. As the reality of a long war became increasingly clear, the immediate consequence was that most European countries suffered widespread shortages of food and coal. The prospect of a winter with less to eat and houses far more expensive to heat did much to cool the initial enthusiasm of the public for war, especially after the shock of the terrible numbers of dead and wounded. The initial zeal for war in the Russian capital rapidly cooled, and even as autumn began, foreign observers noted that some officers who had returned to Petrograd* to recover from wounds or illness showed no particular desire to return to the front line.[13]

---

* The Russian capital St Petersburg was renamed Petrograd in August 1914, as it was felt that the name St Petersburg was too Germanic.

The coming year would see huge changes on the Eastern Front, whereas the situation in the west would remain almost unchanged. Just as important as the fighting on the ground was the bitter fighting within Germany and Russia, as different factions attempted to impose their will upon their nations' policies. Whilst there were already signs by the end of 1914 that many Germans had a low opinion of the value of their alliance with the Austro-Hungarian Empire, this would grow considerably as the year progressed, sowing the seeds for greater misunderstandings in 1916, which would have a major impact upon the course of the war.

As 1915 began, the sector of the Eastern Front that remained most active was also the one least suited to warfare during winter: the line of the Carpathian Mountains, separating Galicia from the Hungarian Plain. It was here that the first major battles of the new year would be fought, and more blood spilled, for almost no tangible gain.

The Eastern Front, January 1915

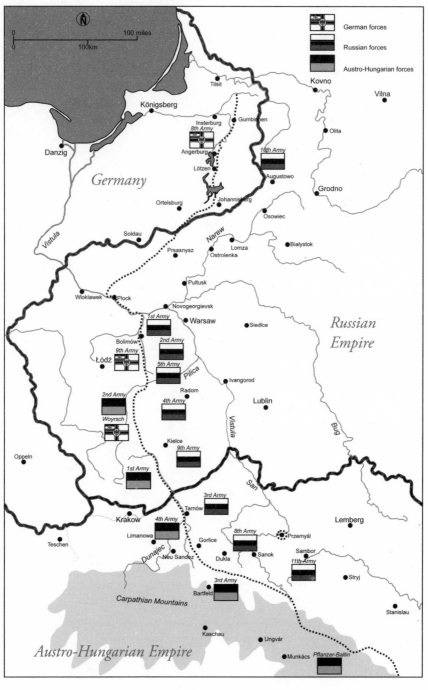

German forces

Russian forces

Austro-Hungarian forces

Germany

Russian Empire

Austro-Hungarian Empire

Carpathian Mountains

0 ___ 100 miles
0 ___ 100km

Tilsit
Kovno
Vilna
Königsberg
Insterburg
8th Army
Gumbinnen
Olita
Angerburg
Danzig
Lötzen
10th Army
Augustowo
Grodno
Germany
Ortelsburg
Johannisburg
Osowiec
Soldau
Narew
Prsasnysz
Lomza
Ostrolenka
Białystok
Pultusk
Novogeorgievsk
Wloklawek
Plock
1st Army
Warsaw
Siedlce
Bolimów
2nd Army
9th Army
Łódź
5th Army
Pilica
Ivangorod
2nd Army
Radom
4th Army
Lublin
Woyrsch
Kielce
9th Army
Oppeln
1st Army
3rd Army
Tarnów
Lemberg
Kraków
4th Army
Limanowa
Gorlice
8th Army
Przemyśl
Teschen
Dunajec
Neu Sandez
Dukla
Sanok
Sambor
11th Army
Stryj
3rd Army
Bartfeld
Stanislau
Kaschau
Ungvár
Munkács
Pflanzer-Baltin

CHAPTER 1

THE COMBATANTS

The Russians entered the war in 1914 with mixed feelings about their prospects. Within the first few months, there was ample evidence to support almost any opinion about the Russian Army, and what it might achieve in 1915.

Shortly after the turn of the century, Russian and Japanese rivalries in Manchuria plunged the two nations into war. There was almost universal expectation amongst the Great Powers that Russia would rapidly overwhelm its Asian opponent, but events turned out very differently. By the time the war was over, the Russian Navy had lost both its Pacific and Baltic Fleets; the latter sailed all the way around the world and was then destroyed in the Battle of the Tsushima Straits. On land, the Japanese besieged Port Arthur (now known as Lüshun Port), and after capturing the strategic harbour drove inland to defeat the Russian Army in a series of bloody encounters. No combat arm of the army – infantry, artillery or cavalry – emerged with any credit, and the turmoil that followed brought the tsar's empire to the edge of chaos. It took many years and huge investment before the Russian Army began to rise from its nadir.

One of the problems that Russia faced in the years between the end of the Russo-Japanese War and 1914 was that almost every part of its armed forces required massive expenditure. The navy had almost ceased to exist, and the huge army required re-equipment with modern rifles and guns. Even within the army, there was endless argument on where money should be spent. A series of fortresses had been built to protect the western border of Russia, but were now widely regarded as obsolete in the face of modern artillery, and required substantial refurbishment. In 1908, fortress enthusiasts drew up a plan for modernisation; it was estimated that this would cost at least 800 million roubles, a sum equivalent to the entire army budget for two years. The plan would have resulted in 90 per cent of Russia's artillery being deployed in static positions, and the opponents of spending so much money on the seven fortresses drew a little consolation from the fact that although modernisation of the fortresses was approved, it was not on such a lavish scale as originally proposed.[1]

With the benefit of hindsight, it is abundantly clear that the effect of concentrated defensive firepower had repeatedly demonstrated that massed infantry attacks would struggle to prevail. At the time, many observers did draw such a conclusion after the battles of the Russo-Japanese War and the Boer War, but the widespread conviction that it was only through offensive action that wars could be won continued to prevail, despite the desire to spend lavishly on fortresses. Evidence from recent conflicts was used selectively to justify preconceived points of view, with the result that armies entered the First World War with a completely unrealistic belief in what might be achieved by offensive operations. The Russians were by no means immune to this, and had the additional problem that their anti-German alliance with France – which expected to face the bulk of German power – required the Russians to mount early assaults in order to divert German forces to the east. In their own plans, the Germans had relied on relatively slow Russian mobilisation to give them sufficient time to overwhelm France, but there were great improvements in the years before the First World War, largely as a result of French investment in Russian railway lines, meaning that the Germans could now expect the Russians to be ready for war far sooner than they might have hoped. However, the new railways generally stopped at the Russian border. Critically, they did not extend across Russian-occupied Poland, which would ensure that in an era where the movement of supplies was largely dependent upon railways, the Russians would struggle to maintain momentum if they advanced towards Germany. The relative weakness of the railway network in Poland was, to a very large extent, a deliberate policy. It might hinder the Russians, but it would equally impede the Germans if they attacked across Poland. However, the overwhelming imperative of the Russian-French alliance was for Russian pressure on Germany, and the lack of good railways across Poland ensured that the only place at which the Russians could exert any early pressure was East Prussia, where the terrain was greatly in favour of the German defenders.

This failure to look at the consequences of logistic difficulties was more widespread than a lack of investment in railway infrastructure. Russian staff exercises before the war repeatedly ignored logistic aspects entirely, not least because the majority of Russian generals had a very poor grasp of such matters, and preferred to behave as if their armies were always adequately supplied.

Consequently, those planning the exercises – with an eye on their own advancement – ensured that such lowly matters would not embarrass senior commanders. Logistic and supply formations were usually given a low priority in mobilisation plans; typically, the first groups of mobilised troops were combatants whilst logistic units had to wait almost until the end of mobilisation before their ranks were filled, with the result that infantry, cavalry and artillery repeatedly struggled to deploy rapidly, having to pause while mobilisation could be completed. In the meantime, the few overworked units that were available laboriously brought all manner of basic supplies forward.

The most critical supply shortage of all related to artillery ammunition. Immediately before the war, the French held stocks of 2,000 rounds per artillery piece, while the Germans doubted that their 3,000 rounds per gun would prove inadequate; by contrast, Russia had not achieved even 1,000 rounds per gun, and much of this ammunition was held in large artillery parks centred on the border fortresses. The weakness of the army's logistic services ensured that moving these stocks to the front line would be a slow business, and when the Russian armies first crossed into East Prussia in August 1914, they took barely 400 rounds per gun with them.[2] In intense fighting, this would last less than three hours of continuous action.

At the outset of the war, the Russian Army's infantry was organised into divisions of four regiments. Each regiment consisted of four battalions, and the division had an artillery brigade of six eight-gun batteries. In peacetime, divisions had two cavalry brigades with a total of four regiments (each in turn composed of two or three squadrons of horsemen), but after the outbreak of war these were removed to create purely cavalry formations. They were meant to be replaced by reservist formations, mainly Cossacks, to give infantry divisions their own reconnaissance support, but these replacements were generally of poor calibre and the widespread lack of literacy throughout the Russian Empire meant that their usefulness in reconnaissance and communication was limited. The infantry divisions were grouped together in a series of corps, which combined to form armies. These armies were subordinated to two higher commands, Northwest Front and Southwest Front; broadly, these faced Germany and the Austro-Hungarian Empire respectively. Attempts had begun to reorganise the artillery into six-gun batteries, as it was widely accepted that a six-gun battery could provide as effective fire support as an eight-gun battery, but these met resistance in the ranks of the artillery, where the increased number of batteries that would result was regarded as unwelcome. Officially, this was because there might not be sufficient skilled officers to command the batteries, but in addition there were fears that such an increase in the number of batteries might result in their being commanded by captains rather than majors, thus reducing the number of posts available to majors. Attempts to increase the number of howitzers per division from six to twelve also met opposition from unlikely sources. Many artillery officers regarded the howitzers as inferior to conventional artillery, and their usefulness in assaulting fortifications was rejected as somehow being an improper use of artillery.

The opening months of the war resulted in major casualties for Russia. Rennenkampf's First Army achieved a tactical victory at Gumbinnen in August 1914 but failed to exploit it in any meaningful manner, and thus contributed considerably to the freedom with which the Germans concentrated their forces against Samsonov's Second Army, effectively destroying it at Tannenberg just a fortnight later. Although the huge scale of Russian mobilisation, with some 4.7 million men swelling the ranks, meant that even the destruction of an entire army was little more than a setback, the loss of so many officers and NCOs, and of almost all of Second Army's equipment, would have serious repercussions. After their success, the Germans turned east again to chase Rennenkampf's army back to the border in what is now known as the First Battle of the Masurian Lakes. Thereafter, although the Germans attempted a brief advance into Lithuania, they were ultimately forced to fall back to the line of the lakes, where they established a defensive network of fortifications.

The main Russian effort fell on the Austro-Hungarian forces in Galicia, where forces came under the command of Southwest Front. Initially, the Russian Fourth Army marched south immediately east of the Vistula, with Fifth Army on its eastern flank, extending the line as far as the valley of the Bug. Both of these armies met early setbacks and were driven back, but the other two armies of Southwest Front – Third and Eighth Armies – won significant victories in eastern Galicia, leading ultimately to the collapse of the Austro-Hungarian positions throughout the province. Forced into a catastrophic retreat, the troops of the Dual Monarchy were driven far to the west, leaving almost all of Galicia in Russian hands. The fortress of Przemyśl was left isolated and besieged. Although the Austro-Hungarian forces appeared to be on the edge of rout, the Russians had been sufficiently weakened to prevent a crushing pursuit.

Before the war, much had been made of the huge size of the Russian Army. Once its forces were gathered, it would be able to advance and crush all resistance before it. With the Austro-Hungarian forces driven back in disarray, the Russians began to gather their armies near Warsaw with a view to striking west, but the Germans moved first. Showing a level of flexibility that was beyond the dreams of the Russians, the German Army concentrated forces in Silesia and thrust northwest into Poland, advancing to the southern approaches of Warsaw while the Austro-Hungarian forces attempted to recover ground in Galicia. Eventually, the simple arithmetic of the battlefield – a substantial concentration of Russian forces near Warsaw facing a relatively small German force, whose eastern flank relied upon the Austro-Hungarian Army for protection – forced the Germans to pull back. Przemyśl was once more besieged, and the Russians threatened to advance on Krakow.

Again, the Germans showed imagination and flexibility, shifting forces from Silesia and elsewhere into West Prussia. From here, they marched east and southeast in November, attempting to encircle and destroy the rebuilt Russian Second Army in Łódź. Despite early successes, the operation proved to be beyond the ability of the German troops, who had a remarkable escape after being encircled east of Łódź. Attempts by the Germans late in the year to force their way through to Warsaw from the west met with defeat along the lines of the Rivers Bzura and Rawka, but further south, the Austro-Hungarian armies won an important battle at Limanowa-Łapanów, ending the Russian threat to Krakow. For the moment, the Eastern Front ceased to be a theatre of mobile operations. By the end of the year, almost every formation included large replacement drafts, and as in every army in Europe, field officers expressed considerable dissatisfaction at the quality of these men. Their training was rudimentary, many were unfit for front-line service, and the level of equipment was poor.

Command in the Russian Army was a complex affair, greatly complicated by internal politics. The Russian minister for war, Vladimir Alexandrovich Sukhomlinov, was a controversial figure. He had spent many years before the war establishing a faction composed of his supporters and associates who attempted – with variable justification – to portray themselves as reformers. Opposing this faction was the traditional wing of the Russian Army. Historically, a large proportion of Russia's officers had come from families with a Baltic German background – names such as Rennenkampf, von Plehve, and von Saltza speak for themselves. These men formed the heart of the anti-Sukhomlinov faction, with widespread support amongst the Russian aristocracy. The inability of either faction to achieve a decisive advantage over its opponent left the army divided at almost every level, and it was commonplace before the war for army commanders and their chiefs of staff to come from opposing factions, resulting in arrangements that were both farcical and harmful: in August 1914, Rennenkampf was part of the anti-Sukhomlinov camp, but his chief of staff was a supporter of the minister for war, and the two men were frequently not on speaking terms, communicating only in writing even when they were both in the same room.

Once hostilities began, *Stavka* – the Russian high command – was established, and after minimal debate, Grand Duke Nikolai, a cousin of the tsar, was appointed as its commander, and therefore commander of all of Russia's forces. His hostility towards Sukhomlinov ensured that friction between the two camps continued after the declaration of war. There was general agreement that he was the right man for the post, even though his only military experience was in the 1877–78 war against Turkey. He had spent many years helping to modernise the cavalry, and had a reputation for promoting officers on merit, regardless of their background. He was strongly committed to the alliance with France, and pressed for an early attack on Germany; howev   er, he had no part in drawing up the plans for initial Russian operations, and lacked both the strategic vision and the drive to impose himself upon the sprawling armies of Russia. The interventions of *Stavka* were frequently limited to choosing between the different plans of subordinate commands, and despite his personal high standing with his contemporaries, his impact upon the opening months of the war was minimal. Similarly, Nikolai Yanushkevich, the chief of the general staff, was an ineffectual figure; his appointment owed more to patronage than any military skill, and in any case Sukhomlinov had designed the Russian military system in a way that greatly circumscribed the power of the chief of the general staff when compared with Germany or Austria-Hungary. One of the most influential persons in *Stavka* was Yuri Danilov, the quartermaster-general, who struggled to reorganise Russian logistic services in the midst of the fighting. Perhaps his most important innovation was to disperse the stockpiles of artillery ammunition in the fortresses to create depots closer to the front line, in an attempt to ease the desperate ammunition shortage. However, whilst Danilov has generally been treated kindly by history, it is worth remembering that much of his reputation is based upon his own account of the war, which naturally portrays him in the best possible light.

By the end of 1914, Northwest Front was commanded by Nikolai Vladimirovich Ruzsky, who had started the war as commander of Third Army in Galicia. Here, he advanced with utmost caution, constantly urged on by both his front commander and *Stavka*, but when Yakov Zhilinski, commander of Northwest Front at the beginning of the war, was dismissed following the disastrous attempted invasion of East Prussia, Ruzsky was appointed as his replacement. It is difficult to understand the full justification behind this, as Ruzsky had performed at best competently in Galicia. It is probably relevant that the appointment occurred at a time when Grand Duke Nikolai was attempting to move men he trusted into key positions; Ruzsky was a member of the Sukhomlinov faction, and the minister for war probably ensured that such a key role was filled by one of his supporters, rather than allowing Grand Duke Nikolai to strengthen the anti-Sukhomlinov group. It can surely have been no surprise to anyone that Ruzsky's performance in his new role proved to be equally indecisive. During the fighting around Łódź in November 1914, he oscillated between urging his commanders to attack recklessly and sending signals to *Stavka* about the dire state of his armies and their imminent defeat. In the aftermath of the campaign, he demonstrated the political footwork necessary for success in the tsar's army by ensuring that Pavel Rennenkampf, commander of First Army – and, of course, a member of the anti-Sukhomlinov faction – took all the blame for the failure to destroy the German forces that were briefly encircled east of Łódź.

The most northerly formation in Northwest Front was Tenth Army, commanded by Thadeus von Sievers. The son of a Baltic German family, he served in the tsar's armies in fighting against the Turks and Chinese, and commanded troops with distinction in the Galician campaign of 1914. When Tenth Army was then created, he was nominated to take command of it. In October, Sievers led his army into East Prussia, occupying Goldap and the southeast part of the German province, but repeated assaults against the strong German line running from the area to the northwest of Lyck to Wirballen resulted in severe casualties for almost no gain. On paper at least, Sievers commanded a strong army, with fifteen infantry divisions, but none was remotely close to its establishment strength. Relations between him and Ruzsky were inevitably strained, as they represented the two opposing camps in the Russian Army. In early 1915, Sievers repeatedly warned Ruzsky that his line was thinly manned, with almost no reserves held further back; consequently, he warned, his army faced the real possibility of being on the receiving end of the sort of German offensive that had thrown Rennenkampf's First Army back from the Masurian Lakes in September 1914. Ruzsky rejected the warning out of hand.

Some distance to the south was First Army, now under the command of Alexander Ivanovich Litvinov. The divisions of the army had suffered heavily in the fighting around Łódź and the subsequent futile German assaults on the Russian defences to the east of the city, as had Second Army, commanded by Vladimir Smirnov, who inherited the army from Sergei Scheidemann; the latter was judged rightly to have been too passive during the Battle of Łódź.

Another force that had been extensively involved in the Battle of Łódź was Fifth Army, commanded by Pavel Plehve, who had led the formation from the outset of the war. Alfred Knox, the British military attaché, visited Plehve's headquarters in early 1915, and wrote a typically acerbic pen-picture of the man:

Plehve was at this time nearly 65. In appearance he was a little wizened-up rat, but his intelligence was keen and he had an indomitable will. His staff spoke of him with admiration, but it was evident that they feared as much as they loved him. They said he had been a nuisance in peace, constantly interfering in detail and worrying over trifles, but that in war he was quite different, grasping the situation with extraordinary quickness and giving his decision rapidly and firmly. He never, to my knowledge, visited the trenches, chiefly, no doubt, because, though he rode well, he was too infirm for walking. I imagine, too, that to him the men at the front were merely pawns. He expected everyone there to do his duty, as he, their commander, did, by issuing strong and clear instructions ... His strong, dry character, and also, it must be confessed, his strong prejudices on occasion regarding individuals, made Plehve very unpopular with senior Russian officers, who ... could forgive mistakes in strategy sooner than a lack of geniality.[3]

During the often-chaotic fighting around Łódź in December 1914, Plehve was perhaps the only Russian senior officer who clearly understood the overall situation, and his swift march to the aid of the Russian Second Army was decisive in preventing a German victory. Like all Russian armies in the front line, his had suffered heavy losses, but he ordered his formations to keep substantial forces in reserve, both at division and corps level, ensuring that any German attack could be countered before a breakthrough could be achieved. In this respect, he was one of the few commanders in any army involved in the war to understand the importance of such reserves in a war where well-organised defences were almost impregnable. The combined strength of his army, and First and Second Armies to the north, was a little over thirty-three infantry divisions.

Immediately to the south of Plehve's men was Fourth Army. It suffered a serious defeat at the beginning of the Galician campaign, resulting in its first commander, Anton von Saltza, losing his post. His replacement was Alexei Evert, a longstanding friend and ally of Grand Duke Nikolai. Evert's eight divisions were, in the opinion of Quartermaster-General Danilov, in the best location to mount an offensive against the Germans, but they faced entrenched opponents.[4] In any case, none of the units on Evert's flanks were likely to be able to support any such advance, even if he had received sufficient reinforcements to refill his depleted ranks and – more importantly – sufficient supplies of artillery ammunition to make an offensive even remotely possible.

Southwest Front had been commanded from the beginning of the war by Nikolai Ivanov, who was one of the few Russian generals to emerge from the Russo-Japanese War with his reputation enhanced. In the years immediately after the war, he commanded the Kronstadt Fortress near St Petersburg, a centre for dissident activity during and after the 1905 Revolution. Ivanov's suppression of dissenters further increased his standing, and in August 1914, his armies swept into Galicia. Despite initial Austro-Hungarian successes, the Russians won a major victory, capturing Lemberg (now Lviv) and encircling the fortress of Przemyśl. As with other Russian commands, there was dissent in the headquarters of Southwest Front, with Ivanov being a representative of the Sukhomlinov faction and Alexeyev, his chief of staff, being from the opposing group.

The division of the Russian forces facing the Central Powers into two Fronts was to a large extent dictated by geography. The difficult terrain of the Pripet Marshes divided the area into two, each with its own distinct network of roads and railways. Each front also faced a different opponent at the beginning of the war, with Southwest Front confronted by the Austro-Hungarian Empire and Northwest Front by Germany. Inevitably, this resulted in each front regarding its own sector in isolation, with little cooperation between them. Just as first Zhilinski and then Ruzsky wished to concentrate on Germany, Ivanov repeatedly insisted that the best prospects for Russian victory lay in a sustained effort against the Austro-Hungarian Empire, particularly after the opening rounds in Galicia. In the last weeks of 1914, though, such a decisive victory seemed as elusive as ever. Nevertheless, Ivanov remained determined to try to force a conclusion: if his armies could cross the barrier of the Carpathian Mountains into Hungary, there was every prospect of the fragile Austro-Hungarian Empire falling apart.

The boundary between the two Russian fronts shifted during the autumn of 1914, as *Stavka* tried to ensure that the armies operating in the central part of the long Eastern Front were under the command of the same front – without such rearrangements, there was no prospect of effective cooperation. Currently, the most northern army of Ivanov's front was Platon Lechitsky's Ninth Army, created with reservist divisions after the beginning of the war. Unlike their German counterparts, the Russians treated their reserve formations as markedly inferior to regular divisions and corps, sending second-rate officers to them and giving them low priority in terms of equipment and supplies, and perhaps as a consequence, Ninth Army had to date played little more than a linking role, completing the line between its neighbouring formations.

The line continued to the south with Third Army, which had originally been Ruzsky's command in August 1914. It was now led by the capable Radko Dimitriev, but had been badly cut up in the Battle of Limanowa-Łapanów. To his south was Eighth Army, whose commander was Alexei Brusilov. With a history of innovation in the traditionally minded cavalry formations of the Russian

Army, he took command of his army at the beginning of the war, leading it in an unbroken advance of over 90 miles (150km). For much of late 1914, he was left to protect the extreme southern flank of the Russian front line with barely adequate forces. Short of supplies of all sorts, he improvised as best he could, demonstrating that he was perhaps the best Russian commander of his era. To his rear was the Austro-Hungarian fortress of Przemyśl, and the siege was the responsibility of Eleventh Army. This last formation also had to provide troops to cover the southeast section of the Carpathian line. Like Ninth Army, it consisted of mainly reserve formations.

Danilov estimated that the entire Russian Army was about half a million men below strength, and many of its artillery formations were also in desperate need of re-equipment.[5] Whilst there was hope that there would be an improvement by the end of February, the front-line formations would have to do the best they could in the meantime. Such matters had to be taken into account when planning the next operations against the Central Powers. Concluding that the Russian Army lacked the strength and resources to strike at all possible objectives at the same time, Danilov felt that it would be necessary to select a single axis – either against the Austro-Hungarian Empire, or against Germany. Vienna was a little closer than Berlin, and there was a general appreciation that the defences of the Austrian capital were far weaker. Furthermore, a Russian advance on Vienna, even if only partly successful, was likely to encourage Italy and Romania to join the Allies, leading to pressure on the Austro-Hungarian Empire that would surely force its dissolution. Despite this, French pressure remained for further operations against the Germans, as it was felt that this was the best way to force Germany to dilute its strength in the west. But an invasion of Germany was a difficult proposition. As the Russians had discovered in 1914, the German railway network allowed them to move troops rapidly from one part of the front to another to oppose a Russian attack, and the geography of the Eastern Front meant that it was difficult for the Russians to press into Germany without exposing one or both flanks – East Prussia had proved impregnable, and however enfeebled the *k.u.k.* Army might be, it was unlikely to remain passive if presented with the possibility of striking into the southern flank of a Russian advance towards Germany. Therefore, logic dictated that an essential precursor to any such advance was the elimination of the threat to one or other flank, and given that the danger from German forces in East Prussia was greater than the danger from Conrad's battered armies to the south, Danilov returned again to a theme he had championed in 1914, the conquest of East Prussia:

I regarded the occupation of East Prussia in itself as an objective of the greatest importance: the war would be taken into the enemy's territory, the inevitable evacuation of the population would have repercussions to the very heart of Germany, while the capture of one of the most ancient parts of Prussia would serve as compensation for the occupation of part of our territories on the Vistula by the Germans. East Prussia ultimately represented the only sector of Northwest Front where one could expect tactical successes, the rest of the front being already strongly fortified and sufficiently well-held by enemy forces that there would be no prospect of success.[6]

To this end, Danilov wished to group together the three army corps not currently assigned to any army – the Guards Corps, IV Siberian Corps and XV Corps – and strike across the southern border of East Prussia towards Soldau and Ortelsburg. Tenth Army would protect the eastern flank of this force, while a mixed infantry and cavalry force centred on Mlawa would protect the western flank. Alternative options for operations against the Germans included a further assault in central Poland towards Łódź, but although Ruzsky expressed interest in this option, the disadvantages were numerous: the attack would be against perhaps the strongest part of the German line; a similar advance in the previous autumn had not yielded any major success; and there was no clear operational or strategic objective within reach. Consequently, at a conference in Siedlce in mid-January, it was resolved to pursue Danilov's suggestion of another East Prussian campaign. A new Twelfth Army would be created as the main strike force around Mlawa. The commander of this army would be Plehve, currently in command of the static Fifth Army in central Poland.[7]

Inevitably, Ivanov had no intention of allowing his Southwest Front to be allocated a secondary role. He repeatedly raised the need to deliver a knockout blow against the Austro-Hungarian Empire by forcing the line of the Carpathians. Once his troops entered Hungary, he insisted, the Budapest government would sue for peace, triggering the collapse of Germany's ally, and this would leave Germany in an impossible position. In order to prepare for such an operation, Ivanov advised *Stavka* that his front would require at least four additional divisions as reinforcements, because of menacing concentrations of Austro-Hungarian forces and the appearance of German formations in the Carpathians. Danilov, whose own preference was for Northwest Front to strike against East Prussia, later recorded that while the situation was indeed dangerous, this was partly due to the thinly held Russian line – pressure anywhere along it would inevitably create a major threat. Reluctantly, unable as usual to impose its will upon its subordinate commands, *Stavka* agreed to dispatch XXII Corps to the south as reinforcements.

Ivanov had good reasons for believing that the *k.u.k.* Army was close to collapse. Its losses in 1914 had been catastrophic in every respect; the majority of its trained personnel, particularly officers and NCOs, was dead, wounded or taken prisoner, and even if artillery ammunition had not been in short supply, many formations had lost most of their guns. Casualties amongst the mobilised reservists were also appalling, and in any previous war, would probably have forced a nation to sue for peace. It was later estimated that nearly half of the officers and men who joined the Austro-Hungarian front line in 1914 were killed, wounded, sick or prisoners by the end of the year.[8]

Each regiment of the *k.u.k.* Army, recruited in a specific area, was sent reinforcements in the form of 'march battalions', in an attempt to keep the ethnic identity of the regiments intact. By the end of 1914, most regiments had already received four or five march battalions, and a sixth wave was en route for the front; like their predecessors, these battalions consisted largely of poorly trained recruits and reservists, with little in the way of equipment, and weak in terms of officers and NCOs. Given the almost exclusive use of railways as a means of moving large bodies of men to the front, it was inevitable that individual trains often contained more than one march battalion, intended for regiments that were broadly in the same part of the front line. It was equally inevitable that, when these battalions arrived in groups of three or four at the front, they were collectively pressed into use as ad-hoc regiments or brigades to deal with a local crisis. This policy might have been regarded as expedient, but it was badly flawed. Poor levels of training, inadequate leadership, and a lack of equipment resulted in these formations suffering crippling casualties, often shattering their morale even before they had reached their intended regiments. It also undermined the attempts of the *k.u.k.* Army to keep the ethnic identity of regiments intact – these improvised groups of march battalions often spoke very different languages, and this did nothing to engender any sense of unit cohesion. When officers were assigned to these groups, they tended to be exclusively German speakers, further alienating many of the recruits. Wherever possible, staff officers attempted to provide regiments with replacement drafts of the right nationality, but the uneven nature of reservist cadres created further problems. Some regiments in the upper Vistula valley grew from their peacetime strength of four battalions to as many as seven battalions, while regiments in the Carpathians were reduced to only two or three weak battalions, as there were insufficient reservists of the appropriate ethnicity available. Despite this, Conrad and many other senior staff officers consistently treated units as if they were at their establishment strength, making little or no allowance for their losses or equipment levels.

In an attempt to provide sufficient manpower to keep the army in the field, older men in formations intended for defence of the homeland in the event of an invasion – *Landsturm* in Austria, *Honvéd* in Hungary – were dispatched to the front line, where their lack of training, fitness and equipment was cruelly exposed. As wounded and sick men – both from regular units and from the *Landsturm* and *Honvéd* – returned to their homelands, they spread tales of mismanagement and defeat. It is therefore small wonder that of the Great Powers involved in the war, the Austro-Hungarian Empire was the first to show worrying levels of war-weariness amongst the general public.

The artillery complement of the *k.u.k.* Army had been neglected during the period of Conrad's dominance. On the one hand, he was aware from the events of the Franco-Prussian, Russo-Japanese and Boer Wars of the importance in artillery in overcoming defences, but on the other, he believed in the supremacy of infantry pressing home their attack at close quarters, and insisted that this was the most important consideration. Whatever lessons were not learned about the resilience of well-organised defensive lines, all armies rapidly came to appreciate the frequently decisive effect of artillery in 1914, particularly howitzers, which had been generally derided in the years before the war. Once the fighting began, their ability to drop explosive shells into the midst of trenches repeatedly proved decisive in both attack and defence. In October 1914, the *AOK* sent a memorandum to the War Ministry calling for the creation of new light field guns, howitzers and field artillery, but there was no need – there were plenty of thoroughly tested guns available to choose from, and in early 1915, an artillery programme was adopted in which each infantry division would continue to have twenty-four field guns, but would also receive thirty-six light field howitzers, and a battery of four heavy howitzers. In addition, there would be three batteries of heavy artillery at corps level.[9] However, it would take many months before sufficient guns could be produced, and as has already been described, it was proving impossible to provide the existing artillery with sufficient ammunition. Nor was it clear where the trained personnel required for such an expansion of the artillery arm would come from. As an interim measure, several artillery pieces built by Skoda for China and Turkey were appropriated, but by the end of 1914, these had already been dispatched to the front line. Despite this measure, the losses of guns in the opening months of the war left the army perilously short of firepower, even before the ammunition shortage was taken into account.

Although Archduke Frederick was nominally the supreme commander of all Austro-Hungarian forces, the dominant figure remained Conrad, the chief of the general staff. He had been such a huge influence in the years before the war, presiding over training, organisation and war planning, that his reputation survived the catastrophic defeats of 1914. To an extent, he was helped greatly by the fact that there were no clear alternative figures who could replace him at the top of the hierarchy – Oskar Potiorek had been his great rival for many years, but by the end of the year he was a broken man, humbled and disgraced by defeat in Serbia, and his reputation tarnished further by the fact that he had been governor in Sarajevo at the time of the assassinations that triggered the war. Conrad had placed great importance on fostering morale, maintaining that it was this rather than the numerical strength of an army that mattered, and had written extensively about the role of officers at all levels in building morale and confidence in the rank and file, but by the first winter of the war, he was rarely seen even in army headquarters, preferring to remain at *AOK* in Teschen.[10] Indeed, this tendency for senior officers to avoid going to the front line became an increasingly common fact of life in many armies, but particularly the *k.u.k.* Army. It is striking that the first five months of the war saw thirty-nine Austro-Hungarian senior officers, of the rank of colonel or higher, killed in action; in the entire rest of the war, there would only be another thirty-one such casualties.[11] Much of Conrad's teaching had concentrated on the importance of local initiative, but unlike the German Army, the *k.u.k.* Army failed to produce men with sufficient training and knowledge to exercise such initiative effectively. The high losses of officers in 1914, and their replacement by men with even less experience and training, might have suggested the need to alter the doctrine under which the army functioned, but Conrad remained insistent upon delegating decision-making to lower levels. In 1914, this had resulted in officers trying to implement Conrad's own teachings on tactics, almost regardless of local circumstances, such was the reverence with which they treated their chief of staff. By 1915, the replacement officers lacked even the ability to attempt such slavish adherence to doctrine, and the army was left with orders from above that frequently appeared too minimal, while lower ranks lacked the ability to improvise to fill in the blanks according to local conditions.

In order to compensate for the weakened state of the *k.u.k.* Army, the German *Oberste Heeresleitung* (*OHL*, or Army Supreme Command) dispatched many units to reinforce the Austro-Hungarian line, resulting in these units becoming intercalated with the Austro-Hungarian formations. The most northerly of Conrad's armies was Second Army, commanded by Eduard Freiherr von Böhm-

Ermolli, consisting of IV and XII Corps. Unusually for an era where aristocrats still dominated the upper echelons of the armies of most European nations, Böhm-Ermolli came from relatively humble origins; his father was a sergeant in the Austrian Army during the First Italian War of Independence, winning an officer's commission as reward for bravery at the Battle of Novara. The original Austro-Hungarian war plan intended for Second Army to be deployed against Serbia, and although Conrad eventually changed his mind, switching the army to eastern Galicia, it was still sent to the Balkan front on mobilisation, and then transferred to face Russian troops in Galicia. Its divisions arrived in Galicia as the fighting around Lemberg reached a crisis, and were unable to prevent a comprehensive Russian victory. In November, as German troops that had advanced across Poland from Silesia to the southern approaches of Warsaw were forced to withdraw to their start line, Second Army was sent north to ensure continuity with the Germans massing before Łódź. In December, as the Germans advanced and captured Łódź to the north, and the Russians were driven back from the approaches to Krakow to the south, Conrad repeatedly urged Böhm-Ermolli to join the advance and to throw back the Russians on his front. Despite his best efforts, all of his attacks foundered in the face of stout Russian defences. The best that he could achieve was to tie down Russian troops that might have been moved to support the Russian lines in front of Krakow.

Immediately to the south of the Austro-Hungarian Second Army was a German force commanded by Generaloberst Remus von Woyrsch. Predominantly composed of Silesian *Landwehr* reservists, this corps had already distinguished itself advancing to the Vistula – twice – in 1914, before conducting an orderly withdrawal in the face of superior Russian forces. South of Woyrsch's command, which was under Austro-Hungarian control, was the Austro-Hungarian First Army. With II, I, V and X Corps, it was a strong formation on paper, but most of its divisions were barely at the numerical strength of regiments, and their fighting power was still weaker. The commander of this force was Viktor Dankl, who had led his men to an initial success in August 1914 at the Battle of Kraśnik before he was driven back. In October, he was part of the failed operation to secure the entire left bank of the Vistula south of Warsaw; while the Germans threatened the Polish capital, Conrad ordered Dankl to allow the Russians to reinforce their bridgeheads across the river, with a view to counterattacking and destroying them. This obsession with the offensive, when a determined defence along the river would have sufficed, was regarded at the time as a highly risky endeavour by the Germans, and they were not at all surprised when Dankl's counterattack failed with heavy losses. In the weeks that followed, First Army was driven back towards the upper Vistula, and at times appeared in danger of being forced to retreat south, opening the way for a Russian thrust against Krakow, but through a mixture of timely reinforcements and over-extended Russian supply lines, the Austro-Hungarian forces were able to prevent the fall of the vital city. Dankl's successes in Galicia in August – little more than a tactical success – were no greater than those of Moritz von Auffenberg, whose Fourth Army drove back the Russians at Komarów, but while Auffenberg took the blame for the overall Austro-Hungarian defeat in Galicia, Dankl was regarded as a great hero, in an empire desperately in need of heroes to restore its self-respect.

To the south of First Army, the terrain changed. The rugged peaks and passes of the Carpathians formed a natural barrier between Galicia, now in Russian hands, and the great plain of Hungary and the Danube valley. Fourth Army had been on the southeast flank of First Army since the beginning of the war, and after the dismissal of Auffenberg following the September defeats in Galicia, it came under the command of Archduke Joseph Ferdinand. During the initial battles, the archduke had led a corps-sized unit with some distinction, before Conrad assigned him impossible tasks that would have required at least twice as many troops. His army contained XVII, XIV, and XI Corps, as well as improvised groupings of troops. These approximated to the strength of a corps, but were known in the *k.u.k.* Army as 'army groups', a term more often associated with much larger bodies consisting of several armies. These groups, eponymously named after their commanders – Křitek, Ljubičić, Arz and Králiček – were built around regular army divisions, but frequently contained improvised brigades of march battalions, with rudimentary rear area units such as logistics and medical support. Their durability in sustained operations was therefore limited.

Continuing the Austro-Hungarian line along the Carpathians was Third Army. Badly mauled near Lemberg, the army was now under the command of the capable Svetozar Boroević. In recent years, his ethnicity has become a subject of controversy; he always stated that he was Croatian, but many regarded him as Serbian.[12] He inherited a battered and defeated army, but managed to restore its fighting power sufficiently for it to contribute to the Austro-Hungarian advance in October, when the fortress of Przemyśl was briefly relieved. As the armies of the Central Powers retreated once more, Boroević struggled to hold the line of the Carpathians, receiving mutually incompatible orders both to eliminate Russian penetrations through the mountain passes and to strike northwest in support of Joseph Ferdinand's army near Neu Sandez (now Nowy Sacz). This battle marked the beginning of a period of difficult personal relations between Boroević and Conrad. The army consisted largely of VII and XVII Corps, with some improvised groups. On its southeast flank, completing the long front line, was 'Army Group Pflanzer-Baltin', primarily centred on the Uzsok Pass.

About 42 miles (70km) behind the Russian front line was the city of Przemyśl, where the Austro-Hungarian garrison continued to hold out against encircling Russian troops. Built as a bulwark against Russian invasion, the fortress was performing the role that had been assigned to it in Austro-Hungarian plans: to tie down Russian troops and to hinder their lines of communication until it was possible for the *k.u.k.* Army to advance to lift the siege. Already, the city had been reached by an Austro-Hungarian relief column in October 1914, only to be besieged once again as the Central Powers were forced to give up their temporary gains at the end of the month. Now, with rations and other supplies beginning to run low, the probability of the garrison, a substantial force of 120,000 men, holding out until help arrived seemed increasingly unlikely.

Whilst the *k.u.k.* Army had endured substantial setbacks in Galicia, it had encountered complete disaster in its 1914 campaign against Serbia. The small, impoverished nation that was at the heart of the July Crisis after the Sarajevo assassinations had an army that was strong in spirit, but weak in modern firepower, and had not recovered from losses and ammunition consumption in the Balkan Wars of 1912 and 1913. In August 1914, when the Austro-Hungarian Empire unleashed Fifth and Sixth Armies, together with parts of Böhm-Ermolli's Second Army, the expectation was that the Serbs would rapidly be overrun. But the initial Austro-Hungarian assault, across the mountainous and heavily wooded Drina valley, ended in an ignominious withdrawal, and although a second offensive – over the same difficult terrain – finally succeeded in pushing into the heart of Serbia, supplies of guns and ammunition from France and Russia arrived in time to rejuvenate the Serbian Army, which launched a determined counterattack in early December. On 9 December, Oskar Potiorek, the Austro-Hungarian commander in Serbia, had to admit to Vienna that the campaign had run into serious trouble, and that he would be forced once more to retreat to the frontier. The outcome of many weeks of bitter fighting was that the *k.u.k.* Army lost perhaps 224,000 men dead, wounded, taken prisoner or through illness; the Serbs lost 170,000, which as a proportion of their smaller army was a far heavier blow, and during the winter that followed, tens of thousands of Serbs, soldiers and civilians alike, perished from illness. The Austro-Hungarian Sixth Army was disbanded, and Fifth Army was left as the only force covering the Serbian front. Overall command of the Balkan theatre was assigned to Archduke Eugen.

Much as was the case in the *k.u.k.* Army, the nominal commander-in-chief of the German Army – Kaiser Wilhelm – was no more than a figurehead. At first, Wilhelm had been desperate to be involved in military decision-making, and was dismayed and hurt by the brusque way that the professional officers of the army sidelined him. By Christmas 1914, he cut a forlorn figure, ignored by most of the staff of *OHL*, and almost pathetically grateful to anyone who would spend time talking to him about the war. The real power within the army lay in the office of chief of the general staff. At the beginning of the war, this post was held by Helmuth von Moltke, nephew of the great von Moltke who masterminded Bismarck's wars of German unification. After the failure of the German invasion of France, Moltke's nerves failed him, and he was dismissed and replaced by General Erich von Falkenhayn in mid-September. Born in West Prussia, Falkenhayn saw action in China during the Boxer Rebellion, and in the summer of 1914 was serving as minister for war in Berlin. Like many of his contemporaries, he saw the July Crisis as an opportunity to bolster the Central Powers, without necessarily triggering war across the entire continent, but when events escalated, he was perfectly prepared for such a conflict.

In his new role as chief of the general staff, Falkenhayn retained control of the War Ministry, though the German Chancellor, Theobald von Bethmann-Hollweg, successfully argued for the appointment of a new minister for war in early 1915; the new minister, Wild von Hohenborn, was a close ally of Falkenhayn, and had previously served as quartermaster-general.

Overall command of German forces in the east lay with Generaloberst Paul von Hindenburg, acting in the role of *Oberbefehlshaber der gesamten deutschen Streitkräfte im Osten* ('Supreme commander of all German forces in the east', usually abbreviated to *Ober Ost*, a term used for both the commander and his headquarters). In the years before the war, Hindenburg had been considered for the post of chief of the general staff, but was in retirement when hostilities began. After initial German setbacks in East Prussia, he was recalled and sent east to take command of the German Eighth Army, accompanied by his new chief of staff, Erich Ludendorff. It was the beginning of a relationship that would dominate Germany's conduct of the war.

The new command team could not have had a better start. Through a mixture of good judgement, good fortune, Russian mistakes, and wilful disobedience on the part of their subordinates, Hindenburg and Ludendorff won a crushing victory over the Russian Second Army at Tannenberg in August, and then chased the Russian First Army from East Prussia in September. Thereafter, the performance of German forces was less spectacular. The Germans pursued the

Russians from East Prussia, only to overreach their supply lines and fall back, conceding the southeast corner of the province. Hindenburg was appointed as overall commander on the Eastern Front, and a short time later Ludendorff became his chief of staff.

Much has been written about the relationship between the two men.[13] Hindenburg is often portrayed as the genial, calm strategist, the perfect foil for the highly strung genius of Ludendorff. Whilst there may be much truth in this picture, there is also no doubt that both men became the focus of a great deal of mythology and propaganda, and both did much to promote and propagate this. What is inarguable is that the sum was greater than its parts. On their own, neither would have accomplished a fraction of what they achieved together. Their good fortune in winning a glittering triumph at the outset of their partnership at Tannenberg secured them a great deal of prestige, which survived later setbacks and allowed them to become ever more powerful. Hindenburg's own assessment of their relationship is perhaps a particularly succinct summary:

> It has been suggested that these relations [between the two men] find a parallel in those between Blücher and Gneisenau. I will venture no opinion as to how far such a comparison reveals a departure from true historical perspective. As I have already said, I had myself held the post of chief of staff for several years. As I knew from my own experience, the relations between the chief of staff and his general, who has the responsibility, are not theoretically laid down in the German Army. The way in which they work together and the degree to which their powers are complementary are much more a matter of personality. The boundaries of their respective powers are therefore not clearly demarcated. If the relations between the general and his chief of staff are what they ought to be, these boundaries are easily adjusted by soldierly and personal tact and the qualities of mind on both sides.
>
> I myself have often characterised my relations with General Ludendorff as those of a happy marriage. In such a relationship how can a third party clearly distinguish the merits of the individuals? They are one in thought and action, and often what the one says is only the expression of the wishes and feelings of the other.
>
> After I had learnt the worth of General Ludendorff, and that was soon, I realised that one of my principal tasks was, as far as possible, to give free scope to the intellectual powers, the almost superhuman capacity for work and untiring resolution of my chief of staff, and if necessary clear the way for him, the way in which our common desires and our common goal pointed – victory for our colours, the welfare of our Fatherland and a peace worthy of the sacrifices our nation had made.

I had to show General Ludendorff that loyalty of a brother warrior which we had learnt to find in German history from youth up, that loyalty in which our ethical philosophy is so rich. And indeed his work and his determination, his whole great personality were truly worthy of such loyalty ...

The harmony of our military and political convictions formed the basis for our joint views as to the proper use of our resources. Differences of opinion were easily reconciled, without our relations being disturbed by a feeling of forced submission on either side. The hard work of my chief of staff translated our thoughts and plans into action at our army headquarters and, later, at main headquarters when the responsibilities of that post were entrusted to us. His influence inspired everyone ... Around the two of us gathered the wider circle of our colleagues, filled with a resolute soldierly sense of duty and well endowed with ideas.[14]

This wider circle of colleagues in *Ober Ost* regarded the entire Eastern Front as their responsibility, and as the year progressed, there would be growing friction between Hindenburg's headquarters and *OHL*, which was responsible for the conduct of the war on all fronts.

During October 1914, most of Poland west of the Vistula was in German hands, before the 'Russian Steamroller' finally started to grind its way west. As they fell back, the Germans conducted a ruthlessly efficient scorched earth policy to hinder the Russian advance; the greatest impact of the systematic destruction of railways, bridges and many roads was felt by the Polish population. Treated with casual contempt by the three Great Powers, and with many of their men pressed into service in the armies of the occupying nations, the Poles had to endure a bitter winter in a devastated landscape, struggling to find enough food to survive. Before the war, the Austro-Hungarian Empire had attempted to incite armed resistance against the Russians, and a small group of Polish soldiers was serving alongside the *k.u.k.* Army near Krakow as the Polish Legion, but its leader, Józef Piłsudski, had no illusions about the long-term reliability of the Great Powers to grant his people independence. He had already anticipated that Poland's best hope lay first in a victory of the Central Powers over Russia, and then in a victory of the Western Powers over Germany.[15]

Despite its setback in December 1914 in the battles along the Bzura and Rawka, the German Army finished the year in good shape on the Eastern Front. Its formations and command structures had generally functioned well, better than those of any other army in the area, and it had started the war with a better artillery complement supplied with larger ammunition stocks than those of its opponents. The evolution of military philosophy in the German Army, resulting in well-trained junior officers and NCOs who were encouraged to improvise if required in order to fulfil their orders, was far ahead of either the Russian Army or that of the Austro-Hungarian Empire. All leaders in the German Army were trained to be prepared to take over at least one or two levels of command above their own, with the result that German formations were far more resilient in the face of casualties than their opponents.[16]

Although German officers were as concerned as those of other armies about the low levels of training and fitness of replacement drafts, these replacements functioned generally better than expected, not least because they were usually given cadres of experienced officers and NCOs. Even when reservist formations were mobilised and sent to the front line in completely new formations, they performed almost as well as regular army units, though Ludendorff worried that the expectations placed upon them were often beyond their ability to fulfil, particularly in the case of fortress formations that had never been intended for deployment in the field army, but were cobbled together into ad-hoc divisions:

> These divisions were later given numbers like the active divisions, but this did not alter their character. Fighting and marching made demands on them that were different for units made up of younger men. Frequently, in the urgency of the moment, these distinctions were not possible. These troops did more than could reasonably be expected of them; they gave their best for the defence of the homeland and thus their homes, women and children.[17]

The most northern part of the Eastern Front was held on the German side by Eighth Army, which had been the only German army facing Russia at the beginning of the war. Some of its best formations had been used to create Ninth Army, but it remained a powerful force. It had known many commanders during the first few months of the war; originally, it was commanded by Maximilian von Prittwitz, but his apparent loss of confidence after the opening battles on the border resulted in his dismissal and replacement by Hindenburg. When Hindenburg took command of first Ninth Army and then the entire German contribution to the Eastern Front, Eighth Army came under the command of Richard von Schubert, but in October he was replaced by the ebullient and frequently insubordinate General Hermann von François. Just a few weeks later, a characteristic failure to follow orders – in this case, Ludendorff wanted François to release the experienced I Corps for the impending drive towards Łódź, but François sent a reserve corps instead – cost François his post, and he was replaced by General Otto von Below, who had served on the Eastern Front since the beginning of the war, leading I Reserve Corps with some distinction.

To the southwest of Eighth Army was Generaloberst August von Mackensen's Ninth Army. The army had suffered substantial losses in December 1914 when Ludendorff ordered an assault across central Poland towards Warsaw; the Russians withdrew in the face of the first German attacks into prepared positions, and large numbers of German soldiers, newly arrived from the Western Front, were squandered in futile frontal attacks. Nevertheless, with a total of eleven corps, Ninth Army remained a formidable formation, its will to fight undiminished, despite the terrible conditions it had to endure:

> Here, we have the most unpleasant weather, wet, foggy, often raining. The roads deteriorate daily, the fighting trenches grow ever damper, and in this unsuitable weather the use of artillery is unthinkable. The Russians are able to dig in ever deeper ... the endurance of the troops is tested ever more severely.[18]

For many years before 1914, it had been highly likely that a future war involving most or all of Europe's nations would see Germany and the Austro-Hungarian Empire fighting as allies, but very little – if any – formal planning had taken place between the two nations. At the beginning of the war, the venerable General Hugo von Freytag-Loringhoven was appointed liaison officer with Conrad's headquarters. Born in the middle of the 19th century, Freytag-Loringhoven served as an officer in the armies of both Russia and Prussia, and wrote extensively on military matters before the war. He was a close friend and ally of Falkenhayn, and it was no surprise that the latter should call him back to Berlin at the end of 1914, to take up the post of deputy quartermaster-general. His replacement in Teschen was August von Cramon, who started the war as the chief of staff of VIII Corps when it invaded Luxembourg and Belgium. Whilst he found the task of dealing with Belgian civilian authorities problematic, this was rapidly eclipsed by the difficulties in his new role, where the clash of personalities between Conrad and Falkenhayn put huge stresses upon the Alliance. On almost every occasion, the two men held opposing opinions, exacerbated by their very different ways of working; Falkenhayn regarded personal meetings as a waste of time, preferring to discuss things at length by telephone, while Conrad steadfastly refused to take part in telephone conferences. Falkenhayn had a more forceful personality, and frequently came away from meetings with Conrad believing that his point of view had prevailed, only to receive a lengthy written rebuttal from Teschen a day or two later.[19] From the very outset of the war, Falkenhayn showed open disdain for Austria-Hungary, treating Franz Joseph's empire as little more than an encumbrance for Germany; to a very large extent, this reflected his unshakable belief that the war was primarily a matter between France and Germany, and victory in the west would make events elsewhere in Europe irrelevant. At the very start of his time as liaison officer, Cramon discovered fundamental differences of opinion about strategic issues such as the likely conduct of neutral nations:

> General Conrad, who already considered the Italians to be hostile, believed that Rome would be ready for hostilities by March at the latest, and would launch an offensive to decide the fate of the disputed territories [on the border between Austria and Italy]. General Falkenhayn was of the opinion that Italy would be prepared to preserve its neutrality in return for territorial concessions. This difference of opinions is understandable; Vienna had a different relationship with Rome than did Berlin; Vienna had repeatedly warned against placing too much confidence in Italy honouring its alliance, while those in Berlin had been convinced that memories of the past were clouding judgements about the present ... That this could only occur to the cost of Austria-Hungary, and that Berlin wished to trade the land of its ally for [an alliance of] dubious value, caused much ill-feeling in Vienna at that time.[20]

The very fact that Falkenhayn could suggest such a move shows the degree to which he regarded the Austro-Hungarian Empire as subservient to German interests. Conrad did nothing to hide his irritation at such suggestions, and frequently countered by proposing that Germany should hand over Alsace and Lorraine to France in return for securing peace.

Falkenhayn's own opinion of the alliance was, naturally, that German dominance was entirely justified:

> Germany's allies were forced by the pressure of the military situation to subordinate any particular wishes of their own to the common ends.
>
> In order to bring their views into harmony with one another, the German and Austro-Hungarian high command ... had to settle each point as it came up. That the German ... view carried more weight in such cases was only natural in view of the relative strength of the forces.[21]

The fundamental root of the difference of opinion between Falkenhayn on the one hand, and Conrad – supported by Hindenburg and Ludendorff, not least because they regarded Falkenhayn's interventions in the east as interference in their area of operations – on the other was the German chief of the general staff's abiding view that the Western Front remained the most important theatre of the war, where the entire conflict would be won or lost. All that was required, Falkenhayn maintained, was to avoid defeat in the east; the struggle of sustaining its war effort would bring Tsarist Russia to its knees:

> If such a strictly disciplined political organism as Germany, accustomed as she had been for centuries to conscientious work, and having at her disposal an inexhaustible wealth of skilled organising forces in her own people, was only barely able to accomplish the mighty tasks imposed upon her by the war, it was certain that the Russian State, so much weaker internally, would not succeed in doing this. As far as human calculations went, Russia would not be able permanently to meet the demands of such a struggle, and at the same time to effect the reconstruction of her whole economic life, which was necessitated by her sudden isolation from the outer world, owing to the closing of the western frontiers and of the Dardanelles.
>
> … It was a grave mistake to believe that our Western enemies would give way, if and because Russia was beaten. No decision in the east, even if it were as thorough as was possible to imagine, could spare us from fighting to a conclusion in the west.[22]

From the perspective of *Ober Ost*, this last statement ignored the fact that a victory by the Central Powers in the east would release substantial forces for use in the west. Hindenburg on his part also believed that final victory in the war could only come in the west, but he did not discount the importance of the eastern conflict:

> Even to me the decisive battle in the west, a battle which would have meant final victory, was the *ultima ratio*, but an *ultima ratio* which could only be reached over the body of a Russia stricken to the ground.[23]

However, Falkenhayn was following what had been accepted wisdom in German military circles before 1914. Barely a century after Napoleon's *Grande Armée* came to grief in the vastness of Russia, it was widely accepted that Russian forces could retreat almost indefinitely, and forcing a decisive battle on them was almost impossible. As far as Falkenhayn was concerned, the best that could be hoped for was a sufficiently large operational success to neutralise Russia. Whilst this might conceivably force Tsar Nicholas to sue for peace, such an outcome was unlikely.

It had always been Germany's deepest fear that the Central Powers would find themselves involved in a protracted two-front war, and the entire thrust of German planning before 1914 had concentrated on winning a decisive success on one front or the other, allowing Germany to defeat its foes in sequential campaigns. Now that the worst fears had been realised, the priority was to find a way of knocking out one of Germany's opponents as quickly as possible. Four new infantry corps had been raised and were being trained and equipped, and would be ready for front-line service in February. Whilst their training proceeded, discussion centred on where and how they should be used. Falkenhayn favoured sending the troops to the Western Front, though it was unclear where this force could be used to achieve a decisive success. Unsurprisingly, Hindenburg, Ludendorff and Conrad wished them to be sent east. Conrad stressed the importance of lifting the siege of Przemyśl – this would effectively end any threat of the Russians penetrating through the Carpathians into Hungary, and would disrupt Russian communications to the west of the fortress. In order to complement an Austro-Hungarian advance to lift the siege, Conrad suggested, the Germans should attack into Poland from East Prussia while his own armies attacked from the south – effectively, another iteration of his repeated proposals for a simultaneous operation at both ends of the long front line. But without German reinforcements, it would be impossible for the *k.u.k.* Army to continue the war beyond the spring of 1915 unless it received substantial reinforcements, argued Conrad, and in these circumstances Vienna would be forced to sue for peace. Ludendorff generally agreed with Conrad's proposals:

> It seemed to me that reinforcement of the *k.u.k.* Army in the Carpathians was required, on account of its circumstances; all the more so, as the Russian Army could not be engaged energetically elsewhere. Whether this was possible in East Prussia was questionable; it was not yet known whether we would be given the authority to deploy the four corps. I therefore had to accept the dispatch of German troops to Hungary from within the resources of *Ober Ost* ... A number of divisions could be withdrawn from Ninth Army for other tasks. I rejected a resumption of frontal attacks here, or south of the Pilica, as had been suggested in some quarters.[24]

Conrad and Falkenhayn met twice in December 1914, once in Breslau (now Wrocław) and shortly before Christmas in Oppeln (now Opole); neither was particularly impressed by his opposite number. Falkenhayn wished to occupy Poland west of the Vistula, and then to establish a fortified line upon which all future Russian attacks would founder. This would allow him to withdraw troops from the Eastern Front for use in a decisive attack in France early in 1915. Conrad countered that the Russians had been badly weakened, and the time was right for a decisive blow against them, from both north and south. Falkenhayn was unconvinced. In the face of any such attack, he suggested, the Russians would merely pull back further east, drawing the armies of the Central Powers into the vast emptiness of Russia.[25]

The Oppeln conference ended without any agreement. On 27 December, Conrad wrote to Falkenhayn once more urging the Germans to send further reinforcements to the Eastern Front, with a supporting telegram from Hindenburg. A third meeting took place in Berlin on New Year's Day, between Falkenhayn, Ludendorff and Conrad. Ludendorff suggested that the four new corps might be used for an attack towards Białystok from East Prussia; when Conrad raised concerns that his troops might not be able to hold back the Russians in the Carpathians, Ludendorff offered to abandon further attacks with Mackensen's Ninth Army in central Poland, and to release two divisions, a reinforced brigade and some cavalry, which could be sent south to reinforce the *k.u.k.* Army. Falkenhayn was unenthusiastic; the German troops were not trained for mountain warfare, he pointed out, and when Conrad expressed enthusiasm about using the German reinforcements to resume offensive operations, specifically to relieve the siege of Przemyśl, he countered that the rail network in the area would ensure that the Russians could concentrate troops to counter any such move faster than Conrad could advance. Given the strains of a two-front war, Conrad's proposal risked squandering valuable troops on an operation with little prospect of success. Once more, the meeting failed to come to any firm conclusions.

Other figures were also attempting to influence events. From his largely ceremonial post as deputy chief of the German general staff, Helmuth von Moltke added his voice to those opposing Falkenhayn, hoping that he might be given a second chance in the supreme role himself. There was close coordination between Moltke and *Ober Ost* – Moltke's adjutant, Major Hans von Haeften, was also press officer at Hindenburg's headquarters. Leopold Berchtold, the Austro-Hungarian foreign minister, and Prince Gottfried von Hohenlohe-Schillingsfürst, the ambassador to Berlin, visited Conrad in Teschen and suggested that a further attack against Serbia should be made. This could be carried out in conjunction with an agreement to allow the Italians to seize Albania, they suggested, thus appeasing Rome and reducing the likelihood of the Italians joining the Entente. The final defeat of Serbia would also shore up the wavering neutral states in the Balkans, and would open land communications with Turkey, allowing German munitions to reach the only ally of the Central Powers. Conrad was unenthusiastic, insisting that any German reinforcements had to be used against the Russians, not against the Serbs. But there was growing concern about the intention of the neutral states. Archduke Frederick, the nominal commander of the *k.u.k.* Army, wrote to the Emperor on 5 January:

> It is certain that an attack by the Italians and Romanians, or by either of these states alone, would place the Dual Monarchy in an untenable military position. This situation requires urgent attention, with a success against Russia as early as possible.[26]

To this end, Conrad repeated his intention to use the German forces assigned to him by Ludendorff to attack north from the Carpathian line. Falkenhayn remained unconvinced. Any local Austro-Hungarian successes to the north of the Carpathians were hardly likely to have much impact in Rome or Bucharest. Instead, he suggested that the small German force, with additional German and Austro-Hungarian reinforcements, should be sent to Serbia. Although they had defeated Potiorek's armies, the Serbs had been left exhausted by the effort, and would not be able to withstand such an attack. Conrad rejected the suggestion. Italy would only be impressed by a victory over the Russians, he insisted. In any event, the Austro-Hungarian campaigns in Serbia suggested that substantial troops would be required to overwhelm the Serbs, and it was not possible to spare such numbers.

The reasons Conrad gave for rejecting a further assault on Serbia were not persuasive. The defeat of Potiorek's two armies owed much to incompetent leadership, and in any event, had come close to success; four fresh German corps, which were universally regarded as having greater fighting power than an equivalent number of Austro-Hungarian corps, would surely have brushed aside the exhausted Serbian Army. But Conrad refused to give way, and was supported by his emperor. Falkenhayn's suggestion of appeasing Italy by offering Austro-Hungarian territory on the upper Adriatic coast still rankled in Vienna.

By this stage, the animosity between Falkenhayn and Ludendorff was widely known; the former had run up substantial gambling debts as a young officer, and Ludendorff resurrected this minor scandal, with the implication that the man who had gambled so freely with money as a younger man was now gambling with Germany's future. Bethmann-Hollweg added to the mistrust and air of conspiracy by appealing to the kaiser on 3 January for Falkenhayn's dismissal and replacement by Ludendorff. There was a final conference in Breslau on 11 January, marked by bitter arguments. Hindenburg announced that in his opinion as the oldest general in the army, the troops had lost confidence in the chief of the general staff, who should resign.

Falkenhayn had no control over how troops already on the Eastern Front were deployed, and had to accept the plans of Conrad and Ludendorff for the German forces released by Ninth Army – under the command of General Alexander von Linsingen, and rather grandiosely named the South Army – to be sent to the Carpathians. Reinforced by additional Austro-Hungarian units, this force would form the core of the attack to lift the siege of Przemyśl. Somewhat to everyone's surprise, Ludendorff was appointed Linsingen's chief of staff. The precise reasons for this are not clear, and the appointment was not expected by Ludendorff himself:

> During the discussions about the operation I was surprised by a telegram from the High Command that I was to be the chief of staff of the South Army.
>
> Field Marshal Hindenburg did not wish to be separated from me. He wrote a detailed letter to His Majesty requesting that I be permitted to stay in my previous post at his side.[27]

Hindenburg's appeals were in vain. It seems that Falkenhayn wished to weaken the Hindenburg–Ludendorff team; it is also likely that the motive was partly an attempt to make Ludendorff take personal responsibility for a course of action that he had supported, and was contrary to Falkenhayn's wishes. Hindenburg was furious; already, Haeften was working to promote the interests of the pro-Hindenburg-Ludendorff group of officers at *Ober Ost*, and Hindenburg ordered him to increase his activities. Although he succeeded in adding Crown Prince Wilhelm and Grand Admiral Alfred von Tirpitz to his cause, Falkenhayn remained obdurate.

Falkenhayn had previously been warned by Freytag-Loringhoven, the German liaison officer at *AOK* in 1914, to avoid allowing German troops to become entangled in the dense Carpathian forests, but he could do nothing to prevent the deployment.[28] All of his arguments that the artillery and supply trains of the German divisions were unsuited to such terrain were brushed aside. Conrad assured him that remedial work was in hand to ensure good quality roads and rail lines to support the attack. One final suggestion, swiftly vetoed by Falkenhayn, can only have served to irritate him still further: Conrad wished to send some of the German troops allocated to him by Ludendorff to the Italian and Romanian frontiers, to act as a deterrent – any attempt by the neutral powers to launch a surprise attack on the Austro-Hungarian Empire would thus result in conflict with German troops.

On 20 January, Kaiser Wilhelm entered the fray. He had become aware of Haeften's activities in recruiting officers, politicians and members of the royal family to the cause of Hindenburg, Ludendorff and Moltke, and he summoned the major to a meeting, where he angrily rejected all calls for Falkenhayn's dismissal. Such a decision was his to make, and to sack Falkenhayn so soon after his appointment would only give succour to Germany's foes. Growing more enraged, the kaiser warned that he would court-martial Hindenburg and others unless *Ober Ost* ceased its destabilising activities.[29] In an attempt to bring the dispute to an end, Wilhelm ordered that Haeften be removed from his post and assigned to a staff post in Cologne.

Despite this intervention, Falkenhayn could do little to argue against troops being sent east. The defeat at the Marne after the initial invasion of Belgium and France, followed by the failure to break the British lines at Ypres in the autumn, begged the obvious question: if Falkenhayn wished to make a further effort in the west, where would this be, and why should a new effort be any more likely to succeed than the assaults of the previous year? Unable to articulate a persuasive answer to this, Falkenhayn had to accept that the four new corps would be sent east for operations in East Prussia. The best that he could do was secure agreement that they would be released back to him once their tasks there were complete.

Hindenburg had threatened to resign if Falkenhayn remained in his post, and Kaiser Wilhelm begged him to change his mind. The resignation of a man who had been hailed as a great hero after Tannenberg would do great harm to the prestige of Germany, and Hindenburg agreed to remain. Nevertheless, the fact that the kaiser – nominally the commander-in-chief of the army – had been forced to plead with one of his generals did great damage to Wilhelm's personal standing. Ludendorff wrote to Moltke that he now regarded his loyalty as being to the Fatherland rather than to Wilhelm.[30] The failure of either side to prevail left animosity that would continue to interfere with the functioning and decision-making of the German Army throughout the year.

On the battlefield, too, the stage was set for further heavy fighting. The Russians were building a new army in the north with the intention of mounting a further assault on East Prussia, but had also sent reinforcements to Ivanov so that he could apply pressure in the Carpathians. The Central Powers, too, were sending forces to the northern part of the front, whilst Conrad – undeterred by the disastrous losses suffered by his armies in their attempts to execute his offensive plans the previous year – intended to launch attacks along the Carpathians, aimed at lifting the siege of Przemyśl. Neither side was prepared to wait for better weather; an attempt would be made to force a decision in the depths of winter.

CHAPTER 2

THE FIRST CARPATHIAN CAMPAIGN

The city of Przemyśl, now in southeast Poland, on the banks of the River San, has been an important settlement for centuries. It is thought to be the second-oldest city in Poland, reflecting its location close to the Carpathians, astride an important river, in a rich, fertile valley. The city's importance grew with the building of railways in the middle of the 19th century, connecting it with Lemberg (now Lviv) to the east and Krakow to the west. With growing tension between Austria and Russia, fortifications were built around Przemyśl, creating a belt of military installations around a circumference of about 9 miles (15km). The rapid development of artillery in the years that followed soon rendered these fortifications obsolete, and considerable money was invested over quarter of a century before the First World War to modernise the defences. By the outbreak of hostilities, Przemyśl was widely regarded as an excellent fortress, able to accommodate at least 85,000 soldiers.

The purpose of the fortress changed as military thinking evolved. At first, it was envisaged as one of a series of strongpoints along the San, but financial considerations as well as changes in tactical and operational doctrine made such a plan unworkable. The Austro-Hungarian Empire struggled constantly with its dual political arrangements in Vienna and Hungary to agree significant increases in military expenditure, with the result that many of the fortifications planned for Przemyśl were never built, and others were constructed on a more modest scale; fortifications elsewhere along the San did not, in the main, ever get past the planning stage. Even if a line of fortresses had been constructed, the *k.u.k.* Army would have required its entire manpower to defend them, leaving no forces available for the offensive operations that were increasingly in vogue. Instead, Przemyśl was to be used as a military headquarters for operations to the east, and if the Russians succeeded in overrunning parts of Galicia, the fortress could be left to hold out in the rear of the enemy's lines, disrupting communications and supplies until it could be relieved.

As soon as hostilities broke out, additional work began to reinforce the defences of Przemyśl, with miles of trenches and barbed wire being laid out. Undergrowth, buildings and trees were removed to provide clear fields of fire in front of the perimeter forts. At first, as Austro-Hungarian forces advanced confidently against the Russians, it seemed likely that none of the defences would be tested, which was some relief to the engineers working around Przemyśl, as their plans had been based upon having far more time at their disposal. However, the crushing defeats that led to the abandonment of Lemberg and a retreat to the west brought the front line to the region. Conrad's original intention, to pull back to the line of the San, proved to be inadequate; the Russians were following too closely, and were already over the river in some areas before the Austro-Hungarian troops had completed their withdrawal, and the shattered units of the *k.u.k.* Army were in no state to offer much resistance. Instead, the retreat continued, resulting in the first siege of Przemyśl. The first shots were fired near the perimeter on 17 September, and the encirclement was complete nine days later, trapping 131,000 soldiers and civilians in the city.

The Russians were confident that the Austro-Hungarian garrison, mainly drawn from the broken retreating armies, would not be able to put up much resistance, as Brusilov later recalled:

> The investment of Przemyśl was entrusted to the new commander of Third Army, Radko Dimitriev, who when he was in command of VIII Corps of my army, and earlier, in the Turco-Bulgarian War, had struck me as an extremely decisive, intelligent and very talented officer. I did not doubt for a moment that at this juncture he would display these same military qualities and would attempt to take Przemyśl without more ado, which would have freed our hands, established us firmly in eastern Galicia, and given us an opportunity of pushing onward without meeting any hindrance and without leaving behind us an enemy fortress and a besieged city. Indeed, after such a succession of defeats and heavy losses, the

Austrian Army was so demoralised and Przemyśl so little prepared to stand a siege, for its garrison, composed of beaten troops, was far from steady, that I was absolutely convinced that by the middle of October the place could have been taken by assault without any serious artillery preparation. The matter did not concern me directly, because I did not think I had authority to intervene in the decisions of my neighbour and in any way influence his decision.[1]

Initially, the Russians sent an officer under a flag of truce to make an offer to discuss terms of surrender. The garrison commander, Feldmarschallleutnant Hermann von Kusmanek, had six infantry divisions at his disposal, and had no intention of capitulating; the Russian offer was rejected without discussion. Radko Dimitriev began a bombardment of the city, but this had little effect. On 7 October, Russian infantry attacked in strength against the southern fortifications, briefly penetrating into one of the forts before they were themselves encircled and forced to surrender. The following day, another Russian attack was made, this time against the northern perimeter, but it foundered in the face of heavy defensive fire before it had even penetrated the barbed wire entanglements. By this stage, Conrad's armies were advancing from the west towards Przemyśl, and the Russians abandoned their attacks, aware that even if they were able to reduce the garrison, they would be too weakened to hold the city in the face of the advancing Austro-Hungarian forces. On 9 October, the first elements of the relieving army reached the city.

It wasn't long before Conrad was forced to retreat again, and the city was once more surrounded. This time, it was left in a far worse state than before. When they arrived to lift the siege, the Austro-Hungarian field armies, which had outstripped their supply lines, were allowed to replenish their own depleted stocks of ammunition and food from the fortress stores, and as a result, even though thousands of civilians were ordered to leave before the resumption of the siege, the garrison of over 120,000 men – and several thousand civilians, who refused to leave their homes – soon began to run short of supplies. On this occasion, Dimitriev took command of the troops that had moved past the fortress, leaving the conduct of the siege to General Andrei Selivanov.

Matters inside the fortress were not handled well. Originally, it had been intended that the garrison would be largely Hungarian, but owing to the troops within Przemyśl being drawn from a variety of formations that were retreating through the area, the reality was that the mixture of nationalities reflected the polyglot nature of the Austro-Hungarian Empire. Despite substantial supplies being withdrawn from the city's stores by the troops that briefly lifted the siege during the autumn of 1914, there should have been ample supplies, provided they were managed well. The reality was that while officers dined well, their men were often left to face starvation. Large numbers of horses had been left with the garrison, and shortly before the end of 1914, a decision was made to slaughter 7,000 of them – Kusmanek reported that the reduction in demand for fodder, and the additional meat that this would provide, would allow the garrison to survive until at least mid-February. However, this did not come without a price, as it also greatly reduced the potential mobility of the garrison. One of the main reasons for maintaining a garrison in Przemyśl had been to have a force that could strike across Russian supply lines, which required forces able to move swiftly to attack targets of opportunity before withdrawing to the safety of the fortress. One such operation was abandoned on 18 December when a Russian cavalry force succeeded in capturing the city's outer defences to the north. Determined counterattacks over the next few days failed to recapture the positions, and merely produced more casualties for the defenders. On 27 December, Kusmanek assembled a force of fifteen battalions and thirteen artillery batteries in the southwest part of the fortress perimeter for another excursion, but in the face of determined Russian defences, it made no progress. This latest failure appears to have had a marked effect upon the morale of the garrison. Although Kusmanek reported his combat strength as being nearly 84,000 men, fewer than 15,000 of them were regular soldiers. The rest were relatively inexperienced and poorly trained *Landsturm* reservists, whose ability to keep fighting in the face of setbacks was limited.[2] But although the impact of the attempted sorties was minimal, the Russian commander of Southwest Front, Ivanov, was able to use them to justify his demands for additional reinforcements.

When they became aware of the slaughter of horses within Przemyśl, the surrounding Russians took to mocking the defenders by making neighing noises whenever they were within earshot. Within the city itself, the drastic killing of horses became the subject of grim humour:

> What is the difference between the heroes of Troy and those of Przemyśl? In Troy, the warriors were in the belly of a horse, while in Przemyśl, the horse is in the belly of the warriors![3]

Josef Tomann, a young army doctor, recorded his personal observations of life during the siege. In January, he saw the first cases of malnutrition:

> Starvation is kicking in. Sunken, pale faces wander like corpses through the streets, their ragged clothes hanging from skeletal bodies, their stony faces a

picture of utter despair. And then there are the fat-bellied gents from the commissariat, who stink of fat and go arm in arm with Przemyśl's finest ladies, most of whom (and this is no exaggeration) have turned into prostitutes of the lowest order.

The hospitals have been recruiting teenage girls as nurses, in some places there are up to 50 of them! They get 120 crowns a month and free meals. That comes to 17,000 crowns a month! They are, with very few exceptions, utterly useless. Their main job is to satisfy the lust of gentlemen officers and, rather shamefully, a number of doctors, too. None of them go without furs, even though they have dirty underwear. They just get in the way. Meanwhile, I am paid less than 60 crowns for my work as a doctor!

... In the night a few frozen soldiers were brought in from their sentry posts. Starvation is taking its toll on the civilian population. Opposition to the siege threatens to make its presence felt. The situation is critical! Surplus foodstuffs are being taken away from the civilian population. It snows non-stop! Will the field army in the Carpathians be able to advance at all in this snow, which must surely be two or three metres deep there?[4]

By the beginning of 1915, following a further horse cull, Kusmanek estimated that he had enough supplies to hold out until March at the latest.[5] Any relief attempt could therefore not wait until the spring, but would have to be mounted at the worst time of year. To the south of Przemyśl, preparations were already under way for mounting such a relief operation. Slowly, the threadbare ranks of the Austro-Hungarian infantry divisions were brought up to something approaching their establishment strength, but whilst they may have improved numerically, their fighting power remained a shadow of its intended level. Recruits were meant to undergo eight weeks of basic training before being sent to their units, but the desperate need for replacements led to this being reduced in stages, first to four weeks and ultimately to only two weeks. The shortage of rifles meant that most of these recruits received almost no weapons training during this short period, though at first, this was not regarded as a particularly important issue. Conrad's pre-war training manuals had discounted the value of accurate rifle fire, preferring to rush forward in order to get into close combat as quickly as possible, but the first months of the war had already demonstrated the value of accurate infantry fire, particularly when defending. Regardless of the merits of good musketry, the truncated training schedule produced soldiers who had only the most rudimentary understanding of what was expected of them, either with the bullet or the bayonet, and for men drafted from urban areas there was inadequate time to ensure that soldiers acquired an acceptable level of physical fitness. The full equipment of an Austro-Hungarian infantryman came to about 33kg, and even when it was possible for recruits to receive a full set of clothes, overcoat, helmet, shovel, rifle etc, many of them, too unfit to march with such a load, simply discarded much of it.[6]

In any event, most of the troops that were about to fight in the Carpathians had no training for mountain warfare. The *k.u.k.* Army started the war with several divisions that had trained for precisely such a role, and had been equipped with suitable lightweight artillery that could easily be dismantled, transported by pack-animals, and then reassembled, but most of these units had been bled white in the bloody mountain fighting in Serbia. Even though many of the troops in the Carpathians had learned the realities of warfare in such terrain through bitter experience, no army had ever attempted major operations in a mountainous, heavily wooded landscape in the middle of winter. It would be a new experience for all concerned.

The Carpathian Mountains form a daunting obstacle between Galicia and Hungary, and although the average height of the peaks is lower than the Alps, the mountains rise in places to over 8,500 feet (2,600m). The dense woodland on the flanks of the mountains, together with the relatively few roads and railways, ensured that large-scale military operations faced formidable obstacles. At the time, there were five main passes through the mountains, at Wyszkov, Verecke, Uzsok, Lupkov and Dukla from east to west. Of these, the three western passes had the greatest military value. In particular, control of the Uzsok and Dukla Passes was critical; the former was the route of one of the few railways across the mountains, while the latter was a broad route through to the Hungarian Plain, difficult for the *k.u.k.* Army to defend.

Russian forces that had been retreating as a consequence of the Austro-Hungarian success at Limanowa-Łapanów struck back towards the end of December 1914 at several points, bringing the advance of Conrad's troops to an abrupt halt; casualties were heavy on both sides, further depleting divisions that had already lost so many of their men in the battles of the autumn. One Russian attack, in the very last hours of the old year, succeeded in gaining control of the Uzsok Pass in December 1914. The Austro-Hungarian General Jeno Rónai-Horváth's forces had been contesting the pass for several days of bitter fighting, but late on New Year's Eve, a surprise Russian attack succeeded in turning the flank of the Austro-Hungarian line. Rónai-Horváth tried in vain to conduct an orderly retreat, but his men did not rally until they had been driven back at 12 miles (20km). Attempts to restore the situation by a counterattack failed, and it was decided to await sufficient reinforcements to mount a proper offensive.[7] Similar events occurred at the other main passes, where the Russians were left either in control of the passes, or in positions to dominate them. Even before it began, Conrad's plan for a drive northwards from the Carpathians had already become more difficult.

From the Russian point of view, their operations in the Carpathians were motivated both by defensive concerns – they wished to prevent Conrad's armies from marching to lift the siege of Przemyśl, or to threaten their east–west communications across Galicia – and Ivanov's hopes for a drive into Hungary. By securing the Uzsok Pass, any immediate threat of the *k.u.k.* Army relieving Przemyśl was effectively eliminated, but for the moment there was little attempt to penetrate further south. Brusilov's army limited itself to a few Cossack raids into the southern foothills, where a few Hungarian villages were pillaged; just as the *k.u.k.* Army was unable to make any headway without reinforcements, the Russian formations, weakened by their own heavy losses in the autumn and early winter, would need time to recover their strength. Even before the final capture of the Uzsok Pass, Ivanov had ordered his armies to limit their operations to no more than a limited pursuit of the enemy.[8]

Gradually, reinforcements began to arrive on both sides. Ludendorff and Linsingen set up their headquarters in Munkacs (now Mukacheve), about 30 miles (50km) south of the Uzsok Pass, and began a series of visits to the assembly area for their troops, and to establish contacts with neighbouring Austro-Hungarian formations, which would be added to the new South Army. Ludendorff found that Conrad's promises of adequate preparations were far from reality, and obtained an insight into some of the difficulties faced by Germany's ally. His comments also reflect the views about relative values of different cultures that were widely prevalent at the time, as well as a growing feeling about Germany's ally:

Insufficient had been done for the troops, from construction of positions to provision of accommodation. There was a lot of catching-up to be done.

Passing through the mountain forests I came upon an outpost. The soldier reported to me in a foreign language, I can no longer remember which one. Nor could the *k.u.k.* officers accompanying me understand. I thus gained an impression of the difficulties that faced this army. They were greatly amplified because the nationalities in regiments were mixed together, to try to improve their reliability. Czech and Romanian regiments had defected to the enemy. These nationalities were now distributed across numerous regiments. This measure had not helped.

Specifically, it had reduced the value of the brave Hungarian and efficient German [i.e. Austrian] regiments. It had also increased linguistic difficulties to an extraordinary level.

Here, too ... I gained an insight into the utter backwardness of all people who do not belong to the ruling race. I had the same impression from a journey to the villages of the *Hutzels* [an ethic group living in the Carpathians]. I still remember the flimsiness of the houses of these unfortunate people. How different are affairs in Germany, thanks to the measures of their lords, and how cultured and advanced they are with us, compared with Austria-Hungary. Whenever I saw a *Hutzel* house, it was clear to me that these people could not know what was to become of them. Austria-Hungary had failed repeatedly in so many respects; as an allied power, we had to know what hindered us. If the Dual Monarchy and the *k.u.k.* Army had achieved only half of what Germany justifiably and rightly expected from them, then at least German troops would not have been required in such numbers as reinforcements for the Austro-Hungarian front; we would have had more forces available for the west during this period ... ultimately, it was our undoing to be allied to declining states like Austria-Hungary and Turkey. In Radom, a Jew said to one of my men that he could not understand why such a lively and strong nation like Germany should chain itself to a corpse. He was right, but Germany could not gain strong-willed war allies ... I learned about the circumstances of Austria-Hungary for the first time during the course of the war, having had no opportunity before. It surprised me to see such a low state. Our relevant departments had certainly known that the Dual Monarchy had become the sick man of Europe, but they had not drawn the correct conclusions.[9]

For the German troops transferred from central Poland, this was their first experience of warfare in such terrain. They watched with amazement as supply columns negotiated the difficult landscape:

Truly fantastic is the appearance of one of these modern supply caravans, stretching in zigzag, with numerous sharp corners and turns, upward to the heights of the passes and down on the opposite side. Here we see in stages, one above the other and moving in opposite directions, the queerest mixture of men, vehicles, machines and animals, all subordinated to a common military purpose and organization by military leadership, moving continually and regularly along. The drivers have been drummed up from all parts of the monarchy, Serbs, Ruthenians, Poles, Croats, Rumanians, Hungarians, Slovaks, Austrians, and turbaned Mohammedans from Bosnia. Everyone is shouting to his animals and cursing in his own language. The whole mix-up is a travelling exhibition of most variegated characteristic costumes, for the most part, of course, extremely the worse for wear. Common to all these are the little wagons adapted to mountain travel, elastic and tough, which carry only half loads and are drawn by pony-like, determined little horses. In between are great German draft horses, stamping along with their broad high-wheeled baggage and ammunition wagons, as though they belonged to a race of giants.

Gravely, with a kind of sullen dignity, slow-stepping steers drag at the yokes of their heavily laden sledges. They are of a powerful white breed, with broad-spreading horns a yard long. These are followed in endless rows by carefully stepping pack animals, small and large horses, mules and donkeys. On the wooden packsaddles on their backs are carefully balanced bales of hay or ammunition boxes or other war materials. Walking gingerly by the edges of the mountain ridges they avoid pitfalls and rocks and walk round the stiff, distended bodies of their comrades that have fallen along the way ... In the midst of this movement of the legs of animals, of waving arms, of creaking and swaying loaded vehicles of manifold origin, there climbs upward the weighty iron of an Austrian motor battery, with an almost incomprehensible inevitability, flattening out the broken roads like a steam roller.

From the first pass the baggage train sinks down into the depths, again to climb upward on the next ridge, to continue striving upward ever toward higher passages, slowly pushing forward toward its objective against the resistance of numberless obstacles.

The road to the battlefield of today crosses the battlefield of recent weeks and months. Here there once stood a village, but only the stone foundations of the hearths are left as traces of the houses that have been burned down. Sometimes falling shots or the terrors of a brief battle in the streets have reduced to ruins only a part of a village. The roofs of houses have been patched with canvas and boards to some extent, and now serve as quarters for troops or as stables. In the narrow valleys the level places by the sides of streams have been utilised for encampments. Here stand in order wagons of a resting column and the goulash cannons [German military slang for field kitchens] shedding their fragrance far and wide, or the tireless ovens of a field bakery. Frequently barracks, hospital buildings, and shelters for men and animals have been built into the mountainsides. Here and there simple huts have been erected, made of a few poles and fir twigs. Often they are placed in long rows, which, when their inmates are warming themselves by the fire at night turn the dark mountain road into a romantic night encampment, and everywhere fresh crosses, ornamented at times in a manner suggestive of the work of children, remind us of our brothers now forever silenced, who, but a short time before went the same road, withstood just such weather and such hardships, talked perhaps in these same huts of the war, and dreamt of peace.

The saddest spectacle, however, were the lightly wounded, poor fellows, who might under ordinary conditions have readily walked the distance from the first aid station to the central gathering point, but who here on account of the ice or muddy roads require double and three times the usual time.[10]

The great reliance upon horses, mules and oxen to move heavy loads through the mountains was not without a price. The presence of these animals necessitated additional supply movements of fodder, and inevitably, this occurred in a haphazard and disorganised manner. Hard-pressed logistics personnel resorted to feeding their animals with whatever provisions they could get, resulting in a rapid increase in the number that died or became too unwell to continue working.[11]

The entire region had been regarded by Austro-Hungarian theorists as merely a route from one area of operations, the Hungarian Plain, to another, the Galician theatre. There had been no consideration of fighting in the Carpathians, but Conrad brushed aside any reservations on the grounds that he expected his forces to fight their way clear of the mountains very quickly. The failure of Austro-Hungarian forces to achieve such rapid success in far more favourable conditions should have led to caution about making such claims, but there was no sign of Conrad even questioning the validity of his theories, let alone accepting that they were wrong. His plans for the offensive centred on Third Army. Reinforced by six infantry divisions – two within V Corps, two within XIX Corps, and two additional reservist divisions – Boroević received orders as early as 2 January to group his forces so that his right flank would strike towards the Uzsok Pass, his centre would advance against Sanok, while his left flank, which was believed to face the strongest Russian defences, would join the general advance as it gained pace. In addition to his infantry reinforcements, Boroević had been assigned several cavalry formations, and he recommended their return to the front line in Poland, as the terrain that he would be crossing was completely unsuitable for cavalry. *AOK* disagreed; once his men were clear of the Carpathians, Conrad argued, the cavalry would play an important reconnaissance and exploitation role. Leaving aside the difficulties that had to be overcome before Third Army could expect to be free of the mountains, this was another example of Conrad refusing to learn from experience. The performance of the cavalry of all armies, but particularly of the *k.u.k.* Army, had been far weaker than expected in 1914. The value of mounted units in raiding operations and reconnaissance had been minimal in summer conditions, and it was surely another triumph of rigid doctrine in the face of evidence to suggest that things might be different in midwinter.

Linsingen's South Army began to assemble on the eastern flank of Boroević's Third Army. While *Gruppe Szurmay* on Third Army's eastern flank attacked directly towards the Uzsok Pass, Linsingen would force the Verecke and Boskid Passes about 12 miles (20km) further east, and would then continue towards the northeast, aiming for the town of Stryj. On Linsingen's right flank, *Gruppe Pflanzer-Baltin* would also cross the mountains and would protect the eastern end of the long battle line. After he and Ludendorff had visited their neighbouring units, Linsingen concluded that *Gruupe Szurmay* was far too weak to be able to achieve much success in its attack towards the Uzsok Pass. The Austro-Hungarian 6th Infantry Division had been assigned to Third Army; it had been serving with *Gruppe Pflanzer-Baltin*, and was therefore accustomed to mountain warfare, and Linsingen recommended that it should be assigned to Szurmay's force. He further suggested that the attack on the Uzsok Pass should be subordinated to his command. Always reluctant to allow the Germans to take control of his front-line troops, Conrad disregarded this latter suggestion. Furthermore, instead of giving Szurmay 6th Infantry Division, he assigned him 7th Infantry Division, which until now had been in Third Army's reserves, and in contrast with the troops suggested by Linsingen, had little or no experience of mountain warfare. As well as failing to provide Szurmay with troops that were likely to be most effective, this move also reduced the forces available to Boroević in the event of a crisis developing.[12]

On 20 January, Linsingen and Boroević met to discuss the coming battle. The latter informed his German counterpart that Szurmay was to start moving towards the Uzsok Pass on 22 January, a day before the rest of Third Army began its assault, and in order to assist this initial movement, Linsingen offered to advance with his left flank a day earlier in an attempt to tie down as many Russian forces as possible. Meanwhile Hindenburg had been working to reverse Falkenhayn's attempt to break up the power base of *Ober Ost*. After only a few days in his new post, Ludendorff headed back to Posen to resume his duties as Hindenburg's chief of staff. He was replaced in South Army by Generalmajor Paulus von Stolzmann.

The Russian forces made little effort to interfere with the preparations of their opponents. While Ivanov turned a blind eye to the wishes of *Stavka* and Grand Duke Nikolai, who had already declared that priority was to be given to operations against East Prussia, Brusilov recorded in his memoirs that he regarded an attack towards Hungary as more important than the Southwest Front commander, though for different reasons. Brusilov calculated that his army, which had suffered crippling losses in the Battle of Limanowa-Łapanów, would be unable to withstand a concentrated blow at any point on its long front, and it was therefore necessary to mount an attack to tie down as many Austro-Hungarian forces as possible, thus preventing them from massing for an attack of their own. According to Brusilov, Ivanov was against this, but Mikhail Alexeyev, chief of staff of Southwest Front, sided with Brusilov.[13] To an extent, one can detect elements of the ongoing feud between different factions within the Russian Army in these nuances. Brusilov was too good a commander to believe that a spoiling attack could achieve much in such difficult terrain, and he correctly points out later that there were huge risks involved in an invasion of Hungary:

> It was not difficult to foresee that if my army descended to the Hungarian plains with inadequate supplies of munitions, it would be forced to surrender or face destruction. I therefore dissimulated that I wished to attack through the Carpathians, and actually tried to pin down as many enemy forces as possible, so as not to give them the opportunity to be deployed on other operations. Conditions in the mountains were extremely tough, the movement of supplies was difficult, and there were shortages of winter clothing.[14]

The modest reinforcements that Ivanov had been able to extract from *Stavka*, primarily XXII Corps, took far longer to arrive than anticipated, and in the meantime, Brusilov's depleted formations had to do their best to cover the long front line. The original demand for reinforcements had been to allow Brusilov to strengthen his line east of the Uzsok Pass, which was covered by only four divisions, three of which were made up primarily of reservists; it was only the comparable weakness of General Karl von Pflanzer-Baltin's command that prevented a serious setback. Artillery ammunition remained in critically short supply, and like their Austro-Hungarian counterparts, the Russians found that the replacement drafts arriving at the front were poorly trained and completely unprepared for winter warfare in the mountains. Even if Brusilov's Eighth Army should succeed in forcing its way onto the Hungarian Plain, this would in the short term result in a considerable lengthening of the front line. In these circumstances, there was the threat of the Central Powers using their excellent railway network to concentrate forces in southern Poland, which could then strike at the exposed western flank of the attack into Hungary; if that were to occur, Brusilov might find himself attempting to conduct a retreat under pressure through the Carpathian passes.

The First Carpathian Campaign, January–February 1915

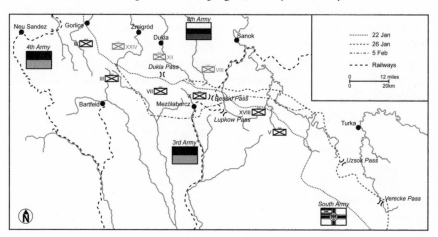

Whilst the Central Powers had agreed their overall strategy – albeit with great misgivings on the part of Falkenhayn – there continued to be very little strategic coordination between the German and Austro-Hungarian commands; each was aware of the other's intentions and plans, but took few steps if any to alter their own plans to help. There were similar problems on the other side of the front line, where *Stavka* proved incapable of imposing its will upon the two Front commanders. Although all priority was meant to be towards the renewed attack on East Prussia, Ivanov continued to demand – with mixed success – that all mountain artillery units be moved to the Carpathians from the entire Eastern Front. Brusilov was ordered to prepare his forces for their attack on 25 January, regardless of his continuing shortages of men, ammunition and practically everything else. On the other side of the front line, the forces assembled by Conrad – the remnants of Boroević's army, reinforcements from southern Poland, troops transferred from the Serbian Front, reservists and replacement drafts, and the German element of South Army – struggled to move themselves and their equipment into position along inadequate, snow-covered roads. Much of the artillery of the assault formations failed to reach the front line, and was abandoned where it slipped off icy roads or encountered other obstacles; those guns that did reach the front line were often so short of ammunition that commanders had to order that the guns could fire only in the event of a major Russian attack. The consequence was that the assault troops, who in the main had little or no experience of mountain warfare, and in the case of the replacement drafts had no experience of any kind of warfare, would have to launch their attacks with minimal or often completely absent artillery support. But despite Conrad's rigid insistence that the offensive should go ahead, other officers quietly recorded their doubts about the wisdom of the plans. One senior staff officer in the Operations Bureau of *AOK* wrote in his diary that the operation amounted to 'methodical mass murder', and that the high command was showing a degree of 'headlessness' in its approach.[15]

The *k.u.k.* Army launched its assault two days before Brusilov's proposed start date. The difficult approach marches ensured that Boroević's men were already tired by their exertions before the operation even began, and in many cases not all elements of each formation had arrived; one consequence was that the push towards the Uzsok Pass, intended to begin a day before the rest of the campaign, had to be delayed. Although accounts of the fighting describe operations launched by individual divisions, the reality was that with a few exceptions, particularly in the case of the German divisions, none of the formations possessed their normal complement of men, artillery and supporting equipment, and the terrain often resulted in ad-hoc groups fighting isolated actions, unable to support groups just a short distance away. Nevertheless, *Gruppe Puhallo* encountered only Russian cavalry when it advanced to the west of the Uzsok Pass and edged forward cautiously. To its east, *Gruppe Szurmay* struggled forward towards the Uzsok Pass itself, hindered perhaps more by the snow-covered terrain than by Russian resistance; it took three days to reach and then secure the pass, in the face of growing resistance from the Russian 34th Infantry Division and 65th Cavalry Division.[16]

Already, the different rates of advance and the mountainous terrain were causing difficulties, with a substantial gap opening between *Gruppe Puhallo* and *Gruppe Szurmay*, forcing reserves that would otherwise have been held ready to keep up the momentum of the advance being deployed to complete the front line. A similar gap developed on General Paul Puhallo's western flank. The advance towards Baligród was assigned to 44th Rifle Division, supported by 43rd Rifle Division from the neighbouring *Gruppe Krautwald*. It was characteristic of the lack of detailed Austro-Hungarian staffwork in preparing for the offensive that it had not been anticipated that the attack lay precisely at the seam of the two Austro-Hungarian commands, and belatedly, 43rd Rifle Division was transferred to Puhallo's command. Feldmarschalleutnant Josef Krautwald was meant to advance with the rest of his force to keep pace with Puhallo's advance, but as 43rd Rifle Division was drawn away to the northeast, a gap opened up between it and Krautwald's remaining units. To add to Krautwald's frustration, the two divisions tasked with capturing Baligród succeeded in taking the town in the face of only minimal resistance; it is likely that Puhallo's troops would have sufficed without the transfer of Krautwald's right flank division, which would have allowed Krautwald to concentrate forces for his own operation. On this occasion, there were no more reinforcements available to cover the gap, and Puhallo and Krautwald simply had to resort to hoping for the best. To make matters worse, Krautwald's western flank failed to make the anticipated progress, forcing him to stretch his line ever further to try to keep contact.

The constraints of the landscape greatly limited the ability of local commanders to attempt to manoeuvre around the flanks of their enemies, with the result that the only option was to launch bloody frontal assaults, made all the more difficult by the diversion of reserves. In addition to Russian resistance, the attacking troops had to face almost impossible weather as conditions deteriorated rapidly; Conrad had banked on perhaps a week of clear weather, but snow was falling across a wide area as early as the second day of the offensive. Georg Weith, an artillery officer and historian, recorded the difficulties that he and his men faced in the opening days of the battle:

> On 23 January, we pushed forward into the frozen hell of the Carpathian battlefield. We assaulted the Uzsok, Verecke and Wyszkov Passes, but on the northern slopes of the mountains, a blizzard engulfed the troops. The reports from those days are terrible. Hundreds froze to death every day. The wounded that were unable to drag themselves along were left behind to die.
>
> … Pack animals couldn't advance through the deep snow. The men had to carry their own supplies on foot. The soldiers went without food for days. Food rations froze solid at -25°C. For an entire week, 43rd Infantry Division struggled against superior Russian troops, without any warm food. Almost no battalions in the front line had even 200 men as the lines grew ever thinner. Battle-weary troops were repeatedly pulled out of one position and sent elsewhere to plug a new gap. Medical personnel and those not seriously ill or injured were pressed into action. There was constant, widespread confusion, which was greatly detrimental to military command. Apathy and lack of concern grew, and could not be contained.[17]

On the right flank of the Austro-Hungarian Third Army, Linsingen's South Army struggled forward through similarly difficult conditions to take the Verecke Pass. With no prior experience of winter warfare and without adequate winter clothing, the German component of South Army suffered as much as Austro-Hungarian forces, with hundreds suffering from frostbite. To make matters worse, there were repeated episodes of warmer weather, resulting in sudden floods from melting snow that swept away roads and even bridges. As they secured their hold on the Verecke Pass, the troops of South Army found themselves confronted by the barren slopes of the Łysa Góra, a modest mountain that lives up to its name (in Polish, 'Bald Mountain'). Without any cover and almost no artillery support, Linsingen's men launched repeated futile attacks on the Russian defences, each assault leaving the slopes littered with the dead and dying.[18]

On the left flank of Puhallo's force was Krautmann's X Corps, and together with the adjacent VII Corps, it was meant to join in the advance as it gained momentum. With little sign of any momentum developing, first VII Corps ground to a halt, and then the neighbouring X Corps came under attack on 24 January as Brusilov's forces launched local counterattacks. Just as the terrain had forced the Austro-Hungarians to make costly frontal assaults, so the same applied to the Russian VIII and XII Corps. Casualties mounted on both sides for little gain, but the immediate consequence was that the two Austro-Hungarian corps, covering against any Russian attempt to descend into Hungary via the Dukla Pass, were unable to make any attacks of their own to assist the right flank of Boroević's army in its advance.

By 26 January, Conrad's great offensive, which was intended to break out of the Carpathians quickly to avoid prolonged mountain fighting, had effectively ground to a halt in Third Army's sector. The weather remained atrocious, with heavy blizzards reducing visibility to a minimum; even when they weren't crippled by ammunition shortages, the German and Austro-Hungarian gunners were unable to see far enough to offer fire support to the infantry. In any event, the Russians had not been standing still. Reinforcements in the form of the Russian XXII Corps and several batteries of mountain artillery had been dispatched – with some reluctance – to the region by *Stavka*, and as they began to arrive, Brusilov started to apply pressure to the Austro-Hungarian line. Ivanov remained convinced that the key to winning the war was to inflict a crushing defeat upon the armies of the Dual Monarchy; he was certain that this would trigger the entry of Italy, Romania and Bulgaria into the war on the side of the Entente, and would lead to the dissolution of the Austro-Hungarian Empire. Germany would not be able to stand alone against the rest of Europe, and isolated from its only ally, Turkey, would be forced to come to terms. The first step in this great plan was to seize the important railway hub of Mezőlaborcz. Once this town was taken, the supply situation for Boroević's army would become almost impossible.

Accordingly, Brusilov's troops launched their own determined attacks on the western part of Boroević's line. At first, Boroević judged the attack as no more than an attempt to tie down his troops, but he was rapidly disabused. Far from being able to continue their advance and remain linked up with the centre and right flank of Third Army, the forces defending the main approaches to the Dukla and Beskid Passes – on the left, Archduke Joseph's VII Corps, and on the right, Krautmann's X Corps – found their own lines under strain from attacks by the newly arrived XXII Corps and the reinforced VIII Corps. Casualties mounted steadily, but the seam between the two Austro-Hungarian corps came under ever-greater pressure. Finally, VII Corps' right flank was forced to yield ground, and Brusilov's men turned on the exposed left flank of X Corps. Casualties soared on both sides as the terrible conditions and bitter frontal assaults wore formations down at a shocking rate. VII Corps began to fall back even further, despite Conrad's repeated instructions that positions had to be held to the last man. Desperately, Boroević requested reinforcements – at least a full division would be required for him to restore the situation. Conrad had no reserves available, and turned to Archduke Joseph Ferdinand's Fourth Army. Joseph Ferdinand replied that his army had already been stripped of its reserves in an attempt to build up Third Army prior to the offensive, and therefore he could spare nothing; eventually, he was able to release a single brigade. Conrad then urged him to launch attacks of his own – if he couldn't send troops to Boroević's aid, he could at least tie down the Russians in his sector. Grimly aware that such attacks would only result in more casualties without any lasting benefit, Joseph Ferdinand assured Conrad that he would do his best to comply:

> If in the weeks that followed [the end of the Russian counterattacks of early January] the opposing front line of General Dimitriev's forces was slowly weakened, this did not alter the situation, as Fourth Army also had to send ever more troops to the Carpathians. An isolated attack by Fourth Army remained futile. It was completely unthinkable that, with the limited forces available, any attack would result in major successes, and thus have an impact on the situation in the eastern Carpathians; any such offensive would certainly be extremely costly and would call into question the continued occupation of the Dunajec–Biaiala line.[19]

Just as morale on the German and Austro-Hungarian side sagged, there was suddenly some positive news from the extreme right flank of the operation, where South Army and Pflanzer-Baltin's forces faced perhaps the weakest

Russian positions. A local success by the German XXIV Corps, on the right flank of South Army, led to a sudden advance towards the north, and for a moment, it seemed as if the Russian defences might be unpicked. But as the troops approached the Wyszków Saddle, the main route across one of the many ridgelines of the Carpathians, they encountered fresh Russian defences, and the advance ground to a halt again. Nevertheless, the nearby Verecke Pass was captured, and Szurmay's men were finally able to fight their way clear of the Uzsok Pass towards Turka. As resistance stiffened, Boroević asked Linsingen for help; Szurmay's troops were clearly exhausted, and their depleted ranks could not expect to force a way out of the mountains on their own. The German 3rd Guards Infantry Division was available, and Boroević requested that it be used to clear the way for his men to continue their advance. Linsingen was unenthusiastic, wishing to use the troops on his right flank, where he felt he could make the most of the recent successes. After some prevarication, *AOK* supported Linsingen, but as Szurmay's push towards Turka was brought to a standstill, Linsingen was ordered to support Szurmay by dispatching a strong column to the area. By this stage, the troops of 3rd Guards Infantry Division, who had been in the right area to mount such a push just a day earlier, were already heading east to Linsingen's other flank.

Unable to advance down the Turka road with a frontal attack, Szurmay attempted to extend his line to envelop one or both flanks of the Russian position. His troops struggled through deep snow to attempt the operation, only to find that the Russian defenders had countered with an exactly equivalent redeployment. On 2 February, Szurmay gave up. There was no point in remaining in exposed positions in front of the formidable Russian defences, and he pulled back towards the Uzsok Pass to try to give his men a chance to rest and recover.

This withdrawal came at a bad moment for Linsingen's South Army; 3rd Guards Infantry Division and 1st Infantry Division had succeeded in advancing at the eastern flank of South Army's position, and seemed poised for further success. From their distant viewpoint, Hindenburg and Ludendorff tried in vain to extract details from *AOK* about the events on the battlefield. From their perspective, only the German troops of South Army had actually achieved any significant advance, and this was now placed in jeopardy by Szurmay's withdrawal. Conrad had few details to add – his hands were full dealing with the growing crisis on Third Army's front. In an attempt to help Szurmay recover the ground he had conceded, Conrad requested that Linsingen send 3rd Guards Infantry Division back towards Turka. Having already argued against such a proposal, Linsingen was unwilling to do this. His army and Pflanzer-Baltin's men on the extreme right flank of the offensive faced only weak Russian forces, whereas resistance elsewhere was steadily strengthening. He urged Conrad to allocate troops to his command from both Pflanzer-Baltin and Szurmay, so that South Army could fight its way clear of the mountains and then begin to manoeuvre effectively. Conrad rejected this, preferring to stick to his own plan. Boroević's Third Army was to remain the main force for the offensive.

As Archduke Joseph Ferdinand commented on 27 January, his troops weren't alone in suffering from the elements:

> A new enemy appeared today, but a rather even-handed one because it hinders the Russians as well as us. This is the heavy snow and appalling cold. Terrible reports have come in, especially from 10th *Honvéd* Infantry Division, about the number of frostbite cases, many of them serious. This evening, it started snowing heavily, which may help us as the Russians will find it difficult to move supplies to their advanced positions.[20]

Even when the temperature rose a little, it brought additional problems to the exhausted soldiers on both sides, as Weith recorded:

> At the end of January, there was a sudden thaw, with rain. Everyone was soaked to the bone, with no opportunity to dry themselves. In addition, men's clothes froze to their bodies overnight, like an icy suit of armour. Then, the Russian counterattack struck. Already half-maddened before this tribulation, the soldiers retreated in listless resignation to their starting positions. By now, even the enemy had had enough of fighting. On their side, too, entire companies surrendered. The slaughter finally subsided. There we were, where we had started in the middle of January; but in the intervening time, another army had perished.[21]

By the end of January, the Austro-Hungarian forces had been driven back to their start line on almost all the front, and in some areas – particularly near Mezőlaborcz – had been forced to concede some of their original lines. Briefly, they had marched as far north as Baligród, before Brusilov's counterattacks drove them back in disarray. The Austro-Hungarian VIII Corps, currently in the Balkans, was ordered north without delay, but Conrad issued instructions that its deployment and use was to await the arrival of the entire corps, rather than allow elements to be committed piecemeal. Aware that his front line was stretched perilously thin, Boroević simply ignored this, sending units into action as reinforcements whenever they arrived. Additional troops were ordered to the area from Fourth Army, but in the meantime, VII and X Corps would have to hold the key sector of the line south of the Dukla and Beskid Passes.

István Tisza, the prime minister of Hungary, was growing increasingly alarmed by developments in the Carpathians. Before the war, his parliament had often been seen by Vienna as obstructive and difficult, but Tisza had always remained committed personally to the Austro-Hungarian Empire, and fearing that a Russian invasion of Hungary might trigger secessionist pressures he urged Conrad to do all that he could to hold back Brusilov's troops. Conrad's response was to berate Boroević for failing to achieve victory, given that he had fifteen divisions at his disposal, faced by only twelve Russian divisions.[22] With his divisions reduced to barely the strength of a regiment, and with no artillery support to speak of, Boroević's reaction to this can only be imagined. Relations between Conrad and Boroević, never particularly good, deteriorated further.

The reality was that Boroević's troops were disappearing at a terrifying rate. Over four days, V Corps – part of *Gruppe Puhallo* – reported that its fighting strength had fallen from 10,500 to barely 2,000.[23] Near Mezőlaborcz, 2nd Infantry Division, part of X Corps, had started the battle with 8,150 men, but was now left holding a front line running through forested mountains that stretched 3 miles (5km) with only 1,000 survivors.[24] By 4 February, rail movements through Mezőlaborcz had become impossible due to Russian artillery fire. The defenders of the town were at the end of their strength, and were no longer able to hold back the Russian attack, primarily by VIII Corps. It would be wrong to talk of a retreat; the scattered survivors of the *k.u.k.* Army's X Corps simply faded away, struggling south on their own initiative until they could regroup. Only 2nd Infantry Division seems to have continued functioning as a coherent unit, forming a rearguard. Russian troops entered Mezőlaborcz late on 5 February, where their advance stopped for the moment, largely through exhaustion.

The capture of Mezőlaborcz had serious implications for Boroević's eastern forces. Most of the supplies for *Gruppe Puhallo* and *Gruppe Szurmay* had been brought forward using the railway line that ran through the town, and with this line now in Russian hands, there was little prospect of any campaign to relieve Przemyśl. Given that this was one of the main purposes of Conrad's entire strategy, Boroević cannot have been surprised to be ordered to intervene personally to recapture Mezőlaborcz. Conrad added his displeasure at the fact that Boroević had ignored instructions to hold troops arriving in the theatre back until they were fully assembled, rather than committing them piecemeal. Stung by *AOK*'s criticism of his forces for the setback, he responded angrily that his entire army had no reserves available, and that as the emergency had developed, he had had no choice but to use whatever troops were present. In any event, he added, if he had held the troops back, they still would not have been completely assembled in time to launch the decisive counterattack that Conrad had wished.

Casualties in Boroević's army had been dreadful, even by the standards of the battles of 1914. At the start of the operation, his formations had a total strength of a little under 135,000 men; by the end of the first week of February, nearly 89,000 were dead, wounded, sick or prisoners.[25] Despite the arrival of nearly 31,000 reinforcements, most of whom were poorly trained recruits, the defensive lines were stretched to the limit to hold back Brusilov's troops. Any assistance from the weather, regardless of its effect on their own ranks, was welcomed by the men of Third Army.

Conrad's entire strategy had been based upon swift success, largely brought about by surprise. He had completely failed to take into account the constraints resulting from operating in mountainous terrain in the depths of winter, and throughout the fighting repeatedly behaved as if the symbols on his maps were full-strength formations, despite a steady stream of information about losses and setbacks. His insistence upon attacking in all situations greatly increased casualties, and when the Russians began to gain the upper hand, the repeated refrain of 'defend to the last man', like his refusal to accept that divisions and regiments had been seriously degraded by combat, is very reminiscent of Hitler's behaviour with regard to the Eastern Front in the Second World War. At the height of the fighting, he wrote to his mistress, Gina von Reininghaus:

> The privations of the troops are certainly indescribably hard, but I would rather endure them a thousand times over than the nerve-wracking mental work of high command.[26]

This seems a remarkable statement for a man who refused to allow the realities of conditions on the front line to influence his plans, and never left his headquarters in Teschen even to visit Boroević, let alone the front line itself.

The first campaign in the Carpathians was over. Although it had been a clear victory for the Russians, Ivanov and Brusilov were in no position to capitalise upon their success, as their own ranks had suffered nearly as much as those of the forces they faced. Nevertheless, there seemed no prospect of any lifting of the siege of Przemyśl, and the glittering triumph that Conrad had expected, which would prevent any deterioration of the political situation, remained as remote as ever.

Chapter 3

WINTER IN MASURIA

It was with considerable reluctance that Falkenhayn agreed to the deployment of four additional corps on the Eastern Front in early 1915. Whilst he remained convinced of the primacy of the Western Front, the failure to win a decisive victory there left him unable to counter the arguments of Hindenburg and Ludendorff, who could claim – with variable justification – that their troops had won several important battles, and might be able to inflict a sufficiently heavy defeat upon Russia to end the conflict in the east. Clearly, they had to date been unable to progress from these triumphs to a war-deciding conclusion, but they were able to argue that this was precisely because they had lacked the resources to do so. The counter-argument was that the vastness of Russia made impossible the conversion of tactical and operational successes into a war-winning victory. Whatever Falkenhayn's personal scepticism about such claims, he had no choice but to allow the precious troops to be sent east, though he added a caveat that they were to be released for service in the west as soon as they had achieved their immediate objectives. After some last-minute changes, it was decided to send one experienced corps – XXI Corps – and three of the four new corps to the Eastern Front, where they would arrive in early February. It seems that the decision to send XXI Corps to the east was made at least partly because this formation contained significant numbers of men who had been recruited in Alsace and Lorraine, the parts of France occupied and annexed by Germany at the end of the Franco-Prussian War. It was felt that they would be more likely to fight reliably against Russia than against France, though there was no evidence that they had failed to fight well in the west.[1]

One of the new corps was XL Reserve Corps, under the command of the redoubtable General Karl Litzmann. During the fighting around Łódź, he had commanded a Guards division with distinction, and was awarded the *Pour le Mérite* for his role in the escape of the German forces that were briefly encircled to the east of the city. As was frequently the case, the German general staff provided him with the best possible help in establishing his new formation:

> My chief of staff, at that time Major but later Oberstleutnant Mengelbier, was incomparable as I rapidly discovered, and the longer I worked with him, the more I appreciated this … He was a Rhinelander, from Fusilier Regiment 39, an honest and upright character, an outstanding soldier and a talented and gifted general staff officer, a clever, skilful helper and soon the truest of friends, a caring superior to his subordinates and an excellent comrade. He had earlier held the post of Ia in the staff of II Corps and had already had useful experience in the west and the east. He soon demonstrated a useful talent for organisation in the establishment of my corps, with the gift of guiding his subordinates in such a way that they quickly took up the tasks in their new posts and were filled with enthusiasm. They looked to him with devotion and complete trust. The staff of the subordinate formations and the troops of our corps soon found that the chief of staff was a man of great expertise in all military fields, with a clear and determined mind, and a warm heart.[2]

The German experience with reserve formations in the autumn had been a mixed one. Whilst some – for example, during the Battle of Łódź – performed with the courage and expertise of regular units, others proved far less effective, capable of little more than bloody frontal assaults that achieved nothing more than adding to the already terrible casualty lists. In contrast with the continuing disdain with which the Russians treated their reserve formations, and the chaotic way in which Conrad's armies were forced to throw reservists into the front line to replace losses, the Germans took a more organised approach. Every step was taken to ensure that the creation of this latest wave of new formations would learn from previous experiences. A solid cadre of veteran junior officers and NCOs joined seasoned officers like Litzmann and Mengelbier to improve the likelihood of success. The workload for those tasked with bringing the new formations up to combat-readiness was huge, as Litzmann recorded:

> Every day, I received briefings in Corps Headquarters and soon saw how under the unceasing, pragmatic work of Mengelbier and his assistants the preparation of the corps in all respects and its equipage with horses, vehicles, military equipment of all sorts, ammunition, and ration reserves was taken forwards. A huge amount

of work was of course necessary to be ready for deployment by the designated date.[3]

Assured of reinforcements, Hindenburg and Ludendorff – reunited again at *Ober Ost* – considered where these troops could achieve maximum effect.

> It was agreed with *OHL* to use the four corps to strike against the enemy forces deployed against Eighth Army as soon as they arrived. The experiences of Tannenberg and the Battle of the Masurian Lakes had shown that a great and swift victory in battle could only be achieved if the enemy were attacked from two sides. There was an opportunity here to use a strong group of three corps that had been assembled between the Niemen and the Insterburg–Gumbinnen road to thrust from Tilsit through Wladislawow to Kalwaria [now Kalvarija in Lithuania], and another, XL Reserve Corps, to which 2nd Infantry Division and 4th Cavalry Division were assigned, would advance from between the Spirding-See over the border near Bialla to Raigrod and on to Augustowo and the area to the south. At the same time, the enemy was to be held in position by frontal attacks.
>
> The enemy was weak on both flanks. We could hope to gain considerable ground before the main enemy force could break contact from the attacks along its front. Both assault groups were to encircle the enemy; the sooner this occurred, the better.
>
> If it were possible to destroy the enemy, the question would then arise of attacking towards Osowiec and Grodno while guarding towards Kovno [Kaunas], gaining a crossing over the Bobr at Osowiec. A prerequisite was that the long flank from Wloclawek through Mlawa, Johannisburg and Osowiec remained intact.[4]

In addition to this, Ludendorff wished to attack across this long southern flank of the operation, so that a second German force could threaten Osowiec from the southwest, but Hindenburg judged this to be beyond the strength of the forces at his disposal. The operation would be limited to the encirclement of the Russian forces facing the German Eighth Army; this was ambitious enough in the middle of winter.

The Russians were of course preparing their troops for an operation of their own against East Prussia. Artillery ammunition remained in short supply, but by the end of January, the staff of the quartermaster-general estimated that they could raise stocks in the front line in the north to about 430 rounds per gun, which they estimated would be enough to carry out the planned strike into East Prussia.

Nevertheless, there was a requirement to avoid battle in all areas where it could be avoided, something that proved to be the case on both sides of the front line:

> The commander [of Fourth Army], General Evert had been ordered by General Ivanov to retire from the Pilica if the river froze [and thus ceased to be an obstacle]. Evert sent a party of sappers to destroy a long dam which made freezing more probable. This party was at work at night preparing the lodgements for the explosives when it was alarmed by suspicious noises on the opposite bank. Tools were thrown down and rifles seized, but reconnaissance revealed the fact that the enemy was at the same game. Apparently they lived in terror of a Russian advance in this sector of the front, and also wished to prevent the Pilica from freezing. It is said that both sides blew up sections after dawn. So the Pilica did not freeze and both generals slept in peace.[5]

In January, General Oranovsky, the chief of staff of Northwest Front, was appointed as commander of the cavalry of the new Twelfth Army, which would strike into East Prussia from the south. His replacement on Ruzsky's staff was Arseny Gulevich, a member of Grand Duke Nikolai's anti-Sukhomlinov circle, perhaps as a counterweight to Ruzsky himself. The account left by Knox of his appointment speaks volumes about the gulf between staff officers in the Russian Army and their equivalents on the other side of the front line:

> Gulevich was very clever and a man of charming manners, but lazy – in fact, 'a gross, fat man', who had put on much flesh since the war started, for he 'rested' in bed daily from 2 to 5pm and never took any exercise. It is said that he was present when the telegram informing him of his new appointment was deciphered. Russians use the same word for 'chief' in 'chief of staff' and for 'commander' in, for instance, 'commander of a division'. When the words 'Gulevich is appointed commander' were deciphered, he held his head in his hands in despair, for he had a horror of the comparatively active life he would have been forced to lead as the commander of a division. He was greatly relieved when the context revealed the nature of his new appointment, and at once gave orders for a thanksgiving service. My cynical informant added that few officers attended this service, for they had all rushed off to scribble memoranda for the general's guidance of the honours and rewards they wished to receive.[6]

The Russian Tenth Army, which was the target of the German attack, was still recovering from its futile attempts to storm the German defences along the

81

Lyck–Wirballen line. As has already been described, the Baltic German Thadeus von Sievers, commander of Tenth Army, had tried in vain to alert Northwest Front to the problems caused by lack of reserves behind his front line; nearly all of his men were committed to the long front, and if the Germans were to break through anywhere, it would prove almost impossible to intercept them. The southern flank of Sievers' Tenth Army was protected by a thin screen of infantry and cavalry, behind which Plehve's new Twelfth Army was beginning to assemble. The cavalry along the border was due to be reinforced into a substantial body prior to the proposed invasion of East Prussia, but as Ludendorff began to issue orders in early February, these troops were only partly assembled, lacking supplies and adequate logistic support to function effectively. In the main, Sievers would have to face the new German attack alone.

After discussing matters with his staff, Sievers decided that the forests in front of his northern flank would provide good cover for the Germans to assemble an assault force, and ordered Nikolai Epanchin's III Corps to secure this area. Like other Russian officers – and, indeed, officers in many European armies – Sievers was concerned that prolonged spells in static trench warfare would sap the morale and offensive spirit of his men.[7] The fact that committing a significant part of his strength to this attack would further increase the problem of inadequate reserves was something that Sievers either ignored, or regarded as worth the risk. In order to give this operation any chance of success, Sievers had to scrape together reinforcements from the rest of his army, leaving the line greatly denuded. The operation made very little headway, and was abandoned after six days; it merely resulted in more troops being tied down in a front line that grew ever longer.[8] Even if it had succeeded in clearing the Germans from the wooded area, this would have been of questionable value, as a Russian officer later wrote:

> For Epanchin to 'take action to clear the forest' [the orders he had received from Sievers] says nothing about the overall operational concept. It intuitively begs the question – what was to be done once the forest was cleared? The task assigned to Epanchin's corps was vague, unrelated to any overall concept of time, purpose or direction.[9]

Writing after the war, Danilov blamed Sievers for not preparing a secondary line of defensive fortifications, and for failing to position adequate reserves behind his front line.[10] Whilst the former seems to be a reasonable criticism, the latter is less so. Sievers barely had enough men to hold his long front line, let alone free up sufficient units to create the reserves that would be essential to prevent a German breakthrough, though his attempts to advance in the forests south of the River Niemen – with the knowledge and approval of Ruzsky's Northwest Front – exacerbated the lack of troops. When Sievers requested reinforcements from Northwest Front, his concerns about his line were simply disregarded.

Ruzsky's rejection of Sievers' warnings about the weakness of the front was probably part of the ongoing feud within the Russian Army. Sievers was popular with Grand Duke Nikolai and was a member of the anti-Sukhomlinov faction, whereas Ruzsky was a firm adherent of the Russian minister for war. If *Stavka* had functioned as a proper high command, it would have suppressed such factionalism, but *Stavka* itself was a product of the Russian military system that Sukhomlinov had designed and developed before the war; even if Grand Duke Nikolai had been a sufficiently forceful person to attempt to impose his will, the minister for war had ensured that the rules by which it worked would prevent Sukhomlinov himself from losing his grip upon matters.

Morale in Tenth Army was not good. The troops spent prolonged periods in waterlogged trenches, harassed by German night raids. Despite the assurances of the quartermaster-general's office, artillery ammunition remained in short supply, leaving the infantry feeling that they were unsupported by their gunners. Sievers repeatedly ordered his formations to keep up local attacks, but if these were intended to prevent the men from becoming too accustomed to static warfare, they failed; their only result was a steady increase in casualties, and further loss of morale.[11]

In addition to the four corps being sent to the Eastern Front, Ludendorff intended to redeploy formations already facing the Russians. XX Corps, I Reserve Corps, 6th Cavalry Division, 3rd Infantry Division, and 1st Guards Reserve Division would all find themselves drawn into the new campaign at some point. This would leave other parts of the German sector of the Eastern Front thinly held, but this was a risk that Hindenburg and Ludendorff freely took – they had done so before with impunity, relying on their faster speed of lateral movement to allow them to react before the Russians could take advantage of any local weakness. In addition, Falkenhayn's experiences on the Western Front, and to a lesser extent the experiences of the autumn fighting in the east, were put to use. Many recent battles had shown how a suitable defensive position, with adequate reserves in support, could beat off almost any attack without requiring large numbers of men to hold it. With much of the German part of the Eastern Front now switching to a defensive posture, it was possible to release formations for use in the critical sector. The Germans were aided in this by an awareness that the Russians, too, were running down their central sector, in line with the growing demands of the fighting in the Carpathians and the need to build up Plehve's

Twelfth Army and its flank supports for the forthcoming attack on East Prussia.

Partly to hinder such redeployment by the Russians, *Ober Ost* still wished to attack with Mackensen's Ninth Army in central Poland. It was also possible that a powerful attack might encourage the Russians to believe that the Germans were planning a major effort in that sector, and this might even result in Russian troops being diverted away from East Prussia. To mount this attack, Mackensen concentrated I Reserve Corps, XIII and XVII Corps, reinforced by other formations, near the village of Bolimów, a little to the east of Lowicz, with a sizeable body of artillery. Mackensen planned for most of the preparatory work to be done by the guns, and he had some justification for feeling confident that this might give his attacking infantry a decisive edge: his gunners were about to deploy a new weapon.

It is likely that the first use of chemical weapons in the war was as early as August 1914, when French guns fired shells containing a tear gas agent, probably ethyl bromoacetate, which had previously been used against rioters by the French police in 1912. The use of poison gases was banned by the 1899 Hague Declaration Concerning Asphyxiating Gases, but the French argued, as did other European nations, that this treaty did not ban the use of an irritant agent like tear gas. Although the military effect of this bombardment was zero – at the time, the Germans didn't even detect the presence of the gas, which was fired in 26mm grenades – it was used as justification by the Germans for their own chemical warfare programme, which first saw use in October 1914 against British troops near Neuve-Chapelle. Again, there was little major impact, but research and production continued, and the guns that Mackensen assembled for use at Bolimów received about 18,000 shells filled with xylyl bromide, another tear gas agent.

On the last day of January, the German guns began their bombardment. It was a bitterly cold day, with snow lying on the ground, and many German shells failed to detonate when they landed. Those that did explode released their potentially lethal chemical, but in the freezing air, very little vaporised. To make matters worse, the prevailing wind was from the east, and small amounts of gas drifted back over German lines, though once more, its effect was minimal. Aware that the bombardment had failed, Mackensen called off the infantry attack that was to follow. Smirnov's Second Army had gathered five infantry divisions in the area under the command of Vasily Gurko's VI Corps, and these forces now launched a counterattack. In his memoirs, Gurko, who had previously commanded cavalry forces in the war, relates that several of his men were overcome by the German gas attack, but he drove back the Germans and inflicted heavy losses on them; by contrast, Mackensen recorded that his troops smashed the Russian counterattacks with heavy artillery fire and took several thousand prisoners.[12] But despite this success, Mackensen continued, his men failed to gain as much ground as he might have hoped:

> I would have hoped to take fewer prisoners and to gain more ground. The Russians are the toughest opponents when defending. That is to their credit. Men's lives play no part in their calculations, and they thus endure the heaviest losses … our losses are not heavy, but on our side we value every man, and I grieve for every infantryman rendered unfit for combat. The best of them are already lying in large numbers on the battlefields. As before, the troops remain full of high spirits, and I am certain will persevere.[13]

It was an inauspicious start to major use of chemical weapons in the modern era. The impact upon Gurko's men was so minimal that few reports reached *Stavka*, and almost no information reached the other Entente Powers about the incident. German planners looked at the battle as a learning opportunity, and the next time that the German Army deployed chemical weapons, when it used chlorine in its assault on the Ypres salient a few months later, the impact was far greater.

The Russians had also started to consider the use of chemical weaponry. General Grigory Zabudsky was appointed the head of the army's new Central Scientific and Technical Laboratory, and just a few days before the German attack at Bolimów, on 26 January, he called a meeting, in which several matters were discussed including the use of suffocating and intoxicating gases in shells. Most of the officers present were against the idea, regarding it as both distasteful and something that the Russian Army had never attempted before. Despite this, Zabudsky ordered research and development to begin, with a view to beginning production rapidly should the need arise.[14] Shortly after, Nikola Zelinsky, a scientist in Moscow University, started experiments with gas masks using charcoal filters. After additional input from an engineer, Eduard Kummant, the first practical masks appeared in 1916, though it would be many months before they were available in significant quantities.[15]

The experience of the front-line soldiers at Bolimów was dominated by the terrible conditions created by the weather rather than the novel weaponry being used, as one German veteran later recalled:

> It was 27 degrees below zero in Bolimów … We wore only thin coats, which left us constantly frozen. Consequently, we also had head, wrist and chest wraps,

kneepads, and woollen jackets. It grew dark at 3 p.m. and it was generally light again at 9 a.m. We had to go out and stand watch every two hours. It was so cold that when you had to go out from your foxhole, where you could attend to your needs, your trousers were already full because you wore them all the time, as your fingers were rigid from the bitter cold.[16]

Inevitably, there were casualties due to frostbite, and the men often had to improvise as best as they could to cope with the weather. The environment also created problems other than the cold:

I had second and third degree frostbite of my ears. I was taken to a field hospital, and the field surgeon cut off my ears. I thought nothing of it. We really weren't equipped for this country. We had coats and blankets, but these were inadequate for there. Those on watch were often relieved every hour. In any case, we had mounted double watches. One man constantly had to come out of the dugout just to check that the watchman was still there. We had to shovel the drifting snow out of the dugouts before we could go back into them … for each of us who had to stand watch outside, there was a Russian fur. We had a very young Jew in our battery, whose father owned a clog factory near Itzehoe. He got clogs for our battery. So, we stood with our normal boots inside felt boots, and with giant clogs over these felt boots. We had to deal with the dreadful wind whenever we did anything. We had to build field positions in the winter. It's no exaggeration to say that the ground was frozen up to two metres down. You could only hack at it with pickaxes. By the evening, when we had broken through the frozen layer, we filled everything with snow to stop it freezing again.

But the worst thing that I experienced in the east as well as the cold was the vermin. You really can't believe what we endured there. A few older comrades thankfully knew how to build dugouts, and we learned from them. We used timber from Russian farm buildings. But the Russian buildings were full of bugs, lice and fleas. They were full of vermin. Whenever you saw someone who suddenly started to scratch himself, there would be a cry of 'You've got lice, you pig!' But everyone else had them, they just didn't know yet. The beasts hid in the recesses of your body.[17]

The area in which the Germans were deployed was in fact Polish rather than Russian, but it was part of the Russian Empire, and such distinctions meant little to the soldiers on the ground. De-lousing stations were set up, but even when the treatment succeeded, the troops were rapidly re-infested.

Although conditions before Bolimów were grim, some soldiers counted their blessings amidst the horror of war:

The fighting was comparable with France in terms of violence and intensity. In the far distance, we could see reflected light from Warsaw, our ultimate objective. I often stood there in January 1915 and thought, 'You're 19 years old and this is your life.' As a reasonable thinking person, you had to admit to yourself, 'You're stupid to be in the military.' But one thing I must say is that it was also fortunate that I had volunteered. As a result, I was sent east from Breslau, and at least wasn't stuck in a supply depot but was in the real war, but still not as awful, as technical and mechanised, with flamethrowers and gas shells, as in the west. In the east, you could acclimatise as a young soldier and become familiar with the equipment. If I had been sent west, I wouldn't have lasted long.

… We learned from the food-bearers that many guns were forming up behind us. We were in swampy ground in which you couldn't dig in deep, but had to shelter behind a forward-facing wall. I lay with my group at the end of a rifle trench that ended at the swamp. A machine-gun had been set up there to cover the open area. But the others, which were positioned further to the right, had to be hauled up onto the wall if the enemy attacked. After we had been there for four or five days, there was a huge thunder one morning with close-range and long-range guns firing, large and small calibre. We had already been told that we were to attack at such-and-such a time. My comrades from Breslau, with whom I had undergone three months' training in barracks – there were students and teachers amongst them – all had to go. I was lucky in that with the machine-gun crew, my group was able to leave the foxhole and run towards the enemy. And my guardian angel looked after me again. We didn't have to run across the meadow, because there was a drainage ditch about a metre wide that had frozen, and we were able to run along it. I had my gun in my hands, and ran bent over, hearing again and again the 'Snap! Snap!' of machine-gun salvoes overhead. We got across without casualties. And the others, who had to cross the open ground, were dead. We hadn't reached Warsaw, and were in a village where we received replacements, all youngsters of 19 or 20 with brand-new uniforms. They came from Paderborn. Far in the distance, if you had binoculars you could see a Russian tethered balloon in the sky. Things had been set up in the village square. A few people had set out their cooking gear, lit fires and were frying bacon. I kept an eye on the tethered balloon and thought to myself: 'Leave your bacon for now, even if it burns.' I moved to the shelter of the wall of a house. It didn't take long. The Russians aimed right at the cooking setup in the square. There were screams, twenty or thirty dead. And I too was hit by shrapnel from a shell. My right ear bled, that was all. I was so shocked. I saw heads that had been blown off. Or the side of the body was torn away. It was a slaughterhouse.[18]

Preparations continued for the main German attack against the Russian Tenth Army. By 6 February, the four corps of reinforcements had finished their initial formation and were beginning to assemble in East Prussia, and Hindenburg and Ludendorff moved their headquarters to Insterburg to be closer to the coming battle. The new German Tenth Army was now established under the command of General Hermann von Eichhorn. Max Hoffmann, a staff officer who had played an important part in the Tannenberg campaign – he would later claim that he had devised the critical orders that placed German forces on the flanks of Samsonov's Second Army – and, during Ludendorff's brief absence in the Carpathians, had served as Hindenburg's chief of staff, had suggested the crown prince as the commander of the new army, but his suggestion was not adopted. Prince Wilhelm was currently in command of Fifth Army on the Western Front, though he had very little genuine military experience, but by contrast, Eichhorn was a career officer, who had missed the opening phases of the war as a result of injuries sustained in May as a consequence of falling from a horse. He recovered in time to take part in the fighting at Soissons, and was thus familiar with the nature of fighting in this new war. Whilst he was a newcomer to the Eastern Front, he was greatly aided by his chief of staff, Emil Hell, who had been chief of staff of XX Corps at Tannenberg, and had extensive experience of fighting the Russians.

A further advantage held by Eichhorn over a royal appointment was that he was part of the close brotherhood of German officers. He had been a classmate of Litzmann during their time in the *Kriegsakademie*, and had remained a friend ever since; Hell, too, had a link with Litzmann, having studied under him when the latter was an instructor at the academy. Regardless of the bitter conflict between *Ober Ost* and Falkenhayn, the sense of military brotherhood in the German Army remained strong, and relationships built up over many years remained far more important in the eyes of most officers than any recent disagreements.

The suggestion of a royal appointment was clearly political. Whilst Haeften's intriguing on behalf of Hindenburg and Ludendorff had been brought to an abrupt end, the feud was far from over, and it seems that Hoffmann wished to build on Haeften's recruitment of the crown prince to the cause of *Ober Ost*. The kaiser's repeated backing of Falkenhayn – whose rapid promotion and advancement had been at least partly due to Wilhelm's support – led Hoffmann to record at a later date that Wilhelm had little love for the senior commanders on the Eastern Front.[19] The appointment of one of Wilhelm's family to high command in the east, particularly if he could be kept 'under control' by a suitably skilful chief of staff, would therefore have been a move calculated to enhance the standing of *Ober Ost* in the kaiser's eyes.

Whilst it could have been possible for all troops in the forthcoming campaign to be assigned to a single command, Ludendorff was keen to have two headquarters, with one responsible for each arm of the grand encirclement; experience of trying to coordinate troops during the Tannenberg campaign, and again during operations in Poland, had shown the difficulty of communications over large distances. Eichhorn's new army deployed in the most northern part of East Prussia, from the River Niemen to the area northeast of Insterburg, with XXI Corps in the north, XXXIX Reserve Corps in the centre, and XXXVIII Reserve Corps to the south. In front of them, masking their presence from the Russians, were 1st Cavalry Division, which had operated in this area with some distinction at the very beginning of the war, and 5th Guards Infantry Brigade. The southern flank of Tenth Army consisted of reservist formations containing large numbers of *Landwehr*, mainly from the East Prussian capital, Königsberg; Eichhorn wished to avoid using these men in the toughest of the fighting.

Below's Eighth Army would form the southern group in the planned encirclement operation. Its most northerly formation was 2nd Infantry Division, immediately to the west of Johannisburg, with XL Reserve Corps to its south. As was the case with Eichhorn's army, a cavalry formation – this time 4th Cavalry Division – was deployed forward of the main group to cover its presence from the Russians. XX Corps, transferred from Ninth Army further south, covered Below's right flank at Ortelsburg. The main thrust would be delivered by Litzmann's XL Reserve Corps. On its southern flank, General Max von Gallwitz would attempt to take advantage of the main operation in order to thrust south into Poland, in a somewhat truncated version of Ludendorff's original intention of a major thrust towards Osowiec.

Even as Litzmann and the men of his XL Reserve Corps set out for the Eastern Front from their barracks in Altona, just outside Hamburg, they still had no clear idea of their destination, such was the secrecy with which the Germans made their preparations:

In addition [to keeping plans secret], the deployment of my corps was masked perfectly by the terrain; it took place in and behind the excellent forestland that was also deeply covered in snow. The eastern approaches were naturally covered by the line of the lakes, in addition to which the border positions were blocked by barbed wire and fortifications. Determined East Prussian *Landsturm* held off the enemy's reconnaissance; the Russians couldn't spot us.[20]

The German plan was ambitious by any standard. Although Hindenburg's formations had broken through the Russian lines during the advance to Łódź, and earlier had achieved great success at Tannenberg and – to a lesser extent – during the September fighting at the Masurian Lakes, they had failed to penetrate the prepared Russian defences outside Warsaw in October, and again in central Poland in December. The new campaign would require two breakthroughs, one on each flank of the Russian position. Then, in the depths of winter, the two assault groups would have to press home their advance with alacrity in order to close the trap before the Russians could withdraw. After their brief invasion of Lithuania in the previous autumn, the Germans knew first-hand that the quality of roads they would be using did not compare with the roads on their side of the frontier; yet there appeared to be no doubt amongst the planners, all of whom seemed confident that they would be able to achieve their aims, in stark contrast to the disastrous failures by Austro-Hungarian (and also German) troops in the Carpathian Mountains. In some respects, the coming battle would be an examination of the arguments on strategy between *Ober Ost* and *OHL*. Would it be possible to repeat the victory of Tannenberg, as Hindenburg and Ludendorff planned, or would Falkenhayn be proved right by a rapid Russian withdrawal?

On 4 February, after a two-day train journey from Hamburg, Litzmann and Mengelbier met Below at the headquarters of Eighth Army, where they received a full briefing on the situation. In addition to his own corps and 2nd Infantry Division, Litzmann was assigned additional combat engineers and five batteries of heavy artillery. Below confirmed Litzmann's fears that the Russians might attempt to interfere with the advance by attacking from the south – there was already evidence of Russian troops moving into this area, in accordance with Ruzsky's plans for Plehve's new army to strike into East Prussia. But the German officers agreed that risk was manageable, particularly as the Russians were clearly far from ready to mount their attack. Litzmann would take steps to protect his flank, and additional forces were already moving into the area from Mackensen's Ninth Army.

Unlike Conrad's assault in the south, there were considerable efforts to allow for the weather. All troops had been issued with adequate winter clothing, and many horse-drawn vehicles had been converted into sledges with wooden or iron runners. But when Litzmann led the first elements of the German forces forward on 7 February, heavy snow had already been falling for two days. Deep drifts

The Masurian Campaign, February 1915

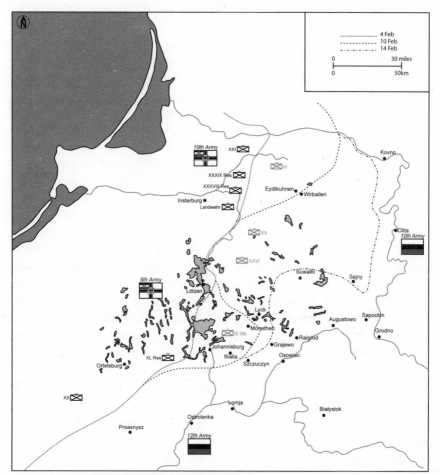

often blocked the way and despite the careful preparations of the German planners, movement on roads was difficult, across country almost impossible. Throughout his memoirs, Ludendorff frequently erred on the side of over-emphasising the difficulties that he and others on the Eastern Front had to overcome, but on this occasion, some of his hyperbole seems justified:

> The achievement of men and horses in the following days is indescribable, and a glorious deed for all time. The spearheads of the march columns laboriously

worked their way through the drifts. Vehicles became stuck, columns were stalled, and grew ever longer. The infantry pushed past vehicles and guns and tried to link up with those further ahead. Guns and ammunition wagons were pulled by ten to twelve horses. The march routes thus became full of infantry pressing forward, with only a few guns amongst them, and little ammunition. At night, or when encountering resistance, the columns drew together a little again. After a few days the weather broke, the roads became bottomless, and on the still-frozen ground away from the roads and on the swamps stood deep water. It was fortunate that over a wide area, we captured the enemy's supply columns and food, as the entire advance would otherwise have been forced to stop due to food shortages.

For the high command and lower commands, there were extraordinary difficulties. Whenever we ran into the enemy, it took time until combat-worthy formations could be gathered. Orders didn't get through, wires were torn away in the storms, and messages did not get through. Despite this, the greatest goals were attained.[21]

The first day of the German attack began with Litzmann's corps advancing through the forests to the east of Johannisburg. The three infantry divisions lined up side by side, with Adalbert von Falk's 2nd Infantry Division on the northern flank, 80th Reserve Infantry Division in the centre, and 79th Reserve Infantry Division on the southern flank. Falk had commanded his division from the beginning of the war, leading it in the battles of Stallupönen, Gumbinnen and Tannenberg; taking advantage of a heavy snowstorm, his men surprised the Russian 57th Infantry Division, which was holding a strong position just to the west of Johannisburg, and took the first haul of prisoners from the battle. Immediately, Falk divided his division in two, sending half to cut the road to Johannisburg from the north, and the rest straight towards the town. Labouring forward through the heavy snow, 80th Reserve Infantry Division reached and crossed the River Pisseck, which ran south from Johannisburg. The following day, Litzmann set the objective for his corps as the town of Bialla, about 10 miles (17km) east of Johannisburg. As the day progressed came news of further successes by Falk; he had stormed Johannisburg, capturing about 3,600 Russians. On the right flank, 79th Reserve Infantry Division crossed the line of the Pisseck, and had to contend with repeated attacks on its southern flank from parts of the fragmented Russian 57th Infantry Division. Nevertheless, the advance continued, with 80th Reserve Infantry Division reaching Bialla towards the end of the day.

This counterattack from the south was made by elements of the Russian 57th Infantry Division, which had borne the brunt of the initial German attack.

Largely made up of reservists from the city of Kaluga, the morale and fighting power of the division demonstrated the gulf in the approach of the two armies to their reservists. Like all reserve divisions, this formation had been treated with disdain by the Russian Army before the war began and given low priority in terms of supplies, equipment and good officers, whereas the German reserve formations with their cadre of experienced officers and NCOs demonstrated the improvements that the German Army had made to such units since the beginning of the war. In vain, Omelyanovich, the commander of the Russian 57th Infantry Division, gathered together what men he could, and attempted to launch a counterattack through the steadily falling snow, but the German flank guard beat off the attack with ease. Omelyanovich was forced to retreat towards Osowiec, sending a report to Sievers that he had been driven back by at least two German divisions, which were advancing towards Szczuczyn.

Sievers' reaction to the news of the German attack was concern, but it was limited to worrying about whether this attack might be part of a German plan to drive his army away to the northeast after turning its southern flank. This would then potentially create an opportunity for the Germans to drive south into the rear of the Russian forces spread across central Poland, and Sievers attempted to contain the situation. In accordance with orders sent to him by Ruzsky, he sent instructions to General Evgeny Radkevich, commander of III Siberian Corps, to regroup and to pull back to a new line running from Lyck towards the southeast; the northern formations of Tenth Army would also pull back to conform with this. In addition to his own corps, Radkevich was to take control of the neighbouring XXVI Corps, and using elements of this he was able to cobble together an extra improvised division.

The German force advanced in the face of little resistance until it encountered the new line being established by the Russians. At the junction of III Siberian Corps and XXVI Corps, the improvised division that Radkevich had created took up positions in the town of Lyck, determined to hold on at all costs; the roads leading east and southeast from here were vital lines of retreat for the Russian forces. Despite being significantly below their establishment strength, the regiments in Lyck had reasons for confidence. The western approaches of Lyck were protected by the waters of the Lyck-See, with the Gross Selment-See to the southeast. As a result, the only route by which the Germans could enter the town was across the relatively narrow neck of land to the south of Lyck, between the two lakes.

At the northern end of the battlefield, the new German Tenth Army joined the offensive on 8 February. During the abortive attempts to attack the German positions in late January, Epanchin's III Corps had noted that there were fresh German troops in the area, but the report sent to Sievers merely spoke of a solitary battalion of Germans, later upgraded a little, though not sufficiently to cause concern. The sector chosen by the Germans for their attack was held primarily by Levitsky's 73rd Infantry Division and the Leontovich detachment, the latter composed mainly of the cavalry of III Corps. Throughout the war, the cavalry of every nation had failed to live up to expectations of its prowess, and this battle was no different, with Leontovich making little effort to slow down the German outflanking movement around the northern flank of III Corps. Elements of the Russian 56th Infantry Division were driven back in disarray, and the German advance gathered pace on the following day, helped by Sievers' order for all of his army to pull back in conformation with III Siberian Corps' withdrawal on the southern flank. Even as Epanchin sent reports that in addition to being driven back, his position was being outflanked to the north, Sievers – perhaps still believing the initial reports that the German forces involved were modest in strength – replied:

> There is no reason to attach great importance to the movement of enemy forces bypassing your right flank. You can parry this movement with cavalry and the brigade of 68th Infantry Division [held in army reserve] that has been sent to you.[22]

But far from being able to parry the German advance, Epanchin was rapidly losing control of events. With confusion spreading quickly, Levitsky's 73rd Infantry Division fell back to a secondary defensive line in an uncoordinated manner, only to find that some German formations had got there first. As the retreat turned almost inevitably into a rout, most of the division's guns were abandoned on the snowbound roads, and throughout 9 February the orders from corps headquarters, delayed by the difficulties of movement in the prevailing weather, were unable to keep up with developments on the battlefield. Levitsky's withdrawal exposed Yuzefovich's 56th Infantry Division, which had already been driven back in confusion, and Sievers could only watch in frustration as Epanchin's increasingly disorganised corps was herded back to the east. By the end of 9 February, Eichhorn had advanced a remarkable 25 miles (40km), and covered nearly as much ground again in the next two days. Having lost much of his corps' equipment and support columns, Epanchin ordered a withdrawal towards the fortresses of Kovno (now Kaunas) and Olita (now Alytus). Eichhorn was able to leave only modest forces facing east, mainly the *Landwehr* that he had not wanted to use in his main attack, and turned the rest of his army south in strength as planned. Epanchin's battered III Corps had effectively been knocked out of the battle, which was a serious blow to Sievers' army, but it was made far worse by the failure – as was so often the case in the Russian Army – of the withdrawing elements of III Corps to warn the formations to their south, from XX Corps, of their movements.

Alfred Töpfer, a German infantryman with the Königsberg *Landwehr* later recalled the experience of fighting and marching in the snow:

On the first day – there was about 40cm [16 inches] of snow on the ground – we had to undertake a march of 40km [25 miles]. We crossed the Russian frontier and in darkness entered a snowy landscape, with scattered woodland all around, where we spent the night. One of us stood watch and had to prod everyone every ten minutes to make sure nobody had succumbed to the cold. When it grew light the next morning, we had a huge surprise. Just a few metres from us lay a few hundred Russians. Just like us, they had slept in the snow out there. Strong, young Siberian guys, who were bigger than us. In terms of clothing, they were much better equipped than us. Naturally, both sides were surprised, the Russians as well as us. Who would be the first to summon their courage and take the others prisoner? We were the first to shout out: 'Hands up!' We told the Russians, 'Give us your good boots, we'll give you our jackboots.'

... Late in the afternoon, we were involved in a fight, but we continued without a pause ... I was a machine-gunner and had an assistant rifleman with me. Our machine-guns were set up 10–20m apart. At first light, several ranks of Russians marched up on a frontage of 800–900m and I fired on them with the machine-gun. The assistant rifleman to my left said, 'Töpfer, let me have a go with the gun.' He took my arm and pulled me out of the way. Then he began to fire. It saved my life. Less than a minute later, the machine-gun took a direct hit and he was killed by a head wound. The machine-gun was destroyed. I said to my guys, 'We have to retreat, we can't hold on any longer.' About 1km [half a mile] to the rear the division commander asked us, 'So, what's going on?' Because of an intervening hill, he hadn't been able to see. I told him of the advancing Russians and showed him the remains of my machine-gun, and explained how the gunner had been killed. Then the general said, 'That's fine, we'll pull back now. We're here to protect the encircling forces, and we've been successful until now. We can pull back safely.'[23]

Pressure inevitably now fell upon the Russian XX Corps. With the German XXI Corps and XXXIX Reserve Corps bearing down on his northern flank, the commander of XX Corps, General Pavel Bulgakov, was forced to deploy 27th Infantry Division in a line facing north, trying in vain to retain contact with the retreating elements of III Corps. Having achieved their breakthrough, the German infantry did not get bogged down in a fight with Bulgakov's divisions; instead, they simply marched on through the widening gap between XX and III Corps. In such circumstances, the doctrine that Conrad had preached to the *k.u.k.* Army would have required the attacking forces to attempt to destroy 27th Infantry Division, but the Germans had no intention of wasting their strength in such attacks. Their officers preferred to win the battle by encirclement rather than physical destruction of the enemy's troops.

The message from Ruzsky to Sievers specifying the new defensive line for Tenth Army was predicated upon a belief that this German attack could be repulsed without upsetting Russian plans for an offensive into East Prussia. To this end, Augustowo was to be held at all costs, as it would provide a good base for the planned invasion of East Prussia. In response, Sievers pleaded for reinforcements; III Corps had been driven from the battlefield, and III Siberian Corps had suffered serious losses. Although he could not offer any reinforcements, Ruzsky was able to tell Sievers that the new Twelfth Army's vanguard had arrived and was ready to attack the German positions on the right bank of the River Narew. Whilst this was welcome, and might have sufficed to neutralise the threat to his southern flank, Sievers knew that it was not enough to salvage the situation now that there was another threat from the north.

Litzmann's corps headquarters moved into the ruins of Bialla on 9 February on the heels of 79th Reserve Infantry Division, finding much of the town ablaze. A little to the north, 80th Reserve Infantry Division and parts of 2nd Infantry Division ran into retreating elements of III Siberian Corps in Drygallen, whilst the rest of 2nd Infantry Division, covering the northern flank of Litzmann's advance, beat off a thrust by Alexander Gerngross's XXVI Corps from the north. This flank of the German thrust was meant to be supported by the troops of 3rd Cavalry Brigade, but despite Litzmann's constant urging, the German cavalry made only slow progress through the snow. On 10 February, losing patience at what he perceived as a lack of urgency, Litzmann dismissed the brigade commander, assigning command to Oberstleutnant Graf von Schmettow. There was, recorded Litzmann, an immediate improvement in the performance of the cavalry brigade.[24]

A growing concern for the Germans was their lack of knowledge about Russian movements. In battles the previous year, they had benefited from intercepting Russian radio signals, many of them sent uncoded, but for the moment, at least, it seemed that the Russians had learned from their earlier mistakes and were taking better precautions about security. The best information available to Litzmann came from his intrepid aerial observers, who repeatedly risked life and limb to fly over the front lines to try to spot Russian movements. In their fragile and unreliable aircraft, completely exposed to the elements and aided by only rudimentary instruments, they repeatedly ventured forth whenever the weather allowed. At 2 p.m. on 10 February, they reported that substantial Russian forces were falling back from Arys to Lyck, and that other columns had been seen further north, all heading east. Litzmann decided that he needed to continue his own drive eastwards before trying to turn north to link up with Eichhorn's Tenth Army; if he were to turn north too soon, there was far less likelihood of surrounding significant Russian forces. Within an hour of receiving the aviators' reports, Litzmann issued orders requiring 79th Reserve Infantry Division to press on from Bialla to cut the Lyck–Grajewo road, with 80th Reserve Infantry Division to its north. Falk's 2nd Infantry Division would have to drive its way into Lyck alone, while the reinvigorated cavalry attempted to intercept Russian columns retreating east from Lyck.

The weather worsened on 11 February, with heavy snow driven by a strong eastern wind. In temperatures of -15°C, the soldiers of both sides struggled as best they could to keep moving. Rather than confine themselves to defending Lyck, the Russian troops of the garrison deployed a short distance to the southwest of the town, in order to allow full use of the roads leaving Lyck for the southeast and east. Falk's 2nd Infantry Division ran into these defences, and found its northwest flank under increasing Russian pressure; luckily for Falk, his reserve formation, 4th Grenadier Regiment, was one of the toughest and most prestigious in the entire army. Known throughout its history by its full title of *König Friedrich der Grosse*, it was arguably the oldest formation of the old Prussian Army, and rapidly defeated and routed the Russian move against Falk's flank. But when the regiment attempted to outflank the Russian line that had stopped Falk's advance towards Lyck, it made little headway. From his new headquarters location in Monethen, less than 3 miles (5km) behind Falk's division, Litzmann dispatched General von Buttlar's 5th Infantry Brigade, his main corps reserve, to support Falk's southeastern flank, and the Russian line, made up mainly of surviving elements of III Siberian Corps, began to fall back.

At this stage of the battle, Litzmann found himself dealing with an unexpected request for help:

The fury of the snowstorm drove us to shelter in the roadside inn east of Monethen; it was impossible to use maps outside. The inn was full of seriously wounded men;

we found only one small room free, with a wobbly table, on which Mengelbier spread his map. But before he could begin his report, there was a knock on the door from the neighbouring kitchen; the division pastor, Dr Seeberg, entered and asked permission to baptize a little girl whose father was serving in the field with us, and whose young mother had been robbed by the Cossacks and was in great need. She wished for nothing more than the baptism of her child, who had been born eight days earlier, and the evangelical pastor of the region had been taken away by the Russians and perhaps might never return. I gave Seeberg four minutes, and in this short interval the holy task was fully carried out, with the thunder of guns in the background, as well as the quiet groans of the badly wounded men in the next room. The little one was my godchild, and was named Klara Alice Judka, after my wife and Mengelbier's wife.[25]

Sievers had little doubt that his position was rapidly moving from serious to catastrophic, but Ruzsky continued to believe that the planned Russian offensive into East Prussia would still be possible. During the course of 11 February, Sievers' chief of staff, General Budberg, spoke to Gulevich in Ruzsky's headquarters. He informed Gulevich that Epanchin's corps was effectively out of the battle, but the southern flank of the line was holding firm at Lyck. Gulevich stressed the need for all units to hold their positions so that the planned offensive could proceed; increasingly aware of the chaotic state of the area immediately behind their front line, with all manner of rear area units trying to move east along the frozen roads, Budberg and Sievers could only repeat their doubts that they would be able to comply with their orders.[26]

Sievers now spoke to Gulevich directly, emphasising that the retreat of Epanchin's corps had allowed the Germans to bypass his northern flank. In these circumstances, he stressed, it was too dangerous to allow XX Corps to remain west of the Rominte Heath. The reply from Ruzsky, via Gulevich, was that regardless of Epanchin's retreat, the rest of Sievers' army had to remain ready to advance. Sievers repeated that he felt it important to retreat to the line of the Niemen, and grudgingly, Northwest Front granted him freedom to act upon developments as he saw fit, provided that he did not retreat beyond the original line that Ruzsky had decreed – some considerable distance short of the Niemen, where Sievers felt he might have a chance of stopping the Germans.[27] Part of the problem was that although Sievers acknowledged that the northern flank of XX Corps had been bypassed, he remained completely ignorant of the scale of the German threat, estimating that the German forces in the area amounted to no more than one or two divisions of *Landwehr* – in other words, the relatively weak formations that Eichhorn had assigned to protect his eastern flank. The reality was that a German force almost as strong as his entire army was now advancing into the wide gap between the northern flank of XX Corps and the retreating elements of II Corps. As a result of his ignorance, Sievers failed to make Ruzsky aware of the magnitude of the threat that was rapidly developing. Bulgakov, commander of XX Corps, pleaded in vain for permission to withdraw immediately southeast to Augustowo. Instead, Sievers ordered that if retreat became necessary, XX Corps would fall back eastwards to Suwalki, where it would attempt to hold up any German forces advancing from the north.[28]

The fighting for Lyck continued on 12 February. Falk's division remained held at arm's length to the west of the town, and 80th Reserve Infantry Division now formed up to the south. Meanwhile, 79th Reserve Infantry Division was now some distance to the east, and Litzmann worried about the lack of reports about its situation. But the Russians were just as much in the dark about the exact situation, and although Sievers and the commander of III Siberian Corps, Radkevich, were aware that the position at Lyck had been bypassed, they did not know the strength of the advancing German forces. Nor of course did Gulevich, who could only telegraph Radkevich with orders to attack towards the south in order to hold up the German advance.[29] Accordingly, the Russian forces in Lyck launched determined assaults, which Litzmann's troops beat off in the midst of a further heavy snowstorm. Further north, Eichhorn's Tenth Army continued its relentless advance, and its XXXIX Reserve Corps, led by Generalleutnant Otto von Lauenstein, overwhelmed a Russian force in Eydtkuhnen and Wirballen, capturing several thousand prisoners and six guns. It seemed that everywhere other than at Lyck, Sievers' formations were withdrawing as fast as possible. Such a rapid withdrawal while under pressure from a pursuing enemy is a difficult operation to pull off in any circumstances, and given the weather conditions, it became even harder. Additional problems were created by the use of a withdrawal plan that had been drawn up in advance, as a contingency; many of the roads that this plan designated were either impassable or already covered by German guns. Danilov's description of conditions matches that given by Ludendorff:

For several days, snow squalls of unbelievable force raged unabated; snowdrifts left roads through the forests impassable, while ice made it very difficult to move off roads. The retreat was carried out under great pressure from the enemy, who had the advantage of being able to advance by following along roads cleared in the snow by our retreating columns. Our troops were starving, lost contact with each other, and finding no shelter, frequently spent the night out in the open.

Nevertheless the retreat was conducted in good order and all of the heavy artillery that had been assembled before Lötzen was withdrawn to Osowiec. But clearly, a retreat under such conditions was only possible due to the tremendous efforts of officers, men and horses.[30]

Whilst the German advance might have been aided by the snow trampled by the retreating Russians, it was only possible at all because of the food abandoned by the retreating Tenth Army; the movements of German supply columns were as restricted by the weather as everyone else. With its flanks threatened, the improvised Russian division in Lyck pulled back to the edge of the town, allowing Litzmann to transfer 80th Reserve Infantry Division elsewhere – worrying reports suggested that Russian troops were concentrating in Grajewo, from where they could threaten the southern flank of his advance. Already fatigued by the fighting around Lyck, the German reservists trudged south towards Grajewo, where further German reconnaissance had identified strong Russian defences to the north of the town. Rather than launch a costly frontal attack, Generalmajor Max Beckmann ordered his men to bypass the Russian positions to the west, so that they could then attack from the southwest. Inevitably, this added to the fatigue of the men, leaving no possibility for any further attack on 13 February.

Although the attention of Sievers and Ruzsky was centred on the threat created by Litzmann's advance, the real danger to the Russians came from Eichhorn's Tenth Army. After his success in driving off the Russian III Corps, Eichhorn had turned his forces south, and reached the town of Suwalki on 14 February, only 15 miles (25km) from Augustowo. The retreat of Epanchin's III Corps had been so rapid and chaotic that all contact with Fritz von Below's XXI Corps had effectively been lost, and the German force marched onwards with barely a shot fired. Sievers issued orders for his cavalry to cover the northern flank of his remaining forces, but the Russian cavalry remained as ineffective as it had been throughout the war.

With an encirclement of XXVI, XX and III Siberian Corps apparently within reach, Eichhorn pushed forward with Below's XXI Corps on his eastern flank, cutting the road from Augustowo to Sejny on 14 February. Even if Bulgakov were able to pull back to Suwalki, the Germans had already cut communications to the east from Suwalki. Radkevich, who had been planning another counterattack against the southern flank of Litzmann's advancing forces, abandoned these plans and dispatched what troops he could spare towards Sejny, in order to keep open the lines of retreat for Sievers' army. Finally realising the magnitude of the danger facing his army, Sievers now issued orders to his embattled subordinates that effectively eliminated any possibility of a future offensive. Instead of retreating east towards the Niemen, as he had originally intended, the commander of Tenth Army directed his forces to withdraw towards the southeast, the only escape route that remained open. XXVI Corps was to pull back towards Grodno via Sapockin, while XX Corps withdrew first to Suwalki, and then southeast to form up on XXVI Corps' northern flank. It was anticipated that XX Corps might have to fight its way through the advancing German forces.[31] In conditions that remained almost impossible, with roads being little more than narrow corridors between high walls of snow, XXVI Corps staggered back towards Augustowo, but lost contact with XX Corps to the north. Finally becoming aware that XX Corps was already surrounded on three sides, Sievers ordered Bulgakov to move energetically to defeat the German forces that had bypassed his northern flank and now lay to his east. Time was of the essence, stressed Sievers, as it was likely that Bulgakov would enjoy numerical superiority over the German spearheads, but this would soon change as the main body of the German forces arrived. The reality was that Bulgakov was probably already outnumbered, and the weather and movement conditions prevented the Russian corps commander from gathering sufficient strength to be able to exert any significant pressure upon the Germans. Instead, his columns collided with equally exhausted groups of German troops, with no decisive success for either side. But at this stage, the Germans did not need such a success: the two pincers of their advance were closing in on Augustowo, and if they met, all the Russian troops to the northwest of the town would be encircled.

Within hours, new orders reached Bulgakov. He was now to operate as a rearguard for XXVI Corps, which would retreat through Augustowo; XX Corps would then follow the same path. Time was running out, though, with the Germans also closing in on the vital town. Below's XXI Corps pushed on after securing Sejny and entered the northern edges of the Augustowo Forest, where it encountered Russian troops attempting to retreat, mainly from XXVI Corps. Confused fighting spread throughout the area, for the moment bringing the German advance to a halt. Further to the west, Falk's 2nd Infantry Division finally captured Lyck on 14 February, seizing perhaps 5,000 Russian prisoners, many of them wounded. The following day, Litzmann's southern formation, 80th Reserve Infantry Division, moved forward through Grajewo towards Raigrod, where 79th Reserve Infantry Division fought off a local Russian counterattack. Concerned that this attack might prove too strong for the German division, Litzmann tried to organise reinforcements. The weather, which had played such a big part in the campaign, now changed again:

There was a sudden change in the weather, rain and thaw. The immense masses of snow on the roads turned to knee-deep mud. Beckmann's troops [80th Reserve Infantry Division] were badly affected. And yet, I had to request that 80th Reserve Division hurried to help its sister division. I set off for Grajewo to discuss the situation with my division commander and to ensure that a strong vanguard reached Raigrod – some 18km [11 miles] from Grajewo – during the night. I couldn't know that 79th Reserve Infantry Division would overcome the significant danger that it faced with its own resources.[32]

Late on 16 February, Litzmann's leading elements reached Augustowo, which Ruzsky had ordered to be held at all costs. As heavy fighting developed around the western approaches to town, the Germans were forced to divert forces – 3rd Reserve Division, 5th Infantry Brigade, and 11th *Landwehr* Division – to cover the southern flank of Eighth Army. This mixed force was ordered to advance on and surround Osowiec, a fortress that the Germans had unsuccessfully attacked in the autumn. At the same time, further to the west, I Reserve Corps, under the command of Curt von Morgen, would attack from Chorzele towards Przasnysz. German intelligence reported the presence of substantial Russian troops in this area, with XIX Corps in Ciechanow, I Siberian Corps near Pultusk, and II Siberian Corps near Ostrolenka; Morgen's wry observation that he was about to prod a veritable wasps' nest was no exaggeration.[33]

Despite the concerns with the long southern flank of the German advance, the main focus now centred upon Augustowo and the surrounding area, where Sievers' remaining forces – the remnants of III Siberian Corps, XXVI Corps, and XX Corps – had retreated, with Eichhorn's Tenth Army bearing down from the north and Below's Eighth Army, primarily Litzmann's corps, still pushing forward from the west. Litzmann described the terrain for the last phase of the battle:

[The battlefield] was bordered on the north by the edge of the Augustowo Forest, in the east by the road from Kopciowo to Sapockin, in the south by the swamps of the Bobr and in the west by a line from the Bobr north through Barglow and Raczki. This entire area of 2,500 square kilometres [965 square miles] is mainly composed of thinly populated wood- and scrubland, with few roads. There is open and sometimes strikingly hilly land along the edges: in the west in the area from Raczki to Augustowo and Barglow, in the southeast at Sapockin, Holynka and Lipsk, in the south on the right bank of the Bobr at Fastrzembna, Krasnybor and Ramien. The interior has only small clearings around the scattered villages.

The Augustowo Forest, February 1915

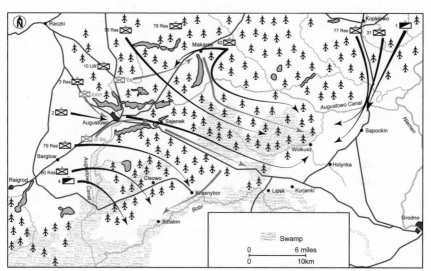

In this difficult terrain and especially in the weather conditions prevailing at the time, the main roads were of the greatest importance; they were of particular military value in that they all came together at Augustowo where they passed between several lakes ... The main line of retreat for the Russians was the main road that passed across a narrow neck of land southwest of Sajenek and then continued 30km [18 miles] through woodland and swamps, passing to the north of Lipsk and Kurjanki and running to the Niemen fortress of Grodno. The country roads were of limited use, icy on high ground and swampy in low-lying areas.

... The most significant waterway is the Augustowo canal. For its first third, it runs from the Bobr north to Augustowo and along this section is parallel to the River Netta. Swampy terrain on either bank turns it into a major obstacle ... In Augustowo, the canal turns to the east, runs through a chain of three lakes, and then into woodland. For its last third it follows the course of the Czarna Hancza until it reaches Lake Wigri southeast of Suwalki. The canal opens into the Niemen 23km [14 miles] north of Grodno. The Bobr runs through a swampy area, at least 1.5 and in the west up to 20km [one mile up to 12 miles] wide. As a result, a major crossing would be a most difficult undertaking ... The entire southern part of the Augustowo Forest is a grim area of alders and a few pines. In this landscape, near Wolkusz to the northwest of Holynka, the tragedy of the Russian Tenth Army came to its conclusion.[34]

Litzmann's XL Reserve Corps entered the area from the direction of Raigrod, with Eichhorn's formations pressing down from the north. In this context, the terrain described by Litzmann was very significant. For his forces, advancing from the west, any attempt to bypass Augustowo to the south, by attempting to advance between the town and the Bobr swamps, would involve the use of poor roads and would be hindered by the substantial obstacle of the Augustowo canal. On 16 February, 79th Reserve Infantry Division deployed for a full-scale assault towards Augustowo, with 2nd Infantry Division to its north and 80th Reserve Infantry Division moving up in support from Raigrod. At the same time, two small detachments consisting of two or three infantry battalions with artillery support were ordered to cross the canal and push forward to cut the Augustowo–Grodno road. The reservists had been in almost constant action since 7 February, and the exertions of marching and fighting in such hostile conditions began to show their effects; it took the two detachments the entire day just to reach the canal as they advanced along snow-choked tracks. Litzmann's cavalry, dispatched forward on a similar mission, fared no better. The main force advancing on Augustowo ran into Russian defences about 4 miles (7km) from the town, and although the Germans rapidly widened their front line in an attempt to find and turn the flanks of the Russian position, the advance came to an abrupt halt. In his quarters in Barglow, in a room that had been occupied by Russian officers the previous night and still smelled strongly of cigarettes, Litzmann reflected on the terrain over which his men were struggling to advance:

> On this day, the battlefield had a singular appearance. As the ground was still frozen by frost, the water from the melting snow couldn't soak into it, and instead formed extensive lagoons, with high ground forming small islands. On one such large island, accessible by a footbridge, prisoners were gathered. It was amusing to watch as the guard detachment replaced their shredded boots with the excellent felt boots of the Russians: an entirely appropriate measure, as my brave young men needed good footwear more than the Russian prisoners did for their rail trip to Germany.[35]

The fact that the Russians would have to march for at least a day across the frozen roads before they could board trains was something that Litzmann either did not realise, or regarded as irrelevant.

From the north, Eichhorn's units also began to make their presence felt. XXXVIII Corps captured Suwalki early on 16 February, seizing 5,000 prisoners and several guns, and pressed on towards Augustowo. To its east, XXXIX Reserve

Corps could make little headway into the dense woodland, hindered by a lack of roads, but XXI Corps' 31st Infantry Division made good use of one of the few good routes through the area to reach Sapockin by the end of the day. This placed the Germans directly east of Augustowo; if Litzmann could break through south of the town and advance to link up, the encirclement of the Russian Tenth Army would be complete. Closer to Augustowo itself, a single brigade from 42nd Infantry Division pushed right up to the northeast outskirts, but then ran into strong Russian defences and was brought to a standstill.

Coordination between the Russian forces was now minimal. Sievers continued to issue orders, but these were almost always far behind the course of events on the battlefield. A substantial gap was opening up between Bulgakov's XX Corps and the rest of Tenth Army, and Bulgakov now attempted to fight his way out on his own, past the lakes to the north of Augustowo. As they tried to march east, Bulgakov's troops found the German brigade from 42nd Infantry Division in their path, and confused fighting erupted in the forest. For a while, the Germans were isolated and surrounded, but Bulgakov's men were not interested in forcing their surrender; their priority was to escape to the east.[36]

Nevertheless, the initiative lay firmly on the German side. Litzmann urged his forces to cross the canal as early as possible on 17 February. Although the bulk of XL Reserve Corps continued to be held at arm's length west of the town, a small German force of *Landwehr*, attached to XXXVIII Corps, penetrated into Augustowo from the northwest. There was no longer any point in the Russian III Siberian Corps holding its positions facing Litzmann's main force, and these were now abandoned. The two Russian divisions in the town itself – one from XXVI Corps, the other from XX Corps – tried to fight their way out to the east. Order broke down, and XXVI Corps effectively ceased to exist as a coherent formation. Both Radkevich and Gerngross had been in Augustowo earlier but had left, and in their absence, their subordinates had to improvise as best they could. Unaware of the precise locations of their own forces, let alone the Germans around them, they attempted to press down the road towards Grodno. The original plan – to hold on until Bulgakov's XX Corps could retreat through Augustowo – was completely abandoned.

Bitter fighting continued in the woodland north and northeast of Augustowo as the Russian XX Corps attempted to make its escape to the east. Casualties were heavy on both sides, particularly around the village of Makarce, where the leading elements of the Russian 27th Infantry Division launched a dawn attack on the German troops in the village. The approach march was executed without incident before dawn, but as soon as it began to grow light, increasingly accurate German fire brought the attack to a standstill. Artillery from both sides joined the fighting, but the German guns were rapidly silenced and the Russian infantry was able to close with Makarce from the north and east. By the end of the day, Makarce was back in Russian hands, with many Germans killed and perhaps as many as 700 taken prisoner, including the commander of 131st Infantry Regiment.[37] The Russians also captured a set of orders on the body of a German officer, revealing the locations of many of Eichhorn's troops, but the information came too late to be of much use; XX Corps was now isolated and acting on its own.[38]

Bulgakov ordered 27th Infantry Division to form a blocking position in Makarce, while the rest of his corps attempted to continue retreating to the southeast. Unfortunately, this resulted in almost no significant move to the east for a day. The Russian regiment that had taken Makarce was still in good shape, and might have made further progress, but by the time that other elements of XX Corps arrived, the Germans had recovered from their setback. Meanwhile, unaware of XX Corps' positions, Radkevich ordered what remained of his XXVI Corps to fight its way down the road from Augustowo towards Lipsk and on to Grodno, while III Siberian Corps pulled back to the south over the Bobr. Parts of 64th Infantry Division would form a rearguard, destroying bridges and other vital positions as they fell back. Radkevich had already made good his personal escape, reaching Grodno the previous day and spreading tales of the complete destruction of his corps.[39] The reality was that, despite the spreading chaos, XXVI Corps was still fighting. Amidst scenes of confusion and muddle, some parts of the Russian rearguard took the wrong road, marching directly into the arms of the Germans. A few forceful officers attempted to make the best of things, abandoning any attempt to disentangle the various formations and improvising them into ad-hoc columns. The leading formation of XXVI Corps, a regiment from 64th Infantry Division – which should actually have been part of the rearguard – reached Lipsk late on 17 February, ensuring that the line of retreat remained open.

Sievers had not received any news from XX Corps for over a day, and Radkevich's report that the Germans had cut the road behind him was manifestly incorrect, as further stragglers continued to pass through Lipsk and thence to Grodno. In an attempt to find out what was really happening, the army commander dispatched several staff officers to the area. To his alarm, they returned with the news that German forces were threatening Lipsk from the north. The report he sent to Northwest Front painted a bleak picture:

> The situation is almost hopeless. The Germans have taken the Augustowo–Sapockin road and are threatening the Augustowo–Grodno road … there has

been no news from XX Corps for two days ... the fortress of Grodno lacks an adequate garrison, and [the situation] is dangerous.[40]

It was only now that Northwest Front finally dropped its lingering hope of launching its own offensive. Ruzsky telegraphed *Stavka* that Osowiec was now under threat, and even if Sievers' army could escape, it would be in no state to hold an extended line. Meanwhile, buoyed by his success at Makarce, Bulgakov continued to try to move east, intending to reach Sapockin – unaware that the town was already in German hands. On his southern flank, parts of 29th Infantry Division succeeded in making a tenuous connection with XXVI Corps, but Bulgakov decided to stick with his original plan rather than turn south. This decision effectively sealed the fate of his troops.

To the south of Augustowo, some of the German XL Reserve Corps' detachments managed to cross the frozen canal on 17 February, but a vital bridge had been destroyed by the retreating Russians, preventing artillery from crossing. Construction work continued throughout the day despite harassing fire from the Russians, and during the afternoon, it was possible for more substantial German forces to advance. Immediately, they ran into a further obstacle in the form of the River Netta, running parallel to the canal. Its swampy banks were covered by Russian artillery fire and once again, the German advance stalled. The increasingly frustrated Litzmann deployed 80th Reserve Infantry Division in support of the crossings, with 79th Reserve Infantry Division to its north. During the night of 17/18 February, the Germans penetrated as far as the village of Cisowo, southeast of Augustowo but still a considerable distance short of linking up with XXI Corps further east.

On 18 February, Litzmann's command was assigned to Tenth Army in order to allow for better coordination of the troops that were concentrating around Augustowo. Eichhorn called for Litzmann's cavalry to secure crossings over the Bobr, but the advance to the east to complete the encirclement of the retreating Russians continued to make only slow headway. Further east, additional German troops linked up with 31st Infantry Division around Sapockin, and continued south to cut the road between Lipsk and Grodno; even if the Russians were able to hold Lipsk, the route to the east was blocked. The Russian troops of III Siberian Corps and XXVI Corps now had German forces closing in on them on three sides, with only the south left open, and after a brief discussion between officers of the two divisions of XXVI Corps, a decision was made to march as fast as possible to Sztabin on the Bobr, where III Siberian Corps was already concentrating its remaining formations. The first troops to reach the town and its vital ferry were from 8th Siberian Rifle Division, and by the end of 17 February most of the troops of III Siberian Corps had successfully crossed to the south bank. Belatedly, the Germans realised that large numbers of Russians were escaping at the very last moment, and 80th Reserve Infantry Division was ordered to attack Sztabin immediately. After several days of exhausting marches, such a task was beyond the strength of the reservists, and the division commander informed Litzmann that he would be unable to attack until 19 February – in addition to needing rest, his men had to wait until the division's artillery caught up.[41] By then, it was too late. During the night, the disordered columns of the Russian XXVI Corps reached Sztabin and crossed to safety. When the Germans prepared for their attack the following morning, they found that the Russians had escaped, and the bridgehead had been abandoned.

Sievers had started the battle with four corps. Epanchin's III Corps had been driven off to the east in the initial German assault at the northern end of the battlefield, and III Siberian Corps and XXVI Corps had succeeded in escaping across the Bobr, albeit after suffering heavy casualties and after abandoning much of their equipment. The remaining formation, Bulgakov's XX Corps, was still trying to reach Sapockin. By the end of 18 February, Bulgakov realised that the German forces between him and his intended destination were too strong, and he decided to turn south. It seems that even at this stage, Bulgakov remained confident that he would be able to reach Grodno; despite having a force of perhaps 200 Cossacks at his disposal for reconnaissance, he made little effort to determine the position and strength of the surrounding German forces, and appears to have made little use of the valuable intelligence that had been gained by the capture of German documents in Makarce.[42]

The troops of 108th Infantry Regiment, part of 27th Infantry Division, were to lead the way to safety. Commanded by Vladimir Belolipetsky, the regiment had started the battle at only 75 per cent of its establishment strength, and many of its personnel were replacement drafts with only limited training and no real combat experience. Its four battalion commanders, too, were of limited quality; one was an elderly colonel, while the other three were captains, temporarily assigned to their posts in the absence of their seniors due to sickness. Nevertheless, prudent measures by the regiment commander ensured that his troops spent much of the winter in good trenches, regularly rotated to rear areas for rest, with plentiful supplies of hot food.[43] During the opening phases of the February fighting, the regiment frequently found its northern flank threatened by the German advance, and like all troops it found the weather conditions almost impossible:

When the main column reached the village of Praslauken ... it encountered an unexpected obstacle. Due to a lack of local knowledge, the regiment's rear area units were using only a single road. With the winter snow, the other roads had merged with the surrounding fields, and only two rows of willows, which were planted along nearly all the minor roads of East Prussia, marked their route on the snowy plain ... The artillery battalion commander decided that moving along the uncleared snowbound roads with guns could be fatal for his horses, and suggested first sending a mounted detachment to trot down the highway to the south along the former front up on Daken [to flatten the snow so that the guns could follow], and there turn to the east to rejoin the infantry. There was little risk of encountering German patrols, and in the hope that the blizzard would keep the Germans from pursuing during the night, it was decided to send the artillery separately. One infantry battalion moved forward on the snow-covered road. It was hard going at the front, but most of the column found the snow was already flattened [by the leading formation].

The wind grew ever stronger. The wind blew off one officer's hat, and it was impossible to find, so he had to wrap his head in a blanket, as suggested by one of the soldiers. Near the village of Valdaukadel the road was lost, as it was not fringed by trees at this point and turned to one side – consequently, the road was covered with snow and indistinguishable from the surrounding terrain. A burning inn on the road made a terrible impression. Smoke and sparks, fanned by the wind, were visible from afar and alerted the Germans to the Russian withdrawal. Some thought that Germans hiding somewhere in the empty villages had set it on fire for this purpose.[44]

For much of the retreat, Belolipetsky's regiment only knew about his neighbouring formations because he sent out patrols to investigate; command and control from above remained haphazard. At one stage, Belolipetsky established contact with 29th Infantry Division on his flank, and then received orders to withdraw. He sent an officer to inform his neighbours, and to enquire whether they too had been ordered back; the officer returned and reported that 29th Infantry Division had already withdrawn, and he had found a single battery of artillery in the process of packing up.[45] Through a mixture of good fortune and forceful leadership, 108th Infantry Regiment succeeded in remaining relatively intact, though much of the rest of the division disintegrated. Nevertheless, the regiment became separated from its supply columns, which pulled back into Augustowo before the town fell to the Germans, taking with them several wagons belonging to Belolipetsky's headquarters. In addition to leaving the regiment without supplies, there were other complications:

The absence of the staff wagons put the regimental commander in a difficult position: he had no maps of the area of forthcoming operations ... Fortunately, the commander of the 3rd Battalion was the regimental hoarder, and was carrying maps of the ground to Grodno. Learning about the absence of maps in the headquarters, he immediately made them available to the regimental commander.[46]

After days of hard marching and the tough battle at Makarce, the officers and men of 108th Infantry Regiment were approaching the end of their endurance. Belolipetsky struggled to stay awake as his division commander issued him orders on 18 February, but at first the Russians brushed aside the relatively small German force in their path. As they attempted to exploit their initial success, the Russians realised that the Germans had merely pulled back to stronger positions that were far too strong to be forced. The retreat of the other two Russian corps opened the way for the German troops that had captured Augustowo to close in on Bulgakov's corps from the south, and Falk's 2nd Infantry Division now stood in the path of the encircled Russians. Despite its losses and the need to cover both a segment of the Bobr and a possible threat from the Russian forces in Grodno, Falk's division beat off all Russian attempts to break out on 19 and 20 February.

Within the encirclement, all supplies – ammunition, food, and medical stores – were almost exhausted. The Russians continued to make desperate attempts to escape, and some groups of infantry – and a small group of Cossacks – managed to reach the Bobr, where they were ferried to safety on the south bank. The northern and eastern perimeter of the encirclement collapsed under heavy German pressure, and Bulgakov and his staff were captured during the afternoon of 21 February. With order breaking down completely, Belolipetsky's regiment – reduced to perhaps 800 men – broke into small groups and attempted to infiltrate through the German lines. Most were captured, but a few reached Grodno over the coming days.[47]

Belolipetsky had no intention of surrendering. Accompanied by a group of his men, he hid from German patrols in a thicket until the evening of 21 February, intending to try to escape to the east during the night. The weather, which had been such a hindrance to both sides during the battle, now turned against the Russians; rising temperatures melted the ice on small rivers and streams and turned their banks into almost impassable quagmires. Finding that all the bridges over one such stream were guarded by Germans, Belolipetsky's group improvised a bridge of their own, using timber from a nearby bunker. The next obstacle was the Augustowo canal, but they managed to find an unguarded crossing and, dodging German columns on the road running south towards

Grodno, approached the Niemen. Here, they found a substantial German presence in the villages near the river, but local villagers provided them with shelter and food and told them of a substantial ice floe on the Neman, by which it might be possible to cross. Late on 4 March, the small group successfully reached the east bank, where they encountered a cavalry patrol. Like many infantrymen, Belolipetsky had a low opinion of his army's cavalry, and was not at all surprised that the cavalry had no idea that the ice across the river was still intact. He and his men were amongst the lucky ones to escape the encirclement of XX Corps. Some elements of 29th Infantry Division managed to reach safety before the German ring closed, and after adding small groups like the one that accompanied Belolipetsky, an estimated 1,400 men from Bulgakov's corps managed to reach Russian lines.[48] The Germans captured 30,000, including 11 generals and 200 guns.[49]

From Grodno, Sievers attempted to reach XX Corps before it was overwhelmed. Several attacks were launched, but the German forces facing Grodno defeated them without any apparent difficulty. The bulk of these German units belonged to 1st Cavalry Division, and given the relatively poor performance of cavalry throughout the war, the ease with which the relief attempts were beaten off suggests that they did not amount to much.

On the southern flank of the German advance, the German I Reserve Corps attempted to pre-empt any Russian attack, and set off on 19 February in three columns. The distance from Chorzele to Przasnysz was only 18 miles (30km) but although Morgen's troops made rapid progress at first, they then ran into determined Russian counterattacks. The Russian garrison of Przasnysz was surrounded, but refused to surrender. As more Russian troops approached from the south, Morgen issued orders to 1st Reserve Infantry Division that the town was to be taken without delay:

After a one-hour heavy bombardment, particularly of the churchyard and the barracks near the southern end of the town, Przasnysz was stormed at 4 p.m. on 24 February, 10,000 unwounded prisoners, thirty-six guns, fourteen machine-guns, a regimental flag, 500 horses, several field kitchens, and other war materiel fell into the hands of the brave division which, under the command of its skilful and energetic commander, Generalleutnant von Foerster, did not fail in any respect, here as in other difficult situations. Our losses were clearly heavy and the physical exertions had been great. Men sank up to their knees in the deep clay, and all across the battlefield one saw boots stuck in the mud. The Russians had suffered heavy losses. In view of the brave conduct of the garrison, I allowed the commander to keep his sword. Like two other colonels who were captured, he was disappointed that the relief column had not arrived in time.[50]

More Russian troops, particularly II Siberian Corps, began to assemble opposite Morgen's troops, and heavy fighting continued in the coming days, resulting in Przasnysz being abandoned. Despite the growing Russian strength and the threat of encirclement, the German formations, largely made up of reservists and *Landwehr*, conceded ground in good order, withdrawing along several diverging roads with almost no interference by the Russians. Morgen regarded the operation as a remarkable success:

> I Reserve Corps' expedition to Przasnysz was one of the most daring in all the accounts of the war. To take a strongly fortified town with one corps, defended by a division and supported by another division, while three fresh enemy corps attacked from further afield, was adventurous. I attribute our success in extracting our head from the noose, and carrying out a retreat 'under the nose of the enemy' to the slowness of the Russians and the energy and skill of my subordinate commanders, and the courage and endurance of my men.
>
> The Przasnysz operation once more demonstrated a principle: 'concentrate in attack, withdraw by dispersing'. The Russians in Przasnysz could not endure the concentrated fire and wholesale attack, and the Russians couldn't hinder the withdrawal along different axes. They milled about in Przasnysz and could not determine where the main strength of their enemy had gone. For me, as a commander, the Przasnysz expedition was the most interesting and challenging of the entire war.[51]

Morgen's description is slightly misleading. Not all parts of his corps succeeded in withdrawing intact, and in addition to the casualties suffered in storming Przasnysz, several hundred German troops were captured in the Russian counterattack.

As part of their operation on the southern flank of the battlefield, German troops returned to the Osowiec fortress on the Bobr, scene of fighting the previous autumn. Here, there was a major threat to the overall Russian position: if the fortress were to fall quickly, the Germans would be able to advance on Białystok and thus cut the main railway line that ran to Warsaw. At first, the garrison of Osowiec consisted of only a few battalions, and Russian expectations were that the best they could hope for was to delay the Germans while further defences were improvised, but as was repeatedly the case in the opening phases of the war, troops in defensive positions proved able to repulse assaults by their enemies even when outnumbered. On 14 February, the Germans began a heavy bombardment that lasted two days in an attempt to crush the defences, and after a brief pause to bring up more guns and ammunition, launched a second bombardment in the last week of the month. Despite this, when the German infantry attempted to storm the fortress in early March, they were once more repelled. Reluctantly, the attackers had to give up and the front settled down in positional warfare, which would last for several months.

The Germans estimated that the total losses suffered by Sievers' Tenth Army exceeded 150,000, with two thirds of that total made up of prisoners. In addition, over 300 guns were captured, together with large quantities of small arms and other war *matériel*.[52] Russian estimates were rather less, suggesting a figure barely over half the German estimate.[53] German losses, both sides agreed, were far lighter, and amounted to fewer than 20,000. However, sufficient Russian formations had escaped to allow the Russian line to be rebuilt, particularly as reinforcements – originally intended for the planned Russian offensive into East Prussia – continued to arrive. The destruction of the Russian Tenth Army was intended to be a prelude to a German advance that would roll up the entire northern part of the Eastern Front, but repeated attempts by Litzmann's corps to secure crossings over the Bobr failed, partly due to the growing strength of the Russian Twelfth Army and partly due to warmer weather. The swamps on the banks of the Bobr, frozen solid just a week or two before, now became almost impassable.

Even before the destruction of XX Corps, Ruzsky had decided to move the bulk of his forces away from their positions in northern Poland. Aside from the stricken Tenth Army, his forces had eighteen corps at their disposal, and he advised *Stavka* that he intended to leave only five corps on the right bank of the Vistula, concentrating the rest along the Bobr to the west of Grodno.[54] The arrival of the Russian XV Corps near Grodno at the end of February brought to an end any lingering possibility that the Germans might be able to crown their victory by seizing the fortress. Repeated Russian attacks forced the Germans onto the defensive, and in the first two weeks of March, the front line moved a short distance towards the west.

For Hindenburg and Ludendorff, the Second Battle of the Masurian Lakes – known in Germany as the Winter Battle of Masuria – was undoubtedly a victory, but it fell short of what had been intended. Much of Sievers' Tenth Army escaped the German attempts to create an encirclement to rival Tannenberg, albeit with substantial losses. Although *Ober Ost* emphasised the considerable tactical success that had been achieved, there was little doubt that Falkenhayn's scepticism about being able to force a decision in the east had been proved correct. However, his intention to allow the precious new formations to be used on the Eastern Front for only a short time was also thwarted; the speed with which the Russians restored their line, and the pressure that Plehve's Twelfth Army exerted, ensured that the reserve corps that had fought so well were unable to be withdrawn for use in the west. Nevertheless, the consequences of the victory were substantial, as Danilov recorded:

> This offensive by the German Eighth and Tenth Armies in February 1915 was definitely a great success for our enemies. Our Tenth Army was forced to withdraw from the territory of East Prussia, this time permanently. Once more, we suffered very severe losses of men and military materiel, in addition to which we suffered a substantial blow to our prestige in East Prussia for the third time. Our plan to secure this province in order to anchor our right flank and to advance on the lower Vistula was rendered impossible by the German tactical victory.
>
> However, subsequent attacks along the Bobr were foiled, at least as far as our Northwest Front was concerned. The [German] intention to carry out a deep envelopment of the right flank of our armies had to be abandoned. The forces that were to carry this out did not try to hold the positions they had reached and withdrew to a front a little to the rear.
>
> From the point of view of our western allies, the immobilisation of four German corps on our front, three of which had been recently and carefully established, was certainly a major advantage, as we had brought upon ourselves a blow that was to have fallen upon them. The British Army was able to continue to increase its forces, while the French high command was able to continue its offensive in Champagne.[55]

These concluding sentences seem to be an attempt to find crumbs of solace from a bleak situation. The fighting in Champagne was, like so many battles on the Western Front, completely inconclusive with little ground changing hands; a series of attacks and counterattacks merely resulted in steadily escalating losses on both sides. It seems highly unlikely that the four German corps deployed in East Prussia would have made much difference, and even if a local success had been achieved by the German Third Army, it is likely that the French would have been able to seal off any German gains without difficulty, given the troop densities along the front line.

In a similar vein, Ludendorff too reflected upon the winter fighting:

> For me, the days until the beginning of April were difficult. I had to put aside the hopes I had held of an immediate strategic exploitation of the winter battle. We

had succeeded tactically, and I had to content myself with this. I was pleased that the great attacks planned by the Grand Duke [Nikolai] collapsed and we stood on enemy territory everywhere. But a conclusion with Russia ... was only one step closer. The great deployment of Russian forces against East and West Prussia would prove to be useful later in operations in Galicia. The Russians' losses were extraordinarily high in comparison to our own. Even Russia's huge manpower resources could not readily sustain this.

The individual tactical situations had required my full mental energy. Not everything can be written down – the proud hopes, the trembling of one's heart, the disappointment, the struggle to reach a conclusion, displeasure at this and that. One cannot describe the friction that had to be overcome in so many cases, nor can one adequately describe what I felt for the troops who had to endure the hardships of a winter campaign in unfavourable weather.[56]

Ludendorff's frustrations transcended purely military matters; the failure of *Ober Ost* to deliver a decisive victory was a major setback in its struggle against Falkenhayn's *OHL*.

Both sides contemplated the questions that the battle raised. Could the Germans have accomplished more? However much they might claim to have won a major victory, the reality was that it fell short of their intentions, and what was needed either by *Ober Ost* – a crushing victory, or a dislocation of the entire Russian line – or *OHL*, where Falkenhayn wished merely to damage the Russians sufficiently to allow for troops to be moved west. Russian accounts describe the difficulties faced by their troops in moving and fighting in such conditions, but at the same time frequently comment on the slowness of the German pursuit – which was, of course, hindered by the same appalling conditions. Epanchin's III Corps retreated out of the battlefield at an early stage, but there was a real possibility of the remaining three corps being encircled in and near Augustowo; in order to achieve this encirclement, though, either or perhaps both pincers of the German operation would have had to move faster. Given the exhaustion brought by struggling through deep snow, shortages of ammunition and food, stubborn Russian resistance (particularly against Litzmann's XL Reserve Corps at Lyck) and the final obstacle of the Augustowo canal, a faster advance was surely impossible. In many respects, the overall German plan was as unrealistic as Conrad's attempt to advance quickly through the Carpathian Mountains in the middle of winter. Indeed, given that so many of the German troops were reservists with little or no combat experience, their achievements in the battle were remarkable.

The greater German plan to follow up the destruction of Sievers' Tenth Army by rolling up the northern flank of the Russian position on the Eastern Front was surely beyond the resources available. Even if a superhuman effort by Eighth and Tenth Armies had succeeded in enveloping III Siberian Corps and XXVI Corps near Augustowo, the physical exhaustion of the troops was such that a continued major operation would surely have risked disaster. Nevertheless, the last possibility of a Russian assault on East Prussia had been eliminated.

Like many battles on the Eastern Front in the First World War, this winter engagement gave rise to its share of legends. In particular, there was a widespread belief that Bulgakov's XX Corps was deliberately sacrificed to ensure that most of the Russian Tenth Army escaped encirclement. There is no doubt that the combat between the retreating Russians and the leading elements of Eichhorn's forces delayed the German advance, and given how close the Germans came to trapping III Siberian Corps and XXVI Corps, this delay was probably crucial. However, there is nothing to suggest that anyone – Ruzsky, Sievers or Bulgakov – consciously made a decision to sacrifice XX Corps for the greater good. Rather, it was largely a matter of chance that Bulgakov lost contact with his southern neighbours in the final phase of the battle, and chose to strike out directly towards the east, inadvertently placing his men in the path of Eichhorn's columns. Nor is there anything to suggest that once they found themselves in this position, the troops of XX Corps fought the Germans around them for any reasons other than self-preservation.

While the Germans had to satisfy themselves with a tactical victory, the Russians had no doubt that they had suffered another heavy defeat. It was inevitable that heads would roll. Epanchin was an obvious candidate, following the ignominious performance of his corps; he was replaced by Alexander Zegelov. Bulgakov, the commander of XX Corps, was taken prisoner when his men were finally overwhelmed east of Augustowo, and remained in German captivity until the end of the war. Despite the growing legend of his corps' contribution to the escape of III Siberian Corps and XXVI Corps, Bulgakov was dismissed from service during his imprisonment. There is little doubt that his corps repeatedly made mistakes during the battle, but this was at least partly due to poor command and control by Tenth Army. Whilst he made little or no use of his attached cavalry for reconnaissance, the same was true of a great many of his contemporaries.

Radkevich and Gerngross, the commanders of III Siberian Corps and XXVI Corps, were also the targets of much criticism. Radkevich conducted a good defensive withdrawal on the southern flank, but when their troops became concentrated around Augustowo, both corps commanders made for the safety of

Grodno, leaving their men leaderless at a critical moment. The division commanders had to make decisions on their own, and Sievers demanded an explanation for this apparent dereliction of duty, as did Nikolai Yanushkevich, chief of the general staff.[57] Both men survived in their posts, though clearly under a cloud.

Inevitably, the finger of blame was also directed at Sievers. The orders under which he was attempting to function were frequently contradictory, but he made little attempt to make the best of them. The decision to try to clear the German-occupied forests in front of his northern flank was poorly conceived, with no clear end-point that would allow the troops gathered for the task to be released. He lacked sufficient troops to prepare for a defence in depth, but his men were in position for sufficient time to have constructed a secondary line to which they could withdraw if they came under attack. His orders were to prepare for the invasion of East Prussia, but the deployment of his troops did little to provide the sort of concentration that would have been necessary to break through the German positions. Once the battle began, he failed to recognise the magnitude of the threat to his northern flank, continuing to believe that the main German effort was opposite III Siberian Corps. For the moment, he remained in command, though Ruzsky ensured that he came in for considerable criticism, if only to divert blame away from Northwest Front.

Ruzsky's role in the battle was minimal. He continued to demand that Sievers hold back the Germans so that the planned invasion of East Prussia could go ahead, but he could argue with some justification that this was based upon Sievers' reports about what was happening at the front. Nevertheless, the concentration of Twelfth Army was slow, and he made little attempt to accelerate this, or to send any reinforcements to his hard-pressed front-line troops.

It was only at the lowest levels – battalion and company command, and the individual soldiers – that the Russian Army performed well. The stubborn resistance that had been a hallmark of previous battles was seen again, even on occasions when the situation was hopeless, as was the case in XX Corps' last stand to the east of Augustowo. But it was increasingly clear that unless higher levels within the Russian Army could match the commitment and determination of lower ranks, there was little prospect of winning a victory against the Germans.

CHAPTER 4

SPRINGTIME

SLAUGHTER AND DISAPPOINTMENT

At the beginning of the war, the *k.u.k.* Army attempted to invade Serbia across the inhospitable Drina valley, and suffered a surprise defeat at the hands of the numerically inferior Serbian Army. A few weeks later, on 8 September, rather than attack via the far more favourable route from the north across the River San, the Austro-Hungarian commander Oskar Potiorek opted for a repeat of his failed initial invasion. The result on this occasion was less immediately disastrous, but still resulted in huge casualties.

In early 1915, as described above, Conrad elected to try to force the Russian lines along the Carpathian Mountains, despite the terrain being singularly unfavourable for offensive operations at any time of year, let alone in winter, and suffered a setback to rival that of his former rival Potiorek in Serbia. Now, after a pause for breath, he decided to try again, in exactly the same area. It seemed to the Germans that their ally had failed to learn from failure in Serbia, and were now determined to fail to learn from their setback in the Carpathians; however, the plight of the besieged fortress of Przemyśl left Conrad with little choice. He lacked the strength to try to lift the siege by anything other than the shortest route.

After the failure of the first Carpathian assault, Falkenhayn and *OHL* resurrected their proposals for a renewed campaign against Serbia. Italy was still neutral, but the Germans were increasingly convinced that this would soon change, opening a new front on the southwest borders of the Austro-Hungarian Empire. Consequently, a timely defeat of Serbia would allow Austro-Hungarian troops to be available to face any new threat from Italy, and once more Berlin urged Vienna to consider ceding territory to Italy and Romania with the aim of bringing both nations into the war as allies rather than enemies. At the same time, the conquest of Serbia by the Central Powers would allow for direct rail communications with Turkey, particularly as there were increasing signs that the British and French were preparing an operation to try to open the gates to the Black Sea.[1] As if to highlight the threat to Turkey, an Anglo-French flotilla began a bombardment of the Turkish forts defending the Dardanelles on 19 February. It was clearly the first step of a much larger operation.

Conrad had no more intention of agreeing to this than he had earlier in the year when Falkenhayn made the same suggestion, not least because it implicitly required the abandonment of the Przemyśl garrison. Even before the end of the fighting in Masuria, he was already congratulating Ludendorff on his victory and urging him to exploit the successes of the German Eighth and Tenth Armies by mounting a deep thrust towards Warsaw from the north. Falkenhayn acted swiftly to counter this proposal, reminding Hindenburg on 19 February that he still expected most or all of the four corps he had reluctantly committed to East Prussia to be sent west in the second half of March. The advance on Przasnysz and the subsequent withdrawal in the face of Russian counterattacks spoiled the plans of both Conrad and Falkenhayn. There was now little prospect of turning the German victory into the prelude for an advance into the rear of the Russian centre, but at the same time, the strength of the Russian counterattacks ensured that Falkenhayn would have to leave the forces he had temporarily assigned to Hindenburg where they were.

The Russian counterattacks were possible only because of the commitment of the Russian Guards Corps and XV Corps, which had been held in reserve by *Stavka* until then. From his headquarters in Southwest Front, Ivanov had repeatedly demanded that additional forces be sent to him, both for a resumption of his attempts to break into the Hungarian interior and to protect his extreme southeast flank. There now followed a period of great prevarication, during which Grand Duke Nikolai appears to have changed his mind repeatedly. First he advised Ivanov that no further reinforcements would be forthcoming, and he would have to make do with the troops at his disposal, perhaps by switching units away from central Poland. Even III Caucasian Corps, previously promised to Southwest Front, would be required elsewhere and would not be available. On 14 February Ivanov began to issue orders for his formations to regroup with a view to resuming offensive operations at the end of the month. Brusilov's Eighth Army was to push forward with its western elements towards Homonna (now Humenné), while the eastern flank held back the German and Austro-Hungarian forces trying to advance north.

At the same time, Third Army in southern Poland – reinforced by XXIV and XII Corps from Brusilov's army, and an additional infantry division from central Poland – was ordered to advance on Neu Sandez. In the southeast, where the forces of the German South Army and *Gruppe Pflanzer-Baltin* posed a considerable threat, he had to confine himself to defensive arrangements, and attempted to accelerate the transfer of Ninth Army from central Poland to a position on the very southeast end of the front line. After repeated representations to *Stavka* about the weakness of the Russian forces in this area, Ivanov was finally assigned XXXIII Corps as reinforcements for Ninth Army.[2]

If Ludendorff's plan to envelop Sievers' Tenth Army had been ambitious and had exceeded the resources available, Ivanov's orders for the resumption of offensive operations were even more so. The Austro-Hungarian forces facing him might have been substantially weakened, but the same was true of the Russian units in Ivanov's armies. Artillery ammunition remained in short supply, the weather in the Carpathians was hard to predict and frequently switched from bitter cold to rain, each bringing its own difficulties, and even if his subordinates could break the resistance of the *k.u.k.* Army, there simply weren't enough Russian troops to exploit any success. In the short term, any advance into Hungary would result in a far longer front line and extended supply lines running across the Carpathians. Nevertheless, Ivanov clung to his repeated belief that the Austro-Hungarian Empire would not survive a Russian invasion. The Hungarians would break away from Vienna, and the various Slav nationalities of the empire would rise up.

The evidence to support such an argument was thin, at best. There had been some defections of Slav troops during the first months of the war, particularly by Czech formations, which on occasion had deserted en masse. Although this had led to widespread and often unjustified suspicion of Czech formations, there had been little sign that the empire itself was looking like disintegrating. The initial surge of goodwill and patriotism around the outbreak of war had long since vanished, partly as casualties soared and defeat followed defeat and partly through insensitive repressive measures taken by both Austrian and Hungarian authorities, but István Tisza, the Hungarian prime minister, remained a devout supporter of the Dual Monarchy. Whilst he repeatedly highlighted the dangers of a Russian invasion of Hungary, at no point did he suggest that he would support – still less lead – a Hungarian secessionist movement. Within the *k.u.k.* Army, there were repeated concerns about the wavering loyalty of all Slav elements of the army, not just the Czechs, but much of this appears to have had little firm foundation. It seems that Ivanov's persistent argument that the Austro-Hungarian Empire could

The Carpathian Front, February–April 1915

be brought to collapse with ease was little more than a manifestation of the widely held opinion throughout Europe before the war that the empire was in its twilight years and that its demise was merely a matter of time.

Tisza was in many respects a typical example of the political class of the Austro-Hungarian Empire. He was undoubtedly a Hungarian nationalist, and had a strong following, particularly amongst the Hungarian aristocracy and middle classes, who retained control of the limited franchise within Hungary. A pressing concern within Hungary in the years before the war was Transylvania, which was ruled by Hungary but had a substantial Romanian population. Tisza strongly advocated a negotiated settlement with the Romanians, allowing them substantial autonomy and nationalist rights, but within the Hungarian state – in a similar manner to the relationship between Hungary and the empire as a whole. Such complex arrangements were completely alien to observers in autocratic Russia, and it is unsurprising that some officials in the tsar's administration interpreted Tisza's opposition to many policies originating in Vienna as signs of a fracture line that might be exploited. The fact that Ivanov was able to pursue his plans at a time when all priority was meant to be going towards the proposed invasion of East Prussia highlights yet again the inability of *Stavka* to control those who were notionally its subordinates.

On 17 February, even before the German offensive around Augustowo had finished, Grand Duke Nikolai summoned the commanders of Northwest and Southwest Fronts to a conference at Siedlce. Once again, the planned attack on East Prussia by First, Tenth and Twelfth Armies was discussed and approved, even though by this stage Tenth Army was in danger of being completely destroyed. Despite this, Ruzsky was confident that he could concentrate twelve corps for his own offensive. In order to achieve this, he told the conference, he intended to pull back his forces on the left bank of the Vistula in central Poland to a shorter line. Ivanov objected strongly to this, as any withdrawal by Northwest Front's forces in central Poland would necessitate that his own armies also withdrew. Eventually, he was able to persuade the grand duke to order that the armies of Northwest Front in central Poland should attempt to hold their positions rather than retreat as Ruzsky had proposed, but only by promising that if the Germans attacked, Southwest Front's forces in central Poland would support Ruzsky's troops energetically.[3]

Ivanov remained adamant that his front should be allowed to carry out its planned attacks. With each front commander implacably opposed to the proposals of the other, there was even discussion about a third option, to attack in central Poland, but this was rapidly rejected as the Russian armies in this area were regarded as weak – most of their regular formations had been moved away to north and south, leaving them with large contingents of reservists. Eventually, Grand Duke Nikolai concluded that, given the shortage of artillery ammunition and the losses in the recent fighting, both in East Prussia and the Carpathians, the capacity of the Russian Army to mount a major offensive was greatly reduced. In order to preserve forces from unnecessary casualties, he suggested that operations in southern Poland and the Carpathians should be limited to counterattacks to wear down the enemy.[4] This was reiterated in a telegram sent to both fronts:

> Given the current state of our armies, we will not be able to cross the frontier and conduct an invasion of East Prussia … His Imperial Highness [Grand Duke Nikolai] concludes that the forces assigned to the operation should be limited to the northwest of the battlefield and with short thrusts should advance only to the frontier for now, retaining our large bridgehead on the left bank of the Vistula.[5]

Inevitably, Ivanov did not accept these restrictions, and *Stavka* proved unable to enforce them. On 2 March, he advised *Stavka* that the *k.u.k.* Army was preparing another attempt to push through via Sanok to relieve the siege of Przemyśl, and that substantial forces threatened his southeast flank. Once more, he repeated his belief that a decisive defeat of the Austro-Hungarian forces in the south would knock Germany's ally out of the war.

The planned invasion of East Prussia, originally conceived as a two-pronged attack with the new Twelfth Army thrusting north and Sievers' Tenth Army attacking from the east, went ahead in a somewhat modified form and with rather different intentions. It was clearly no longer possible to expect the battered Tenth Army to participate in an operation intended to conquer an entire German province, and the new intention was to reverse some of the gains made by the Germans during their offensive, in keeping with the Grand Duke's closing suggestions at the Siedlce conference. There was considerable concern in Russian circles that the Germans might exploit their success by attempting to strike south in order to threaten Warsaw, or even northeast to pose a threat to Petrograd, though it must have been clear to anyone that *Ober Ost* lacked the resources to conduct anything other than local operations. The promised supplies of artillery ammunition had also not appeared, making any sustained Russian offensive operation impossible.

Ruzsky's assault started on 2 March, and for the next four weeks, the Russian infantry slowly advanced. The Augustowo Forest changed hands once more, and though they suffered substantial casualties – Danilov later estimated the haul of prisoners alone as approaching 12,000 – the Germans fell back in good order.[6] As exhaustion and rising casualties brought the fighting to a close in early April, the towns of Mariampol, Kalwaria, Suwalki and Augustowo remained in German hands.

During the fighting, further communications from *Stavka* arrived at the front line, suggesting a radical change of emphasis. The previous priority assigned to Northwest Front, with a view to overrunning East Prussia, had already been abandoned in favour of more local operations, and was now reversed completely in favour of increased emphasis in the south where a major effort was to be made to invade Hungary with a view to knocking the Austro-Hungarian Empire out of the war.[7] In addition to weakening Germany by eliminating its main ally, this would induce Romania and Italy to enter the war against the Central Powers. Inevitably, given the rivalry between Ruzsky and Ivanov, the former did not approve of this. At the very least, he demanded that he should attempt to regain the line of the Masurian Lakes, which would provide good defensive positions. Merely pushing forward to the frontier would leave his men in a potentially disastrous position in the spring, when the increasing floodwaters of the Bobr and Narew would create substantial marshy areas in their rear, and the Germans would still have the unrestricted use of their railway network to shuttle troops to wherever they might be able to launch an attack under advantageous circumstances. He wasn't the only senior officer to question the wisdom of this change of plan. Writing after the war, Danilov, the quartermaster-general of the tsar's armies, wrote about the grand duke's decision:

Personally, I was not an enthusiast for this sudden turnaround. I remained convinced of the necessity of directing our main effort against Germany and only to take account of the Austrian Army insofar as it affected the execution of our principal plan. I was also of the opinion that once Germany was defeated, all the aims pursued by the [Entente] would be achieved ... Consequently, it seemed to me that political considerations should not dominate strategy. I was certain that the most effective plan of action, pursued rapidly to its conclusion, was to conduct an offensive on the left bank of the Vistula towards Berlin. But in view of the lack of skill in manoeuvre in our army and our poorly developed rail network, I thought that this offensive could only succeed when our position was securely consolidated on both flanks of our front line, [which were] pulled back too far to the rear and consequently were greatly threatened. This was why I had always devoted so much attention to the East Prussian sector.[8]

Danilov insisted that failing to secure the northern flank by reducing the German forces in East Prussia left the entire front line vulnerable, particularly given the force-multiplying effect of the German railway network that allowed rapid redeployment in the northern half of the long front. Of course, a similar argument could be made for the southern flank, where there was always the danger that a powerful drive by the armies of the Central Powers might threaten the Russian line from the south; Conrad and Ludendorff had mounted such an operation in the autumn of 1914, advancing along the left bank of the Vistula. Danilov, though, remained convinced that any diversion of effort away from East Prussia was a serious strategic error. In his opinion, the northern flank of the Russian position was more vulnerable than the southern flank because the railway network in East Prussia was far superior to that in southern Poland or the northern parts of the Austro-Hungarian Empire; in addition, the Carpathians provided a natural line that could be defended against any threat from the Central Powers. Ultimately, the war would be won by defeating Germany, not the Austro-Hungarian Empire, and to talk of the road to Berlin being via Budapest was – in Danilov's opinion at least – absurd. Ruzsky raised an additional potential complication of Southwest Front's plan: the Germans had concentrated substantial forces in Silesia in a short time in October 1914, and had used them to advance to the outskirts of Warsaw. If Russian troops became embroiled in fighting in the Carpathians, or ventured into Hungary, the Germans could easily repeat the exercise, and then advance along the northern edge of the mountains, trapping any Russian forces that had crossed into Hungary.[9]

Although Ivanov had been advocating increased priority for his front throughout the winter, the change of emphasis by *Stavka* is still striking. Why did Grand Duke Nikolai, who was a fervent Germanophobe and had advocated the strongest possible attack on Germany as soon as it could be organised, now opt for marking time in the north while his armies attempted to knock out Germany's ally? It seems that the lack of progress by Ruzsky's armies played a major part in his thinking. Like all high commands in Europe, the Russians were struggling to come to terms with this war, in which battles stubbornly refused to proceed as pre-war doctrine and planning dictated. Hamstrung by the losses suffered by Sievers' Tenth Army, the assault by Northwest Front showed no signs of producing any significant victory; indeed, none of the Russian Army's attacks on the Germans in the war to date had produced any major results. There was also a firmly established sense of inferiority within the Russian Army with regard to the Germans. Before the war, the German military machine had been both admired and feared in Russia, and the events of the war to date had confirmed the potency of the German Army. Even when the Russians had been in an advantageous position, for example during the Battle of Łódź during November 1914, the Germans had turned the tables on them. The only significant successes the Russians had enjoyed against the Germans had been defensive operations, outside Warsaw in October and in central Poland in December. Rather than waste resources in another offensive that showed so little promise, it was understandable that a defensive posture might be preferred against such a formidable foe.

By contrast, almost every Russian operation against the *k.u.k.* Army had succeeded. The Russians were also under constant pressure from their French allies. The pre-war strategy of the Entente had been for France to bear the brunt of German attacks, while Russia crushed the Central Powers in the east. The French felt they had delivered their part of the bargain, and repeatedly made the Russians aware of this. It was high time that Russia delivered some worthwhile results. With no prospect of a major success against the Germans, the grand duke had little option but to look to the south.

Other political issues also played a part. Both the Central Powers and their enemies placed great importance on attracting neutral states – specifically Italy, Bulgaria and Romania – to their side. Whilst the relatively small and poorly equipped armies of the latter two nations would not make a major difference to the outcome of the war, the extension of the front lines to incorporate these areas would put a great strain on one or other side, perhaps creating weaknesses elsewhere. If Russia could win a major victory over the Austro-Hungarian Empire in the Carpathians, it seemed likely that Italy and Romania in particular could be persuaded to join the Entente Powers. Both nations had territorial claims on land held by Austria-Hungary, and would surely take advantage of any weakening of the *k.u.k.* Army. The entry of Romania and Italy into the war might also further destabilise the internal integrity of the empire, which had substantial minorities that might side with these two nations.

Danilov was not alone in opposing this change of emphasis. Some, like Mikhail Bonch-Bruyevich, a rising star in the infantry, saw deeper problems:

> The high command did not set general objectives for the war and the resultant tasks for each front. This lack of clear, firm goals resulted in no coherent plan of action, and on our part the war became a bloody mess, without any promise and with no understanding by its participants of the part that their actions played in any overall scheme. It can certainly be argued that at this stage, not only the ordinary soldiers but also the senior officers did not understand their missions.[10]

This was partly due to the structure of the Russian Army, and partly due to the personalities within that structure. Vladimir Sukhomlinov, the minister for war, had played a large part in designing the command arrangements of the army, and in doing so had been driven as much by a desire to establish and consolidate his own position as by any wish to improve the functioning of the army – indeed, the development of capable, strong-minded staff officers along the lines of the German Army would have been a distinct threat to his own authority. The appointment of Grand Duke Nikolai as supreme commander after the outbreak of war was perhaps inevitable, given the lack of any other obvious candidate, but despite his administrative skill and experience, he was not a strategist capable of devising a new master plan when the pre-war plans failed to function as expected; nor was he a man with sufficient personal authority and forcefulness to bring the various factions within the army into closer cooperation.

Away from the battlefield, there were some notable casualties. Perhaps in protest at the change in priority, Ruzsky announced that he was unwell on 26 March and was unable to continue as commander of Northwest Front. His replacement was Mikhail Alexeyev, who had been chief of staff in Southwest Front. He and Ivanov had frequently been at loggerheads, being representatives of different factions within the Russian military establishment; Ivanov was a member of Sukhomlinov's circle, while Alexeyev came from the ranks of the minister for war's enemies. The appointment of Alexeyev to command Northwest Front was therefore hardly likely to result in more harmonious relations between the two formations. Nevertheless, as a leading proponent of assigning primary importance to Southwest Front, Alexeyev might be expected to ensure that Northwest Front no longer demanded more troops and resources than was absolutely necessary, allowing for the switch of Russian efforts to Ivanov's front.

Some of the men who had come under critical scrutiny in late February also found themselves in new posts. Sievers was dismissed from command of Tenth Army, and replaced by Evgeny Radkevich, who had commanded III Siberian Corps during the February fighting. Although he and his corps fought well, Radkevich had been criticised for abandoning his corps towards the end of the battle and reaching the safety of Grodno while his men were left to find their own escape route over the Bobr; nevertheless, this was overlooked in the face of the pressing need to find a replacement for Sievers. In turn, Radkevich was replaced by Vladimir Onufreyevich Trofimov as commander of III Siberian Corps. Sievers disappears from records at this stage, and one account suggests that he was overcome with grief at his defeat in Masuria and his dismissal, and committed suicide.[11] There are no other accounts that confirm this, and some documents suggest that he was still alive in 1920, as part of the White Russian forces. Regardless of his ultimate fate, he played no further part in the First World War.

Despite its vast resources, Russia was struggling to provide sufficient troops to man the huge front line and to make good the terrible losses of the opening months of the war. This was at least partly due to the inadequate arrangements for reservists and other reinforcements to be prepared for war; the training depots repeatedly failed to perform as expected, and matters were worsened by the chronic shortage of rifles, guns and other equipment, with the result that troops arriving at the front line frequently had completed almost no proper training. On 20 February, the French ambassador in Petrograd, Maurice Paléologue, wrote:

As I had to call on Sazonov [the Russian foreign minister] this afternoon, I brought him away in my car.

As we were crossing the Field of Mars we noticed several companies of infantry who were drilling. The men had difficulty in marching in the snow. The yellow fog which hung over the great parade ground gave the whole scene a most gloomy and funereal aspect. Sazonov remarked with a sigh:

'Look! There's a sad sight for you! I suppose there's about a thousand men there, and they're not conscripts being put through their paces but trained men who are no doubt leaving for the front in a few days. And there's not a rifle among them! Isn't it dreadful! For Heaven's sake, Ambassador, stir up your Government to come to the rescue. If they don't, where shall we be?'

I promised him to press them again, and with the greatest vigour, to accelerate the dispatch of the rifles expected from France, for the sight of these poor *moujiks* on their way to the slaughterhouse tore my heart.

As we were continuing our drive in silence a scene from Shakespeare came to my mind – a scene in which the great dramatist seems to have concentrated all the ironic pity with which the spectacle of human follies filled him. It is at the beginning of *Henry II* [Paléologue is mistaken, the quote is from *Henry IV Part 1*]. The merry Falstaff is presenting to Prince Henry of Lancaster a troop he has just recruited, a gang which is simply a collection of ragged beggars without arms. 'I never did see such pitiful rascals!' cries the Prince. 'Tut, tut!' cries Falstaff; 'Food for powder, food for powder; they'll fill a pit as well as better. Tush, man! Mortal men, mortal men!'[12]

Whilst steps were in hand to improve matters, the army would have to live within its resources for the moment. In such circumstances, the Russians turned their attention to the forces still besieging Przemyśl. Ivanov concluded that the sooner that the siege could be brought to an end, the better, as this would release a substantial body of men with which he could counter any threat to his extreme southeast flank, or alternatively use the troops for renewed assaults across the Carpathians. *Stavka* had promised to transfer four infantry divisions from Northwest Front, but for the moment, it was difficult to identify areas of the front line from where they might be extracted. The Russian artillery around the fortress resumed its bombardment on 9 February, while attempts to reduce the outer fortifications began at a higher intensity. A further slaughter of almost all the remaining horses allowed Kusmanek, the garrison commander, to put off the moment when he would have to admit defeat, but the arrival of a relief column was now critically needed.

From his headquarters in Teschen, Conrad continued to urge his commanders to make preparations for a renewal of offensive operations. The reality from the front was that the losses of the first attempt to force the Russian line in the Carpathians had left the divisions of the *k.u.k.* Army unable to contemplate any major attack. At first, following the bitter fighting of late January, much of the Carpathian front went over to positional warfare, and it was only at the extreme southeast end of the line that movement continued. Pflanzer-Baltin managed to attack and capture the town of Kolomea (now Kolomyya) on 16 February, but lacked the strength to pursue the retreating Russians energetically. After a pause for rest, the Austro-Hungarian forces attempted to renew their advance towards Stanislau (now Ivano-Frankivsk), but soon ran into renewed Russian resistance.

Linsingen urged his South Army to resume its attacks, but his men were approaching the limits of their strength; in combat since 23 January, they had spent all but three days out in the open, often with limited or no supplies.[13] Fortunately for Linsingen, reinforcements arrived at the critical moment in the form of the Austro-Hungarian 5th Infantry Division and the German 4th Infantry Division, the latter transferred from the German forces in East Prussia. Rather than allow these formations to wither away in further pointless mountain warfare, Linsingen dispatched them to reinforce Pflanzer-Baltin's western flank. Meanwhile, he attempted to turn both flanks of the Russian position that had blocked his advance.

On 19 February, the cautious optimism amongst Austro-Hungarian officers about Pflanzer-Baltin's advance fell sharply, albeit temporarily. The Russian forces opposing the German XXIV Reserve Corps hurled back the attempts by Linsingen to encircle them. A week later, when the Germans tried to advance again, they were rapidly brought to a halt by tough resistance, and closer cooperation between Linzingen and Pflanzer-Baltin remained unattainable. Nevertheless, the Austro-Hungarian forces reached and captured Stanislau on 20 February; the official Austro-Hungarian history of the war records that the local population greeted them with jubilation, and whilst this may be true of some parts of the population, it is likely that other elements were less enthusiastic.[14] With Czernowitz also back in Austro-Hungarian hands, there now seemed a real possibility of prising open the Carpathian position from the east – if Pflanzer-Baltin could maintain his advance, the Russians holding up Linsingen would be forced to retreat.

Ivanov had been worried about his southeast flank for some time, and had already put in place a plan to remedy the problem. The formations of Ninth Army had been withdrawn from central Poland and transferred to the critical sector, and on 20 February, they launched an attack on Stanislau from three directions. The Austro-Hungarian 36th Infantry Division succeeded in fighting off the initial assault, but the overall situation had changed almost instantly from one of some promise to something far more threatening. Fortunately for the energetic Pflanzer-Baltin, who immediately travelled to the front line to see the battlefield and to meet his subordinate commanders, reinforcements were at hand. In addition to being able to move elements of his own command towards Stanislau, he managed to persuade *AOK* to give him a free hand with the newly arrived 5th Infantry Division, which had been intended to reinforce Linsingen's South Army immediately to the west. Heavy fighting continued around the town for several days, and though Pflanzer-Baltin's forces slowly edged forward, the price they paid was heavy; 6th Infantry Division reported that one of its regiments had been reduced to only 320 combatants, another to fewer than 100.[15]

An officer involved in the fighting described the attritional nature of the constant battles after the war:

It was the nature of the Carpathian war this winter that the fighting did not cease when the actual battles ended. The front line continued to fluctuate greatly, and the terrible misery continued without interruption. Today, it is almost incomprehensible how it was possible to have no protection against the cold of winter and its consequences, in a land in which timber for construction and firewood was available in greater abundance than almost anywhere in Europe. The explanation of the matter is the total absence of arrangements due to lack of foresight on the one hand, and no provision of work parties on the other. The combat troops themselves ... were in any case numerically far inferior to their opponents, more so every day as a result of their terrible losses, and consequently the most urgent priority was for every rifle to be deployed at the front; and with the almost continuous fighting, troops could at best dig in a little during the few short lulls, but couldn't fell trees and cut planks. The labour battalions stationed behind the front faced a daily increasing burden of maintaining roads, which might be under a metre of snow today, frozen tomorrow, and the day after awash as a result of a sudden thaw and turned to bottomless mud, and were finally used to support the front line provided that they weren't starving or were rendered defenceless due to a shortage of ammunition. It became increasingly rare for the few reserves to get some actual peace and rest, or even to be under a roof. Thus the misery grew steadily worse; in the front line, the soldiers were held firmly in combat, with the possibility of relief and replacement prevented by escalating losses, which rose to new records, and prevented any rest and recuperation behind the front. All of this was exacerbated further by the wretched supply situation. The railways in the Hungarian-Galician border area were extremely sparse and very inefficient, and were inadequate for the needs of the large military forces that had now assembled here; the road network was also too thin and of extremely poor quality, and did not stand up to the sudden huge increase in demands. Other routes through the thinly populated forested hills were few and of the most primitive type. As a result, entire corps were repeatedly left all of a sudden with no usable communications to the rear for days at a time; one does not have to be a soldier to appreciate the consequences.

It can be no surprise that the physical suffering paved the way for a collapse of morale. One must not forget that this was no longer the original army, rather a more or less improvised 'replacement army'. The replacements who arrived with the march battalions could not usually be sent to their regular troop formations and incorporated into them, but instead were deployed as independent tactical formations as they arrived, which was of course not ideal, but the tactical situation could not be avoided. And with these march battalions there also came the most fatal first signs of defeatism and political unreliability in certain parts of the hinterland behind the front. First the Czechs; during the Carpathian winter, the 28th Prague Regiment 'allowed itself to be led away from its positions by an enemy battalion without a shot fired'. There were even treasonous plots amongst the Romanian troops; it is known that a Transylvanian priest had called on arriving recruits to give an oath that they would desert to the enemy at the first opportunity. At the same time, the enemy conducted a most intensive propaganda campaign. Their greater numbers allowed regular relief and rotation; they were also better supplied and clothed, and their medical services worked perfectly ... and the great hopes that we placed in corruption that had been seen in their services in earlier times proved completely unfulfilled. As a result of the comprehensive propaganda, the entire indigenous peasant population stood almost unanimously on the side of the Russians and did their best to spy on us. The Jews were the only exception; they spied equally on both sides.

For our troops that remained loyal, and this was by far the larger proportion, continually being surrounded by treason and espionage became steadily more unbearable, and the men became increasingly panicky just as their officers became increasingly nervous, undermining the last remnants of confidence in the future.[16]

It was inevitable that troops in such terrible conditions would see the enemy as being in a far better position; the reality was that the Russian troops suffered just as much, and their medical services were far from the level of perfection that are described here.

There is no doubt that the morale of the *k.u.k.* Army collapsed during the Carpathian campaign, and it is worth considering how much of this was avoidable. The entire campaign had been initiated with the expectation of advancing quickly out of the mountains, and by the end of January it must have been clear that this was not going to be achieved; to persevere with the operation in such inhospitable circumstances was to court disaster. Perhaps the only justification for Conrad's stubborn perseverance is that there seemed to be a faint glimmer of hope in Pflanzer-Baltin's sector of the front line. But even if the Russians had been driven back from the mountains, the question has to be asked: 'What then?' The supply lines of the Austro-Hungarian and German forces, running through the mountains, would have been severely stretched just to hold any gains, let alone allow for the build-up of sufficient strength to continue an advance towards the north. The relief of the Przemyśl garrison would barely compensate for the huge losses being suffered in trying to break through the Russian lines. The entire operation lacked any clear strategic purpose, and was part of Conrad's abiding belief in the necessity to mount offensive operations to break the enemy's will to continue the war. The folly of continuing such operations in terrain that was so unsuited to offensive operations was clear even at the time, and the outcome was precisely the opposite of what Conrad intended: the morale of his men was dealt a huge blow, from which it would never recover.

In addition to the advance across the relatively open right flank, Conrad wanted to make another effort to break out of the Carpathians. To an extent, this was inevitable. One of the primary purposes of the entire Carpathian campaign was the relief of Przemyśl, and Pflanzer-Baltin's units were too far from the fortress to be able to achieve this. Every attempt to use their advance to unlock the Carpathian positions had failed to date, and Conrad returned to his previous plans for frontal assaults against the Russian positions. Seven infantry divisions were transferred from Poland to Böhm-Ermolli's army, while additional troops were also assigned to Pflanzer-Baltin, but it must be remembered that none of these formations was remotely at full strength. Given that the formations they reinforced had been ground down by January's battles, they barely restored the front line to the levels achieved prior to the previous disastrous offensive.

Böhm-Ermolli's plan was to push north along the road through Baligród to Lisko (now Lesko) with a force of about 50,000 men, taking the most direct path to Przemyśl. The entire attack force of five divisions, added to General Karl Tersztyánszky's group, would be dependent upon a single mountain road for its supplies, and it was therefore vital to try to recover the railway line running into the mountains via Mezölaborcz. Boroević would have to recover Mezölaborcz itself with X Corps, while XIX Corps attacked two days before the main drive in order to clear the railway line. The planned start date of 19 February for the main thrust had to be postponed by three days, as Boroević was still struggling to assemble sufficient forces to attack Mezölaborcz, particularly given the serious losses that the divisions of X Corps had suffered. Two of X Corps' divisions collectively amounted to only 4,662 men, barely the equivalent of one third of the establishment strength of a single division.[17] Even with this delay, the commander of Third Army rated the prospects of a successful assault on the town as poor, and without the railway line Böhm-Ermolli doubted that his drive would have any chance of success. Consequently, Boroević concluded, the entire operation was highly likely to fail. To make matters worse, there was incessant rain for two days before the start date, and the single road upon which everything currently depended began to deteriorate. Böhm-Ermolli requested a further delay until the weather improved, but even if Conrad had been minded to agree, a delay was to be avoided at all costs; unless a relief column arrived by mid-March, the garrison of Przemyśl would be forced to surrender.

Regardless of the pressing urgency, a delay became inevitable. The rain effectively washed away the supply road, and guns, wagons and horses became bogged down in thick mud. Only two of the five divisions assigned as reinforcements for Tersztyánszky managed to detrain at their designated deployment areas; the rest were forced to form up somewhat further back, adding to the congestion and chaos in the rear areas of Second Army. Conrad sent further impatient messages to Böhm-Ermolli, demanding that Second Army reach Przemyśl by 12 March. In addition to the military pioneers struggling to restore the supply road, Böhm-Ermolli now pressed some 7,000 civilian labourers into service in a desperate attempt to allow the offensive to start. Tersztyánszky insisted on a further day's delay while supplies were brought forward, and, belatedly, Böhm-Ermolli declared that the entire attack could not possibly succeed without heavy artillery to smash the Russian positions. However, even when such artillery could be found in other parts of the front and dispatched to the key area, there was little prospect of the guns struggling forward to Tersztyánszky's group, and even the batteries that were already present were hugely hampered by the ongoing shortage of ammunition.[18]

Finally, as the weather turned snowy again on 27 February, the adjoining units of Second and Third Armies made their opening assaults to try to reach the vital railway line. The following day, Boroević attempted to capture Mezőlaborcz. Casualties piled up in both battles, but the Russian lines held. At one stage, the commander of the Russian VIII Corps, Vladimir Mikhailovich Dragomirov, reported to Brusilov, his army commander, that one of his divisions was hard pressed and would have to retreat. Brusilov replied that a retreat was unthinkable, and that the division commander should be told that if he did not feel able to hold his positions, he would be replaced.[19] Whether this sufficed to stiffen the resolve of the wavering division commander, or whether the Austro-Hungarian attacks foundered in the face of impossible conditions, the Russian line held.

The main drive, commanded by Tersztyánszky, continued to be hampered by the weather. The force had few proper mountain howitzers, and none of the additional guns demanded by Böhm-Ermolli had arrived. The bulk of its artillery proved difficult to manoeuvre into position, due to both the conditions underfoot and the terrain. Only a small proportion of guns actually fired in support of the attack, and even these were of very limited value as low cloud and fog made accurate artillery fire almost impossible. From their trenches, the Russians faced mass attacks by Austro-Hungarian troops, and crushed them with defensive fire; their own guns had ranged in on likely targets in the preceding weeks, and had little difficulty in raining shells down on the advancing infantry.

Conditions for the Austro-Hungarian forces struggling to reach the front remained appalling, taking a huge toll on men and animals, as an artillery officer recorded:

> When the artillery unit reached Lopienka, men and horses collapsed immediately. They all sank into the snow and drifted into a deathly sleep. It had taken forty-eight hours to travel 40km [25 miles] … There had been no sleep for the men.
>
> … My horse, which had saved my life so often, could neither be set free to die in misery from hunger along the road, nor be sent to the so-called 'horse hospitals' … The course of action that was required was quite clear, but this would be the hardest shot I fired in the entire campaign. I prepared my pistol; my hand wavered. My thoroughbred, the noblest of creatures, lay exhausted on the ground. He greeted me with a faint whinny … I dropped my pistol, but the horse whinnied again, so I raised the weapon and fired. I collapsed in the snow, and wept for only the second time in the war.[20]

At the eastern end of the battlefield, Pflanzer-Baltin's forces faced growing Russian resistance. Brusilov had no intention of staying on the defensive; instead, he planned an attack of his own, with the intention of cutting off Pflanzer-Baltin from the rest of the front and then destroying him in isolation by combining his attacks with those of Ninth Army from the east. When the attacks commenced, the Austro-Hungarian forces enjoyed some notable defensive successes, but the Russian pressure showed no signs of letting up and on 1 March, Pflanzer-Baltin's line began to give way. By throwing their last reserves into the battle, the battered units of the *k.u.k.* Army were able to prevent a disaster, but all thought of further advances had to be abandoned. Instead, Pflanzer-Baltin ordered a withdrawal to defensive positions that had been prepared in haste a short distance to the rear.

Over the coming days, it became increasingly clear to Pflanzer-Baltin that his force stood no chance of resuming its advance. Intercepted Russian messages revealed that further Russian cavalry forces had been dispatched to try to turn the eastern end of the line, and whilst it was relatively straightforward to block this move – the cavalry of both sides continued to make very little impact – the messages also revealed that with most of the Russian Ninth Army now deployed in the area, the Russians enjoyed a superiority of 2:1 in infantry and 3:1 in cavalry. On 10 and 11 March, heavy snow brought movement by both sides to a standstill, but two days later the Russian cavalry launched its attack against the eastern part of the Austro-Hungarian line and succeeded in gaining some ground before bloody counterattacks brought them to a halt. Finally, on 18 March, the fighting died down and both sides were able to catch their breath. A little to the west, Linsingen's South Army had also been involved in heavy fighting. On 7 March, the Germans launched a major attack, but made minimal progress in the face of heavy casualties. Two days later, further heavy snow brought all activity to a halt; two companies of infantry had to be dug out of their trenches after they became buried in snow. Russian counterattacks followed, adding further to the terrible losses; again, there was almost no change of battlefield positions.

Amongst the German formations struggling through the snow was 1st Infantry Division, originally recruited in East Prussia. The division had fought with great distinction in its home province in 1914, but was now beginning to show signs of strain. Dominik Richert was an Alsatian who was conscripted into the German Army, and after brief service in the west he was sent to 1st Infantry Division as part of a group of replacements. They reached the front line late at night:

> We joined our company. Most of the men came from East Prussia and spoke in a dialect which was difficult to understand, while others were German Poles. As it dawned I was able to see that they were all very run-down and looked in a bad state. They told us how much they had suffered from the cold, and warned us that it was very dangerous to raise your head above the snow as the Russians, Siberian marksmen, would shoot anyone who dared to do so.
>
> ... The East Prussians then told us that they had already made several attacks on the Russian positions, but that they had been beaten back each time with heavy losses. Their dead were still lying up there and had been buried by the snow. I raised my head for a moment and was able to see a number of rigid hands and bayonets sticking up out of the snow. I also saw a number of mounds in the snow, under which lay the bodies of the fallen. Food could only be fetched at night-time. As it was not possible for a field kitchen to get up here, the cooking was done down in the valley in small portable pots. By the time that the people who had been given the task of collecting the food had climbed back up ... both the food and the coffee were cold ... As a result of the cold conditions, almost everyone was suffering from stomach pains and diarrhoea ... It drove you to despair, and there was no way out; we were threatened either by death, injury and frozen limbs or by being taken captive. There was an incredible lack of courage among the soldiers, and it was only the terrible force of circumstances which forced us to bear it.

... On particularly cold nights several soldiers would have frostbitten feet, noses or ears. One morning they found two sentries in a listening post who had frozen to death in the snow.

...We were all suffering from lice, and it seemed a mystery where they had all come from. As it was impossible to get undressed because of the cold, the lice were able to nest and breed in our clothes.[21]

The number of men having to leave the front line in South Army averaged 400–700 per day, and in two weeks the total reached over 6,700.[22] Given his failure to make any headway, Linsingen sent a telegram to Berlin stating that the forces available were simply too weak to force their way out of the Carpathians. Instead, any future offensive should commence from near Krakow, and proceed towards the east along the northern edge of the mountains. This would take advantage of the better road and rail network in that area; given that this was Austro-Hungarian territory before the war, it is remarkable that Conrad and the rest of the Austro-Hungarian high command had not given more consideration to such an approach at an earlier stage.

As much in desperation as any other reason, Conrad now looked at just such an offensive north of the Carpathians. If the Russians had been stripping their front line of troops to reinforce the units fighting in the Carpathians, there might be an opportunity for the Austro-Hungarian Fourth Army to advance. Archduke Joseph Ferdinand wished to wait until there was clear evidence of Russian forces withdrawing, arguing that his army was simply too weak to force its way forward in a frontal attack; he argued that if the Russians did not show any signs of reducing the strength of their front, some of the troops he had assembled for an attack should be transferred to Pflanzer-Baltin at the eastern end of the line. *AOK* disagreed, on the grounds that the railway line for such a transfer could run only twelve trains a day and the move would therefore take far too long. Wrangling between Conrad and Joseph Ferdinand, and a deterioration of the weather, delayed matters until 8 March, when 8th Infantry Division attacked the Russian lines. At first, there was encouraging progress towards Gorlice but the weather intervened again in the form of heavy snow. Joseph Ferdinand was in favour of waiting for better weather, but once more Conrad insisted on a resumption of attacks. The Russians responded with energetic counterattacks, and Joseph Ferdinand rapidly scaled down his efforts to the minimum that would satisfy *AOK*.

Back in the Carpathians, attack followed counterattack as the Austro-Hungarian forces tried in vain to deliver a breakthrough to Przemyśl. The first two weeks of March cost Second Army over 51,000 casualties, many from frostbite and exposure.[23] Georg Weith, an officer in the front line, later described the appalling conditions in the mountains:

> On 1 March there was heavy snowfall and fog, all sense of direction disappeared, and entire regiments lost their way, resulting in catastrophic losses. On 6 March, the weather changed again: clear sky, a thaw during the day, and as low as -20°C at night, with the result that all slopes were completely covered in ice, so that even in the absence of enemy activity, any attack became the most energetic of ventures. And although this meant that at least during daylight hours the combatants were warmed a little by the sunshine, an icy storm from the northwest drained the last heat from their bones and joints. Throughout the entire attack area, for days and weeks nobody in any part was able to take off their clothes, which for the most part formed frozen layers of ice; the ground, frozen as hard as stone, hindered the attackers from digging in when under enemy fire, casualties climbed enormously. The wounded, whose evacuation was almost impossible, died en masse after suffering appallingly; throughout the weeks of fighting and endurance, the men couldn't sleep at night, out of fear of rapidly freezing to death.
>
> ... On 10 March, a snowstorm such as is only known in the glaciers broke loose. All advances stopped, every attempt to evacuate the sick was impossible ... the icy ground, covered in snow, was completely impassable, and all attempts to dig in were abandoned; without cover and unable to move, the infantry were left stranded in front of the enemy's positions, the bulk of the artillery was still three or four marches behind the front line! And the troops held on; despite the reports from their commanders that had told of complete exhaustion for weeks, despite the constant [enemy] propaganda, despite everything, they persevered in this hell.[24]

As if this was not bad enough, Brusilov's troops now began a series of attacks aimed at driving back Boroević's battered formations. In his memoirs, Brusilov maintained that he had no real expectation of being able to conquer Hungary, but mounted the attacks in order to tie down as much of the strength of the *k.u.k.* Army as possible, and thus to prevent the gathering of sufficient forces to break through to Przemyśl. It is difficult to confirm this, but it seems consistent with the prevailing belief in most armies of the day that offensive operations were the preferable way of conducting war. At first the Russians gained some ground but as was consistently the case in the First World War, defensive firepower inflicted crippling losses on the attackers. Before long, the Russian advance came to a halt, and even in their distant headquarters the senior commanders of both sides had to conclude that – for the moment, at least – further advances in the Carpathians were beyond the strength of the exhausted soldiers. Casualties had been terrible; Böhm-Ermolli's army fielded nearly 149,000 men at the beginning of March, and in the following two weeks reported that he had lost nearly 24,000 dead and wounded, and nearly 17,000 forced to leave the front line through ill health.[25] By mid-March, most front-line commanders in the *k.u.k.* Army had grown used to their attacks faltering when neighbouring units failed to make their own promised attacks, and many planned assaults simply didn't take place, with battalion and regimental commanders waiting to see if the supporting units were going to make any move. In such circumstances, whatever tiny hope of reaching Przemyśl disappeared completely. The heavy-handed replacement of such commanders by others who might show more resolve only made matters worse, as complete strangers struggled to impose their will upon exhausted and demoralised soldiers. The only consolation was that the Russians had fared little better.

To the north of the blood and snow of the Carpathian battlefields was the besieged city of Przemyśl, the objective of all the bloody Austro-Hungarian assaults. By March, the situation for the troops within the fortress was rapidly becoming desperate. Although losses through death, wounding and particularly illness – worsened by food shortages amongst the ordinary soldiers – had reduced the garrison by perhaps 24,000, there simply weren't enough rations for continued resistance, and thoughts began to turn to life as prisoners of war. Josef Tomann, a doctor in the garrison, recorded on 5 March:

> Gunpowder and ecrasite [the propellant in Austro-Hungarian artillery rounds] are being taken to the weapons factories so that the fortress can be blown up if our defences fall, which could happen any time now. Despondency is widespread. We are preparing for a trip to Tomsk, Irkutsk or Tashkent. Our rucksacks are packed. I have sent postcards to Landskron and Petersdorf. Will they be my last? I hope not! I won't write anything about my state of mind.[26]

By this stage of the siege, men were dying at a rate of about 300 per day, mainly from malnutrition and associated diseases, though officers continued to live well. Over the coming days, Tomann continued to make entries in his diary:

> A terrifying number of people are suffering from malnutrition; the starving arrive in their dozens, frozen soldiers are brought in from the outposts, all of them like walking corpses. They lie silently on their cold hospital beds, make no complaints and drink muddy water they call tea. The next day they are carried away to the morgue. The sight of these pitiful figures, whose wives and children are probably

also starving at home, wrings your heart.

... New officers are coming in almost daily with cases of syphilis, gonorrhoea and soft chancre. Some have all three at once! The poor girls and women feel so flattered when they get chatted up by one of these pestilent pigs in their spotless uniforms, with their shiny boots and buttons.[27]

The plan to relieve Przemyśl had always anticipated that the garrison would attempt to fight its way out in order to help any approaching relief column, and even though it was now clear that no relief column would reach the fortress, Kusmanek made preparations for a breakout anyway. Initially, Kusmanek proposed to break out with as many troops as possible, suggesting to *AOK* that he would field about 20,000 men organised in twenty-four battalions, but Conrad insisted that sufficient troops should be left behind to ensure that the fortress continued to hold out. This reduced the scale of the breakout to less than half the original figure.[28] The attempt would be made towards Sambor, even though Böhm-Ermolli advised Kusmanek that there was no possibility of his men making any further headway through the Carpathians. He and his subordinates estimated that they would need at least 40,000 men to make such an assault, and only 31st Infantry Division – already significantly below its establishment strength – was available. Even as this formation began to take up positions for an almost suicidal attempt to break through to Sambor, the Russian VIII Corps renewed its attacks on the left flank of Böhm-Ermolli's army, where XIX Corps found itself in serious difficulties. In these circumstances, with Russian forces threatening to turn his flank, Böhm-Ermolli had no choice but to redirect 31st Infantry Division to the endangered sector. The last lingering hope of linking up with the Przemyśl garrison at Sambor had gone.

Even as the siege was entering its closing stages, Conrad left *AOK* to travel to Schönbrunn for a meeting with the crown council. Despite the almost universally bad news – the ongoing slaughter in the Carpathians, the imminent fall of Przemyśl, and the likely defection of the Italians to the camp of Austria-Hungary's enemies – Conrad was surprisingly animated and optimistic during the meeting, all the more remarkable given his reputation for pessimistic melancholy. The reason was a personal one. Hans von Reininghaus, the husband of his mistress Gina, had decided to divorce her, raising the possibility of Conrad achieving the long-held dream of marrying her.[29] In his headquarters in Teschen though, the mood remained bleak. In keeping with Conrad's instructions, Tersztyánszky ordered his officers to use the full weight of their authority to drive their men forward. The futility of such exhortations must have been clear to all concerned.

After a series of futile assaults on the outer fortifications of Przemyśl in autumn 1914, the Russians had largely restricted themselves to containing the garrison and allowing starvation to wear down the defenders. At one stage, heavy naval artillery had been ordered to the area from Sevastopol, but none of the guns reached the siege perimeter, becoming bogged down on muddy roads or being sent elsewhere. Late on 14 March, the Russians surprised the garrison by attacking and overrunning the outer fortifications to the north of the fortress. Kusmanek ordered a force to be assembled for a counterattack, but preparations were repeatedly held up, not least because the garrison had almost no horses left with which to move artillery, and eventually the planned attack was abandoned.

Two days after the Russian attack, Kusmanek signalled *AOK* that he intended to break out towards the east rather than the southeast. Conrad replied that the original plan should be followed, as Böhm-Ermolli's Second Army was making a further effort to get through – though he must have known at this stage that any such effort was doomed to failure. Kusmanek doggedly stuck to his guns. He would attempt to break through the Russian perimeter towards the east, and hope that he could link up with Pflanzer-Baltin. The reason for this change of plan was that Kusmanek was increasingly aware of the very limited mobility of his forces, and regarded fighting in mountainous terrain as beyond their strength. If he could penetrate the siege lines as he planned, his troops might capture the Russian supply depots at Mościska (now Mostys'ka) and Sądowa Wisznia. After the initial breakout on 19 March, the rest of the garrison would attempt to follow.

Even if there had been no prospect of major Russian resistance, a march to link up with Pflanzer-Baltin over a distance of over 60 miles (100km) in poor weather conditions and along roads that had been badly damaged by the passage of armies in recent months would have been a near-miraculous achievement for men weakened by starvation and lack of activity. Nevertheless, Kusmanek was determined to make the effort. Immediately before the breakout, he sent a signal to Vienna:

> Your Majesty:
> Undefeated by the enemy after six months' continuous fighting, but driven by hunger, the garrison of Przemyśl will attempt to break the encirclement tomorrow morning, 19 March, even though the personnel are almost completely exhausted after months of deprivations of all kinds, so that before its probable defeat it is able to give some service to the field army.
> In this fateful moment we lift up our hearts in love and unswerving loyalty to Your Majesty.[30]

Even as the attempt began, a reply arrived from Franz Joseph:

> The report of this heroic attempt that the hitherto undefeated garrison of Przemyśl has resolved to make has moved me deeply and from the bottom of my heart, I send my blessings to the heroes who are commencing upon a last great deed for the honour of the Fatherland and the glory of our armed services. The achievements of the garrison of Przemyśl will live in memory forever, and every individual deserves a leaf from the wreath of laurel that the Fatherland and I dedicate to the brave, self-sacrificing garrison.[31]

Late at night, as the weather turned first to rain, then sleet, the troops designated to attempt the breakout assembled in the eastern part of the fortress. It had been Kusmanek's intention to attack shortly before dawn, but the plan rapidly ran into difficulties. Exhaustion amongst the troops delayed their movement to the start-line, and matters were made worse by the fact that they had to move through the city via narrow roads and alleys within the fortress. Even when they were out of the city, they had to cross an area that was heavily mined, resulting in still further delays. In any event, there was no possibility of surprise; the Russians had been monitoring Austro-Hungarian signal traffic for some time, and had deciphered the codes currently being used. Consequently, Selivanov, the commander of the besieging forces, had ample time to make his preparations. Several batteries of guns had been deployed in anticipation of the garrison's attempt, and these now opened fire on the gathered troops. The main effort was made by the reservists of 23rd *Honvéd* Infantry Division, which managed to advance perhaps a mile into the Russian defences before its exposed southern flank came under strong counterattack by the Russian 58th Cavalry Division. For once, the Russian cavalry managed to exploit its manoeuvrability, and although 23rd *Honvéd* Infantry Division succeeded in retreating, it lost over two thirds of its personnel. By mid-afternoon, the attempt was over, with the survivors retreating to their fortifications.[32]

There was now no hope for the garrison. Kusmanek considered fighting on until he was overwhelmed, but there was little point, as food was almost exhausted. Russian attacks followed on the two days after the breakout attempt, and although they were beaten off, it was clear that the troops would not be able to resist for long, and such resistance would simply result in heavy casualties for no material gain. Plans for a possible capitulation had been prepared some time before, and were now put into effect. Large stocks of paper money and official documents were burned, the remaining horses were slaughtered, all equipment that might be useful to the Russians was destroyed or disabled, and demolition charges were laid around the major fortifications. Late on 21 March, the fortress guns fired their last rounds, and some were destroyed; others were prepared for destruction.

The following morning, two hours before dawn, Oberst August Martinek, commander of one of the *Landsturm* brigades in the fortress, and Kusmanek's chief of staff, Oberstleutnant Ottokar Hubert, left Przemyśl and travelled under a flag of parlay to Mościska, the headquarters of the besieging Eleventh Army. Their intention was to negotiate terms for the men of the garrison, but Selivanov was not in the mood for any such discussions, and had them disarmed and treated as prisoners of war. It took the personal intervention of the tsar before they received the courtesies they had expected. As it grew light on 22 March, even as Martinek and Hubert were being detained, the charges placed in the fortifications and in the last guns were detonated in a rolling series of explosions. White flags were raised, and Russian forces entered Przemyśl. About 117,000 men went into captivity, including no fewer than nine generals.[33]

Within Przemyśl, anti-Semitism had been as prevalent as it was through much of Europe at the time, with many suspecting the Jewish population of profiteering during the siege. Helena Jabłońska, a civilian living in the city, recorded on 18 March:

> The Jews are taking their shop signs down in a hurry, so that no one can tell who owns what … They've all got so rich off the backs of those poor soldiers, and now of course they want to run away![34]

The Jews had good reason to fear the coming of the Russians. By 1 April, they were already being singled out for harsh treatment:

> The Catholic shops are open and are already fairly well stocked with goods. The Jews have been allowed to see only what they still have in stock. The Russians make fun of them, saying they'll let them eat their matzos in peace, but after the festivities they'll take them in hand, send them to Siberia. They're saying they will confiscate their houses and property … the Jews pretend they don't believe all this talk. They suck up to the Russians.[35]

It is worth noting that although the Catholic Jabłońska commented on the Jews making money during the siege, she did not remark on how the non-Jewish shops had managed to retain substantial stocks of goods despite the siege. For the Jews, worse was to come, and a pogrom commenced two weeks later:

The Jewish pogrom has been under way since yesterday evening [i.e. 16 April].
The Cossacks waited until the Jews set off to the synagogue for their prayers
before setting upon them with whips. They were deaf to any pleas for mercy,
regardless of age. They were taken away from the synagogues, from the streets and
from their doorsteps and driven towards some enormous barracks at Bakończyce.
What are they going to do with them? Some of the older, weaker ones who
couldn't keep up were whipped. Many, many hundreds were driven along in this
way. They say this round-up is to continue until they've caught all of them …
Some Jews are hiding in cellars, but they'll get them there too.[36]

The fall of Przemyśl was a huge disaster for the Austro-Hungarian Empire. The
great victory that Conrad had hoped would restore the empire's political fortunes
had instead turned into another humiliation. Inevitably, the enemies of the
Central Powers made much of their victory, particularly in Russia, where the
pressing need for good news was as great as in Vienna, as Stanley Washburn, who
was in Petrograd, recorded:

On the 23rd it snowed heavily in Petrograd and a biting wind was sweeping
through the streets … And then came the announcement that the great fortress in
Galicia had fallen. In an hour the news was all over the town and in spite of the
inclement weather the streets were thronged with eager Russians, from Prince to
Moujik, anxiously asking each other if the news which had been so long promised
could really be true. The fall of Przemyśl it must be remembered, had been
reported at least a dozen times in Petrograd before this.

… If ever a people genuinely rejoiced over good news it was the citizens of all
classes of Russia's capital when it became known that Przemyśl was at last in
Russian hands. By three in the afternoon, crowds had organised themselves into
bands, and with the Russian flag waving in front, and a portrait of the tsar carried
before, dozens of bands marched through the streets chanting the deep-throated
Russian national anthem.[37]

Troops that might have been put to decisive use elsewhere had spent the winter
languishing in the fortress and had accomplished little, even in the negative sense
of tying down Russian forces. To make matters worse, Conrad's repeated attempts
to relieve Przemyśl cost several times as many men as there were in garrison he
was trying to rescue, but having allowed such a large force to be left in the fortress,
he probably felt that he had no choice but to try to reach them. But this
immediately begs the question: was it necessary to try to hold the fortress in the

first place? The issue of the usefulness of fortresses is a curious one. Throughout the 19th and early 20th centuries, several fortresses – Sevastopol, Port Arthur, Sedan, even Paris – had played important parts in battles, but on none of these occasions had the defenders of the fortress been able to use it to win the war. Despite this, huge amounts of money were spent on massive fortifications, with the expectation that they would prove to be of huge benefit. Przemyśl was arguably obsolete by 1914, yet Conrad still allowed it to be occupied. Once that decision was taken, and particularly after the first siege was lifted in October 1914, the attempts to reach the city in order to lift the siege were inevitable.

Even if it is accepted that a relief attempt was required, there is little doubt that it was badly managed. Troops were committed on a variety of axes on a broad front, in which the terrain ensured that even neighbouring units would struggle to offer each other any support, let alone cooperate over larger distances. As a consequence, there were isolated tactical successes, but at no point were sufficient forces mustered to allow for the exploitation of these successes. Conrad remained obsessed with attempting a relief by the shortest route possible, even though this required an advance through the mountains at the worst time of year, with the attacking troops dependent upon poor communications for their supplies.

It was argued at the time that by denying the Russians the use of the railway junction in Przemyśl, the garrison imposed considerable delays upon Russian movements for the duration of the siege. This may have been true, but it would only have any value if it could be demonstrated that these delays had an effect upon Russian operations. However, in the middle of winter, the shortages experienced by troops in the front line were far more due to consumption of ammunition and supplies of all sorts exceeding the ability of the Russian Empire to replace them than due to the limited ability of the Russians to move supplies to the front line.

The fighting around the city was costly for both sides. By the end of the siege, the Russians had suffered over 100,000 casualties, though over a third of these occurred in Radko Dimitriev's failed attempt to storm the defences in autumn 1914. But any analysis of casualties should include the men who died in the Carpathian battles in early 1915 – without the existence of the fortress, there would have been no rationale for those battles. And whilst both sides had suffered heavily, Russia could afford the casualties far more than Austria-Hungary.

An important consequence of the fall of Przemyśl was the release of the Russian troops that had been besieging the fortress. XXVIII Corps was assigned to Eighth Army, and XXIX Corps to Third Army. Together with other formations that were arriving from other sectors, Ivanov was finally in a position to consider his long-planned advance into Hungary. His plan was to break through the Austro-Hungarian and German lines south of the Uzsok Pass; once clear of the mountains, Eighth Army was to strike southeast into the rear of Pflanzer-Baltin's forces, while Radko Dimitriev's Third Army turned southwest into Hungary. At the same time, Ninth Army would attempt to turn the eastern flank of the enemy line, raising the possibility of an envelopment of Pflanzer-Baltin and possibly the German South Army. *Stavka* was unenthusiastic about this plan, preferring to make the main effort in the east, thus avoiding the need to commit large numbers of men to force their way through the Carpathians.

Danilov – who remained opposed to any diversion of resources away from the north – accepted that Ivanov's plan held great promise if it were to succeed, but regardless of the quartermaster-general's support, the plan contained within it several factors that reduced the likelihood of success. Firstly, the proposed attack did not correspond to the current deployment of troops, and would stretch resources to the limit. Secondly, it would extend the overall front line considerably, exposing the western flank of the forces pushing into Hungary to a counterattack from the west.

Starting on the eve of the surrender of Przemyśl, Ivanov's subordinates struggled to get their troops into positions. XII and XXIX Corps from Third Army assembled in the mountains to the west of the Beskid Pass, with VIII, XVII, XXVIII and VII Corps from Eighth Army to their east. Out on the very eastern end of the long front line, the Russian II and III Cavalry Corps found themselves in action against a mixed force of Austro-Hungarian infantry and cavalry. Amongst the formations of the Russian II Cavalry Corps was the so-called 'Wild Division', recruited from indigenous tribes of the Caucasus. The corps was commanded by Huseyin Khan Nahitchevanski, who had failed miserably as commander of Rennenkampf's cavalry in the first invasion of East Prussia in August 1914; on this occasion, he fared rather better, driving off Pflanzer-Baltin's flank guard. This should have allowed the Russians to turn the flank of the Austro-Hungarian positions, but the Russian cavalry was supported by XXXII and XXXIII Corps, both made up of low-grade troops. Although they had a limited amount of front-line experience, they failed to make the most of Nahitchevanski's success.[38] Nevertheless, with *AOK* unable to find reinforcements from elsewhere, Pflanzer-Baltin had no option but to shuffle troops from one part of his front line to another. The consequence was that while he might be able to prevent the Russian forces on his flank from rolling up the line, Conrad's dream of forcing the Carpathian position by an advance by Pflanzer-Baltin and the German South Army remained no more than wishful thinking. There were tense moments along the line of the River Dniester as well as on the extreme flank, but through a mixture of good fortune, poor Russian coordination and astute juggling of his limited resources, Pflanzer-Baltin managed to hold his positions. For his achievements, he was awarded the Commander's Cross of the Military Order of Maria Theresa; it could be argued that given the desperate need in the Austro-Hungarian Empire for good news, this was an overly lavish award, but there can be no doubt that he prevented a perilous general situation from turning into a disastrous one. Had his 'army group' been dislodged and driven back, the German South Army too would have been forced to retreat, conceivably followed by the entire line of forces in the Carpathians.

Falkenhayn might have hoped that the fall of Przemyśl would result in Conrad abandoning his bloody attempts to advance through the Carpathians, but on 14 March, before the city surrendered and at a time when it was clear that no relief of the garrison was possible, the Austro-Hungarian chief of the general staff sent a message to his German equivalent stating that he wished to continue with his attempts, as it was important to tie down Russian forces rather than allow them to be gathered elsewhere. Over the next few days, a series of orders from *AOK* to Second, Third and Fourth Armies eliminated any remaining hope amongst the Germans that there might be a change of emphasis. As soon as the next draft of march battalions had arrived, all three armies were ordered to conduct operations in accordance with Conrad's pre-war doctrine of attacking at all costs, at every point of the front; no sector was to be allowed to remain quiet.

August von Cramon was the German liaison officer in *AOK* at the time. He had worked hard to build good relationships with his hosts, and proved to be a valued and able liaison officer for both the Germans and the Austro-Hungarians. His memoirs provide an interesting illumination on events in Teschen.

The fighting in the preceding weeks had adequately demonstrated that the intentions of the army leadership could not be reconciled with the effectiveness of the troops. Only when all the formations committed to an attack are adequately trained and equipped, only when commanders of all ranks and at every level fully carry out their duties [can success be expected] – there was no meaningful answer for the complexities created by the weather, and the Central Powers could not keep up with the growing defensive strength of the Russians. The troops in the front line realised the futility of their endeavours earlier than the army leadership. Many orders for attacks remained merely orders. Conrad tended to think through his operations without regard to the troops; his orders to some extent reflected this and overlooked the fact that every decision could only be realised through the living will of the masses. Troops of whom more is constantly expected than they can achieve with their best efforts lose enthusiasm and trust, and in this manner, ideals too found their graves, and their disappearance was blamed upon the troops.[39]

In vain, Falkenhayn suggested on 22 March that the entire Carpathian sector should go over to the defensive, releasing troops to be sent south for a spring offensive against Serbia. He reiterated that this would also create sufficient reserves to cope with any Italian intervention, and would open the route for support to reach Turkey. Conrad responded by stating that eight to ten German divisions would be required to overcome the Serbs; Falkenhayn suggested that only three or four would be needed. The two were still wrangling when Ivanov's offensive made the argument irrelevant.

The first attacks began on 20 March, even before Kusmanek and the Przemyśl garrison had surrendered. XVII Corps, on the left flank of Boroević's Third Army, came under heavy pressure from the Russian XXIV Corps, part of Radko Dimitriev's Third Army, and was driven back over the following days. The Russians extended their attack to the east, with the Austro-Hungarian VII and X Corps hard pressed to hold their positions. Although Russian progress was limited, this was a sector of the front from which Conrad had intended to draw troops that could be sent to Pflanzer-Baltin on the eastern flank, and this was now clearly impossible. Troops of 4th Cavalry Division, some of whom had already boarded trains, were hurriedly sent back to shore up the sagging front line.

Although their advance was slow, the Russians felt confident, knowing that further reinforcements were due to arrive over the coming days. On 28 March, Ivanov sent a cautiously optimistic telegram to *Stavka*:

> Advancing with valour, our troops have pushed the enemy back over the main ridgeline in the Carpathians at many points … [but] have encountered fresh enemy formations, resulting in stubborn fighting.[40]

He went on to admit that there would have to be a pause while reinforcements and supplies were brought forward. In short, Ivanov was now experiencing exactly the same problems that Conrad had faced earlier in the year. The terrain made anything other than head-on attacks impossible; deploying sufficient artillery to give such attacks any chance of success was extremely difficult; and getting reinforcements and supplies to the front line was dependent upon just a few roads with limited capacity.

Within hours of Ivanov sending his telegram, he received a reply from Yanushkevich in *Stavka*:

The Supreme Commander [Grand Duke Nikolai] has instructed me to ask you ... to deliver a more detailed report on the state of the armies entrusted to your front, their current requirements, and the causes of the delay in progress in the Carpathians. He also wishes to know when you intend to recommence your unfinished operations, bearing in mind that the current pause is extremely disadvantageous – both politically and militarily – as it enables our enemies to bring up reinforcements and strengthen their new positions.[41]

Conrad was already attempting to bring such reinforcements to the front line. Aware that his own resources were almost exhausted, he turned again to Falkenhayn, requesting that two or three German divisions be sent to the mountains. At first, Falkenhayn declined the request, not wishing to commit more troops to the futile and bloody fighting in the Carpathians, but the increasing pressure upon Conrad's line forced his hand. General Georg von der Marwitz, who had commanded XXXVIII Reserve Corps in the winter fighting in Masuria, would form a new *Beskidenkorps* in the Carpathians, built around 25th and 35th Reserve Infantry Divisions and 4th Infantry Division. The move confirmed Falkenhayn's fear that the reserve formations that he had allowed to be sent east on a temporary basis would not be available for operations in the west for the foreseeable future. However, he insisted that together with the limited Austro-Hungarian forces being sent to the area, the personnel of the *Beskidenkorps* were not to be committed piecemeal as they arrived. Instead, they were to be held back until fully assembled, and then used in a decisive counterattack to smash Ivanov's forces.

Boroević was not enthusiastic about this proposal. Even once the new corps was fully assembled, he feared that there would be insufficient forces available – perhaps 50,000 men – with which to overcome the Russians, who had at least 40,000 troops in the area. The mountainous terrain would limit the ability of troops to manoeuvre freely and would prevent artillery from being used properly, and in any case, the Germans had no experience of mountain warfare. It would be better, he suggested, to allow the Russians to spend their strength in further attacks. The time for a counterattack would come once they had been worn down. *AOK* agreed in principle, but added that the *Beskidenkorps* should not be used to support the existing front line; instead, it should be held in reserve until the time came for a counterattack. The only troops that should be used to bolster the line should be those transferred from the neighbouring Second Army. Even this, though, proved to be impossible, as renewed attacks by Brusilov's Eighth Army resulted in Böhm-Ermolli demanding the return of the troops, together with an additional division.

This new Russian pressure proved to be short-lived, as once more Ivanov's divisions outstripped their supplies, and had to pause while reinforcements struggled forward along the mountain roads. Inevitably, questions arose about the wisdom of continuing the operation, but remarkably, one of the prime critics was Alexeyev, Ivanov's former chief of staff. From his headquarters at Northwest Front, Alexeyev complained that the plan had been for a swift and heavy blow in the Carpathians, not the battle of attrition that was now being fought. It is typical of the way in which personal, factional and regional command rivalries dominated the Russian Army that he argued that the operation should be brought to an immediate halt, and priority given to preparing an attack in central Poland.[42]

For the moment, though, Ivanov still had permission to prosecute his offensive. Once supplies and reinforcements had been brought forward, his troops once more renewed their attacks. A gap developed at the seam between the Austro-Hungarian XVIII and V Corps, and in order to release troops to help bridge the gap, Böhm-Ermolli had to ask Linsingen to extend the front held by his South Army towards the west, thus releasing elements of Böhm-Ermolli's army for use elsewhere. Whilst Linsingen – who had for the moment given up any intention of further offensive operations of his own – was willing to help, the move would take several days before it yielded results. In the meantime, *Korps Schmidt*, on the left flank of the hard-pressed XVIII Corps, launched a counterattack of its own to try to restore the situation; as was almost always the case, the attack faltered and stalled without significant gain. By the afternoon of 1 April, Second Army had no choice but to issue orders for a gradual withdrawal from the Carpathians.

The orders were greeted with dismay. Karl Tersztyánszky, in whose eponymous group *Korps Schmidt* was fighting, objected to the withdrawal on the grounds that some of his forces were still holding their positions on the high ridgelines. From Teschen, too, came objections. Conrad wanted Böhm-Ermolli to continue to hold the Uzsok Pass, something that would be impossible if his troops withdrew from the mountains. Böhm-Ermolli replied that he had no option but to give up the pass and its approaches; if he attempted to stand and fight, his weakened forces in the area would be overrun, and the Russians would be able to threaten the supply routes of Szurmay's group to the east. On 2 April, Boroević joined the criticism, pointing out – with some justification – that if Second Army was finding it difficult to hold the Russians at bay in the mountains, which greatly favoured defensive fighting, things would only be worse south of the Carpathians. He suggested that it was inevitable that Böhm-Ermolli's proposed retreat would result in a gap opening between his troops and Boroević's eastern flank, offering the Russians a multitude of opportunities against both Austro-Hungarian armies. In vain, Second Army Headquarters pointed out that fighting in the mountains brought its own disadvantages – the weather was atrocious, and there was nowhere for troops rotated out of the front line to rest and recuperate in dry and warm surroundings. The new line would also be rather shorter than the existing front line, and the troops would no longer be dependent upon inadequate roads for supplies. Linsingen, too, was amongst the ranks of those who objected. If the Uzsok Pass were conceded to the Russians, all the ground that his men had captured at such high cost would have to be conceded; even if Second Army had to pull back further west, it should hold its positions around the vital pass. To add to Linsingen's irritation, the Austro-Hungarians had initially agreed to the transfer of 38th *Honvéd* Infantry Division to his army from the neighbouring group commanded by Szurmay, but had then proved reluctant to allow the transfer to take place, not least because the increasing Russian pressure made any such withdrawal difficult. Perhaps in an attempt to put Böhm-Ermolli under pressure both to release the promised troops and to change his plans for a retreat, Linsingen sent him an uncoded signal:

> Up to the present time, despite repeated requests to *AOK* in Teschen, no order for the subordination of 38th *Honvéd* Infantry Division to the South Army has been received. As the South Army regards the complete retreat of Second Army as unnecessary, it sees no reason to allow a division to retreat with another army and thereby become complicit in the retreat.[43]

Conrad decided to side with Böhm-Ermolli's critics. The whole of *Gruppe Szurmay* – a little over three infantry divisions – was subordinated to Linsingen's South Army, with orders to hold the area around the Uzsok Pass. Inevitably, the transfer of such a substantial body of troops, together with the widespread criticism of Böhm-Ermolli, was received badly at Second Army Headquarters, and it can have come as no surprise when Böhm-Ermolli offered his resignation. The offer was turned down, and *AOK* explained to Böhm-Ermolli that the reassignment of *Gruppe Szurmay* was purely so that it could stay in place, allowing the rest of Second Army to pull back. Almost immediately after, Linsingen apologised for his outburst. It is not known whether he was prompted to do so by another agency.

The withdrawal of Second Army's centre and western flank proceeded in the first days of April with almost no Russian interference. Although the intention had been to withdraw to a shorter line, the requirement to continue holding the Uzsok Pass nullified this and the withdrawal resulted in a longer front line, leaving the mountainous sector between Second Army and *Gruppe Szurmay* – about 6 miles (10km) – held by a single under-strength division. The feelings of the soldiers, pulling back along the few mountain roads past the debris of abandoned wagons, dead horses and stranded artillery, must have been decidedly mixed. On the one hand, they were leaving behind the misery of mountain warfare in winter; on the other hand, they also left behind tens of thousands of comrades, who had perished for no significant gain.

Meanwhile, Ivanov issued further instructions to his armies. Radko Dimitriev's Third Army was to safeguard the western flank of the offensive, while Brusilov's Eighth Army completed the descent into Hungary. A combination of a shortage of time, resources and lines of communication ensured that it was impossible to build up sufficient reserves behind the front line to mount a sustained offensive; Ivanov had to hope that one more surge by the troops facing the *k.u.k.* Army would be sufficient to make a final breakthrough. As the Austro-Hungarian Second Army completed its withdrawal, new Russian attacks opened along the front of Boroević's Third Army towards the town of Zboró (now Zborov). This was close to the seam between the Austro-Hungarian Third and Fourth Armies, and both armies rushed whatever reserves they could to the area to prevent a gap from opening up. At the same time, X Corps on Boroević's right flank came under increasing pressure, and it seemed to be in danger of having both its flanks driven back.

The commander of X Corps was Hugo Meixner, whose twin brother Otto had been forced into retirement the previous autumn following the setbacks in Galicia. Meixner had only just returned to X Corps after being absent through illness, during which period command passed to Josef Krautwald. During the weeks following the Russian capture of Mezőlaborcz, Krautwald had warned Conrad that his troops were near the end of their strength, but received no response.[44] Now, Meixner requested permission to pull back in order to prevent his troops from being encircled. This earned him a sharp rebuke from *AOK*, to the effect that local Russian penetrations must not result in a general withdrawal. This signal was followed by one that dismissed Meixner from his post for failing to show adequate resolve to hold the front line. Krautwald was appointed as his replacement, with clear instructions not to countenance a withdrawal. This was not the first or the last time that Conrad reacted to requests for withdrawal by dismissing the officer concerned, though it seems that the final straw came in the form of an angry message from Marwitz, commander of the *Beskidenkorps*, denouncing Meixner for wanting to make an unnecessary retreat.[45] In Meixner's case, it marked the end of his career and he retired with considerable bitterness and resentment about the way in which he had been treated by a distant headquarters whose representatives never visited the front and therefore had little idea of the reality on the ground.

Just as it seemed as if the entire front line might collapse, the German *Beskidenkorps* arrived, and Boroević immediately subordinated X Corps to Marwitz. Easter Sunday fell on 4 April, and on quiet sectors of the long Eastern Front, soldiers from both sides exchanged gifts; in the Carpathians, there was no such pause. One of the few Austro-Hungarian units still in position on the Beskid Ridge was 34th Infantry Division, and throughout the day it had to beat off repeated Russian attempts to dislodge it. Marwitz's *Beskidenkorps* was now ready for its counterattack, and the Russian forces were rapidly driven back across much of the ground that they had recently conquered. At first, *AOK* failed to recognise the importance of Marwitz's counterattack; a little to the west, VII Corps had been driven back, and this latest setback seemed to dominate Conrad's thoughts for the moment. Boroević rejected criticisms of VII Corps on the grounds that his subordinate formation had been left with no choice – it would have been preferable to assign a division from the *Beskidenkorps* to support this part of the line, but Conrad had insisted that the German corps be deployed as a single group.

In any event, the crisis passed as swiftly as it developed, as the Russians lacked the strength to follow up any gains in VII Corps' sector. Marwitz briefly considered continuing his counterattack, but concluded that unless his neighbouring formations were able to advance, his gains would be too localised to make any major difference, and instead he decided to hold the ground he had captured, pulling some of X Corps' troops out of the front line for some much-needed rest. Inevitably, the Russians attempted to launch local counterattacks, but Marwitz beat them off with ease.

After spending much of the preceding weeks in transit from one front to another and back again, the Russian III Caucasian Corps was finally assigned back to Southwest Front and arrived in Lemberg at the end of March. However, after demanding reinforcements for an assault through the Carpathians for weeks, Ivanov now had a sudden change of heart. Perhaps as the details of the Easter fighting became clearer – the Austro-Hungarian estimates of Russian losses put the figure of dead, wounded and prisoners at over 45,000 – Ivanov ordered Third, Eighth and Ninth Armies to go over to the defensive. *Stavka* demanded an explanation, and Ivanov sent a telegram to Grand Duke Nikolai on 14 April:

After the fighting at the beginning of March, Ninth Army urgently needs rest and reinforcements. Without this, attacks have no chance of success ... the shortage of artillery ammunition has also contributed to halting the general offensive.

... Overall, I believe that the Galician front may begin a general offensive after 20 April [Russian calendar, 7 April in western calendar]. The exact start date depends on adequate supplies.[46]

The problems faced by Ivanov were similar to those that Conrad's armies experienced when attempting an assault through the same terrain: shortages in the manufacture of ammunition were made worse by the extremely limited capacity of the local road and rail network. Even though III Caucasian Corps had finally arrived, getting it into a position where it could make a difference created additional problems, as the movement of so many troops would clog the roads still further, delaying the arrival of food, ammunition and reinforcements for units already in the front line.

After weeks of bloody fighting, the intensity of operations throughout the Carpathian region diminished as both sides took stock. Casualties had been devastating. The *k.u.k.* Army had suffered over 800,000 casualties – dead, wounded, sick or prisoner – trying to batter its way through the mountains, with over 100,000 more lost as a result of the surrender of Przemyśl. Much of the original trained core of the army had died in 1914, with a devastating effect on unit cohesion. With so many different nationalities within the empire, the Austro-Hungarian forces were particularly dependent upon close relationships between officers and their men, and this delicate structure had almost disintegrated by early 1915. Officer losses had been disproportionately high, and replacement drafts frequently ended up in formations of different nationalities, as crises along the front line prevented them from being sent to their intended destinations. By the end of the Carpathian fighting, this state of affairs had worsened still further, with the additional devastating impact of the appalling conditions on troop morale.

Whilst some of the suspicions about Slav populations within the Austro-Hungarian Empire may have been overstated in early 1915, the fracture lines were much clearer after the pointless slaughter of the first three months. In the final phases of the battle, half of the Czech 28th Infantry Regiment, part of Boroević's army, surrendered to the Russians without firing a shot near Zboró, immediately north of Bartfeld; the rest of the regiment was disbanded and its personnel distributed to other regiments, further diluting linguistic and cultural ties between the men in the front line.[47]

There were also concerns about the nature of Austro-Hungarian casualties and what it revealed about the army itself. The proportion of officer casualties reported as missing or lost – which usually meant that they had been taken prisoner – was 48 per cent of the total, compared with only 16 per cent for German officer casualties and 25 per cent for Russian officer casualties, suggesting that Austro-Hungarian officers were less prepared to fight on in the face of adversity than officers of other armies. This was confirmed by the fact that officer casualties for 1915 constituted only 8.7 per cent of total casualties, compared with 18 per cent for the German Army and 25 per cent for the Russian Army. In addition, junior officers made up a disproportionate amount of officer casualties, partly because even at this stage of the war they were often in distinctive uniforms, attracting the attention of Russian snipers, and partly because the new drafts of ill-trained officers at the lowest levels had simply not learned the basic skills required to stay alive.[48]

Overall, the fighting power of the army was hugely diminished, reducing it to little more than a barely-trained militia. The latest march battalions had trained with wooden rifles due to a shortage of firearms, receiving real weapons only when they reached the front line. Artillery, never a strong component of the *k.u.k.* Army, had failed to make any significant impact in the fighting, and large numbers of guns had been lost both as a result of Russian action and while attempting to drag them through the mountains in winter.

The Russians, too, had suffered grievous losses, perhaps as great as those suffered by the *k.u.k.* Army. Although these did not have the same consequences in terms of unit cohesion, the diversion of troops to the mountains, especially from Southwest Front's sector in southern Poland, would have serious implications in the coming weeks. The fighting itself had a marked effect on the troops who were involved, who frequently felt that their huge efforts were not appreciated by higher commands, as Brusilov recorded:

We must remember that these troops were in the mountains in winter, neck-deep in snow with severe frosts, involved in incessant bitter fighting, day after day, and had to try to conserve munitions at all costs, particularly artillery shells. They had to fight with the bayonet, counterattacking almost exclusively at night without artillery preparation or excessive rifle-fire, in further attempts to preserve ammunition.

I am in awe of the heroes who endured the terrible ordeal of the winter fighting in the mountains without adequate protection from the weather, against an enemy that frequently outnumbered them three to one. I was constantly surprised that the outstanding work of the troops was not sufficiently appreciated by higher commands

... I felt that the heroic self-sacrifice of our troops and officers who had been subordinated to me should receive recognition, that our mother country should know what her sons had done for the benefit, glory and honour of Russia.[49]

Despite their losses, the Russians remained determined to press on with operations in the Carpathians. Britain and France were about to launch their operation against the Dardanelles with the aim of knocking Turkey out of the war, and were this to succeed, it seemed inevitable that Bulgaria and Romania would join the Entente, as well as Italy; British diplomats were already hard at work to ensure that Italy joined the cause against the Central Powers sooner rather than later, and any further weakening of the Austro-Hungarian Empire would help both the defeat of the Turks and the entry of neutrals. There was also concern in Russia that unless the Russian Army was seen to have played a substantial role in the defeat of the Dual Monarchy, the 'spoils of war' might go elsewhere and Russia would receive inadequate compensation for its losses.

Writing about Tannenberg after the war, Hindenburg reflected that victory has many parents, while defeat is an orphan. Whilst many people scrambled to take credit for the German victory in August 1914, nobody on the Russian side was prepared to step forward to accept responsibility for their failure to penetrate through the Carpathian Mountains. Ivanov had loudly and persistently demanded priority of supply to mount a major thrust, but in an encounter nearly two years later, Ivanov told Danilov – who was quartermaster-general in 1915 – that the proposed operation to advance through the Carpathians had been presented to him 'like a perfectly cooked roast joint', and all that was required of him was to execute the plan.[50] This raises intriguing questions. If the plan did not originate with Ivanov, who proposed it? Brusilov claimed in his memoirs that Ivanov had never been keen on advancing into Hungary, and that Brusilov and Alexeyev – Ivanov's recently departed chief of staff – had been the main proponents of such a plan. But even here, Brusilov wrote that he had always doubted the ability of his army to mount any meaningful invasion of Hungary, and had merely tried to bind as many of the enemy's forces as he could to his own front. However, this argument would only make sense in the context of a major Russian effort elsewhere – the only point of tying down the forces of the Central Powers in the Carpathians would have been to create an exploitable weakness elsewhere. It is possible that after the planned penetration of the Carpathians failed, Ivanov attempted to distance himself from it as much as he could. At the time, he gave no indication that the plan was anything other than his own idea.

On the opposite side of the front line, there could be no question about where the main responsibility for the campaign lay. Conrad had been urged repeatedly by Falkenhayn to abandon the Carpathian operation in favour of a renewed campaign against Serbia, but the chief of the Austro-Hungarian general staff had obstinately pursued his own plans. The continued attacks had been based upon a completely unrealistic expectation of being able to achieve a quick breakthrough, and when it became clear that such a breakthrough was not possible, troops were thrown into the fight with complete disregard for the realities and difficulties of mounting operations in such terrain. Throughout his professional life, Conrad had been a staunch proponent of offensive operations to be conducted at all costs; his armies paid a huge price attempting in vain to turn his rhetoric into reality.

A glance at the maps of the campaign shows the futility of such operations for both sides. The bloodshed was enormous for the modest gains and losses, ranking the Carpathian fighting as amongst the most ineffective of the entire war. For the Germans, the outcome was confirmation that their ally would be unable to achieve anything without substantial German support – indeed, if it hadn't been for the arrival of the German South Army and *Beskidenkorps*, Conrad's lines would have disintegrated. Regardless of Falkenhayn's belief that the only way to win the war was in the west, there was now a pressing need for a further operation in the east to try to reduce pressure upon the Austro-Hungarian Empire.

CHAPTER 5

MACKENSEN'S BREAKTHROUGH

The failure of either of the Central Powers to conduct an advance through the Carpathians came as no surprise to Falkenhayn, who had been opposed to Conrad's proposals from the outset. He had repeatedly shown great reluctance to allow German troops to be sucked into the fighting, only relenting when there was a high likelihood of a Russian breakthrough. His observations in his memoirs are consistent with the views he had stated on numerous occasions at the time:

> The appeals of the allies [Austria-Hungary] for assistance, in constantly new forms, never ceased. To be sure the attentive observer was able to notice on the Russian side symptoms favourable to the Central Powers. The persistence of the enemy's offensives diminished from week to week. Even where success was obtained, the attacker was no longer in a position to exploit them fully. The enormous losses which the Russians had suffered in their reckless attacks during the winter in the Carpathian Mountains could only be made good by bringing up ill-trained troops. Signs of an incipient shortage of arms and ammunition among them were reported in many cases. But even in this state they threatened the Austro-Hungarian front in a way which could not be borne for any length of time on account of the decreasing morale of certain sections of the allied troops. Symptoms of disintegration became more and more evident in formations of Czech and Southern Slav recruits.[1]

Like many Germans, Falkenhayn regarded the Austro-Hungarian Empire increasingly as a burden, and his opinion of the fighting ability of the *k.u.k.* Army, never high, declined still further after the Carpathian fighting. To an extent, this was not entirely justified – Linsingen's South Army had performed little better than its Austro-Hungarian neighbours, and had suffered just as heavily. Nevertheless, there were serious concerns in Berlin that Vienna might seek a separate peace. An Anglo-French force numbering about 80,000 had disembarked on the island of Lemnos, near the approaches to the Dardanelles, and it was expected that once the Entente navies had forced the straits, these troops would then be used to threaten Istanbul, forcing Turkey out of the war. Were that to happen, Romania and probably Bulgaria would have little option other than to side with the Entente. With Italy already heading towards declaration of war against the Central Powers, the pressure upon the resources of the Austro-Hungarian Empire would become unmanageable; at the outset of the war, Conrad had warned that a conflict against Russia, Serbia and Italy at the same time was impossible, and beyond the resources of the *k.u.k.* Army – and if that was true in August 1914, it was doubly so by the end of the first winter of the war, given the murderous losses suffered by the Austro-Hungarian forces.

After the war, many Russians claimed that *Stavka* had never been enthusiastic about an operation against Turkey by the French and English.[2] At the time, though, there appeared to be considerable demand for the Western Powers to establish firm contact with their Russian allies. Danilov wrote that greater efforts could have been made to use the sea route past northern Scandinavia to Murmansk and Archangel, as was the case in the Second World War, but in 1915, rail access to Russia's northern ports was simply not good enough to allow significant western aid to reach the tsar's armies by that route. With regard to Istanbul, the Russians had assurances from Britain and France – repeated in the middle of March – that any post-war settlement would be in accordance with Russia's aspirations. Many within the Russian establishment, including Danilov, interpreted this as meaning that Russia's long-term desire to control the gates to the Black Sea, and therefore Istanbul itself, would finally be realised. However, the breadth of the discussions about the outcome of operations against Turkey were, to say the least, somewhat premature:

The Dardanelles operation ... initiated discussion of a series of difficult issues and caused considerable difficulties for the diplomats of the [Entente] allies. One of them observed with complete justification that one was hastily trying to divide up the hide, before the bear had even been killed. The details of a ceasefire with Turkey were debated in case the latter should sue for a separate peace; this led to preliminary talks about the fundamentals that would be required to establish a general peace ... in their optimism, diplomatic circles went so far as to discuss the ceremonial arrangements for the entry of allied forces into Istanbul and the dispositions that should be taken to prevent the pretensions of second-rank powers from playing too important a role in these ceremonies.[3]

This last comment appears to have been directed in particular at Greece, which seemed to want to be involved in the entry of Christian troops and officials into St Sophia's Cathedral. This created pressures within Greece; King Constantine remained opposed to entering the war, whereas Prime Minister Eleftherios Venizelos was in favour of military assistance of the planned British operation in the Dardanelles. This disagreement led to Venizelos' resignation, though any relief felt by Constantine would have been short-lived, as Venizelos won the subsequent election.

The attempt by the British and French navies to force the Dardanelles, and the landings at Gallipoli, are beyond the scope of this work. For the moment, the failure of these operations took away at least one of the concerns of the Central Powers. Whilst there appeared little doubt that Italy would enter the war against Germany and Austria-Hungary, the Germans still hoped that Vienna might be persuaded to make sufficient territorial concessions at least to delay this. Conrad, though, remained adamantly opposed to any such concessions. He advised a meeting attended by Emperor Franz Joseph on 8 March that if Italy was not serious about going to war, then concessions were pointless; if, on the other hand, Italy was determined to go to war, concessions would only delay the inevitable. Understandably, the emperor was as unenthusiastic about making any concessions to Italy as Conrad.[4] Such an argument ignored the possibility that there might be shades of grey between the two extremes that Conrad described. In any event, Italian mobilisation was likely to be a protracted business, which would allow time for deployment of Austro-Hungarian troops along the frontier. The pressing need was to achieve a situation on the Eastern Front that would allow for such a deployment.

The relative ease with which the *Beskidenkorps* drove Brusilov's troops back, and then beat off the last attempts by the Russians to penetrate into Hungary, was noteworthy. Regardless of the alleged better fighting quality of German troops – and by this stage of the war, this high opinion of the German Army prevailed on all sides on the Eastern Front – it did seem as if the Russian Army had been gravely weakened by the recent campaigns. Additional intelligence came in the form of intercepted Russian communications; as August von Cramon, the German liaison officer in *AOK* recorded, even coded messages were relatively easy to decode, and as a consequence, both *AOK* and *OHL* knew about Russian losses and difficulties with ammunition supply.[5] Provided a suitable force could be gathered at a suitable point, the prospects of achieving a success seemed favourable.

The question that now arose was how to exploit the perceived weakening of Russian forces. Falkenhayn remained convinced that his view that the war could only be won in the west was correct, but in order to do so, Germany needed to be free to concentrate against France and Britain without the constant threat from Russia. Therefore, merely reducing the pressure on the *k.u.k.* Army would not be sufficient; Falkenhayn wished to strike a blow that would permanently diminish the ability of the Russian Army to mount offensives in future:

> This [objective] could only be expected from a breakthrough, and not from operations against the Russian wings. Operations against the Russian right wing were prohibited, and they could not even be considered against the left wing, owing to the technical difficulties in their way – mountains and bad communication.
>
> Thus the choice of the place of breakthrough was from the beginning limited to a few sections of the front. It could only fall either on the sector between the Pilica and the Upper Vistula, or on that between the Upper Vistula and the foot of the Carpathians. The Chief of the General Staff decided in favour of the latter.
>
> This allowed for a sharper concentration of the breakthrough troops. Their flanks here were exposed to considerably less danger of encirclement – in consequence of the restrictions imposed upon the movements of the Russian troops by the valley of the Vistula in the north, and the ridge of the Carpathians in the south – than is usually the case with breakthroughs, and as would have been the case between the Pilica and the Upper Vistula from the direction of Warsaw ... The Russians had just withdrawn such strong forces from western Galicia for their Carpathian offensive that they were no longer able to replenish this front in time, even if they did perceive the danger which threatened it. We could hope with some certainty to appear at the decisive spot with undoubted superiority. There was even a probability that this favourable proportion could be preserved for some length of time, if the operations were conducted with energy.[6]

This brief summary, written by Falkenhayn after the war, fails to give the full story. The suggestion that further operations in the north were 'prohibited' is loaded with nuance. Clearly, there were no objectives within striking range that would force Russia to sue for peace, and the northern sector of the Eastern Front was too far from the Austro-Hungarian section to relieve pressure upon Germany's ailing ally. However, the internal politics of the German Army undoubtedly

In addition to being chief of the Austro-Hungarian general staff, Franz Conrad von Hötzendorf, pictured here (left) in 1914 with his adjutant Oberstleutnant Rudolf Kundmann, was responsible for almost all aspects of *k.u.k.* Army doctrine and training before the war. (IMAGNO / Austrian Archives / TopFoto)

Archduke Frederick was the nominal commander-in-chief of the *k.u.k.* Army, but was in many respects no more than a figurehead. (©2003 Topham Picturepoint)

Felix Graf von Bothmer, a Bavarian officer, took command of the German South Army and proved to be a far more congenial colleague for the Austro-Hungarian officers than his predecessor, Alexander von Linsingen. (©ullsteinbild / TopFoto)

Infantry General Otto von Emmich, Commander of X Corps (centre, front) and Ernest Augustus, Duke of Brunswick, alongside other officers in the field. (©ullsteinbild / TopFoto)

Erich von Falkenhayn became chief of Germany's general staff after the failure to defeat France in 1914. (©ullsteinbild / TopFoto)

Grand Duke Nikolai Nikolayevich, commander-in-chief of Russia's armies until his dismissal in the summer of 1915. (©Print Collector / HIP / TopFoto)

August von Mackensen, pictured here riding to inspect German positions, enjoyed a hugely successful year, first in Galicia and Poland, and later in Serbia. (©ullsteinbild / TopFoto)

Alexei Andreyevich Polivanov replaced Vladimir Sukhomlinov as War Minister in 1915. Though unpopular with Tsarina Alexandra, he was instrumental in rebuilding the Russian Army after its defeats during the year. (©ullsteinbild / TopFoto)

Alexander von Linsingen, photographed here after the war, was an uncompromising old-school Prussian who made little attempt to be diplomatic towards the Austro-Hungarian officers with whom he worked. (IMAGNO / Austrian Archives (S) / TopFoto)

General Mikhail Vasiliyevich Alexeyev started the war as chief of staff of Southwest Front and then took command of Northwest Front; by the end of 1915, he was chief of the general staff. (©TopFoto)

Alexei Brusilov was one of the few Russian generals to emerge from 1915 with an unblemished record. (Allied Army Leaders of the Wills's Cigarettes, 1915–1916). From a private collection. (Fine Art Images / Heritage Images / TopFoto)

Marshal Radomir Putnik was chief of Serbia's general staff. He led his forces to victory in 1914, but was forced to flee his homeland in 1915, and died in France the following year. (©2003 Topham Picturepoint)

Nikola Pašić, Serbian Prime Minister, photographed here after the war. (IMAGNO / NB / TopFoto)

A Russian trench in the siege perimeter around Przemyśl during the winter of 1914–1915. (©Topfoto)

Russian artillery moving into Przemyśl after the capture of the fortress. (©Topfoto)

played a part. For Falkenhayn, it was out of the question that his opponents at *Ober Ost* should be given a further opportunity to increase their prestige.

Relations between Falkenhayn and Conrad had never been good, and in late March, after further Austro-Hungarian requests for German reinforcements, Falkenhayn wrote to Cramon asking for confirmation that *OHL's* estimate of thirty-four German and Austro-Hungarian divisions faced by twenty-four Russian divisions in the Carpathians was correct. Cramon confirmed the estimate, but added that the Austro-Hungarian divisions were greatly depleted in strength and morale, and that each Russian division started with a greater establishment strength than divisions of the Central Powers. Cramon added that the addition of the *Beskidenkorps* would only provide additional defensive stability, and would not be enough to allow for offensive operations to be resumed. The following day, a longer message reached Falkenhayn from his representative in Teschen. Although the Russian offensive appeared to have been contained, the Austro-Hungarian armies were all close to collapse. A decisive German effort was therefore needed in order to pre-empt this, and Conrad had requested either German reinforcements for the Carpathian front – something that Falkenhayn wished to avoid at all costs – or a relieving attack elsewhere. Cramon added that Conrad had suggested an attack on the Russian lines north of the Carpathians, in the region of Gorlice.[7]

Discussion about where to make an attack on the Russians had already begun, and Cramon's message came at a time when attention was already turning to southern Poland. This was the precise region that Linsingen had suggested as being a better area for an attack on the Russians than the Carpathians. Further discussions between Falkenhayn and Oberst Wilhelm Groener, head of the German general staff's railway section, in the following days concentrated increasingly on the logistics of gathering substantial forces in Upper Silesia, at first with the possible intention of launching a counterattack should Russian forces penetrate into Hungary, but then increasingly towards a possible drive eastwards into Russian-occupied Galicia.[8] On 4 April, Falkenhayn wrote to Cramon:

> The question of a powerful thrust in the Gorlice area towards Sanok has interested me for some time. The execution depends upon the overall situation and the preparation of the necessary forces – four army corps. Apparently, the limited capacity of the railway to Tarnów and through Neu Sandez poses great difficulties. However, I would greatly value your early thoughts about such an operation. Information about the capacity of the railways, and options for the use of local roads by our vehicles, are essential.[9]

The precise location for the offensive was almost entirely dictated by geography. Repeated German successes in and near East Prussia had done nothing to reduce pressure upon the Austro-Hungarian Empire, and Falkenhayn didn't need Cramon's report to know that further operations in the Carpathians would achieve nothing. Prompted by Falkenhayn, Cramon sent further information to *OHL* in early April, confirming that the Russian troops between the Vistula and the Carpathians amounted to perhaps 56,000 men. The *k.u.k.* Army had slightly more troops, and if Falkenhayn could add an additional four corps as he had suggested to Cramon, the Central Powers would be assured of a substantial superiority. Once warmer weather dried out the ground, an offensive could be undertaken with some confidence.[10]

After further discussions with German officers, Falkenhayn wrote to Conrad on 13 April:

> Your Excellency knows that I do not consider advisable a repetition of the attempt to surround the Russian extreme (right) wing. It seems to me just as ill-advised to distribute any more German troops on the Carpathian front for the sole purpose of supporting it. On the other hand, I should like to submit the following plan of operations for your consideration ...
>
> An army of at least eight German divisions will be got ready with strong artillery here in the west, and entrained for Muczyn–Grybow–Bochnia, to advance from about the line Gorlice–Gromnik in the general direction of Sanok. This army must be joined by von Besser's division, which must be relieved by Austro-Hungarian troops ... and by one Austro-Hungarian cavalry division. This army and the 4th Austro-Hungarian Army would also be united in one command, and naturally a German one in this instance. If, during the concentration of the attacking forces, the Second and Third Austro-Hungarian Armies could give way step by step, drawing the enemy after them ... such a movement would considerably increase and facilitate the success of operations.[11]

The message went on to ask for assurances that *AOK* would be able to provide logistics columns for the German forces, and to request details of the capacity of the vital local railways; Conrad was invited to Berlin to discuss matters further. The concluding words returned to a subject over which the two men had disagreed many times:

> Apart from the strictest secrecy there remains a further preliminary condition for the execution of the operations, and that is, that Italy is kept quiet by meeting her

as far as possible, at least until we have dealt the blow. It is indeed well known to your Excellency that no sacrifice seems to me too great if it keeps Italy out of the present war.[12]

Conrad replied the same day that he too had wished to mount an operation in this area, but that the required forces had not been available. He omitted to mention that such forces might indeed have been available had he not chosen to squander them so wastefully in the Carpathians. Until now, he had considered an operation in southern Poland purely as a local tactical measure, and he remained in favour of a much more grandiose pincer movement, with forces advancing from both ends of the Eastern Front with the intention of meeting somewhere in eastern Poland. Given the appalling losses suffered by his armies, it says much about how detached he was from realities in the front line that he could even consider such an operation.

Conrad travelled to Berlin on 14 April for further discussions, in which he rejected the additional suggestion from Falkenhayn of trying to draw the Russians further south by Second and Third Armies conceding ground. This was at least partly out of a natural reluctance to concede territory of the Austro-Hungarian Empire to the Russians, and as Falkenhayn speculated in his memoirs, also influenced by the fear that once a withdrawal began, it might prove difficult to stop it from continuing further than intended. Nevertheless, the general shape of Falkenhayn's plan received Conrad's support and two days later, *OHL* issued orders for the creation of a new Eleventh Army, consisting of the Guards Corps reinforced by 119th Infantry Division, XLI Reserve Corps reinforced by 11th Bavarian Infantry Division, and X Corps. Archduke Joseph Ferdinand's Fourth Army would be subordinated to the new German army. Eventually, 119th Infantry Division and 11th Bavarian Infantry Division were grouped together in *Korps Kneussl*, and additional troops in the form of the Austro-Hungarian VI Corps were added to Eleventh Army.

The creation of divisions for the new army had been a considerable piece of work. Impressed by the resilience of German troops on the Western Front when the French attacked in late 1914 and again in early 1915, Falkenhayn had adopted the proposal of Oberst Ernst von Wrisberg, a senior official in the German war ministry, and ordered some divisions to give up one of their four regiments and to reduce their artillery batteries from six guns to four. The forces released would be used to create new divisions, while the 'donor divisions' would receive additional drafts of new recruits and additional machine-guns. This would leave the existing divisions able to carry out their defensive duties without difficulty, while the new formations would contain significant numbers of experienced personnel. The process was originally intended to take place in only a few selected areas, but was rapidly extended to the entire Western Front. However, its implementation proved difficult, not least due to the inability of Germany to provide sufficient replacement drafts for the 'donor divisions' and adequate equipment for the new formations. Nevertheless, by Easter, Falkenhayn had fourteen new divisions at his disposal.

While the staff officers assigned to the new army began their meticulous preparations, attention turned to the appointment of the commander of the operation and his chief of staff. The German system was designed around the concept of commander and chief of staff operating almost seamlessly, but in some cases – the most notable being Hindenburg and Ludendorff – there has been a considerable body of opinion to the effect that the chief of staff was the driving intelligence of the partnership. There is no question that the calibre of German staff officers was almost universally very high, but many commanders had served as staff officers in their turn, and the arrangement undoubtedly worked best when both men were of a high calibre and moreover were able to cooperate closely. For the role of chief of staff, Falkenhayn had already made his choice. Hans von Seeckt was the son of a Pomeranian officer, and like many of his contemporaries he had spent most of his adult life in uniform. He had served as chief of staff to III Corps in 1914, earning a reputation for innovative and effective use of artillery, and Falkenhayn had no hesitation about appointing him as Eleventh Army's chief of staff.

The next consideration was the commander of the army. Germany and the Austro-Hungarian Empire had cooperated to a degree in previous operations; during Hindenburg's advance to the Vistula and the outskirts of Warsaw in October 1914, for example, Austro-Hungarian cavalry had served to protect the northwest flank of the German forces, and of course Linsingen's South Army and Marwitz's *Beskidenkorps* had played their parts in the fighting in the Carpathians. However, this new operation required cooperation on an entirely different scale. Falkenhayn's agreement with Conrad stipulated a German commander for the planned assault, but Conrad only agreed to this on condition that the new commander would be subordinated to *AOK*. However, it was further agreed that *AOK* would only issue instructions to the German commander that had been approved by Falkenhayn. This cumbersome arrangement was not without its advantages for Falkenhayn – the new army would be outside the remit of his opponents at *Ober Ost*.

Although both Germany and Austria-Hungary had only one other ally – Turkey, isolated in the southeast corner of Europe – there was considerable mistrust between the high commands of both nations. Conrad felt that he had been deeply misled by the Germans at the beginning of the war. Moltke the Younger, who was at that time chief of the German general staff, had led him to believe that Germany would make a greater effort in the east than was actually the case. Even when it became clear that there would be no German assault into Russian Poland to complement Conrad's own offensive from the south, the *k.u.k.* Army had still proceeded to draw the full weight of the Russian Army upon itself in order to give the Germans every opportunity to defeat France before turning east. In this respect, too, Conrad felt deeply let down. His armies had sacrificed hundreds of thousands of men, yet the Germans had not delivered the promised victory in the west. The Germans, too, felt disappointment at the performance of their main ally. They showed increasingly open disdain for the fighting abilities of the Austro-Hungarian forces, particularly for the senior officers, who they regarded as lacking all the professional values that they – with much justification – considered the strongest features of the German military machine. The choice of which German officer was to take command of the new operation was therefore more than simply a question of a man with suitable military skills; the appointee would also be required to show adroit diplomatic footwork.

Fortunately, just such a person was available. Since the abortive gas attack at Bolimów, Mackensen's Ninth Army had seen almost no significant action beyond intermittent exchanges of fire across the static front line. For a cavalryman in an era in which offensive doctrine reigned supreme, this was a deeply frustrating experience, and in early March he greeted orders to push forward his southern flank with enthusiasm. This advance proved to be only modest, and once more his troops went over to positional warfare, to the irritation of their commander:

> The course of events on my front does not please me. For several days we have had muddy conditions. This change does not help with further [offensive] operations. I fear the onset of illness. The determination and greater numbers of the Russians in their field fortifications hinder any attempt to strike a decisive blow. My troops are faced by fortifications along the entire line. Their resolve is unbroken, their courage is above all praise, but I am answerable for their losses and therefore cannot attack again ... Staying in a situation from which there seems no escape, where any operational consideration is nipped in the bud, is frankly unbearable. We Prussians are – with justification – accustomed far too much to successful offensive operations. As in the west, we in the east too are forced onto the defensive![13]

Late on 16 April, Mackensen received a signal from the kaiser, bringing his time with Ninth Army to an end:

> Trusting in your so frequently demonstrated leadership skills, I have selected you for a different post and hereby name you as commander of Eleventh Army. I do this in the certain knowledge that you will succeed in the tasks expected of you as admirably as you have done in the past. I wish to take this opportunity to offer you my warmest thanks and my particular recognition for what you have achieved in your previous commands as I assign you a new post, and also ask that you pass on these thanks to the brave troops of Ninth Army.[14]

Inevitably, the *Ober Ost–OHL* feud also played a part in the decision. Whilst Mackensen was not an enemy of the Hindenburg–Ludendorff faction, he had clearly resented being sidelined during the first months of 1915, in command of a secondary sector of the front after playing a leading role in the fighting of 1914. His transfer away from *Ober Ost* deprived Hindenburg and Ludendorff of perhaps their best army commander.

Leaving his army in the hands of its new commander, Prince Leopold of Bavaria, Mackensen travelled to Charleville in northern France, passing the battlefield of Sedan where, in 1870, he had fought for Prussia as a junior officer in the *Leibhusaren* regiment. Falkenhayn briefed him about his new task, and on 19 April he headed east again to Neu Sandez to take up his new appointment. He travelled via Teschen where he met Archduke Frederick, the nominal commander-in-chief of the *k.u.k.* Army, and Conrad, and immediately demonstrated a keen understanding of the diplomatic aspects of commanding Eleventh Army:

> The soldierly, great-hearted Archduke Frederick, who probably owed his high position not so much to his military abilities as to his high birth, greeted me warmly and frankly, as the circumstances of the alliance and the serious situation required. General Conrad was more reserved. I had the impression that this brilliant man was burdened by heavy moral responsibility and the unfavourable recent events, but strove to master his oppressively heavy task. In keeping with the agreement reached by the two high commands after lengthy negotiations, I would be bound by the directives of the Austro-Hungarian military leadership, who in turn would make all important decisions in agreement with their German counterparts ... Given how the military situation had unfolded since the beginning of the war, it was entirely understandable that the chief of the general staff of the German Army had to have decisive influence in overall conduct of the war. But the prestige of our allies should

and must not be forgotten, which in this context had particular importance. As a German soldier, I had until then only been directly subordinated to my own supreme command and at first found it an unfamiliar burden to have to take account of the preservation of prestige. It meant that I had to serve two masters. The tactful, chivalrous, and comradely personalities of the *k.u.k.* Army with whom I worked during the course of the war made this burden much lighter.[15]

Mackensen went on to describe his first meeting with his new chief of staff:

I had already been acquainted with him in peacetime during my time as a brigade commander in Danzig, when he was the youngest staff officer in XVII Corps. His commander at the time, General von Lentze, referred to the young Hauptmann [Seeckt's rank at the time] as 'a character', something that said a great deal about [his] high achievements ... Much as I was unhappy to be parted from my outstanding chief of staff General Grünert [in Ninth Army], I still knew immediately from my first experience of working with him how excellently suited my new chief of staff was for difficult duties. Militarily gifted and flexible, possessing a penetrating intelligence, clear, precise and decisive, Seeckt had completely mastered all branches of general staff duty and army command ... Of all the German officer corps, Seeckt was probably the most knowledgeable about the Austro-Hungarian armed forces.[16]

Cramon gives an illuminating description of the personality who would be leading the joint operation, particularly in comparison with others who might have been appointed to the task:

[Mackensen] was one of those people whose affection you value, on whose lips the word 'No' sounded better than the 'Yes' of others. His elegant, youthful appearance [Mackensen was actually 65 at the time, but well known for his physical fitness], his amiable yet determined manner, his understanding engagement of other peoples' characters allowed him to win over all Vienna in a heartbeat. There was no German commander to compare with him. Woyrsch, Bothmer [commander of an eponymous corps in the German South Army] and Heye [Woyrsch's chief of staff] were as well-loved as he was; Hindenburg was regarded by the Austrians as too serious and awe-inspiring, Falkenhayn as too restless and strong-minded, Ludendorff as too cutting and hard.[17]

Almost immediately after visiting Teschen, Mackensen and Seeckt drove to the headquarters of Joseph Ferdinand's Fourth Army to establish personal contact, thus furthering the important task of protecting 'prestige' that Mackensen had already identified. But whilst there was a considerable advantage in appointing a commander with a good diplomatic touch, it was also important that he was a skilful commander, and Mackensen had already proved that on several occasions. After a shaky start at the Battle of Gumbinnen in August 1914, he had led his XVII Corps with distinction during the Tannenberg campaign, combining a determination to get his men into battle with an adroit touch when it came to tactical deployment. Similarly, he had been appointed to lead the drive towards Warsaw in October 1914, and had held the Russian forces at bay even though outnumbered and outflanked. The ultimate failure of his army at the Battle of Łódź was a disappointment, but not due to any mistake on his part; he was popular with those he commanded, and as good a choice from a purely military perspective as he was from a diplomatic perspective. In many respects, he embodied the Prussian principle of leading by example and placing the welfare of his men as his primary concern.[18]

His corps commanders in the new Eleventh Army were all men with established military credentials. The foremost of them was the ebullient Hermann von François, who had commanded I Corps at the beginning of the war. Just as Mackensen's XVII Corps had formed the northeast pincer of the German encirclement at Tannenberg, so François' I Corps had provided the southwest pincer; much of the credit for the German victory rests with him, not least for his repeated refusal to obey instructions from Ludendorff in favour of doing what he believed to be right on the battlefield. Whilst such independent thinking was, to an extent, encouraged by the German military system, it ultimately cost him his post; after he became commander of the German Eighth Army in East Prussia, he disobeyed an instruction from Ludendorff to release the veteran I Corps for the Battle of Łódź, and was dismissed. After a short time languishing without an appointment, he was assigned to command of the newly formed XLI Reserve Corps, which was deployed on the Western Front. Now, he found himself back in the east, and partly as a result of the German security arrangements, he arrived without having had sufficient time to learn about the area in which his troops would be operating:

> [We arrived in Galicia] completely unexpectedly, without any prior study of the region. Galicia was not covered in tourist publications; few of us had had any opportunity to know much about it. In the Dual Monarchy, the land either side of the Carpathians was not valued highly. They had a low opinion of all the towns with their lack of culture, with houses full of dirt and infestation, and where the Galician Jews in their shabby kaftans and their hair in characteristic ringlets

dominated commercial life. The Austrian officers were not fond of either the Galician garrisons or the Galician populace.[19]

François' attitude to Jews in Poland was unremarkable for the era. Within Germany, most of the Jewish population was effectively assimilated into society, and functioned far more as part of the nation than was the case in Russia and parts of Poland. Indeed, the Jewish population provided proportionally more men for the army than any other part of German society. Further east though, for a variety of reasons, Jews still lived in far more segregated societies, and tended to be much more recognisable. For many Germans, the Jews in the east were simply a distinctly alien race, and given the widespread casual anti-Semitism throughout Europe, even amongst French and British travellers in Eastern Europe, the reaction of François would not have been regarded as unusual by any of his contemporaries, in all its contradictions:

In Galicia, a particularly eye-catching group of people is the Jews. Their large number, compared to other territories, is due to the fact that the Jews were received hospitably in Poland, whereas elsewhere they were at the mercy of the fanaticism and exploitation of the rest of the population. The Jews are mainly involved in commercial trade and running public houses. They manage all the goods produced by the estates. Wherever there is money to be earned, the Polish Jew shows a creeping servility, and yet he has a deep contempt for those of other faiths. This is an odd two-sided aspect of his character. In addition to high ethical principles he has contradictory morals, he has a high opinion of his own faith but utterly lacks self-esteem, his food and drink is refined and clean but contrasts with endless filth on his body, clothes and in his house. Their strength lies in their unbreakable community and subordination to the laws of the rabbis. We were entirely dependent upon the Jews in Galicia for food and supply services ... through their mediation, anything was possible.[20]

Generally, the Jews of Poland favoured the Germans – the alternative was rule by Russia, where pogroms against Jews were relatively commonplace. However, some Germans behaved as badly towards the Jews as the feared Cossacks:

One day, a young, beautiful Jewish girl came to our unit to get payment for some horses that we had bought from her father, a horse-trader ... [The senior NCO] was an older man from Saxony. He took her, strung her up on a bed, and raped her. She was 18 years old, as pretty as a picture. War is really grim.[21]

The attitudes of the three Great Powers on the Eastern Front to civilians showed some similarities, but many differences. All three armies were greatly exercised by fears about armed civilian resistance, spying activity, and saboteurs, and undoubtedly these fears led to arbitrary killings and the taking of hostages. The Germans committed several such acts in Belgium as they advanced in 1914, but after the initial burst of activity, occupied areas under German control on both fronts generally settled down to a peaceful, if strictly regulated, existence. On many occasions, German officers punished soldiers – even enforcing executions – for crimes such as the rape described above. But sometimes, they turned a blind eye. Given their conduct in a future war, it is remarkable that during the First World War, civilians on the Eastern Front regarded the Germans generally as better than Russian or Austro-Hungarian soldiers.

Polish and Ruthenian civilians in the war zone rightly believed that Russia was the most repressive of the Great Powers, and there was considerable support for the Dual Monarchy in southern Poland and Galicia, but this was greatly damaged by the conduct of the *k.u.k.* Army. As a result of past experiences – for the Austro-Hungarian forces, suppression of insurgents in the Balkans, and for the Germans, long memories of French *Francs tireurs* during the Franco-Prussian War – both armies issued instructions that those suspected of being or aiding armed civilian fighters were to be treated harshly. The Germans were no strangers to summary justice, but their allies were far worse. The regulations of the *k.u.k.* Army allowed officers in the field to dispense justice including the death penalty after minimal legal process, and in many cases even this was ignored and executions were carried out purely on the basis of suspicions. During the campaigns of 1914, Austro-Hungarian forces regularly executed civilians and left them on display in an attempt to dissuade others from helping the Russians. Before the war, there had been great concern about pro-Russian groups in occupied Poland and eastern Galicia, and although the populations of these areas largely favoured the Dual Monarchy – even if this was purely as the lesser of evils – the soldiers of the *k.u.k.* Army were told to treat civilians with deep suspicion. Hostages were taken regularly, and often executed when Austro-Hungarian troops were ambushed, even if the attackers were not civilians.

Even within the *k.u.k.* Army, some units behaved worse than others. Troops from Hungary, particularly those in second-line *Honvéd* formations, rapidly acquired a notorious reputation for random acts of brutality. There were many factors that drove this. Firstly, nationalist movements in Hungary openly discriminated against non-Magyars, and this attitude was widespread throughout a country that consciously made clear distinctions between itself and the rest of the empire. Secondly, there was the problem of the language barrier. Although German was the official common language of the first-line formations of the *k.u.k.* Army, this was not the case in *Honvéd* formations; unable to communicate easily with civilians outside their own country, Hungarian soldiers in these formations found it easy to regard all such civilians as potential enemies and behaved accordingly.[22]

In particular, the Ruthenian population of eastern Galicia, ethnically related to the people of the neighbouring Ukraine, was singled out for brutal treatment by the *k.u.k.* Army. Conrad told an Austrian politician in September 1914 that 'Everywhere Ruthenes are being executed under martial law.'[23] By the time that the Russians had seized the region, it is estimated that as many as 25,000 Ruthenians had been killed in less than three months, most without any legal process at all.[24] The Polish population played a major part in the killings – many of the administrators of the region were Poles, and as they were responsible for drafting the lists of those who might be disloyal to the Dual Monarchy, many took the opportunity to add the names of personal enemies and rivals.

When they entered East Prussia, the Russians suspected German civilians of being involved in both spontaneous and planned resistance activity. Some of this was based on the vast gulf between the two nations. Very few Russians owned bicycles, and their use was associated with official or military activity. As a result, any German civilian riding a bicycle in occupied areas ran the risk of being executed out of hand as a spy. Whenever Russian forces were ambushed by German troops, there was a tendency to punish the local populace, either by direct executions or punitive artillery bombardments of entire towns, as occurred at Neidenburg in August 1914. Looting and rape were frequently punished by Russian officers, but equally frequently ignored. Second-line and rear area units of the Russian Army rapidly acquired a reputation for particularly ill-disciplined conduct, and civilians in all parts of the Eastern Front rapidly learned to avoid them.

Both Russian and Austro-Hungarian forces deported large numbers of civilians. In the former case, this was allegedly to improve security in the region immediately behind the front line, while the Austro-Hungarian authorities deported those suspected of having anti-Dual Monarchy tendencies and interned them in camps. One such camp was at Theresienstadt [now Terezin], where a concentration camp was established in the Second World War. Those deported by the Russians from East Prussia were dumped in the area between the Volga and the Urals, where they were frequently used for forced labour. Food supplies were completely inadequate, and perhaps a quarter of those deported died. Although the Germans also had concerns about security, they dealt with it by issuing draconian warnings to the civilian population.

It is therefore little surprise that most civilians regarded the Germans as the least bad occupiers. This is not to suggest that the German Army behaved impeccably; there were plenty of occasions when civilians were killed or mistreated, but this was usually in the first weeks of occupation when there were fears of attack by guerrilla fighters. There was little of the racial intolerance displayed by Austro-Hungarian troops or the casual indiscipline associated with some elements of the Russian Army.

Notwithstanding the attitude of urbane Germans and Austrians to the poverty of culture and civilisation in Galician towns, the province was noted for its beauty. Several rivers ran from the Carpathians in the south to the Vistula in the north, forming picturesque valleys between low hills. The main roads across the area were a cause of concern for the Germans, who regarded them as poor, with inadequate foundations and liable to break up if subjected to heavy traffic; the smaller roads were unmetalled, and would rapidly degenerate into muddy tracks in poor weather. But the largely agricultural province also offered opportunities: in pre-war years, there had been a thriving trade in exported livestock, so any rapid German advance could expect to capture substantial stocks of food should the leading troops outstrip their supply lines. However, the greatest value in Galicia lay in its crude oil production, with Russia the only European territory with a larger output. Its re-conquest by the Central Powers was therefore of considerable economic value, in addition to forcing the Russians to abandon their positions in the Carpathians.

As soon as the German divisions began to move from their detraining areas towards the front line, their worst fears about the Galician roads were realised, as they rapidly broke up under the weight of the heavy German supply wagons. Given the failure of the Austro-Hungarian authorities to deliver on Conrad's logistical promises to the Germans before the South Army deployed in the Carpathians, the hard-pressed German staff officers experienced both considerable relief and more than a little surprise when they found that, in accordance with the agreement between Falkenhayn and Conrad regarding logistical support for the forthcoming operation, each division had been assigned nearly 200 light Austrian wagons. Each was drawn by two animals; although their capacity was inferior to the German wagons, they did far less damage to the roads, allowing deployment to proceed smoothly. The combination of local people with his own supply personnel made a striking impression upon François, though some of the animals were ultimately put to a use for which they had not originally been intended:

As the wagoneers were retained to provide specialist care for the horses, our baggage-trains rapidly took on a most singular appearance. Krakowians, Masurians, Goralians in their assorted colourful costumes amongst the logistics troops in field grey; strong German military horses, small long-maned Galician ponies, and oxen. The columns were very long, and the strict requirements that we expected from the baggage trains came under threat. The ox-drawn wagons were useful in the hill roads, but on the plains they could not keep up with the march tempo and they gradually disappeared into the field kitchens.[25]

Seeckt rapidly got to grips with preparing for the new offensive. In order to maximise the chances of success, Falkenhayn ensured that Eleventh Army received additional artillery in the shape of heavy guns and mortars. It was hoped that these would help blast a path through the Russian field fortifications, allowing the offensive to get off to a good start. Generalmajor Alfred Ziethen, an artillery specialist who had commanded heavy batteries on the Western Front at the outset of the war, was appointed to Mackensen's staff to oversee planning for the initial bombardment. Careful reconnaissance identified the main Russian strongpoints, and in addition to organising a precise plan for his guns, Ziethen also ensured that significant numbers of guns were held in reserve, ready to move forward with the advancing troops. This, it was hoped, would prevent any advance from having to pause while guns were brought forward.

Although the offensive had been predicated upon the creation of new divisions, only two of them – 11th Bavarian Infantry Division and 119th Infantry Division – would take part in the planned attack. The other units were made available by using the new divisions to take their place in the front line. However, it must be remembered that even the two new divisions were largely made up of experienced troops, and by using complete regiments, unit cohesion at lower levels was preserved. By contrast, many of the reinforcements arriving in the Russian front line were of a far poorer standard. One of them was Nahum Sabsay, a man of 25, who described his train journey from Russia. The draft of forty-five officers and 2,100 men was commanded by Lieutenant Colonel Serugin, who had been left behind by his regiment to train replacements, and was now summoned in his turn. At first, Sabsay observed, Serugin was shocked that he too would have to go to war – a portly man in his fifties, he had perhaps hoped to serve out the duration in a training post. However, he put a brave face on matters, until the day after departure:

At dinnertime the train halted at a station where a Red Cross train loaded with wounded had stopped, too, on its way from the front. As he walked towards the restaurant, accompanied by his adjutant, [Serugin] recognised in one of the soldiers saluting them the orderly of another lieutenant colonel in his old regiment, now a full colonel and in command of the regiment. Questioning the man, he learned that the colonel had been wounded a few days earlier, quite badly, and was now among those on the Red Cross train.

Assured that the train would be there for at least another hour, he had his dinner, then went to see if he could visit the colonel. He could, if he wanted to, the doctor told him, but it would be better if he didn't. It wouldn't do any good either to him or to the wounded man. The colonel had got it in the face, the doctor said. They ended up sending one of the Red Cross sisters to ask the colonel if he would like to see Lieutenant Colonel Serugin, and the colonel said no, he didn't want to see anyone.[26]

Crestfallen by this, Serugin kept very much to himself for the rest of the journey. His officers were largely the product of the hasty and inadequate four-month wartime training that was now the norm, while the rest of the draft was made up of raw recruits and reservists, some in their forties. The senior officers had a generally low opinion of them:

> They were mostly peasants – Great Russians, Ukrainians, White Russians – sprinkled with the natives of the many lands Russia had captured over the years, some of them still nomads and others, even if settled, still very much primitives. There wasn't a skilled or semiskilled worker in the whole trainload. Those who were had to be kept in plants and shops and mills that couldn't produce a tenth of what the army at the front needed.
>
> There were not many among those in the train who could read and write well enough to make a company clerk. Those who could had been snatched up long ago while still in training. There were the Jews, of course. There were plenty of literates among *them*, and quite a few were well educated. But *they* weren't allowed to be used in the army except as combatants, though sometimes the regulations had to be disregarded to get things done.[27]

As the German troops moved into their allotted front-line sectors, François, who had experience of warfare on both the Eastern and Western Fronts reflected upon the differences between them:

> The sector assigned to XLI Reserve Corps on the River Ropa southwest of Gorlice as far as Podliesie had a width of 9km [5.5 miles]; each division thus had 4.5km. On the

Western Front, the divisional frontage for a breakthrough was a maximum of 3km [nearly 2 miles]; here it was rather more. It is clear that in our sector an attack in close order was not possible. The most beneficial points for attack had to be identified by reconnaissance and then tackled in depth. Extensive deployment in depth at the assault points was all the more important as at first there were no reserves behind the front, as the divisions of X Corps had not yet arrived.

Many who came from the Western Front had pause for thought at the thin lines of the assault troops without reserves; but those who knew the Russians were aware that one could trust this approach.

... in the eyes of German officers, coming from the trenches in the west, the Austrian trenches looked rather unsatisfactory. Their construction was patchy, they were very neglected and in need of refurbishment. The Austrian liaison officers attracted some puzzled looks. Oberst Kaupert, a brigade commander, said to his opposite number: 'You clearly don't place much value in Galicia. The Ruthenians lean towards Russia, the Poles strive for independence. It seems unlikely that the Dual Monarchy will be able to hold onto this land.' The troops on either side of the front showed little hostility towards each other. The trenches were 800m or more apart. For weeks, there had been no significant fighting. Traffic on the approach roads conducted itself with the greatest lack of care. Supplies were brought up by small railways right behind the trenches and distribution proceeded without interruption [by the enemy]. They told us about a Russian priest who crossed the front line with about sixty Russians on Easter Sunday and handed out Easter presents. In conjunction with this, a three-day ceasefire was agreed and was conscientiously observed.

Such fraternisation also occurred on the Western Front, perhaps more frequently than was realised by higher commands. It is a typical consequence of positional warfare, which has a greatly weakening effect upon the warlike spirit.[28]

The apparent lack of activity that François observed was far from universal. In the sector occupied by Guards Corps, Russian snipers killed several officers in late April, including a battalion commander.[29]

On 25 April, Mackensen visited Teschen again, where he outlined his hopes for the operation. The initial objectives for his formations would be fairly modest, he explained, but the intention was to continue the attack without pause. Once he reached the River San, he would push on towards Lemberg and Rawa Ruska, in eastern Galicia:

I will never forget the shrugs and smiles that greeted me when ... I outlined this idea, naming the two locations. At that time, in view of the highly critical overall war position, it seemed that achieving this was beyond the boldest plans and hopes.[30]

Two days later, Seeckt informed Falkenhayn that preparations for the offensive were nearly complete, and that the artillery preparation would begin on 1 May. It was clear that the Russians now expected an attack, and Mackensen was keen to strike before Russian reinforcements could arrive.[31] Given that Conrad's visit to Berlin on 14 April marks the starting point from which German preparations began in earnest, it speaks volumes about the expertise of the German general staff that in barely two weeks, a new army had been created, troops had been moved from one side of Europe to the other, artillery ammunition and other stores had been stockpiled, and preparations had been made for the assault.

Throughout the German preparations, it was important to try to prevent – or at least delay – the Russians from becoming aware of the concentration of German troops in southern Poland. Trains carrying the troops were dispatched on circuitous routes, with the troops themselves usually unaware of their final destinations. Attacks were also launched elsewhere in an attempt to distract attention. There had been fighting along the northern border of East Prussia through much of March, with Russian troops seizing the port of Memel (now Klaipėda); a German telephonist continued to send bulletins from the main post office even as Russian troops entered the building, and Ludendorff later wrote that he tried in vain to award her the Iron Cross for her devotion to duty.[32] A swift counterattack by troops hastily gathered together drove the Russians back across the frontier, and later this was followed by an operation that saw German cavalry and infantry, under the command of Generalleutnant Otto von Lauenstein, penetrate into Lithuania and Latvia, to the north of East Prussia. With the cooperation of the German Navy, the force was able to seize the Baltic port of Libau (now Liepāja). Taken by surprise, the Russians could not prevent the German cavalry from reaching and capturing Šiauliai, but once they had reinforced their own cavalry in the area, they recaptured the town and drove the Germans back towards the East Prussian frontier. Ultimately, additional German reinforcements had to be sent to the area to prevent further Russian successes, which somewhat undermined the value of an operation that was originally intended merely to divert Russian attention. The German forces gathered together in Lithuania – largely cavalry, with improvised infantry support – were now merged together under the title of the *Njemen-Armee* ('Army of the Niemen'), under the command of Otto von Below. His previous command, Eighth Army, passed to Fritz von Scholtz, who had played an important part in the Battle of Tannenberg the previous year. Nevertheless, even though the Lithuanian operation ended up with more German resources being committed than had originally been intended, Russian attention had been diverted from southern Poland.

In the assembly areas of the German Eleventh Army, most civilians had been evacuated, in order to reduce the risk of reports of the troop build-up reaching the Russians. Aware that the limited number of Russian aerial reconnaissance planes were usually active in the early afternoon, German commanders avoided marching large bodies of men in the open during the middle of the day. In the immediate rear areas behind the front line, all significant troop movements took place at night.[33]

The concentration of German forces for the new offensive in the east had consequences elsewhere. After the failure of the German gas attack at Bolimów at the end of January using xylyl bromide, further refinements had been made, and in April, over 5,700 cylinders of chlorine gas were laboriously carried to the German trenches near Ypres on the Western Front. On 22 April, the gas was released over a 4-mile (6.5km) stretch of front line; this was a dangerous manual process, and cost the lives of many German soldiers involved.[34] Nevertheless, the gas cloud caused heavy casualties in the French lines, and resulted in a substantial gap opening up as many men fled in the face of this new weapon. Unfortunately for the panicking soldiers, carried by an easterly wind, the gas cloud accompanied the retreating men, causing far more casualties than if they had stayed in their positions. However, the Germans had not anticipated the effectiveness of their new weapon and had not positioned sufficient men to take advantage of the success – even had they wanted to do so, it would have been beyond the resources of the German Army to provide adequate support for the gas attack at the same time as preparing for the offensive in southern Poland.

Despite the attempts to distract the attention of the Russians, it was impossible to hide the scale of the build-up. Brusilov, commander of Eighth Army, later wrote:

There was another dark cloud on our horizon. Reports continued to come in from Third Army of the continuous build-up of the enemy's heavy artillery and troops. As I recall, these alarming reports began to arrive in the second half of February [end of February to early March in the western calendar], and on the basis of reports from reconnaissance troops and observation aircraft, General Radko Dimitriev anxiously reported to the [front] commander that a powerful German attack group was concentrating on his front. It was clear that, after the failure of his efforts in the Carpathian Mountains and after the loss of Przemyśl, the enemy now planned to break through our front elsewhere. Any defeat of Third Army threatened to allow the enemy to penetrate into my rear areas, and it seemed to me that it would be very difficult and dangerous to conduct a retreat from the mountains in the face of a powerful enemy. Radko Dimitriev remained concerned about the situation on his front, and repeatedly pressured Ivanov about the need for a strong reserve to counter the danger that threatened him. Unfortunately, it seems that General Ivanov did not trust the reports from Radko Dimitriev and clung to the belief that the greatest danger facing us was not along the River Dunajec but on our left flank.[35]

Brusilov's claim that the concentration of German and Austro-Hungarian forces had been detected as early as the end of March is contrary to the known movements of German forces, especially as Conrad and Falkenhayn did not meet to agree the operation until 14 April. In a similar vein, Danilov too claimed that the Russians had been aware of growing enemy concentrations near Krakow since mid-February.[36] Nevertheless, it would have been impossible to hide the preparations that were being undertaken, and although the Russians may have picked up early signs of activity, they were certainly aware of the gathering German forces by the last week of April. German troops replaced Austro-Hungarian soldiers in the front line, and attempted to hide their presence by avoiding wearing their distinctive *Pickelhaube* helmets, but interrogation of captured prisoners – first by the Russians, and then by the Germans – revealed the presence of German troops, and the Russian awareness of them. On 12 April, Danilov wrote a memorandum on a probable German attack:

> It is possible, indeed probable, that the Germans have the intention of massing considerable forces on Austro-Hungarian territory to bring our offensive in the Carpathians, which troubles them both for military and political reasons, to a halt. Indications lead us to believe that the main shock of the German attack will be directed against the centre of Third Army with the intention of turning the right flank of our troops who have crossed the main chain of the Carpathians; such an attack could well succeed, as the front line in question has been extended too far.[37]

By then, there was little the Russians could do. Reserves at a strategic level, in the shape of III Caucasian Corps, had already been sent south into the Carpathians, and it now became subject to arguments about whether the corps should be used to revive the offensive against the Austro-Hungarian armies, or whether it should be sent west. Locally, Dimitriev had few reserves with which to reinforce the front line. In any event, he appears to have been concerned mainly that the southern flank of his army

Breakthrough at Gorlice, May 1915

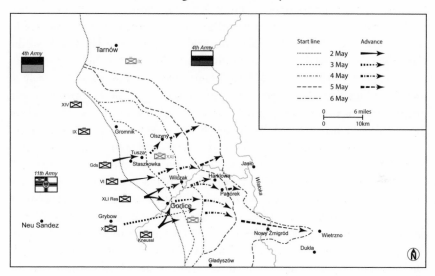

would come under attack, and sought to concentrate whatever troops he could spare in that area, particularly the bulk of the formations that had formerly belonged to XXI Corps.[38] Belatedly, III Caucasian Corps – delayed for a day in Chyrów when it paraded in front of the visiting Tsar Nicholas – was dispatched to reinforce the critical area. The limited railway lines running parallel to the line of the Carpathians, which had not been fully repaired since the fighting of the previous year, meant that as the moment for the German assault approached, the first of the critical reinforcements had barely reached Jaslo, still at least 12 miles (20km) from the threatened front. The bulk of III Caucasian Corps was still strung out along the rail lines to the east.[39]

The troops of the Central Powers were now in position. Over 500 trains had carried Mackensen's army to the front, and they deployed with *Korps Kneussl* in the south, immediately to the southwest of Gorlice, and XLI Reserve Corps to the west of the city. The Austro-Hungarian VI Corps was next in line, with Guards Corps on the northern flank. In reserve, still in the process of assembling, were the two divisions of X Corps. To the north of Eleventh Army was Joseph Ferdinand's Fourth Army. IX Corps was deployed either side of Gromnik; the two divisions of *Gruppe Roth* stood to its north; and a new *Gruppe Stöner-Steiner*, assembled from a variety of *Landsturm* and a few battalions assigned from First Army, formed the most northern formation. A single brigade from XII Corps formed Joseph Ferdinand's reserve.

179

Facing these formations were the divisions of Radko Dimitriev's Third Army. Nikolai Ivanovich Protopopov inherited X Corps and its three divisions when Sievers, who commanded the corps at the outbreak of the war, was promoted to take command of Tenth Army. X Corps held the front from Gładyszów in the Carpathians to Rzepiennik; two of its divisions – 9th and 31st Infantry Division – were regular formations, while 61st Infantry Division was made up largely of reservists. Much of the corps had been in action in the Carpathians, and interrogation of prisoners suggested that its morale remained low as a result of the casualties it had suffered. To its north was what remained of XXI Corps, under Jakov Feodorovich Shchkinsky, with little more than the four regiments of reservists from 70th Infantry Division. At the northern end of the line was IX Corps, commanded by Dmitri Gregorovich Shcherbachev, with a further three divisions. Anticipating an attack by Austro-Hungarian and German forces to try to turn his line from the south, Dimitriev had stationed an additional two infantry divisions and five cavalry divisions behind the southern flank of his army, and intended to dispatch III Caucasian Corps there as soon as it arrived. On the very eve of the German offensive, prisoners and deserters informed the Russians of the real location of the attack, to the west and northwest of Gorlice. It was now far too late to respond.

In the opinion of the Germans, the Russian positions were a formidable obstacle:

The Russians between the Carpathians and the Vistula were in positions that had been fortified over five months of labour. With their customary skill, the Russians had used every feature of the landscape. Steep slopes and hilltops had positions often seven deep in stages, with good flank protection and frontal obstacles, strongpoints and machine-gun nests.[40]

The reality was somewhat different. Although there were undoubtedly many positions that were constructed with care, others were woefully inadequate, and the second and third lines of defence existed more in the minds of staff officers than in reality. During the winter, X Corps had actually wished to prepare better positions to which it might fall back in the event of an attack, but Dimitriev refused permission, on the grounds that if troops could be spared for such activity, they were clearly surplus to requirements and Ivanov would force him to transfer them elsewhere. Instead of being allowed to prepare secondary positions, Protopopov was forced to give up two regiments of 'surplus' troops, which were promptly dispatched to the slaughter in the Carpathians.[41]

Russian problems over artillery ammunition would also play a major part in the fighting. On the face of it, Third Army should have had sufficient shells to defend itself, but the endemic rivalries within the tsar's army remained unresolved. Large stocks of shells continued to be held in fortresses and rear areas, where they were guarded jealously; there was a widespread opinion amongst higher commands that the front-line gunners would squander them if they were allowed to have them. Fedor Petrovich Rerberg, who was Protopopov's chief of staff, later wrote that during his time with X Corps, there was never any significant shortage of ammunition; however, whilst this point of view may have been correct from the perspective of corps headquarters, which was just as guilty as higher commands when it came to hoarding supplies, it was not true for the forces in the front line.[42]

At the time, Brusilov too complained of a shortage of artillery ammunition:

The steadily declining supply of ammunition worried me greatly. I had fewer than 200 rounds [per gun]. I tried to get information on when it would be possible to rely upon a plentiful supply of gun and rifle ammunition, and to my dismay was notified by the staff of [Southwest] Front that an improvement in this field could hardly be expected earlier than late autumn 1915, and even then it was an assurance in which they had little confidence. With the paltry amount of ammunition in my possession, and the hopelessness of obtaining enough, it was utterly pointless to take active steps to push onto the Hungarian plain. In fact, rifle ammunition might be sufficient for only one battle, and the army would then be completely helpless, unable to advance further and facing great difficulty in withdrawing through the Carpathian Mountains, armed only with bladed weapons.[43]

Just as rivalries and mistrust interfered with the distribution of ammunition, turning a substantial problem into a potentially catastrophic one, similar rivalries prevented troops from being sent from one command to another. At a time when Ivanov was ostensibly being given priority for the ongoing fighting in the Carpathians, Northwest Front actually had more infantry divisions at its disposal than Southwest Front, and although he had originally been chief of staff in the south, Alexeyev used every possible excuse to block any attempt to transfer troops to Ivanov. When his excuses were overruled, he complied as slowly and as incompletely as possible. One of the reasons for his appointment had been a hope that, as he had come from Southwest Front, he would be more inclined to cooperate with Ivanov than his predecessor; however, much like Ruzsky, he proved to be a willing player in the ongoing game of rivalry that *Stavka* proved incapable of stopping.

In order to launch their opening attacks from the most advantageous positions possible, the regiments of 11th Bavarian Infantry Division launched limited attacks on 29 April, taking up new positions barely 200m from the Russian trenches. The following day, the Austro-Hungarian VI Corps also made a preparatory attack, which went less well. Local Russian counterattacks and determined resistance had to be overcome, but nevertheless, the desired positions were secured on time.

It seems that the Germans had intended to use every means possible to achieve their planned breakthrough, as François recorded:

> Gas cylinders, our most modern means of destruction, had also been given to me for use [in the initial attack]. I had no enthusiasm for this un-chivalrous means of killing men, and was most pleased that the wind direction prevented their deployment.[44]

In the last days before the attack, François carried out personal reconnaissance of the area where his forces would attack. He later recalled some memorable incidents:

> [There were] two Austrian 120mm guns. A small lieutenant presented himself and told us he was the battery commander. I explained to him that he would be under my command, and asked if he could hit a Russian position, which was about 3km [nearly 2 miles] in front of us. He immediately fired a few shells with such good effect that a number of Russians could be seen fleeing from there. This led to lively firing from the Russian trenches along the entire line. As we climbed towards Szalowa, we encountered a Hungarian soldier in the woods, who stared at us in fright and then signed to us to follow him. He led us to a watch-post and reported that he had found 'Russian deserters'. The sentry rushed out immediately with his detachment, and saluted when he saw us; his comrades laughed at our 'captor', who had never seen a German soldier before.[45]

As a result of the experiences of attacking prepared positions in central Poland in December 1914, and particularly on the Western Front, the Germans were keen to maintain the momentum of their initial attack. Mackensen's orders concluded with paragraphs that allowed a degree of freedom that would have been impossible in any other army of the era:

If it is to achieve its objective, the attack by Eleventh Army will have to push forward quickly. This is required as a fundamental part of the operation; but protection against the enemy putting up further resistance in rear area positions and the hindrance of organised deployment of strong reserves is not just to be achieved by speed. It is thus desirable at every level to sustain a steady advance within the allocated sectors of attack. Two factors contribute to this: deployment in depth of the assaulting infantry; and swift progressive artillery support. Therefore, it is not possible to give the army's attacking corps and divisions daily objectives, the securing of which might hold up the possibility of further advances.

But on the other hand it is vital that the unified nature of the army's assault is constantly maintained. It cannot be expected that the attack will proceed smoothly across the entire front. Already, the requirement for the front line, starting off facing northeast, to swing to the east, places additional demands upon the left flank. Faster advances of one section of the front will often facilitate progress in harder sectors, where the advance may have come to a halt, particularly when the deployment in depth allows successful units to take over parts of the neighbouring front line. But conversely, there is the possibility that a further advance will expose units to being outflanked. This might then expose the troops – who, through their rapid advance, deserve it the least – to suffer setbacks. This consideration means that it is necessary for the army to define lines that should be reached in a uniform and if possible simultaneous manner, without preventing the troops from collectively moving on to secure the next sector where possible. Every advance of the attack will be gratefully received by the army, and will be highly praised. There is at the same time consideration for the requirement for corps and divisions to retain contact with their neighbours, not just by telephone but with liaison officers. Beyond that, corps and divisions are bound to keep army command up to date on developments, in order to ensure coordination between the different parts of the battlefront and to be able to dispatch and deploy reserves as the situation warrants.[46]

Without officers of the high calibre of the German Army, such instructions would have risked complete chaos. François' own orders to his troops culminated in a typically rousing finale:

Soldiers!
His Majesty the Kaiser and King has given us the task of freeing Austria alongside our Austro-Hungarian brothers in arms. Your devotion to duty and true German ethos and your courageous bearing against the French are for me a guarantee that

you will energetically carry out the great duty assigned to us. The coming days will make great demands upon your physical strength and your military skills. Ensure that you will be able to look back at your efforts with the same pride as you can at your heroic conduct in previous battles.[47]

After dusk on 1 May, Ziethen's meticulous artillery plan was put into effect. The first phase involved sporadic shelling for an hour, followed by a pause of a similar period. Flares were fired into the night sky in an attempt to lead the Russians to believe that an attack was actually underway, and to encourage them to try to put more men into their front-line trenches. At first light, heavier artillery fire commenced and continued for four hours, with the heavy mortars joining in for the last hour; then, as the infantry launched its attack, the artillery commenced bombardment of the Russian rear areas. Many steps had been taken to try to minimise the possibility of troops coming under 'friendly fire'; troops in the front line had stitched white squares to their backpacks, so that artillery spotters could recognise them, and the assault companies carried placards that were grey on the side facing the Russians, red and white on the side facing the rear.

François' headquarters was on a low hill a little behind the front line. To the south, the snow-capped peaks of the Tatra range were visible in the dawn light, and ahead, the rolling hills of Galicia stretched away towards the east. As it grew light, the Germans watched the artillery preparation:

Six o'clock! The 120mm gun by Hill 696 fired the signal shot and all batteries, from field guns to heavy howitzers rapidly fired a salvo at the Russian positions. It was followed by rumbles and thunder, crashes and hammering; 700 guns opened their fiery throats and spat steel and iron, which hissed and whistled through the air. Over there, the shots bored into the ground, hurling lumps of earth, fragments of wood, and broken obstacles high into the air. Either side of the Russian lines, smoke and flames erupted from the farms and villages. Here and there, one saw Russians fleeing from their trenches and strongpoints, though our deadly shrapnel still pursued them. Heavy guns on railway flatcars held the enemy's approach roads under fire. North of Gorlice, a great pillar of flames rose as high as a house, black masses of smoke climbed upwards to the clouds. An unforgettably striking spectacle. The tanks of a naphtha factory were ablaze, whether through our fire or intentionally set alight by the Russians, it was impossible to tell.

The Russian artillery took some time to reply, and its fire remained feeble.

The clock stood at nine o'clock! A new sound joined the artillery bombardment. The mortars began their destructive work. Small and large shells flew in high arcs, visible as they climbed over the assault positions and fell on the enemy lines. The explosions were sharp and nerve shattering. Trees burst apart like matchwood, huge roots were hurled aloft, the stone walls of houses collapsed into rubble, fountains of earth rained down on the ground. The ground trembled, hell seemed to be let loose.[48]

After the mortars had done their work for an hour, the German barrage lifted onto the next line of Russian positions and the assault troops set off. At the most southern part of the attack was 11th Bavarian Infantry Division, part of *Korps Kneussl*; its southern regiment encountered determined resistance, requiring a further bombardment before the Russians could be dislodged, but the northern regiment made better headway. During the afternoon, the division encountered the second line of Russian defences and overran them, beating off a Russian counterattack. Losses were substantial, with one regiment losing over 700 men, almost a third of its strength; nevertheless, compared to losses suffered on the Western Front, the casualties were acceptable.[49] The northern half of *Korps Kneussl*, 119th Reserve Infantry Division, reached the southern outskirts of Gorlice. Although it, too, suffered substantial losses, Kneussl could be satisfied with the first day's progress by his men, pushing the Russians back over a mile. Their opponents were from General Vladislav Napoleonovich Klembovsky's 9th Infantry Division, part of X Corps; by the end of the day, it had suffered serious casualties, including several hundred prisoners, and its component regiments were barely in contact with each other.

To the north of *Korps Kneussl* was XLI Reserve Corps. François had positioned 81st Reserve Infantry Division on the northern part of his sector, with 82nd Reserve Infantry Division to the south. The latter made good progress towards the outskirts of Gorlice, reaching its first objective – a Jewish cemetery on a small hill – in less than an hour and capturing numerous prisoners. From there, Generalmajor Friedrich Fabarius turned his attention to Gorlice itself. Fighting continued throughout the day, but by dusk, most of the town was in German hands. Fabarius' division lost 142 officers and men killed, and a further 365 wounded; in addition to their dead, the Russians lost over 3,600 prisoners, including one general.[50] It was the first major success of the campaign, and the seam between the Russian 61st Infantry Division and 9th Infantry Division had been forced open.

The northern part of François's corps, 81st Infantry Division, found itself facing determined resistance. In addition to the trenches and fortifications that they had built in the preceding months, the Russians were protected by a railway embankment immediately in front of their defences, and machine-guns positioned in the cover of a nearby village cut into the flank of every attempt by the German division to storm the steep embankment. Just before noon, a further 15-minute artillery bombardment rained down upon the Russians, who nevertheless repulsed the next assault. Once more, the German gunners attempted to subdue the defences; in the early afternoon, Generalmajor Leo von Stocken, the commander of 81st Infantry Division, made another attempt to overrun the embankment. Accurate defensive fire drove many of the attackers to ground, but part of one battalion, supported at close range by an artillery battery, succeeded in penetrating into the Russian positions. Finally, the resistance was broken, and Stocken's division was able to secure the railway embankment. Over a thousand Russian prisoners were taken at the embankment, the total rising to 4,000 by the end of the day, but losses were heavy; 269th Infantry Regiment, which had formed the main assault force at the railway embankment, suffered nearly 170 officers and men killed, and a further 571 wounded.[51] Nevertheless, François had every reason to be happy with his corps' work. By mid-afternoon, his two divisions had already exceeded their objectives for the first day of the campaign, and the remaining hours were put to good use gaining further ground and bringing forward supplies.

François' neighbour to the north was the Austro-Hungarian VI Corps, commanded by Feldmarschallleutnant Arthur Arz. He had inherited command of his corps when the previous commander, Boroević, took over Third Army, and had led his troops with some distinction in the fighting at Limanowa-Łapanów the previous December. He watched his men set off on their attack, acutely aware of how many times Austro-Hungarian troops had commenced such attacks, and how little success they had enjoyed:

> Our tension peaked as the infantry set off from their assault positions precisely at 10 o'clock. Soon they disappeared into the dust and smoke that was rapidly spreading. Would they succeed? The question was on everyone's lips. When the smoke began to clear, we saw just a few individuals on the southwest slope, then entire lines hurrying down. The attack seemed to have failed. But the retreating lines grew steadily denser, gathering together into masses that were much stronger than those deployed for the attacks. Now we saw it clearly: the masses pouring down the slopes like lava were – Russians. There were thousands of prisoners, who counted themselves fortunate to have escaped hell. The mountain was ours, the first breach in the enemy positions had been made.[52]

The southern part of his corps, 12th Infantry Division, made good progress attacking the Pustki plateau, at one stage moving significantly ahead of the German 81st Infantry Division as the latter struggled to overcome the Russian defences at the railway embankment. By the end of the first day, Feldmarschallleutnant Paul Kestranek was able to report that his division, too, had taken significant numbers of prisoners; the Russian forces opposing him, he wrote, had effectively been destroyed and would not be able to put up further prolonged resistance.[53] There was a particular sense of satisfaction in this success; many of the troops of 12th Infantry Division were from western Galicia, and were therefore fighting on the terrain of their home province. The other part of Arz's corps, 39th *Honvéd* Infantry Division, fared far worse, trying to advance through hilly terrain. The bulk of VI Corps' artillery support had been concentrated in support of 12th Infantry Division, and the initial attack by the *Honvéd* division, with large numbers of reservists in its ranks, made little headway until further artillery fire was directed into its area. Eventually, the division was able to reach its objectives, at least partly because the opposing Russian forces pulled back through fear of both their flanks being turned by German successes to the north and the advance of the Austrian 12th Infantry Division to the south.

The most northern element of Mackensen's army was formed by Guards Corps, commanded by General Karl von Plettenberg. He had led his elite troops since the beginning of the war, and like many senior German commanders, his family had a long history of military service. His oldest son was serving as a lieutenant in a regiment of the Guards as part of his father's corps, and was killed in August 1914 at St Quentin. In their latest battle, Plettenberg's guardsmen would have to advance across hilly terrain to capture their objectives. As was the case with Arz's corps, artillery support was assigned unevenly, with the result that part of the advance of 2nd Guards Infantry Division was held up until fire support could be switched to its sector. After heavy and costly fighting, the village of Staszkowka was captured during the afternoon, allowing the Germans to push forward towards Tusza by the end of the day.[54]

The northern part of the corps, 1st Guards Infantry Division, encountered minimal resistance; the German artillery preparation in this sector had been particularly effective, and the division was eventually forced to stop more out of fear that it was getting too far ahead of its neighbours than because of Russian resistance. Like the rest of the assault troops, the Guards had suffered substantial losses, particularly in the tough fighting around Staszkowka, with nearly 500 killed. Hermann von François, commander of XLI Corps, had particular reasons for feeling the losses personally; he had served in the Guards himself as a young man, and many former comrades were amongst the fallen. He also had personal relatives serving in the Guards:

> One death that particularly touched me was that of Major Freiherr von Wangenheim, who was once my regimental adjutant. He was a man of the noblest bearing, outstanding character and great military ability. The 17-year-old youngest son of my brother also died for the Fatherland. His oldest brother had already preceded him, falling at Buquoy in 1914, and the last brother followed them later.[55]

In his headquarters, Mackensen anxiously followed the day's reports. That evening, he wrote:

> So far, everything is proceeding well. But the tactical situation will come to a head tomorrow morning when the enemy will deploy his reserves. He was barely able to do so today. I am therefore happy with the day's results, provided that no contrary reports are received overnight. This morning, a Russian aircraft paid a visit to our headquarters, but departed rapidly without dropping any bombs when it was greeted by gunfire. It was probably observing the railway station. Somewhat later, Archduke Frederick, accompanied by the heir to the throne [of Austria-Hungary] and his chief of staff visited me. I burst from my office and was able to give them the first good news from the front just as it had arrived. He stayed here over an hour and then drove towards Gorlice with his entourage in order to see the fighting for himself. Unfortunately, I was stuck in Neu Sandez. My thoughts were full of the countermeasures that the Russians could take.[56]

Mackensen needn't have worried about contrary reports ruining the day's news. By first light on 3 May, he recorded, the count of prisoners had reached 12,000, an impressive total for what amounted to a frontal attack; François' account gives an even more impressive – if unlikely – 17,000.[57] On both flanks, the neighbouring Austro-Hungarian armies had been able to make sufficient ground to protect the flanks of the main assault. On the Russian side, the news reaching higher commands was far less favourable. Two regiments of 70th Infantry Division had been effectively knocked out of the battle, and the northern flank of 31st Infantry Division had been turned. Contrary to Mackensen's fears, Dimitriev had insufficient local reserves to restore the situation; all now hinged upon the arrival of III Caucasian Corps, the main elements of which remained over a day's march to the east. The position of X Corps in particular was critical; the Russians could only hope that the German assault would have to pause long enough for III Caucasian Corps to be able to reinforce the line.[58]

In Berlin, the news of the initial successes was received with huge jubilation. In a war in which little had gone well, even the modest successes of 2 May were lauded and celebrated. By contrast, the Russians were faced with a situation that was ominous, and likely to get far worse. As reports of the fighting began to spread around the world, the Russians instructed their ambassadors to try to limit the damage, particularly in Washington:

> The Imperial Russian legations are authorised to deny categorically all the reports from Berlin and Vienna of the supposed great German–Austrian victory in Western Galicia. The fighting that is going on in this area cannot even be described as a partial success for the German–Austrian armies.[59]

The following morning, François rode over the ground his corps had captured:

> At the railway embankment near Kaminiec lay many bodies, stiff and silent; the brave men of 269th Infantry Regiment, who were not destined to experience the triumph. In the nearby woods and in Kaminiec was a scene of destruction the likes of which I had never seen before. The heavy artillery and mortars had wreaked devastation here; the ground was roughed up by shellfire, the huge trees splintered, with stricken Russians here and there under them. In the northern part of Kaminiec, there were hundreds of huts made from raw logs; there was a great deal of military equipment there, as well as dead Russians, whose cheerful rear area existence had been utterly wrecked by our shells. Then [I rode] on to the Jewish cemetery to the north of Gorlice, a bulwark built by the Russians with all their skill, now a field of craters, filled with corpses, guns, cooking implements, and cartridges. On to Hill 357: trench after trench with barbed wire fortifications; here too our shells had done their work. Thick black clouds of smoke still rose from the naphtha tanks and rolled over the battlefield. Gorlice was almost demolished; the section of the town that had seen fighting resembled a sea of ruins. By a shot-up wall there were fifteen bodies, apparently a headquarters unit that had set up here; in a three-metre trench, we counted thirteen dead Russians. Staying in Gorlice under the crashes of shellfire and the din of collapsing buildings must have shredded their nerves. A hail of steel and iron had stormed over the town for four hours. Nevertheless, one encountered residents everywhere, mainly kaftan-wearing Jews, who emerged from foxholes and cellars and sorted through the dead Russians.[60]

With the first line of Russian defences effectively overrun, Mackensen issued orders for the advance to the next objective, the River Wisłoka. As the troops of X Corps had now arrived, he sent one half – 20th Infantry Division – to the southern end of the battlefield, where General Otto von Emmich, commander of X Corps, now took command of the forces that had previously been led by Kneussl, allowing the latter to return to command of his 11th Bavarian Infantry Division. The southern sector would now be the main effort for Eleventh Army, and Emmich directed Kneussl's division to move up to the Russian second line of defences. Further north, 119th Reserve Infantry Division was to march east from Gorlice, and as the battle developed, 20th Infantry Division would be inserted between the two formations that had already endured tough fighting. Whilst the terrain around Gorlice was hilly, it was increasingly so further south, and a mixture of poor roads, the landscape, and rain prevented the Bavarians from making early progress. Under heavy fire from the Russian artillery that had been deployed in the second line of defences, 11th Bavarian Infantry Division struggled to make much progress. By contrast, 119th Reserve Infantry Division pushed forward quickly and finally stopped for the night having covered half the ground to the Wisłoka; even if the Russians were able to hold up Kneussl, they were in danger of being outflanked.

Despite a delayed order from Mackensen telling him to extend his corps' line a little further south in order to allow *Korps Emmich* to concentrate its forces, François was confident that his men would continue to enjoy success. Aerial reconnaissance reported disorganised columns of Russian troops withdrawing towards the east, while fresh troops attempted to move west towards the front line; correctly assessing this as a sign that the Russians were struggling to organise their defences, François ordered 82nd Reserve Infantry Division to push forward to capture the Russian positions on Mount Wilczak, part of the second line of defences. It was a formidable objective, with five lines of entrenchments, strongly supported with artillery and machine-guns. At first, the advance went well, and by midday, XLI Reserve Corps' artillery was beginning its work on the Russian positions on the mountain. A few hours later, the heavier guns were also in position and joined the bombardment. Despite determined Russian resistance, 82nd Reserve Infantry Division fought its way forward, eventually securing the vital mountain in the evening. A final Russian counterattack was repulsed by the timely intervention of the division's infantry, and as darkness fell, the remaining Russian forces withdrew to the east, albeit in good order. François' troops were content to let them go.[61]

The Austro-Hungarian forces on François' northern flank continued to battle forward through the Russian positions. Whilst their progress was unspectacular, they kept pace with François, ensuring that there was no threat to his men from the north. At the northern end of Mackensen's front, Plettenberg's Guards Corps faced a similar obstacle to XLI Reserve Corps, in the shape of heavily fortified hills north of Olszyny. Despite the difficulties they faced, the guardsmen succeeded in securing the ridgeline by the end of the day.

Confident that his formations were making good progress, Mackensen issued further orders during the afternoon, to the effect that crossings over the Wisłoka should be secured the following day, thus dislocating the third and final Russian defensive line. As a prelude to this, the objectives for 3 May were moved further east; unfortunately, this order reached the front line at about the same time that Russian resistance slowed the advance of 11th Bavarian Infantry Division in the south, 82nd Reserve Infantry Division in the centre, and the Guards in the north. Consequently, by the end of the day, many of the new objectives had not been reached. Nevertheless, progress remained satisfactory. The formations of Eleventh Army had advanced perhaps 6 miles (10km) through the Russian defences, and though casualties had not been light, they were acceptable. These gains were modest compared with those seen at Tannenberg or the Masurian Lakes, but given the strength of the Russian positions, and by comparison with attacks upon fortified lines on the Western Front, they were nevertheless impressive.

On the Russian side, Dimitriev knew that his army's resistance was crumbling. Late on 3 May, he sent a telegram to Ivanov that Protopopov's X Corps was under attack by substantial German forces, and might not be able to hold on until the arrival of III Caucasian Corps. The minimal reserves available had already been dispatched to the front in the hope that this would buy time for a major counterattack to be organised. However, Dimitriev warned that if X Corps was unable to hold its positions, it would have to pull back to the final line of defences along the Wisłoka, necessitating a matching withdrawal by all forces on its flanks. Although he had not given orders for such a withdrawal, Dimitriev felt that it was his duty to make Ivanov aware of the possibility. He concluded with a request for additional reinforcements from as far afield as Northwest Front, on the grounds that if the Germans were concentrating here in southern Poland, they must have weakened their lines elsewhere.[62]

Ivanov's response was unhelpful: the units of III Caucasian Corps should be sufficient both to bolster the front line and to mount a counterattack, and no other reinforcements were being sent. Accordingly, Dimitriev committed the elements of III Caucasian Corps to the front line as they arrived, instead of concentrating them into a force that might have had a chance of making an impact. To a very large extent, he had no choice. His front line was about to collapse, and he had no other reserves with which to shore it up. However, the loss of troops was accelerating faster than they could be replaced. A German breakthrough was only a matter of time.

Rain had hindered the German advance on 3 May, but the weather improved the following day. At first light, German aircraft were aloft again, and reported that the Russians had abandoned their positions in front of 11th Bavarian Infantry Division. However, they also spotted new columns of Russians hurrying forward as the elements of III Caucasian Corps were fed into the battle piecemeal. Kneussl immediately got his men moving, rapidly advancing to Rozdziele. A little further east, though, the Bavarians ran into organised defences and had to wait for their artillery to catch up. During the afternoon, the Russian position was overcome, and Kneussl ended the day having advanced perhaps 3 miles (5km) during the day. On his northern flank, 119th Reserve Infantry Division faced a serious Russian counterattack but succeeded in defeating it, ensuring that Emmich's corps was ready to press on towards the Wisłoka.

François dispatched 82nd Reserve Infantry Division to try to penetrate the line of hills on the west bank of the vital river. By the end of 4 May, the division was firmly established in Pagórek, in the midst of the Russian positions. A short distance to the north, 81st Reserve Infantry Division encountered tougher resistance at Harklowa, where the Russians were aided by dense woodland, which made coordination of the German formations difficult. Nevertheless, the German troops – often acting on their own initiative in the best traditions of German devolved decision-making – worked their way through the difficult terrain. Attempts to take Harklowa itself repeatedly foundered due to flanking fire from positions on a nearby hill; although the hill was meant to be in the Austro-Hungarian VI Corps' sector, 81st Infantry Division took it upon itself to try to force the position. Increasing confusion between different regiments, though, hindered the Germans as much as Russian resistance, and as darkness brought a lull to the fighting, Harklowa remained in Russian hands.[63]

Arz's VI Corps had continued its slow progress, pushing through Biecz in the morning of 4 May. As it advanced into the same line of hills that had halted XLI Reserve Corps, 39th *Honvéd* Infantry Division was involved in several bloody assaults before it finally took its objectives; late in the day, 12th Infantry Division succeeded in overrunning the Russian positions that had outflanked the German attacks on Harklowa, but too late to allow a decision to be forced before the end of the day. Further north, Guards Corps was forced to pull back its left flank, as the Austro-Hungarian forces alongside Mackensen's army had failed to keep up with the advance. François recorded approvingly that the guardsmen advanced in exemplary fashion, as if on parade, and overran the Russian defences; he did not mention whether their dense formations made tempting targets for Russian artillery and machine-guns.[64]

That evening, Dimitriev sent a further telegram to Ivanov. The deployment of III Caucasian Corps had failed to restore the situation, and X Corps had been reduced to barely 5,000 combatants. The pressure upon the Russian line began to have an effect elsewhere. Near the Dukla Pass, XII Corps began to withdraw, and nearer Nowy Żmigród, XXIV Corps received orders to move east. Far earlier than Falkenhayn and Conrad might have expected, the advance was beginning to destabilise the Russian positions in the Carpathians.[65]

On 5 May, Emmich finally committed 20th Infantry Division to the fighting. The fresh troops swiftly overcame the Russians opposing them, and seized the town of Nowy Żmigród before the Russians had completed their withdrawal. Importantly, a bridge over the Wisłoka in the town was captured intact, and the division pushed on almost unopposed to Wietrzno, over 7 miles (12km) further east. With 11th Bavarian Infantry Division protecting the southern flank of the advance and 119th Reserve Infantry Division pausing to rest in Żmigród, Emmich had good reason to be satisfied with the outcome of the fighting. A little to the north, François found himself held up by elements of III Caucasian Corps, and although his men eventually overcame the resistance of the Russians, only a few reconnaissance patrols reached the Wisłoka. Similarly, Arz's VI Corps also spent the day gaining only modest ground, as further elements of III Caucasian Corps were fed into the battle. The divisions of the Guards, too, laboured forward slowly. Nevertheless, with *Korps Emmich* firmly established beyond the Wisłoka, Mackensen could claim that he had successfully broken through the Russian defences. The roads running south to the Dukla Pass were now in German hands, and the Russian forces in the western Carpathians had no choice but to start withdrawing east. By midday, Mackensen had already sent a triumphant signal to Berlin, announcing that he had successfully completed the task assigned to him, and would now seek to exploit it further.[66]

There was nothing that Dimitriev could do to stop such exploitation. Any hope of concentrating III Caucasian Corps into a single force with which to mount a counterattack was now impossible, with the component regiments scattered along the entire front. X Corps had been reduced to less than the establishment strength of a single rifle regiment, and the disparate elements of III Caucasian Corps had lost over two thirds of their troops. Even the forces that remained were disorganised and demoralised, and in desperate need of time to rally; in the face of a confident German Army, such time was unlikely to be available. German losses had not been light – François recorded that his corps had lost 13.5 per cent of its strength, with similar losses amongst the other German corps, and heavier casualties in the Austro-Hungarian VI Corps. However, when compared with the huge casualties incurred by both sides in the Carpathians, and by the Austro-Hungarian Army in almost all of its battles, these losses were acceptable, particularly given the difficult terrain through which Mackensen's troops had advanced.

The conduct of the campaign from its inception to the moment of breakthrough is worth reviewing in some detail. Falkenhayn's thoughts turned to the possibility of an offensive some time in March 1915, and detailed planning began in mid-April. Using railways that had never been intended for mass movement of troops, the Germans and their Austro-Hungarian allies moved eight German divisions, additional artillery, ammunition and supplies, and reinforcements for the Austro-Hungarian troops, into position in less than three weeks. Many of the troops were also given the opportunity for training, relating to assaults on fortified positions. Despite this being the first time that the two Central Powers had cooperated on this scale, matters were managed smoothly, even when François, Kneussl, Emmich and Plettenberg found themselves relying on civilian Austro-Hungarian supply services. The attack itself was planned with meticulous care and attention to detail, making the most of what had been learned from similar attacks on the Western Front, and using information gained through all routes – intelligence, aerial reconnaissance, and prisoner interrogations – to build up as complete a picture of Russian positions as was possible. Once the troops set off, Mackensen had the confidence to allow his subordinates to conduct operations as they saw fit, provided that this complied with his overall objective, and Emmich in particular put this to good use, shifting the point of emphasis of his corps to achieve a breakthrough – in other words, an exemplary demonstration of both the theory and practice of *Auftragstaktik*.

In just a few days, the Germans achieved what amounted to a tactical victory, albeit a substantial one. They had broken the Russian defensive line and inflicted heavy losses, but they had done this on several occasions during the war; the bigger test still lay ahead, to turn this tactical success into a strategic one. Inevitably, there were conflicting claims for who should take credit. Conrad's *AOK* had nominally been in command of the operation, and had organised logistic support as well as providing considerable numbers of men, and Conrad later claimed that he had always intended an offensive in this area. However, given the number of occasions that he suggested offensives almost anywhere on the Eastern Front, this is unsurprising. Similarly, his assertion that it was the bloody fighting in the Carpathians that had weakened the Russian Army sufficiently to allow Eleventh Army to break through successfully at Gorlice–Tarnów ignores the fact that his own armies suffered far heavier casualties, and this weakening of the Russians was thus bought at a huge price. Falkenhayn perhaps had greater justification for claiming credit, as he envisaged the assault, moved troops swiftly to the area, and created a new army with which to mount the attack. The manner in which Mackensen delegated responsibility to his subordinates is also worthy of mention. Perhaps if a single entity is to be recognised, it should be the German staff officer system, from *OHL* down to the chiefs of staff of every formation in the battle. Their flexibility, resourcefulness, and sheer professionalism put the performance of their equivalents in the Austro-Hungarian and Russian armies to shame.

The tactics used by the Germans also played a substantial part in their success. This was the first major operation on the Eastern Front where there was a conscious attempt to apply the lessons that had been learned in fighting elsewhere. The careful preparation and planning of the preliminary bombardment in particular was greatly influenced by experiences on the Western Front, both in German attacks and when defending against attacks by the British and French. Once the Russians were driven from their main defences, the poor standard of their second and third lines left them increasingly vulnerable to artillery fire, and a vital element of the German plan was for rapid forward movement of their guns to ensure that momentum was sustained. The importance of that momentum was repeatedly stressed, both during planning and execution; the experiences on the Western Front suggested that overcoming a fortified defensive line was a tough task, but exploiting any success was even tougher. It was therefore crucial to ensure that the Russians were given no opportunity to establish a new line with fresh troops being brought up from the rear. In the event, the Russian losses in the front line – one estimate is that perhaps a third of the defenders were killed by the artillery bombardment alone – and the lack of adequate reserves behind the front line combined to prevent the sort of rapid stabilisation that repeatedly occurred in the west.[67] Once the attack began, the use of artillery to smash isolated strongpoints that held up the advance was also flexible and innovative, contributing significantly to the breakthrough.

Whilst the use of artillery by the Germans was new and imaginative, the same could not be said of their infantry. As had been the case in almost every battle since August 1914, the soldiers advanced in line abreast – though perhaps these lines were slightly more extended than before – to try to reduce the impact of defensive fire, particularly from machine-guns. Perhaps the only attempt to learn from recent battles was in the manner that jump-off positions were established as close to the Russian lines as possible, to limit the exposure of the infantry. François regarded his casualties as acceptable, but if fighting were prolonged, even these losses would have a significant effect on the ability of the Germans to exploit their breakthrough. Nevertheless, their tactics were superior to those of their opponents, in the opinion of Alfred Knox, the British military attaché accompanying the Russian Army:

> The Germans win against anything like equal numbers if the Russians have not time to entrench. They manoeuvre more boldly and are not nervous about their flanks, having a wonderful mutual trust in the command. The Russians have less idea of manoeuvre. Units do not trust one another, and each is constantly nervous regarding its flanks. This prevents all dash and initiative. Every commander expects to be let down by his neighbour, and of course consequently generally is. The Russians suffer from the lack of shell, of heavy artillery and of machine-guns. It is believed that the Germans have four machine-guns per battalion, and they do not spare shell. They use their machine-guns to form pivots for manoeuvre, keeping up a deadly fire in front from a group of machine-guns while the infantry works round one or both flanks. The number of these machine-guns makes the capture of a trench once lost a very costly business.[68]

By contrast, the Russians struggled from the outset. Although second and third lines of defence had been designated, few preparations were made, with the result that there were isolated positions of great strength, but the lack of attention to the intervening areas allowed them to be outflanked. With troops constantly being dispatched to the apparently endless fighting in the Carpathians, it was impossible both to man the front line and station adequate reserves behind it. This ensured that once the Germans broke through the line, it would be difficult to prevent a major retreat.

Although the Russians correctly recognised the imminent German attack, they took few if any steps to improve their positions. Ultimately, III Caucasian Corps – the only significant force available for redeployment in Southwest Front – was dispatched to the threatened sector, but the huge inefficiencies of the Russian railway system across the entire Eastern Front, combined with poor quality railroads, ensured that these reinforcements would arrive too late, as did whatever additional ammunition was ultimately dispatched to Dimitriev's army. The Russian railways had functioned better than many anticipated when the tsar authorised mobilisation in 1914, but thereafter, they consistently failed to perform at a level remotely comparable with those of Russia's enemies, and the reasons for this are characteristic of failings throughout Russia. Compared with Germany and the Austro-Hungarian Empire, Russia had far fewer railway engineers who could maintain and repair railways. Although railway formations had formed part of Russia's mobilisation plan, these were often poorly trained and illiterate. Unlike the substantial logistic and staff support available for railway planning in both Vienna and Berlin, the Russian system relied almost entirely upon one individual, Sergei Alexandrovich Ronzhin, who was head of *Stavka's* railway office, to coordinate all railway activity at a central level. With only two subordinates and a clerk, he was effectively powerless to intervene when railway officers at the headquarters of Northwest and Southwest Fronts refused to cooperate. To make matters worse, the two fronts controlled only about one third of Russia's railways, engines and rolling stock; the rest remained within the control of the civilian authorities. Cooperation between the civilian and military railway commands was as bad as cooperation between the two fronts, with the result that substantial quantities of trains and rolling stock sat idle while the various parties squabbled over precedence and control. At a time when Falkenhayn devised, planned and executed the redeployment of the troops that would form Mackensen's army in less than two weeks, the Russians proved unable to move III Caucasian Corps from one end of Galicia to the other.

Nor is it sufficient to blame the discrepancy between Russian and German railway performance on the relatively primitive Russian railways when compared with those of the Central Powers. When the Russians were forced to retreat, the Germans succeeded in running far more trains on the same railway lines that had failed to move troops and supplies for the tsar's armies. To a considerable extent, this reflects the far greater skill and numbers of German railwaymen and engineers, who were able to extract levels of performance that were undreamed of by the Russians.

Perhaps one of the factors that effectively guaranteed that Ronzhin and other officials would struggle to move troops and reinforcements in a timely manner was the greater dependence of the tsar's armies upon horses. All armies of the era used horses as their main means of pulling wagons and guns, but from the beginning of the war there had been great expectations of the ability of the Russian cavalry to have a major impact upon the campaigns on the Eastern Front. When their cavalry singularly failed to achieve anything of note, other armies rapidly downgraded their cavalry, often dismounting them and using them as infantry as the war continued, but the Russians persisted in maintaining large mounted formations. More trains were required to move a cavalry formation than an infantry unit of the same numerical strength, and matters were even worse in terms of logistic needs – the Russians consistently needed more wagons to move fodder for horses than to move food for troops. The combination of all of these factors – poorly trained railway personnel, no proper central authority to enforce coordination and cooperation, and disproportionate amounts of rolling stock serving the needs of the least effective element of the Russian Army – ensured that the German and Austro-Hungarian railway networks would serve the needs of their armies far more efficiently.[69]

The quality of staff officers in the Russian Army also contributed greatly to the inefficiencies of its performance; their lack of professionalism was apparently widely known amongst their colleagues. Writing a little before the beginning of the Gorlice–Tarnów campaign, Knox recorded his opinion of Grigory Ivanovich Nostitz, chief of staff of the Guard Corps:

> Nostitz is a very interesting character. He writes everything to his wife. Generally he is writing to her, but he has other relaxations. One day I found him reading a French book, *Quelques Pages de la Vie d'une Diplomate à Teheran*. This when the guns were distinctly audible. I told Engelhardt [another officer in the headquarters of the Guard Corps] that I was glad to have met Nostitz, for no staff officer of such a type would appear in any future campaign. He said: 'And thank God for that.'[70]

When he observed an officer conducting an interrogation of a captured German officer, Knox again noticed a complete lack of professionalism:

> He was doing Engelhardt's work as Corps Intelligence Officer during the latter's absence at the Imperial Duma. The cross-examination, which should be carried out by a good German scholar with a barrister's acuteness, was, as usual, being conducted haphazard. Bridge was in progress in the next room and 'Dummy' always strolled in and tried his German on the prisoner, the same questions being asked many times. These people play at war. As Rodzianko said, it makes one furious – a favourite expression of his – to think of the poor devils in the hospitals who have given their all, their health and their limbs, for their country, while the cause is being sacrificed by such childishness in the rear.[71]

On the Russian side, many blamed Radko Dimitriev for the setback, as it was his army that was effectively torn apart. His case was worsened by the embarrassing fact that when the battle started, he was absent from his headquarters, celebrating the award of the Order of St. George.[72] Brusilov was of the opinion that while Dimitriev had to take some responsibility, much of the blame lay elsewhere:

The blame for the breakthrough in Third Army's sector cannot in any way be placed entirely on Radko Dimitriev, and must be laid upon Ivanov. However, Radko Dimitriev must answer for the fragmented and chaotic retreat of the army. He was aware of [German] preparations, and he knew the area where they would attack. He also knew that no reinforcements were available and that he would not therefore be able to resist this attack. Consequently, it seems that he should have ordered the timely gathering of all possible reserves in his army at the threatened point and at the same time he could have given precise orders to his troops regarding the sequence and direction of withdrawal if necessary, and where they should stop and renew their resistance in order to reduce the speed of the enemy advance if possible, and to allow troops to retreat systematically and in good order. To achieve this, it was necessary to withdraw all rear area units without delay … under such circumstances, Third Army would not have been completely broken.

In addition, Radko Dimitriev lost control during the unfortunate retreat of the army, which would not have happened if he had made appropriate arrangements in advance for his communications services, without which the army could not operate. Instead, he drove from one location to another by car, issuing orders that were often contradictory to unit commanders via liaison officers, frequently bypassing the chain of command. Such attempts at command and control merely increased the confusion and disarray in the retreat … commanders at every level did not know what to do, nor what their neighbours were doing.[73]

Criticism that Dimitriev failed to establish proper reserves ignores the fact that any such reserves were likely to be dispatched to the Carpathians, but the lack of any plan for retreat certainly contributed to the disaster that befell Third Army.

Yuri Danilov, the Russian quartermaster-general at the time, also wrote an interesting assessment of Dimitriev:

Later, I had the opportunity to become a close acquaintance of General Radko Dimitriev during the course of my service with the Northern Front. There, he commanded Twelfth Army in 1916–1917, in the Riga sector, where I started by serving as chief of staff for the front, and later as commander of Fifth Army on the

Dvina, close to Dvinsk [now Daugavpils]. There, I learned to value and respect him profoundly. Very gifted, persevering, with great personal courage and never losing his calm in any circumstances, he was certainly a remarkable commander, with perhaps the single fault that he attached too little importance to the techniques of modern warfare.[74]

Unfortunately, Danilov does not define precisely which modern techniques were ignored by Dimitriev. Although he repeatedly warned his superiors that his position was weak and that he lacked artillery ammunition, he was very much a product of the Russian system in which officers at all levels colluded with their superiors in order to avoid having to face hard truths. Danilov himself criticised this tendency, yet he too was guilty of refusing to accept facts from Third Army if they were not palatable to *Stavka*.[75] Ultimately, the failures of leadership in Third Army highlight the gulf between the Russian and German staff systems.

Detailed analysis of credit and blame still lay in the future; for the moment, both sides were more concerned with what would follow the first days of May. The German and Austro-Hungarian troops could look forward with anticipation; aware of how badly Dimitriev's army had suffered, the Russians must have viewed the immediate future with dread.

CHAPTER 6

THE EXPLOITATION

Mackensen's orders for the beginning of the campaign were deliberately couched in terms that avoided discussion of long-term objectives; securing a breakthrough was a task that was tough enough. Nevertheless, Mackensen had already made clear during his visit to *AOK* – to the polite ridicule of his hosts – that he regarded this as merely the first phase of the operation. Even a modest tactical victory would force the Russians to give up their positions in the Dukla Pass, thus ending a major threat to Hungary, and if the advance were to continue, Russian positions north of the Vistula would also have to pull back. The prospects were encouraging, but achieving them remained a formidable task.

The breakthrough itself produced major gains in the areas immediately to the north and south of the main thrust. With German and Austro-Hungarian troops advancing beyond the Wisłoka, the Russians had to consider their positions in the western Carpathians. Conrad had always taught that any success should be exploited and followed up as energetically as possible, but to date he had failed to achieve a sufficiently important success. Mackensen's Eleventh Army was notionally under the overall command of *AOK*, even though Conrad had to seek Falkenhayn's approval before issuing instructions. Now, despite this complex chain of command, there was general agreement. Mackensen would attempt to cut the roads running north from the Dukla Pass, while the Austro-Hungarian formations, supported by the German *Beskidenkorps* and 4th Infantry Division, would attempt to pin down the Russians to hinder their withdrawal. There was a possibility that if events went favourably, two Russian corps could be destroyed.

The two Russian formations at risk were Afanasy Andreyevich Tsurikov's XXIV Corps, immediately to the south of Mackensen's breakthrough, and XII Corps, commanded by Leonid Vilgelmovich Lesh, in the area of the Dukla Pass and

Mezölaborcz. A combined attack by the German *Beskidenkorps* and the Austro-Hungarian VII Corps near Mezölaborcz rapidly put the Russian 12th and 19th Infantry Divisions under pressure, but they were able to carry out an efficient fighting withdrawal through the town and into the mountains; by 6 May, they had pulled back over 12 miles (20km), with casualties that were only a fraction of those suffered during the winter fighting for far smaller movements of the front line.

Although the Russian withdrawal was carried out skilfully, it did not remove the threat of envelopment. Ivanov continued to insist that the reinforcements dispatched to Dimitriev would be sufficient to stop the German advance along the line of the Wisłoka, but Vladimir Mikhailovich Dragomirov, who had moved from command of VIII Corps to become chief of staff at Southwest Front, did not accept his superior's assurances. He proposed to *Stavka* that Fourth, Third and Eighth Armies should pull back together to a line running from Radom to Przemyśl and Turka, while Ninth Army launched an attack at the southeast end of the long front. This line would be far shorter than the current front, and would allow the armies that had been bled dry in the Carpathians and hammered by Mackensen to regain their strength. Such a withdrawal would have been a formidable undertaking, especially given the pressure being exerted in southern Poland, but Grand Duke Nikolai was not interested. The line of the Wisłoka was to be held, and the reinforcements dispatched would be sufficient.[1]

The problem for Dimitriev was that the reinforcements were fed into the front line as they arrived; the casualties suffered in the opening days of Mackensen's offensive ensured that there was no possibility of massing III Caucasian Corps for a decisive operation. To make matters worse, the Wisłoka line was already untenable, with Mackensen's troops crossing the river in strength at the southern end of the German offensive. In combination with the Austro-Hungarian troops of Third Army to the south, these forces were now in a position to exert potentially lethal pressure upon the western end of the Russian line in the Carpathians.

On the other side of the German offensive, the Russian IX Corps was also withdrawing rapidly. Feldmarschallleutnant Josef Roth's group from the Austro-Hungarian Fourth Army attempted to pursue, but was unable to pin down the Russians:

> As a result of continuous marching, constant fighting, a lack of sleep, shortages of supplies, as the support columns could not keep up with this pace, the troops were significantly degraded and often collapsed from exhaustion … For almost 18 hours, the regiment stumbled rather than marched to Zwiernik [immediately south of Dębica].[2]

The Advance to the San, May 1915

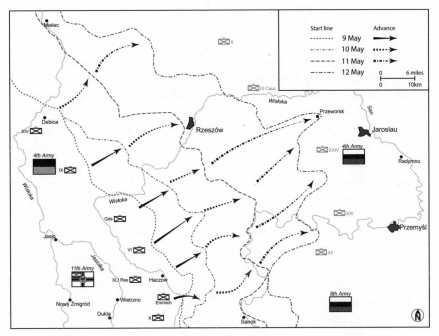

The retreating Russians gave up Tarnów, which had been badly damaged by artillery fire, almost without a fight, though the high ground to the east and south of the town was contested fiercely. However, the Austro-Hungarian advance on the northern flank of Mackensen's forces was held up more by internal issues than enemy action. In the opening days of the offensive, Fourth Army advanced less than 18 miles (30km) before its commanders asked for a halt to allow the men to rest and for supplies to catch up. It seems that although Mackensen's supply lines – provided by the Austro-Hungarian authorities – functioned efficiently, the same clearly could not be said for those of Fourth Army.[3]

In the centre of the battlefield, Mackensen now brought the rest of his army forward towards the line reached by Emmich's corps on the southern flank. It was clear that, regardless of the wishes of *Stavka*, the Russians were in full retreat, as Mackensen recorded on the evening of 6 May. His observations about his Austro-Hungarian allies are also of interest:

Along the entire line from the Vistula far into the Carpathians, the enemy is retreating. His entire Carpathian front line appears to be pulling back. In a few locations, he puts up determined resistance, because the terrain is particularly suitable, or a vital road junction needs to be protected, or an important retreat has to be secured. The longer he halts, the greater our tactical success. Today I calculate we already have 60,000 prisoners. Over 25,000 have already passed through Neu Sandez alone. My troops are doing everything to exploit their success. One doesn't need to urge them on, one even has to rein them back here or there; all I have to do is assign to them the sectors within which each corps operates … X Corps, reinforced by the Bavarian infantry division, which has fought with great distinction, has already blocked the enemy from using the road running east from the Dukla Pass and the Carpathian range. There and at Dukla, even more military materiel was seized today. We have already captured huge amounts of ammunition. Without doubt, our attack has surprised the Russians, or at least the force with which it has been carried out; they did not regard us as being this strong.

The Austrian troops have fought well in the battles. It is striking to see how the proximity of the *Pickelhaube* has an effect upon their bearing in battle. Their confidence in battle depends upon it. The actual Austro-Hungarian leader is General Conrad von Hötzendorf, a man whose heart and mind have grown with his position. Archduke Joseph Ferdinand is a good soldier; he does his job with deliberation and decisiveness, issues orders promptly, and therefore I appreciate him, as his subordinate. General von Arz, too, who commands VI Corps (consisting of one Austrian and one Hungarian division), which has been assigned to Eleventh Army, has turned out to be a skilled commander.

I have every reason to be satisfied with my Prussian generals and I believe I also have their confidence. The same applies to my staff … a report has just arrived that Jaslo has been taken. I will move my headquarters there in the morning.[4]

The final paragraph speaks volumes about the continuing dominance of the German Army by Prussians. This tightly knit brotherhood might have been derided and disliked by many, both within and without Germany, but the quality of the officers that it produced was beyond question, and was clearly something that the Germans themselves regarded as a certainty.

For the Russian troops at the western end of the Russian line, the situation remained precarious. XXIV Corps now found its lines of retreat cut by the German and Austro-Hungarian advance. Its northern formation was 49th Infantry Division, and despite losing much of its equipment, it succeeded in fighting its way through to its designated line. It was followed by Lavr Kornilov's 48th Infantry Division, which found that the roads it intended to use for its retreat were still choked with rear area elements of XXIV Corps. Attempting to find an alternative route, Kornilov ran into the troops of 11th Bavarian Infantry Division and turned back, only to find that the guns of the pursuing Austro-Hungarian 45th Rifle Division were now within range. Order rapidly broke down, and the bulk of the division's infantry fled into nearby woodland. Most of the division's artillery was captured by Austro-Hungarian cavalry that had advanced through the Dukla Pass.

On 7 May, Kornilov's remaining troops gathered their strength for one last attempt to reach safety. Struggling through the mountains along inadequate roads and pursued by Austro-Hungarian units, 48th Infantry Division was no longer able to function as a coherent unit. Eventually, fragments of eight battalions succeeded in retreating through the mountains, but the rest of the division was killed or captured. Kornilov, two colonels, and five other officers tried to make their way to safety, but on 12 May they ran into an Austro-Hungarian munitions column and were taken prisoner.[5]

Nevertheless, despite the destruction of 48th Infantry Division, most of the Russian troops in the western Carpathians managed to withdraw safely. Pursuit was hindered by the same problems that had hindered all fighting in the mountains – the terrain did not allow for rapid advances, and even the slow rate at which the German and Austro-Hungarian troops were able to move forward was checked by the inability of supply columns to keep up. Badly degraded by so much activity during the winter, the poor winter roads simply broke up.

The high tempo of Mackensen's operations now diminished a little, as the various formations secured crossings over the Wisłoka and pushed on towards the line of the River Jasiołka. François had no doubt that he was pursuing a beaten enemy:

> The route of march bore clear signs of a hurried retreat: discarded wagons, weapons and pieces of equipment, dead Russians and horses littered the road. Stretching away for 2km [1.5 miles] either side of the road were trenches full of weapons and munitions.[6]

On 8 May, François' men moved forward to advance from Haczow to attack the next village to the east. It was in many respects an unremarkable operation, but his account shows the degree to which infantry tactics remained locked in the doctrine of a previous era:

> The attack was carried out over a field without any cover over 3km [nearly 2 miles]. In exemplary order, the lines of riflemen moved forwards at a calm pace.

The smoke of exploding shrapnel often covered them, but the advance continued without pause. Despite strong enemy artillery fire, the first wave reached the Morawa valley with really light losses. But after crossing, the riflemen came under heavy rifle and machine-gun fire from houses and hedges, and there now began a laborious and costly fight to advance. After breaking into the village, every farmhouse had to be taken in bitter hand-to-hand fighting. The battle raged throughout the night, and it was only at dawn that the village and the high ground to the east were in the division's hands. Fresh Russian forces had again fought with remarkable courage. Our men were proud of their success and named the day 'the parade attack from Haczow'.[7]

It was impossible for Dimitriev's retreating units to prevent the Germans from securing crossings, let alone to adhere to instructions from both Ivanov and *Stavka* to hold the line of the Wisłoka, and Dimitriev was now forced to consider where he might be able to stop the Germans. In addition to the pressure from Mackensen, he was aware that although XII and XXIV Corps had managed to pull back from the western Carpathians, the losses suffered – particularly the destruction of 48th Infantry Division – meant that there was the possibility of another breakthrough in his front line to the south. Even as Kornilov's division was disintegrating in the mountains, Grand Duke Nikolai summoned his two front commanders to a conference to discuss the situation. Despite having ordered Dimitriev to hold the line of the Wisłoka, Ivanov was pessimistic, and suggested an immediate withdrawal to the line of the San. Supported by Quartermaster-General Danilov, Nikolai rejected this out of hand, demanding that a line extending south from the lower Wisłoka was to be held at all costs. Discussion then turned to the creation of sufficient reserves behind Third Army to prevent further setbacks. A new XXIX Corps was to be created at Mielec, consisting of the 13th Siberian Rifle Division and 63rd Reserve Division. In addition, 8th Infantry Division was dispatched from the Narew and assigned to XXI Corps. But Nikolai's concerns did not end with Third Army. Despite receiving substantial reinforcements – in particular, XXXIII Corps – the Russian Ninth Army had shown little inclination to move onto the offensive. Ivanov was given permission to redeploy XXXIII Corps if he saw fit, and in addition V Caucasian Corps, held back in Odessa in anticipation of possible deployment by sea against Turkey once the British and French had forced their way through the Dardanelles, was ordered to prepare for dispatch to Galicia.

Another outcome of the conference was a reversal of previous exchanges between France and Russia. Throughout the fighting of 1914, the French had urged the Russians to attack Germany with as much force as possible, in order to force the Germans to switch troops away from the Western Front. Now, Nikolai made a request for the French to accelerate their plans for an offensive. At the very least, this would prevent the Germans from sending more men to the east; at best, it might force Falkenhayn to divert resources back to the west. The French and British had planned a major offensive for some time, with converging attacks – a combined Anglo-French operation from the northwest and a second French effort from the southeast – to try to reduce the great salient at Noyon. Even as the fighting in Galicia was escalating, the French opened their planned offensive against Vimy Ridge; although they gained three miles (4.8km) of ground, the subsequent German counterattacks drove them back with heavy losses. The existing German forces in the west, it seemed, were sufficient to hold the line. There was no significant prospect of these battles reducing pressure upon the Russians.

The fighting in the west would, though, prove to have a lasting consequence. During a local counterattack, the Germans captured French documents that described a new way of fighting a defensive battle. To date, all armies had concentrated on forming a strong front line that was defended against enemy attacks; the French proposal was for a series of positions arranged in depth. This elastic defence, it was argued, would be more effective, and less likely to result in heavy casualties. After evaluation of the documents, the Germans concluded that the proposal represented a significant advance, and steps were taken to adopt German defensive positions in line with this new approach. However, through a mixture of limitations imposed by terrain and the resistance of some senior officers to embrace such change, traditional fixed linear defences were still widely used throughout the war, and implementation of the new ideas was patchwork.[8]

However welcome the victories in southern Poland were for *AOK*, the increasingly threatening reports from Italy continued to cause concern. As early as 4 May, an intelligence assessment suggested that the Italians had already committed themselves to the Entente against the Central Powers. The reports were correct – Italian officials had signed the Treaty of London on 6 April, committing themselves to war against Austria-Hungary within a month and Germany by 1916 in return for territorial concessions after the defeat of the Dual Monarchy. For the moment, the dispatch of Austro-Hungarian troops to another front was unthinkable, and the mood in Teschen plunged with the news. Further reports followed suggesting that a declaration of war would occur towards the end of May, in line with the provisions of the secret Treaty of London. Inevitably, this raised the possibility – in many people's eyes, the likelihood – that with the Austro-Hungarian Empire faced by possible dismemberment, the Romanians would also throw in their lot with the Entente, in order to secure their territorial ambitions in Transylvania. In these circumstances, it was all the more important to achieve some sort of decisive result elsewhere in order to free up troops for potential new fronts. On 9 May, *OHL* moved from its base in Mézières in the west to Pless in the east, only an hour's drive from Teschen, a clear indication of the importance now placed on the Eastern Front. On the same day, discussions began about how to exploit the successes of Mackensen's army. Predictably, Conrad suggested a complex and energetic widening of the offensive. Mackensen should pursue the retreating Russians towards and beyond the line of the River San, while the Austro-Hungarian Fourth Army on Mackensen's northern flank also joined the assault. In order to do this it would require reinforcements, and Conrad requested that the Germans provide these additional troops, not least because he had none of his own to spare. Reinforcements would also be required for Pflanzer-Baltin's group in the southeast.

These suggestions did nothing to improve the already difficult relationship between Conrad and Falkenhayn. The latter summed up the issues succinctly:

> The decision will be made here in West Galicia. It will make no difference whether or not Pflanzer-Baltin's group is driven back a few kilometres. If the blow that we have initiated succeeds, the question of Pflanzer-Baltin will be settled, and if it fails, then it will not be possible to hold Bukovina. But it is certain to succeed if undertaken with all available troops.[9]

Further troop movements from the west were out of the question in view of the fighting raging around Vimy Ridge; however, it would be possible to move two divisions from the German armies currently enjoying a relatively quiet time in the northern part of the Eastern Front, and two new German divisions that had been completing their formation in Syrmia on the northern borders of Serbia, where they had freed up Austro-Hungarian troops that were being sent to the Alps in preparation for war with Italy, would also be transferred to Galicia. Any troops that Conrad might wish to send to Pflanzer-Baltin, Falkenhayn suggested, could be better employed alongside Mackensen.

Conrad countered by raising the wider political context. Any setback for the Central Powers in Bukovina would have a negative impact upon relations with the Romanians, and consequently he had to reinforce Pflanzer-Baltin. Despite their agreement on the current primacy of the Eastern Front, the two chiefs of staff remained unable to come to a clear agreement on how to proceed. In the meantime, although resistance before Emmich's troops on the southern flank of Mackensen's army stiffened, the other formations were able to make good progress.

On 10 May, with the aid of Austro-Hungarian troops to the south, Emmich was able to overcome Russian resistance along the line of the River Wisłoka. The same day saw other developments, as the Russian XII Corps, withdrawing from the Carpathians, turned on its pursuers and drove them back a short distance. At the same time, Dimitriev pushed XXI Corps forward in a counterattack to try to restore the line along the Wisłoka. Shchkinsky divided his corps into two thrusts to the northwest of Sanok. One of these discovered a gap between 11th Bavarian Infantry Division and 119th Infantry Division, but Emmich had 20th Infantry Division available in reserve and threw this into the flank of the Russian attack. At the same time, the Austro-Hungarian X Corps to the south threatened to envelop the Russian forces. Just in time, Shchkinsky dispatched his reserves to hold off the threat from the south, and pulled back to Sanok. The counterattack – effectively the last hope of holding a line west of the River San – had failed to make any significant impression on the campaign.[10]

German aerial reconnaissance reported a widespread Russian retreat towards the San, and Emmich ordered his men to overcome their fatigue and losses and push on. The exhausted columns laboured forward through the hills perhaps half the remaining distance to Sanok before they were forced to halt. To their north, François continued the rapid progress that his corps had achieved in the preceding days, reaching the San during the evening of 11 May. After an advance of over 60 miles (100km) in ten days, often in the face of determined Russian resistance, François had good reason to be pleased with his XLI Reserve Corps. He issued a congratulatory order to his men:

> The corps stormed and broke through the fortified Russian positions at Gorlice and in daily – often heavy – fighting has thrown the enemy back over the River San. The troops of our young corps have thus fought with outstanding courage and have borne their great tests with proper German determination and resolution. The soldiers of our young corps are fully justified in standing alongside the battle-hardened troops of older corps.
>
> I extend my thanks and acknowledgement to all formations of the corps and hope that it is granted to them to achieve even greater accomplishments in the continuation of the campaign.[11]

The German and Austro-Hungarian formations had taken heavy losses, but the gains were considerable. By the end of 11 May, *OHL* estimated that 100,000 prisoners and eighty guns had been captured. Despite the reinforcements that it had received, Dimitriev's army was clearly in no state to halt Mackensen's advance. From the point of view of the Central Powers, it was therefore all the more important to reach a conclusion about how to continue operations. In the meantime, Mackensen intended to continue his advance with as much energy as possible. The immediate objective was to secure the line of the San, and to press on towards Rawa Ruska. If the Germans succeeded, they would in turn threaten Lemberg, the former Austro-Hungarian capital of Galicia. This, at least, could be agreed by OHL and AOK. Conrad had no objections, despite still sending troops to Bukovina; however, he insisted that it should fall to the Austro-Hungarian Third Army to recapture the fortress of Przemyśl, the objective of so much bloody fighting during the winter. Mackensen's army was therefore ordered to remain north of the fortress.

In keeping with this, Eleventh Army was to regroup and realign its forces a little to the north. Ammunition was brought forward, and as had been the case before the initial assault at the beginning of May, extensive aerial reconnaissance was carried out to identify the dispositions of the Russian forces. The reports that Mackensen's pilots brought back highlighted the damage suffered by Dimitriev's units. Large columns were reported to be moving east from the San crossings as shattered formations were pulled out of line, while fresh troops appeared to be replacing them. The reality was that despite a few fresh formations, such as V Caucasian Corps from Odessa, Dimitriev's Third Army was a greatly reduced force. X and XXIV Corps had effectively ceased to exist, while IX Corps had lost 80 per cent of its establishment strength. III Caucasian Corps, fed into the battle in fragments, was – until the arrival of V Caucasian Corps –perhaps the strongest remaining element, despite losing two thirds of its troops and guns west of the San.[12] Ammunition had been either expended or lost to the advancing Germans, and Dimitriev pleaded in vain for more supplies to be sent; even if *Stavka* had been willing to help, there simply weren't sufficient shells to be dispatched in the quantities that Third Army demanded. At first, Dimitriev had hoped that the arrival of III Caucasian Corps would allow him to restore his army's fortunes, but his mood was now far more pessimistic. At Southwest Front Headquarters, Ivanov was also increasingly despondent. He no longer made much effort to influence events, resorting simply to passing messages from Dimitriev to *Stavka* and orders in the reverse direction. His chief of staff, Dragomirov, telegraphed Danilov, the Russian quartermaster-general, on 9 May to repeat his previous request for a withdrawal beyond the San; Danilov's response was uncompromising. Dimitriev's army would have to hold a line from the middle Vistula to the

Carpathians. Relief would come in the form of Lechitsky's Ninth Army in Bukovina, at the southeast end of the front. Danilov assured Dragomirov that a successful attack here would force the Germans to divert troops away from southern Galicia.[13]

The mood in Southwest Front headquarters was clearly very low. One of the formations being transferred to the critical sector was VI Corps, which had been facing the Germans in central Poland as part of Northwest Front. Its commander, Vasily Gurko, preceded his troops by car:

> Having absolutely no knowledge of the position of affairs in the southwest combat area, I continued my motor-car journey to the staff of this front to see General Ivanov in hopes of receiving the necessary information from him. From the staff and from General Ivanov I personally heard, I am sorry to say, nothing reassuring … The general impression I took away with me from my stay … was that General Ivanov himself and his staff had to a great extent lost heart and faith in the possibility of bringing the Austro-German advance to a stop.[14]

Aware of the desperate state of Third Army and the growing disorder as Brusilov's Eighth Army began to withdraw from the Carpathians, Dragomirov attempted on 10 May to send an apocalyptic appeal to Grand Duke Nikolai via the chief of the general staff, Yanushkevich, foreseeing a retreat into the depths of Russia:

> The strategic position of our forces is hopeless. Our line is greatly over-extended, we are unable to shift forces along it with any speed, and the weakness of our armies renders them even more immobile. In our opinion, it is not possible to collect and concentrate reserves … our armies urgently require reinforcements. The poorly trained men who are sent to us arrive barely dressed, and are completely unsatisfactory … We need to consider the possible loss of Przemyśl, and should not seek to prepare the fortress for battle. We have neither the time nor the means for this. Instead, we should make every effort to supply Brest-Litovsk … Kiev, Rovno, Mogilev, Cherkassy, Kremenchug should all be fortified … the army should abandon any serious military operations until its strength has been restored.
>
> … I assure Your Excellency that this is not written in a pessimistic mood, but is dictated by calculation. We must now establish a plan of action and adhere to it firmly without thoughts of unfulfilled hopes. In particular, I consider it my duty to note the position of Fourth Army, which will become very dangerous if the enemy breaks through along the lower San. Its withdrawal to the Vistula is required at the first sign of this development.[15]

In addition, Dragomirov recommended that reserve battalions currently being used to train new recruits might be better used in the front line; however, whilst this might have alleviated the short-term shortage of properly trained troops, it would surely have exacerbated the problems with poor training of new drafts. In any event, the telegram was completely unacceptable to *Stavka*. Two days after it was sent, Dragomirov was dismissed on the grounds of 'nervous exhaustion'.[16]

The only concession in response to Dragomirov's telegram was an acceptance that Przemyśl was not to be regarded as a fortress, and was to be assigned no greater importance than any other sector. This was a timely acceptance of reality. Many of the fortifications had been badly damaged by demolition explosions carried out by the Austro-Hungarian garrison immediately prior to its surrender, and few had been rebuilt. Even if they had been in a defensible state, Dimitriev's army simply lacked the men to allocate sufficient forces for the defences to be manned properly. Nevertheless, this was a remarkable departure in thinking for *Stavka*:

> For the first time, this directive sanctioned a new opinion amongst us about the practical role of fortresses and other permanent fortifications. Their defence was not to be envisaged as having an intrinsic value other than that which they derived from the point of view of operations with the field army; if this value were diminished, the defence of a fortified position in modern conditions was not only useless but actually harmful, in that it would weaken the field army by immobilising its troops and artillery for its defence. Naturally, this is not to say that an isolated fortress should not defend itself to the end – even until the end of the war; such a conclusion would be profoundly erroneous. But it meant that the high command ... would not hesitate to decide to order the evacuation [of a fortress] if it judged it more advantageous to save the garrison and its ammunition reserves rather than leaving them in place for continued defence. The only criterion was what was in the interests of the field army, the most important factor in war.[17]

If the line of the San could be held, there was some prospect of stabilising the front. Overall, the new line would be about 60 miles (100km) shorter than the front held at the beginning of May, and given Dimitriev's losses, such a reduction in demand for troops could only be welcomed. However, the San could only be defended if Dimitriev had time to organise his defences. His shattered divisions needed to reorganise, ammunition had to be brought forward, and field fortifications had to be prepared. But unfortunately for Dimitriev, Ivanov and *Stavka*, Mackensen had no intention of allowing Third Army any pause to catch its breath. Differences of opinion between Falkenhayn and Conrad were settled in a conference in Pless on 12 May, and Mackensen issued orders for his army to move up to the San in strength. Bridgeheads were to be secured at Jaroslau and Radymno, to the north of Przemyśl. The Austro-Hungarian armies on the flanks would move forward in support, while Third Army was given the additional task of seizing Przemyśl itself. With 56th Infantry Division joining Emmich's corps, Mackensen assigned 11th Bavarian Infantry Division to XLI Reserve Corps. As part of the general reorganisation, X Corps was pulled out of its position on the southern wing of Eleventh Army and moved to the northern wing.

For the moment, François' corps had little to do, having largely reached the line of the San on 11 May. The Bavarians were awarded a welcome day of rest, while a bicycle battalion attached to corps headquarters busied itself with reconnaissance duties. Such cycle-mounted troops had been part of most German divisions at the beginning of the war, but, without any clear idea of how to use them to best effect, many commanders converted them back to regular infantry. François though chose to gather them together in his corps to form a single battalion, and at a phase of the campaign where horse-mounted units were struggling to maintain their mobility due to shortages of fodder, the bicycle patrols proved to be an effective means of continuing operations.[18]

To the north, the Russian retreat in Galicia began to have consequences for the troops in central Poland. On 9 May, the Russians had attacked the right wing of the German Ninth Army, but the following day a radio intercept revealed to the Germans that Alexei Evert's Fourth Army, holding the Russian line from the Pilica valley to the Vistula, had been ordered to withdraw in order to prevent its southern flank from being turned. Facing the Russians were the troops under Remus von Woyrsch and – immediately north of the Vistula, along the line of the River Nida – Viktor Dankl's 1st Army. The demands of the fighting in the Carpathians had resulted in many of Dankl's troops being moved elsewhere, and his army was now reduced to slightly less than four infantry divisions and a single cavalry division. None of these formations were at full strength, and after months of trench warfare they pursued the retreating Russians cautiously. Similarly, Woyrsch's southern flank moved forward to occupy Kielce, but there was little serious fighting. For a while, *AOK* had hoped that the relatively rapid advance of the troops south of the Vistula would offer the possibility of Archduke Joseph Ferdinand's Fourth Army attempting a thrust from the right bank of the Vistula into the rear of Evert's army, but clearly this was no longer an option. Despite the Russian withdrawal, Dankl still had some difficult moments. On 16 May, a sudden assault by the Russian

3rd Grenadier Division caught the Austro-Hungarian 25th Infantry Division by surprise, throwing it back with heavy losses.[19]

In the centre of Mackensen's Eleventh Army, Arz's VI Corps approached Jaroslau from the southwest on 11 May, and a day later Plettenberg's Guards Corps captured Przeworsk, only 6 miles (10km) west of Jaroslau. It was still not clear to the Germans whether Dimitriev intended to make a determined stand along the San, and on 14 May, aerial reconnaissance reported a Russian column stretching over 12 miles (20km) moving east from Przemyśl; but any doubts were dispelled on 14 May, when the German advance encountered renewed resistance.[20] Despite their struggles, Dimitriev's troops had succeeded in reaching the line of the San. From the Vistula, IX, X and III Caucasian Corps took up their new positions, while the line extended further south with XXIV, XXI and XII Corps. The closest formation of Brusilov's Eighth Army, VIII Corps, was also assigned to Dimitriev's command. Exhausted and ground down by their fighting in the Carpathians, the troops of VIII Corps could hardly be regarded as adequate reinforcements for the shattered Third Army.

Mackensen now directed his troops to reduce the Russian bridgehead across the San at Jaroslau. The perimeter of the bridgehead was defended by 62nd, 41st and 45th Infantry Divisions, and these put up strong resistance when Plettenberg's Guards Corps made its first attempt to capture the town. Deciding that it would not be possible to storm Jaroslau with a quick attack, Mackensen reshuffled his forces, once more detaching 11th Bavarian Infantry Division from XLI Reserve Corps and reforming *Korps Kneussl* by reuniting it with 119th Reserve Infantry Division. François' corps was ordered to advance against Radymno, while Guards Corps and the Austro-Hungarian VI Corps concentrated on Jaroslau. Throughout 14 and 15 May, Plettenberg's and Arz's troops attempted to overcome the Russian defences; although the Austro-Hungarian formations succeeded in making some progress, they came under artillery fire from Russian guns on the east bank of the San, holding up their advance. Nevertheless, it was not possible for the battered Russian forces in Jaroslau to sustain the battle, and by the end of 15 May, Plettenberg could report that his troops had entered Jaroslau and were approaching the San itself. Arz reached the river immediately south of Jaroslau, and the remnants of the garrison withdrew to the east bank.

It appears that the fall of Jaroslau further diminished Dimitriev's confidence in the ability of his men to hold their bridgeheads west of the San, and he ordered XXI Corps to abandon Radymno on the western side of the river. Before the order could be executed, it was countermanded by *Stavka*. The Radymno bridgehead had at least been more extensively prepared than many other parts of

The San Battles, May–June 1915

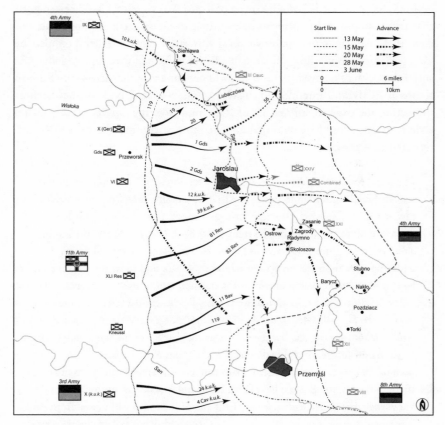

the San line, though François' description is probably a little exaggerated:

Once more, the Russians had created a masterpiece of field fortifications in front of Radymno: a triple line of fieldworks. A major position had been dug into Hill 202 west of Ostrow [about a mile northwest of Radymno], like an outthrust bastion, with multiple rows of barbed wire, forming a strongpoint of the defence running over the railway embankment along high ground. Then there was a well-constructed secondary position, which ran through the centre of Ostrow, and a third line of dugouts from Zagrody, which could bring all the roads running from Radymno over the San bridges under fire. Our pilots had repeatedly photographed all of these positions; the outcome lay in the hands of the troops.[21]

Whilst the positions at Radymno may have been formidable, the San line was generally in poor condition. The speed of Third Army's retreat had been so great that there simply hadn't been sufficient time to construct good positions, nor were there sufficient materials available; this latter issue was compounded by local garrison troops selling off large quantities of barbed wire captured after the surrender of the Przemyśl garrison to local civilians.[22] Nevertheless, the Russian troops in Radymno intended to make a stand, not least because the defences protecting the western approaches of Radymno were the only point at which a serious defence could be mounted, as Shchkinsky, commander of XXI Corps, reported to Ivanov:

> I personally went to Radymno to assess the situation … the position occupied on the left [west] bank is quite strong due to local conditions and has good fields of fire, has been intensively strengthened, and much work has been carried out. There are no fortifications on the right [east] bank of the San, and the position along the bank is not advantageous for our troops, as the enemy will fire on them with impunity from the higher left bank of the San, and to withdraw from the bank will mean an abandonment of the defence of this line … the enemy will follow us closely, and I doubt that we can hold on in the flat terrain on the right bank of the San valley … all the division commanders earnestly requested me to report to Your Excellency that they consider the defence of the right bank of the San as hardly feasible, but abandonment of the San is undesirable … We have not been broken, we are just exhausted, many soldiers are barefoot, but our numerical strength has improved as we have fallen back, and morale has improved with the knowledge that we are halting on the left bank of the San; a withdrawal from the San would worsen the overall situation, as it would deprive us of the powerful artillery support of the field positions [west of Radymno]. A voluntary withdrawal of the bridgehead would entail great losses in crossing the San, not to mention the fact that it would deprive us of our freedom of manoeuvre and our ability to conduct reconnaissance [on the west bank]. Finally, a retreat will have a bad effect upon the local population.[23]

By the end of 16 May, François' main concern was a shortage of artillery ammunition. There was sufficient to repel any Russian counterattack, but not enough to mount an assault on the prepared Russian positions around Radymno. To his great frustration, he had to limit the activities of his troops to preparatory actions. On 17 May, in bright sunshine, Plettenberg's corps crossed the San at Jaroslau, with Emmich securing a bridgehead a little further north. By contrast,

François had to content himself with issuing medals to wounded soldiers in the rear area of his corps. The only good news was that with no clear threat from the direction of Przemyśl, there was no need for *Korps Kneussl* to shield the southern flank of Eleventh Army with two divisions, and the Bavarians were returned to XLI Reserve Corps. Nevertheless, an assault on Radymno remained impossible without more artillery ammunition. To the north, Arz and Plettenberg expanded their bridgehead, planning to turn south against Radymno, enveloping it from the northeast. Perhaps in response to the unravelling of their positions along the San, the Russians mounted attacks during the night of 18–19 May on François' corps outside Radymno; all were repulsed with ease. To their surprise, the Germans discovered that many of the attackers were armed only with hand grenades and clubs – the shortage of rifles that had plagued Russian expansion of the army in late 1914 had now reached a critical stage. More importantly, several hundred prisoners were taken, and interrogation revealed plans for a larger Russian attack on 19 May.

With time to prepare themselves, the Germans were able to crush this attack with ease during a heavy thunderstorm, the crash of lightning adding to the roar of the guns.[24] The day saw Russian attacks against the German and Austro-Hungarian forces that had crossed the San further north in an attempt to reduce their bridgehead; a new combined corps had been improvised, using the troops of 3rd Caucasian Rifle Division, newly arrived from Lemberg, and 77th Infantry Division, recently arrived from the Narew. In total, the force consisted of about twenty-four infantry battalions, and these attempted to push into the seam between the Prussian Guards and VI Corps. The attack was fought off with minimal difficulty. The attacks against the northern part of Plettenberg's corps were particularly disjointed, and the German 56th Infantry Division became aware of a gap in the Russian line between XXIV and III Caucasian Corps, and took advantage of this to push north and secure a bridgehead across the River Lubaczówa. With the troops of the Austro-Hungarian IX Corps, the most southerly of Archduke Joseph Ferdinand's formations, pushing forward from the west, III Caucasian Corps was in danger of encirclement. Dimitriev reacted with speed, ordering the corps to abandon its attack and to pull back beyond the Lubaczówa. In addition, the two southern components of Dimitriev's Third Army, XXI and XII Corps, were passed to the control of Brusilov's Eighth Army. These, too, were meant to join the general assault towards the west, but their contribution proved to be minimal.

During the preparation for these battles, Grand Duke Nikolai sent Brusilov a telegram expressing his great confidence in Brusilov's abilities, urging him to continue to hold not only Przemyśl, but to stop the slow advance of the Austro-

Hungarian forces in the Carpathians. Brusilov replied that he had perhaps 124 battalions available for the task, faced by an estimated 200 Austro-Hungarian and German battalions, and that he urgently needed two corps of reinforcements. Even when he wrote this, he must have known that no such reinforcements were available.[25]

Mackensen's diary entry states that he was not expecting the Russian attacks to succeed, but was nevertheless aware of the importance of taking appropriate defensive measures if required.[26] As is demonstrated by the difficulty in getting sufficient artillery ammunition to XLI Reserve Corps, Eleventh Army was operating at close to the maximum sustainable distance from its railheads, and until railway lines west of the San were brought back into use, any determined Russian attack might pose considerable problems for the troops that had crossed the river. Mackensen raised this issue with Falkenhayn and Conrad, stressing that an urgent solution to the supply issues was required, and until then he would have to restrict himself to limited operations.

The failure of the attacks against the San bridgehead led Dimitriev to send a further telegram to Southwest Front stating that the current line was indefensible, and that his army would have to withdraw further; the San could not be held, given the substantial bridgehead occupied by the Austro-Hungarian VI Corps and the German Guards Corps. His assessment was quite correct, but Grand Duke Nikolai decided that Dimitriev was no longer the right man to command Third Army. Consequently, the only outcome of Dimitriev's telegram was his dismissal. His replacement was Leonid Lesh, whose XII Corps had retreated from the Dukla Pass earlier in the campaign.

Conrad continued to urge his Second and Third Armies to make faster progress as they pursued the Russians from the Carpathians. Boroević's Third Army in particular received repeated messages demanding greater speed, as the agreement between Conrad and Falkenhayn allocated the recapture of Przemyśl to the *k.u.k.* Army. On 19 May, Boroević visited X Corps to assess the situation personally after receiving another order from *AOK* to launch a forceful assault. X Corps was now led by Feldmarschalllleutant Hugo Martiny, who told his army commander that he lacked the resources to launch the sort of frontal assault towards Przemyśl that Conrad demanded. His two divisions had been almost destroyed during the last phases of Ivanov's Carpathian offensive and remained badly under strength, and the replacement drafts lacked adequate training. Ammunition was in short supply, not least because of the difficult supply lines running across the mountains. Perhaps more importantly, Conrad's orders were based upon the supposition that Przemyśl was defended by a mixture of Cossacks and reservists, whereas Martiny's troops were still being held at arm's length by the Russian XII Corps. Unless X Corps could be supported by the sort of heavy artillery that the Germans had used repeatedly to such good effect, any attack would fail. Boroević duly reported back to Conrad that the attack was out of the question. Priority should be given to restoring and improving railway lines to allow his formations to be supplied properly.[27]

On the other side of the front line, there were continuing attempts to devise a plan that might bring the German advance to a halt. On the same day that Boroević visited Martiny, *Stavka* decided to start concentrating forces around Rawa Ruska in order to create a new reserve army.[28] The biggest problem was finding troops for this new army; with great reluctance, Alexeyev had finally released II Caucasian Corps from Northwest Front, and had agreed to send a further three divisions when he could extract them from the front line. V Caucasian Corps, finally arriving from Odessa, and an additional division withdrawn from the Caucasus, would also be available. It was hoped that additional troops would come from the forces retreating from the Carpathians, as the front line shortened. To an extent, the decision to create this new army was due to growing dissatisfaction in *Stavka* with Ivanov's conduct of the campaign. Grand Duke Nikolai wished to concentrate forces for a decisive counter-blow, whereas Southwest Front had to date fed reinforcements into the fire of battle as they arrived. The reality was that Ivanov had little choice. If *Stavka* wished him to stand and fight as it repeatedly ordered, the battered troops in the front line would need reinforcements. In late 1914, faced by an untenable position along the Vistula, the Germans had pulled back across most of Poland, calculating correctly that the lengthening Russian supply lines would ultimately halt the Russians short of the German frontier, and had used this withdrawal to manoeuvre around the northern flank of the Russian advance; Ivanov was not granted any such flexibility by *Stavka*.

Quartermaster-General Danilov later claimed that he was the author of the plan to create this new army. Command of the new army would be assigned to Pavel Plehve, who had fought with some success in the same area in the opening weeks of the war. To Danilov's disappointment, the plan did not develop as he had intended:

> The interest that the idea aroused gradually disappeared, particularly when it was found that the formation of a new shock group could only be effected at the price of certain sacrifices and would require the withdrawal of the armies in the northwest to a shorter line along the Narew and Vistula.[29]

As always, *Stavka* proved unable to assert its will over that of its front commanders. Ivanov opposed the plan, demanding that the reinforcements were needed in the front line. Alexeyev, too, objected, and came up with a completely different proposal. Italy's entry into the war – which as will be seen was imminent – would divert sufficient German and Austro-Hungarian troops to the Alps to make the creation of this new army unnecessary. Indeed, Ivanov should be able to stabilise his front with his existing forces. This meant that it should be possible to concentrate two armies, with a total of eight corps, between the Pilica and the upper Vistula. A thrust by these towards the southwest would place them behind Mackensen's northern flank, and force a German retreat.[30]

To confuse matters further, Brusilov now submitted a different proposal:

> To help my army fight at Przemyśl, I was sent XXIII Corps and II Caucasian Corps ... my opinion was that these two corps should be moved quietly into Przemyśl, and together with the garrison, make a sudden attack from the western fortifications into the rear of the enemy forces who were on the right bank of the San ... I did not know how the shortage of ammunition could be alleviated, but with this plan, I thought I had some chance of success, though it was not possible to be sure of this in advance ... moreover, it is necessary to add that these two corps were poorly trained, like most of the troops that came to us from the north.[31]

Given the complete freedom with which German aircraft carried out reconnaissance missions at the time, it seems highly unlikely that Brusilov would have been able to move two entire corps, together with sufficient ammunition – assuming that it could be found – into Przemyśl without the Germans spotting them. Indeed, the absence of ammunition supplies, which Brusilov freely admitted and for which he offered no solution, made any such proposal little more than wishful thinking. In any event, the Russians were not given enough time to organise their own plans for counteroffensives. The initiative lay firmly with the Germans, and all the Russians could do was react to events.

Late on 19 May, François finally received assurances from Mackensen that heavy artillery was being assigned to his corps, together with sufficient ammunition, to allow an assault on Radymno to go ahead. To his disappointment, supplies continued to trickle forward in only modest amounts; nevertheless, on 20 May, he issued orders for an assault when circumstances allowed. In addition to his original two divisions, François had 11th Bavarian Infantry Division,

119th Infantry Division, and a Hungarian cavalry division available to him. All he lacked was artillery ammunition.

The following day dawned foggy, and opened on a good note for François: he received a handwritten letter from the kaiser, awarding him the *Pour le Mérite*, Germany's highest decoration. Whilst his XLI Reserve Corps had performed well, this was largely a recognition of his achievements in the previous year. As commander of I Corps, he played a major role in the opening actions on the East Prussian border at Stallupönen and Gumbinnen, before his deliberate disobedience to Hindenburg's and Ludendorff's orders contributed greatly to the German victory at Tannenberg. I Corps was in the thick of the action during the Masurian Lakes campaign in September and after he complained about General Schubert's leadership of Eighth Army he was assigned as commander in place of the hapless Schubert. Unfortunately for François, he then repeated his disobedience of earlier months, but this time Hindenburg and Ludendorff had him sacked. Nevertheless, he remained a personal favourite with the kaiser, and the award of the *Pour le Mérite* marked the completion of his rehabilitation. However, the personalities in *Ober Ost* were not inclined to forgive and forget past disobedience, and whilst François might have been riding high in the esteem of the kaiser and *OHL*, Ludendorff and Hindenburg continued to bear a grudge against him.

Finally, at 5 a.m. on 24 May, XLI Reserve Corps was able to commence its attack with a preliminary artillery bombardment. The Russians responded with their own artillery, and at 7.30 a.m. François' heavy mortars opened fire. As Russian fire began to diminish, the German infantry began its assault at 8 a.m. To their relief, the Russians put up little resistance, many surrendering at the first opportunity. A swift advance by a machine-gun platoon from 81st Reserve Infantry Division caught a Russian battery about to withdraw, capturing six out of eight guns. The rest of the division moved forward rapidly, securing the northern half of Radymno, but progress from the south by 82nd Infantry Division was far slower, due largely to artillery fire from the distant fortifications at Przemyśl. Nevertheless, from both north and south, the Germans made steady headway, against a defence that seems to have been completely surprised, despite several days of clear German preparations. François watched the battle unfold from his headquarters:

> The San valley lay before us in the mist, with the domed towers of Radymno and a few houses on high ground in Skoloszow and Ostrow rising above it ... Ostrow, Radymno and Skoloszow began to burn. At 0815 the first reports arrived: 'Fieldworks on Hill 202 taken', then 'Ostrow stormed, many prisoners', 'Guns

captured', and as early as 0900 82nd Reserve Infantry Division reported that the number of prisoners was so large that it did not have sufficient personnel to escort them back. I immediately sent them von Flotow's cavalry regiment, which had been held in reserve. The San bridge in Zasanie was burning, and through field glasses one could see riders, wagons and disordered crowds of fleeing Russians scrambling up the San valley and hurrying to the east.[32]

As the Germans reached the west bank of the San, they rained fire upon the Russians struggling up the far bank. They had the advantage that the west bank was higher, and hundreds of Russians perished before fighting died down. XLI Reserve Corps destroyed much of the Russian XXI Corps, taking 9,000 prisoners and capturing over fifty guns. Its own losses on the day amounted to fewer than 700 dead and wounded.[33] Given the apparent strength of the Russian positions around Radymno, it was a remarkable success, but a clue to the reason lies in the Russian attack that had been beaten off by XLI Reserve Corps in the preceding days. Many of the Russian troops were new drafts, barely trained and with no experience of warfare. The German bombardment before the attack may have been less intense than the initial assault near Gorlice, but it was sufficient to break the fragile morale of the defenders of Radymno.

On the same day that François captured Radymno, news reached the front line that the Italians had declared war upon the Austro-Hungarian Empire, but – significantly – not on Germany. Predictably, the reaction from Vienna was full of outrage and anger:

> Perfidy whose like history does not know was committed by the Kingdom of Italy against both allies. After an alliance of more than 30 years' duration, during which it was able to increase its territorial possessions and develop itself ... Italy abandoned us in our hour of danger.
>
> ...We did not menace Italy; did not curtail her authority, did not attack her honour or interests. We always responded loyally to the duties of our alliance ...
>
> We have done more. When Italy directed covetous glances across our frontier, in order to maintain peace and our alliance, we resolved on great and painful sacrifices ... But the covetousness of Italy, which believed the moment should be used, was not to be appeased.[34]

The German Chancellor, Theobald von Bethmann-Hollweg, was equally forthright, speaking of how 'Italy has now inscribed in the book of the world's history, in letters of blood which will never fade, her violation of faith.'[35] The

Italian response was equally predictable. Italy had not joined the other Central Powers in August 1914 because it regarded the Triple Alliance as a defensive pact, whereas Austria-Hungary and Germany were embarking upon a war of aggression. There was also mention of Conrad's longstanding hostility towards Italy; the government in Rome was clearly aware of the repeated demands by the chief of the Austro-Hungarian general staff for a pre-emptive war against Italy. But leaving aside all of the political and diplomatic rhetoric, the reality was that the Central Powers now faced the necessity of sending troops to another front.

Discussions about how to deal with this eventuality had been held by Germany and Austria-Hungary on many occasions. Inevitably, Conrad wished for an offensive to strike at the treacherous Italians, but from the German perspective, the mountainous frontier and shortage of troops precluded any such operation. It is indicative of Conrad's inability to adapt his ideas that he persisted in proposing his Alpine offensive even after the disastrous experiences of fighting against Serbia and the Carpathian battles. Overruled by Falkenhayn, Conrad then proposed to ambush the Italians as they attempted to advance into Austria. As had been the case on so many occasions, Falkenhayn disagreed, and made no attempt to be diplomatic about his disdain for his counterpart's suggestion. Such an ambush in the Villach–Laibach area needed the Italians to cooperate by advancing tamely in the direction required of them, he pointed out, and there was no guarantee of any such thing. In any event, the Austro-Hungarian Army simply lacked the resources to concentrate sufficient men to make such an ambush succeed. Instead, Falkenhayn urged a strictly defensive strategy. Using the terrain and the experience gained at such great cost in the Carpathians, it should be possible for fairly limited forces to prevent the Italians from making any meaningful intervention in the Alps. Several Austro-Hungarian divisions had already been sent to the area, and five new German divisions had been created through the policy of reducing the strength of pre-war formations; these were forming up in Syrmia, immediately north of Serbia, where the exhausted Serbs showed no signs of aggressive intent. The lack of activity on this front allowed the *k.u.k.* Army to dispatch additional reinforcements to the Alps, and Falkenhayn added a German *Alpinenkorps* to the troops deployed to block an Italian attack.

The battles of the Italian front are beyond the scope of this work. It is sufficient to record that a combination of difficult terrain, the dominance of defensive firepower, and the slowness of Italian mobilisation ensured that the military consequences of Italy's intervention in the war remained minimal throughout 1915. This was a particular disappointment to the Russians, who had hoped at least that the Italians would be able to draw away sufficient troops to alleviate the pressure in Galicia, and at best would be able to combine in a grand strategy involving the armies of Italy, Serbia and Russia to tear apart the Austro-Hungarian Empire. Nevertheless, even though Germany and Austria-Hungary were able to hold off the Italian Army with relative ease, the troops that had to man the Alpine front might have been of value elsewhere, and the supply requirements in the mountains put a further strain upon the resources of two nations already struggling with the burden of war.

One of the consequences of Italy's entry into the war was a change of command in key Austro-Hungarian forces. Svetozar Boroević was dispatched to the Alps to take command of the forces being assembled there under the aegis of Fifth Army. His replacement in Third Army was Feldzugmeister Paul Puhallo.

Back on the Galician battlefield, the Austro-Hungarian forces that had been tasked with moving against Przemyśl from the south made only limited progress. The divisions of the Austro-Hungarian Second and Third Armies were still badly degraded by their battles of the winter, and Brusilov's Eighth Army conducted an efficient and orderly withdrawal, using the mountainous terrain to good effect to prevent the Austro-Hungarian pursuit from turning into a breakthrough. But Brusilov's troops, too, were far short of their establishment strength, and were in little better shape than their pursuers. Furthermore, their command arrangements left much to be desired:

> The troops were little more than militia with few staff officers, their ranks were reduced, some regiments had been reduced to one incomplete battalion, and at that time our numerous cavalry was of almost no value. The commandant of Przemyśl faced defeat because much of the heavy artillery had been ordered to be loaded up for withdrawal by the commander-in-chief [Ivanov], but then at the request of the commandant of Przemyśl was halted a short distance away, and these changes occurred several times. Finally the commandant, General Delvig, begged for a resolution, saying that his staff were constantly being harassed by this time-consuming work, and requested that either the guns should be sent to the rear or left to fulfil the purpose for which fortress artillery had been intended. I too insisted several times on a definitive conclusion to the problem, but received conflicting answers.[36]

The exact status of the fortress on the San remained unclear. On 19 May, orders arrived from Ivanov's headquarters authorising a withdrawal, only to be countermanded less than a day later, perhaps as a result of the news of Italy's entry into the war. To make matters worse for the Russians, their enemies were fully aware of the indecision about the future of Przemyśl; an enterprising Austro-Hungarian signals unit succeeded in tapping the telegraph line linking the garrison with higher commands.[37] Finally, *Stavka* decreed that the fortress could only be abandoned as a last resort.[38] In addition, Lesh offered Ivanov reassurances that a further retreat might be unnecessary, particularly as reinforcements continued to arrive at the front. These stiffened the line, but were only available at the cost of not creating the mass of reserves that Danilov had wished to build around Rawa Ruska. Nevertheless, Arz and Plettenberg encountered increasing resistance as they attempted to push east and southeast in their attempts to isolate Przemyśl; although they continued to advance, their casualties climbed steadily. Both corps had lost up to half their establishment strength since the beginning of the campaign. But the Russian pressure either side of Mackensen's Eleventh Army had far more serious consequences. The Austro-Hungarian Fourth Army's 10th Infantry Division to the immediate north had secured a bridgehead across the San at Sieniawa, but this came under heavy attack by III Caucasian Corps and collapsed, with the loss of all the artillery that had crossed the river; there were accusations that a great disaster had been caused by the defection of a Czech regiment to the Russians.[39] The reality was that a total of only six guns had been lost, but nevertheless, Emmich's X Corps was forced to dispatch help to restore the line. The failure of his allies to hold back the Russians irritated the usually diplomatic Mackensen:

> A critical evening and a night full of concerns lie behind me ... [Our lines were attacked by] fresh troops, who had been brought forward by rail through Lublin. Their losses must have been substantial. But every Austrian division that failed to hold the line at Sienawa has significant losses ... fortunately, my right flank has made good progress, and I was able to draw a new reserve from there. Before everything was put in order, there were some difficult hours in the evening and night. This morning [28 May] there is relative calm and for the time being I have no concerns ... if only I had just German troops in my command! Our operations would then have prospered even more and the haul of prisoners would be even greater. Our troops would not have allowed themselves to be driven from Sienawa. Despite all the advantages that one has to give them, the Austrians are not hardy enough for the demands of war. My neighbours to the right also are not advancing properly and thus also hinder my advance.[40]

In fairness to the *k.u.k.* Army, it should be added that Arz's VI Corps had performed well throughout the campaign, and the German *Beskidenkorps* had proved just as unable to advance quickly as its Austro-Hungarian neighbours. Nevertheless, there could be little doubt that Russian attacks on Austro-Hungarian formations generally enjoyed far greater success than attacks on German formations. The collapse of the Sieniawa bridgehead briefly led Lesh, commander of the Russian Third Army, to speculate about a new grand counteroffensive to restore his army's fortunes: III Caucasian Corps could exploit its success against the Austro-Hungarian 10th Infantry Division, while Brusilov conducted an energetic advance from Przemyśl towards the northwest, with the aim of encircling Mackensen's entire army. But whilst the advances required by each force – perhaps 15 miles (25km) – were not unreasonable, they were undoubtedly beyond the ability of the under-strength forces available. Despite this, III Caucasian Corps was ordered to prepare for such an attack, scheduled to begin on 30 May.[41]

To the south, the Austro-Hungarian troops attempting to advance out of the Carpathians struggled to make any significant headway. Brusilov had pulled back his line, but wherever his men paused, they proved quite capable of halting their pursuers, who continued to be hamstrung by supply problems, exacerbated by the poor mountain roads that had bedevilled operations throughout the winter. Plans for a major assault by the *Beskidenkorps* and the Austro-Hungarian troops of Second and Third Armies out of the Carpathians in order to cut off Przemyśl had to be delayed because of a critical shortage of heavy mortars and howitzers with the required high trajectory to be able to smash the Russian defences. It was only late on 27 May that the weapons finally arrived, and their deployment was then delayed while essential repairs were carried out. Once they went into action, they were still not as effective as the guns of Mackensen's army. Despite their ongoing shortages of ammunition, Eleventh Army's gunners managed to use their limited supplies to good effect through extensive and careful use of aerial reconnaissance. By contrast, the Austro-Hungarian and German formations in the Carpathians frequently found their aircraft were unavailable due to mechanical problems. Given the supply difficulties in the mountains, remedying these problems proved difficult; even the delivery of adequate food to the front line often placed an intolerable burden upon the men of the supply columns. When they finally attacked, the troops trying to push back the Russians perished in their hundreds. After a day of fruitless assaults on 24 May, Generalmajor Rudolf von Willerding, commander of the Austro-Hungarian 32nd Infantry Division, reported that his unit had dropped from 5,200 men early in May (still substantially below establishment strength) to only 1,900 men.[42]

If Przemyśl could not be cut off by a drive from the south, an attempt would have to be made from the north, as a further advance towards the east by Eleventh Army would be impossible while the Russians remained in the fortress. But despite his success at Radymno, François found it difficult to make significant progress towards Przemyśl. The Russians had dug in either side of the San and put up determined resistance, but the forward momentum of XLI Reserve Corps could not be held back. By 28 May, the German 81st Infantry Division had pushed through to Stubno and Nakło, placing it about 9 miles (15km) to the northeast of Przemyśl. Aware of the threat this posed to the fortress, the Russians attempted to storm the village of Nakło on 28 May, as the local German commander recorded:

> The enemy was in trenches west, south and east of Nakło, between 300 and 1000 metres from us.
>
> Until 1030 on 28 May the Russians' fire was minimal, but then rose significantly. Enemy artillery, including heavy guns, fired from the direction of Torki, Poździacz and Hill 213 at Turczyna.
>
> At 1430 the Russians attacked in dense waves from three sides. One assault wave followed another; if one was shot down, another appeared. Our artillery did devastating work, with 2nd Battery ultimately firing with only one gun, the other three having been destroyed by enemy artillery fire. The observation post of the battalion commander, Hauptmann Freiherr von Bredow, at the eastern edge of the village was constantly under the heaviest artillery fire. Bredow remained at his post and oversaw the firing of the [artillery] batteries with great calm.
>
> The Russian attacks on the churchyard and the southeast corner of Nakło were particularly heavy. Here, the Russians broke in and stormed forwards along the village street towards the church in dense groups, near where Hauptmann von Bredow and I had our headquarters. Hastily, I assembled clerks, bicyclists, some young lads, signallers, and medics around me; Hauptmann von Bredow, his adjutant Leutnant Seiffert, and a few gunners, all armed with rifles, also hurried over. The first volley that we fired brought the Russian onslaught up the village street to a halt, and using the resultant confusion, we threw ourselves with loud cries upon the enemy. At the same time, Leutnant Schilling and his 5 Coy attacked from the eastern side of Nakło and two machine-guns under Leutnant Röhrbein and Hauptmann Schmidt-Hern's 5th Battery from 6th Field Artillery Regiment put down an effective fire. The Russians fled back in complete disarray, their attack having failed with heavy losses.[43]

François was operating with one division on either bank of the San, and in an attempt to improve coordination between them, a pontoon bridge was constructed at Barycz. As a result, elements of 82nd Infantry Division were able to cross to the eastern shore of the river, relieving the pressure on Nakło from one side. Nevertheless, a major thrust towards Przemyśl looked unlikely to succeed. To make matters worse, most of 119th Infantry Division was pulled out of the line facing the fortress and moved to a location behind the northern flank of Eleventh Army, where it was able to offer some security in the event of further setbacks in the sector held by the Austro-Hungarian Fourth Army. This was particularly frustrating for François, who had sent a Jewish merchant to Przemyśl to investigate what was happening; the spy returned early on 29 May with news that the Russians had begun to evacuate the fortress. In response, François moved his heavy artillery to Nakło, from where it could interdict the railway lines running east from Przemyśl. At the same time, 11th Bavarian Infantry Division moved closer to the fortress from the north and northwest.

On 30 May, artillery fire erupted all around the western and northern perimeter of Przemyśl. The German heavy artillery in Nakło succeeded in stopping rail and road movements, but brought upon itself a furious counter-bombardment, which detonated much of the detachment's ammunition and devastated the village, also wiping out the heavy artillery battery that had been interdicting Russian rail movements. The rest of the German artillery struck at the defences of Przemyśl where Delvig marshalled his forces, fragments of six different infantry divisions. Originally, 11th Bavarian Infantry Division had intended to attack from the north on 31 May, but an extra day was given over to artillery preparation. However, when a Prussian NCO probed forward with a reconnaissance patrol, he discovered that one of the forts on the northern perimeter had already been abandoned. Swiftly, the German infantry moved forward, securing the fort and its two neighbours. With his troops in holding positions to the northeast, François impatiently asked Mackensen to return 119th Infantry Division to him, so that he could complete the encirclement of the fortress. His suggestion was turned down.

The Russians made yet another attempt to change the course of the campaign by mounting a counterattack. Yanushkevich had issued orders on 25 May to Alexeyev, demanding that an additional corps be sent south; at the same time, the Russian Fourth Army, formerly part of Southwest Front, was now assigned to Northwest Front. Assured of these additional reinforcements, Ivanov ordered Third Army to make a general attack along its entire front, with a preliminary objective of an advance of about 20 miles (32km), even though only one division from XIV Corps, the formation grudgingly released by Alexeyev, had actually arrived. The attack was launched on 1 June, and although the relatively fresh troops of XIV Corps succeeded in dislodging the Austro-Hungarian XIV Corps from Rudnik and, joined by the rest of Third Army's right flank, briefly threatened to roll back Archduke Joseph Ferdinand's Fourth Army, the battle became irrelevant in view of events further south.

Despite François' desire to envelop Przemyśl from the northeast, the troops of 119th Infantry Division would not have arrived in time. More forts on the perimeter of the Russian defences fell on 1 and 2 June, and all counterattacks failed to dislodge the Bavarians. By the end of the day, it was clear that Przemyśl could not be held, and Brusilov ordered Delvig to retreat east before it was too late. Just before midnight on 2–3 June, the last bridge over the San in the city was blown up. Kneussl had planned to storm the last Russian defences on 3 June; instead, his troops marched in unopposed. The Russian occupation of Przemyśl had lasted only 67 days.[44]

Mackensen made considerable show of presenting the city to Emperor Franz Joseph, but could not, and did not attempt to, hide the fact that German troops had effectively recovered an Austro-Hungarian possession that had proved to be beyond the ability of the *k.u.k.* Army to recapture for itself, as he wrote in a letter after the battle:

> To mark the occasion of the fall of Przemyśl, His Majesty [Kaiser Wilhelm] has awarded me the Oak Leaves to the *Pour le Mérite*, and the King of Bavaria has awarded me the Military Order of Max Joseph, specifically the Great Cross. This is an order that in Bavaria is equivalent to the *Pour le Mérite*. I have not yet heard from the Emperor of Austria. He had most reason to celebrate the recapture of the fortress, but his joy is probably diminished that it was not an Austrian, but a German, who laid the fortress at his feet. I would like to have given them the satisfaction of being the first into Przemyśl. But they lacked something that I would characterise as confidence and self-belief. The capture of Przemyśl is a feat of arms that only troops raised in the Prussian spirit could accomplish, and that is also true of the excellent Bavarian troops who were involved.[45]

There was undoubtedly a mixture of chagrin and irritation, both in Vienna and Teschen, that Austro-Hungarian troops had failed to reach Przemyśl first. Nevertheless, this was rapidly put to one side. The relatively swift and painless capture of Przemyśl eliminated an inconvenient salient, and allowed for troops to be made available for deployment elsewhere. It also removed a potential threat to

Mackensen's south flank, thus opening the way for further exploitation towards the east. The question of awards for the capture of the fortress was also put right. A few days later, Mackensen was appointed colonel-in-chief of the *k.u.k.* Hussar Regiment *Friedrich Wilhelm III.* For a man who still proudly regarded himself as a former hussar officer, this ceremonial post to a famous regiment was a high honour.

When they had captured the city in March, the Russians had noted that the population was overjoyed at their arrival. François recorded a similar reaction when he visited Przemyśl on the day of its capture by the German Army:

> The joy of the liberated population was indescribable. Wherever they spotted German soldiers, they surrounded them and embraced them, decking them with flowers. I did not see any Austrian soldiers. The houses were decorated with flowers. Triumphal arches were erected. All the ordeals of the last months were extinguished in unfeigned celebration, and all hearts were filled with great confidence that once and for all, the distress and suffering of Russian occupation was over.[46]

In view of the history of Central Europe in the decades that followed, it is particularly striking that the residents of Przemyśl who showed particular enthusiasm for the arrival of the Germans were the Jews. The Germans might look down upon them, but generally left them free to live their lives; some of the Russian troops, on the other hand, had used their brief occupation to persecute them, as was also the case in other parts of Poland and Bukovina. Whilst some elements of the Austro-Hungarian Empire – for example the Hungarian authorities – treated Jews with contempt and hostility, there was widespread affection in the Jewish community for Franz Joseph as the emperor who had granted them emancipation. By contrast, in addition to the arbitrary violence meted out by elements of the Russian Army, many figures in high positions, including Yanushkevich, the chief of the general staff, made no secret of their anti-Semitism. Many wished to remove all Jews from occupied parts of Galicia, and a policy of deportations was implemented across the region. In March 1915, Grand Duke Nikolai ordered that Jewish civilians should be driven towards the German lines – they would either be killed by German fire, or become refugees on the German side of the front.[47] During their occupation of Przemyśl, the Russians expelled about 17,000 Jews from the city. Many of them moved to Lemberg, where no provision was made for them, resulting in dozens dying from hunger and exposure. Those who survived were deported to the east.[48] As they retreated across Galicia, the Russians frequently burned and looted villages, often concentrating on the Jews.

Whilst the German and Austro-Hungarian governments attempted to make the greatest capital possible from the recapture of the fortress, the Russians tried to describe it as part of a larger picture:

> On 1 June, the fighting in Galicia spread with the same intensity along the entire front from the Vistula to the area of Nadwórna. On the left bank of the lower San, our troops decisively drove back the enemy positions on 2 June and secured an important section of the enemy's fortified positions near Rudnik, where we took about 4,000 prisoners, and captured artillery and many machine-guns; our attack along the entire front as far as the mouth of the Wisłoka was successful.
>
> In view of the fact that the state of its artillery and the destruction of its defences by the Austrians before its fall rendered Przemyśl impossible to defend, its possession was for us only important for as long as the occupation of its fortifications facing north and west aided us in the fighting on the San. As the enemy had taken Jaroslau and Radymno and had advanced onto the right bank of the San, our troops were forced to occupy positions that were very hard to defend … and exposed them to the concentrated fire of the enemy's numerous heavy artillery. On this basis we began to evacuate the varied materiel that we had seized from the Austrians. After the completion of this on 2 June, we pulled out our last batteries and during the following night, in keeping with their orders, our troops evacuated their positions to the north and west of Przemyśl and took up new positions further east.[49]

To a large extent, the Russian account was a reasonable one. The Germans captured only four guns when they took the fortress, and these had been disabled. Given the overstretched Russian line, holding the fortress at the end of a salient served no useful purpose. Indeed, this is what Conrad should have done the previous autumn, instead of allowing a huge garrison to be left behind, ultimately being starved into defeat and costing hundreds of thousands of lives in a doomed attempt to lift the siege. The haul of prisoners taken by the Central Powers was modest, though it would perhaps have been greater if François had been given sufficient resources to threaten Przemyśl from the east; this, in turn, would have involved taking greater risks elsewhere, for example on Fourth Army's southern flank. Nevertheless, the fall of the fortress completed the second phase of the German advance from its original starting line near Gorlice and Tarnów. The losses suffered by the Russians to date were crippling, probably exceeding 400,000; of these, over 170,000 were prisoners. Although Mackensen's divisions had all taken substantial losses and were diminished in strength, many reduced to perhaps 50 per cent of their starting number, they remained confident and intent on driving on.

Throughout this period, fighting continued at the southeast end of the Eastern Front, where both sides had looked to this area as a possible means of outflanking the deadlock in the Carpathians. Even before the beginning of the Gorlice–Tarnów campaign, the German South Army had continued its attempts to push forward, Dominik Richert found when his regiment was ordered to advance up a hillside to dislodge the enemy:

> As soon as we left the trench the Russians appeared above us and welcomed us with rapid fire. Despite this, everyone ran and climbed upwards. While running, we could see the heads of some Russians and fired our rifles at them. That put them off and they did not aim so well ... Suddenly a Russian machine-gun began firing at our flank. Many people were hit ...
>
> At last, out of breath, we reached the Russian positions. Some of the Russians continued to defend themselves, and they were stabbed to death using bayonets. The others either apprehensively held their hands in the air or ran off down the other side of the hill. The Russian positions had not been well manned as they had been busy cooking breakfast in the shelters which were located behind their position. Now we crossed the brow of the hill and could see that the slope on the other side was crawling with Russian soldiers who were fleeing downwards. They were shot down in large numbers. As the northern slope of the mountain was quite bleak, they could not find cover anywhere. It was horrible to look at this slaughter. Only a few of them reached the foot of the mountain. Some of them rolled three or four hundred metres down the mountain.[50]

On 7 May, Pflanzer-Baltin learned from a radio intercept that an attack by Lechitsky's Ninth Army towards Kolomea was imminent. Pflanzer-Baltin – whose own command had just been renamed Seventh Army – dispatched what troops he had available to the threatened sector, but this amounted to no more than a cavalry brigade, five battalions of assorted gendarmerie and reservists, and two regiments of Hungarian *Honvéd*. Overall, Lechitsky had about 120,000 men at his disposal, faced by about 80,000 in the Austro-Hungarian Seventh Army. Ivanov and Grand Duke Nikolai both believed that the best possibility of stopping the German advance in southern Poland was to achieve a success here. It remained to be seen whether this would be sufficient – as Falkenhayn had argued in his disputes with Conrad, it was irrelevant if the front line in this sector moved back or forward, as the centre of decision lay elsewhere.

Bukovina, May 1915

On 9 May, the Russian XXXIII Corps began to cross the River Dniester at Kopaczyńce, brushing aside the German 9th Cavalry Brigade. Reinforcements hastily dispatched to the area arrived too late, and General Wolf Marschall, the German commander of the mixed forces in the area, could do little more than attempt to seal off the Russian bridgehead. At the same time, Russian pressure to the west of Stanislau threatened the seam between Pflanzer-Baltin's Seventh Army and the German South Army, preventing the withdrawal of troops from here with which the line further east might have been reinforced. Two days after they established their bridgehead, the Russians began to drive Marschall's group back. Although Conrad had dispatched III Corps to Seventh Army, contrary to Falkenhayn's wishes, these troops had no time to assemble and were fed into the growing crisis as they arrived; the railway line that they required was also the main supply route for Seventh Army, and its capacity was very limited. Matters were worsened for Pflanzer-Baltin by political interference. Prime Minister István Tisza of Hungary held back some Hungarian reservist drafts that were intended for Seventh Army, on the grounds that he needed to guard against possible hostile action from Romania.[51]

As the fighting continued to intensify, and casualties mounted – the first three days of the battle cost Marschall nearly half his men – Pflanzer-Baltin had no choice but to order a withdrawal back to the River Prut. There was heavy fighting near Kolomea where XXXIII Corps reduced one of the last Austro-Hungarian bridgeheads over the Prut on 13 May, but Pflanzer-Baltin remained determined to resume offensive operations as soon as possible. Linsingen's South Army did actually make some headway against the Russians, advancing towards the town of Stryj despite terrain difficulties hindering the movement of artillery. The ground here was as difficult as elsewhere along the Carpathians:

> We crossed the next mountain and entered a primeval forest which covered the whole side of the mountain. The ground was covered with the trunks of pine trees. The ones underneath were rotten, while those on top were hard and free of bark. At some places it was almost impossible to get through. In between the fallen trees were younger trees of all sizes, together with mature trees which were unbelievably tall and massive. The mountains here were very wild and rugged – no roads, bridges, or human habitation anywhere.[52]

Russian resistance now stiffened. On the left flank of South Army, Szurmay's troops were effectively brought to a standstill. Repeated attacks towards Stryj also failed, and by 20 May, the Russians had halted Linsingen along his entire line.

Further east, the Russians continued their attacks on the Austro-Hungarian Seventh Army. Despite their best efforts at concealment, the Russians were unable to hide their preparations from their opponents, but when XXX Corps assaulted the left flank of Pflanzer-Baltin's forces, it succeeded in taking Nadwórna on 15 May, and then attempted to redeploy forces to strike southeast across the Prut. Again, troops were ordered to move at night in order to try to avoid detection, and heavy fighting erupted on 19 May. Slowly, the Austro-Hungarian defenders were forced from their positions, though the cost was heavy – the Russian 80th Infantry Division alone lost nearly 4,200 officers and men. Further advances were clearly impossible, and ultimately the Russians had little choice but to withdraw.[53] Gradually, exhaustion brought the fighting to a pause as both sides attempted to marshal their resources. Such a pause, though, was far more costly for the Russians than the Central Powers. Ivanov had placed great value on the offensive in Bukovina as a means of reducing pressure in Galicia, but no such relief appeared. Indeed, the diversion of troops and munitions to this sector came at a time when the hard-pressed Third Army could have put them to better use in trying to halt Mackensen's offensive.

After his army was brought to a halt, Linsingen paused to take stock. Rather than spread his effort along his entire front, he decided to concentrate all his efforts at a single point. The objective of this thrust was Stryj, and the assault began on 26 May. Carefully constructed Russian defences proved stubborn obstacles, and casualties were heavy; Richert's company in 1st Infantry Division was reduced from 156 men to only thirty.[54] To make matters worse, a counterattack by the Russian XVIII Corps against the eastern flank of South Army gained considerable ground. While Pflanzer-Baltin launched attacks with his own left wing in an attempt to draw away Russian forces from his neighbour, Linsingen tried again to reach Stryj on 31 May. This time, the town was captured. Richert's regiment was one of the first to enter, and his encounter with a local resident reflects the same anti-Semitic opinions held by so many of the combatants on either side of the front line:

> The inhabitants brought us rolls, cigarettes and so on. An old Jew came up to me and said: 'We have prayed to our just God to give the Germans victory.' He immediately got down to business, pulling out a packet of tobacco and saying: 'Would you like to buy some very good Russian tobacco, German sir, it's not expensive – really cheap.' I told him that I hardly ever smoked, but he kept on following me for a while, pestering me to buy his tobacco. These Galician and Polish Jews were a real pest to us whenever we entered a town or a village.[55]

Fighting continued to consume men and *matériel* at the southeast end of the front line in the coming weeks. But the decisive area of conflict remained further west, where – after their successful forcing of the line of the San, and the capture of Przemyśl – Mackensen, Falkenhayn and Conrad once more pondered how to proceed.

CHAPTER 7

LEMBERG

The Russian Army might have escaped a disastrous encirclement at Przemyśl, but it was still in a wretched state. The last definitive plan for Southwest Front had been to hold the line of the San; this was now clearly an impossibility. The casualties suffered prior to the battles along the San had been bad, but the new formations rushed to the line had now been drawn into the fighting, losing much of their strength either in desperate attempts to stop the German advance or in counterattacks that often failed – particularly against the Germans – or did not materially change the campaign when they made initial headway. Many blamed the failure of these attacks on a shortage of heavy artillery, and repeated instructions to be parsimonious in the use of ammunition; others on poor leadership at every level.[1]

The battlefield that the armies would be contesting in June was bordered by several rivers. The eastern and western boundaries were the Bug and San respectively, with the Dniester to the south and the Narew and Tanew to the north. The southern parts of the battlefield formed the Carpathian foothills, with steep-sided valleys running predominantly north–south, and the central area rose to create a watershed between the various rivers. There were few roads, and most were unmetalled; already degraded by the campaigns of 1914, they were in a poor state, and the hot weather of the summer turned them into dusty tracks, across which the troops of all armies laboured to move their guns and supplies.

On 3 June, Lesh issued orders to his battered Third Army to start to pull back to prepared positions on the right bank of the swampy River Tanew. This was based upon two considerations: the line of the San had clearly been forced, and attempts to drive the Germans back across the river had failed; and Eighth Army to the south had pulled back to a new line closer to Lemberg, and unless Lesh did likewise, his southern flank would be exposed.[2] Ivanov immediately raised objections from Southwest Front headquarters. Even if Eighth Army had withdrawn, he stated, Third Army should be able to pull back just its southern flank for protection without abandoning the rest of its positions. In place of Lesh's proposed withdrawal, he ordered several formations – II and V Caucasian Corps, XXIX and XXIII Corps, and three divisions of cavalry – to concentrate on the southern flank of Third Army, under the collective command of Vladimir Olukhov, though subordinated to Third Army. Ivanov insisted that this force would be sufficient to prevent Third Army's southern flank from being turned, and could also be used to launch a counterattack towards the south if the German and Austro-Hungarian armies attempted to drive Brusilov further east. In addition, the counterattack in the north against the southern flank of the Austro-Hungarian Fourth Army was still showing signs of promise. Ivanov concluded his message to Lesh with a repetition of the demands made throughout the campaign, both by Southwest Front and *Stavka*: no territory should be conceded voluntarily.

The creation of Olukhov's group was to an extent a revival of Danilov's proposal to create a new army in this area, but had several important differences, all of which were to its detriment. Firstly, the new formation would be under the command of Third Army; this would limit its use to missions assigned by Lesh, unless Ivanov intervened from Southwest Front. Secondly, Danilov had proposed concentrating troops further to the rear, from where they might be dispatched en masse in a number of different directions along the threatened front, whereas the new proposal left them massed directly opposite the main force of Eleventh Army, or the 'Mackensen phalanx' as the Russians had come to call it. Thirdly, Danilov had intended to create a new army from formations that were still close to full strength, but the units now assigned to Olukhov had all been involved in heavy fighting, and were badly degraded. II Caucasian Corps had only 5,300 combatants available (compared with an establishment strength closer to 28,000), and only Third Guards Division was remotely near full strength.[3] However, it should be remembered that Danilov's plan also suffered from a fundamental flaw: the concentration of reinforcements in a rear area to create a new army would only have been possible if the front line had at the same time been strong enough to hold off the German advance. In the event, the reinforcements were fed into the front line as they arrived, and even with this additional help, the embattled Russian troops were steadily pushed back by the Germans. It could be argued that a concentrated deployment would have had far more effect, but this would have necessitated a flexible attitude to trading territory for time, and *Stavka* repeatedly demanded that Third Army stop the Germans as far to the west as possible.

Regardless of the views of higher commands about voluntary retreats, Brusilov's Eighth Army began to withdraw after the fall of Przemyśl. The new line was around Gródek (now Horodok), only 15 miles (25km) from the centre of Lemberg, and rear area units were pulled back behind this position. For the moment, many of the troops remained where they had halted after Przemyśl fell, about 24 miles (40km) further west, but Brusilov had no doubt that his weakened formations were in no state to mount a serious defence, not least because of the poor quality of replacement drafts:

> Leaving aside the fact that they were very poorly trained, they came unarmed, and we did not have rifles for them. While we were advancing, all our weapons that were left on the battlefield – and those of our enemy – were gathered by special teams and returned to use after servicing, but now, as we were retreating, the opposite happened: all the weapons from the dead and wounded fell into the hands of the enemy. There were insufficient rifles left in rear areas. Orders were issued for the walking wounded to take their weapons with them to the dressing stations, and even money was offered to encourage this, but these measures had very little impact. Increasingly, groups of unarmed soldiers, who were almost impossible to train, accumulated within each corps. In general, the disorganisation of our army increased rapidly, and our fighting capacity decreased by the hour, and the spirit of the troops plummeted.[4]

One estimate put the number of men without rifles in Southwest Front at 300,000.[5] German and Austro-Hungarian writers described the defences running from Gródek north to Magierów [now Maheriv] as formidable fortifications:

> The Gródek–Magierów position was well laid out from a strategic point of view. From it, a powerful army that understood its task, even if outnumbered, could defend Lemberg for several months. To the south was the Dniester, which with its shore defences created a barrier that could only be overcome with crippling losses and extraordinary materiel commitment. It could be concluded that it would not be possible for the united German–Austro-Hungarian troops to force a crossing here to approach the Galician capital from the south. Therefore, this left only an attack from the west. But this was very difficult, especially as there would be an ongoing threat to the [northern] flank from the Tanew.
>   ... The position was further strengthened by nature. From the Dniester to Cuniow, the valley of the Wereszyca, with its broad area of swamps and lakes, lay before the position. From Cuniow to a point west of Magierów there stretched a

The Advance on Lemberg, June 1915

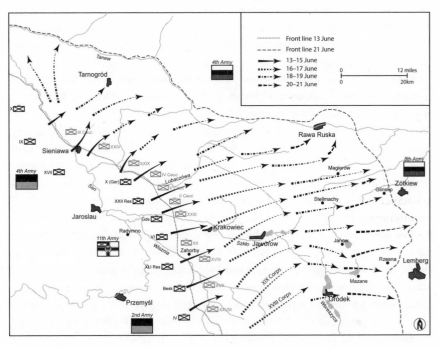

great band of woodland, about 10km [6 miles] deep, of an almost primeval sort, split up by only a few firebreaks. The only proper road running through it was the great Jaroslau–Jawórow–Janów–Lemberg road. In the middle of this woodland that lay before the attacker, the course of the Wereszyca with its swamps and lakes at Janów and Mazane created further natural obstacles. Further north, where the woodland turned west on high ground near Magierów, there was hilly country, characterised by numerous deep gullies with steep sides.

... All parts of the great position were faultlessly laid out from a tactical viewpoint; the attacker encountered flanking fire at every point, and good fields of fire had been cleared. Its construction brought great credit to the Russian engineers. The trenches were well constructed with firing points and strong shelters in abundance. Magierów itself and the ridges between it and the main positions were strongly fortified.[6]

Regardless of the accuracy of this assessment of the fortifications, the key point was that it would require a capable army, with adequate supplies, to hold them, and this was clearly not available to the Russians. As far as Brusilov was concerned, his retreat was forced on him. Ivanov had switched V Caucasian Corps and XXIII Corps from his command to Third Army, and with his forces thus weakened, it was impossible for Eighth Army to continue to hold its positions, particularly given the losses it had suffered in recent fighting. Now, as Brusilov fell back along his supply lines towards the east, Third Army looked as if it would pull back on a divergent path, towards the northeast. Inevitably, a gap would open between the two armies – directly opposite the troops of the 'Mackensen phalanx'. Brusilov immediately raised this with Ivanov, brushing aside Southwest Front's assurances that Olukhov's group would cover the gap; Brusilov knew that the infantry formations of this new group had all suffered heavily during the fighting in May, and would not be able to put up prolonged resistance to a renewed German attack, still less carry out the sort of counterattack into the flank of any German advance against Eighth Army that Ivanov hoped. Given that Olukhov faced the most powerful and consistently successful part of the forces facing Southwest Front, it was highly likely that when the Germans had brought forward sufficient supplies and reinforcements, they would launch an attack against this group and would drive it off; they would then proceed to separate the two western armies of Ivanov's front. Were that to happen, Eighth Army's ability to retreat slowly, let alone hold its positions, would be severely compromised, and in all likelihood a precipitate withdrawal would be required to prevent encirclement and annihilation. Brusilov's protests were in vain; Ivanov insisted that he give up the corps as ordered. A trip to Southwest Front headquarters by Eighth Army's chief of staff, Piotr Lomnovsky, did not alter matters:

> In addition, I sent my chief of staff by car to front headquarters, to find out what they were thinking, what were the assumptions of higher authorities for further action and what we can expect in the near future. Returning from this trip, the chief of staff informed me that he found the front staff deeply despondent, with no plan of action or any ideas about the future; everyone was extremely pessimistic, believing that the campaign was lost. General Lomnovsky also received pessimistic information about reinforcements, replacement weapons, and ammunition supplies.[7]

Ivanov was now functioning as little more than a messenger between those above and below him. When Lesh or Brusilov requested permission for retreats, he raised objections, but ultimately allowed them to do what they wished; when

Grand Duke Nikolai told him to insist on the armies holding their positions at all costs, he passed these instructions on to his subordinates. On the occasions that *Stavka* berated him for retreats, he forwarded reports from the front line about the parlous state of affairs. His only significant intervention seems to have been the creation of the Olukhov group, and in reality this amounted to little more than assigning a single commander to the southern flank of Third Army. The best indicator that he could give to *Stavka* was that, like his forces, the Germans were also struggling with ammunition shortages:

> This fact shows that as the enemy owes his success above all to his immense consumption of munitions, it is reasonable to expect that the enemy will thus be deprived of the means by which he seeks to achieve his ends in the Russian theatre of war.[8]

The Russian setbacks in western Galicia were having consequences further afield, and caused consternation in the capitals of Russia's allies. From Paris, Alexander Izvolsky, the Russian ambassador, reported that many French politicians expressed doubts about the ability of the French Army to endure a second winter in the trenches, and were therefore anxious for the 'Russian Steamroller' to crush the Central Powers, as had been repeatedly promised since the start of the war. Given that it would take several months for Italy to bring sufficient forces into battle, the French now urged the Russians to look elsewhere for allies who might intervene sooner.

The obvious target for such efforts was Romania. For many years, the Romanians had made repeated claims on the province of Transylvania, part of the Austro-Hungarian Empire but with a majority Romanian population. However, a long history of good diplomatic relations with Germany ensured that the elderly King Carol successfully blocked attempts by the *Partidul Naţional Liberal* (National Liberal Party, or PNL) to take advantage of the outbreak of war to try to seize Transylvania, despite strong encouragement by Russia. German and Austro-Hungarian diplomats, on the other hand, urged the king at least to stay neutral, if not enter the war on their side, and the strain on Carol was so great that one of the diplomats, the Austro-Hungarian Ottokar Czernin von und zu Chudenitz, had little doubt that it brought about his premature death in September 1914.[9] Carol's successor was his nephew Ferdinand I, who was less inclined to keep Romania out of the war. He was a close ally of the Romanian prime minister, Ion Brătianu, leader of the PNL, and shortly after he came to power Ferdinand authorised secret negotiations with the Entente Powers about a possible Romanian entry into the war. The price for such an entry would be the disputed territory of Transylvania.

The negotiations proceeded slowly, not least because Romania's interests often conflicted with those of Russia and its ally, Serbia. Romania claimed dominion over parts of Bukovina and the Carpathians that were also claimed by Russia, and laid claim to parts of eastern Serbia, and Sergei Sazonov, the Russian foreign minister, did his best not to dispute these claims for fear of antagonising a potential ally. The Russian setbacks in western Galicia appear to have had a profound effect upon the Romanian leadership. As the prospect of a rapid collapse of the Austro-Hungarian Empire receded, the difficulty of securing – and perhaps more importantly, retaining – Transylvania became proportionately greater, and it became clear to the Entente diplomats that they could not count on an early Romanian entry into the war. Nevertheless, the importance placed on a potential Romanian alliance formed part of the ongoing wish by both *Stavka* and Southwest Front to continue offensive operations against the Austro-Hungarian Seventh Army and the German South Army in Bukovina. The resurgent South Army had to be halted and driven back from the Dniester, while Pflanzer-Baltin's Seventh Army was to be pushed back across the Prut, potentially allowing the flank of the entire Eastern Front to be turned. The use of this section of the front in some grandiose outflanking movement had been a repeated aim of both sides, and it says much about their reluctance to learn from events that this idea continued to resurface in both camps.

But if Romania's entry into the war on the side of the Entente was now a receding prospect, there were factions within Romania who might bring the nation into the camp of the Central Powers. Czernin believed that such an eventuality might have been engineered:

> Brătianu himself would never in any case have ranged himself on our side, but if we could have made up our minds then to install a Majorescu or a Marghiloman Ministry in office, we could have had the Romanian army with us. In connection with this there were several proposals. In order to carry out the plan we should have been compelled to make territorial concessions in Hungary to a Majorescu Ministry – Majorescu demanded it as a primary condition to his undertaking the conduct of affairs, and this proposal failed, owing to Hungary's obstinate resistance.[10]

Such territorial concessions were similar to those urged by the Germans on Austria to keep the Italians out of the war; just as Falkenhayn's proposals were met with brusque rejection by Vienna and Conrad's counter-suggestion that Germany should offer to concede Alsace and Lorraine to France in order to secure peace was rejected by Berlin, so were the suggestions of Czernin and like-minded individuals turned down by Budapest. The outcome of all these offers and counter-offers, and the impact of the fighting in western Galicia, was that for the moment at least, Romania remained neutral. In the words of Danilov, Romania chose to take no risks for the moment with either side.[11]

Although the Russians continued to make some progress in Bukovina, the front line elsewhere generally seemed to be stabilising, not least because Mackensen's forces had been forced to pause while railway communications across western Galicia were restored. Although the Russian Army had suffered a serious blow, Falkenhayn and Conrad knew that the huge resources of the tsar's empire would allow these losses to be made good over time, and it was therefore important to strike another blow with the intention of breaking the ability of the Russian Army to mount significant offensive operations for the foreseeable future. Such a success would allow the Central Powers to turn their attention elsewhere.

This immediately raised three matters. Firstly, there was the question of where this new blow should be struck. Secondly, a resumption of offensive operations would require additional reinforcements. Although German and Austro-Hungarian losses in Galicia had been far lighter than those of the Russians, they were still substantial enough to make further advances much more difficult, particularly as troops had to be diverted to face a possible threat from Italy. Finally, discussions were needed on where the two allies should turn their attention after the Russians had been defeated.

The first matter was settled relatively easily. Hindenburg and Ludendorff advised Falkenhayn that even with reinforcements, they could only expect tactical successes against the Russians in the northern half of the Eastern Front. Such gains, whilst welcome, would fall far short of the crippling blow that was needed if the Central Powers were to be given a free hand to turn their attention elsewhere. The ongoing Russian preoccupation with Bukovina was from Falkenhayn's point of view most welcome – this was a sector that was too far from the centre of activity to have a major effect, and if the Russians wished to divert troops to that area, it would weaken their ability to fight elsewhere. The logical conclusion, easily reached, was to continue attacking in Galicia. The Russians were clearly in disarray in this sector, and their troops demoralised. Once it was possible for supplies to be brought forward, an attack should be launched to the east, with a minimum objective of recapturing the Galician capital, Lemberg. It seems that there was initially a suggestion that rather than trying to force the

Gródek position from the west, the assault should be mounted from the south over the Dniester, but even the most cursory of considerations showed that this would be a far harder undertaking. The only realistic option for an assault would be a continuation of the earlier advance.[12]

Conrad was enthusiastically in favour of this. The defeats in Galicia in 1914 would thus be avenged, and the return of Austro-Hungarian forces to Lemberg would do much to restore the credibility and prestige of his battered armies. Once eastern Galicia was once more in Austro-Hungarian hands, it might be possible to return to another of his long-held wishes: a simultaneous attack from north and south into the great salient held by the Russians in Poland.

A draft of reinforcements arrived for Mackensen's army, allowing at least some of the formations to replenish their ranks, and further reinforcements were now dispatched to Galicia. Conrad could not contribute much, due to the need to cover the Italian front, but there was a significant rearrangement of Austro-Hungarian forces. With the front moving so far to the east, Puhallo's Third Army was broken up. Its X and XVII Corps were assigned to Joseph Ferdinand's Fourth Army on Mackensen's northern flank, and the *Beskidenkorps* and two additional reservist brigades were handed to Second Army on Mackensen's southern flank. Puhallo himself was dispatched to central Poland, where the command of First Army had undergone changes. Viktor Dankl had been sent to take command of the Austro-Hungarian forces in the Tyrol, and was briefly replaced by Karl von Kirchbach; Puhallo now took over from Kirchbach, who resumed command of I Corps. More importantly for Mackensen, a little over two German infantry divisions arrived from the Western Front; although this left the armies facing the French and the British with the bare minimum of reserves, Falkenhayn felt that this was a manageable risk, particularly as the Anglo-French attacks of the first half of 1915 were now dying down. An additional two divisions were extracted from *Ober Ost*, one from Ninth Army in front of Warsaw and the other from the new divisions that had been created by shrinking the pre-war establishment of existing divisions. Finally, two additional divisions were recalled from Syrmia, the region of the Austro-Hungarian Empire immediately north of Serbia. These, too, were formations created using troops freed from existing divisions, and it was now felt that there was little prospect of any Serbian offensive, particularly as the threat of Romanian intervention against the Central Powers had receded for the moment.[13]

Discussion then moved to what might be achieved after a further defeat had been inflicted on the Russians. Conrad made two suggestions. The first was a resumption of the proposals he had made at the start of the war, for a huge pincer movement by the Central Powers against the Russian salient in Poland. Hindenburg and Ludendorff could attack from the north, while Austro-Hungarian forces moved north from Galicia. In addition to shortening the front, Conrad speculated that such an operation would force Russia from the war. His other suggestion was to concentrate on Italy. Large numbers of troops, including Mackensen's Eleventh Army, should be sent to the Austrian Alps, and the Italians should be induced to invade; once they had crossed the border, the massed troops could be used to crush them. If the Italians did not invade as expected, the Austro-Hungarian and German forces should be used to strike into northern Italy.

Falkenhayn had little time for an adventure against Italy. He was aware that Conrad had a long-seated antipathy towards the Italians, and that part of the motivation for this proposal derived from this deep distrust of Austria-Hungary's neighbour; and in any event, the Italians showed little sign of obligingly marching into a grand trap. It was surely a triumph of optimism over experience, given the disastrous conduct of the Carpathian campaign, for Conrad to believe that a major offensive could be mounted across the Alps into Italy, and in any case Falkenhayn had other plans. Once Russia had been humbled, he insisted that attention should turn to Serbia. The elimination of Serbia would open land communications between the Central Powers and Turkey, which would be of far more long-term value than any defeat of Italy, particularly as the Italians showed no signs of making any major intervention. Conrad responded that there were repeated reports that Serbia might be prepared to accept peace terms. There were several exchanges of letters between Conrad and Stephan Burián von Rajecz, the Austro-Hungarian foreign minister, on this subject, but it was by no means clear whether there was any foundation to the rumours about a Serbian desire for peace. In any event, given that the war had broken out over Serbia's refusal to accept Austria-Hungary's ultimatum following the assassination of Archduke Franz Ferdinand and his wife, the diplomatic gymnastics required for the two nations to accept peace while the war continued elsewhere would surely have been impossible to achieve.[14] It is far more likely that Conrad was willing to believe any rumour that furthered his own plans for an attack on Italy.

For the moment, all arguments about where to switch attention after the completion of operations on the Eastern Front could be left for a future date. The priority was to prepare and execute the next advance by Mackensen's army, and plans were drawn up for Eleventh Army to strike from its bridgehead over the San towards Magierów (now Maheriv), towards the area to the northwest of Lemberg. The left flank would aim to secure the vital road and rail junction at Rawa Ruska, control of which would cut the most direct line of communication between the Russian forces under Ivanov and those further north. The two neighbouring Austro-Hungarian armies would protect the flanks of Eleventh Army, with Fourth Army recovering lost ground at Sieniawa before advancing alongside the Germans, while Second Army to the south covered the city of Lemberg itself. Whilst this would – in theory – allow Austro-Hungarian forces to be the first into the Galician capital, this was scant consolation for Conrad; Mackensen asked for, and was granted, overall command of his own army and the two flanking Austro-Hungarian armies. The advance would begin on 13 June, though Joseph Ferdinand would attack at Sieniawa a day earlier.

By 5 June, trains were running as far as Jaroslau, bringing a steady stream of reinforcements and supplies. Once more, German reconnaissance aircraft ranged over the Russian lines, meticulously photographing every position that could be identified. Particular attention was paid to the line of lakes near Gródek and the woodland that extended north; this was identified as the most crucial point on the new battlefield where the terrain would favour the Russian defenders. In the meantime, the infantry of Eleventh Army took the opportunity to rest and recuperate, though commanders at every level grumbled that the poor state of the local villages, worsened by recent Russian occupation, meant that most troops had to bivouac in the open. Despite the best efforts of the German medical services, a few cases of cholera appeared, but major outbreaks of illness were prevented.[15] Some, however, felt that the preventive measures themselves caused problems:

The vaccination itself [against cholera], administered by two injections, brought more illness than the cholera itself. Swollen shoulders, pain in the arm, and fever occurred frequently. I myself suffered after vaccination; convalescence or even rest were not possible because of the responsibilities I carried. I had to endure and suppress the physical ill-health which passed in a few days.

Until then, cases of cholera had been very few. On 12 June, 81st Infantry Division reported eight cholera cases in I/268 [1st Battalion, 268th Infantry Regiment], adding that the regimental doctor had classified the battalion as unfit for operations. That was a complete misjudgement of the situation, a peacetime viewpoint. Whoever went to war had to be aware that he might lose his life from an enemy bullet or through illness. The field hospitals were there for the sick, but the healthy had to fight. There is no such thing in war as a formation unfit for operations with personnel who are capable of fighting. I immediately drove to 81st Infantry Division and expressed my opinion to the division doctor. I/268 played a glorious part in the fighting of the following days. There were no further cases of cholera. In war, advancing is an effective means of maintaining health.[16]

The tensions between the Germans and their Austro-Hungarian allies that had already become visible prior to the fall of Przemyśl continued to resonate in the days that followed. François' XLI Reserve Corps planned to attack towards Medyca and Bucow to the east of Przemyśl in an attempt to cut off the retreating garrison, but the Austro-Hungarian XVII Corps, which was meant to help in the attack, failed to reach its start line in time and the operation was scaled down at the last moment, to the irritation of François, who nonetheless threw his divisions forward without restraint:

> The low-lying land around the Bucow canal, 3km [nearly 2 miles] wide and completely without cover, had to be crossed under fire from Russian artillery, and the canal that cut across the field of attack had to be waded. The bed of the canal was soft, and in places the water was chest-deep. Either side of the canal, Russian infantry fire broke out, but our artillery increased its own fire with such effect that the infantry assault encountered little serious resistance. The [Russian] troops in the trenches surrendered in large numbers and openly expressed their joy that the war was over for them. It became apparent that a large proportion of the prisoners were Jews from Russian Poland. As the columns of prisoners set off, Russian artillery put down accurate shrapnel fire on their captured comrades.
>
> ... Large amounts of weapons and munitions were captured in the trenches, as well as several rolls of barbed wire from American factories.[17]

Throughout the first week of June, XLI Reserve Corps continued to achieve local successes, but the Austro-Hungarian XVII Corps repeatedly failed to keep up on its southern flank. Finally, this led to Mackensen ordering 11th Bavarian Infantry Division to take the place of XVII Corps. A sharp exchange of messages between Mackensen, Falkenhayn and Conrad followed, but it had already been decided to move XVII Corps to the Austro-Hungarian Fourth Army following the dissolution of Third Army, and this redeployment helped calm matters. Finally, Archduke Frederick, the nominal commander-in-chief of the *k.u.k.* Army, sent a personal letter to Falkenhayn. Karl Křitek, commander of the criticised corps, was a valuable and skilful commander, Frederick assured the Germans, and he and his men would fight reliably in future. Others had a different opinion of Křitek. Boroević, in whose army Křitek's XVII Corps had fought during the Carpathian battles, wrote in his final report before leaving Third Army that Křitek was a man who was not fit for higher commands, though he later revised this opinion after Křitek served under his command on the Italian front.[18]

The pause in operations also allowed time for other issues to be raised. On 10 June, Mackensen's headquarters issued an announcement that over 250 men were to be awarded the Iron Cross for their part in the capture of Przemyśl; François was both annoyed and hurt that not a single medal was assigned to men of his corps. They had fought hard to capture Radymno, and had then been involved in heavy fighting in attempting to move closer to the fortress from the northeast. In particular, François felt that his artillery had played a major part in interdicting movements to the east of Przemyśl, and had sustained substantial losses in this task. He wrote to Macksensen to complain, but there is no record of any response; given that most of the staff at Eleventh Army headquarters would have been fully occupied planning the new offensive, this is unsurprising.[19]

During the preparatory phase for the new advance, there was time to reorganise and redeploy Eleventh Army's forces. The left flank, nearest Joseph Ferdinand's Fourth Army, was assigned to a new corps consisting of 119th and 56th Infantry Divisions; Karl von Behr, commander of the former, was also designated as corps commander. To his south was Emmich's X Corps, with 19th and 20th Infantry Divisions, then XXII Reserve Corps with 107th and 43rd Infantry Divisions; the commander of this formation, newly arrived from France, was Eugen von Falkenhayn, the older brother of the chief of the general staff. Plettenberg's Guards Corps was next in line, with Arz and the Austro-Hungarian VI Corps to his south. Finally, on the southern wing of the army was François' XLI Reserve Corps. For the first time since the start of the offensive, Mackensen would have substantial reserves at his disposal – in addition to the tried and trusted men of 11th Bavarian Infantry Division, he also had 8th Bavarian Infantry Division, 22nd and 107th Infantry Divisions, and the Hungarian 11th Cavalry Division. Despite their reinforcements, the Germans were still significantly below full strength. The two divisions of François' corps should have had 3,000 men in each of their regiments, giving a total of 18,000 infantry in the corps; the actual total was 202 officers and 10,620 men.[20] It was perhaps in view of this that Mackensen positioned his units so that Falkenhayn's XXII Reserve Corps, fresh from France and close to full strength, and Plettenberg's Guards, who had received significant replacement drafts, were at the centre of his army. Facing them were the battered formations of the Russian Third Army, weak in numbers, ammunition, and morale.

As had been the case in the days when the Germans approached the San, there was considerable fighting in Bukovina, a continuation of the battles of May. Shcherbachev's Eleventh Army had been driven back towards the Dniester, but Lechitsky's Ninth Army had pushed Pflanzer-Baltin back to the Prut.[21] At

Bukovina, June 1915

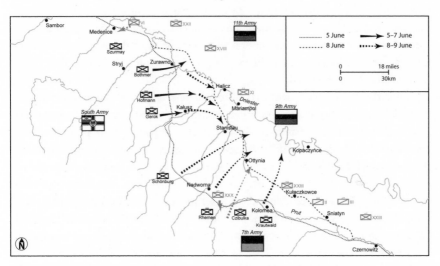

first, Lechitsky tried to alleviate the pressure on his neighbour by continuing with his advance, and in early June he launched several attacks against the Austro-Hungarian forces along the Prut. At the western end of the line, Lieutenant General Andrei Medardovich Zayontchovsky's XXX Corps succeeded in crossing the river and threatened to break through the defensive line, and counterattacks with the few available reserves struggled to stabilise the situation. Eventually, Pflanzer-Baltin concentrated seven infantry battalions and 10th Cavalry Division in order to launch an assault on the Russian bridgehead; the intention was to attack early on 7 June, but late the previous day, it became clear that the Russians were withdrawing.

The reason for this sudden withdrawal was the threat from Linsingen's South Army. Its left flank was firmly established on the Dniester, and Linsingen now directed his troops east, whilst ordering Szurmay, on his left flank, to leave barely an infantry division to hold the line of the river while the rest of the forces attempted to cross the lower Stryj in support of Bothmer's corps. At the same time, the right flank of the South Army was to advance first on Kałusz (now Kalush), and then push on towards Stanislau. At first, the main hindrance to the German advance came from the weather, oscillating between stifling heat and sudden downpours that turned the dusty roads to mud. The first serious Russian resistance was encountered just outside Kałusz on 5 June, but was swiftly overcome. The town itself fell during the following night, and the Russian XI Corps fell back towards Stanislau. On 7 June, the predominantly Czech *Brigade Bolzano* stormed the next Russian positions with great élan, doing much to redeem the reputation of their nationality in the eyes of the Austro-Hungarian high command. Finally, on 8 June, *Gruppe Gerok*, on Linsingen's east flank, reached the town of Stanislau.

It was this last development that forced the retreat of the Russian Ninth Army from the Prut. If Lechitsky continued to advance southwards, he would leave Linsingen behind his western flank, and XXX Corps was now pulled back to cover this threat. Immediately, Pflanzer-Baltin ordered his new group to pursue the retreating XXX Corps. Late on 6 June, the group made an almost unopposed advance of about 9 miles (15km) before encountering resistance the following day. The Russians had established an interim position running from Ottynia (now Otynyia) through Kułaczkowce (now Kulachkivtsi) to Sniatyn (now Snyatyn), but by 9 June Pflanzer-Baltin's troops had already pierced this line at several points. The battling armies were now once more approaching the valley of the Dniester, and Lechitsky ordered his men to try to hold a new line in the hills immediately to the south of the river. Immediately, Pflanzer-Baltin issued orders for his army to mount concentric attacks on what amounted to a long, relatively shallow Russian bridgehead south of the Dniester.

Meanwhile, on the western flank of the Bukovina battlefield, Szurmay's group had been having a difficult time. When they advanced towards the Dniester, they found that the Russian troops facing them were relatively weak, and late on 6 June the Austro-Hungarian forces – 7th Infantry Division and 128th Infantry Brigade – attempted to push ahead to prevent the Russians from withdrawing safely over the river. Unfortunately for them, the operation failed; Gurko's VI Corps had no intention of giving up the south bank without a fight. As other elements of South Army pushed east, Szurmay had to spread his troops ever further along the line of the hills south of the Dniester. When *Gruppe Gerok* reached and took Stanislau almost without firing a shot on 8 June, Linsingen decided that it was time to force his way across the Dniester and ordered his subordinates to secure bridgeheads over the river at Halicz and Mariampol (now Mariyampil). However, Szurmay now reported growing pressure along his thin line to the west. The relatively fresh Russian VI Corps began to apply pressure at several points of the line, threatening to break through at Medenice, and 121st Infantry Brigade was almost wiped out in fighting along the lower Stryj. The Russians now threatened to push on to the town of Stryj, the main railhead for South Army and Seventh Army, and Linsingen realised early on 10 June that the thinly stretched forces of Szurmay's group would not be able to concentrate sufficiently quickly to prevent this. Accordingly, plans for a thrust over the Dniester were abandoned, and the eastern elements of South Army were ordered to move back towards the west in support of Szurmay. Bothmer would thus attack into the eastern flank of the Russian forces threatening Stryj, while a newly assembled group attacked from the west. As was so often the case, on both the Eastern and Western Fronts, the fighting broke down into increasingly costly local struggles for little gain. Around Stanislau, too, the Russians launched an attack on 11 June; alerted by a radio intercept, the Germans were prepared and although they lost ground, they rapidly regained it the following day. For the moment, the threat of a Russian breakthrough towards the south was averted.

Relations between the Austro-Hungarian Seventh Army and the German South Army were not especially cordial. Theodor von Zeynek, Pflanzer-Baltin's chief of staff, recorded that this was due to the personalities of the German officers:

> The two men [Linsingen and Stolzmann, his chief of staff] were exaggerated examples of the Prussian character: they seemed cold-hearted and did not engage our sympathies, and seemed to us to behave like actors; as a result, communications over operations were lacking.[22]

Regardless of the temperamental differences of opinion, the commanders had to do what they could to get along. Nevertheless, Zeynek could not resist recording Linsingen's inability to treat his Austro-Hungarian counterparts as equals, and his refusal to admit that his South Army needed assistance from Pflanzer-Baltin's forces.[23]

On 11 June, Pflanzer-Baltin's central formations secured crossings over the Dniester, but every attempt to exploit this into a general rolling up of the Russian position failed to make headway. The following day, at the very eastern end of the front line, the Austro-Hungarian XI Corps crossed the frontier into Russian territory, but rather than allow the front to extend even further east, Pflanzer-Baltin ordered Edler von Korda to halt his advance, even though the opposing Russian XXXII Corps was making little attempt to resist. All along his front, Pflanzer-Baltin had reason to be satisfied; his forces had once more reached the Dniester, and this time the Russians appeared too weak to drive him back. However, the neighbouring South Army continued to struggle. The constant fighting had ground down Linsingen's divisions with some reduced to as few as 1,000 combatants, and the entire army only having about 19,800 German and 24,700 Austro-Hungarian soldiers available. The Russians made further attempts in mid-June to breach Linsingen's lines, with further bloodshed on both sides for little gain. The Austro-Hungarian 37th Infantry Regiment, part of *Gruppe Szurmay*, was reduced to a mere 150 men, effectively a single company. Szurmay reported to *AOK* that the intensity of the fighting matched anything that he and his men had endured during the long winter in the Carpathians, but the worst was over. Events in central Galicia forced the Russians to turn their attention elsewhere.

Everything was now ready for Mackensen to resume his offensive operations. On 12 June, the preparatory operation on the northern flank commenced, with *Korps Behr* and the German 22nd Infantry Division, temporarily assigned to the Austro-Hungarian XVII Corps on the southern flank of Joseph Ferdinand's Fourth Army, launching an attack to recover Sieniawa. After their successful capture of the town, the Russians had developed a salient about 3 miles (5km) towards Jaroslau, but this was rapidly overrun and most of Sieniawa occupied. The Russian XXIV Corps launched several counterattacks towards the end of the day, but all were fended off, and the Germans had good reason to be satisfied with their day's work, having captured another 5,000 prisoners.[24] At the same time, the Austro-Hungarian troops of XVII Corps also crossed the river.

The following morning, the main assault began, with the same pattern of artillery preparation that had served Mackensen's army so well in previous battles, on this occasion delivered by some 700 guns of all calibres. François reached his field headquarters before dawn and watched the morning assault:

At 0530, the infantry launched their assault. They had a tough task; they had to advance over open ground under fire from enemy machine-guns and shrapnel to and across the Wisznia, which was an excellent obstacle in front of the Russian trenches. Russian machine-guns, cleverly dug in, could fire along the length of the river.

For 81st Infantry Division, the objective was Zahorby, north of the Wisznia, and the assault groups of 267th and 268th Infantry Regiments led the way; 267th Infantry Regiment followed as a second line. The attack proceeded as far as the Wisznia without pausing, though casualties were not light. As the first men of 268th Infantry Regiment prepared to wade across the Wisznia, they were cut down by Russian machine-gun fire. Once again, the artillery probed the area for the machine-gun nests. The second assault across the river also foundered under Russian machine-gun fire. General von Stocken [commander of 81st Infantry Division] stood on the heights at Turczyna. Again, every bush on the riverbank was brought under artillery fire, and then the third assault began at 1300. The brave men of the 268th now succeeded in reaching the northern, steep bank of the Wisznia. The regiment sent a report back to the division and requested a 15-minute bombardment of Zahorby ... by 1400, Zahorby was in their hands.[25]

By evening, 81st Infantry Division had fought its way forward perhaps 3 miles (5km) in the face of tough resistance, and had suffered substantial losses. To the south, 82nd Infantry Division also struggled to cross the Wisznia, again requiring two further artillery bombardments before being able to advance late in the day. The formations to either side of XLI Reserve Corps – *Beskidenkorps* to the south and Arz's VI Corps to the north – similarly made only modest progress. For a total of about 1,000 dead and wounded, François' men took about 1,400 prisoners from the Russian VIII Corps. The neighbouring Austro-Hungarian divisions had similar fortunes.

Further north, Plettenberg's Guards had been given additional artillery support for their attack. The southern formation of the corps, 1st Guards Division, had to request further artillery support before it was able to penetrate the first line of Russian defences, but 2nd Guards Division to the north had an easier time; its attack struck at the seam between the Russian XXIII and II Caucasian Corps, and it rapidly advanced 3 miles (5km), taking prisoners throughout the day.[26] On Plettenberg's north flank, Falkenhayn's XXII Reserve Corps and *Korps Behr* also made good progress, and by the end of the day, Mackensen was confident that the hard work had been done.

Now, the emphasis for Mackensen was to prevent the Russians from establishing a new defensive line that would halt his troops. At first light on 14 June, François ordered his two divisions to launch new attacks on the Russians, only to find that they had retreated during the night. After pushing forward perhaps 4 miles (6.5km), the Germans ran into a new Russian position; one of François' brigade commanders, Oberst Wilhelm Kaupert, carried out a personal reconnaissance towards a nearby wood:

A few hundred metres from the edge of the wood, I clearly saw Russian trenches. The rifles lay on the breastwork, and the troops were perched on the edges. There were no shots. Staying parallel to the trench line I rode further until I spotted the left flank and behind it some reserves. As I took the road back, I suddenly came under brisk fire, which I avoided by speeding up.[27]

It transpired that Kaupert was wearing an unusual hat, similar to that worn by Russian cavalry, which was presumably why the Russians had not shot at him, but his own troops had. Once the confusion was over, he organised a swift assault. After brief but determined combat, his men overcame the Russians and took the positions that Kaupert had reconnoitred. Although losses were lighter than the preceding day, XLI Reserve Corps was feeling the strain of having been in combat since early May without reinforcements; its infantry strength had fallen to less than 10,000 men, compared with an establishment of 18,000.[28]

On the southern flank of the battlefield, the Russian Eighth Army pulled back rather than risk getting outflanked by the German advance. Mackensen and Conrad both urged Böhm-Ermolli's Second Army to pursue the Russians harder, in order to try to stop their orderly withdrawal. On the army's left flank, the *Beskidenkorps* had attacked energetically on the first day of the operation, sustaining considerable losses, but elsewhere, the Austro-Hungarian formations, badly weakened by their winter fighting in the Carpathians, had shown less energy. On 14 June, they attempted to put this right, and XVIII, XIX and IV Corps moved up alongside the *Beskidenkorps*. Casualties were, inevitably, as heavy in these attacks as almost any such operation in the First World War, and the *Beskidenkorps* had to pause when it encountered a new Russian defensive line; the Russian XVII Corps was determined to cover the main road leading east to Gródek for as long as possible. Nevertheless, as was the case with Eleventh Army the previous day, there was a growing sense that the hard work had been done.[29]

On François' northern flank, the Austro-Hungarian VI Corps also had a day of hard fighting. Krakowiec (now Krakovets) was the first sizeable town in the path of the assault, and it lay in the southern part of VI Corps' sector. As they approached the town, the troops of 39th *Honvéd* Infantry Division could see that the Russians had set the bridges over the Szkło ablaze, but although they could see columns withdrawing to the east, the Hungarians ran into determined resistance around the small lake immediately outside Krakowiec, bringing their advance to a halt. North of the town, there was easier progress. In close cooperation with Plettenberg's Guards, the Austrian 12th Infantry Division overcame determined resistance from the Russian Caucasian Grenadier Division and 34th Infantry Division. A little further north, XXII and X Corps and *Korps Behr* had a difficult day advancing through woodland, which made effective use of artillery difficult, but nevertheless maintained their progress, driving the Russians back towards the northeast.[30]

Although Mackensen's troops had made progress, they generally fell short of the day's objectives set by him. Nevertheless, the central formations had pushed through the second line of Russian defences, and Ivanov struggled to devise a solution to the problems that his front faced. His preferred option was to use

Olukhov's forces for a counterattack, but many of the components of this group were already tied down in battle, and consequently were unable to manoeuvre or concentrate. Nor were there sufficient reserves behind the line to help restore the situation; although the German and Austro-Hungarian troops reported the appearance of new formations on the second day of the assault, there were little more than the local reserves, most of which had been badly degraded in fighting the previous month. It was only in the north, where Joseph Ferdinand's Fourth Army was attempting to expand its bridgehead over the San, that the defences continued to hold.

The general advance continued over the coming days. At first, difficult terrain – a wide swampy area, overlooked by wooded high ground – held up XLI Reserve Corps, but the retreating Russians put up little more than token resistance; François characterised the fighting as little more than dislodging rearguards that withdrew when daylight revealed their small numbers.[31] By 17 June, the front line had moved perhaps 18 miles (30km) from the starting position, and now ran along what was known as the Gródek position, recognised by both sides as the last significant barrier before Lemberg.

On this day, there was a conference of senior Russian figures in Khelme, involving *Stavka* and Southwest Front. The overall situation was bad, with the front-line divisions collectively short of half a million combatants, and ammunition stocks significantly below 50 per cent of what had been planned before the war – and the experiences of 1914 and 1915 had shown that these peacetime stocks were in any case inadequate. Morale had plummeted, and Brusilov told the conference that he had issued orders for machine-guns to be used if necessary to force men to remain in their positions. Everyone agreed that there was no possibility of the Russian Army mounting major offensives in the near future, and instead the troops would be exhorted to fight for the protection of Mother Russia. As for the situation in the front line, the inevitable consequence of the loss of Lemberg – and perhaps more importantly the north–south communications running through the city – would result in divergent paths of retreat, and in these circumstances, it was agreed that all forces falling back north would pass into the control of Northwest Front, not least because they would be entirely dependent upon Alexeyev's front for their supplies. Southwest Front would be left with Brusilov's Eighth Army, Shcherbachev's Eleventh Army, and Lechitsky's Ninth Army.[32]

Within hours of the conference coming to an end, tensions within the Russian camp came to a head when Brusilov objected to increasingly critical telegrams from Ivanov's new chief of staff, Sergei Savich. The latter was a man who had no significant experience of high command, having risen to prominence since the start of the war, and Brusilov clearly felt that he lacked the authority to criticise the conduct of his army. In protest, Brusilov wrote to Grand Duke Nikolai, offering his resignation:

> However, I received a reply from the supreme commander in which he flatly refused to allow me to resign, and expressed his gratitude to me for past military service, but with the caveat that I was obliged to carry out the instructions of my superior. This last phrase, to be honest, was incomprehensible to me, because I had always complied with orders of higher commands. If I occasionally protested against them, it was only when I had considered that in the interests of our objectives, I needed to explain the situation that was apparently not understood by front headquarters.[33]

Brusilov travelled to Ivanov's headquarters in Rovno, where the front commander attempted to allay his irritation, with limited success. Regardless of the disagreements between commanders, the harsh reality on the ground was that the Russian Army was close to breaking point. Ivanov insisted that the main problem was a shortage of artillery and ammunition, without which counterattacks were unlikely to make any headway; he continued to argue that the German successes were solely due to their superiority in artillery. A young British officer with Third Army sent a series of reports to Alfred Knox, the British military attaché, who was not with the front-line forces at the time:

> This army is now a harmless mob ... Here are some of the strengths even after reinforcements have arrived since 14 May at a rate of 2,000 to 4,000 a day: 12th Siberian Division, 18 officers and 3,000 men; X Corps, all three divisions together, 14,000 men ... XXIII Corps lost more than half its strength in an attack. IX Corps lost 3,500 men in three days ... we are very short of ammunition and guns. All realise the futility of sending men against the enemy, they with their artillery and we with ours.
>
> ... All the late advances have been pure murder, as we attacked against a large quantity of field and heavy artillery without adequate artillery preparation.[34]

But even had sufficient ammunition and guns been made available, it is likely that the poorly trained and poorly equipped recruits reaching the front line, led by a mixture of elderly officers and inexperienced cadets, would have made no impression on the irresistible advance of the 'Mackensen phalanx'. The opening phase of this new assault had already been a decisive success for the German and Austro-Hungarian forces; the haul of prisoners alone was in excess of 34,000.[35] One more drive could see the severing of the most direct lines of communication between the Russian Northwest and Southwest Fronts.

The German and Austro-Hungarian gunners spent 18 June bringing forward the heavy artillery that had been such a feature of the campaign. There was plentiful evidence from reconnaissance, civilian reports, radio intercepts and prisoner interrogations that the Gródek position had been extensively fortified, and Mackensen did not intend to take any chances. It was clear that a position like this would make the post of the traditional Russian strengths in stubborn defence, but if the line could be breached, the Russians would be forced to fight a battle of manoeuvre, and the losses they had suffered – particularly amongst their officers – would count heavily against them.

Despite the damage done by the retreating Russian forces to the roads and bridges in the battle zone, it seems that the artillerymen encountered no significant problems. While they and Eleventh Army's pioneers rebuilt bridges and moved their guns and ammunition, German aircraft continued their careful pre-bombardment reconnaissance; the Russians could do little other than wait for what was to come. On 19 June, after a prolonged artillery preparation, Mackensen's troops attacked again. On this occasion, he had no reason to reproach Böhm-Ermolli's Second Army; elements of its XVIII Corps stormed the town of Gródek, attacking long before dawn in order to take the Russians by surprise. Bitter house-to-house fighting continued into the day before the Russians withdrew, setting up a new position immediately to the east with the remnants of four regiments from different divisions. Exhausted by their exertions, the Austro-Hungarian troops were in no state to push on without a pause.[36] To their north, XIX and IV Corps also attacked, turning the northern end of the line of Russian defences along the lakes near Gródek and making modest progress either side of the lake at Janów.

The German 81st Infantry Division, part of François' XLI Reserve Corps, faced a difficult task, not least because its reconnaissance had not been as complete as General von Stocken had hoped, and the attack proved difficult to execute:

> Reconnaissance of the front line before the regiment, particularly the swampy meadows by the lake, was difficult, with all patrols driven back on 18 June with casualties. It was discovered that entrenchments with barbed wire obstacles ran through Stellmachy, there was another entrenchment with wire on the slope at Krolowa and the wooded hill was fortified with strongpoints. It was later

discovered that the trenches and shelters were dug deep into the limestone. The swampy meadows north of the lake and at the southern end of Stellmachy appeared to be impassable. There were machine-gun nests in the undergrowth on the northern shore of the lake, covering the entire swampy area. There were similar nests, completely invisible, on the Krolowa slope.

The assault began at 7 a.m. By 10 a.m., the right flank of the regiment had taken the farm west of Stellmachy and the right flank had broken into the first Russian position, but the centre had not been able to advance, the powerful enemy fire suppressing every attempt to attack. In addition, a battalion on the right flank was in the swamp, where men sank up to their hips.[37]

After a further artillery bombardment, including the use of a smoke barrage to obscure the line of sight for Russian machine-gunners, an assault in the evening succeeded in taking the Russian fortifications. In a similar manner, all of the elements of Eleventh Army were able to advance, even though in most sectors the ground gained was not great, not least because a chain of several fortified hills had to be overcome; most units required the artillery to renew their bombardments to suppress determined pockets of resistance. Plennenberg's Guards, however, succeeded in overcoming all the Russian defence lines in their path. Badly weakened during its retreat, Nikolai Alexandrovich Kashtalinsky's XXVIII Corps fought a determined battle all day, mounting repeated counterattacks even after its main positions had been overwhelmed, but by the end of the day the Germans had advanced an impressive 7 miles (12km) to reach and cut the railway line running north from Lemberg to Rawa Ruska.

Both Kaiser Wilhelm and Falkenhayn visited the front line to witness the attack, though the wooded terrain made the battle harder to observe than many previous advances. François was disappointed that neither visited his headquarters, largely because of the difficulties of moving through the wooded terrain, but he received a surprise visit from the Swedish explorer Sven Hedin.[38] When they spent time with the *Beskidenkorps*, the visitors from Berlin might have been disappointed by the pessimistic tone of the report they received; it seems that Marwitz, the corps commander, was not convinced that a further major victory could be achieved. By contrast, when they met Mackensen in Radymno on 20 June, the mood was far better. Reports from the entire front suggested that the main line of the Gródek position had been forced, and the gains made by 1st Guards Division were of particular value. Nevertheless, Mackensen was summoned back to Radymno that evening for further discussions with the kaiser; although he recorded that these went well, he added that the result was that it was past midnight before his day came to an end.[39]

The importance of the advance of the Guards was that if the Russians were forced further back, their inability to use the vital north–south railway would ensure that their front line split in two, with one part falling back north and northeast and the other retreating due east, much as Brusilov had feared from the outset. It was therefore no surprise when the Russians launched determined but ultimately futile counterattacks on 20 June to try to recapture the railway. On either flank of the Guards Corps, German and Austro-Hungarian troops moved up alongside, and further south, François' two divisions made better progress, covering most of the ground to Zótkiew (now Zhovkva). Here, they encountered new Russian defences, and paused while the heavy artillery caught up with the advance. Perhaps the most important gain of the day though, came in X Corps' sector, where 19th Infantry Division moved almost unopposed into Rawa Ruska. In François' opinion, there could be little doubt about the scale of the overall success:

> Once more, we had successfully fought a breakthrough battle, the fourth in the Galician campaign. The Russian positions had lacked nothing in scale of preparation, but the moral and psychological strength of the Russian soldiers had been weakened by their constant setbacks and heavy losses. The contentment of the prisoners was a clear sign of this. They willingly drove their own transports to the assembly areas that were marked out for them. We had to economise with escorts, as the infantry regiments had been reduced to the strength of battalions and replacements had not appeared.
>
> … I accompanied 81st Infantry Division and saw the Russian fortifications against which our artillery and mortars had made great efforts. There were heaps of shattered corpses in the trenches, smashed machine-guns, deep shell craters, everywhere were strewn bits of bodies, the ground torn up. It was a picture of all the horrors of war.[40]

The Russians had already started to consider the abandonment of Lemberg when Mackensen attacked the Gródek position, and by 21 June it had become inevitable; realising as much, Brusilov ordered his troops to delay the enemy for as long as possible to ensure an orderly retreat, but to avoid being overrun or isolated.[41] The Austro-Hungarian formations of Second Army were closing in on the city from the south and west, and during the night of 21–22 June, XLI Reserve Corps, supported by 11th Bavarian Infantry Division, forced its way through the defences to the west of Zótkiew at Glinsko, taking Zótkiew itself early on 22 June. At the same time, the *Beskidenkorps* and Austro-Hungarian

IV Corps penetrated the outer line of defences to the northwest of Lemberg itself. The village of Rzesna, perhaps 2 miles (3km) to the northwest of the city, came under artillery bombardment at dawn on 22 June, and an early assault by the Austro-Hungarian XIX Corps took Rzesna shortly afterwards. In Lemberg itself, there was frantic activity as Russian rear area units attempted to evacuate to the east, while the defenders, from the ranks of XVII and VII Corps, attempted to buy as much time as possible, through a combination of determined defence and repeated, though futile, counterattacks. The leading elements of the Austro-Hungarian 13th Infantry Division, part of XIX Corps, penetrated into Lemberg itself at midday. The morning's fighting had exhausted the Russian defenders, and they now faded away. After intercepting a radio message from Brusilov's headquarters calling for his men to break off combat, the Austro-Hungarian forces pressed on with renewed determination. Eduard Böhm-Ermolli, whose Second Army had been heavily involved in the ultimately doomed attempts by the *k.u.k.* Army to hold Lemberg in 1914, was with his men when they marched into the city centre in mid-afternoon.

At the outbreak of the war, Lemberg was the fourth-largest city of the Austro-Hungarian Empire. The loss of the Galician capital was a major blow in 1914, both politically and in terms of its industry and resources; similarly, its recovery in 1915 was a suitable crowning moment for the entire campaign that commenced with the original attacks near Gorlice and Tarnów.

When the Russians occupied Lemberg in early September 1914, they recorded that at least part of the population greeted them as liberators. Over a quarter of the population were Orthodox Christian Ruthenians, and it is likely that it was this segment that was particularly enthusiastic. Although most of the Catholic Christian population was Polish and therefore Slav, most Poles had bitter memories of Russian repression over the previous century, and had no illusions about how the Russians would treat them. Now, when Böhm-Ermolli made his triumphant entry into the city, he and his men were also greeted with great enthusiasm.

In a similar manner, Hermann von François and the men of his XLI Reserve Corps were given a warm reception when they entered Zótkiew:

> The residents of Zótkiew were overcome by boundless joy. The troops were given flowers and refreshments, and the town was covered with celebratory decorations. During the afternoon a deputation of the town elders visited me. The mayor gave a long speech, closing with a 'Hurrah!' for the German kaiser. I gave a speech in reply and wished long life to the Emperor Franz Joseph and the ancient town of Zótkiew.

... The Russians were in Zótkiew for ten months, and before their departure they looted the shops and set fire to the barracks, railway station and the old Sobieski Castle. When I entered the town, the castle was still ablaze.[42]

There were many reasons for both the popularity of the Russians – at least amongst Orthodox Christians – when they took Lemberg, and the rejoicing on their departure. The Jews, who formed nearly 20 per cent of the town's residents, had little reason to welcome the tsar's soldiers; many left with the retreating *k.u.k.* Army, while others endured the occupation as best they could. The fears of Jews, Poles and others were increased when Brusilov issued a declaration immediately after his troops captured the city in 1914 that this was a Russian land, populated by Russian people.[43] This was a widespread view amongst Russians, but the first Russian governor of the province, Sergei Sheremetev, took a pragmatic approach, cooperating with the Polish residents – particularly the minority that was pro-Russian – and allowing them to open Polish schools. There were immediate objections from many in the Ukrainian community, and Sheremetev was immediately replaced by Count Georgi Alexandrovich Bobrinsky, who took a much harder line. Insisting that Galicia was Russian territory, he pursued a policy of Russification, including the imposition of Russian laws and language; this cost him the support of many of the Ukrainians in the city in addition to the Poles. Schools were closed temporarily while teachers were sent on courses so that they could then teach in Russian, and all thought of allowing Polish to be used in education disappeared. Originally, it had been the intention of the Russians to proceed with Russification at a gentler pace, and to allow Austro-Hungarian institutions to continue to function, but too many civilian officials had fled with the retreating *k.u.k.* Army, and their replacements – either local Russophiles or personnel brought in from nearby Russian cities – proved to be heavy-handed.

Perhaps one of the issues that played a leading part in the increasing disaffection with the Russians was the question of religion. Many of the Ukrainians in Galicia were part of the Ukrainian Catholic Church, and its leader, Metropolitan Andrei Sheptytskyi, was arrested and exiled to the interior of Russia.[44] Although the tsar issued a decree forbidding the compulsory imposition of Orthodox Christianity, Archbishop Evlogyi of Volhynia and Zhitomir attempted to do precisely that, arranging for hundreds of Russian Orthodox priests to replace Ukrainian and Polish priests who were arrested. Not all Russians were blind to the consequences; one Russian general told the British military attaché Alfred Knox with perhaps a little exaggeration that the activities of the Orthodox Church in Galicia were worth four army corps to the *k.u.k.* Army.[45]

Inevitably, the residents of Galicia that suffered the most during the Russian occupation were the Jews. The military authorities almost universally regarded them as Austrian sympathisers and at least potential spies; when shots were fired during the night shortly after the Russian occupation of Lemberg, Cossacks stormed through the city's Jewish quarter, killing between twenty-four and fifty Jews and wounding many more, on the thin pretext that the shots had been fired by an unidentified Jewish woman. Bobrinsky's authorities subsequently held an enquiry that cleared the Jews of any blame, but despite this, Yanushkevich, the chief of the Russian general staff, ordered further reprisals and repression. In November 1914, Grand Duke Nikolai even issued a proclamation declaring that the Jews were amongst Russia's most resolute enemies, ignoring the fact that tens of thousands of Russian Jews were fighting and dying for Russia at the time.

The city governor of Lemberg was Yestafy Nikolayevich Skalon, who had previously been Kiev's police commissioner, where he had established a reputation for ruthless corruption. He rapidly took advantage of his new appointment in the Galician capital and threatened literally to decimate the Jewish population unless the community paid a thousand roubles.[46] Movements and activities by Jews were increasingly curtailed, badly disrupting commercial concerns owned and operated by Jews; they then found themselves accused of deliberate sabotage, because they were unable to sell their produce to the occupation authorities. In early 1915, Shcherbachev suggested to Bobrinsky that as the Jews of Galicia were enemies of Russia, they should be forcibly collected together on the Romanian border and left to starve; they would then cross over into Romania, from where the Romanians could expel them to the Austro-Hungarian Empire. Bobrinsky recoiled from such a suggestion, pointing out that it would hugely undermine the delicate negotiations to bring Romania into the war against the Central Powers, and might even trigger a widespread Jewish backlash against the Russians.[47] Nevertheless, the Russians passed a Liquidation Law in February 1915, which authorised the seizure of land within 98 miles (160km) of the frontier belonging to Jewish citizens of the Central Powers.

In such circumstances, it should come as little surprise that so many residents of Lemberg and Zótkiew were pleased to see the Russians leave. Others, however, were less enthusiastic. Many thousands of Russophiles fled with the Russian Army, their additional numbers on the roads adding to the traffic problems east of the city. There was an opportunity for the Austro-Hungarian authorities to capitalise on the bitter experience of Russian occupation, but somewhat characteristically they chose a different path. There were widespread arrests of those suspected of collaborating with the Russians, and the result was that many of the local population, regardless of their ethnicity and religion, were increasingly inclined to believe that their best hopes for the future lay in self-rule rather than as citizens of either Russia or Austria-Hungary.

For the moment, there was a pause to the campaign. From his headquarters at *Ober Ost*, Hindenburg described the operation that had started in early May:

> Like an avalanche which apparently takes its rise in small beginnings, but gradually carries away everything that stands in its destructive path, this movement began and continued on a scale never seen before, and which will never again be repeated.[48]

This description is simplistic. On several occasions, Mackensen's advance came to a halt, but he was able to resume operations by resorting to the same measures on each occasion: a pause for artillery and ammunition to be brought forward, modest realignments of limited front-line resources, and careful artillery preparation directed by equally careful reconnaissance. It is a measure of the rapidly waning strength of the Russian forces that each assault succeeded in re-establishing the German advance with little difficulty. The operation had begun as an attempt to alleviate the pressure on the Carpathian front, where a collapse of Austro-Hungarian forces had seemed imminent, and although Mackensen claimed to have foreseen the possibility of an advance as far as Lemberg, few others appear to have considered such a heady possibility, though Conrad claimed that this had always been his intention. As is always the case, there were many who attempted to take credit for the victory. Conrad insisted that the success was largely due to the losses that he had inflicted upon the Russians, starting with the Battle of Limanowa-Łapanów in December; he conveniently ignored that his own armies had almost bled to death in the process, and such attrition had never been his stated intention at the time. Mackensen, of course, was widely regarded by all sides as having been instrumental in the success of the Central Powers; the kaiser was only one amongst many to take this view, though his position allowed him certain privileges:

> With their constant advances and true brotherhood of arms, the German and Austro-Hungarian combat forces subordinated to you have thrown back a tough and hard-fighting enemy from his fortifications in one sector to the next. With masterful leadership, always focussed upon your objectives, you have led your proven, incomparably brave troops, who courageously endured every deprivation and effort, from victory to victory. After the superlatively swift capture of Przemyśl

... the enemy has now been driven from the capital of Galicia.

I wish to show my Royal thanks and the high regard I have for you and all troops under your command by promoting you to Field Marshal. May God, who steers all battles, accompany you further on your victorious campaigns.[49]

It should be pointed out that Mackensen had shown no innovative flair during the campaign; his forces had performed outstandingly well, but this was largely due to the exemplary quality of the staffwork that preceded every battle. In recognition of this, Hans von Seeckt, his chief of staff, was promoted to Generalmajor. Conrad, too, was promoted to Generaloberst, and an array of medals: his emperor awarded him the Order of the Iron Crown and the Grand Cross of the Order of Leopold, to which Kaiser Wilhelm added the Commanders Cross of the Order *Pour Le Mérite*. Additional medals followed from Saxony, Turkey, Bavaria, Württemburg and Mecklenburg-Schwerin, and even the Grand Cross of the Most Exalted Order of the White Elephant from distant Siam.[50]

Falkenhayn was keen to bring matters to a close so that he could concentrate once more on the Western Front, and was not the sort of personality to attempt to derive any personal glory from the fighting, even though he had played such a large role in devising the plan and providing the forces for its execution. Nevertheless, he must have derived considerable personal satisfaction from the awareness that his deployment of fairly modest forces to Mackensen's command in late April had yielded such astonishing successes. François' XLI Reserve Corps suffered a total of about 10,500 officers and men killed, wounded and missing; it took nearly 57,000 prisoners and killed and wounded many thousands more, and captured sixty-nine guns.[51] In all, the haul of prisoners was in excess of 240,000 just in Eleventh Army's sector, rising to over 400,000 if the flanking armies and those on the Dniester are included. The Russian Third and Eighth Armies had been effectively eliminated as significant formations, and the overall mission of the German and Austro-Hungarian forces – to strike a decisive blow that would eliminate the threat of Russian offensives – had been achieved in less than two months.

In any earlier war, such a blow would probably have proved fatal to a nation's ability to continue fighting. It was a measure of the new territory into which the world's powers had strayed that even a victory on this scale was not enough to allow Germany to achieve a resolution. Inevitably, the same question arose on both sides of the front line: what now?

CHAPTER 8

DECISIONS AND DEPARTURES

The original intention of Falkenhayn's proposed Eastern Front offensive in May 1915 was to relieve pressure upon the Austro-Hungarian Empire, and to eliminate any serious threat to the Central Powers from Russia, allowing forces to be concentrated against Britain and France. Falkenhayn's plans did not specify how long the operation would continue, or where it would stop; from his discussions with Conrad as matters progressed, it is likely that he would have been satisfied with pushing the Russians back to the line of the San and Dniester, where it would be possible to establish robust defences against any future Russian attacks. Instead, the advance continued into eastern Galicia, drawn on by its own success.

When Kaiser Wilhelm and Falkenhayn visited the front shortly before Lemberg fell, there were extensive discussions on what the next step should be. All of the successors of Moltke the Elder, the first chief of the German general staff, had held the same fundamental opinion about war with Russia: the vast scale of the Russian countryside, together with relatively few major objectives within easy reach, would allow the Russian Army to retreat almost without consequence, drawing an invader behind it until his supply lines became hopelessly overextended. Any advance against Russia had to be with a precise purpose in mind. To date, that purpose had been the destruction of Russia's ability to mount offensive operations, and to a large extent this had now been achieved. Hans von Seeckt, Mackensen's highly capable chief of staff, summarised the situation:

> The actual military objective on the Eastern Front [must be] the early and complete defeat of Russia. The Russian southern front has been crushed. The northwest section remains unbroken. It can only be beaten if it is forced to abandon its strong front line and is enveloped from the south as it retreats.[1]

As will be seen, though, this was not a view that was shared by *Ober Ost*, facing the undefeated elements of the Russian Army.

Falkenhayn also felt a pressing need to transfer forces back to the west. Although the major assaults by the British and French in the first half of 1915 had been beaten off, fighting continued at a lower level along the entire Western Front, straining the limited resources of the German reserves that had been left there, and the chief of the general staff decided that it was now time to withdraw XLI Reserve Corps, 8th Bavarian Infantry Division, and 56th Infantry Division from Mackensen's command. Orders were issued the day after the fall of Lemberg for the troops to proceed to embarkation points; a few days later, François was appointed to command of VII Corps on the Western Front. He would never serve on the Eastern Front again, and left behind him an impressive record of successes, and after his latest triumphs he might have expected promotion in the coming months. However, any further progress in his career was effectively brought to an end as Hindenburg and Ludendorff, who had clashed with him repeatedly in 1914, became increasingly powerful within the German hierarchy; memories in *Ober Ost* were long. François effectively retired from the army in July 1918, and wrote several books about the war; inevitably, these all put his own activities in a favourable light. He died in 1933, aged 77.

Conrad and Archduke Frederick visited Lemberg the day after its capture, and like the first Austro-Hungarian troops to enter the city, they were greeted with enthusiasm by the local population. Conrad took advantage of the journey to travel the short distance to Rawa Ruska, the scene of bitter fighting in 1914. Here, he finally had the opportunity to visit the grave of his son Herbert, who had been killed in the battles of September. He found that the grave had been carefully tended, and was marked by a simple birch cross.[2] Herbert's death had had a profound effect on him and continued to haunt him for many years, which makes his continued near-indifference to the appalling casualties suffered by his armies even more remarkable.

Conrad continued to seek revenge on the Italians. Throughout the Austro-Hungarian Empire, the sense that Italy had turned its back on its alliance with Germany and the Dual Monarchy in return for the promise of territorial gains led to a brief surge in patriotic outrage, and given his longstanding antipathy and distrust of Italy, the chief of general staff made no secret of his desire to punish what he regarded as a treacherous former ally. He repeatedly raised the possibility of luring the Italians into a grandiose ambush on the Austrian side of the Alps, but Falkenhayn rejected this on every occasion that it was suggested. If troops were to be deployed en masse on a different front, he argued, it should be against

Serbia. There was a very real prospect of successfully knocking Serbia out of the war entirely, and such a move would open a direct link with the Turks, who continued to impress by pinning down the British Empire forces that had landed at Gallipoli.

However, before attention could be turned elsewhere, there was still unfinished business on the Eastern Front. Seeckt resumed his suggestion of a drive to the north, into the rear of the Russian forces in Poland. Supported by Mackensen, he argued that such an operation was more likely to force a decisive battle upon the Russians than further advances into eastern Galicia. A series of meetings followed in the last week of June, and Conrad gradually allowed himself to be persuaded; aware that any immediate operation against Italy would require substantial German support, which was not forthcoming, he opted for an operation that might allow sufficient Austro-Hungarian forces to be freed for him to carry out an assault on Italy without Falkenhayn's approval. He could also hope that *Ober Ost* might launch an attack from the north, resurrecting his long-cherished hope of a grandiose pincer movement to destroy the Russians before they could retreat from Poland.

Whilst Mackensen had been enjoying such success in Galicia, Hindenburg and Ludendorff, the former rising stars of the Eastern Front, had been playing merely a minor role. The incursion of German troops into Lithuania certainly drew Russian forces away from southern Poland, but the scale of the German forces involved had also grown steadily. Originally, the main force was Generalleutnant Otto von Lauenstein's XXXIX Reserve Corps, which together with attached formations became first *Armee-Abteilung Lauenstein* on 22 April, and then the Army of the Niemen on 26 May; at this stage, Lauenstein reverted to command of his corps, while control of the army was assigned to Otto von Below, formerly commander of Eighth Army. His place in Eighth Army was taken by Friedrich von Scholtz, who simultaneously commanded his own XX Corps.

At first, the German forces in Lithuania and Latvia faced little more than third-line reservist formations. These were rapidly driven off, but they were replaced by regular troops when three cavalry divisions and XIX Corps disembarked from trains in Riga and Mitau (now Jelgava). In addition, the Russian XIII and XV Corps – reformed after being destroyed at Tannenberg in 1914 – began to concentrate in Kovno. At first, the German forces attacked the Russian forces and succeeded in winning some ground and taking some prisoners, but the balance tilted steadily in favour of the Russians, and the Germans began to fall back slowly, albeit inflicting stinging attacks upon the cautiously advancing Russian troops. By the time that Below took command of the Army of the Niemen, it was clear that the German forces were badly overstretched, and in the face of a major new Russian attack, Curt von Morgen's I Reserve Corps began to withdraw. Morgen noted that the resistance of his men was not the most significant factor in limiting Russian progress:

> It was just as well that my opponent, the commander of XIX Corps [Vladimir Gorbatovsky] was a very cautious gentleman. In every withdrawal by elements of my forces, he suspected a probable trap. He always probed forward deliberately, dug in on every hill, and attacked only when all his forces had assembled. We thus won time, which was in keeping with my mission.[3]

General Vladimir Nikolayevich Gorbatovsky was a veteran of the Russo-Japanese War, and had struggled to adapt to the realities of the war when leading his XIX Corps in the opening months:

> The description of him given by 'Victor Ivanovich', one of the junior officers of the general staff of the corps, was interesting. He said that Gorbatovsky was 'quite unprepared' when he took command of the corps, that he used to try to command companies in the firing line instead of directing the whole from the rear. The chief of staff was too old and weak in character to effect anything. 'It therefore devolved on us youngsters to educate the corps commander! At first we had our work cut out for us, and we had constant quarrels, but after a month we could say to each other: "Well, we have trained him now!"'[4]

On 4 June, the Germans had gathered sufficient forces to launch an attack on the cautiously advancing Russians. As was almost always the case, the Russians reacted by launching immediate counterattacks, which were cut down by German artillery and machine-guns with heavy losses. The original German advance had reached the town of Schaulen (now Šiauliai) before falling back in the face of Gorbatovsky's cautious advance, and the fighting once more shifted to this area. After further heavy though futile battles, with losses on both sides, the front line stabilised.

The staff at *Ober Ost* had watched the developments in Galicia with mixed feelings. On the one hand, they rejoiced in the victories of their compatriots; on the other hand, there was an understandable sense of frustration that they were unable to contribute other than by trying to pin down Russian troops to prevent their transfer to the south. In addition, there was the intense irritation that their credit as Germany's saviours in 1914 was now being shifted to Mackensen and Falkenhayn, and of course the enmity between Falkenhayn and *Ober Ost* was never far from the surface. Contrary to Seeckt's views, some in the Hindenburg–

Ludendorff entourage doubted that the operations in the south would be sufficient in themselves to force a decisive outcome, and their inability to come up with an alternative plan earlier in the year perhaps provided some of the impetus to new thinking:

> Our discussions at Headquarters on this subject often became very lively. From the beginning I supported the opinion that we had now perhaps for the last time the possibility of dealing the Russian Army an overwhelming blow. General von Mackensen's offensive would gradually wear itself out as he had always to make frontal attacks; the continuation of this advance could never result in an overwhelming blow for the Russian Army. The only enemy wing which was still open to our attacks on the whole of the continent was the right Russian wing that lay opposite the army of *Ober Ost*. Against this wing a large outflanking operation ought to be made to the north or the northeast, so that the middle of the Russian line which was still before Warsaw on the Ravka and the Bzura would not be able to escape the blow by retiring, but would be cut off.
>
> I therefore supported the opinion that all the forces that the *Ober Ost* could spare from the sphere under his orders, as well as all the troops that could be obtained from the General Headquarters, should be brought into action in the left wing of the Tenth Army. Kovno should be taken in the shortest time possible and the offensive attack be carried over Vilna to the rear of the main Russian forces.[5]

Aware that the advance of Mackensen's forces in the south would raise suggestions – particularly from Conrad – that *Ober Ost* should launch an attack towards the southeast to complement Mackensen's advance, the personnel at *Ober Ost* concluded that such an attack would pose considerable difficulties. Their armies had already attempted to force the line of the Bobr near Osowiec, and regarded this line of advance as particularly difficult, as the widespread presence of swamps would allow the Russians to concentrate their forces in relatively narrow areas. It would also be relatively straightforward for the Russians to abandon the western parts of their salient if the German forces began to make significant headway, thus escaping from any potential encirclement. Similarly, an attempt to force a breakthrough between Osowiec and Grodno would encounter tough Russian defences. A straightforward thrust to the east ran the risk of the German forces finding themselves in a salient that would invite Russian counterattacks, and as Hoffmann described, Ludendorff and the staff of *Ober Ost* therefore proposed something far more elaborate:

It seemed better first to take Kovno, with Tenth Army from the west and at the same time with the Niemen Army outflanking it to the north. If this fortress, the keystone of the Russian defences on the Niemen, were taken, the road to Vilna and into the rear of the main Russian forces would be open. They would therefore be forced to make a huge withdrawal to the east. If the Niemen Army and Tenth Army were to receive only modest reinforcements in a timely manner and be equipped adequately with supply columns and support units, it was hoped that this advance from the north through Vilna could envelop the [Russian north] flank, and that the summer campaign of 1915 would end with decisive losses for the Russians.[6]

Such considerations had arisen long before the war. The frontier between Germany and the Russian Empire invited convergent attacks on Russian Poland, but there had always been the concern that the Russians would simply retreat to the east, drawing German forces after them, and consequently Moltke the Elder, drawing up contingency plans shortly after German reunification, highlighted that it might be necessary for the German troops to advance further east before attempting to converge with Austro-Hungarian forces operating to the south of the Russian salient. Ludendorff's proposal added an additional nuance: if German forces in the north advanced further east before turning south, they would have a greater dislocating effect on the Russian railway system, accelerating the collapse of a unified Russian front line, much as Mackensen's advance had effectively broken Southwest Front into two parts, forced to retreat in diverging directions.

Although Ludendorff recorded that the kaiser seemed in favour of such an operation, Falkenhayn unsurprisingly rejected it, on the grounds that it was far too ambitious. Even if it had reached its objectives, the gains – the dislocation of Russian rail movements – were, in Falkenhayn's opinion, too small a return on such a risk. A final conference was held in Posen, involving Falkenhayn, Conrad, Hindenburg, Ludendorff, and the kaiser. Although the Western Front was relatively quiet for the moment, German aerial reconnaissance had spotted preparations for a new French offensive in Champagne, and it seemed likely that this would commence in the early autumn. Falkenhayn advised the conference that it would therefore be necessary to transfer substantial numbers of troops from the Eastern Front to France before this date. Time for further operations against Russia was therefore limited, and the objectives of such operations had to be realistic.[7] Instead of Ludendorff's major operation in the north, *Ober Ost* was to conduct a drive by Twelfth Army, commanded by Max von Gallwitz, to the northeast of Warsaw, while the German Ninth Army, Woyrsch's forces, and the

Austro-Hungarian First Army drove the Russians back across central Poland to the Vistula.

This conference was a further test of wills between Falkenhayn on the one hand, and Hindenburg and Ludendorff on the other. Given Mackensen's successes, it was inevitable that the kaiser would support Falkenhayn, especially as the last major operation mounted by *Ober Ost* – the attempted strategic encirclement in Masuria in the winter – had ended with relatively modest successes. Ludendorff recorded that he came away from the conference still believing that once the operation towards the rear of the Russian salient in Poland was over, there would still be time to launch the planned thrust to take Kovno and Vilna. He had left for the Posen conference confident that his plans would be approved, and his staff waited for a telephone call that would allow them to issue the orders that they had already drawn up. Instead, they were forced to adopt the plan that they regarded as less favourable, a drive towards the southeast. Max Hoffmann, one of the senior staff officers in *Ober Ost*, recorded in his diary how the news was received in Hindenburg's headquarters:

> Bockelberg, who had travelled [to the conference] with the chief of staff, just telephoned to tell us what we are to do – naturally, it was somewhat different from what we wished. I was so disheartened, I regarded our proposal as better and more likely to be effective ... The chief of staff returned this evening at 2300, he was furious.[8]

The conference at Posen also marked a complete divergence of doctrine. Hindenburg, Ludendorff and Conrad continued to seek a larger version of the encirclement victory of Tannenberg, whereas Falkenhayn preferred the grinding advance that Mackensen had made since early May. It has been argued that the former group was still seeking a 19th-century battle of grand manoeuvre, whereas Falkenhayn had concluded that such operations were anomalies in the conditions of the First World War.[9] Whilst the German encirclement of Samsonov's Second Army at Tannenberg had seemed to be a huge victory, it had not delivered a lethal blow to the Russian Army, and Mackensen's series of frontal assaults across Galicia had actually inflicted greater losses on the Russians. The likelihood of breaking through the enemy front line in sufficient force, with sufficient freedom of manoeuvre to achieve an encirclement that could trap the Russian forces in central Poland, was in Falkenhayn's opinion mere wishful thinking. Despite his superior artillery, Mackensen had repeatedly been forced to pause while supplies were brought forward, and on every occasion the Russians had recovered and reorganised their lines, albeit in a weakened state. The problem was not necessarily the achievement of a breakthrough; it was sustaining an advance in an era in which only railways could transport sufficient volumes of *matériel*.

But if Falkenhayn's viewpoint was correct, the German victory at Tannenberg stood out as anomalous. The reality was that it had occurred through a mixture of Russian mistakes, German good fortune, and the dispersal of troops over a large area, allowing both sides considerable freedom of manoeuvre; in the case of the Russians, they used this freedom disastrously, concentrating their troops in the centre of the battlefield, whereas the Germans placed their main strike forces on the flanks. The battle was also fought entirely on German territory, where the Germans made excellent use of their intact railways and good quality roads to deploy troops at the key points of the battlefield; such advantages would be conspicuously absent on Russian territory, as it was certain that the Russians would devastate the countryside and destroy the poor quality infrastructure as they retreated, much as the Germans had done in Poland in autumn 1914. Even on German territory, every attempt to reproduce the victory of Tannenberg – notably in the two battles in Masuria – had failed, because the Russians had simply fallen back faster than their flanks could be turned. For Falkenhayn, the lesson was simple. Leaving aside the unarguable disadvantages of advancing across terrain in which the Russians would destroy all bridges and railways as they fell back, a repeat of Tannenberg was almost impossible. The great victory had been won because the Russians had not made any attempt to escape the encirclement until it was too late. There was little prospect of this occurring again.

There were wider divergences. From the moment when it became clear that the German dream of a swift victory in the west had disappeared, Falkenhayn had overtly sought to bring the war to the earliest possible conclusion on terms favourable to Germany. With regard to Russia, he repeatedly told his colleagues that a settlement that involved reparations paid to the Central Powers would be sufficient. By contrast, Hindenburg and Ludendorff were increasingly associating themselves with those who saw a future with Germany dominating a central and eastern European empire, with considerable territory seized from Russia. These political considerations played a part in shaping strategic proposals. In order to force Russia to accept peace terms with financial reparations and few if any territorial concessions, it would be sufficient to eliminate the ability of the tsar's armies to threaten the Central Powers. On the other hand, major territorial gains at the expense of Russia would require a more comprehensive defeat, and the physical occupation of the territories that were to be annexed.

For the moment, Falkenhayn's more limited proposals prevailed and it was agreed to strike at the Russian salient in Poland. While Hindenburg and Ludendorff advanced towards the southeast, Mackensen's forces would turn north, while the Austro-Hungarian Second Army – removed from Mackensen's 'army group' – pushed Brusilov's Eighth Army east. Whilst some – particularly Conrad and the staff of *Ober Ost* – might hope that the Russians would make a determined attempt to defend their fortresses at Novogeorgievsk and Ivangorod, and thus give the armies of the Central Powers time to encircle them, the more likely outcome was that the Russians would continue their retreat. If sufficient pressure was applied, their losses would continue on the scale of the fighting in Galicia, and Germany and Austria-Hungary would be left in a position of great power: the capture of Poland might be sufficient to force the Russians to consider peace, and even if they continued the war, they would be too weak to mount any serious threat for at least a year.

On the Russian side, there was widespread gloom in military circles. The army was already badly weakened, and the replacement drafts were inadequately trained and poorly equipped. Although Southwest Front had sustained the bulk of the casualties, first in the Carpathian battles and then in its doomed attempts to stop the 'Mackensen phalanx', Alexeyev's Northwest Front was also significantly weakened, as it had been forced to transfer substantial troops to the south in order to prevent a complete collapse. There was little prospect of help from Russia's allies; the French and British had few munitions or guns to spare, as they were concentrating on building up their own forces, and after the failure of their assaults earlier in 1915 they lacked the strength to mount further relieving offensives. The Italians too were in no position to help, with their slow mobilisation delaying their entry into hostilities. When the Italian Army was finally ready, it lost huge numbers of men in a series of futile assaults along the Isonzo front, with no significant impact on events elsewhere. Nor was there any help forthcoming from the Serbs; after expelling the Austro-Hungarian forces that had invaded Serbia in 1914, the Serbs had slowly rebuilt their strength, but instead of using this against the Austro-Hungarian forces facing them, they mounted an invasion of northern Albania. Despite constant requests from Russia, the Serbs showed great reluctance in committing their forces for an invasion of Syrmia, to the immediate north of Serbia. This was at least partly due to British recommendations for caution, on the grounds that such a move by Serbia might attract a substantial response by the Central Powers, and it was probably better to wait until the British forces in Gallipoli had achieved a victory and had opened the route for a strike against Istanbul, which it was hoped would knock Turkey out of the war.[10]

The defeats in Galicia had major consequences away from the immediate battlefield. Any prospect of Romania entering the war on the side of the Entente disappeared for the time being, though the value of such nations to either cause seems to have assumed an importance out of proportion to their military power. Romania had a common border with both Serbia and the Austro-Hungarian Empire, and would thus facilitate communications with one while increasing the defensive concerns of the other, but this was clearly not going to happen in the near future. Sergei Sazonov, the Russian foreign minister, did his best to ease the concerns of the allies, telling the British ambassador that there was no immediate threat to Warsaw; Alfred Knox, the military attaché, thought this was overly optimistic and doubtless briefed his ambassador accordingly.[11]

On 24 June several senior figures, including the tsar, met in Baranovichi. There was general agreement that the main priority for Russia was to buy time for its armies to be rebuilt. The critical period would be the summer; come the autumn rains, campaigning would become much more difficult for the Germans. The Germans would have been disappointed to learn that the conference rapidly concluded that prolonged defence of the Polish salient was out of the question. Instead, it was agreed that Russia's armies would fall back to a line running from Riga through Kovno, Grodno, Brest-Litovsk, along the upper Bug and finally along the Dniester to the Romanian frontier. Both flanks were effectively already on this line, so they would have to hold their positions while the centre fell back. As Southwest Front's defeated forces north of Lemberg – Fourth and Third Armies, and the Olukhov group – would be unable to fall back along Ivanov's supply lines, they were transferred to Alexeyev's Northwest Front.[12] In addition, the Olukhov group would be given the designation of Thirteenth Army, under the command of the cautious Gorbatovsky, brought south from Lithuania.

There were other changes too. The Russian Fifth Army was effectively disbanded, and its troops distributed to its neighbouring formations. Alexei Evgravovich Churin, who had inherited command of the army from Plehve, was assigned to lead Twelfth Army, and Plehve himself was dispatched with his staff to the north, to take control of the troops facing the Germans near the Baltic coast. A new Fifth Army was created here, consisting of III, XIX and XXXVII Corps, with seven cavalry formations. The mission assigned to Plehve was a daunting one; he was to cover the terrain from the Niemen to the Baltic coast, specifically to eliminate any German threat towards Riga. By the time that Plehve arrived, the German efforts in the area – which had originally been intended to be no more than a demonstration to draw away Russian forces from Galicia – were dying down, but Plehve found it almost impossible to carry out the second part of the task that had been assigned to him, to drive the Germans back.[13]

A few days after the conference in Baranovichi, Grand Duke Nikolai chaired a further discussion, this time in Khelme. The parlous state of the army was discussed at length; there seemed to be a shortage of everything, from soldiers and officers to rifles, guns, ammunition, field telephone equipment and mobile kitchens, with a great deal of equipment having been degraded or simply lost during the months of fighting. In the summary that Nikolai sent to the tsar, he lamented the poor quality of the replacement drafts:

> They are no more than barely trained peasants, who on account of the shortage of rifles barely know how to shoot.[14]

Alexeyev now controlled the great bulk of Russia's forces, and met Grand Duke Nikolai in Siedlce on 5 July. It was agreed at this conference that the most critical sector of the long front line remained in front of Mackensen's forces. Reluctantly – in accordance with the earlier meeting with the tsar – approval was given for a retreat elsewhere in order to preserve the strength of the remaining armies as much as possible. Accordingly, Alexeyev began to prepare plans for a slow withdrawal from the Polish salient. As this occurred and the front line shortened, troops would be freed for service elsewhere, or to create the reserves that would be needed to stop the German advance. In the meantime though, Alexeyev once more raised the question of the danger in the north. The German presence in Courland, he maintained, was a serious threat to Russia, as German troops there might strike east to sever the lines of communication running south from Petrograd, or might even threaten the Russian capital itself. To counter this, he insisted that he would require more troops to reinforce Plehve's Fifth Army. Even when he made the request, he must have known that such additional forces simply did not exist.

It wasn't just the army that was showing signs of strain. Earlier in June, there was violent disorder in Moscow. Official communiqués attempted to blame this on hatred of the Germans, but even within Russia, this explanation lacked credibility, and for some the riots were the first sign of trouble to come:

> Personally, I attributed the disorder in Moscow to a simple explosion of popular sentiment that had been profoundly wounded and humiliated by the setbacks that we had suffered. In their own way, everyone sought a way out of the untenable situation in which they found themselves. But nobody in Russia wished for peace, nobody dared utter the odious word. However, there was an exception to the rule,

represented by a small number of revolutionary extremists who knew no limit to their efforts against a regime that they detested. Since the beginning or the war, these people had adopted a completely defeatist attitude; some of them, a few of whom formed part of the Duma, had tried in December 1914 to organise strikes in factories and had attempted to spread defeatist propaganda in the training battalions.

We knew that a representative of the Russian socialist parties, who attended a conference of socialists from the Entente nations in 1915, had revealed their viewpoint in the following terms: 'The victory of France, Britain and Belgium will bring peace and contentment to Europe, but this would involve saying that Russia too will be victorious. Can one imagine that a victorious tsarist Russia, with its regime thus strengthened, will be willing to consider reforms? Or will it increase its oppression in its own country, as well as in newly-acquired territories that were until then relatively liberal?'

... Some of the resolutions of the socialist conference in London that were directed against the internal politics of Russia were publicised in Parisian newspapers.[15]

For the moment, Ivanov survived as commander of Southwest Front, despite widespread criticism. Only a few weeks earlier, he had been lauded for the capture of Przemyśl, receiving the Order of St Vladimir (1st Class, with Swords) to add to the Order of St George (2nd Class) that he had been awarded the previous year after conquering Galicia, and this may have played a part in his retaining his office – to sack him so shortly after he received such a high honour would have been embarrassing, to say the least. There was also no obvious replacement, and his repeated insistence that his armies had failed because of a shortage of shells, heavy artillery and good quality recruits resonated with the views of many in the Russian hierarchy. Consequently, attention turned elsewhere and focussed on Vladimir Sukhomlinov, Russia's war minister.

If a single person could represent all the contradictions, strengths and weaknesses of Russia's war machine, it would be Sukhomlinov, not least because he played such a large part in creating the army that went to war in 1914. During the years preceding the outbreak of hostilities, he was involved in shaping almost every part of the Russian military system, including the byzantine arrangements that caused so many difficulties in asserting any command and control on the entire edifice. Sukhomlinov was a man about whom his contemporaries rarely had neutral opinions. Many – particularly those who prospered during his time in power – regarded him with huge enthusiasm as a man of rare genius. Others detested him with remarkable intensity, including many foreign officials who encountered him, such as Maurice Paléologue, the French ambassador:

> There is something about General Sukhomlinov that makes one uneasy. Sixty-two years of age, the slave of a rather pretty wife thirty-two years younger than himself, intelligent, clever, and cunning, obsequious towards the tsar and a friend of Rasputin, surrounded by a rabble who serve as intermediaries in his intrigues and duplicities, he is a man who has lost the habit of work and keeps all his strength for conjugal joys. With his sly look, his eyes always gleaming watchfully under the heavy folds of his eyelids, I know few men who inspire more distrust at first sight.[16]

Others, particularly those who benefited from his patronage, had a very different opinion; one such person wrote about him in 1914, after the war had begun:

> His affability, his simplicity of manner, the absolute accessibility of the Minister, coupled with a just and honest uprightness and truthfulness, are well known to the army.[17]

Before and during the first year of the war, Sukhomlinov was protected to an extent by the tsar, who continued to have faith in him despite his unpopularity with many others, including Grand Duke Nikolai. The division of the entire Russian military hierarchy into two broad camps – the supporters of Sukhomlinov and their enemies – also did a great deal to insulate him from personal criticism, but in the aftermath of the disasters in Galicia he was no longer able to deflect blame. The system that he had created, from the field army and its equipment, through its officers and doctrine, and on to the logistic mechanisms and replacement training system, had failed in almost every respect. Even at this stage, Tsar Nicholas attempted to protect his old friend, telling him on 23 June that he would retain his post; the following day, Grand Duke Nikolai persuaded him that Sukhomlinov had to go, and reluctantly the tsar agreed, writing the letter of dismissal personally.

This fall of such a powerful figure, who was a virtuoso player of the military-political machine – after all, he had created much of it – was an involved process. Sukhomlinov had plenty of enemies within the army, and they made common cause with factions within the Duma who were hostile to Sukhomlinov. Further support came from Russian industrialists, who resented the war ministry's inflexibility in terms of pricing for military contracts, and the hostility of the ministry towards private enterprise. Sukhomlinov refused to pay private firms more than a minimum amount for shell manufacture, despite the fact that these industries needed the money to invest in the infrastructure required for expansion. Instead, he preferred to build state-owned factories, which to his credit managed to perform far more efficiently than the private firms – shells for 3-inch guns appeared to cost less than half as much if manufactured in the new factories than if they were made by the private sector.[18] Indeed, there was plentiful evidence of corruption and inefficiency in the private sector, with one industrialist diverting advances that had been paid in the expectation of investment in expanded production into speculative schemes that tried to take advantage of wartime inflation in the price of everyday goods.[19] However, at a time when the war was going badly, being able to prove that many industrialists were profiteering did nothing to strengthen Sukhomlinov's position – it merely created more powerful enemies.

Some of these criticisms of private industry in the tsar's empire should be treated with caution. They are based upon documentation that was published during the Soviet era, when there was a natural tendency to highlight the achievements of state-owned industry in comparison with private industry. Such documents often fail to acknowledge that there were plenty of cases of corruption in the state-owned factories.

Sukhomlinov's standing was further weakened by the Myasoyedov Affair. The details of this affair say a great deal about the internal politics of the Russian Army and senior government officials, and therefore are worth examining in some detail. In the years before the war, Sukhomlinov kept a close eye on potential political enemies, and appointed Sergei Myasoyedov, an intelligence officer, to command a special military police unit to spy on Russian officers. The activities of this unit were denounced in the Duma by Alexander Guchkov, a powerful political opponent of the war minister, who also added allegations – quite without foundation – that Myasoyedov was passing intelligence to the Austrians. After an increasingly acrimonious series of private and personal exchanges, the men agreed to fight a duel; there does not appear to be agreement in accounts about who made the challenge. From Myasoyedov's point of view, the duel did not go as planned:

> Guchkov coolly awaited his opponent's shot and discharged his revolver into the air and walked off, without shaking hands, to show that he did not regard his opponent as worthy to take part in a combat of honour.[20]

The scandal involving a military unit dedicated to spying on fellow officers, and the allegations that he was also spying for Austria-Hungary, led to the tsar telling

Sukhomlinov to remove Myasoyedov from his post. He was immediately reassigned to other duties, though protected from any other untoward consequences of both his spying on his fellow officers and the ill-judged duel. The allegations regarding Austria-Hungary were proved false, but Myasoyedov remained tainted by the incident.

When war broke out, Myasoyedov's alleged misdemeanours were put to one side, and Sukhomlinov – who regarded his protégé as a personal friend – secured him a post as an intelligence officer in Northwest Front. The Russians made extensive use of espionage before the war, running an agent in Vienna for many years to good effect, and naturally suspected that their enemies would do the same.[21] In early 1915 a young Russian officer, Lieutenant Kolakovsky, voluntarily gave himself up to the authorities, telling them that he had been sent back to Russia from Germany after agreeing to spy for the Germans; he added that there was a high-ranking spy working for the Germans in Northwest Front. At some point during Kolakovsky's interrogation, Myasoyedov's name was suggested – by the interrogators – as the man working for Germany.

Due to his activities on behalf of Sukhomlinov, Myasoyedov had made plenty of enemies in the army, and these figures now saw an opportunity to damage Sukhomlinov via his protégé. Myasoyedov's case was presented to Grand Duke Nikolai, himself a leading member of the anti-Sukhomlinov camp, and an investigation started. Copious documentation was gathered, and Myasoyedov was arrested, charged, and swiftly executed. Due to his association with Myasoyedov, Sukhomlinov's standing with the tsar was fatally weakened by the affair, and when the war minister's enemies called for his dismissal in late June, Sukhomlinov found that he was defenceless. His replacement was General Alexei Polivanov, a long-time political opponent.

The alacrity with which Sukhomlinov's opponents – who included Alexeyev, the commander of Northwest Front, in their number – moved against Myasoyedov is itself remarkable, and could be construed as a desire to eliminate him before contradictory evidence could be gathered. Despite the voluminous evidence gathered against Myasoyedov, there was no damning testimony against him. Some of the evidence presented at his trial – two soldiers were produced by Mikhail Bonch-Bruyevich, who had risen to become chief of staff of the Northern Front, to state that they had driven Myasoyedov to a farm where they saw him hand secret documents to a German agent – was later shown to be entirely fabricated, and many of those involved in his arrest later admitted freely that the entire affair had been little more than judicial murder.[22] Ironically, many documents bearing Bonch-Bruyevich's name found their way into the hands of

Lenin, in exile in Switzerland at the time; these documents probably reached Lenin via German intelligence channels, suggesting that Bonch-Bruyevich or someone close to him was spying for the Germans.

Sukhomlinov's impact on the Russian Army was huge. On the one hand, he challenged many of the long-established centres of power and influence in the army, campaigning with mixed results for a dilution in spending on fortresses in favour of expanding the size and power of the field army; on the other hand, he was without question extensively engaged in power politics within the Russian government and army, and this created tensions and pressures that greatly hampered the ability of the army to fight effectively. Perhaps the most balanced judgement is that he created the army with which Russia went to war in 1914, in all its contrasts of strengths and weaknesses.

Sukhomlinov's misfortunes did not stop with his sacking. His enemies continued to seek evidence against him; a witness was produced who testified that an Austrian, Alexander Altschüller, was a leading Austro-Hungarian spy and that Sukhomlinov was working closely with him, deliberately passing him secret documents. Even the most cursory examination of the allegations would have thrown up discrepancies – the witness claimed to have seen Altschüller creeping into Sukhomlinov's office and rummaging through his documents, which is hardly likely if he and Sukhomlinov had been working together.[23] Further allegations of spying followed, including against Vasili Doumbadze, to whom Sukhomlinov had given details of Russia's pre-war military reforms in order to help Doumbadze with the task of writing a biography of Sukhomlinov. In March 1916, Sukhomlinov himself was arrested and charged with treason and abuse of power; whilst the latter was certainly true, he had probably done little worse than many other figures in the Russian government, and there was little hard evidence regarding his alleged treason. Nevertheless, he was imprisoned for six months before being allowed home on house arrest, and was then re-arrested in February 1917. On this occasion, his case proceeded to court, where the prosecution evidence of treason disintegrated in the cold light of day. By the end of the trial, the behaviour of the prosecutors was so widely ridiculed in the Russian press that there was considerable public sympathy for Sukhomlinov; nevertheless, although the court acquitted him of all charges of treason, he was found guilty of abuse of power, and sentenced to penal servitude for his part in the army's lack of preparation in 1914. In May 1918, he was released when he turned 70 and left Russia, travelling first to Finland and then to Germany, where he lived in poverty. In 1926, he was found on a park bench in the Tiergarten in Berlin; he had frozen to death overnight.

Sukhomlinov was not the only target of those who sought high-ranking scapegoats for Russia's misfortunes. When he was appointed supreme commander, Grand Duke Nikolai was hailed as the obvious and only choice, but his performance had been decidedly mediocre. Partly because of the constraints built into the Russian command system by Sukhomlinov and partly as a consequence of his own personality, Nikolai struggled in vain to impose his will upon the two front commanders, oscillating between supporting the ambitions first of one, then of the other. By the summer of 1915, there were many within the Russian government who felt that he should be replaced. The tsar himself became increasingly disenchanted with the performance of his cousin but for the moment the grand duke remained in post; like Ivanov, he had been awarded a prestigious decoration (the Order of St George, 2nd Class) after the fall of Przemyśl, and it would have been too much of a contradiction for him to have been sacked immediately after. Polivanov, the new minister for war, was a close personal ally of the grand duke as would be expected from someone prominent in the anti-Sukhomlinov groups, and campaigned tirelessly for his retention. In doing so, he earned the enmity of the wife of the tsar, Alexandra Feodorovna, who at this stage was urging the tsar to take personal control of the army. The tsarina's close links with Rasputin, a friend of Sukhomlinov, further increased her antipathy towards the new war minister.

There were other changes, too. The ultra-conservative prime minister, Nikolai Longinovich Goremykin, had been brought out of retirement in 1914. His hostility to the opinions of both the Duma and the public, combined with his apparent inability to coordinate government in any meaningful way, resulted in his position coming under increasing scrutiny but for the moment his fawning attitude towards the tsar allowed him to survive. However, the equally autocratic minister of the interior, Nikolai Alexeyevich Maklakov, was removed from his post.

Back in the war zone that stretched from the Baltic to the Romanian border, the first steps for the Germans were to rebuild their supplies, and to secure the flanks of Mackensen's army. The railway line running across Galicia was steadily restored to use as the front line advanced, and would reach Lemberg in mid-July, but thereafter the advancing troops would be dependent on lines of far lower capacity. In particular, the single-track line running north from Lemberg to Kovel would be critical, as this was broadly the axis along which Mackensen would be advancing. Until the railway reached the old frontier where it crossed the Bug near Sokal, it was still constructed on the standard central European gauge; thereafter, there would be additional problems, as the railwaymen would need to re-pin the rails as the front line moved north. As supplies began to arrive, Mackensen tentatively set the start date for the resumption of the advance as 26 June.

Protection of Mackensen's eastern flank would require the combined forces of Linsingen's South Army, with the Austro-Hungarian Second and Seventh Armies on its flanks, to push forward to eliminate any possibility, however remote, of the Russians threatening a decisive counterattack from the Tarnopol area. The German *Beskidenkorps* had been detached from the Austro-Hungarian Second Army and was now assigned to Mackensen's Eleventh Army as its most eastern formation, but despite losing these forces and the terrible losses of the winter, Böhm-Ermolli was aware that Brusilov's Eighth Army, too, was in poor shape. On 23 June the Austro-Hungarian forces attacked in strength. Resistance was variable, but by the end of the day, the Russian bulge in the centre of the sector had been effectively eliminated.

A little to the east, Linsingen's South Army had received reinforcements in the shape of Generalleutnant Robert Kosch's X Reserve Corps, consisting of 101st and 105th Infantry Divisions, which had been formed from regiments released by the process of reducing the size of existing divisions. These new formations had been forming up on the Serbian border and there was a delay while they were carried by train to the Dniester front; originally, they were intended to be present in full strength by 20 June, but three days later, when Linsingen ordered his men to press forward across the Dniester, perhaps two thirds had arrived. The attack was made with *Korps Bothmer* on the left, X and XXIV Reserve Corps in the centre, and *Korps Hofmann* on the right, along a broad front from Zurawno to Halicz. In conjunction with Böhm-Ermolli's Second Army, the South Army moved forward across the river on 23 June, rapidly running into strong Russian defences.

The German 1st Infantry Division found itself forcing a crossing of the Dniester close to Zurawno, at almost exactly the same point that it had attempted to cross a few weeks earlier. Dominik Richert's description of the second attempt gives a graphic picture of the assault, as well as highlighting the critical role played by the German artillery:

> Our engineers had built two footbridges across the river ... The crossing started at midnight. Our first battalion went first then we were the next. In order not to overload the swaying bridge we had to leave a gap of four paces between one man and the next. It started to rain too, and it got so dark that it was difficult to see the silhouette of the man in front. With each step that you took you had to check your feet to make sure that you did not miss the footbridge and plunge into the

water. In the middle, the bridge sank down under our weight, causing the water to run into the top of our boots.

... The Russians, who were occupying exactly the same places on the rocky hill as at the time of the first crossing, fired in the direction of the river all night, but almost all their bullets went over our heads. When the whole regiment had crossed, we were quietly given the command to advance slowly, and to dig ourselves in if we came under fire. As the meadow between the river and the Russian position was only 200m wide, the Russians soon noticed us and fired a few shots off. I immediately threw myself to the ground, in order to dig myself in with my spade ... I felt around with my hands and discovered that I was in a foxhole which had probably been made during the first crossing ...

When the Russian artillery started to fire [after dawn] it became less comfortable. Three men from Lorraine had dug themselves in to the embankment of the road quite close to us. A shell landed in their hole and flung their mutilated bodies out onto the grass. It was a gruesome sight. Our artillery remained silent until, at about 8 o'clock in the morning, we heard the crash of a gun. This heralded the bombardment that was going to soften up the Russian position in preparation for the attack. Suddenly a terrible din tore through the air as all the German batteries of different calibres hurled their shells at the Russian position. There was a crashing and a roaring and the earth shook. Lying there on the ground we were able to feel the impact of the heavy shells quite clearly. How they wooshed and roared over us! ... I lifted my head a little to watch the fearful spectacle. The whole of the rocky hill looked like a mountain breathing fire: shells were landing everywhere, throwing bushes, earth and lumps of rock all around ... Everywhere you could see the heads of our infantrymen sticking up out of their holes to watch the terrible sight. Some of them stood upright, offering the Russian infantrymen a good target, but the Russians were probably all lying in terror at the foot of their trenches, as they could not defend themselves while this hail of iron continued to drum down on them. After about half an hour there was movement in the front Russian trench, which followed the bottom of the hill. Making their way between the exploding shells all the occupants of the trench who were capable of marching came over to us with their hands in the air. They were almost all as pale as death from fear and were shaking violently as a result of the terror they had survived. They were made to lie down on the meadow behind us to give them better cover from the Russian shells, which still flew over from time to time. The troops occupying the top Russian trench saved themselves by fleeing. This meant that only the middle trench, which was on the slope, was still occupied.

We were given the order: 'Get ready! Fix bayonets!' ... The German artillery moved its fire further forward. The command rang out: 'For attack, forwards. March! March!' We all shot out of our holes and, yelling 'hurrah', stormed off in the direction of the Russian trenches. But our artillery had already done most of the work; we only encountered minimal resistance. In the bottom trench there were only dead and wounded. A few shots came out of the middle trench and one of the bullets smashed our first lieutenant's knee ... We climbed up the steep slope. Some of the Russians from the middle trench wanted to flee and climbed upwards as fast as they could, but they were shot down like rabbits and rolled back down into the trench.[24]

Six days of bloody fighting followed as the Russians were driven back to the line of the Gniła Lipa. This was the terrain where the Austro-Hungarian successes of the early weeks of the war had been brutally reversed in September 1914; on this occasion, there was no prospect of such a setback. Nevertheless, moving forward through difficult terrain, Second Army struggled to achieve its objectives, potentially leaving the eastern flank of Eleventh Army vulnerable. Its efforts depleted many of its formations severely; 27th Infantry Division, part of IV Corps and closest to Mackensen's army, was left with only 4,000 men, and 40th *Honvéd* Infantry Division could only scrape together 2,600. Persistent Russian counterattacks against the northern part of Böhm-Ermolli's army and the shortage of supplies added to the problems faced by field commanders, who asked repeatedly and in vain for their formations to be pulled out of the front line for a few days in which they might be able to absorb fresh drafts into their ranks in a more organised manner. The centre and right flank of Second Army fared somewhat better, driving back the Russians in damaging battles east and south of Lemberg. But the fighting had been costly for both sides, and the Russian forces were now too depleted to put up prolonged resistance. By the end of the first week of July, the front line had moved east to the valley of the Złota Lipa.

With François' former command, XLI Reserve Corps, preparing for departure to the west, the eastern flank of the German Eleventh Army was formed by the *Beskidenkorps*, and it was anticipated that as Mackensen advanced towards the north, it would be increasingly stretched to cover the east along the valley of the Bug. It was therefore important for the Austro-Hungarian Second Army to continue to advance, and Seeckt made a request to this effect to *AOK*; his proposal was a repeat of what he had suggested before, for Fourth Army, Eleventh Army and Second Army to continue to operate in a coordinated assault on the Russian line. The response wasn't encouraging; Conrad professed concern about the Russian forces in eastern Galicia, and doubted that Böhm-Ermolli would be able to widen his front without major risk. In any event, he wished for Second Army to drive the diverging Russians east, while the Germans and Archduke Joseph Ferdinand's Fourth Army continued to advance north. After further discussions, agreement was reached on 28 June at a meeting in Pless. As the front line shortened in central Poland, the Austro-Hungarian First Army was to be withdrawn from its positions south of Woyrsch's troops and reinserted into the front line between the German Eleventh Army and Böhm-Ermolli's army. In the meantime, the *Beskidenkorps* would have to suffice. Paul Puhallo received orders on 28 June to push forward with his First Army towards Tarłów and the Vistula, but at the same time to prepare for the imminent departure of his troops. The following day, I Corps reached the Vistula at Zawichost. The Russian XXV Corps withdrew to a bridgehead around Józefów, and finally pulled back to the right bank of the Vistula on 2 July, leaving Józefów in the hands of II Corps. The remaining Austro-Hungarian troops boarded trains for Galicia, satisfied to be able to report that the entire left bank of the Vistula south of the mouth of the Kamienka was in their hands.

On the Austro-Hungarian Fourth Army's front, the Russians retreated to a line that followed the lower San to the Vistula. Throughout central Poland, a slow withdrawal began, and Mackensen was relieved when his troops started moving forward on 26 June – the longer the delay, the greater the opportunity for the Russians to pull back in good order. At first, the right flank was held back to ensure contact was maintained with Böhm-Ermolli's troops, and after initial resistance in front of *Korps Emmich* to the west, Eleventh Army began to move forward. The formations in the centre of Mackensen's line met little resistance, but whatever reserves were available had to be fed into the right flank, which slowly began to take on an increasingly extended appearance. In the last days of June, the Germans reached and crossed the old frontier between Austro-Hungarian Galicia and Russian Poland, but there were also several major Russian counterattacks, particularly against the long eastern flank. None of these made any major impression on the German advance, but responding to a request from Eleventh Army, Falkenhayn authorised elements of François' former command, XLI Reserve Corps, to postpone their departure for the west and to resume duties on the eastern flank.

Both sides continued to reorganise their troops. The Russians had not contested the German advance largely because they were content to fall back to a shorter line near the River Wieprz, where they hoped to be able to stop the Germans while the troops in central Poland pulled back across the Vistula. The growing concern for Mackensen's eastern flank resulted in the creation of a new

Army of the Bug, consisting of the *Beskidenkorps* and Friedrich von Gerok's XXIV Reserve Corps, with the German 107th Infantry Division and the 11th Bavarian Infantry Division. Linsingen and Stolzmann, the chief of staff of the South Army, were appointed to command the new Bug Army. Given the poor relationship between the officers of the Austro-Hungarian Seventh Army and the two Prussians, this was welcome news for Pflanzer-Baltin and his staff:

> The supreme commander of the army, Archduke Frederick, visited us at the beginning of July ... [he] brought us the pleasant news that Linsingen and Stolzmann were to be replaced by General Freiherr von Bothmer and Oberst Hemmer. In an instant, the relationship with the German South Army took on a character of friendly cooperation, something that was urgently needed.[25]

Bothmer and Hemmer, his chief of staff, were Bavarians, and Pflanzer-Baltin and Zeynek clearly found them far more agreeable colleagues than their cold, austere predecessors.

These changes triggered a further series of messages between Conrad and Falkenhayn. The former made no secret of his resentment of the subordination of Austro-Hungary to German authority, and took these changes as an opportunity to try to assert some influence and control. He questioned the assignment of Linsingen, perhaps feeling that he should have been consulted in advance, and stated that the Austro-Hungarian troops serving with Mackensen's Eleventh Army – VI Corps and the Hungarian 11th Cavalry Division – should not be assigned to the new Bug Army. In response to Falkenhayn's suggestion – in reality, more of an instruction – that Mackensen should have overall command of the Austro-Hungarian First and Fourth Armies in addition to Eleventh Army and the Bug Army, Conrad objected to the addition of First Army, and proposed that the South Army should be subordinated to Pflanzer-Baltin, commander of the Austro-Hungarian Seventh Army.

If Conrad had any doubts about the growing imbalance in the alliance with Germany, it was dispelled by Falkenhayn's blunt response. The chief of the German general staff told his Austro-Hungarian counterpart that the assignment of commanders to German armies was not a subject in which Conrad had any say. The Hungarian 11th Cavalry Division and Arz's VI Corps had already been assigned to German control as part of Mackensen's Eleventh Army, and if it was felt appropriate to reassign them to another formation under Mackensen's control, this would be done without seeking further assent from *AOK*. Nor did Falkenhayn accept the suggestion that the Austro-Hungarian First Army should

The Second Battle of Kraśnik, July 1915

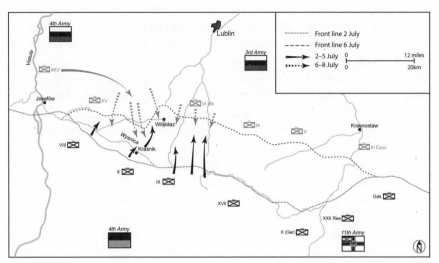

not be under Mackensen's command; and the proposal that the South Army should be subordinated to Pflanzer-Baltin was dismissed out of hand.[26]

In vain, Conrad attempted to raise the matter with Archduke Frederick, the nominal commander of the *k.u.k.* Army. The only crumb of comfort that he received was that VI Corps and 11th Cavalry Division would not be assigned to the Bug Army; in every other respect, Falkenhayn's wishes prevailed. Even if Frederick and other officials sympathised and agreed with Conrad, they were more willing to accept the reality that the Austro-Hungarian Empire was unquestionably the junior partner in the alliance.

From the German perspective, this relationship was based upon the relative performance of the two armies in the field, and this viewpoint was strongly reinforced by the events of the next few days. Archduke Joseph Ferdinand's Fourth Army, operating between Mackensen's left flank and the Vistula, estimated that it faced no more than five to eight battered infantry divisions and two cavalry divisions, and attempted to push forward on 1 July to the high ground north of Jósefów, where the Russians were withdrawing from the left bank of the Vistula. From there, it would be able to advance towards Lublin. Almost immediately, the advance stalled along the line of the relatively small River Wyznica. Some troops from X Corps who had penetrated into Kraśnik were forced to withdraw late in the day. To the east of the town, the Austro-Hungarian troops made better progress, and the following day, Joseph Ferdinand ordered a resumption of attacks, believing that he was facing only modest rearguards. Feldmarschallleutnant Roth, gathering together XIV and IX Corps, was to break through the Russian lines east of Kraśnik as soon as possible. It was rapidly becoming obvious that the determined Russian resistance was much more than a rearguard action, but Roth organised his men into two assault groups for what he hoped would be the decisive breakthrough. The attack began on 3 July, and after a day of hard fighting, Roth's two corps had managed to advance on a broad front of about 9 miles (14km). Over the following day, the advance continued, albeit slowly, accumulating a haul of over 8,000 prisoners. The Russians had suffered substantially, and Alexeyev reported to *Stavka* that X Corps, facing the left flank of Mackensen's Eleventh Army, was reduced to only 4,000 men, with few officers.[27] Nevertheless, the withdrawal from central Poland released troops that could be sent to the threatened sector, and XXV Corps, II and VI Siberian Corps began to assemble behind the shaking front line. The western sector of the area through which Joseph Ferdinand was attempting to advance now passed to the control of Evert's Fourth Army.

On 5 July, the first Russian reinforcements launched a powerful counterattack against the Austro-Hungarian X Corps with 3rd Grenadier Division from XXV Corps, supported by the Ural Cossack Division. The initial Russian attack made good headway, but by the end of the day, Joseph Ferdinand had restored the line by deploying his reserves. Heavy fighting continued the following day as Joseph Ferdinand urged his men to achieve a decisive breakthrough, but although they managed to gain some ground, it was at a considerable price, and the Russian lines remained unbroken. Almost all of the Austro-Hungarian Fourth Army's troops were now deployed in the front line; only two brigades remained as reserves, and Joseph Ferdinand reluctantly ordered a cessation of attacks for two days while supplies – particularly of artillery ammunition – were brought forward.

Unfortunately for Joseph Ferdinand, the Russians had no intention of allowing his men a two-day rest. Alexeyev's reinforcements had been arriving in large numbers, and with the full resources of XXV and VI Siberian Corps available, Evert and Lesh ordered their armies to launch counterattacks against the Austro-Hungarian forces that were attempting to advance on Lublin. Preliminary attacks began before dawn on 7 July between Wilkołaz and Kraśnik against the tip of the Austro-Hungarian advance, where 106th *Landsturm* Infantry Division put up determined resistance for several hours before being forced back. Further to the west, 24th Infantry Division also retreated under pressure from the Russian 3rd Grenadier Division, with the result that the two divisions in the front line between these Russian attacks now found their flanks exposed. In these circumstances, Feldmarschallleutnant Hugo Martiny, who had replaced the ailing Krautwald as commander of X Corps, had no alternative but to order the two exposed divisions to retreat. Although 21st Rifle Division in particular suffered substantial casualties attempting to pull back while still in contact with the Russians, the line appeared to stabilise during the afternoon after a withdrawal of perhaps a mile; Roth dispatched his modest reserves to reinforce the positions of 106th *Landsturm* Infantry Division.

Even this setback would have been bad enough, with the ground that had been gained at such cost being lost again, but the Russians weren't finished for the day. XXV Corps launched renewed assaults on the Austro-Hungarian X Corps late in the day, driving in the left flank of 24th Infantry Division. Joseph Ferdinand reacted by ordering VIII Corps, to the west of X Corps, to assign its reserves to Roth so that the retreat of X Corps could be checked, but the initiative remained firmly with the Russians. The most westerly formation of X Corps, 37th *Honvéd* Infantry Division, was the next unit to feel the full weight of the Russian assault and was driven back in disarray. The seam between X and VIII Corps remained fragile.

Martiny reported to Joseph Ferdinand that he doubted his troops' ability to hold back further Russian attacks. They had been worn down by their own costly assaults towards the north, and the lack of reserves, combined with the ongoing shortage of artillery ammunition, greatly reduced their capacity to resist. Other commanders reported similarly, and Joseph Ferdinand anxiously asked Mackensen if he was able to offer any help, either by drawing Russian forces away with an attack of his own, or by providing reinforcements for the Austro-Hungarian Fourth Army. Conrad remained untroubled, merely suggesting to *OHL* that the German 103rd Infantry Division might be transferred from the Serbian front and assigned to Joseph Ferdinand. Yet again, the *k.u.k.* Army had to ask its stronger and more capable ally to come to its aid.

On 8 July, The Russians resumed their assaults. Vasiliev's VI Siberian Corps surged forward against 106th *Landsturm* Infantry Division and 8th Infantry Division, and although the advance seemed to be checked in the morning, there was a further incident that raised questions of the loyalty of some elements of the *k.u.k.* Army; the Czech 21st Infantry Regiment appeared to put up little resistance, resulting in 8th Infantry Division retreating from its positions. A counterattack in the afternoon ran into a further Russian advance, and fighting continued long into the night. The following day saw further determined Russian attacks, but even though the Austro-Hungarian line was perilously stretched, it managed to hold. However, its formations were at the end of their strength; the Russians later estimated the Austro-Hungarian dead and wounded as in excess of 20,000, though inevitably these figures were subject to inflation.[28] Several days of intense combat had exhausted their supplies, but *AOK* continued to urge Fourth Army to hold its positions at all costs:

> We need a whole week until everything is ready to the east of [Fourth] Army for a resumption of an advance by all forces; until then, the line must be held. Unless everyone from the highest command downwards works incessantly day and night, this cannot be achieved. Landgraf, be strong![29]

Reluctantly, Mackensen transferred his reserves to his left flank in order to be ready to support Joseph Ferdinand's faltering line, aware that the weakness of the Austro-Hungarian forces was compromising his own ability to attack. However, the crisis had passed; although the Russians attacked again on 10 July, they were beaten off, and the arithmetic of warfare in 1915 began to work against them, much as it had against the Austro-Hungarian Fourth Army. Short of artillery ammunition and after suffering substantial casualties in their attacks, the Russians were unable to sustain their efforts. For Conrad, this came as welcome relief, but the Germans chose to interpret the events of what became known as the Second Battle of Kraśnik – the first battle had been fought in this area the previous August – as a further sign that as soon as it came under pressure, the *k.u.k.* Army would need German forces to be made available to restore the situation. Although on this occasion the German contribution was modest – a few battalions from Woyrsch, and the precautionary deployment of Mackensen's reserves – the battle reinforced belief in all three armies on the Eastern Front that the Austro-Hungarian forces were the weakest in the sector, and would struggle without their German allies. And of course it was no coincidence that Alexeyev chose to throw his counterattack against Joseph Ferdinand's army, rather than Mackensen's. In an attempt to make good the losses suffered in the fighting, *AOK* assigned the Austro-Hungarian II Corps, formerly part of First Army, as reinforcements to Fourth Army.

Despite the alarm that the Russian attack caused in Fourth Army headquarters, its purpose was purely to stop the offensive towards the north. The losses suffered in Galicia meant that, while discussions continued about how far the Russian armies in Poland should retreat, the retreat itself was now almost universally accepted as inevitable. Arguments now focussed on the fate of the great fortresses that had been built in the 19th century to defend Poland, and as was almost always the case, political and factional issues both played their parts. In the first decade of the century, Sukhomlinov had proposed the abandonment of the fortresses at Ivangorod and Novogeorgievsk, on the grounds that they would be hugely expensive to modernise and were of little benefit to field armies, but he had been overruled by the artillerists and other fortress enthusiasts in the army. Amongst those who had argued against Sukhomlinov were Grand Duke Nikolai and his inner circle; now, with Sukhomlinov in disgrace, it was difficult for the army to adopt a policy that the discredited former war minister had championed. Although fortresses had generally proved to be negative assets – Liège and others in the west, and Przemyśl in the east had failed to have any positive impact on operations – the fortresses at Ivangorod and Osowiec had resisted German attacks, and many within the Russian Army simply refused to accept that all fortresses should be abandoned without a fight. An additional argument in support of the fortress enthusiasts was that there simply weren't enough trains available to remove all the artillery and other equipment, particularly precious artillery ammunition, that was stored in the fortresses. If the fortresses were abandoned, some 11,000 guns of assorted calibres and ages, together with millions of rounds of ammunition, would be lost. In the end, no clear decision was made. Instructions were sent to the fortress commanders that they should prepare for evacuation, but at the same time they were advised that there was no hurry.[30] Grand Duke Nikolai would have defended this approach as being flexible; in reality, it was a further example of indecision at the highest level.

Alexeyev interpreted his instructions with a degree of flexibility. Ivangorod would cease to have any value once the Russian Army had retreated east of the Vistula, and it was therefore only to be held until the withdrawal across the river was complete. For the moment though, Novogeorgievsk was to be held, even if encircled. Initially, Alexeyev assigned this task to Dmitri Vasiliyevich Balanin's XXVII Corps, but later changed his mind. Instead, the garrison would be formed from 58th, 63rd, 113th and 114th Infantry Divisions; the last two were in reality merely groupings of territorial forces, and in no way approximated to the fighting power of a regular division.[31]

Wider political issues also influenced the reluctance to implement the agreement to abandon Poland. The British and French continued to launch attacks in Gallipoli, and those within the Russian establishment who remained wedded to an eventual Russian occupation of Constantinople were concerned that further retreats would weaken their bargaining position with their Entente partners. Similarly, the Italians might break through on the Isonzo, and Russia would have less of a say in the carving up of the Austro-Hungarian Empire. And finally, there remained the issue of the neutral Balkan states. The Russians were aware that Germany was actively wooing Bulgaria, and further German successes in Poland were certain to aid the German cause. Similarly, Romania remained reluctant to throw its weight behind the Entente, and the abandonment of Poland would only increase this reluctance.

The Posen conference at the beginning of the month had set the date for *Ober Ost* to attack from the north on 13 July, and Mackensen intended to resume his own advance two days later; his objective would be the Russian railway line running from the east to Lublin and on to Ivangorod. An early priority was the capture of Władimir Wołynsk, in front of Mackensen's right flank. This town represented a vital railhead for the Russians, and its capture would seriously compromise the ability of the Russians to sustain their defences. Falkenhayn and Conrad disagreed strongly about the forces required to capture the town; Conrad felt that three divisions would suffice, while Falkenhayn regarded this as completely inadequate. Ultimately, there was a compromise; additional troops were allocated, though the overall force fell short of Falkenhayn's wishes.[32] As attention turned back to the battlefield, and the commanders on both sides awaited the resumption of major operations, they must have done so with very different emotions. The Russians could only face the future with concern at best, dread at worst. The Austro-Hungarian leadership continued to believe in achievements that were far beyond the power of their army, and resented greatly the increasingly undisguised superiority of the Germans. The kaiser's generals were the ones with the highest expectations. Those at *Ober Ost* could hope that they would finally play a part in the decisive events of the year, while in *OHL* and Mackensen's armies they looked forward to another series of short, decisive drives. Falkenhayn himself probably had the best reasons for confidence: the Russians had suffered huge losses, and he would soon be able to turn his attention to the west.

CHAPTER 9

THE GREAT RETREAT

All units laboured to bring forward supplies, particularly of artillery ammunition, in preparation for the next great assault. On 13 July, *Ober Ost* attacked as planned, and Gallwitz's Twelfth Army launched its attack on Litvinov's First Army. It was almost impossible in the First World War to assemble men and supplies undetected – Gallwitz's gunners had stockpiled some 400,000 rounds in preparation – but it seems that Litvinov's men were taken by surprise. Immediately, the Russian general ordered his men to hold their positions at all costs; this lack of flexibility doomed thousands to perish under artillery fire, and within two days the Germans had pushed forward 9 miles (14km) and captured 7,000 prisoners. Hindenburg and Ludendorff spent the opening days of the battle in Gallwitz's headquarters, noting with approval the mood of both the officers and the troops of the army. In two days, Twelfth Army and the neighbouring Eighth Army fought their way through the entire depth of the Russian defences. They reached the Narew two days later, and forced the Russian First and Twelfth Armies to retreat along diverging axes. But just as had been the case in the May fighting in western Galicia, the Germans now had to pause while supplies were brought forward. Whatever the senior generals might have wished, it was simply not possible in 1915 to manoeuvre large bodies of men sufficiently quickly to exploit such opportunities.

Far to the southeast, the Austro-Hungarian Seventh Army and the German South Army began operations on 13 July, with the main effort – made by the Austro-Hungarian III Corps – commencing the following day. Despite Russian counterattacks and determined resistance, Pflanzer-Baltin's chief of staff, Zeynek, felt able to advise *AOK* on 16 July that the bulk of the serious fighting was complete, and there was every prospect of further successes.[1] But if III Corps seemed poised for further successes, the attempts by the left flank of Seventh Army to advance merely triggered powerful counterattacks by the Russian XXXIII Corps, forcing *Gruppe Begnini* onto the defensive. The battlefield slowly calmed again, and very little had changed, other than further heavy losses for both sides.

The contrast between this attack – indeed, so many attacks in this part of the Eastern Front – and Mackensen's repeated advances is striking. The decisive difference seems to have been in the use of artillery. The Austro-Hungarian commanders lacked sufficient heavy firepower to dislodge the Russian defences in front of their men. As a result, when they advanced, the troops of the *k.u.k.* Army expended most of their energy battering through the initial defences, after which they were at the mercy of Russian counterattacks. By contrast, the Germans had perfected the art of demolishing the initial Russian defensive line with concentrated heavy shellfire. It is a further demonstration of the adherence to outdated tactics that cost such heavy losses on every front throughout the First World War.

The combined forces of Mackensen's army group consisted of a little over forty-one infantry divisions – most of which were significantly below establishment strength – and five cavalry divisions. They were opposed by thirty-three Russian infantry divisions and a little over six cavalry divisions; again, most had been badly weakened in the preceding weeks. Even assembling this force had involved taking risks for the Russians; their line facing Woyrsch in Poland had been thinned dangerously and barely mustered five infantry divisions and a few cavalry. Mackensen's attack began with preliminary operations on his eastern flank. The Austro-Hungarian First Army, consisting of the German XLI Reserve Corps and the Austro-Hungarian *Gruppe Szurmay* and I and II Corps, was to seize the town of Sokal and secure a substantial bridgehead to the east. Linsingen's Bug Army, with the *Beskidenkorps* and XXIV Reserve Corps, was a little further west, and would attack towards Khelme. The main effort of Mackensen's thrust lay further west, but these advances in the east would protect his flank against Russian counterattacks.

The Austro-Hungarian I and II Corps were tasked with capturing Sokal, while the rest of Puhallo's First Army advanced towards the north. The defenders of Sokal were the troops of Alexei Maximovich Kaledin's XII Corps, part of Eighth Army. The attack would involve crossing the Bug, which was swollen by a summer rainstorm immediately before the attack, and the only gain from the first assault on 14 July was a modest bridgehead. Early on 16 July, two Austro-Hungarian battalions fought their way across the Bug, establishing a further

The Eastern Front, July 1915

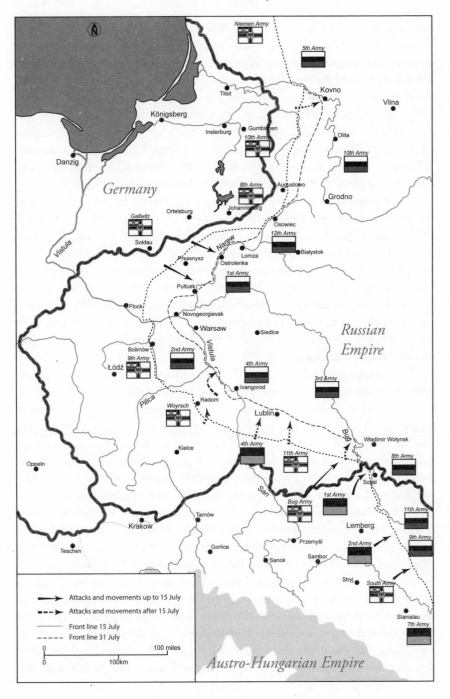

foothold, but the combination of the high water level in the river and the fact that the east bank was steep and overlooked the west bank made the prospects of success for I and II Corps remote. Nevertheless, on 18 July the two corps attacked Sokal directly from the west. The Russians had established three lines of defence, but these were overcome in a determined attack, and by the afternoon Puhallo's troops had secured the town and the high ground to the southeast. Despite its slow start, the Austro-Hungarian First Army had achieved its objective and thus anchored Mackensen's eastern flank. The next stage was to push on towards Władimir Wołynsk, and First Army's three cavalry divisions, under the collective command of General Hans von Heydebreck, began to cross the river.

Linsingen's Bug Army found itself facing tough Russian defences. For perhaps the first time in the war, Russian aircraft performed effectively, spotting German artillery batteries and reporting their location to Russian gunners, who were able to put down accurate counter-battery fire. By contrast, the German aviators struggled, encountering anti-aircraft fire that accounted for several planes.[2] Linsingen expressed doubts that he would be able to penetrate the Russian lines, but Mackensen refused to send him any reinforcements. Despite its slow start, though, the Bug Army succeeded in overrunning the first line of Russian defences on 15 July, and after a further four days of tough fighting, the Russians were in retreat across the entire front.[3]

The main assault by the German Eleventh Army faced two lines of Russian positions, built behind the streams of the Rivers Wolica and Wokslawka. There were two attack groups, the stronger to the west, with most of Plettenberg's Guards, XXII Reserve Corps, and 20th Infantry Division, and a smaller group to the east, with the Austro-Hungarian VI Corps, which was to cooperate with the neighbouring Bug Army. Despite all their preparations, the Russians could do little to hinder the effect of Mackensen's artillery, and the first assault on 16 July overwhelmed the first line of Russian defences. About 6,000 prisoners were taken, but the overall Russian front line remained intact. The following day, repeated attacks secured much of the Russian second line, but the defenders had bought sufficient time to construct an improvised line further back, thus denying Mackensen his breakthrough. Nevertheless, as had been the case in earlier assaults by Eleventh Army, the Germans remained confident that they were making progress; their previous experiences suggested that once the Russians were driven from their prepared positions, their ability to resist would be greatly diminished. In particular, the capture of the town of Krasnostaw by Plettenberg's Guards late on 17 July was a critical success, as it effectively outflanked the Russian forces that were holding up the eastern half of Eleventh Army. For 18 July, Eleventh

Army's eastern flank would be strengthened by the deployment of reserves, so that the line of the Wolica could be forced.

Alexeyev also deployed his reserves, releasing II Siberian Corps and the Guards Corps to Third Army. Bitter fighting raged across the entire battlefield as the German and Austro-Hungarian units continued to grind their way north; by the end of 18 July, they had advanced a total of a little over 7 miles (12km) on a front of about 19 miles (32km), and had taken some 15,000 prisoners as well as inflicting major losses on the Russians; their own losses, though, were substantial.[4] Similarly, the Austro-Hungarian Fourth Army suffered heavy losses as it attempted to pick its way through the Russian defences to the west of Eleventh Army. Already weakened by the losses suffered in the Russian counterattacks of early July, Joseph Ferdinand's troops made minimal progress, except on the flanks of the army. Inevitably, Falkenhayn interpreted this as another failure by his allies, and dispatched Generalmajor Gerhard Tappen, the head of the operations bureau at *OHL*, to Teschen in an attempt to extract better performance from the *k.u.k.* Army.[5]

With progress relatively slow, both in Mackensen's command and in *Ober Ost*, it was important for the German 'army detachment' between the two attacking groups, under the command of Woyrsch, to try to pin the Russian troops that they faced in order to prevent them from retreating. By the end of the first week of July, the Russian line facing Woyrsch's forces ran from southwest of Radom towards the southeast until it reached the Vistula. Although he had been obliged to transfer substantial forces to other commands, Woyrsch still had substantial numbers of troops at his disposal; the northwest part of his line was formed by the Austro-Hungarian XII Corps, the centre by 4th *Landwehr* Division, and the southeast segment by 3rd *Landwehr* Division and Bredow's eponymous division. Woyrsch was aware that the Russian troops facing him had been reduced in strength as troops were diverted elsewhere, and decided to try to break through the Russian lines rather than simply trying to pin them down. Reconnaissance suggested that the most promising point for such a breakthrough was northeast of Sienno, and he concentrated both *Landwehr* divisions and a brigade from Bredow's division in this area, a total of twenty-six battalions. This was achieved by taking considerable risks elsewhere; the only regiment of *Landwehr* not committed to the assault was left to hold a segment of front that extended about 15 miles (24km). The assembly of the German troops was restricted to night movements, in order to evade detection. After a heavy artillery bombardment – extended along much of Woyrsch's front, in order to try to hide the point of main effort – three German columns moved forward at dawn on 17 July. They found that the Russian barbed wire entanglements were still intact, and a further bombardment was ordered, but the leading infantry decided to press on, firing flares to alert the gunners to shift their fire onto deeper positions. Despite heavy losses, the *Landwehr* exploited a 20-metre breach in the barbed wire to penetrate into the Russian positions. They took 2,000 prisoners and put the rest – largely made up of elements of the Grenadier Corps – to flight; many of the defenders had not survived the prolonged artillery bombardment.

Woyrsch gave orders for an energetic pursuit, hoping to catch significant numbers of Russians to the west of the Vistula. As they moved forward, the *Landwehr* found itself on familiar ground; they had advanced along these roads in September 1914. The Russian forces opposing them made little attempt to establish a new line, abandoning Radom and pulling back towards Ivangorod. A new line was established near Zwoleń; the Germans attacked this on 21 July, driving the Russians before them.[6]

Despite the heavy fighting that Mackensen's forces in particular had endured, the overall German plan – to inflict a crushing defeat on the Russians before they could retreat from Poland – appeared to be moving forward smoothly. Nevertheless, the two thrusts were still separated by about 160 miles (257km), and in the coming days, neither was able to make fast progress, as a result of a mixture of increasing Russian resistance and difficult terrain. The Russians took measures to ensure that the pursuing Germans would find their task difficult, as Hoffmann recorded in his diary on 19 July:

> It seems that the Russians are actually repeating [the events of] 1812 and retreating along the entire front. They are setting fire to hundreds of their own villages, whose inhabitants have been evacuated. It's a dreadful nonsense, a huge shame for the country and of no military value.[7]

These comments are more than a little disingenuous. During their retreat across Poland in the autumn of 1914, the Germans had conducted a similar scorched earth policy with no regard for the consequences for the Polish inhabitants of the countryside. As a result, the Russians had experienced considerable difficulties in mounting their pursuit, and it was inevitable that they would take similar measures. However, these measures were patchy. Many rich property-owners managed to bribe the retreating troops into sparing their property, and as the Russian retreat continued and became increasingly disorderly, it seems that much of the damage inflicted by the withdrawing troops was concentrated on the property of the Jews.[8] Nevertheless, as they advanced, the German soldiers saw first hand the consequences of the Russian policy:

More than once, we stood shocked before the moving sight of a scene reminiscent of the flight from Egypt: a small family – were they left behind on their own when everyone else fled, or had they turned back after finding that there was nothing better to flee to? They had assembled a sort of shack from timbers they had dragged together in the garden of a looted farmhouse, living there as poor as gypsies. They had tied their cow to a shrub, a donkey rooted through some shredded vegetables. The mother sat there, a baby at her breast. Father and son prodded at a smouldering heap of ashes, heating a few potatoes, a frugal meal.[9]

The advance by *Ober Ost* rapidly slowed as it approached the swampy terrain of the Bobr and Narew valleys. A bridgehead was secured across the Narew at Pultusk on 23 July, barely 30 miles (50km) north of Warsaw, but then had to pause in the face of determined Russian resistance along what was effectively the last defensible line short of the Polish capital, and also as a consequence of lengthening German supply lines. In Latvia, Below's Niemen Army appeared to secure a decisive victory over the Russian Fifth Army at Schaulen, leading Hoffmann to ponder what might have been had the plan put forward by *Ober Ost* been accepted by Falkenhayn.[10] In a similar fashion to the events north of Warsaw, Mackensen found that he too faced greater difficulty than before in maintaining his rate of advance. After their initial positions were forced, the soldiers of Lesh's Third Army pulled back into a series of hills immediately south of the vital east–west railway that was Mackensen's objective. Confident that his eastern flank was safe, Mackensen ordered the transfer of XLI Reserve Corps back to Eleventh Army, in an attempt to maintain momentum along the main axis of operations.

On 19 July, Alexeyev was summoned to yet another conference with Grand Duke Nikolai, and was given permission to order the abandonment of Warsaw should this become unavoidable. The following day, Archduke Joseph Ferdinand attempted once more to push forwards towards Lublin; his left flank made some progress, but his right flank failed to penetrate the Russian defences. The Russians immediately launched counterattacks along the entire front, and as was usually the case in the First World War, these were beaten off in heavy fighting, with major casualties on both sides. The next two days saw hard fighting along the entire front of Mackensen's army group, and exhaustion forced Mackensen to order a cessation of attacks by Eleventh Army for 22 July. It was now the turn of the Austro-Hungarian Fourth Army to succeed where others failed; Joseph Ferdinand's troops to the west of the main road to Lublin made considerable headway against the Russian Fourth Army, dispelling any suggestions that they lacked fighting spirit and capturing over 12,000 prisoners. Any remaining doubts that Alexeyev might have had about the necessity for retreat were now dispelled, and he issued orders late on 22 July for a general withdrawal to the line running almost due east from Ivangorod – effectively conceding Lublin. A swift pursuit by Joseph Ferdinand might have achieved considerable results, but several days of tough fighting had left the Austro-Hungarian Fourth Army as exhausted as its German neighbours, and it was ordered to halt; given the criticisms that he had faced from the Germans, Joseph Ferdinand could be forgiven if he felt any sense of irony when he advised his corps commanders not to advance when neighbouring German formations were clearly not able to keep pace.[11]

It was time for Mackensen and the entire German high command to face reality. Operating at the end of extended supply lines, the troops of Eleventh Army, who had swept all before them until now, were simply exhausted. On 22 July, Mackensen wrote in his diary:

> My tactical situation is ever more critical. The enemy stands before me with considerable numerical superiority. I must restrict myself to defensive operations until advances in other battlefields give me freedom for manoeuvre. My troops' fighting strength has been greatly reduced in the recent fighting.[12]

It was an exaggeration to claim that the Russians possessed significant numerical superiority; their forces were equally exhausted, and if anything their ammunition supply situation was even worse. The Russian Guards Corps had been extensively involved in the fighting in the previous days, finding itself facing the Prussian Guards, and Bezobrazov, the corps commander, had tried in vain to secure permission and resources for an attack on 18 July. By the time that Lesh granted permission for an attack on 23 July, the Russian Guards had lost too many men for the assault to succeed, and Bezobrazov imperiously refused to waste further lives on what he regarded as an absurd attack. He was probably right, but such insubordination cost him his post. He was replaced by Vladimir Apollonovich Olukhov, who had been in command of XXIII Corps. A British observer wryly recorded that the headquarters staff of the Guards Corps, who were used to overmanning and a relatively indolent lifestyle, awaited the arrival of their new commander with some trepidation.[13]

Aware that Mackensen was in danger of grinding to a halt, Falkenhayn had already put pressure on *Ober Ost* to achieve exactly the sort of advance that might weaken the resistance in front of Mackensen's army group; on 21 July, he signalled Hindenburg in an attempt to urge him to press forward more energetically:

Army Group Mackensen is faced by a superior enemy. Those of his troops that are trying to advance have been significantly degraded by three months of mobile warfare and their right flank continues to be a cause for concern. It cannot therefore be assumed that the army group will be able to advance without aid.[14]

Gallwitz's troops were now gathered in strength along the Narew, but despite initial optimism that there might be a swift breakthrough towards Warsaw, forcing their way further was a difficult task. Litvinov's leadership of the Russian Second Army had been inept to date; he had simply insisted that his troops hold their positions at all costs, and had thrown reinforcements into counterattacks as they arrived, with the result that much of his command had simply ceased to exist. However, with his troops now protected by the swampy Narew valley, he managed to assemble a line that could stop Gallwitz's advance and dash hopes of a swift drive towards Warsaw. Once more, Ludendorff raised the suggestion of a deep penetration directly east, suggesting that this would at least draw away Russian forces; he maintained that it could be launched by diverting troops from Woyrsch's forces and from Ninth, Twelfth and Eighth Armies. Falkenhayn remained unimpressed, insisting that the reduction of the Russian salient in Poland by concentric attacks had to continue. Writing his memoirs after the war, Ludendorff could not resist drawing attention to the problems that resulted:

> As I had expected, the advance of the allied armies in Poland east of the Vistula resulted in frontal assaults and continuous fighting. Here, too, there were repeated futile attempts to encircle the Russians. The Russian Army was certainly forced to move [back], but it escaped. It launched constant determined counterattacks with powerful forces and in the numerous swampy rivers and streams it found repeated opportunities to reorganise and successfully mount prolonged resistance. In view of the constant movement over several weeks, the bad roads, and for the most part unfavourable weather, the efforts required of our troops were extraordinarily severe. Clothing and footwear disintegrated. Food supply became difficult. There was almost no shelter, as the Russians systematically destroyed or burned food supplies and villages.
>
> … After the peace treaty with Russia, a high-ranking Russian officer said to me that he did not understand why we had not advanced quicker, as the Russian Army would have been finished. The leadership and troops did everything to reach their objectives, but when despite excellent discipline and the best efforts and exertions of every man there is insufficient strength [to continue], the urging of the leadership can achieve nothing.[15]

Had *Ober Ost* been given permission to mount the attack that Ludendorff had suggested towards the east, it seems highly likely that it would have encountered precisely the same difficulties.

The German troops of Woyrsch's army detachment were now approaching the Vistula south of the fortifications and crossings at Ivangorod, and Woyrsch considered pursuing the retreating Russian Grenadier Corps across the river. Reconnaissance revealed that the Russians had pulled back to the river, and that there was no prospect of achieving surprise. Instead, Woyrsch's chief of staff suggested redeploying the bulk of the army detachment further north with a view to launching a surprise assault over the Vistula north of Ivangorod. The proposal was submitted to Teschen – Woyrsch was technically subordinated to *AOK* – but in the absence of any clear response, plans were made for an assault at Nowo Alexandria (now Puławy). Late on 24 July, even as the first pontoons were being launched for the crossing, orders arrived from *AOK*: there was to be no assault at Nowo Alexandria. Instead, approval was given for the army detachment to redeploy as suggested north of Ivangorod.[16]

This change of plan was the result of further arguments between Falkenhayn and Conrad. The former concluded that the planned operation faced great difficulties, whereas the alternative crossing to the north offered the prospect of helping disrupt Russian resistance in the northern half of the Polish salient. Conrad, on the other hand, feared that unless Woyrsch attacked at Nowo Alexandria, the Austro-Hungarian Fourth Army's forces would be unable to continue advancing. Ultimately, Falkenhayn's opinion prevailed, though as a concession, it was agreed that the Austro-Hungarian XII Corps would seal off the Russian fortress from the west, while the *Landwehr* divisions attempted to secure crossings over the Vistula.

This was not the only bone of contention between Conrad and Falkenhayn. As early as 21 July, Falkenhayn sent a signal to his Austro-Hungarian counterpart suggesting that Woyrsch's forces should be combined with Prince Leopold's Ninth Army to create a new central army group, which would be answerable to *OHL* rather than *AOK*. Conrad's immediate response was to dismiss the suggestion out of hand; the role of Woyrsch's troops, he insisted, was to cooperate with Austro-Hungarian forces attempting to drive the Russians off the west bank of the Vistula, and overall command should therefore remain with *AOK*. However, with Woyrsch now moving his forces further north, this became a harder line to maintain. Conrad had no choice but to agree, though he was able to retain control of the disputed forces until the completion of operations to reduce the Russian bridgeheads along the middle Vistula.

Another argument broke out about the transfer of Austro-Hungarian forces to the Italian front. On 23 June, the Italians had launched a major offensive along the Isonzo, but two weeks of fighting saw no significant gains. On 18 July, the Italians tried again, and at first seemed to be gaining ground, and Conrad ordered XIV Corps to be dispatched from Joseph Ferdinand's Fourth Army to the Isonzo front. Falkenhayn immediately objected, pointing out that Conrad had agreed that there would be no such transfers without the consent of the Germans. Once again, Conrad had to back down. In any event, the fighting on the Isonzo slowly ground down over the next two weeks, with the only result being over 90,000 casualties amongst the combatants.

Woyrsch's redeployment took four days, not least because his staff took considerable pains to try to hide the movement of several trains of bridging equipment from the Russian observers on the east bank of the Vistula, who used tethered balloons to watch for enemy movements. Shortly after midnight on 29 July, three groups crossed the river in pontoons, hindered by frequent groundings in the shallow water. Resistance was at first minimal, and throughout the day further troops were ferried across into the growing bridgehead. Russian reinforcements arrived from Ivangorod, Warsaw and Lublin, gradually increasing pressure on the German perimeter, but with the first pontoon bridge established before the end of 29 July, a steady stream of reinforcements and ammunition ensured that the Russian attempts to drive the *Landwehr* back into the river were beaten off. However, the Germans found it equally difficult to exploit their bridgehead, but the Russians had no intention of holding Ivangorod indefinitely. Once all Russian troops who could reach the fortress had safely crossed to the east bank, the defenders set off demolition charges in the western fortifications on 3 August. Further north, the Russians withdrew to the forts around the western perimeter of Warsaw.

On the same day that Woyrsch's troops attacked across the Vistula, the German Eleventh Army concentrated its efforts on a narrower front in an attempt to force its way forward. The initial artillery bombardment once more had a devastating effect on the Russian defences, and II Siberian Corps, now under the command of Radko Dimitriev, suffered heavy losses and was forced back. This created a crisis, worsened by the refusal of the neighbouring Guards Corps to provide timely support. Just as it seemed that a German breakthrough might be achieved, the remnants of the Russian X Corps succeeded in halting the advance, until the belated arrival of several battalions of troops from the Guards restored the front line.

Although the eastern part of this latest German attack made little headway, the gains further west once more destabilised the Russian line. With Woyrsch's bridgehead established north of Ivangorod, Alexeyev concluded that a further retreat was necessary. Mackensen's troops reached and secured Lublin on 31 July, but this city, which had been the objective of the drive to the north, was now far less significant, as the Russians had abandoned Ivangorod. A little to the east, the Bug Army, in almost constant fighting, drove forward to Teratyn and broke through the Russian line. Moving forward as fast as they could, the Germans reached and captured Khelme, where the Russians had held so many conferences throughout the war, on 1 August.[17]

A German advance had threatened the city of Warsaw in the autumn of 1914, and some of the troops now advancing towards the city found grisly evidence of the previous campaign:

> I rushed forward with my rifle ready, and suddenly there were two skulls staring at me from the stubbly growth in a hole. The [bodies] were wearing coats. Apparently they had been there since the previous August and had mummified in the meantime.[18]

On another occasion, the same soldier experienced the use of the new weaponry of war:

> At the time, the Russians were in front of Warsaw about 200m from us in a well-constructed position. We watched as combat engineers came into our positions and at dusk positioned pipes on the breastwork facing the enemy, with their mouths pointing in their direction. A couple of days later large bottles, like oxygen bottles, containing gas, were attached to them. One morning – just as the sun was coming up – medics brought bowls containing a blue liquid, like potassium permanganate. We still didn't have gas masks at that time. A cotton wool ball was dipped in the liquid, wrapped in a small bag and bound around the mouth and nose ... the Russian machine-gunfire steadily slackened, and we still hadn't reached them when we heard coughing and wheezing, then silence. We now leapt into the Russian trenches. We had hardly any losses. Perhaps three or four men were killed, who in their haste leaped onto the bayonets attached to Russian rifles. The officers lying in the dugouts were partly naked ... where they had torn their clothing from their bodies trying to breathe.[19]

The fall of Warsaw was now only a matter of time. With his troops struggling to hold back the Germans on the Galician, Vistula and Narew fronts, and the near-collapse of Russian defences in Latvia, Alexeyev took advantage of the freedom granted him by Grand Duke Nikolai to abandon the Polish capital. As with so

Austro-Hungarian troops in foxholes near Przemyśl, April 1915. (©ullsteinbild / Topfoto)

An Austro-Hungarian dugout in Przemyśl after the fall of the city. (©Topfoto)

This postcard from 1915 is entitled 'The heroes of the East, the South, the West – a united band, beat the enemy with an iron fist in the sand – Liège, Warsaw, Przemyśl'. It has Kaiser Wilhelm II in the centre; on his left, Emperor Franz Joseph; on the right the Turkish Sultan Mehmet VI and above him Crown Prince Wilhelm. At top left, Mackensen presents Franz Joseph with Przemyśl after recapturing the fortress, and at top right, German generals indicate the progress of the Central Powers across Russian Poland during the summer. (©ullsteinbild / Topfoto)

A machine-gun team of the *k.u.k.* Army in the Carpathians in early 1915 awaits the next Russian attack. (The Granger Collection / TopFoto)

Russian cavalry moving forward through the Carpathian Mountains in 1915. (©Topfoto)

An artist's impression of Austro-Hungarian troops being attacked by Russian infantry in the Carpathians in early 1915. (©Artmedia / HIP / TopFoto)

The use of motorised vehicles was still in its infancy in 1915, limited by the unreliability of engines and the lack of adequate roads. Here, a tractor is attached to a 305mm mortar in the Carpathians in 1915. (©2003 Topham Picturepoint)

German cavalry fording the River Drina in late 1915. Even after a year of fighting, the lance remained in widespread use on the Eastern Front. (©ullsteinbild / Topfoto)

A German infantry column marches past Bulgarian officers in Serbia in late 1915. (©ullsteinbild / Topfoto)

Serbian troops waiting for orders to move up to the front line in 1915. This photograph shows the rugged terrain over which the campaign was fought. (The Granger Collection / TopFoto)

As Poland changed hands in the summer of 1915, many Poles tried to flee the fighting. (©ullsteinbild / TopFoto)

An artist's impression of Russian trenches in mountainous terrain in southern Galicia, 1915. By the standards of the Western Front, these fortifications were relatively primitive. (©Print Collector / HIP / TopFoto)

Troops of the *k.u.k.* Army in a trench in eastern Galicia in the autumn of 1915. Compared to earlier entrenchments, these are more elaborate. (©ullsteinbild / TopFoto)

A German machine-gun company during the Second Battle of the Masurian Lakes.
(©Artmedia / HIP / TopFoto)

An Austro-Hungarian telegraph station, photographed here in the Alps in 1915;
like motor transport, this was a form of technology that was badly hamstrung by unreliability.
(IMAGNO / Austrian Archives / TopFoto)

many things, the Central Powers had divergent views on how to take advantage of this, and at the heart of the matter was Falkenhayn's view of the outcome of the war in the east. The chief of the German general staff was certain in his mind that it was impossible for Germany to prevail in a multi-front war; consequently, it was vital that one or other of Germany's enemies be forced to negotiate peace as soon as possible, leaving Germany to continue a single-front war that it could win. There was clearly no prospect of the implacably Germanophobic French accepting terms, but Russia might be forced to negotiate – hence Falkenhayn's determination, despite his conviction that the war could only be decided in the west, to inflict sufficient damage on the tsar's armies that Russia would have no choice but to leave the conflict. Like his predecessors, Falkenhayn was dead-set against pursuing a war to the bitter end against Russia; it was barely a century since Napoleon had attempted such a war, and the fate of his *Grande Armée* continued to dominate military thinking.

The Austro-Hungarian foreign minister, István von Burián, requested that a cavalry regiment of the *k.u.k.* Army should be the leading formation into Warsaw. This was a totally unacceptable suggestion for Falkenhayn, who anticipated that such a move would be certain to harden Russia's resolve. The request from Burián came via Conrad, and when Falkenhayn expressed his disapproval, he must have been relieved to discover that – at least on this one matter – he and Conrad were in agreement.[20] The suggestion was put aside, and Prince Leopold's Ninth Army was left to march into Warsaw on 5 August, the day after the Russians abandoned Ivangorod, with as little pomp as possible. At Falkenhayn's request, the celebrations even within Germany were muted.

From the German point of view, pursuing peace was a sensible and pragmatic policy, but it underestimated the commitment of the Russians to the Entente. After discussions with Falkenhayn, Chancellor Theobald von Bethmann-Hollweg asked King Christian X of Denmark, a cousin of Tsar Nicholas, to make an approach to the Russians. The Danes asked the tsar for a meeting, but although Nicholas agreed to meet Hans Neils Andersen, the Danish envoy, this was merely to inform him that Russia had given a pledge to its allies in September 1914 that it would not pursue a separate peace, and had reiterated this pledge when Italy joined the Entente.[21]

Whilst this rebuff left Germany facing enemies on all sides, there were those within the German establishment who were not overly disappointed. In the heady days of late August and early September 1914, when it seemed as if a decisive victory over France was within reach, a document was drawn up by Kurt Riezler, who was working on Bethmann's staff, describing the changes that

Germany would demand at the end of the war.[22] In the east, these called for the German occupation of Poland and the creation of a series of buffer states across Russia and the Ukraine, effectively dismembering Russia's European empire. In the months that followed, the concept of *Mitteleuropa* as a German-dominated counterweight to Britain's overseas empire steadily gained ground, particularly amongst right-wing politicians in Germany and many officers in *Ober Ost*. The peace proposals offered in 1915 would have meant abandoning this plan, and those who believed in *Mitteleuropa* were relieved that the war would continue. It is worth noting that even the peace offer of 1915 would have involved Russia conceding some territory along the Polish–Prussian border.[23]

Karl Litzmann's XL Reserve Corps had been involved in fighting to the west of Kovno and Olita since the end of the Masurian campaign and its aftermath, and in a series of attacks and counterattacks had moved the front slowly east. On 11 July, XL Reserve Corps was ordered to join the general offensive, and late on 15 July Litzmann received reports from aerial reconnaissance of increased Russian rail traffic in Kovno. It was clear that Russian troops were being moved from the city to try to block the German advances elsewhere, and Litzmann decided to take advantage of this with an immediate thrust towards Kovno. Initially, the Königsberg *Landwehr* Division faced a regular Siberian formation, but reports now arrived that the Siberians had been withdrawn and replaced by reservists, and plans for a major assault were drawn up.

In his memoirs, Litzmann described the terrain for the coming campaign:

Linking the great fortress of Grodno and Kovno and passing through the fortified [town of] Olita the Niemen runs north with numerous curves, 200m wide, to a point 20km [12 miles] east of Kovno. There, turning west, it forms a sharp angle, joined from the right at Kovno by the Wiliya and further downstream by the Niewjasha and – now 300m wide – flows towards the northwest to Wilki.

Just above the city of Kovno, where a memorial marks the crossing of Napoleon's *Grande Armée* in June 1812, the Yesya flows into the Niemen. The stream, bordered on both banks by woodland, divides the land to the left of the Niemen into two areas of differing characters: to the west of the Yesya it is flat, and hilly to the east ...

The actual city of Kovno lies in the angle between the Niemen and Wiliya. The city ... was a Russian government centre with 74,000 inhabitants, of whom half were Jews.

... The ring of forts, intended as the main defence, were between 7 and 14km [4 and 9 miles] from the centre and consisted of forts I to V on the south bank of

Kovno, July–August 1915

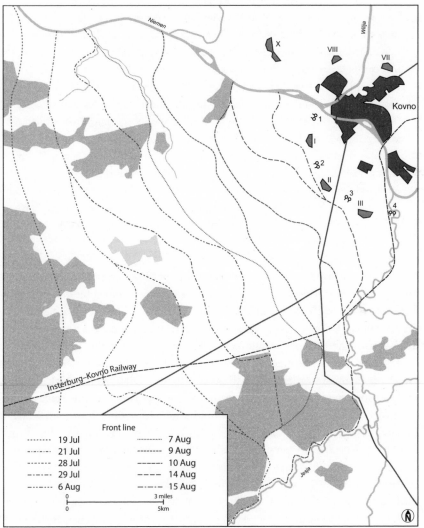

the Niemen and six artillery batteries in the gaps between them. Forts VI to X
were on the north bank. Fort X was constructed after the beginning of the war
and positioned so far forward on the high edge of the river valley that it
commanded the approaches to Forts I and II.

The southwest sector between the Yesya and the lower Niemen, with Forts I to III, had been designated by the Russians as the 'most likely battleground'. The railway line from Insterburg running through the Kovno Forest ensured this, as on account of enormous amounts of materiel – including artillery ammunition – required for modern siege warfare, an existing adequate rail line to the battleground was needed if time-consuming construction of field railways was to be avoided. The approaches to this sector had been carefully prepared for defence. Between the Kovno Forest and the ring of forts there were no fewer than eight field positions that would have to be forced, and these were sequentially stronger as they approached the fortress. The last had tough strongpoints and minefields and was supported by middle-calibre artillery ... The approaches north of the railway had been cleared of woodland and most of the villages had been razed in order to improve the fields of fire.

Kovno had a strong garrison of 90,000 men ... with plentiful artillery and military supplies of all kinds. The stocks of ammunition and food would have sufficed for prolonged resistance.[24]

Litzmann's assessment of the strength of the fortress was accurate, but incomplete. Like all fortresses of the era, the physical defences were only a hindrance if they were defended with determination, and even then they were vulnerable to modern heavy artillery. Given their general retreat across the entire front, it was unlikely that the Russians would contest Kovno with any real resolve.

In order to take advantage of the weak forces facing the Königsberg *Landwehr* Division, Litzmann ordered 79th Reserve Infantry Division to attack through the positions held by the *Landwehr* and force a crossing of the Yesya to the southwest of Kovno. The *Landwehr* would attack to the north of 79th Reserve Infantry Division, with cavalry operating north of the railway line from Insterburg. The artillery preparation, intended for 19 July, had to be abandoned due to heavy rain, forcing a postponement of a day. After a bombardment that continued through the night, the Germans attacked at first light on 21 July. They made swift gains, clearing all the woods to the west of the river, but in mid-morning the weather deteriorated again and the planned assault across the Yesya had to be put off. In the face of the strong Russian defences, Litzmann requested reinforcements from Tenth Army; the reply was disappointing, but not unexpected. There were no troops available, particularly as heavy artillery had already been earmarked for an assault on Novogeorgievsk. Litzmann therefore abandoned his plans for enveloping the fortress from the southeast as well as the southwest; he would have to limit his assault to a much smaller battlefield. This brought its own problems, and Litzmann shared his concerns with Mengelbier, his chief of staff. There was the constant threat that the Russian forces behind the Yesya might attack, and by angling their attack to the northwest they could crush any German group attempting to march on Kovno against the lower Niemen. But whilst such a risk was a theoretical possibility, the reality was that the Russians had little intention of mounting any such attacks; even if the will had existed, their troops were simply too weak.

The clearance of trees and undergrowth in order to improve fields of fire for the Russian defenders was not the only preparation that had occurred in the area. There was a general policy to expel Jews from major towns as the Germans approached, partly through a belief that the Jews would aid the Germans. This policy was justified by the publication of stories such as the alleged 'Kuzhi incident', which took place in modern-day Lithuania:

> During the night of 28 April 1915, Germans attacked the village of Kuzhi, located on the northwest side of Shavl [Siauliai], not far from Kurshan [Kursenai]. Several detachments of the 131st Piatogorsky Infantry were in the village at the time. An event occurred that revealed the terrible betrayal of our army by the *zhids*. As our soldiers retook the village from the Germans, some German soldiers who had been left behind were hidden by the *zhids* in their cellars. Then the *zhids* set fire to the village by shooting, to serve as a signal to the enemy. The Germans quickly came out of their hiding places in the cellars and began shooting at the house where Colonel Dovilev was quartered. This unfortunate case shows the necessity of being careful in places previously occupied by the enemy where the majority of the population is Jewish.[25]

The Duma ordered an investigation of the incident, led by Alexander Kerensky. He found that it was – at best – a gross exaggeration. There had only been eight German soldiers in the village, who left immediately before the Russians arrived. Civilians in the village, including Jews, warned the Russians that the Germans were not far away, but these warnings were ignored and no sentries were deployed; as a result, the return of the German patrol during the night was not detected, and in the resulting firefight the house occupied by the Russians – which belonged to a Jew – was burned to the ground. In any event, it was preposterous to suggest that the Jews would burn down their own village purely as a signal to the Germans.

Nevertheless, pervasive anti-Semitism ensured that there were widespread expulsions. One estimate places the number of Jews expelled from Kovno province as greater than 160,000, and describes how Jewish soldiers were removed from the garrison on the grounds that their loyalty might be suspect, even though there had been no occasions when Jewish soldiers had failed to do their duty.[26] Whilst this figure might have been an exaggeration, the expulsions were substantial enough to create problems. A disproportionate part of Lithuania's intelligentsia was Jewish, and their departure brought commercial activity almost to a halt; there were also widespread protests at the sudden absence of doctors and other essential professionals.

On 23 July, Litzmann received orders from Eichhorn, the commander of Tenth Army, to proceed with his assault on Kovno. He was also assigned modest reinforcements in the form of General von Zenker's infantry brigade, made up of replacement drafts from Saxony, but lost control of the Königsberg *Landwehr* Division, which was dispatched towards Augustovo; by way of compensation, a large part of XL Reserve Corps' sector to the south was reassigned to the neighbouring XXI Corps. In addition, a single 420mm mortar was dispatched to Litzmann, arriving on 26 July. A day later the advance on Kovno began, a direct thrust from the southwest. Despite Litzmann's concerns about the strength of the Russian defences, progress was steady, and casualties relatively light. The arrival of more heavy siege artillery on 30 July gave the Germans a further boost, but two days later the news was less favourable: although *Ober Ost* remained in favour of a thrust against Kovno, Falkenhayn did not approve, rating the probability of success as too low. Litzmann protested that the heavy guns had turned the balance in his favour, and Eichhorn and Hell, Tenth Army's chief of staff, visited the front shortly after to judge for themselves. After surveying the battlefield in the company of Litzmann and Mengelbier, Eichhorn was persuaded to allow the assault to continue. However, the delay caused by these hesitations was not without consequence. The Russian withdrawal from Warsaw released significant numbers of troops, many of whom were dispatched by train to Kovno, and Litzmann was anxious to press on before even more arrived.

In order to secure good observation posts for the artillery, 79th Reserve Infantry Division moved forward early on 6 August, with further gains the following night. On 8 August, the massed guns of XL Reserve Corps bombarded the ring of Russian forts around Kovno and targets within the city. The defending artillery returned fire, but on 9 and 10 August the German infantry advanced, allowing the light and medium artillery to move forward; the heavyweight mortars were less mobile, and would have to be taken apart before they could advance. In a vain attempt to disrupt the apparently inexorable approach of enemy forces, the Russians counterattacked at the southern end of the German advance, but a deserter had alerted the Germans, who crushed the attack in most sectors; only in one area, where the attackers were faced by a *Landsturm* battalion, did any ground change hands.

As in so many battles, there was a steady stream of deserters, and on 12 August one of them brought the Germans further good news. The artillery bombardment had almost completely wrecked Fort I; aerial reconnaissance added that Forts II and III had been severely damaged. Two days later, the last Russian defences outside the girdle of forts were penetrated. Litzmann described the decisive weaponry of the battle:

> During these days, I watched the fighting together with Mengelbier and my son from the attic of an abandoned hut far to the front near Mostaitzy. It was worth the effort to move so far forward: through a hole cut in the straw we could see Fort II and Battery 3 right in front of us, and just as I raised the binoculars to my eyes a 420mm shell delighted me by striking in the centre of the fort. A burst of fire was followed by huge clouds of smoke and a column of concrete rubble, timber and earth that rose at least 200m into the air. Then followed the crash of the huge shattering shell. The mortars that had been set up to our right rear south of the road thundered away. Right behind us, the heavy field howitzers fired rolling salvoes. To our left rear, mortars and howitzers were firing. But from in front of us the Russians fired back. It was the singular music of battle: the prelude to the final act of the drama of Kovno. We had the distinct impression that the force of the fortress artillery was slackening. The conclusion of the duel was turning in our favour!
>
> Sadly, my dear Hauptmann von dem Knesebeck, commander of 12 Coy, 261st Infantry Regiment, fell during the capture of the fortifications at Janutzje. The company lay under heavy fire from the enemy facing them. Knesebeck stood up in order to be able to observe effectively behind a tall bush which more or less hid him, though only from sight. He told his men to lie flatter in order to be better protected. His Feldwebel, lying next to him, shouted 'Only when Herr Hauptmann takes better cover himself!' 'Ach,' laughed Knesebeck, 'They won't hit me.' Right afterwards, an enemy bullet pierced his brave heart. We interred him in the small cemetery in Poshery in front of the black wooden church under beautiful old trees, where three other officers of 261st and 262nd Infantry Regiments had already found their last resting place. The final hymn of the burial ceremony was accompanied by the thunder of the giant mortars from the nearby woodland – a mighty graveside salute.[27]

The Russians made a final attempt to launch a counterattack on 14 August, briefly recapturing the fortifications at Sagroda at the southern end of Litzmann's assault. Although XL Reserve Corps was steadily approaching the forts from the southwest, the northern flank of the assault made little headway, being outflanked by Fort X to the north of the Niemen. At the same time, there was strengthening Russian fire from beyond the Yesya, once more raising the spectre of a major Russian counterattack into the right rear of the attacking troops. Nevertheless, Litzmann gave orders for his men to press on, and during 16 August the infantry stormed Forts I, II and III.

The same evening, Grigoriev, the governor of Kovno, sent a signal to Tenth Army:

We are pulling back behind the Niemen. [We have suffered] huge losses. Telegraphic communication with Vilna [has been] lost. [I] await orders by radio.[28]

The message was intercepted by the Germans, and Litzmann ordered his divisions to press on with all speed. During the night there were loud detonations as the garrison tried to blow the bridges over the Niemen; although some were destroyed, others remained passable. The following morning, the remaining defences to the southwest of Kovno were captured without a fight. Still fearing a Russian attack across the Yesya, Litzmann dispatched his chief of staff to lead XL Reserve Corps into the city and across the Niemen; when no Russian assault appeared, he joined Mengelbier in the outskirts of Kovno. He was shocked to find that few senior officers had accompanied the infantry in their advance. Further enquiry revealed that they had remained in their headquarters for fear of losing contact with higher commands. Mengelbier had taken advantage of the authority granted him by Litzmann to ensure that the absence of senior command did not hold back the troops, and by the end of the day several battalions had been ferried across the Niemen. Towards nightfall, heavy fighting erupted at the eastern end of the bridgehead, but the Russian counterattack was soon beaten off. The following day, as Litzmann's engineers laboured to construct pontoon bridges over the river, the remaining forts fell into German hands. When Eichhorn visited Litzmann, the triumphant corps commander was able to inform his superior that the operation had yielded over 20,000 prisoners and over 1,300 guns. In addition, most of the fortress's considerable stockpile of shells and other war *matériel* had also been captured.[29]

Despite lacking sufficient troops to attempt an encirclement of Kovno, and with only limited heavy artillery, Litzmann had succeeded in attacking and capturing one of the key fortresses on which so much money and resources had been lavished in the years before the war. It turned out that despite the likely axis of attack being fairly obvious, the forts in that part of the perimeter had not been as extensively modernised as they might have been, and they rapidly collapsed under shellfire. The troops deployed to hold Kovno proved to be too few to stop the Germans, but at the same time represented a force that Russia could ill afford to lose, even if they were merely second- or third-line reservists. A lack of clear decision-making at all levels of the Russian command prevented a timely evacuation of the guns, ammunition and other stores in Kovno, and the Germans were handed another relatively straightforward triumph. Litzmann summarised the factors that he thought played a part:

> ... the moral superiority of my troops, the great effect of our heavy high-trajectory artillery, the constant activity of my staff, particularly the chief of staff, the skill of my subordinate commanders and – by no means least – the ineptitude of my opponent, General Grigoriev.
>
> He could have done anything to defend Kovno if he had possessed resolve and strength of purpose. I don't know if the Russian troops along the Yesya were under his command. If that was not the case, he should have urged his superiors to carry out a decisive flanking attack.[30]

Alfred Knox later encountered a young officer who had been in Kovno:

> He had been drafted with four depot battalions from near Baranovichi to Kovno a week before the commencement of the German advance. He said that there were many guns in the fortress, but the defences were beneath contempt. 'The only concrete emplacement was occupied by the Commandant, General Grigoriev, who never left it except at night!' This youth said that in his company of 250 men he had only 68 rifles. A single 16-inch shell destroyed three whole sections. He was contusioned and went to hospital, where he consoled himself with the reflection that at all events the bridge over the Niemen would be blown up and he would have time to escape. The bridge was not blown up, and he only escaped in dressing-gown and slippers on the last crowded train. In his opinion the Russian guns had sufficient shell, and the place might have been held if the commandant had not been a coward. At the very beginning of the attack he had created a half panic by telling officers who had no intention of running away that 'the first man to bolt would be shot!'[31]

The failure of Plehve to coordinate matters in the critical sector undoubtedly contributed to the Russian setback, but blame inevitably fell upon the hapless and incompetent Grigoriev. Accompanied by a priest, he left his fortress on 17 August without informing his chief of staff and travelled to Vilna to report the loss of Kovno. Here, he was arrested under the orders of Grand Duke Nikolai and court-martialled; interestingly, one of the charges he faced was that – contrary to Litzmann's account – he had failed to clear adequate fields of fire in front of his positions. He was sentenced to eight years' hard labour, but the enquiry and court-martial studiously avoided another issue: if the defences of Kovno were in poor condition, as claimed by Knox's ensign and others, what had happened to the money allocated for improvements before the war?

To date, Alexeyev had managed to play the poor hand that he had been dealt with some competence, notwithstanding the loss of Kovno; a combination of lengthening German supply lines and difficult terrain, combined with determined resistance, had slowed the German advance to a crawl compared with its earlier progress, and even the lack of cooperation between armies on the Bobr–Narew front had proved to be less serious than it might have been. With Poland being abandoned, he now had to make a decision about the last major fortress, Novogeorgievsk. Lying to the north of Warsaw where the Narew meets the Vistula, the fortress was on the site of an original fortification built by the Swedes in the 17th century and then rebuilt by Napoleon. In 1832, it was extensively modernised, but by 1883 was once more obsolete. As part of Russia's increased preparations for a possible war with Germany, further work commenced including the creation of eight additional forts in a ring around the central fortress.

Novogeorgievsk was one of the prime targets for Sukhomlinov's proposed changes in the first decade of the new century. The minister for war regarded all such fortresses as obsolete and of little use in mobile warfare and he wished to have it demolished, releasing valuable resources for the field army. He was overruled and large amounts of money were spent on modernisation; however, these new refurbishments were of limited value. The eight forts built as a new perimeter in the 1880s might have been adequate at the time, but the greatly increased range of modern artillery meant that they were now too close to the main fortress, which could be bombarded without having to take the outer ring first. Nor was there sufficient money to modernise all the forts; nevertheless a network of some eighteen outer forts, including the original eight, had been created by 1915, lavishly equipped with about 1,600 guns. Novogeorgievsk was also a major depot, with hundreds of thousands of rounds of artillery ammunition stockpiled within its walls – at a time when the field armies were crying out for more ammunition.

In 1914, as the *k.u.k.* Army retreated in disorder across Galicia, the Austro-Hungarian fortress of Przemyśl had been given a substantial garrison with the intention of serving as a drag on the advancing Russians. To an extent, it was effective in this role, and was relieved when Conrad's armies advanced again in the spring; however, when the Austro-Hungarian forces withdrew once more, Przemyśl was again allowed to be encircled with a substantial garrison. On this occasion, every attempt to lift the siege failed, with disastrous losses in the Carpathians, and ultimately the substantial garrison was forced to surrender.

Alexeyev now faced a similar issue with Novogeorgievsk. His staff calculated that over 1,000 trains would be required to evacuate the guns and supplies stored in the fortress, and many urged that the fortress should be used in a similar manner to the Austro-Hungarian use of Przemyśl in 1914; the German forces required to invest it would not be available for the continued drive across Poland, thus improving the chances of the Russian Army being able to halt the advance of the Central Powers. The obvious flaw in this argument was that when he had allowed Przemyśl to be encircled with a substantial garrison, Conrad believed that he would be able to lift the siege before supplies ran out. By contrast, there was no prospect of the Russians being able to drive back the Germans in order to rescue the garrison of Novogeorgievsk. Nevertheless, Alexeyev decided that the fortress had to be held. Three divisions – 11th Siberian Division and 58th and 63rd Infantry Divisions – were allocated to the garrison, together with the gunners already in the fortress. The total force exceeded 90,000, but 11th Siberian Division had already suffered badly in the opening phases of *Ober Ost's* offensive, and the other two divisions were made up of second-line reservists, mainly older men who had expected to be spared front-line duty. It is estimated that only 55,000 of the garrison were actually fit for combat.[32] The garrison commander was Nikolai Pavlovich Bobyr.

The German forces that advanced on and surrounded Novogeorgievsk, completing the encirclement on 10 August, were themselves largely reservists, mostly from XVII Reserve Corps. Unfortunately for the Russians, they were accompanied by a modern siege train commanded by General Hans von Beseler, who had already achieved fame at the successful siege of Antwerp in 1914. He was sent east specifically to help with the rapid reduction of the fortress, and brought with him seventeen batteries of modern high-calibre siege guns and mortars, as well as several batteries of field artillery. He immediately went to work, planning to reduce the northern forts prior to an assault. To a large extent, his choice was limited by the local railway network; the line from the north was the only one in German control, and therefore the only route by which the heavy guns could be brought forward. Nevertheless, Beseler put his experience at Antwerp to good use – the fire of his artillery would be directed at only a small part of the fortifications in order to maximise its effect, not least because there was only sufficient ammunition available for an intensive bombardment of perhaps three hours.

At this stage, the Germans had a stroke of astonishingly good fortune. A reconnaissance patrol from 10th *Landwehr* Regiment near the northern forts stumbled upon a group of Russians and swiftly subdued and captured them; to their surprise, the Germans found that their prisoners included several senior officers, including Colonel Korotkovich-Notschevnoi, the fortress's senior engineer. Even more remarkably, a search of his car revealed a detailed map of the Russian fortifications, complete with annotations about their strengths and weaknesses; he had been touring the defences to collect information on where additional troops might be needed to compensate for deficiencies. For the Germans, this was all the more valuable a find, as their intelligence on recent improvements in the fortress was very poor.

Armed with this piece of intelligence, Beseler changed his plans. Forts 15 and 16 on the northeast perimeter had not been modernised for many years, and the German siege guns were massed against them. On 13 August, after a delay due to fog that was slow to clear, the artillery commenced a heavy bombardment that rapidly pulverised the obsolete fortifications. When the German infantry advanced in the early afternoon, they found trenches full of dead and wounded Russians; other defenders had already pulled back to the main fortress, but there were still sufficient men manning the defences of the wrecked forts to repulse the first attack with heavy German losses. However, other German units succeeded in penetrating the defensive lines where they had been completely crushed by the artillery bombardment, and the determined defenders were forced to surrender at the end of the day when they found themselves surrounded. The fortifications in the critical sector that remained in Russian hands were abandoned overnight.

Beseler now moved his guns forward to commence a bombardment of the inner fortress. The garrisons of the outlying forts continued to put up fierce resistance, but one by one they were forced either to abandon their positions and pull back to the central citadel or were overrun. The commanders of these garrisons had been ordered to hold their forts, but while many fought to the end of their strength to do so, there was a singular lack of cooperation between the forts; prisoner interrogations later revealed that this was because no such orders had been issued by garrison commanders to their subordinates, and in the absence of any such clear instructions, local officers lacked the initiative to act for themselves. Whilst many Russian units had shown a similar lack of improvisation throughout the war, the lowly status of most of the reservist formations in the garrison ensured that their officers were of particularly poor quality, resulting in these units frequently performing badly, thus damaging their reputation still further.

Belatedly, Bobyr realised that it would be impossible for his garrison to hold out and he ordered the destruction of the stores within Novogeorgievsk. The work had barely begun when the German guns opened fire on the inner fortifications on 18 August. The garrison began to surrender piecemeal, and Bobyr ordered the rest to lay down their weapons two days later. Together with 29 other generals and the survivors of the garrison, he joined the growing number of prisoners taken by the Central Powers during their successful summer. The prisoners were not the only reward for the Germans. Almost all of the fortress guns were captured, together with over one million rounds of artillery ammunition and large quantities of food and military supplies, including nearly 200 tons of copper, bronze and brass. The Germans were not the only ones to be astonished by the scale of their haul; the news that so much *matériel* had been stored in the fortress without the apparent knowledge of any higher commanders seemed to come as a considerable surprise to *Stavka*, despite widespread knowledge in the army about the hoarding of stores in fortresses.[33]

Whilst fortresses like Kovno had not been modernised as planned – through a mixture of incompetence and corruption – Novogeorgievsk had been the recipient of lavish expenditure, though the sheer scale of the fortifications meant that only some areas had been modernised. The capture of the plans of the fortress allowed the Germans to concentrate their efforts on the weaker areas, but as was the case with Kovno, the likely axis of German attack was dictated by the layout of local rail lines, and the Russians should have been able to anticipate the sectors of the perimeter that should receive priority. The decision to allow such a large garrison to be trapped within Novogeorgievsk was extraordinary, given that there was no real likelihood of the field army being able to lift the siege. In any event, the speed with which the Germans overcame both Kovno and Novogeorgievsk demonstrated how obsolete the entire concept of fortresses was by 1915. After a summer in which the Russian Army had lost so many men and so many guns in Galicia, the wanton squandering of so many troops and guns in attempting to defend an ultimately indefensible series of fortresses was an extravagance that Russia could ill afford. Whilst the removal of the guns would have required huge numbers of trains, at least some, and all of the garrison troops, could have been saved – if the will and resolution to do so had existed.

The few remaining Russian fortresses were also now under threat. Osowiec on the Bobr had first come under German attack in 1914, and again early in 1915; on both occasions, the assaults were beaten off. Although the fortress did not lie in the direct path of the advance of *Ober Ost*, a decision was made to make a third attempt to reduce the fortifications. In addition to a force of about 7,000 *Landwehr* and heavy artillery, the Germans deployed thirty cylinders of chlorine gas, and waited until the wind was in the right direction to make their attack on 6 August. It was expected that the gas would permeate through the bunkers and trenches of the fortifications, and after an artillery bombardment, the *Landwehr* advanced in the expectation of meeting little or no resistance. Although an estimated 2,000 Russians had been killed, the attackers were shocked when they came under fire from a small number of guns that had survived the artillery bombardment and were manned by the last survivors of the garrison, many of whom were wearing uniforms stained with blood from their damaged lungs. The Germans withdrew in disarray, and the fortress continued to be held. It was finally abandoned two weeks later, when its continued occupation would serve no further purpose.[34]

The abandonment of the fortresses and most of their artillery had at least one beneficial consequence for the Russian Army: sufficient locomotives and rolling stock were released to allow the army to withdraw faster than the Germans could cut them off. The prospect of the Central Powers encircling a large part of the tsar's forces, or of driving them into the Pripet Marshes where they would be forced to abandon all their heavy equipment, seemed to be disappearing almost by the day. On 3 August, even before the occupation of Warsaw, Falkenhayn wrote to Conrad that as far as Germany was concerned, operations would come to an end when the Russians had been driven back beyond the Bug to a line running approximately from Grodno to Brest-Litovsk. Once this was achieved, substantial German forces would be withdrawn for use elsewhere with the intention of reducing activity on the Eastern Front to no more than sustaining what had been achieved. He added that the Austro-Hungarian forces should assume a similar posture. On this occasion at least, Conrad was in full agreement; he remained anxious to transfer troops to the Alps to deal a decisive blow against the Italians, whom he had regarded with grave suspicion since long before the war.[35] As ever, Falkenhayn continued to be deeply sceptical about any major operation against Italy, remaining in favour of a strike against Serbia. This would serve several purposes, he argued. Firstly, it would open land communications with the Ottoman Empire. Secondly, one of the enemies of the Central Powers would be comprehensively knocked out of the war. Thirdly, negotiations with

Bulgaria had reached an advanced stage, culminating in a resolution on 3 August in which Bulgaria agreed to enter into an alliance with Austria-Hungary and Germany within thirty days, provided a substantial force of twelve divisions – six from each of the Central Powers – was deployed along the Save against Serbia.

There were further discussions between Conrad and Falkenhayn about the best way of continuing operations with Mackensen's army group. For several days, the troops had struggled forward in the face of well-organised Russian rearguards and poor weather before pausing to rest and reorganise, and aware that replacement drafts were en route, Mackensen could look forward to resuming operations at a higher tempo. His preference was to continue to strike directly north, in order to reach the railway line between Brest-Litovsk and Warsaw, and to this end he turned down a request from Linsingen for reinforcements for the Bug Army. He reiterated that Linsingen's mission was not to break through the Russian lines, merely to protect the eastern flank of the German Eleventh Army. In any event, he added, the swampy terrain around the Bug would make it almost impossible for Linsingen to advance at sufficient speed to prevent the Russians from withdrawing:

> At the moment I think it is highly doubtful that stronger pressure on the east bank of the Bug will allow me to advance faster. As things are at present, my efforts must be – in conjunction with Hindenburg's offensive on the Narew – to act as quickly as possible against the Russians retreating east from the Vistula. The shortest route for this and the best terrain is on the west bank [of the Bug].[36]

On 8 August, Conrad suggested changing the axis of advance for Mackensen's group towards the northeast, in an attempt to catch the Russian troops before they could withdraw further east. The drive directly north was already running into difficulties, largely because of delays in bringing forward sufficient ammunition, and Mackensen agreed to the change after a conversation with Falkenhayn in Lublin on 12 August. In order to facilitate this, there was a general rearrangement of troops. As a result of the rapid reduction of the great Russian salient, many of Joseph Ferdinand's troops were now redundant, and were transferred to Puhallo's First Army; the solitary German division was assigned to Eleventh Army, while the Austro-Hungarian X Corps, 22nd Infantry Division and the Guards Cavalry Division were moved to the Bug Army. At the same time, in an attempt to coordinate matters in the central sector, Woyrsch's formations and the German Ninth Army became part of a new army group under Prince Leopold. News of this was greeted by gloom in *Ober Ost*; they saw the creation of Leopold's command as a further weakening of their own remit.

On the Russian side, there was a growing concern that the front might start to break up entirely. There was particular concern with Thirteenth Army, at the southern end of Alexeyev's long front line; as it retreated, there was a distinct danger of both its flanks losing contact with their neighbours. In an attempt to prevent this, Ivanov ordered Brusilov to ensure that he kept a mixed force of cavalry and infantry available on the northern flank of Eighth Army, ready to close any gap that might develop. It was increasingly clear to *Stavka* that Northwest Front had now grown too large to be managed by a single headquarters, and plans were put in place for the creation of a new Northern Front to take control of Fifth, Sixth and Twelfth Armies in the Baltic region. Immediately, this raised the question of who should be placed in command; few senior Russian officers had shown themselves in a particularly good light, and the few who had – such as Brusilov – were desperately needed in their existing roles. Finally, Grand Duke Nikolai turned once more to Ruzsky, apparently recovered from the illness that had forced him to resign his post earlier in the year.[37] Inevitably, Alexeyev was not in favour of such a diminution of his own command; Danilov wrote later that discussions about the new front dragged on, because Grand Duke Nikolai 'greatly valued the work of General Alexeyev and did not wish to insist and hurt his feelings'.[38] Once again, *Stavka* proved incapable of asserting its will over its subordinates.

On 14 August, Mackensen's forces advancing towards Brest-Litovsk ran into fresh Russian positions. Aerial reconnaissance confirmed Mackensen's suspicion that this was likely to be only a temporary halt to buy sufficient time for rear area units to continue their retreat, and he urged his men on. The weather turned a little cooler as the fighting drew closer to Brest-Litovsk. Linsingen's Bug Army forced a crossing over the Bug at Włodawa – about 27 miles (45km) south of Brest-Litovsk – on 15 August, but determined Russian counterattacks prevented exploitation of the bridgehead. Although Eleventh Army continued to fight its way towards Brest-Litovsk, it was clear that the bulk of the Russian Army had succeeded in pulling back across the Bug. There were further discussions between Falkenhayn and Mackensen, and both men agreed that there was little to be gained by driving on into Russia. The line of the Bug was to be held, and operations limited to local attacks.

Mackensen interpreted this as allowing him to order Linsingen to expand the Włodawa bridgehead and to push north and northeast, with a view to enclosing Brest-Litovsk from the south. The operation proceeded slowly, hindered by repeated Russian counterattacks. Nevertheless, even if it had proved impossible to force Russia to make peace, there were clear signs of disintegration in the armies that had been forced to retreat for so many weeks:

Lublin to Brest-Litovsk

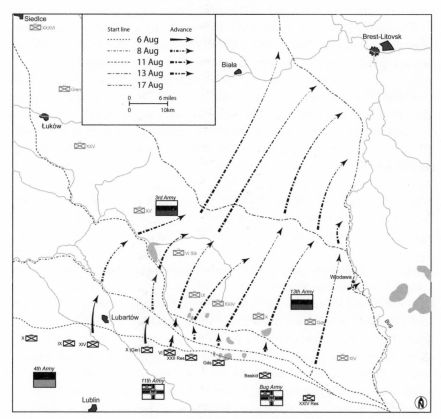

They offer resistance where they find field positions, or the terrain is particularly favourable. A few corps still conduct themselves well. But large numbers of troop formations are already showing signs of disintegration. Prisoners, including officers, frequently tell us that they regard the war as hopeless and that the troops grow tired of fighting.[39]

The mood in *Stavka* was as bleak as that in the Russian front line. Grand Duke Nikolai had once again urged the French to launch attacks in the west in order to force Germany to divert troops, but the response was disappointing: there could be no new offensives before mid-September. Nikolai finally moved to create the new Northern Front under Ruzsky's command on 17 August, to come into effect two weeks later, with the rest of Alexeyev's command now designated

Western Front, with First, Second, Third and Fourth Armies. The pessimistic mood amongst all officers ensured that the retreat continued even though there were increasing signs that the German and Austro-Hungarian forces were struggling to maintain their advance. The further east they moved, the poorer the roads and railways, and although they had suffered fewer casualties than their opponents, the cumulative effect was increasingly severe. Gallwitz's army had lost over a third of its strength, with perhaps another 20 per cent incapacitated through illness, and guns and other equipment were wearing out.[40]

Nevertheless, Linsingen slowly closed in on Brest-Litovsk from the south. By 22 August, there were clear signs that the Russians were abandoning the city and its fortifications. The heavy siege guns allocated for the reduction of the defences were still at least a week away, and Linsingen decided to press on without them. Arz's VI Corps overran the outer defences on 25 August, and XXII Reserve Corps broke through to the city further north. The following day, German troops occupied the citadel. In the days that followed, the Germans pursued the retreating Russians east, eventually stopping through exhaustion and at the very end of their supply lines along a line running roughly from Pinsk to Slonim.

Fighting continued all along the front. Kovel was abandoned by the Russians on 21 August, but as was the case elsewhere, the pursuit was increasingly hindered by the logistic difficulties of moving men and equipment forward. The attention of the Central Powers was already turning elsewhere, and it was time to take stock of the campaign – as far as Falkenhayn was concerned, he had achieved all that he could expect to achieve on the Eastern Front. Russia was clearly not going to accept a separate peace, and the complete destruction of the Russian Army had never been his intention. With so much territory gained and so much damage done to the Russians, it was highly likely that there would be no threat from the east for the foreseeable future.

Ludendorff had other ideas. He continued to believe that even at this late stage, a breakthrough in the north could unhinge the entire Russian line and perhaps knock Russia out of the war completely. Below's Niemen Army had advanced swiftly into southern Latvia, leaving Ludendorff to lament what might have been possible had the drive been given greater priority.[41] The Niemen Army was ordered to advance to seize crossings over the Western Dvina (now Daugava). Ludendorff was frequently criticised after the war for inflating his own achievements, but his logistic feats were quite remarkable; using railways with very limited capacity, twenty-eight of *Ober Ost*'s forty-one infantry divisions and five of its six cavalry divisions were concentrated in the Baltic region for this operation.

Below's troops marched on Friedrichstadt (now Jaunjelgava), reaching the river and securing a substantial part of its left bank in the last days of August, but were unable to cross to the right bank, along which ran the railway line to Riga. Similarly, Scholtz attacked towards Vilna, brushing aside the weak Russian Tenth Army. A frontal attack failed to break through, but largely through errors the Russians had left only a thin screen of troops to the north of the city, and a German force of four cavalry divisions under the command of Otto von Garnier brushed aside the defenders and penetrated as far as Sventsiany (now Švenčiónys), reaching the town on 12 September and cutting the railway line. Fearing further German advances, Alexeyev ordered a wholesale withdrawal of the line further south, in order to release troops that could be concentrated east of Sventsiany as part of a newly reconstituted Second Army in preparation for a counterattack.

Despite his hopes of a deep penetration to the east, Ludendorff had no intention of pushing on with only the limited firepower of Garnier's cavalry, and it proved impossible to move infantry forward to support them in any significant numbers. Instead, the Sventsiany salient was expanded south in order to put pressure upon the defenders of Vilna. With their lines of retreat threatened, the troops of the garrison had no choice but to withdraw, abandoning the city on 17 September. The Germans entered Vilna the following day.

At the end of the month, as the weather deteriorated, the exhausted German infantry reached and captured Baranovichi, the former location of *Stavka* and an important rail junction. There was bitter fighting southeast of Vilna when the German 1st Cavalry Division succeeded in reaching Smorgon and cutting the main railway lines on which the Russian armies depended; this triggered a series of Russian counterattacks, and it proved impossible for German infantry to reach the relatively lightly armed cavalry division in time to prevent a withdrawal, thus reopening the railway. One final German surge towards the northeast in Latvia, aimed at Dvinsk (now Daugavpils) ran out of steam about 10 miles (16km) short of the town, and a frustrated Ludendorff had to call off operations, not least because Falkenhayn insisted on the transfer of thirteen infantry divisions to the Western Front – there were clear signs that the French were preparing a new attack, and in any case, Falkenhayn refused to lose sight of his ultimate objective of winning the war by a victory in the west, not the east.

Stavka left its base in Baranovichi only a short time before the Germans reached the town. Danilov, the quartermaster-general, wanted to move to Borisov on the grounds that it had good railway communications, but Grand Duke Nikolai refused, apparently because he owned several large estates close to Borisov and did not wish to be seen as moving to a location that was convenient to him personally.[42] Instead, *Stavka* moved to Mogilev on 20 August, where there was a large civic reception followed by a service in the cathedral. Danilov regarded the location as less than ideal:

> The inconveniences of this position in a relatively important town did not take long to make themselves felt. A certain section of the headquarters staff established themselves in the town, and the familiar intimacy that had been established in the old headquarters seemed to be lost. The Grand Duke with his entourage and his chief of staff occupied the ground floor of the house of the provincial governor. The first floor was left free in case the tsar should visit *Stavka*. As for me, together with my staff and the telegraph section of headquarters I occupied a nearby house.[43]

Although Danilov wrote that normal activity resumed very quickly, it was not for long. One day before *Stavka* left Baranovichi, a telegram arrived to advise that War Minister Polivanov wished to visit. Shortly after the move to Mogilev, Polivanov arrived and went straight to see the grand duke; at midnight, he departed with several bundles of documents for Volkhovysk (now Vawkavysk), where Alexeyev's Western Front headquarters was located. Somewhat to the surprise of the staff at *Stavka*, he made no attempt to speak to Yanushkevich, the chief of the general staff, or to Danilov.

Polivanov had endured a difficult few days. About a week before, he had learned that the tsar intended to dismiss the grand duke, and take command of the army personally. There were many in Petrograd who were opposed to Nikolai; although Sukhomlinov had fallen from power, his faction continued its struggle against the conservatives, and Tsarina Alexandra had repeatedly urged the grand duke's dismissal. Although Nikolai's appointment had been greeted with general approval and acclaim, he had singularly failed to assert his will upon his various subordinates, and the pressure from his critics was becoming irresistible. Polivanov sent an urgent message to the tsar, pleading with him to reconsider; the war minister was acutely aware of the tsar's almost non-existent military experience, and given that the criticism of Grand Duke Nikolai had been largely that he lacked strategic vision and the forcefulness and skill to impose this vision on the factions within the army, it was inconceivable that the tsar would do any better. The only effect that Polivanov's intervention had was to earn him the hostility of the tsarina, and his protests were brushed aside.[44]

The day after Polivanov's visit to *Stavka* started with the usual morning meetings and discussions. Danilov was then summoned by Grand Duke Nikolai:

The Grand Duke received me on the first floor, in the unoccupied apartments. With a voice trembling with emotion, he told me to read the imperial edict that the minister for war had given him. It stated that at that terrible moment, when the enemy had invaded numerous provinces, the tsar had resolved to realise his old wish to take personal command of the army and the fleet. Affairs in the Caucasus required the leadership of a strong and experienced hand; given that the governor of that province, Count Vorontsov-Dashkov, was ill, Grand Duke Nikolai was assigned the post of commander-in-chief of the army in the Caucasus and governor-general of the Caucasus.[45]

Despite his ineffectual term as commander-in-chief, Grand Duke Nikolai was widely popular, and students in Petrograd staged a strike in protest when his dismissal was announced, while the Moscow city council passed a motion supporting him.[46] At the same time, Yanushkevich was dismissed as chief of the general staff, and replaced by Alexeyev. This was a change that attracted far less criticism; Yanushkevich was widely derided as nothing more than a toady of Sukhomlinov. Alexeyev had served as chief of staff at Southwest Front before taking command first of Northwest Front, then of the new Western Front, and had generally performed competently; his replacement at Western Front headquarters was Evert.

The dismissal of Grand Duke Nikolai was one matter; his replacement by the tsar was quite another. Danilov's thoughts on the matter were probably widely shared:

I will not examine in detail the reasons that persuaded Tsar Nicholas II to assume command of the active army in the situation that prevailed. These reasons are of too complex an order and can only be considered with great caution. At the time, I was convinced that the principal reason was the sovereign's mystic belief in his own abilities, his tendency to dwell on the great history of Russia, which had perhaps been presented to him in a false light; although certain human weaknesses may have played a role. But what I do not understand at all is how persons in his entourage, those in his confidence, could have sought deliberately to strengthen his conviction of the necessity and the opportunity to pursue this idea instead of dissuading him. How blind were they; could they not see the grave events that were developing and did they not understand that they risked compromising the already shaky authority of the head of state?[47]

Danilov might have been bound by the rules of military discipline to keep his doubts to himself, but others were more forthright. A letter signed by the

Procurator of the Holy Synod and eight of the thirteen ministers of the government warned the tsar that 'to the best of our judgement your decision threatens with serious consequences Russia, your dynasty, and your person.'[48] Foreign Minister Sazonov added that 'The war could be won only through the achievement of a harmonious and steady collaboration between the government and the public', judging that the tsar's decision would jeopardise this.[49]

One of the most prominent amongst the inner circle around the tsar was his wife Alexandra. She was widely disliked in Russia for several reasons. She was suspected of pro-German sympathies because of her ancestry – she was the child of Grand Duke Louis IV of Hesse, though the fact that her mother was Princess Alice, the second daughter of Queen Victoria, was generally overlooked. It was also widely known that she had not been a popular match, the marriage being opposed by both of Tsar Nicholas's parents; indeed, the Dowager Tsarina Maria continued to have a poor relationship with Alexandra after the marriage, and matters were not helped by the fact that Russian court protocol treated the dowager tsarina as the senior of the two. Alexandra was perceived as being cold and uncommunicative by many Russians, though others who were close to her felt that much of this was due to her deep-seated shyness. Although she embraced Orthodox Christianity with huge energy, she made no secret of her dislike of most other aspects of Russian culture, and through a mixture of her own personality and her sense of isolation in the Russian court, she associated with a series of other 'misfits', the last and most notorious of which was Grigori Rasputin. At the time that Tsar Nicholas dismissed Grand Duke Nikolai, Rasputin had great influence over Alexandra, and it is probably no coincidence that he repeatedly urged her to persuade Nicholas to take personal control of the war.

Much has been written about Rasputin. George Buchanan, the British ambassador in Petrograd, shared the same low opinion of him that prevailed in almost all of the diplomatic corps:

The role actually played by Rasputin at court is still veiled in a good deal of mystery. His ascendancy over the Emperor was not so absolute as that which he exercised over the Empress, and concerned questions of a religious or ecclesiastical kind rather than of policy. He interested himself chiefly, at first, in securing for his friends and adherents high appointments in the Orthodox Church and in dispossessing any prelate who had ventured to speak disparagingly of him …

Gradually, however, he began to take a hand in the political game. He was on intimate terms with several of the more reactionary ministers, who were at one and the same time his patrons and clients. A few words written on a slip of paper sufficed to secure the granting by these ministers of the requests of his protégés. He would, on the other hand, in his conversations with the Empress and Madame Wyroubova, speak in the sense which they desired, or he would advocate the appointment of some reactionary friend of his to a vacant ministry. He thus indirectly influenced the Emperor in the choice of his ministers, and consequently in the course of his policy. This was more especially the case when, after the assumption by the Emperor of the supreme command, the Empress became all powerful.

... Uneducated, and engrossed by the pursuit of carnal pleasures, he was hardly the man to conceive or formulate any concrete policy. He left that to others, and was content to follow their lead. Self-interest was his guiding principle through life.[50]

The importance of Alexandra's support and her probable influence in his decision-making is highlighted in a letter from the tsar to his wife dated 25 August:

I know of no more pleasant feeling than to be proud of you, as I have been all these past months, when you urged me on with untiring importunity, exhorting me to be firm and to stick to my own opinions.[51]

It seems that Nicholas had no illusions about his own military prowess, but was motivated by a desire to show that the imperial family was taking a lead, and hoped that it would raise morale if the head of state were seen to be at the head of the army. Instead, it plunged the professional soldiers of the army into gloom, as Brusilov recorded:

The whole army, indeed all of Russia, believed in [Grand Duke] Nikolai Nikolayevich. Of course, he had his flaws, even significant ones, but they were more than compensated by his merits as a military leader ... In any case, even if there was a need to move Nikolai Nikolayevich ... nobody expected that the tsar would take over the responsibilities of supreme commander at this difficult moment. It was common knowledge that Nicholas II knew absolutely nothing about the army, and that taking this title was only nominal, with all decision-making left to his chief of staff.[52]

Nor did Brusilov approve entirely of the appointment of Alexeyev as chief of the general staff:

He possessed a good mind with great military knowledge, was quick of thought and certainly a good strategist. I believe that he would have been perfect as chief of the general staff, but as a supreme leader [given that Nicholas would always defer to his decisions and advice] he constantly wavered, and was totally unsuitable because he did not have a strong and determined will.[53]

To make matters worse, Nicholas appointed Alexandra to act as his regent while he was with the army; any improvement in general morale that he might have expected from his assuming command was more than countered by the hostility to the notion that his wife was now such a powerful figure.

It was the end of Grand Duke Nikolai's involvement with the Eastern Front. He stayed on in *Stavka* until the tsar arrived to take command, and then left for the Caucasus. Although he was nominally the commander in the region, General Nikolai Nikolayevich Yudenich was the true authority. The two men combined very effectively and won some local victories against Turkish forces, penetrating into Turkey itself, but the mountainous terrain and lack of railways made it impossible to sustain any momentum. In order to rectify this, the grand duke proposed building a railway across the Caucasus, but work had not started when the tsar was forced to abdicate in 1917. Immediately before his abdication, the tsar appointed Nikolai to the post of commander-in-chief again, but by the time he reached *Stavka* in Mogilev, the Russian prime minister, Prince Georgy Yevgenyevich Lvov, had cancelled his appointment. He withdrew to the Crimea, and in 1919 he boarded a British warship and sailed into exile. He took up residence in France, where he remained involved in anti-Bolshevik activity until his death in 1927.

CHAPTER 10

VOLHYNIA

THE END OF THE LEASH

As the days began to shorten, Conrad attempted to pursue further gains in Galicia and the province of Volhynia to the northeast. After the capture of Lemberg, Mackensen's forces had turned north, with the result that the Russians remained relatively close to the city towards the east. In order to eliminate this threat, and to take advantage of the gap that had opened in the Russian front when the retreating forces were forced to fall back along diverging axes, it was proposed to launch an attack to overrun eastern Galicia and Volhynia. The codename of the attack was the Black–Yellow Offensive, so-called after the black-and-yellow flag of the Austro-Hungarian Empire. This would be the first major operation to be mounted under the leadership of the *k.u.k.* Army without the aid of the Germans since the disasters in the Carpathians, but Conrad planned the operation with his usual enthusiasm and high expectations. The Austro-Hungarian First Army was to attack from Władimir Wołynsk towards Lutsk and Rovno (now Rivne) while Second Army moved east from Lemberg; the two armies would then converge, intending to isolate and crush a significant portion of Brusilov's Eighth Army. In order to increase the chances of success, Conrad proposed to move Fourth Army to support the northern flank of First Army, and to extract VI Corps from the German Eleventh Army, with which it had been serving for several months.

Falkenhayn had his doubts about the likelihood of success of Conrad's operation, especially given the difficult terrain over which it was to be mounted – several rivers lay across the path of the proposed advance, barely a day's march apart and often surrounded by swampy ground, and each would provide the Russians with the opportunity to put up determined resistance. Attempts to restore the railway lines destroyed by the retreating Russians were progressing slowly, but until the repairs were complete the limited capacity would make it difficult to sustain any advance, particularly if the Russians were able to erect successive defensive lines that would require artillery preparation before assaults could be launched. He was also concerned that the operation would be a largely Austro-Hungarian affair, without a large German contingent and particularly without German leadership. However, even a partial success would move the Russians further from Lemberg and any victory would help restore the self-confidence of Germany's ally, and on 27 August the troops of Fourth Army and VI Corps began their transfer.

The comparative quiet on this sector of the front for the previous few weeks had allowed most of the Austro-Hungarian divisions to absorb new drafts and bring their ammunition stocks up towards full strength. The Russians, too, had been able to get some desperately needed rest, and although this sector of the front was accorded a lower priority by *Stavka*, divisions that had been reduced to fewer than 4,000 men were able to replenish their companies and battalions, though they still remained significantly below establishment strength. Like their Austro-Hungarian opponents, their biggest weakness remained in the crippling shortage of fully trained officers and NCOs – Brusilov estimated that some regiments had as few as five officers.[1] In addition, the Russian shell shortage was a constant issue. Staff officers at *AOK* estimated that Ivanov's forces in the area amounted to twenty-nine infantry divisions and fourteen cavalry divisions, none at full strength, whereas the *k.u.k.* Army had thirty-eight infantry divisions and eight cavalry divisions at its disposal for the attack.[2] Even if some of them were also still below their establishment strength, *AOK* characteristically treated them as if they were fresh and their ranks completely filled.

Brusilov was acutely aware of the weakness of his northern flank, but he had been forced to divert so many troops to other parts of the front that he lacked the reserves to resolve the situation. He requested permission to pull back from the Bug, and was relieved when Ivanov finally assented, albeit after a delay of three days. It was not a moment too soon: on 26 August, Szurmay's troops attacked east of Władimir Wołynsk, pushing back Brusilov's rearguards about 15 miles (25km) over two days. The Russians intended to contest the line of the River Sierna, but reinforcements that had been dispatched to Brusilov's northern flank – XXXIX Corps, which was made up almost exclusively of reservists with few experienced officers and NCOs – were still en route, leaving much of the front in

Black–Yellow Offensive

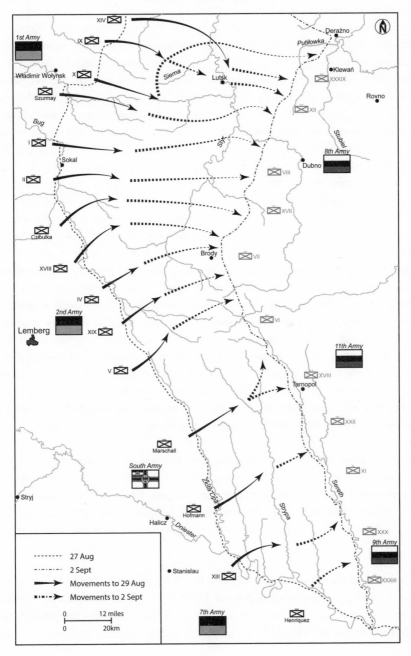

this sector covered only by cavalry. Nevertheless, resistance was determined, with repeated counterattacks all along the line.

Despite the costly Russian counterattacks, the northern wing of Conrad's planned encirclement of the Russians had made an encouraging start. On 27 August the southern wing, consisting of Böhm-Ermolli's Second Army and Bothmer's South Army, began its advance. The Austro-Hungarian Second Army faced a difficult advance across the steep, wooded valley of the Złota Lipa; despite a heavy preliminary bombardment, the attackers suffered heavy losses as they pressed forward into the positions of the Russian VI Corps, but managed to secure most of the eastern side of the valley by nightfall. South Army, the only German contingent in Conrad's operation, also made progress, pushing forward a couple of miles beyond Buszcze where the assault fell on the seam between the Russian XVIII and XXII Corps.

The first major objective of the advance was the town of Lutsk in the north. Brusilov had hoped to deploy XXXIX Corps here, but there continued to be delays with its arrival, leaving the defence of Lutsk largely in the hands of the Russian cavalry. To make matters worse, most of the defences around the town had been built with the expectation of an attack from the south, whereas the threat was now from the west. Nevertheless, General Sergei Fedorovich Stelnitsky, commander of XXXIX Corps, deployed the cavalry and the few formations of his own corps that were available and succeeded in giving the impression that he intended to stand and fight. As Szurmay's troops probed forward cautiously from the west, Stelnitsky launched a few limited though energetic counterattacks, and the commander of the Austro-Hungarian First Army, Paul Puhallo, decided to bring up his heavy artillery rather than risk a setback. Conrad impatiently urged his subordinate to show greater energy and to bypass the Russian defences:

> AOK expects binding orders to corps commanders to adhere completely to its wishes and the achievement of the overall objective, which is certainly achievable in view of our significant superiority [in numbers] if powerful forces are not deployed in pointless frontal attacks as the enemy wishes. The enemy's defence [of the line around Lutsk] must be rendered impossible by thorough envelopment of his northern flank.[3]

The heart of the problem was the doctrine that Conrad had instilled into the *k.u.k.* Army in the years before the war. He believed passionately that the enemy should be engaged and destroyed on the battlefield, and this lay behind the repeated frontal attacks that his subordinates launched throughout the war.

Exploiting weak points in the enemy line to carry out sweeping manoeuvres around exposed flanks had been encouraged, but only with a view to falling upon the enemy centre once the flank had been turned rather than pressing on into the rear areas, yet now Conrad criticised the men he had trained for not showing more imagination. And, of course, the successful campaigns of the summer had been a series of deliberate assaults on the Russian Army, concentrating on solid, pragmatic advances. Now, when an opportunity arose for a swift flanking movement, the opportunity seemed to be ignored. In keeping with Conrad's instructions, Puhallo ordered XIV Corps on 29 August to bypass Lutsk to the north and to push forward towards Rovno; in addition, X Corps was pulled out of the front line due west of Lutsk and sent to reinforce the thrust north of the town. However, Puhallo could not hide his irritation at Conrad's message, responding that his orders had been to drive back the northern flank of the Russian forces and to take Lutsk as quickly as possible. Immediately, Conrad sent a further message to Puhallo, stating that speed was of the essence if the Russians were to be caught before they could withdraw. As they abandoned their positions, he told the commander of First Army, it should be possible to move ever stronger forces to the northern flank.[4]

Fighting steadily intensified at the end of August. Austro-Hungarian cavalry succeeded in coming within a few miles of the northern outskirts of Lutsk on 30 August, but elsewhere the advance was held up by determined resistance. Aerial reconnaissance reported long columns withdrawing to the east behind these strong rearguards, and interrogation of prisoners from the battles north of Lutsk revealed the arrival of more elements of Stelnitsky's XXXIX Corps. Conrad continued to demand rapid advances in the north and greater energy against the Russians along the entire front. While Puhallo attempted to reinforce his northern flank in the hope of turning the Russian position on the last day of August, Brusilov decided that prolonged resistance along the current front line would play into his opponent's hands and ordered a withdrawal behind the River Styr to the south of Lutsk. As the centre and southern flank of Puhallo's army moved forward into the abandoned Russian positions, fighting continued north of Lutsk, and the town fell to Austro-Hungarian cavalry and elements of XIV Corps on 31 August.

It was a considerable success for the Austro-Hungarian First Army to have captured Lutsk, but the chance of outflanking Brusilov's forces and rolling them up from the north had effectively gone. South of Lutsk, the Russians paused along the Styr and then resumed their steady withdrawal, striking back whenever the opportunity arose. A strong Russian counterattack against the centre of

Bothmer's South Army caused panic on 30 August, and similar events further south brought Pflanzer-Baltin to a halt, where Zayontchovsky's rejuvenated XXX Corps entered the fray. A prudent choice would have been to decide that, at the end of a long year's fighting and after first the catastrophic losses in the Carpathians, then the sustained offensive to the Bug, it was perhaps time to settle for what had been gained to date. On this occasion, as on so many others, Conrad's choice was far from prudent. The offensive was to continue.

September brought rain, and with it the majority of the roads in the region turned to mud, further hindering movement, particularly of supplies. Nevertheless the southern flank of the Austro-Hungarian attack reached and secured Brody on 1 September, but attempts by Pflanzer-Baltin to outflank the Russians repeatedly failed. It was only when the South Army was able to resume its advance that the Russians pulled back from the line of the River Strypa. But despite the modest successes that his forces had achieved, Conrad remained determined to strike a telling blow at the Russian Southwest Front; Joseph Ferdinand's Fourth Army was to join with Puhallo's First Army to outflank the Russians from the north. In principle, the forces gathered under Joseph Ferdinand's overall control – his own army, with IX, X, and XIV Corps and two additional divisions in *Gruppe Smekal*, and First Army with I and II Corps and *Korps Szurmay* – represented a powerful concentration, but it would take time to gather the formations together and none was remotely close to full strength. Brusilov was aware that his northern flank had been mauled in the fighting around Lutsk, and decided not to attempt to stop a further Austro-Hungarian advance. As a result, when the Austro-Hungarian XIV Corps moved forward from its start line about 6 miles (10km) east of Lutsk, it encountered almost no resistance. Rapid exploitation of the unexpected Russian withdrawal proved difficult – before they abandoned Lutsk, the Russians had destroyed the bridges over the Styr in the town, and Joseph Ferdinand's army struggled across the river via improvised footbridges.

On 2 September, Joseph Ferdinand ordered his troops to pursue the Russians energetically. Brusilov had pulled back to the line of the River Putiłowka, and when the Austro-Hungarian XIV Corps ran into the new Russian defences, it was ordered to pin the Russians in position while X Corps moved up to outflank them to the north by penetrating into the high ground near Derażno. Unfortunately, this was precisely the area where Brusilov had decided to concentrate XXX Corps, transferred from further south where it had already checked Pflanzer-Baltin's advance. Together with several cavalry formations, Zayontchovsky was to launch a powerful counterattack against the northern wing of the Austro-Hungarian advance – a mirror image of Conrad's plan. At the same time, Puhallo's First Army reached the outskirts of Dubno, but Russian positions along high ground immediately to the west of the town brought the advance to an abrupt halt. Worse was to follow as Brusilov launched powerful local attacks at the northern end of the battlefront; with all his troops committed to trying to break through the Russian line, Joseph Ferdinand found himself with almost no reserves to send to the critical northern flank.

It was a major setback for Conrad, for all sorts of reasons. He had already allocated VI Corps to the forthcoming invasion of Serbia, but now had to hold this formation on the Eastern Front in case it was needed to block the Russian counterattack, resulting in a humiliating request to the Germans to provide additional troops for the Serbian invasion in place of VI Corps. Despite this, a pragmatic policy would have been one of securing the ground already gained and building a strong defensive line to beat off further Russian attacks. Instead, Conrad insisted that his planned outflanking of the Russian line from the north was to proceed, even though this would require an advance through the very sector where the Russians appeared to be gathering their own forces. To a large extent, this was driven by a continuing belief – based upon intelligence from immediately before the operation began – that the Russians had fewer divisions than was actually the case. The Russian attacks, *AOK* assured the local army commanders, were unlikely to be sustainable. Once they had been beaten off, the Russian line was to be turned from the north.

On 3 September, intense fighting continued in the northern sector without Joseph Ferdinand's troops achieving a breakthrough, and casualties continued to mount up. Major Karl Scheller, an officer on Conrad's staff, summed up the irritation of the officers at *AOK*:

This entire operation belongs among the most shameful in the annals of what we have been able to accomplish in leadership. An entire army is held up by two brigades.[5]

At the same time, repeated Russian attacks in First Army's sector created a series of local crises. Conrad vented his anger in a message to the front line:

AOK arranged the assembly of the strongest possible forces for the attack against the northern wing of the Russian Southwest Front, to create the conditions for a rapid, thorough success. This requires Fourth Army to achieve its battlefield objectives through resolute leadership and the assertion of its will. The battlefield situation may become difficult due to the thinly held front on the southern flank of First Army, but these must be overcome through decisive battlefield leadership by subordinate commanders and determined attacks by the superior Fourth Army against the opposing enemy.[6]

The message is entirely characteristic of Conrad's continuing belief in the ability of willpower to overcome all difficulties. Despite all his setbacks over the preceding thirteen months, he clearly remained convinced of the paramount importance of determination by his subordinates to assert their will, beyond all considerations of firepower and numerical strength. However, Conrad had a valid point; any Austro-Hungarian formation of any size consistently performed worse than German or Russian formations, and this was true at every level, from commanders to ordinary soldiers, and it could be argued that more energetic leadership was desperately needed. The converse argument, though, is that the army had been badly degraded as a result of its terrible losses since the outbreak of the war – and Conrad was ultimately responsible for the mistakes that had led to those losses, from the doctrine and equipment of the army through to its deployment.

As had repeatedly been demonstrated throughout the summer, any advance through strongly defended positions required substantial supplies to be brought forward. Now that the chance of bypassing the Russian northern flank was gone, Joseph Ferdinand was faced with the sort of assault that Mackensen had made on several occasions, and the inadequate railway and road communications from the rear areas became critical. Despite their losses, the Austro-Hungarian formations would perhaps have prevailed had sufficient ammunition and food been available for them, and the 'decisive' attack ordered for the concentrated forces of Fourth Army for 4 September might have succeeded. On the designated day, X Corps struggled forward through the rain, its southern flank exposed to Russian artillery, and gained minimal ground before it was brought to a standstill, its flanks exposed. The casualties on both sides were similar to those experienced on the Western Front, but even this state of affairs would have been acceptable, in that it tied down significant Russian forces, if the outflanking movement to the north proved successful. The Austro-Hungarian 4th Infantry Division had moved into position by forced marches, and together with XIV and IX Corps it threw itself forward.

It was a battle that would have been familiar to the combatants in Flanders and northern France. The Austro-Hungarian troops waited for their artillery to complete its bombardment, and then climbed out of their trenches and plodded forwards through the rain and mud towards the Russian lines. In places, the barbed wire had been broken by shellfire, but elsewhere it remained intact, and Russian artillery and machine-guns steadily reduced the attackers' numbers.

Nevertheless, there was encouraging progress in some sectors, and the troops paused to regroup before continuing. At this point, they received repeated demands from X Corps to the north for an attack to relieve the pressure on its southern flank. Roth, commander of XIV Corps, doubted that any such attack was possible, given the losses his men had sustained. On 5 September, X Corps attempted to advance further east, despite the threats to its flanks; by the end of the day, most of its surviving troops were back in their starting positions, having suffered heavy losses as they struggled to reach and penetrate the main Russian positions, which were protected in some regions by large expanses of swampy ground where a small river, swollen by autumn rain, had burst its banks. The Austro-Hungarian 4th Cavalry Division had been moved to try to protect the northern flank of X Corps, but it ran into the Russian 3rd Don Cossack Division and made limited progress; even more alarmingly, the Austro-Hungarian cavalry reported other Russian mounted units moving into position against X Corps' northern flank. At the same time, reports arrived of Cossacks raiding as far as Kovel, some considerable distance to the west.

All along the battlefront, the advance seemed to be slowing, through a combination of supply shortages, muddy terrain, and casualties – both from Russian action and illness, which was widespread due to the constant rain and lack of adequate food and rest. Nevertheless, by the end of 5 September it seemed that the Russian resistance before Second Army and South Army was weakening. Bothmer suggested to his neighbour that the two armies should take a day to gather their strength for a major attack on 7 September, but Böhm-Ermolli didn't wish to delay, and ordered his troops to try to achieve a definitive breakthrough a day before the Germans would be ready. After a powerful artillery bombardment, Böhm-Ermolli's troops stormed the Russian positions, and achieved considerable gains, but as had often been the case, Brusilov's commanders pulled back before the local successes could be exploited, and set up new defences further east. Nevertheless, the fighting was taking its toll on the Russians. The only reinforcements that Ivanov could send to replenish the battered divisions facing Böhm-Ermolli were half-trained recruits who had not yet finished their basic training.[7]

But if the Russians were badly weakened, the forces that Conrad had dispatched were also haemorrhaging away their strength. The original intention had been to try to encircle a large part of Brusilov's Eighth Army before it could retreat, but in reality there had probably never been any prospect of that succeeding – the poor roads and rainy weather would have impeded any attempt to bypass Brusilov's northern flank, even if such an attempt had been made instead of repeated bloody frontal assaults, and there were no vital cities or positions that the Russians could be forced to defend. Had Conrad's subordinates shown as much imagination as he demanded of them, it is likely that Brusilov would have been able to pull back further east to safety.

Bothmer's South Army might be close to the southern outskirts of Tarnopol, but it remained to be seen whether it had the strength to take the town. A little further south, the advantage had already swung back to the Russians, who finally had sufficient supplies of ammunition. This, combined with the shortened supply lines as a result of their retreat, gave them an important advantage. On 6 September; the Russian XI Corps, part of Ninth Army, attacked the Austro-Hungarian *Korps Hofmann* and the neighbouring formations of Pflanzer-Baltin's Seventh Army. As was so often the case, the Austro-Hungarian line proved to be brittle, and fell back in considerable disarray. Heavy fighting erupted around Tarnopol, where Bothmer's forces – planning to attack the town on 7 September, as he had discussed with Böhm-Ermolli – ran headlong into a powerful Russian attack coming the other way. Whilst this battle raged on, with the Germans ultimately gaining the upper hand, the line to the south continued to disintegrate, and Bothmer's formations fell back towards the west, leaving behind several guns and thousands of prisoners. Only the reluctance of the Russians to follow energetically, combined with determined resistance from two regiments of the German 3rd Guards Infantry Division, prevented a complete rout.[8] Nevertheless, the ground that the Russians had gained created a large salient projecting towards the west, giving them ample options for further exploitation.

On 8 September, Pflanzer-Baltin's *Gruppe Benigni* crossed the Dniester and managed to advance about three miles (5km) at the southern extreme of the battlefield, but it lacked the strength to achieve more than local successes, and in any case was too far from the centre of events. Two cavalry divisions that attacked a little further north also made some promising progress at first, capturing perhaps 3,700 Russians and several machine-guns, but the main effort was against the threatening Russian bulge south of Tarnopol. While Bothmer attacked from the north, Pflanzer-Baltin attempted to create a southern attack group, but as was so often the case, these attacks foundered in the face of powerful defensive fire.

Throughout this period, Joseph Ferdinand had not given up hope of breaking through to Rovno. While Puhallo's First Army tied down the Russians immediately west of Rovno, Fourth Army would try once more to turn the northern flank of Brusilov's Eighth Army. Once more, it was more in hope than expectation that the Austro-Hungarian infantry struggled forward on 8 September over terrain that the constant rain had turned into little more than a swamp; inevitably, the gains were small, whereas the losses were great. That evening, Conrad complained

Russian Counterattacks, September 1915

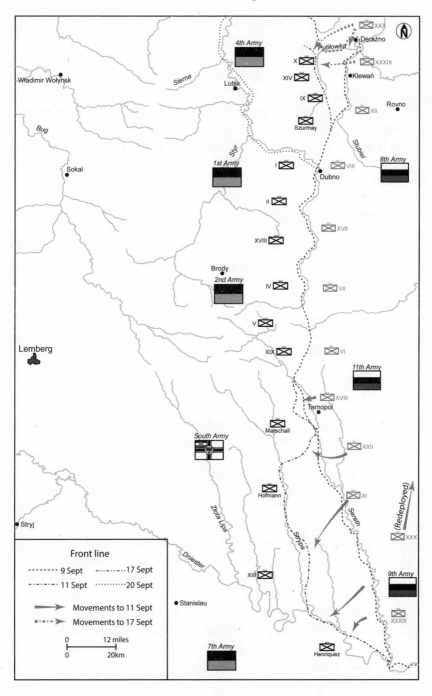

bitterly about the lack of progress, berating Joseph Ferdinand that he had been given fourteen divisions to achieve his objectives and was faced by perhaps half a dozen Russian divisions; this concentration had left the rest of the line dangerously weak, and it was therefore all the more important that the attack succeeded.[9] Joseph Ferdinand responded by ordering his subordinates to press on at all costs, and at first – overnight and early on 9 September – it seemed as if the Russians were withdrawing in front of his forces.

The Russian salient south of Tarnopol represented a serious threat to the forces of the Central Powers. If the Russians should attack in either direction, they might succeed in rolling up a significant portion of the front, much as Conrad had hoped to do with his attempt to outflank Brusilov further north. Consequently, Böhm-Ermolli dispatched first Feldmarschallleutnant Maximilian von Csicserics' 14th Infantry Division, then Generalmajor Julius Ritter von Birkenhain's 34th Infantry Division, to support Bothmer's northern flank by attacking north of Tarnopol; if this were to succeed, the Russian defence of the town would become impossible, and this in turn would force the Russians to withdraw from their new gains south of Tarnopol. Further troops were committed to the group commanded by Csicserics, on 8 September, but although this weakened Böhm-Ermolli's centre, he remained determined to attack here too, with V Corps – he was constantly reminded by *AOK* that he outnumbered the Russians facing him, and should be able to overcome them.

These repeated instructions from Conrad flew in the face of military doctrine that had prevailed for over a century. Simply outnumbering an enemy was no guarantee of success, particularly when that enemy was deployed in a defensive posture. In order to ensure that the attack succeeded, it was generally accepted that odds of 3:1 or greater in favour of the attackers were needed, either in numerical terms or by the use of 'force multipliers' such as heavy artillery, and although his forces outnumbered the Russians, it was not by a sufficient margin to ensure success. Nor did Conrad take into account the degraded state of his formations. However, Csicserics was less inclined to ignore the realities on the ground, and chose not to attack on 8 September as originally intended, in order to give those formations that had arrived a chance to rest and recuperate. Many formations, particularly artillery, were still en route, held up by the poor roads which had effectively disintegrated in the constant rain.

Others took a different view of the situation. The longer Csicserics delayed, Bothmer protested, the stronger the Russian defences would be, and his hard-pressed army desperately needed the support that the planned attack north of Tarnopol would provide. Böhm-Ermolli agreed, and ordered Csicserics to hand over command of his forces to Feldmarschallleutnant Ignaz Trollmann, commander of XIX Corps. Trollmann was ordered to launch the attack on 9 September without further delay; Csicserics pleaded in vain for a start date of 10 September, as this was in keeping with his plans and preparations.

The day of the attack was rainy, with mist obscuring much of the battlefield and making effective artillery preparation impossible. When the weather improved a little in the afternoon, Trollmann ordered the infantry to launch its attack. As Csicserics had feared, many of the designated troops were still not ready, and without artillery preparation – many guns were trapped on the muddy roads, and the weather prevented the others from giving proper support – the attack failed completely, as did the attack by V Corps, a little to the north. But whilst the attacks gained no ground, they forced the Russian forces that were threatening South Army – primarily Aleksandr Fridrikhovich Brinsen's XXII Corps – to pause for a moment; Shcherbachev, commander of Eleventh Army, wished to ensure that no threat would develop to the rear of his army if the Austro-Hungarian forces continued their attack. But if *Korps Hofmann* had a little breathing space, the same was not true on the southern flank of the Russian salient. Here, the Russian forces consisted of Vladimir Mikhailovich Dragomirov's IX Corps, part of Lechitsky's Ninth Army, and they resumed their attacks on 9 September, swiftly driving back the Austro-Hungarian XIII Corps, the formations of which had been too badly depleted in the preceding battles to offer much resistance; since the start of Conrad's ill-fated offensive, its divisions had lost 17,000 men, more than half its establishment strength.[10] By the end of the day the Russians had advanced about 6 miles (10km).

The last major line of defence west of Rovno ran along yet another waterway, the River Stubiel, and it seemed as if the Russians intended to make a stand here. Conrad urged Joseph Ferdinand to avoid a costly frontal attack and to try to turn the northern flank of the Russian position. Such a move would have been the most likely option to succeed – but only if the attacking troops had been fresh and strong, with good roads at their disposal to allow rapid movement, and if the terrain had been suitable for such an operation. The exhausted Austro-Hungarian infantry plodded forward through the endless mud in pursuit of the Russians, at the end of supply lines that would have struggled to cope merely to keep them adequately supplied, let alone to bring forward sufficient *matériel* to allow for high-tempo offensive operations. As expected, the advancing troops rapidly ran into the last Russian line of defence before Rovno on 10 September, and 62nd Infantry Division succeeded in pushing northeast as far as Derażno, hindered as much by the swamps and dense forests as by Russian resistance. Far from outflanking Brusilov's line, the division found itself in a dangerous salient, threatened from the north and east, not least because the cavalry formations that were meant to be protecting Joseph Ferdinand's northern flank had made almost no headway against their Russian counterparts. Attempts by Szurmay to advance towards Rovno from the west made no progress whatever; desperate to fulfil Conrad's orders, Joseph Ferdinand dispatched further reinforcements to Derażno with orders to break the Russian line on 12 September. This completely ignored the swampy terrain and the lack of heavy artillery without which any attempt to break through the Russian defences was doomed to failure.

Events elsewhere were also not going Conrad's way. Following the failure of the Austro-Hungarian attacks north of Tarnopol, Shcherbachev ordered Brinsen's XXII Corps to resume its attacks against South Army. The German 3rd Guards Infantry Division, which had already put up stout resistance, succeeded in holding off most of Brinsen's attacks, but immediately west of Tarnopol an attack by the Russian XVIII Corps forced the South Army to give ground. To the south, other elements of Lechitsky's army joined the attacks, levering Pflanzer-Baltin's troops back from the Sereth valley. Large parts of the front were now held by the thinnest of lines – a gap of 15 miles (25km) between XIII Corps and *Korps Henriquez* was defended by only half of a cavalry division – and reinforcements were desperately needed. This couldn't have come at a worse time for Conrad, who had agreed only a few days before with Falkenhayn to transfer troops south for the forthcoming invasion of Serbia, and now had to tell his German counterpart that he would not be able to provide as many troops as he had promised. Although Falkenhayn agreed to make up the shortfall, he did so on condition that Conrad abandoned further offensive plans in Volhynia.[11] For the avoidance of all doubt, he sent a characteristically precise message to *AOK*:

> Your Excellency will agree with me that further unfavourable developments in Galicia must be prevented, as even without the serious current degradation of both *k.u.k.* and German troops, the overall situation will be influenced unfavourably. Unfortunately, there are already signs of this. In my opinion, the only remedy for the loss of strength already suffered by the troops is to refrain from further attempts at offensive and a complete switch to defence in strong positions which should be constructed immediately with all means available.[12]

Following the agreement with Falkenhayn – which to a large extent was imposed upon him, as he required the Germans to make good his own inability to release troops for the planned invasion of Serbia – Conrad discussed matters with

Böhm-Ermolli on 10 September. If the two attacks north of Tarnopol were not going to succeed, Second Army was to send at least an infantry division south to reinforce the line held by *Korps Marschall*. Böhm-Ermolli assured him that the attacks would succeed, and given the time that it would take to transfer a division to the threatened sector further south, it was better to use the troops where they currently stood ready for attack. Both he and Conrad knew from radio intercepts that the Russians were moving XXX Corps – the entire operational reserve of Southwest Front – north, and if a decisive breakthrough towards Rovno was to be achieved, it had to be done quickly before these additional Russian troops further reinforced the defences.

Böhm-Ermolli's confidence in achieving a breakthrough was of little relevance unless the attack succeeded in forcing a general Russian withdrawal. It was an optimistic point of view, given the failure of either attack to make any headway, and it can surely have come as no surprise when no success came on 10 September – indeed, Russian counterattacks actually drove the attackers out of the minimal gains that they had made to date. With the position of South Army growing worse by the day, Böhm-Ermolli's hand was forced, and he ordered Trollmann to transfer troops to the south immediately; however, the attempts to break the Russian line north of Tarnopol were to continue. The responses from the front line were rather more realistic. Neither Trollmann nor Feldmarschallleutnant Goglia, commander of V Corps, regarded further attacks as possible. Their formations had lost too many men, and such attacks could only succeed with extensive artillery support. With great reluctance, Böhm-Ermolli allowed both attacks to be abandoned. Conrad signalled Falkenhayn that he had given the order for his troops to take up defensive positions, with the exception of the extreme north of the battlefield, where he still clung to the hope that a breakthrough might be achieved.

The Russian attacks south of Tarnopol had been remarkably successful, and by mid-September Lechitsky and Shcherbachev reported that they had collectively taken about 36,000 prisoners and had captured over thirty guns.[13] Until now Bothmer, the Bavarian commander of the German South Army, had shown the diplomatic touch needed to command a force that contained both German and Austro-Hungarian formations, but even he was forced to express his concerns about the *k.u.k.* elements of South Army, writing to Conrad about the worrying tendency of the troops – no longer just those from the Czech parts of the Austro-Hungarian Empire – to surrender too easily.[14] Meanwhile, Ivanov urged on his army commanders, seeking to maximise his gains. Lechitsky's Ninth Army now tried to create a breakthrough between the German South Army and Pflanzer-

Baltin's Seventh Army, attacking *Korps Henriquez* on 12 September, and drove back its left flank in disarray. Pflanzer-Baltin was visiting the front at the time, and personally supervised the dispatch of all available reserves to the threatened area. Fighting continued through the night into the next day and ultimately the Russians held onto their gains, though the concentrated fire of Pflanzer-Baltin's artillery managed to bring their advance to a halt. *Korps Henriquez* struggled to reorder its battered formations; it had started the month with a little under two divisions, and had lost at least half its strength.

Shcherbachev, too, continued to try to exploit his recent successes. When his troops moved forward to assault *Korps Marschall*, they found that their opponents had already withdrawn to fresh positions further west along the Strypa, and they followed cautiously. A little further north energetic attacks by the Russian VI Corps on the southern flank of Trollmann's XIX Corps at the seam of the Austro-Hungarian Second Army and South Army threatened to penetrate the main defensive line. But although both its flanks were turned, 14th Infantry Division showed unusual stubbornness, holding its central position until its flank formations could rally and move back into line. Although the northern divisions of XIX Corps were forced back, Trollmann's divisions at least avoided a major setback. By contrast, V Corps a little to the north was unable to resist the pressure of the Russian VII Corps and fell back in considerable disarray, and only the slowness of the Russian pursuit prevented a complete rout.

Brusilov was now ready to start attacking the exposed Austro-Hungarian forces to the west and northwest of Rovno. XXXIX Corps moved forward on 13 September at Klewań; the official Austro-Hungarian history of the war records that thick fog allowed the Russians to secure crossings over the stream of the Stubiel, and it is worth remembering that when the *k.u.k.* Army had attempted to attack it had frequently blamed fog for preventing its artillery to function effectively. For much of the day, there was a danger that the Russians would achieve a deep penetration at the seam between the Austro-Hungarian X and XIV Corps, but counterattacks late in the day restored the situation. A little further north, X Corps continued to try to break out of its salient into the area north of Rovno, and in desperation Joseph Ferdinand committed the half-trained replacement drafts that had just arrived into the battle. However, he had run out of time, and orders arrived in the evening for the cessation of offensive operations. The situation elsewhere along the front required the urgent transfer of forces away from the northern flank.

There was little relief in the coming days. Further heavy Russian attacks followed against South Army and Second Army on 14 September, but the

Russians were now facing the same difficulties as their opponents had faced throughout the summer: sustaining offensive operations was almost impossible without good roads and railways to move the vital stockpiles of ammunition and other *matériel*. Nevertheless, *Korps Hofmann* was forced back once again, potentially exposing the flanks of its neighbouring formations to further Russian attacks. Reserves were now almost non-existent, and – as had repeatedly been the case since the start of the war – the *k.u.k.* Army found itself facing disaster.

On 14 September, Falkenhayn travelled to Teschen to meet Conrad personally. Bluntly, he told the chief of the Austro-Hungarian general staff that he should consider a major withdrawal to the line of the Złota Lipa, effectively abandoning all the gains that had been made in eastern Galicia since the capture of Lemberg. Conrad was naturally reluctant to consider such extreme measures, and insisted that the situation could be remedied with modest reinforcements – XVII Corps had been intended for the Serbian invasion, but would now be sent to Galicia, while troops could be extracted from the Bug Army for deployment in the Balkans. This would allow the Russians to be halted further east, and in the meantime he hoped that Ludendorff's operations in Lithuania would draw away sufficient Russian forces to reduce the pressure upon his own front. He concluded that the total strength of the units under his command in the south, including replacement drafts, amounted to about 400,000 men, faced by an estimated 360,000 Russians. Falkenhayn had far less faith in the ability of *Ober Ost* to produce a decisive outcome, but agreed to the diversion of XVII Corps to Galicia.[15]

On 15 September, Bothmer and Pflanzer-Baltin made another attempt to deal with the Russian forces that were threatening to drive their armies apart with a coordinated attack from north and south. Although both attacks gained ground, it was insufficient to force a general Russian retreat. Nevertheless, aware that his troops faced little prospect of advancing further west, Ivanov ordered both Lechitsky and Shcherbachev to pull back a little towards the east; their attacks had achieved a great deal, and Ivanov rightly calculated that further assaults were unlikely to yield as much benefit. Further north, the Russians also had to face disappointment as their attacks against Böhm-Ermolli's Second Army were beaten off, albeit in some cases with considerable difficulty. By the end of the day, Böhm-Ermolli estimated that his army had lost 45,000 men since the end of August.[16]

But whilst fighting at the southern end of the battlefield was now dying down, it was about to rise in intensity in the north. A steady flow of reinforcements had reached Brusilov while Joseph Ferdinand's divisions struggled to break through to Rovno, and the redeployment of Austro-Hungarian forces to the threatened sectors further south had not gone unnoticed. On 12 September, Brusilov wrote to Ivanov:

> There were 22 enemy divisions facing Eighth Army, [but] now the enemy only has 14 divisions here. This means that we have approximately equal strength and we are faced by the Austrians, who we have already defeated several times. I am of the opinion that we have already retreated far enough, and we will soon have regrouped and replenished our ranks, allowing us to strike at them once more.[17]

As already mentioned, Brusilov had been considering such an attack since the beginning of the month, hoping to strike at the northern flank of the Austro-Hungarian forces much as they had attempted to strike at his northern flank. Ivanov was not enthusiastic about a major attack, and it took several conversations between the two officers before Brusilov secured permission for 'limited attacks to straighten the front'.[18] One of his formations, XXXIX Corps, had secured a foothold on the western bank of the Stubiel on 13 September, and orders were now issued for a comprehensive assault along the entire front of Eighth Army – far more than the local straightening of the front to which Ivanov had agreed. Even as XXXIX Corps crossed the river, the first formations of XXX Corps arrived at the northern end of the front and immediately went into action against the exposed Austro-Hungarian salient that stretched as far as Derażno.

Until now, Joseph Ferdinand – urged on by Conrad – had been pushing his subordinates to continue the advance in an increasingly futile attempt to break through towards Rovno. The disposition of troops in the front line was therefore more suited to attack than defence, and local commanders now raced to adopt a new defensive posture. At first, the front line remained quiet on 14 September around Derażno and the local troops started construction of defensive positions in the woodland around the town, but the main problem was to the north of Derażno, where a relatively small cavalry force screened a large area of swampy ground. Russian cavalry infiltrated through this area throughout the day, and with the whole of Fourth Army's line under Russian pressure, Joseph Ferdinand felt that he was unable to send army-level reserves to the north. On 15 September, the Russian XXX Corps – supported on its northern flank by cavalry – attacked Derażno from the east and north. The commander of the Austro-Hungarian X Corps, Hugo Martiny, told Joseph Ferdinand that he intended to evacuate the Derażno salient, and the withdrawal took place during the following night. Once the troops reached their new positions, Joseph Ferdinand hoped that they would be able to beat off any further Russian attacks, while he tried to move reinforcements to protect his northern flank.

If fresh troops had been available and the road network had been sufficient to allow a rapid transfer of men to face the threat, Joseph Ferdinand's plan might have succeeded. The Russian forces that had already crossed the Stubiel broke through the Austro-Hungarian lines, and Martiny shuffled his exhausted troops with increasing desperation to shore up the front line. The Austro-Hungarian 62nd Infantry Division was positioned at the northern end of what had originally been the base of the Derażno salient, and it came under heavy attack early on 17 September; it disintegrated and fell back to the west. Elsewhere, the Russians also gained ground, and by the end of the day the front line ran about 3 miles (5km) west of the Stubiel.

With his entire corps under such pressure, Martiny could do little to safeguard his northern flank, where the weak forces of *Kavallerie Korps Berndt* – about 2,600 troops supported by nine field guns – struggled to cover a gap of about 8 miles (13km). Outnumbered by the Russian cavalry under the command of Jakov Fedorovitz von Gillenschmidt, Berndt could do little to hold back his opponents, and as Brusilov had intended, the northern flank of Joseph Ferdinand's army was completely exposed. With no reserves available, the commander of Fourth Army had no choice but to order a further withdrawal to the line of the Styr and Ikwa, and the exhausted troops trudged back across the ground that had been captured at such cost in the preceding weeks during the night to 18 September.

Conrad's original plan had been the swift outflanking of the exhausted and defeated Russian Southwest Front and a rapid advance upon Rovno. Now, Brusilov carried out precisely the sort of manoeuvre that *AOK* had envisaged, with the main objective being the town of Lutsk. The Russian pursuit caught up with the retreating formations during the afternoon when cavalry appeared with several field guns and brought the crowded roads immediately east of Lutsk under fire. A swift counterattack by elements of 21st Rifle Division drove off the Russian cavalry, and the rest of Fourth Army managed to complete its withdrawal, though many of its divisions were reduced to less than half their establishment strength.[19]

In just a few short weeks, the situation on the southern part of the front had changed dramatically. A little further north, Linsingen's Bug Army captured Pinsk on 16 September, and Conrad immediately proposed that it should attack towards the south into the flank of the Russian Eighth Army. Falkenhayn agreed to dispatch two divisions from the Bug Army to the south, but this came at a price: Fourth Army and the cavalry formations on its northern flank would come under Linsingen's overall command. Having had to ask his German allies yet again for help, Conrad was in no position to object, and the only crumb of comfort he was able to extract from the situation was that the new army group would technically be subordinate to the command of Archduke Frederick, the Austro-Hungarian commander-in-chief. At the same time, First and Second Armies were grouped into another new army group, this time commanded by Böhm-Ermolli.

Linsingen had been a difficult partner for Pflanzer-Baltin earlier in the year when the armies commanded by the two men fought along the Dniester, and the dour Prussian wasted no time in asserting his authority. Joseph Ferdinand was ordered on 18 September to prepare his forces for an attack towards the north, in an attempt to close the gap between Fourth Army and the Bug Army by concentrating three infantry divisions behind its northern flank. With his units badly intermingled as a result of their precipitate retreat, Joseph Ferdinand had his hands full simply bringing order to his army. He replied to Linsingen that he could only spare 4th Infantry Division for the moment, but was pulling half of 21st Rifle Division and 10th Cavalry Division out of the front line in preparation for sending them north; he added – sending a copy of the message to *AOK* – that unless he was sent the Austro-Hungarian XVII Corps from Conrad's strategic reserve, Fourth Army would be unable to concentrate sufficient forces for Linsingen's plans.

Brusilov had no intention of giving his opponents time to rally and reorganise. Stelnitsky's XXXIX Corps was ordered to advance due west, while XXX Corps attacked Lutsk from the northeast. The initial attack on 19 September was made by Anton Ivanovich Denikin's 4th Infantry Division, and repulsed in fierce close-quarter fighting; in his report about the action, Stelnitsky criticised Denikin for not showing sufficient energy. Late on 20 September, after a brief artillery bombardment, Denikin probed the defences again but was once more driven off; an exasperated Stelnitsky ordered the rest of his corps to assemble to attack Lutsk from the southeast, and heavy artillery fire rained down on the town, already badly scarred by the Austro-Hungarian assault earlier in the campaign, while XXX Corps attempted to outflank the Austro-Hungarian positions from the northeast. On 22 September, Denikin's 4th Infantry Division tried again. It swiftly penetrated the southern flank of the defences of Lutsk, and the premature destruction of bridges in the town resulted in half of the Austro-Hungarian 24th Infantry Division being completely destroyed. Fighting continued long into the following night before the Austro-Hungarian XIV Corps abandoned Lutsk and fell back; determined resistance by troops along the northern perimeter succeeded in holding off the Russians long enough for the majority of the troops and guns in the town to pull back to safety. Denikin personally led his division into the devastated town, claiming credit for its capture.

Zayontchovsky, the commander of XXX Corps, reported that his troops took some 12,000 prisoners as a result of the fighting around Lutsk, and criticised Denikin for taking so long to seize Lutsk; he claimed that the fall of the town was only possible because of the outflanking movement carried out by his troops to the north. Brusilov noted that both men had some merit in their arguments, but showed little tact in their dealings with each other, resulting in lasting enmity between them as a result of the battle at Lutsk:

> I cite this incident as an example of how sensitive military units and their commander are with regard to their distinguished service in wartime ... Denikin was a good wartime general, very clever and decisive, but he always tried to get his neighbours to work to his advantage ... and they often complained that he wished to take the credit for their achievements.[20]

Denikin was the son of a former serf, who had risen to become an army officer. He succeeded in qualifying for entry to the General Staff Academy at the second attempt, only to be thwarted by a change of rules; he complained, and was offered a place if he withdrew his complaint, but he refused to do so. He served in the Russo-Japanese War, and the outbreak of the First World War saw him assigned to Brusilov's Eighth Army as a logistics officer; however, he requested a transfer to a combat unit, and was given command of a rifle brigade, which was subsequently expanded to the division that he led at Lutsk. His argument with Zayontchovsky is entirely in keeping with his previous disputes with authorities.[21]

The fall of Lutsk was a further blow to *AOK*. Even more important was the threat of the Russians advancing to the north of the town and continuing to outflank the entire line. Joseph Ferdinand wanted to scrape together four divisions to launch a counterattack to recapture Lutsk, arguing that this was the only way to prevent total collapse, but Linsingen disagreed. His assessment was that the Russians lacked the resources for a sustained advance from Lutsk, and the proposed counterattack would simply waste valuable troops. In the following days, there were numerous Russian attacks along the front – some, such as an assault on the Austro-Hungarian 51st *Honvéd* Infantry Division late on 24 September achieved considerable local success, with the division losing three of its regiments when they were encircled and forced to surrender. However, there were no further major threats, and the battered formations of the *k.u.k.* Army were able to regroup and absorb replacement drafts. In the critical sector to the north of Lutsk, German and Austro-Hungarian cavalry fought running battles with their Russian counterparts while the German XXIV Reserve Corps moved into position from the north. Linsingen ordered this formation to prepare for an attack on 26 September, while the Austro-Hungarian XVII Corps attacked from close to Lutsk. Under the overall command of the German Karl Friedrich von Gerock, the two corps would then strike at the northern flank of Brusilov's army, possibly opening the way to Rovno. Other elements of Joseph Ferdinand's Fourth Army would join the attack as it developed.

In essence, this was what Conrad had attempted to do for much of September, with far more favourable odds. When Linsingen informed AOK of his intentions, there were concerns that Fourth Army was far too weak to be able to offer much help. In any case, before the operation could develop, events unfolded in an unexpected way. Brusilov was aware of the advance of German and Austro-Hungarian cavalry north of Lutsk and of the arrival of elements of XXIV Reserve Corps, and intended to block this threat with XXX Corps, but Ivanov disagreed, and sent Brusilov orders that came as some surprise:

> During the evening, I received a long coded telegram from the commander [of Southwest Front] ... the right wing of my army was ordered to withdraw from Lutsk that night back to the Stubiel and thus return to its old positions, while XXX Corps was to move swiftly to the forests east of Kolkov [i.e. to the north of the expected attack by the German XXIV Reserve Corps] so that when the Germans advanced [towards Rovno] it would launch a surprise attack into their flank ... I was ordered to implement this astonishing plan immediately and unconditionally.[22]

Brusilov replied that the orders had arrived late in the day, and their implementation would take considerable time. It would be impossible for XXX Corps to reach its intended destination quickly enough, given the difficult road conditions, and in any event he wished to continue holding the line of the Styr. Ivanov remained insistent: his plan was to be implemented in full. Late on 25 September, Denikin and his 4th Infantry Division were ordered to leave Lutsk, and the town was evacuated overnight. The following morning, Joseph Ferdinand's troops cautiously reoccupied Lutsk without a fight.

Despite this unexpected turn of events, Joseph Ferdinand remained concerned about the state of his troops. They required further rest and time to recover from their recent setbacks, but despite this they were ordered to cross the Styr as quickly as they could in pursuit of Brusilov's Eighth Army. With Fourth Army unable to offer much support for his planned attack, Linsingen appealed for help from First Army. Conrad turned him down, not least because Linsingen wished to have First Army assigned to his army group, and Conrad had no intention of allowing yet more of his troops to be placed under German command. In any event, Ivanov's insistence on a rapid withdrawal had effectively eliminated any chance for Linsingen to turn the northern flank of Southwest Front. Fighting continued for several days, but at diminishing intensity. Both sides settled down to lick their wounds and prepare for the winter.

The fighting in Volhynia had cost the Austro-Hungarian Empire another 231,000 casualties, including over 100,000 prisoners. The worrying trend of mass surrenders by troops of certain ethnicities, such as the Czechs and Ruthenians, seemed to be worsening, and the quality of the officer corps clearly left much to be desired – Fourth Army estimated that one third of its officer casualties were prisoners, compared with German Army estimates for the Eastern Front in 1915 of only 5.2 per cent. Clearly, there was much chagrin at the poor performance of the officers of the *k.u.k.* Army's officers, and official accounts repeatedly and consistently avoided addressing the issue.[23] Russian losses were also substantial, though less than those of Austria-Hungary; given the manpower resources of Russia, the casualties were acceptable in view of the damage inflicted upon the *k.u.k.* Army. The overall gains of the offensive were modest – as was so often the case on the Eastern Front, the battle-lines moved first one way, then the other, before coming to a halt not far from where they had started. It was characteristic that few of Conrad's staff from *AOK* bothered to visit the front line, relying instead on messages sent by teleprinter. Despite Conrad's constant urging, the initial enthusiasm for the 'Black–Yellow Offensive' rapidly faded, and the operation became known to most at *AOK* as *Herbstsau* ('autumn swinery'). Conrad was furious that his subordinates had failed to land a decisive blow on the exposed northern flank of Ivanov's Southwest Front, as his adjutant told Scheller:

> The Chief says: with our troops one cannot plan an offensive. In this war we never had something as simple, as certain as this offensive, and even this we messed up.[24]

Much of this irritation and anger reflected a growing sense of humiliation, and the clear German attitude of dominance that frequently crossed the line into overt arrogance. At *Ober Ost*, Ludendorff had no illusions about the reliability of Germany's ally; as early as April 1915, he wrote to Moltke, the former chief of the German general staff, that there was little prospect of Austria-Hungary continuing as a Great Power and that it was inevitable that Germany would become the dominant power. This opinion was increasingly widespread, and the Bavarian envoy in Berlin, Hugo von Lerchenfeld, repeatedly advised his superiors in Munich that the Austro-Hungarian Empire could not be regarded as a reliable military ally.[25] Matters were not helped by the poor impression that *AOK* made on German visitors; it was now normal for wives and even mistresses to live with senior Austro-Hungarian officers in a manner that would never be tolerated by the Germans. Cramon, the German liaison officer in Teschen, later wrote about the growing criticism even within the Austro-Hungarian Empire:

> 'With few exceptions, the dreadful events [of recent campaigns] have their roots in the leadership' – so ran the theme of sharp attacks in the Hungarian parliament. Many in Vienna, too, were pensive. The foreign minister [Stephan Burián von Rajecz] suddenly discovered such a keen interest in military matters that one could clearly read doubts and reflections between the lines of his documents. Government ministers took up the same issues and demanded standardisation of all parts of command on the Eastern Front. There was opposition to the chief of the general staff amongst the army high command, as he was no longer regarded as being entitled to his general independence in light of recent events ...
>
> To these criticisms of leadership were added criticisms of private arrangements; Conrad had married for the second time and allowed the Baroness to move to Teschen. Strictly ecclesiastically minded groups regarded the marriage with a divorced woman as invalid; but generally it was thought that the chief of the general staff was distracted from the duties of his office by family matters.
>
> ... The marriage was an entirely private matter outside all criticism, [but] the intrusion of family life into the standing of the army high command was to be avoided. Whether official interests were thus damaged or not is not really the issue; it was regrettable that the army high command became the subject of popular gossip and its previously high prestige became damaged by spiteful comments.[26]

Conrad and his colleagues could not fail to be aware of the low esteem in which they were collectively held, and there was increasing talk of a unified command for the entire front. Given the failures of Conrad's armies, such a command would inevitably mean German control, and for the moment, Conrad managed to retain sufficient influence to prevent this.

Fighting now wound down along the entire Eastern Front. The conditions facing the men on both sides were varied, as one German officer later described:

> The army did not actually restrict itself to defending solid, dry, sandy areas. In the north and south, it descended into low-lying swamps and also pushed the front

line as far to the east as possible. But the solid rear area of the Pinsk promontory provided a base from which the troop formations operating in the lowlands could be supported.

It was an extraordinary and foreign landscape in which wartime life played out for the army in the following months. There was a clear difference between the high northern bank of the Jasiolda and the lower southern bank of the Pina. Beyond the Jasiolda one found oneself in a confused tangle of birch woods and cattle meadows. Proper roads were completely lacking, and even country roads were scarce, and the incessant movement of columns of vehicles through the woods and meadows could be seen from the deep ruts they had left behind. On either side of the Jasiolda one ran into the flood area of the Pinsk marshes. In some areas the oak woods held sway. Their mossy branches provided building material for the underground and hutted tents of the rear areas. But the rowing boats tightly secured to posts at the few farmhouses served as a reminder of the rapidly changing circumstances that one had to reckon with when the season submerged the entire area with floods and rain.

On the other hand, the Pina bank gave a different picture on the southeast side of the promontory. Here, we drove for hours through a sandy wasteland between huge dunes. There were only a few oaks and here and there small clusters of old, worn-down pines around a tiny chapel and a large cluster of graves. From on high we looked down on the swamps as if on a still sea; at high water, this illusion changed and we actually had an ocean before us as far as the distant wooded shores, far away …

On the dunes, our soldiers had to deal with the same circumstances as those at Ostend on the North Sea. They could dig quickly into the sand, as any child who has built castles by the sea knows. But their work rapidly collapsed if it wasn't reinforced, and sudden rainfall washed away the edges of their walls in short order; this too, every child knows. Consequently all the fighting trenches, supporting lines, observation posts and gun positions had to be reinforced internally with sods of earth, fascines and boards.[27]

With all of Poland now in the hands of the Central Powers, it was time to organise governmental matters. The territory was divided between Germany and Austria-Hungary, broadly along the Pilica to the west of the Vistula and the Wieprz to the east; at Falkenhayn's instigation, the German sector was governed from Warsaw by Beseler, and the Austro-Hungarian sector from Lublin. Once more, this arrangement did not please *Ober Ost*; Ludendorff had expected his staff to retain control over the region, rather than having it pass to Beseler. This seems to have been another deliberate attempt by Falkenhayn to limit the power of Hindenburg and Ludendorff.

By any standards, the Central Powers had good reason to be pleased with the outcome of the year's fighting, even allowing for the Austro-Hungarian setbacks in Volhynia. From a low point at the end of winter, after the fall of Przemyśl and the threatened invasion of Hungary by Brusilov's Eighth Army, the forces of Germany and the Austro-Hungarian Empire had enjoyed almost continuous victories. As a result, any threat of a Russian invasion of either Hungary or Silesia and East Prussia had been eliminated. To a degree, the memoirs of the main protagonists show the value of hindsight – Mackensen is by no means alone in suggesting that he always believed that the initial advance at Gorlice–Tarnów might ultimately lead to the recapture of all of Galicia. The reality is that the original operation was planned purely to relieve pressure on the *k.u.k.* Army in the Carpathians, and Falkenhayn repeatedly considered pausing or even stopping the advance. Barely a century after Napoleon's disastrous invasion of Russia, the Germans remained acutely aware of the fate of earlier attempts to push into the vastness of the tsar's empire.

The entire campaign can be considered in two sections. The first commenced with Mackensen's original breakthrough, and continued until the advance reached the San, and Przemyśl was recaptured; the second section started with the main axis of advance turning north, until the end of the campaign. It is worth looking at the performance of the two sides to assess how they performed in each phase, and whether they might have done better.

The first phase saw Mackensen methodically demolishing the Russian defences, both those in the original front line and then those in every line that was established. The Russian commitment to defending each line with stubborn determination ultimately only added to their losses. There was nothing that Radko Dimitriev could do to halt the initial German breakthrough; his troops were simply too weak. Conrad later attempted to claim credit for this, pointing out that this weakness was a direct result of the terrible bloodletting in the Carpathians, but again, there is more than a touch of hindsight to this. The intention of the repeated Austro-Hungarian assaults in the Carpathians was to prevent a Russian advance into Hungary, and to try to lift the siege of Przemyśl, rather than to bleed the Russian Army white. Conrad's only justification for this claim lies in the fact that the doctrine he had promulgated throughout his army before the war was to attack the enemy tirelessly to destroy his will to continue the struggle. The price that the *k.u.k.* Army paid was immense. To his credit, Dimitriev repeatedly reported the weakness of his position to his superiors; they failed to respond adequately to his warnings.

An additional factor that greatly increased Russian casualties throughout both phases of the campaign was the doctrine of immediate counterattacks. It should be added that this was a widespread attitude at the time, and accounts of fighting on the Western Front are also full of examples of counterattacks that did little more than increase the already terrible losses suffered by both sides. By the second phase of the campaign, when the Russians were steadily withdrawing, these doctrinal counterattacks could only be justified if they bought more time for other units to withdraw; on most occasions, this was not the case.

During the second phase of the campaign, the alacrity with which the Russians withdrew kept their losses to a more manageable level, and the only occasions when they deviated from this policy – for example when they chose to defend Novogeorgievsk – their losses soared. An earlier decision to abandon the line of fortresses would have allowed for the timely evacuation of their enormous stocks of ammunition and other *matériel*, but the internal politics of the Russian military system probably rendered this impossible. Sukhomlinov had campaigned unsuccessfully for the demolition of the fortresses before the war, and after his dismissal, his opponents were hardly likely to embrace one of his policies.

From the point of view of the Central Powers, the most controversial issue centred on the rivalry between Falkenhayn and *OHL* on the one hand, and Hindenburg and Ludendorff at *Ober Ost* on the other. Having won a spectacular victory at Tannenberg in the opening weeks of the war, Hindenburg and particularly Ludendorff spent much of the rest of the war trying to repeat their feat, constantly attempting to turn the flank of Russian forces; whenever they succeeded, the Russians simply withdrew rather than allow another huge encirclement. By doing so, they prevented *Ober Ost* from achieving much more than local tactical victories, but Ludendorff remained convinced that the key to victory lay in exploiting an open flank. This was largely the logic behind the plan put forward by *Ober Ost* to roll up the entire Russian line from the north. If such a policy had been followed, it seems likely that it would have been no more successful than Falkenhayn's decision to continue the thrust over the San and ultimately to Brest-Litovsk and beyond.

Both Ludendorff and Hoffmann felt that if their plans had been given more support, there might have been far greater success than was ultimately achieved. Conrad also remained convinced that the only way of defeating the Russians was by a huge pincer movement from north and south, encircling their armies in central Poland. Although Falkenhayn finally approved such an operation, it was not on the scale that Conrad had wished, and the Russians proved capable of retreating faster than they could be encircled. As for the suggestions from *Ober Ost* that they might have achieved more in the north had they been given more support: the facts suggest otherwise. Below's advance into Latvia was constantly hampered by supply shortages, and every attempt to circumvent these failed – barges delivering supplies along the Niemen ran aground, and seaborne transport to the small port of Libau (now Liepàja) and then further by rail could not deliver sufficient volume to sustain the advance. Had even more troops been deployed in the Niemen Army, the supply requirements would have been still greater.

Ober Ost also proposed a decisive thrust due east across Lithuania to cut the main north–south railways in Russia. Whilst this would have dislocated Russian movements, it is questionable whether such an advance was achievable. In October 1914, the Germans predicted – with accuracy – that the Russian advance towards Silesia would be forced to stop once they had moved more than 70 miles (112km) from their railheads; similar constraints applied to all armies of the era. By contrast with Ludendorff, Falkenhayn attempted to destroy the forces before him using the technique that Mackensen perfected: assemble sufficient heavy artillery and ammunition to suppress the Russian defences, and then advance in steady stages until encountering further resistance, when the entire process would begin again. Falkenhayn summed up his approach in a message to Conrad on 9 August:

> It is utterly irrelevant where Eleventh Army and the Bug Army break through, so long as they actually break through somewhere.[28]

The differences of opinion between *Ober Ost* and *OHL* are neatly summarised in an exchange of messages between the two headquarters. On 13 August, Hindenburg wrote to Falkenhayn:

> In spite of the excellent results of the thrust on the Narew, the operations in the east have not led to the annihilation of the enemy. As was to be expected, the Russian has drawn out of the pincers and is allowing himself to be driven back frontally in the direction desired by himself. With the help of his good railways he can concentrate just as he wishes and lead strong forces against my left wing which is threatening his communications … A decisive blow is only possible now from the Kovno region … I once more stress the fact that I regarded an offensive by my left wing against the enemy's communications and his rear as the only possibility of annihilating him. This offensive is probably even now the only means of avoiding a new campaign unless it is already too late for it.[29]

The description of the Russian railways as 'good' is an exaggeration, but they were certainly adequate to allow the Russians to withdraw faster than they could be pursued. Falkenhayn's response was entirely in character with his personality:

> The annihilation of the enemy has never been hoped for from the current operations in the east, but purely and simply a decisive victory in accordance with the aims of *OHL*. Nor should annihilation, on the whole, have been attempted in the present instance, for it is impossible to try to annihilate an enemy who is far superior in numbers, must be attacked frontally, has excellent lines of communication, any amount of time and unlimited space at his disposal, whilst we should have been forced to operate with a time limit in a district destitute of railways and roads.
>
> That the enemy has already been decisively defeated for our purposes cannot be doubted by anybody ... There exists a further prospect that the results of the operations will be intensified further, as we have succeeded in driving no fewer than five thoroughly beaten enemy armies into the space between Bialystok and Brest-Litovsk.
>
> It is to be assumed that the operations would certainly have been more decisive if it had been possible to deliver a simultaneous blow across the Niemen. But *OHL* had no forces at its disposal for this purpose, and Your Excellency considered the employment of the Niemen Army in Courland to be more necessary. This is not intended as a criticism, but merely as a statement of the facts.[30]

Falkenhayn rejected Hindenburg's assertions that the northern wing of the German position was threatened; indeed, he regarded the diversion of troops to the Niemen Army as an unwelcome distraction from the decisive theatre in the centre.

There were further disagreements between *Ober Ost* and *OHL* after the capture of Vilna. Hindenburg asked for a delay in the transfer of two of his divisions to the west, as he would be hard pressed to hold all his gains at Vilna and Smorgon without swift reinforcements. Falkenhayn emphatically rejected this suggestion, arguing the precise location of the front line in the east was not particularly important:

> Whether our line stretches from the Smorgon region through Dvinsk to Bausk, or goes in a more or less straight line from Smorgon direct to Bausk, is of no importance to the general course of the war. The loss of our positions in the west can mean an unfavourable conclusion of the war. Owing to the tension which prevails permanently in the west, and to the numerical superiority of the enemy in personnel and materiel ... every division counts on the Western Front.[31]

Hindenburg's response was equally forthright:

I have always taken the general situation into consideration by relinquishing as
many troops as I could ... and also dispatched one [division] belonging to XI
Corps prematurely, an action which was described as a mistake at the time. The
fact that the further relinquishment of divisions is now meeting with difficulties
is due to the plan of campaign favoured in the summer, which was unable to
strike a deadly blow at the Russians, in spite of the favourable circumstances and
my urgent entreaties. I am not blind to the difficulties of the general military
situation, and ... I shall relinquish further divisions as soon as it seems possible
for me to do so ... but I cannot bind myself to a definite time. A premature
relinquishment would give rise to a crisis.[32]

Tempers were rising on both sides of the argument. Falkenhayn's response is full
of incompletely suppressed anger:

Much as I regret that Your Excellency should without any cause consider the
present moment suited for explanations of events of the past, which are therefore
unimportant at the moment, I should not trouble to refute your statements if
they concerned only me personally.

But as it concerns a criticism of orders issued by *OHL* which, as is well known,
have in all important cases met with the previous consent of His Majesty, I am
unhappily compelled to do so.

Whether Your Excellency agrees with the views of *OHL* does not matter once
a decision has been made by His Majesty. In this case every portion of our forces
has to adapt itself unconditionally to *OHL*.

... The attack by the Narew Group can scarcely come into question, for Your
Excellency admitted personally in Posen that it was more a matter of sentiment
whether the Narew or the Niemen operations were decided upon. After the
plentiful experiences of last winter, however, I am unable to rely on the feelings of
other persons with regard to my proposals, but must depend solely on my own
convictions ...

I do not hesitate to say that the acceptance of your proposal [to divert troops
to the Niemen Army in August] would have been disastrous for us.

Direct proof of this lies in the irrefutable fact that, if we had accepted the
proposal, we should never have been in a position to transfer in time those forces
which are urgently required for the support of the Western Front.

... Exactly what I feared and prophesied took place [in the advance to Vilna].

One cannot hope to strike a comprehensive and deadly blow by means of an encircling movement at an enemy who is numerically stronger, who will stick at no sacrifices of territory and population and, in addition, has the expanse of Russia and good railways behind him ... The surprise required for success is, as this war has often shown, never successful enough to prevent the enemy from taking counter-measures in time.[33]

For the moment, Falkenhayn's will prevailed, but the ill feeling between *Ober Ost* and *OHL* continued to simmer in the background; it would erupt with full force the following year. In his own memoirs, Hindenburg was generous in his assessment of the disagreements:

In judging the plans of our high command, we must not lose sight of the whole military situation. We ourselves then saw only a part of the whole picture. The question whether we should have made other plans and acted otherwise if we had known the whole political and military situation must be left open.[34]

For Falkenhayn, the best outcome would have been a separate peace with Russia, but such an outcome was always going to be difficult, given the public pronouncements of the Entente Powers after the outbreak of war. The second-best outcome – Russia sufficiently weakened to allow Germany to concentrate on other theatres, without having to worry about the frailty of the Austro-Hungarian Empire – was perhaps the best that could be expected, and this was achieved. Conrad's desire was for a decisive military victory that would knock Russia out of the war; given the vast open spaces of the Eastern Front, and the reliance of all armies upon railways for logistic support, such a victory was almost certainly impossible, unless the Russians cooperated by making disastrous errors. Once Italy entered the war, Conrad's attention turned to a different objective – the defeat of a nation that he had suspected for years of harbouring hostile intentions towards the Austro-Hungarian Empire. He repeatedly urged his German allies to join in what he expected to be a swift and chastening blow, but he had little or no justification for this belief. Previous Austro-Hungarian operations in mountainous terrain, in the Carpathians and in Serbia, gave no indication that it would be possible to advance swiftly through the Alps, and Conrad's suggestions that the Italians might be lured into a grandiose trap on the Austrian side of the frontier were nothing more than wishful thinking. The summer's outcome – Russia weakened and unable to mount further attacks, and most of Galicia recovered – was realistically as much as he could have hoped for, particularly given how badly the *k.u.k.* Army had been weakened in the fighting in the Carpathians. The price for this was that it was clear to both Germany and Austria-Hungary that the relationship between the two powers was not one between equals.

The Russian Army finished the campaign in tatters. Its losses were terrible, even by the standards of the First World War, and all its shortcomings had been exposed mercilessly – the tactical insistence on immediate counterattacks, the deteriorating quality of its artillery due to the loss of so many pre-war officers, the crippling logistic failures, and the lack of any clear strategy and command at the highest level. Any prospect of a victorious outcome to the war disappeared for the foreseeable future. The pressures within the tsar's empire that still lingered on from the 1905 Revolution were now fed by discontent and growing war-weariness. Unless Russia's fortunes changed rapidly, matters would only worsen.

Casualties on all sides were heavy, even amongst the victorious armies of the Central Powers. The *k.u.k.* Army lost nearly 1.8 million men on the Russian Front in 1915; of these, nearly 800,000 were lost in the bloodbath of the Carpathians. The breakdown of these losses is typical of the era: approximately 146,000 dead, 510,000 wounded, 247,000 sick, and 328,000 prisoners.[35] The result was a further deterioration in the quality of the formations of the army. The delicate relationship between officers and men of differing nationalities, built up so carefully in the years before the war, collapsed almost completely in formations that were not predominantly Austrian or Hungarian, and like all armies involved in the conflict, the loss of irreplaceable experienced and skilled officers and NCOs represented a huge blow. German losses in all theatres exceeded 600,000, with the Eastern Front contributing somewhat more than a third. Russian casualties were devastating. Nearly a million men had been taken prisoner, and about 500,000 killed or wounded. Even the huge resources of Russia could not afford such losses; at the very least, the Central Powers could look forward to a prolonged period of greatly reduced activity by their opponents in the east.

CHAPTER 11

THE FALL OF SERBIA

In August 1914 Oskar Potiorek commanded an invasion of Serbia, using two armies that attacked across the rugged valley of the River Drina and elements of a third army that was meant to be redeploying in Galicia, as a result of Conrad's botched attempt to alter Austro-Hungarian mobilisation plans at the very last moment. The initial invasion was repulsed with heavy losses, but despite this being in part due to the singularly poor choice of invasion route – Potiorek's choice of crossing the Drina for his main assault, through hilly forested terrain that was almost devoid of decent roads and completely lacking in railway lines – the second assault in September followed almost exactly the same pattern. This time, the Austro-Hungarian forces managed to establish themselves in Serbian territory, and began a slow battle of attrition. Eventually, the vastly superior resources of the Austro-Hungarian Empire ground down the Serbian defenders, and as autumn turned to winter, the front line moved steadily east until Belgrade fell to the invaders on 2 December. However, this proved to be the high-tide mark of the invasion. Just as it seemed that the battered and exhausted units of the *k.u.k.* Army were about to prevail and crush the Serbs, a vital influx of arms and ammunition from Russia gave the Serbian armies a sudden boost. The counterattack that followed tore apart the invading armies, and resulted in the complete withdrawal of Austro-Hungarian forces from Serbia and the sacking of Potiorek.

The winter that followed was a tough one. The armies of both sides lost tens of thousands of men through illness, and there were similar deaths in the Serbian population of northwest Serbia; as was the case in Poland, the armies that marched repeatedly through the region left ruined villages and towns, wrecked bridges and roads in their wake. The epidemics of typhus and cholera that swept the land finally abated through a combination of spring weather, strict movement controls to stop the spread of disease, and a steadily growing flow of international aid. An American journalist visiting Serbia described it in graphic terms as 'a country of death'; he then went on to visit the Drina battlefields:

> ... An awful smell hung over the place ... we walked on the dead, so thick were they – sometimes our feet sank through into pits of rotting flesh, crunching bones.[1]

The conduct of the *k.u.k.* Army towards civilians during its brief occupation of northwest Serbia was frequently bad. The atrocities carried out in Potiorek's first invasion were the subject of a report by a Swiss academic; although the Serbian government invited him specifically to study the subject with a view to portraying the Austro-Hungarian forces in the worst possible light, he appears to have tried his best to gather evidence in a rigorous manner.[2] In addition to random and systematic killings, there was widespread looting and rape. There appear to have been many reasons for this, ranging from racial stereotyping of the Serbs as enemies of the empire to a deep-rooted fear of guerrillas – this latter was fed by the fact that the Serbian Army lacked sufficient uniforms for all the men who were mobilised to defend the nation. This extra aspect of the fighting added both to the devastation of the region and to the determination of the Serbs to continue fighting as long as they possibly could.

Slowly, the Serbs recovered some of their strength, though the financial burden on the country was immense. Albin Kutschbach, a German agent in the city of Niš, reported in mid-March:

> The army again numbers between 250,000 and 260,000. After a break of three months ... it has recovered totally.[3]

Kutschbach went on to report that whilst the civilian population in some regions – notably, not those occupied by the *k.u.k.* Army in 1914 – was showing signs of war-weariness, the desire to prosecute the war to the bitter end remained strong amongst the military. The personal standing of the elderly Radomir Putnik, the chief of the Serbian general staff, was at an all-time high. With no resolution to the war with France or Russia in sight, the Germans considered making a separate peace with Serbia, even though their Austro-Hungarian allies remained set on crushing the nation that they blamed for starting the war. At first, Vienna seemed to regard the proposal as something that might be acceptable, but the terms the Germans were prepared to offer were far more generous than anything that the

Dual Monarchy could accept; the deal would have handed territory in Albania, Montenegro, and even Bosnia-Herzegovina – which was Austro-Hungarian territory – to Serbia. In exchange, Serbia would have to assign other territory to Bulgaria and Austria-Hungary, allowing for land contact between the Central Powers and Turkey.[4] Partly due to objections from Austria-Hungary, and partly because some of the intermediaries in the negotiations proved to be interested purely in personal financial gain, the tentative steps towards separate peace were effectively abandoned during the summer of 1915. Kutschbach made one last approach to Prime Minister Nikola Pašić in September, warning him that if he did not accept the terms being offered, his nation faced attack. Pašić declined, later saying that he suspected that the Germans and Austro-Hungarians would have gone back on their word if they had won the war.[5] Serbia would have to hope that its allies could win the war and thus save it from conquest. In the meantime, its armies would do all they could to prevent the nation from being overrun.

When it became clear in early 1915 that Serbia's Russian allies were not going to crush the Central Powers, there were growing calls from Petrograd for a Serbian offensive into Bosnia, in the hope that this would force Conrad to divert troops to the area. The Serbs were not keen on such an offensive; they had mounted a series of attacks across the River Save after expelling Potiorek's first invasion at the beginning of the war, but had failed to make any progress. Aware that his armies were too weak to face another major enemy assault, Prime Minister Pašić and Putnik agreed that there was little to be gained by provoking Austro-Hungary; any attack across the Save was unlikely to secure lasting gains, and if it had the outcome that the Russians desired – the diversion of forces to the Serbian front – the outcome might be disastrous for Serbia, especially as the Russians appeared unable to deliver a killing blow against the Central Powers. Instead, the Serbs used the relative peace along their front line to rebuild their battered armies.

By the end of the summer of 1915, the Serbian Army had reached a numerical strength of about 250,000, perhaps 10 per cent greater than at the outset of the war. To some extent, this was possible through the provision of rifles, a shortage of which had prevented Serbia from deploying as many troops as she might otherwise have done in 1914. Despite the serious casualties of 1914, it seems that the quality of Serbia's army remained high, with officers and NCOs making up with motivation and energy what they might lack in training and experience. Supplies arrived in an intermittent stream from Russia, France and Britain, but not consistently; nevertheless, given the performance of the army in stopping Potiorek's invasions of 1914, there was reason for hoping that any new offensive could be blunted until help could arrive from Serbia's allies.

Local political issues also played a major part during the months of rebuilding, diverting some of Serbia's limited military resources. Serbia's only connection with the coast was via Montenegro, or the single-track rail line through Greek territory to Salonika; the Greek authorities repeatedly interrupted or delayed transport along this line, justifying this as exercising even-handed neutrality. There were also repeated concerns about Austro-Hungarian agitation in Albania, and in an attempt to settle this issue and at the same time open a new route to the sea, the Serbs joined with Italy, Greece and Montenegro to seize parts of Albania, attacking on 29 May. There was considerable resistance, but the Albanians were outgunned and outnumbered, and swiftly overrun. This occupation was then incorporated into the Treaty of London, drawn up in secret in April 1915; Serbia and Montenegro, who were not present at the negotiations in London and were not signatories of the treaty, would be permitted to retain control of northern Albania, while southern Albania passed to Greece and the rest was either taken by Italy or became part of an Italian protectorate. It is characteristic of the era that the Albanians were not consulted during the negotiations.

The other neighbours of Serbia were the subjects of intense diplomatic activity. Romania seemed on the verge of joining the Entente in the first months of the war, but Russian setbacks in Galicia led to a cooling of Romanian ardour for attacking the Central Powers. For the moment, the passage of supplies from Russia to Serbia was the limit of Romanian involvement. Bulgaria, by contrast, moved from a position of neutrality to increasing closeness to Germany. In the First Balkan War of 1912–1913, Tsar Ferdinand I of Bulgaria had regarded the venture as being a crusade, aimed at expelling the Turks from Europe. The Bulgarian Army won several major victories over the Turks, and lost more men than Serbia and Greece; this led to a sense of entitlement in Bulgaria, but Serbia refused to give any of the territory of Macedonia that it had seized from Turkey to Bulgaria, on the grounds that the Bulgarian forces had required more support from Serbia than had originally been planned. This eventually led to the Second Balkan War in 1913, in which Bulgaria initially made gains at the expense of Greece and Serbia, but was eventually defeated when Romania and Turkey also entered the war against Bulgaria.

Because of Russia's support for Serbia, sentiment in Bulgaria turned markedly against Russia after this defeat. Prime Minister Vasil Radoslavov settled his nation's differences with Turkey and steadily moved closer to Germany, not least because France – under pressure from Russia – refused to grant Bulgaria a substantial loan to finance the debts that had been run up during the Balkan Wars. Eventually, on the eve of the outbreak of the First World War, a loan was agreed with a group of German banks, securing control of several industrial interests in Bulgaria in return for their money.[6] Even after this, the Entente Powers seemed little inclined to make overtures towards Bulgaria.

Neutrality was popular in Bulgaria, and there was little appetite for being dragged into what was largely seen as someone else's war. Nevertheless, Radoslavov was aware that there might be opportunities for Bulgaria to achieve some of its territorial ambitions and thus reverse the losses of the Second Balkan War, and he carefully sounded out both sides to determine which was most likely to support – and deliver – Bulgarian aspirations. When British forces landed in Gallipoli, British diplomats tried to persuade the Russians to put pressure on Serbia to cede territory to Bulgaria; if the Bulgarians could thus be persuaded to commit to the Entente, the Dardanelles operation might be the prelude to knocking Turkey out of the war and out of Europe. The Serbs proved utterly intransigent, but in late May the British and French tried again. In return for Bulgarian involvement in the war against Turkey, they promised Radoslavov substantial territorial gains at the expense of Turkey, and stated that they would put pressure upon Romania to return territory seized from Bulgaria in the Second Balkan War. In addition, Bulgaria was offered portions of territory under Serbian and Greek control; this offer was made without consulting either of the two nations involved, and when they became aware of the proposals, both the Serbian and Greek governments protested strongly, making clear their opposition to any such deal. Radoslavov asked for clarification, and the failure of the Entente Powers to agree how they would deliver the promised territories left the Bulgarians doubting their true intentions. At the same time, Germany approached the Bulgarian government and promised that if Bulgaria were to throw its lot in with the Central Powers, they would ensure the desired territories passed to their new ally.

At the beginning of the war, Vienna was reluctant to encourage Bulgaria to attack Serbia, fearing that this might detract from Austro-Hungarian gains and prestige, but the disastrous invasions of 1914 forced Conrad and others to face reality, and the Dual Monarchy became more amenable to Bulgarian involvement in any future attack on Serbia. The Central Powers were in many respects in a better position to deliver their promises to Bulgaria than the Entente Powers; after all, they were at war with Serbia, and Bulgarian involvement in this war would ensure Serbia's defeat. Thereafter, Greece would be left isolated and was more likely to cooperate. With the growing success of the Central Powers on the Eastern Front, and the failure of Entente diplomats to offer clear answers to Radoslavov's requests for clarification, Bulgaria began to look more closely at the offer made by Germany and Austria-Hungary. In August a mission was sent to

Germany, led by Petar Ganchev, an army officer and former military attaché in Berlin.[7]

It was now increasingly clear to the Entente Powers that they were losing the diplomatic race to secure Bulgaria's allegiance. Faced by their inability to exert sufficient leverage on Serbia and Greece to make territorial concessions, Britain and France resorted to desperate measures. With the help of collaborators in Bulgaria, they attempted to buy up all of Bulgaria's harvest, with the intention of creating a food shortage and using this as leverage to make Bulgaria moderate its demands. It was a clumsy plan, and inevitably failed when its details were revealed to the Bulgarian government, destroying the credibility of Britain and France completely. A final attempt in which the Serbs offered limited concessions was also in vain.

Eventually, on 6 September, a Treaty For Friendship And Alliance between Germany and Bulgaria was signed. In addition, an annex to the treaty guaranteed the territorial gains that Bulgaria desired, and a separate military convention was agreed between Germany, Austria-Hungary and Bulgaria. Within thirty days, the two Central Powers would deploy at least six divisions each along the Danube and Save, and within thirty-five days Bulgaria would field four divisions along its border with Serbia.[8] At first, many Austro-Hungarian politicians had continued to demand that any operation against Serbia should be conducted exclusively by the *k.u.k.* Army, particularly the Hungarian premier, István Tisza, who warned his colleagues, 'Austria-Hungary's influence in the Balkans is destroyed forever if we call on the Germans for help.'[9]

Foreign Minister Stephan Burián – who was a close ally of Tisza – also urged Conrad to mount a purely Austro-Hungarian assault on Serbia; but even Conrad, an inveterate and passionate defender of the Dual Monarchy's prestige and independence from Germany, dismissed the suggestion with the words 'But with what?'[10] The reality was that after the dreadful experiences of Potiorek's campaigns of 1914 and the setbacks in the Carpathians, there was now a widespread belief in the army that it was unlikely to prevail without German assistance.

Ferdinand's decision for war with Serbia was driven largely by his wish for revenge and territorial gain. Maurice Paléologue, the French ambassador in Petrograd, had previously served his country in Sofia, and had no doubts about the Bulgarian ruler's views:

How often has he given vent to his hatred of Russia before me in the old days! Since the second Balkan War that hatred has become a morbid obsession, as it is mainly to the policy of Russia that he attributes his final disaster of 1913. And I remember how in November of that year, meeting King Alphonso III in Vienna, he remarked to him, 'I shall have my revenge against Russia, and it will be a terrible revenge!'[11]

It should be remembered, though, that Paléologue was virulently anti-German, and frequently portrayed those whom he regarded as pro-German in an unfavourable light.

Ferdinand was a cousin of Kaiser Wilhelm, but did not like him personally; nor was he particularly enamoured of the ruler of the Austro-Hungarian Empire, once describing Franz Joseph as 'that idiot, that old dotard'.[12] In an era of haughty aristocracy, Ferdinand was a colourful figure, and annoyed Wilhelm by playfully slapping the kaiser on the bottom during a state visit to Berlin. He was also widely known to be a promiscuous bisexual, having a number of liaisons with young officers and fathering children with women of lowly rank. Despite his conduct being published in German newspapers in 1895 after an interview given by Stefan Stambolov, who had been forced to resign as Bulgaria's prime minister, Ferdinand remained popular with his people. He now committed them to war.

Operational command of the new assault on Serbia was assigned to August von Mackensen, who had shown during the Galician campaign that he was well-suited to the mixture of command and diplomacy required to coordinate troops of different nationalities. Whilst he was the natural choice, and there was no obvious alternative, it was becoming ever clearer to the men of *Ober Ost* that he was increasingly close to Falkenhayn, and there was persisting resentment at the manner in which his command during the summer had overshadowed *Ober Ost*. This led to barbed comments from Hoffmann in his diary entry of 9 September:

> Mackensen is to have command of the expedition. As all achievable honours, titles and medals have already been gathered by him in short order, he can only be lauded as Prince Eugen* after the capture of Belgrade.[13]

Mackensen travelled to Pless and Teschen for consultations with Falkenhayn and Conrad, and on 24 September passed through Vienna on his way to take up his new post. Here, he spent an evening with the 85-year-old Emperor Franz Joseph, once more demonstrating his diplomatic skills:

> [The emperor] is somewhat diminished, and drops his right shoulder a little and

---

* Hoffmann refers to Prince Eugen of Savoy, who achieved great success as commander of the armies of the Holy Roman Empire.

pushes his head forwards, but otherwise looks fresh and has an unusually energetic demeanour ... After dinner the emperor asked me to accompany him to his room ... he spoke to me confidentially for over half an hour about military events, the Austro-Hungarian troops, and the Austro-Hungarian generals who had been subordinated to me ... We parted on the best of terms. The old emperor was most touching in his warmth.[14]

The Entente Powers remained ignorant of the treaty signed by Bulgaria, and made a further offer in mid-September; Radoslavov chose to string them along, asking for further clarification. For Germany, the pieces were now almost in place for the planned attack on Serbia. With Bulgaria's cooperation secured, the only remaining doubts for the Central Powers centred upon Greece. The problem for both the Central Powers and the Entente Powers was that they both had powerful sympathisers within Greece. King Constantine I (whose wife Sophia was German) favoured neutrality with friendly relations with the Central Powers, but the Greek prime minister, Eleftérios Venezélos, was in favour of the Entente; however, to complicate matters still further, Venezélos' desire to help the Entente cause led him to consider territorial concessions to Bulgaria, whereas Constantine was starkly opposed to any such ceding of territory. Inevitably, neither the Central nor the Entente Powers felt that they could predict what Greece might do.

This uncertainty influenced operational thinking in Bulgaria. The Bulgarian First Army, consisting of four infantry divisions – ninety-one infantry battalions and ninety-four artillery batteries – deployed against Serbia as part of Mackensen's army group. At the same time, an additional Bulgarian division, accompanied by the 'Macedonian Legion' – a formation made up of ethnic Bulgarians who had been forced from their homeland when Serbia occupied it after the Balkan Wars – operated independently of Mackensen's command, with the intention of covering any Greek intervention. Ultimately, this would grow into the Bulgarian Second Army.

The command arrangements of the assault on Serbia were as complex as would be expected from an operation involving the armies of three countries. Mackensen would have overall command of the three armies, though as had been the case in Galicia, his group was technically subordinated to *AOK*. However, Conrad would have to clear any changes of plan with Falkenhayn at *OHL* before issuing any orders, and the German elements of Mackensen's army group were directly subordinated to *OHL*.[15] Similarly, although the Bulgarian First Army was under Mackensen's control, he would have to pass any instructions to the Bulgarian general staff, who would then pass them to General Kliment Boyadzhiev.

The operational plans for Mackensen's attack had already been drawn up before he took command, at least in principle. Following the two disastrous Austro-Hungarian invasions across the Drina in 1914, the Austro-Hungarian commander on the Serbian front, Oskar Potiorek, was dismissed; his parting words to his successor were 'If you have to attack Serbia again, only do it via Belgrade.'[16]

It was advice that he would have done well to heed when it was proffered to him in August 1914. From the first occasion that Falkenhayn suggested a new attack on Serbia in order to establish land communications with Turkey, plans had been in preparation for a new assault. As the year proceeded, these plans were rewritten and developed, originally using General Karl Tersztyánszky's Fifth Army until it was ordered to the Italian front. Thereafter, the remaining troops under Tersztyánszky's command were ordered to prevent any Serbian attempt to invade Austro-Hungarian territory, but as the summer progressed and it became increasingly likely that the Central Powers would be able to turn their attention away from the Russian front, the plans for offensive operations were resurrected. As part of this, the *k.u.k.* Army carried out extensive reconnaissance of suitable river crossings and Serbian defensive positions, and as troops began to move south after the conclusion of the agreements with Bulgaria, Tersztyánszky was appointed commander of the newly reconstituted Third Army.

As soon as Germany, Austria-Hungary and Bulgaria started implementing their military convention against Serbia, they encountered significant problems. Conrad had intended to move troops from Volhynia to the Serbian front, but the failure of his troops to win a decisive victory in eastern Galicia ensured that no such redeployment was possible. Once again, the Germans were forced to make good the shortcomings of their allies, further reinforcing their low opinion of the *k.u.k.* Army. At first, Mackensen tried to retain direct control of the additional four divisions that Germany committed to the theatre, but ultimately had to accept that most of them would form part of the Austro-Hungarian Third Army. Despite having carried out most of the planning for the coming operation, Tersztyánszky suddenly found himself supplanted; it seems that he had a major disagreement with Hungarian officials over the use of civilian workers in the army, and his notorious temper resulted in a row that went all the way to Budapest, where Tisza raised the matter in cabinet and ultimately insisted on Tersztyánszky's dismissal. Despite Conrad arguing passionately for his retention, Tersztyánszky was sent on extended leave, and replaced by General Hermann von Kövesz.

The troops assigned to the Austro-Hungarian Third Army consisted of XIX Corps (53rd *Landsturm* Division and assorted *Landsturm* brigades), the German

The Invasion of Serbia, October–November 1915

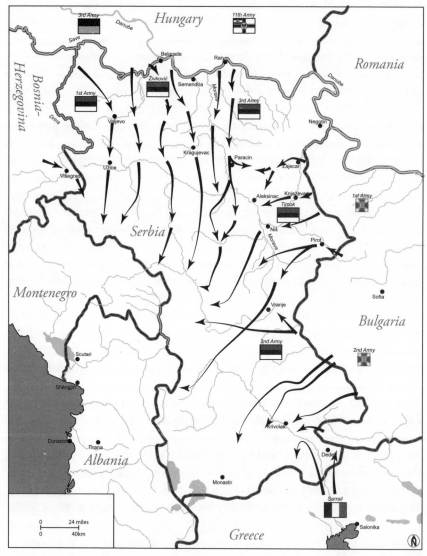

XXII Reserve Corps (43rd and 44th Reserve Divisions) and VIII Corps (57th and 59th Infantry Divisions). The main German contribution to the invasion of Serbia was Max von Gallwitz in command of Eleventh Army, with III Corps (6th

Infantry Division and 25th Reserve Division), IV Reserve Corps (11th Bavarian Infantry Division and 105th and 107th Infantry Divisions), and X Reserve Corps (101st and 103rd Infantry Divisions). In accordance with Tersztyánszky's plans, the intention was to attack from the north. Kövesz would cross the Save and Danube, with his main concentration against Belgrade; Gallwitz would cross further east, between Semendria (now Smederovo) and Ram, on the border between Serbia and Romania. The Bulgarians were to attack due west across their border with Serbia, into the rear of the Serbian Army as it was pushed south; the start date for the river crossings was set as 6 October, with the Bulgarians joining the war five days later.

Facing the forces of the Central Powers were the armies of Serbia. General Živojin Mišić commanded First Army along the Drina and Save, while Mihajlo Živković had a mixed force of about twenty battalions covering a 30-mile (50km) stretch of front around Belgrade. A little further to the east was Pavle Jurišić Šturm's Third Army with twenty-four battalions, and on his right flank, covering the Morava valley immediately to the east of Semendria, were two more divisions. Additional elements formed a newly created Timok Army Group facing the Bulgarian frontier to the south of the Danube, with Second Army, under Stepa Stepanović, continuing the line to the south. At the very southern end of the line, in the disputed Macedonian territories that Bulgaria wished to control, were a further thirty-one battalions, and thirteen were in Albania. The only significant reserve force available to the Serbs was a single division, on the railway line to the south of Belgrade.[17] Despite the apparent imminence of war with Bulgaria, it seems that Serbia failed to detect the build-up of enemy troops to the north. Even in the last week of September, Mackensen recorded that his officers could detect few signs of preparation for renewed fighting in and around Belgrade.[18] Belatedly, the Entente started to take steps against a possible attack on Serbia. Two divisions – one each from France and Britain – that had originally been intended for the Dardanelles were dispatched to Salonika, and on 2 October the Greek government was made aware of the intention to deploy troops on its territory. Although Venezélos made a token protest about Greek neutrality, he informed his cabinet that he intended to honour the treaty with Serbia, committing Greek military support in the event of a Bulgarian attack. However, German diplomacy was also being brought to bear, and Kaiser Wilhelm – whose sister was married to Constantine – assured the Greek king that Bulgarian troops would not enter Greek territory. Constantine now invoked a clause in the Greek constitution that allowed him to dismiss the government; the new government declared that it would not honour the treaty with Serbia, as this was intended only to apply to a war between Balkan powers, not one involving the Great Powers.[19]

It was impossible to hide war preparations in Bulgaria, and the Serbian military attaché notified his government that war was inevitable. The formal mobilisation decree was approved and issued on 22 September, and mobilisation began in earnest the following day; in reality, troops had been moving onto a war footing for over a week. Official mobilisation was accompanied by a declaration from Radoslavov that Bulgaria intended to adopt a position of armed neutrality. In an attempt to deter the Bulgarians, the Serbs now deployed substantial forces on their side of the border, amounting to perhaps half the entire army, and urged the Entente Powers to support a pre-emptive attack. This proposal was supported by the French General Maurice Sarrail, the commander of the force being sent to Salonika, but hoping that it might be possible to keep Bulgaria out of the war, even at this late stage, the British and French governments urged restraint.[20] Their diplomats still placed faith in the Serbian–Greek treaty, and although elements of the Russian government clung to the hope that ordinary Bulgarians would rise up against their government in a Pan-Slavist protest, Foreign Minister Sazonov insisted on a firm ultimatum being presented to the Bulgarians. On 3 October, the first elements of a joint Anglo-French force began to disembark in Salonika, and the following day, Entente diplomats issued a demand that all German officers serving as advisors in the Bulgarian Army must be sent home immediately.[21] Radoslavov made no response, and foreign diplomats began to leave Sofia on 5 October.

Mackensen's plans called for Eleventh Army to secure crossings over the Danube downstream of Belgrade and to push south on either side of the River Morava. At the same time, the Bulgarian First Army was to advance on Paraćin and Niš. The Austro-Hungarian Third Army was to cross the frontier to the west of Belgrade and seize the high ground south and southeast of Belgrade, effectively isolating the Serbian capital. Thereafter, Kövesz was to push south and draw as much of the Serbian Army onto his troops as possible, giving Eleventh Army greater freedom of manoeuvre in order to deliver a killing blow by thrusting down the Morava valley. In order to try to distract Serbian troops from the critical area, the Austro-Hungarian forces in Bosnia were to try to cross the Drina and advance on Višegrad and Užice; the former had been part of Bosnia at the start of the war, but had been occupied by the Serbian and Montenegrin armies in the fighting in 1914. As logistics officers struggled to move troops, ammunition and equipment into place using the limited railways that ran to the region, the Bulgarians informed their allies that mobilisation was proceeding more slowly

The Danube and Save, October 1915

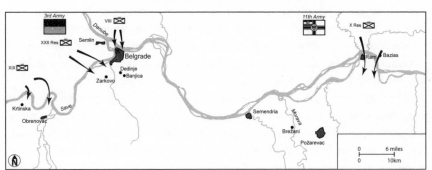

than expected; compared with the enthusiasm in the country during the Balkan Wars, there appeared to be little appetite for this new conflict. Despite thousands of reservists not responding to mobilisation orders, there were widespread shortages of uniforms and footwear. Nevertheless, there was no possibility of delay: Mackensen was operating against a very tight timetable if he wished to complete the campaign before the onset of bad weather.

On 6 October, German and Austro-Hungarian artillery began to bombard the Serbian lines. The first German troops – little more than reconnaissance patrols – crossed at Ram without encountering opposition, with the main force following the next day under the protection of early morning mist. By the end of the day, X Reserve Corps was firmly established on the south bank and moving forwards into the hills where the Serbs had their main defensive lines; the rest of Eleventh Army, too, crossed smoothly and without major incident.

The Austro-Hungarian forces had mixed fortunes. The largest of the formations along the middle Drina, 62nd Infantry Division, was meant to advance on Višegrad, but rapidly called off its advance as soon as it encountered Serbian resistance. Elsewhere, bridgeheads were secured over the Drina and Save, but the advancing troops rapidly came to a halt in the face of defences that had been constructed far enough from the rivers to be relatively safe from bombardment. About 16 miles (26km) to the west of Belgrade, Trollmann's XIX Corps attempted to cross the Save near Obrenovac, supported by the monitor *Szamos*, a vessel built in 1892 and armed with two 120mm guns and two 70mm guns, accompanied by the armoured steamer *Una*.[22] The approach march to the crossings during the night of 6–7 October was hindered by a heavy rainstorm, and there were delays in attempting the morning crossing, but the first brigade successfully established itself on the south bank by 7 a.m. Thereafter, as it attempted to advance on Krtinska, it made little progress on account of swampy ground; this was territory that had previously been controlled by Austro-Hungarian forces during the 1914 invasion of Serbia, and choosing a line of attack that led through such unfavourable ground seems an odd decision. Slightly to the east, another brigade succeeded in establishing a bridgehead, but once more failed to advance in the face of Serbian artillery fire. Nevertheless, at least sufficient ground was gained for XIX Corps to set up a pontoon bridge over the river.

The main attack by Kövesz was against Belgrade itself. The German XXII Reserve Corps had only just arrived from the Western Front and had no time to rest before the assault began. The selected crossing point across the Save, to the west of Belgrade, featured two long islands, marked on German maps as the 'Gypsy Islands' in the middle of the stream, and some of the troops were ferried across first to the island, and then to the south bank. The preliminary bombardment had set parts of Belgrade ablaze, and the few guns that the Serbs had deployed in their front line were rapidly suppressed; under light rain, the troops came ashore on the Serbian south bank, with the terrain lit up by the fires in Belgrade and searchlights on the north bank. Resistance both on the midstream island and the south bank then flared up, and it took until the afternoon for a significant foothold to be secured on the south bank, with both sides suffering heavy casualties. A German officer later recalled the fighting:

> Further west [from Belgrade], XXII Reserve Corps began to cross at 0230, and 43rd Reserve Infantry Division ran into tough resistance on both the larger and smaller Gypsy Islands from the enemy who was supported by fire from the citadel. It was possible to secure the smaller Gypsy Island by midday, with the capture of four officers, 225 men and two machine-guns; but in the thick undergrowth on the larger Gypsy Island, heavy fighting continued until evening. During the morning, a battalion of 44th Reserve Infantry Division's 208th Reserve Regiment passed the larger Gypsy Island and landed by a customs house on the Serbian bank. The Serbian force on the shore was surprised, but rapidly recovered and poured a furious fire onto the Germans who were ascending the bank. This battalion, too, found itself in a precarious position. Laboriously working their way up the bank, the brave soldiers repeatedly had to beat off furious Serbian counterattacks, while it was impossible to bring reinforcements across the river on account of the heavy enemy fire. But at least it was possible to get ammunition to them, allowing them to hold on until dusk when it was possible, albeit with losses, to bring over reinforcements.[23]

The Austro-Hungarian VIII Corps was meant to cross the Danube and Save and attack into Belgrade itself before dawn, but there were delays in setting off, and when the first pontoons attempted to cross, they came under heavy fire. Several boats were sunk, and others were damaged and drifted helplessly downstream. A battalion of 74th Infantry Regiment, commanded by Oberstleutnant Méttelét, passed to the south of the large island at the confluence of the two rivers and succeeded in coming ashore almost intact, and immediately stormed the Serbian positions around the old fortress at the Kalimegdan. While reinforcements struggled to reach the isolated battalion, it came under concentrated fire from the Serbian guns, and a battalion from 87th Infantry Regiment used this distraction to cross a few hundred metres to the east. Two further battalions also managed to establish themselves on the Serbian bank, but with two thirds of the pontoons sunk, further attempts to cross had to be abandoned for the moment.[24]

The troops facing Méttelét's battalion were primarily from the Serbian 10th Infantry Regiment, and their commander, Major Dragutin Gavrilović, rallied them with a call to arms before throwing them into a counterattack:

> At precisely 3pm, the enemy will be crushed by your fierce charge, destroyed by your grenades and bayonets. The honour of our capital Belgrade must not be stained. Our regiment has been sacrificed for the honour of Belgrade and the Fatherland. Therefore, you no longer need worry about your lives: they no longer exist. So forward to glory! Long live Belgrade![25]

Like so many counterattacks in the First World War, this one fell apart in the face of strong defensive fire. Gavrilović was badly wounded, but was carried back by the survivors of his regiment. He survived to see service later in the war, and also fought against German troops in 1941. On this latter occasion, he was captured, and survived imprisonment to return to his homeland where he died shortly afterwards.

The Save and Danube were substantial obstacles, and the Serbs had spent many months preparing for just such an assault. In the circumstances, a trouble-free crossing – particularly so close to the Serbian capital city – would have been too much to expect. Despite the increasing disdain shown by the Germans for their Austro-Hungarian allies, it is worth emphasising that the German XXII Reserve Corps struggled as much as the Austro-Hungarian VIII Corps. Mihajlo Živković, commander of the Belgrade garrison, called up whatever reinforcements were available for a counterattack; two battalions of the division held in reserve south of the city were dispatched with the intention of launching a major assault on 8 October against VIII Corps' bridgehead.[26]

Although losses in capturing the Gypsy Islands had been substantial, this proved to be the turning point of the battle; a footbridge from the larger island to the south bank was seized intact despite the attempts of Serb engineers to detonate pre-positioned demolition charges, and with the islands secured, the German XXII Reserve Corps could ferry troops and supplies across the river far more easily. The Serbs now began to pull back from their defences along the south bank, and during the afternoon of 8 October the Germans captured the southern end of a more substantial Serbian pontoon bridge that connected the larger island to the south bank. Many of the Serbian guns that had made river crossings the previous day so difficult were gradually suppressed by counter-battery fire, and the bridgehead rapidly expanded into the high ground south of the river.

In Belgrade itself, the Austro-Hungarian VIII Corps succeeded in getting more men across the river during the night, but at dawn the Serbian artillery resumed its heavy fire, preventing further reinforcements from crossing. The Serbian infantry also counterattacked and for several hours the troops manning the bridgehead were hard pressed to hold their positions. Nevertheless, the forces on the south bank were sufficiently strong to penetrate into the industrial quarter of Belgrade using a small gully that sheltered them from the guns in the Kalimegdan. Here, they ran into the two battalions of reinforcements that Živković had summoned. Bitter fighting continued throughout the day at close quarters amongst the houses and factories, with the monitors of the Danube River Flotilla adding the weight of their guns to the battle; at nightfall the warships withdrew, several of them badly damaged by Serbian artillery fire. Nevertheless, both through their fire support and by drawing fire upon themselves, they undoubtedly contributed to the successes achieved by VIII Corps.[27]

Gallwitz's Eleventh Army was having an altogether easier time. Troops continued to cross the river and made steady progress into the Serbian positions throughout 8 October. However, the first important success of the campaign came the following morning in Belgrade. As the Serbs pulled back from their defences immediately west of the city, a battalion from the German 43rd Reserve Division penetrated into southwest Belgrade before dawn, and rapidly advanced to the city centre. As it grew light, the German flag was raised over the Konak, the Serbian king's residence. At the same time, VIII Corps assaulted the Kalimegdan, and by evening linked up with XXII Reserve Corps as the Serbs abandoned their capital and withdrew to the south. That evening, Mackensen wrote to his wife:

This is of more political than military value. But in the final analysis it is a rare achievement, considering the river crossing. With God's help, we have begun a victorious campaign.[28]

For the moment, it seemed as if there was more difficulty in overcoming the elements than the Serbs. The stretch of the Danube to the northwest of Semendria was whipped into large waves by the prevailing wind, and combined with the fire of Serbian artillery this prevented III Corps from bringing substantial forces across on 9 October. As was the case with XXII Reserve Corps, the Germans made use of a large island in the river, and the forces at the eastern end of the island enjoyed an easier time in reaching the south bank, partly because the island provided shelter from the wind. By the end of the day two divisions had crossed, and the few troops who had succeeded in crossing further west through the rough waters were withdrawn after dark in favour of concentrating all reinforcements at just one point.[29]

Although the Serbs had contested the crossings, their main defensive line ran through the high ground to the south of the Danube and Save. Further progress of Mackensen's 'victorious campaign' would depend upon how quickly his forces could penetrate through this line. Having linked up with VIII Corps, XXII Reserve Corps now turned south, making steady if unspectacular progress over the next three days; Kövesz and Mackensen agreed that there was little point in haste, as the year's events had demonstrated that success depended on the deployment of heavy artillery, which would now have to be brought across the river. As the front line moved south, pontoon bridges were erected, bringing both reinforcements and supplies forward in larger quantity; Eugen von Falkenhayn, commander of XXII Reserve Corps, had intended to assault the Serbian positions in the Dedinje Heights to the south of Belgrade, but had to wait while the bridges to his rear were strengthened sufficiently for heavy artillery to be brought across; by the time the howitzers arrived, the Serbs had withdrawn. Immediately, Falkenhayn ordered his two divisions to pursue and advanced to the villages of Zarkovo and Banjica. On 11 October, additional troops from III Corps crossed the river to the east and overran the Serbian defenders of Semendria; they then advanced southwest, aiming to link up with the eastern flank of the Austro-Hungarian VIII Corps. Advancing along the Morava valley, the 11th Bavarian Infantry Division encountered tough resistance in the town of Brežani, where elements of the Serbian Cavalry Division made good use of the army barracks to mount a determined defence. This continued through the next day, with many civilians fighting alongside the Serbian Army, but as German artillery began to move south the balance of power swung decisively in favour of the Bavarians. The barracks were abandoned and the cavalry withdrew, accompanied by many of the local population.

The timely withdrawal from Belgrade had prevented the Serbian forces from suffering major losses, but Živković was aware that his forces were outmatched and he sent an urgent message to the Serbian high command:

> It is therefore crucially important that a complete division is sent here immediately, because no purpose is served by sending smaller formations. It is already impossible to pull a single regiment out of the front line as a reserve, as this would leave the line too weak. Some regiments have been reduced to half- or even one third-strength ... One must not forget that we have been in constant fierce combat for five days and have defended every yard of soil of the homeland; all of this within the range of the German heavy guns and the Austrian monitors, whose devastating fire has placed an almost unbearable strain on the nerves of officers and men ... In those sectors where they were not subjected to the devastating fire of the German batteries, our troops have successfully beaten off attacks and also made powerful counterattacks against a superior enemy.[30]

There can have been little disagreement with this assessment, but Serbia was desperately short of troops. Two regiments were dispatched from Second Army, and took up positions on its eastern flank.

The Bulgarian Army also joined the conflict on 11 October, making a few limited attacks on border positions. For the moment though, there was no declaration of war and the fighting was more of the nature of small-scale skirmishes. Given that the Entente Powers remained unenthusiastic about an attack on Bulgaria, the Serbs began to withdraw forces from the Bulgarian border in an attempt to shift resources north to stop the German and Austro-Hungarian advance. Again, it seemed as if the weather was the strongest ally that Serbia had, as storms greatly hindered the attempts to erect bridges to support Gallwitz's Eleventh Army. Mackensen wrote on 16 October:

> A wind is blowing on the Danube, the so-called Kosovo wind, and is creating two-metre waves making supply and bridging operations almost impossible. Also, all rivers, not just the Danube, are running high, many banks and low areas are swamped, and the unsurfaced roads are bottomless mud. The troops who crossed at Belgrade already have bridges over the Save behind them, those who have crossed at Semendria and downstream as far as Bazias are still supplied by barges and ferries. Fortunately we have a few steamers and can thus deliver ammunition and food to our troops on the south bank of the Danube ... The troops are therefore not fully ready for operations and we have to wait until the Kosovo wind

abates. A huge amount of material for two bridges is available and already prepared to bridge the 1200m-wide Danube within twenty-four hours.[31]

The first bridge was erected at Semendria on 20 October, but the troops that had crossed further east at Ran had to wait several more days.

Mounting a major operation so late in the year was always a risky enterprise, and in the second week of October the Serbs completed their withdrawal into increasingly hilly terrain to the south of the Save and Danube. Gallwitz wanted to suspend operations until he could bring ammunition stocks up to full strength, but Mackensen urged him to resume his attacks on 15 October; Gallwitz replied that this was impracticable, as his troops were not deployed for any such attack. In the event, there were modest advances as the Serbs withdrew to a straighter line. Over the next two days, Mackensen's army group consolidated its position. The bridgehead at Belgrade was now perhaps 12 miles (20km) deep, while Eleventh Army succeeded in advancing a little further and secured the town of Požarevac.

After multiple problems during mobilisation, Bulgaria finally declared war on Serbia on 14 October. Numbering nearly 300,000 men, the forces of Bulgaria were divided into two armies. In the north, Boyadzhiev's First Army was to advance on Niš and Aleksinac and thus link up with the German Eleventh Army, while Georgi Todorov's Second Army – operating independently from Mackensen's army group – advanced on Vranje in order to cut communications with Macedonia and Salonika. At first, both forces enjoyed considerable success, overwhelming the weak units along the frontier, not least because the Serbs had started moving substantial numbers of troops to the north. However, after just two days, Boyadzhiev reached the towns of Pirot, Knjaževac and Zaječar, where Serbian troops took up fortified positions. For four days, the two sides struggled along muddy roads through the rainswept hills and clashed inconclusively until the Serbs were forced to pull back. By contrast, Todorov met little significant resistance in the south, reaching Vranje in two days. Even if the Anglo-French force in Salonika was rapidly augmented, its swift redeployment to face the Germans in northern Serbia was now impossible.

Gallwitz was finally able to resume major operations on 18 October. With III Corps operating west of the Morava and IV and X Reserve Corps to the east of the river, he advanced steadily, though supply problems persisted; although it was now possible to move substantial supplies across the Danube, further movement from the riverbank to the front line was hindered by the lack of good roads. Nevertheless, there was a steady weakening of Serbian resistance, and by 22 October the bridgeheads of Eleventh Army and Third Army had merged. With

Pirot and Zaječar in their hands, the troops of the Bulgarian First Army continued their steady progress towards Niš and Aleksinac, and further south, after their successful thrust to Vranje, the Bulgarians diverted some of Second Army north against the Serbs, while the rest of Todorov's command turned south with the intention of pushing along the railway line that led towards Salonika. Aware that reinforcements in the form of the German Alpine Corps were en route for his army group, Mackensen now ordered the Austro-Hungarian XIX Corps to defend the western flank of his forces, while the rest pressed forward with converging axes of advance, aiming to destroy the Serbian Army in the interior of Serbia. Mackensen would have preferred to deploy the Alpine Corps, trained and equipped for mountain warfare, in an attack across the Drina, but the very limited railway capacity in that sector would have resulted in any such deployment taking several weeks, and it was decided that it would be better to get the troops into combat quickly with Eleventh Army.

On 24 October, Falkenhayn visited Mackensen in his headquarters in Temesvár (now Timişoara). The two men agreed on the importance of establishing contact with the Bulgarians as soon as possible, and to that effect the first elements of the Alpine Corps would be deployed on the eastern flank of Eleventh Army for a thrust towards Negotin. Such a thrust would result in the entire south bank of the Danube being in German hands as far as Bulgaria, and it would thus be possible to send supplies to the Bulgarians along the river. As it turned out, Boyadzhiev's northern formations had already captured Negotin, and contact was made on 25 October. Elsewhere, the German and Austro-Hungarian troops maintained their steady advance, and by 29 October had reached a line running from east to west and passing about 6 miles (10km) north of Kragujevac. Here, the Serbs were faced with a dilemma – Kragujevac was a vital manufacturing centre, without which the Serbian Army would not be able to continue fighting, especially as the Bulgarian advance had cut railway communications with Salonika. Further south, the Bulgarians had already captured Skopje, and were about 15 miles (25km) from Niš to the east. Unless help arrived soon, the Serbs faced encirclement.

The only help that might reach the Serbian Army consisted of the British and French forces that had landed in Salonika. The British were reluctant to send their troops too far into Serbia, but General Sarrail decided to push north with the French contingent of two divisions. The most northern formation was 57th Infantry Division, and in the last days of October it clashed with the leading elements of the Bulgarian Second Army. Todorov had anticipated such a move by the forces in Salonika, and at the beginning of November his formations attacked towards the southwest along the entire line held by the French. An advance by the French towards the north clearly ran the risk of being cut off by the Bulgarian attack, and Sarrail now attempted to push back the Bulgarians with 156th Infantry Division, while 57th Infantry Division, reinforced by parts of 122nd Infantry Division, attempted to hold the town of Krivolak, where the vital railway line from the south crossed the confluence of the Vardar and Tcherna rivers. In the weeks that followed, the French were forced to withdraw to the south, and in early December they were back on Greek soil.

The British component of the Salonika expedition was the 10th (Irish) Infantry Division, created in 1914 as part of Kitchener's wave of new volunteer formations. It first saw action in Gallipoli, fighting at both Suvla Bay and Anzac Cove in August before it was withdrawn. After landing in Salonika, the British troops were held back at first on the orders of their government, but in the last week of October a brigade moved north to the Serbian border; the other two brigades followed a few days later. A correspondent described the deployment:

10th Division Headquarters at Dedeli overlooked the half-mile broad valley of the Bojimia river, whose bed, however, was a dry waste of sand and rocks. Cotton, hemp, mulberry trees, withered vestiges of the inevitable Indian corn, witnessed to the fertility of the district whose inhabitants had been driven away by the approach of hostilities – a kind of migration to which, as Macedonians, they were thoroughly accustomed ... A short walk eastwards along the river bed took you to Tatarli, where the General commanding the 31st Brigade had his headquarters. The Bulgarians were understood to hold a line of trenches, blockhouses and sangars along the ridge parallel to ours. It was estimated that there were about 10,000 of them spread out between the Greek frontier and Strumnitza, and believed to belong to the 2nd Philipopolis Division. Deserters would come in voluntarily in little bodies. They complained of shortage of food in the enemy lines. One sheep had to be divided between 250 men. They were generally men between 25 and 35 and seemed to be townspeople. One drew a good contour map to explain how he had come; another mended the watches of the Division Headquarters Staff. They were eager to show that they had not fired their rifles. One deserter had taken off his tunic to make him less likely to be shot at.[32]

The men of the 10th Infantry Division were in poor physical shape as a result of their time in Gallipoli, and as the weather deteriorated in the barren mountains they suffered serious casualties from frostbite and exposure. In early December, as the French troops a little to the west pulled back towards the Greek border, the

British came under increasingly heavy attack and were forced back into Greece. The Bulgarian forces stopped at the border. Some officers in the Bulgarian Army wanted to continue to Salonika, but the Germans urged caution; if fighting were to spread to Greece, they argued, it would undermine the position of King Constantine I and the pro-German faction in the country. It was an ignominious end to the expedition that had been intended to prop up Serbia.

The 'Salonika Front' now became very quiet, but would play a very significant role towards the end of the war. Did the Central Powers miss an opportunity to eliminate this Entente bridgehead in 1915? On the one hand, it seems likely that the defeated French and British forces would not have been able to put up major resistance, and there was only limited shipping available for any evacuation – had the Bulgarians been able to drive to the coast, much of Sarrail's command would have faced destruction or surrender. But on the other hand, such an advance would not have been an easy undertaking:

> But physical conditions alone were enough to hold up the Bulgars at the southern frontier of Serbia. They were as exhausted as the French; they, too, had suffered from the bitter weather conditions, and they had had heavy losses in their successive attacks upon the series of entrenched positions which had protected the French retreat. Moreover the lack of available routes of march was an obstacle even more formidable for the Bulgars than it had been for the French, for the latter had naturally blown up the tunnels and bridges as they came down the railway, so that the enemy could only use the tracks from village to village, which were in an appalling condition and quite incapable of carrying the supply columns and artillery of an army. To press forward yet another fifty miles [80km] with exhausted infantry and only mountain artillery upon an adversary close up against his sea-base with the heavy guns of warships behind to support him would have been a rash undertaking. The Bulgars had won the parts of Macedonia they coveted, and they could afford for the present to pause.[33]

Meanwhile, in Serbia itself, the Serbian high command had to accept that there was no prospect of the Anglo-French force reaching them. The German and Austro-Hungarian armies advancing from the north and northwest made steady ground in the face of resistance that was often tough but not consistent enough to bring the advance to a halt. Mackensen's letters suggest that the terrain and climate were the main obstacles to a swift victory:

> If the roads weren't bottomless mud as a result of the constant rain and the

mountains not wrapped in fog, making it difficult to observe artillery fire, the Serbs would already have been pushed further back and pressed closer together. I hope that fate will soon catch up with them.[34]

Mackensen hoped that the Serbs would make a stand at Kragujevac, but on 31 October, a day after he wrote about fate overtaking the Serbian Army, it became clear that Putnik had decided to withdraw further. While determined rearguards held off the forces pressing down on him from the north, he ordered the rest of the army to pull back towards Kosovo. If the Serbian Army could concentrate here and break contact with the pursuing forces, it might be able to fight its way south to link up with the retreating French forces. Kragujevac was abandoned without a fight, falling to the advancing German III Corps on 1 November. The Austro-Hungarian forces on the western flank were meant to envelop the retreating Serbs and prevent them from falling back to the southwest, but it proved impossible to move swiftly enough to do this. Mackensen urged his forces on, and on 5 November the Bulgarian 9th Infantry Division succeeded in reaching and cutting the main road running south through Niš, effectively isolating any Serbian forces further north in the Morava valley. As the Serbs pulled back into the mountains, their retreat became increasingly chaotic, with large numbers of prisoners, guns and supplies falling into the hands of the pursuing forces. Purely from the perspective of the Serbian Army, matters were worsened by the large numbers of civilians who accompanied the retreating soldiers, blocking roads and preventing military movements.

Mackensen's original intention had been for the Austro-Hungarian Third Army to tie down as much of the Serbian Army as possible, while Eleventh Army advanced down the Morava valley to link up with the Bulgarians before joining in a series of concentric attacks that would destroy the Serbs. As events unfolded, a combination of logistic and movement difficulties prevented his forces from moving fast enough to achieve their objective; the astute withdrawals of the Serbian forces, too, ensured that they did not wait passively to be encircled. Whilst Mackensen expressed frustration that Kövesz was not urging Third Army forward as energetically as he might, he singled out the German XXII Reserve Corps for criticism. Nevertheless, the Serbian Army was effectively eliminated as a fighting force for the immediate future, perhaps permanently, and it was time to consider what to do next. On 6 November, Mackensen wrote that he hoped for an offensive against the French and British who had landed at Salonika. Although Conrad expressed enthusiasm for such an operation, Falkenhayn rejected the suggestion. His overall strategy was to win sufficient victories in the east in order to transfer troops to the west, where he still believed the war would be decided. The first formations – two divisions from Eleventh Army – received their redeployment orders on 7 November, followed by a further two divisions and the staff and corps-level formations of III Corps and IV Reserve Corps a few days later. The Bulgarian First Army, too, was the target of Mackensen's frustrated urging, as it showed little inclination to advance west of the Morava; Boyadzhiev replied to the urgings of the army group commander – via the complicated line of command that led back to the Bulgarian general staff, then to Conrad, and finally to Mackensen – that he had little or no bridging equipment. Whilst this was true, it seems that the Bulgarians were content with the ground they had secured, and now wished to concentrate on the fighting in Macedonia.

Putnik's intention to fight his way through to the French was clearly not possible, though initial attacks in that direction seemed to make a little encouraging progress, driving back elements of the Bulgarian Army. The pursuing German and Austro-Hungarian troops were too close, and there were sufficient Bulgarian forces between his army and Sarrail's troops to ensure that any attempt to break through to the south would proceed slowly at best; Mackensen's armies would then overwhelm the Serbs from the north. In any case, unit cohesion was coming to an end. Faced with the prospect of being driven out of Serbia, many soldiers slipped away and attempted to return to their homes, and on 25 November, Putnik issued a new proclamation to his men:

> The only salvation from this grave situation lies in retreating to the Adriatic coast. There our army will be reorganised, supplied with food, weapons, ammunition, clothing and everything else necessary that is being sent by our allies, and we shall once again be a factor for our enemies to reckon with. The state lives; it still exists, albeit on foreign land, wherever the ruler, the government and the army are to be found, whatever its strength may be … In these difficult days our salvation [lies] in the endurance, patience and utter perseverance of us all, with faith in the ultimate success of our allies.[35]

Over roads that rapidly disintegrated in the rain and after the passage of far more traffic than they could carry, long columns of Serbian soldiers and civilians began to make their way through the mountainous terrain towards the coast. Although some military formations managed to preserve order and discipline, most rapidly disintegrated. Weapons and other equipment were abandoned along the route, with only some being destroyed to prevent them from falling into the hands of the German, Austro-Hungarian and Bulgarian pursuers. Reports from Serbian officers confirmed the growing sense of collapse:

> Huge numbers of soldiers are fleeing; food and fodder are scarce and it is impossible to acquire anything to give to the troops. Communications are difficult; the weather is bitterly cold; clothing and footwear are worn out; men and livestock are totally exhausted as a result of constant fighting and movement; there is no food at all in the directions chosen for retreat.
>
> ... The morale and the material state of our troops are desperate. Despite all the measures to prevent desertion, the number of troops is plummeting, and they are fleeing en masse. Deserters are fighting against our troops to clear their way to the villages of Istok and Mitrovica. They are selling weapons to Albanians. Regiments number only a few hundred men. There is only enough food for the troops for another four or five days. All efforts to acquire food have proved useless.[36]

The weather, terrain and poor roads that had hampered Mackensen's armies now became the main problem for the retreating Serbs. The Serbian occupation of Albania had led to widespread resentment, and many Albanians took up arms – some of them purchased from Serbian deserters, as described above – and attacked the columns as they trudged along the mountain tracks. The only crumb of comfort was that none of the invading armies was particularly anxious to pursue them into the mountains of the border and Albania; the Bulgarians had achieved all of their territorial ambitions, and Mackensen was content to have overrun Serbia itself, with all parties agreeing to stop the pursuit at the Albanian and Montenegrin border at a conference on 16 November involving Falkenhayn, Mackensen, Seeckt, and Nikolaus Jekov, the chief of the Bulgarian general staff. Notably, the meeting took place without any Austro-Hungarian officers present. The Serbian civilian government travelled relatively quickly, reaching the town of Scutari, or Skadar (now Shkodër) on 28 November, over a week before Putnik and the military high command arrived; the ailing Putnik had to be carried most of the way. As early as 20 November, Pašić had sent an urgent message to Serbia's allies, asking for supplies – particularly food – to be sent urgently to the Adriatic ports, but when the Serbs arrived, they found the harbour empty of the foreign ships they had expected and hoped for. Food had been dispatched from France and Britain, but it was in Brindisi, on the other side of the Adriatic, and the Italians had not allocated more than a few small vessels to transport it on to the Serbs, partly through fears of submarines. A convoy was dispatched to Shëngjin, the port closest to Scutari, but it encountered a small group of Austro-Hungarian warships and was destroyed. Some supplies had come ashore in Durrës, but this was more than 36 miles (60km) from Skadar, where the columns of troops and refugees were congregating. Fearing further naval clashes, the British, French and Italians decided that further convoys to the ports closest to Skadar were too risky, and that supplies would only be landed further south. The exhausted, starving Serbs had no choice but to set off on further marches through the mountainous, wintry landscape.

Originally, the Serbs had hoped that they would be able to regroup and replenish along the Albanian coastline, but it was clearly impossible to transport sufficient food to the area, let alone military supplies. Eventually, a decision was made to evacuate the Serbian Army – and its accompanying civilians – to the Greek island of Corfu. This decision, made primarily by the British and French, did not involve any discussions with the Greek authorities. There were delays while shipping was organised, and it was not until early 1916 that the bulk of the Serbian troops was evacuated. Putnik travelled to France for medical treatment, where he died the following year.

The losses suffered by the German and Austro-Hungarian forces during the campaign amounted to about 30,000 men; most of these were killed or wounded in the first two weeks, either along the Save–Danube defences or during the advance to Kragujevac.[37] In addition, the Bulgarians lost about 37,000 men.[38] Serbian losses were far greater; Mackensen recorded that about 150,000 had been taken prisoner, but other estimates put the figure higher at over 170,000.[39] An additional 90,000 men were killed or wounded, and about 155,000 were evacuated from the Albanian coast. Although the Central Powers had intended to destroy the Serbian Army, it had been eliminated as a fighting force, and the main purpose of the campaign – the elimination of one of the many fronts of the war, and the opening of land contact with Turkey – was achieved. With the Russian Army already badly damaged, Falkenhayn could finally begin sending troops west, in the hope of a decisive victory in 1916.

During the planning of the campaign, the Germans had dominated decision-making, but as the campaign progressed Conrad began to be more assertive. During the Potiorek invasions of 1914, there had been discussions within the Austro-Hungarian administration about how to deal with Serbia once victory was achieved, and although these discussions had naturally paused after Potiorek's defeat in December, they now resumed with added energy. Conrad, who had long advocated a war against Serbia, was a member of the hard-line annexationist group. In addition to seizing most of Serbia, this group advocated policies that reflected the German attitude to colonisation, and would recur in a later war: the

Serbian intelligentsia was to be eliminated and the rest of the Serbian population reduced to peasantry, with the area resettled by German, Austrian and Hungarian farmers. The less extreme group was largely centred upon Tisza and other Hungarians; although they too called for substantial annexations, particularly along the pre-war frontier, they imagined a residual Serbian state between the Austro-Hungarian Empire and an enlarged Bulgaria, though this state would be effectively a client of the empire. Now that Serbia had been defeated, these discussions resumed, with Conrad playing a leading role. He sent several memoranda to Foreign Minister Burián advocating that all of Serbia other than the territories promised to Bulgaria should be absorbed into the empire. He also felt that Albania should either be divided between Greece and the empire, or reduced to a client state.

Within Serbia itself, the *k.u.k.* Army continued to display its suspicion of any activity that might be regarded as subversive or hostile. Pál Kelemen, a Hungarian cavalry officer, recorded the treatment of a Serbian straggler who ran into his unit:

> With the aid of a translator, the man was interrogated and we learned the most important matters. It seemed that despite repeated warnings from other villagers he had recklessly fired on our soldiers. As he looked away from those who had gathered, the man seemed half-wild, as if he had been planted here before us from another world.
>
> Soon, judgment was reached: the guerilla was to be hanged.
>
> A man from the kitchen unit, a pig butcher from Vienna, joyfully took up the role of executioner. He brought out a long rope and found an empty case that would provide the required drop. The Serbian guerilla was given the opportunity to say a few last words, but replied that he would not take it. Women cried, children whimpered and stared as if frozen by horror while the soldiers gathered around a tree, slowly and without any apparent emotion, though their eyes were filled with agitation.
>
> The Serbian guerilla was lifted up by two soldiers. He showed no particular emotion, but his accusing stares seemed a little wild. The noose was placed around his neck and the case pulled away from under his feet. It seemed that the rope was too long and with a powerful pull the butcher hauled it up to the correct height. The man's face was contorted for a long time.[40]

Tisza and his supporters had good reasons for their lack of enthusiasm for the widespread annexations proposed by Conrad. Their main concern was that the absorption of so much territory – and in particular the Serbian population – would add substantially to the ethnic problems within the empire. In early December, Tisza expressed his point of view in a memorandum to Franz Joseph:

> Another one and a half to two million Serbs ... will also revive the national aspirations and hopes of Serbs in our state, and the Hungarian state will be threatened with the loss of its true identity ... Hungary will lose its coherence ... An increase in the number of Serb subjects in the Monarchy by unifying all Serbs under the sceptre of one ruler ... will intensify Greater Serb propaganda.[41]

Falkenhayn appears to have had little interest in such matters. Ludendorff and Hindenburg had shown that they supported similar policies as part of a reshaping of Eastern Europe, with large-scale German colonisation and absorption of the Baltic States and other regions, but Falkenhayn was purely interested in winning the war. Discussions of how Europe should be run after an eventual victory by the Central Powers were of little concern to him, and Conrad's enthusiasm for such matters did nothing to improve relations between the two men. Nor did the increasingly forceful attitude of the chief of the Austro-Hungarian general staff. As early as 25 November, Conrad informed Mackensen that he regarded the command arrangements that subordinated the Austro-Hungarian Third Army as being at an end. After Mackensen informed him of this, Falkenhayn expressed his disagreement, but Conrad remained adamant; he intended to concentrate his forces to attack Montenegro. This would prove to be a bitter bone of contention between Berlin and Vienna.

CHAPTER 12

THE BURDEN OF WAR

Before the outbreak of war in 1914, there had been some indications that a future conflict might be long and drawn-out, but despite this, almost everyone – politicians, soldiers, and the general population – planned for a conflict that would be relatively short and would produce a decisive outcome. The reality of prolonged fighting forced all of the Great Powers to adapt, creating considerable strains within each nation.

The first winter of the war saw a wave of patriotic fervour throughout Europe. In Germany, there was a carefully stage-managed setting aside of political differences between different domestic factions in the national interest. The realisation that the boys would not be home by Christmas was tempered by a continuing belief in Germany that victory remained close; the casualties suffered on the fronts were not publicised, and the average German was unaware that the great plan to crush France in a swift campaign had failed, largely because the means by which Germany intended to achieve a swift victory had understandably not been publicised beforehand. Even within military and political circles, only those at the highest levels knew of the Schlieffen Plan, and were additionally aware that there had been no fallback plan in the event of failure. Nevertheless, the ongoing fighting resulted in huge support for all manner of activities; tens of thousands of German women attempted to enrol for first aid courses, or visited exhibitions that showed how to care for wounded men. Civilians sent parcels to front-line soldiers, in many cases to complete strangers. A year later, the mood had changed perceptibly. It was quite clear to everyone that no end was in sight, and it was impossible to hide the casualty figures from the public.

Before the war, Germany had been reliant on imports for a significant proportion of its basic foodstuffs, and although there was a degree of blockade-dodging via Denmark and the Netherlands, there were widespread shortages. The lack of fertiliser – with most chemically generated nitrates being diverted for explosive production – reduced agricultural yields, further exacerbating matters. Some industries purchased additional food supplies to ensure that their workers remained adequately fed; although this was illegal, the authorities tended to turn a blind eye, as the industries involved were vital for the war effort. However, this activity also reduced the amount of food available in the general market. Shortages of food items, particularly those regarded as luxuries, were widespread; compared with 1914, Christmas the following year was a bleak affair, with fewer decorated trees and even the traditional Christmas markets looked austere and rather grim. Evelyn Blücher, the English wife of a descendant of the Prussian marshal who fought at Waterloo, recorded the mood in Berlin two days after Christmas:

> For weeks past, the town seems to have been enveloped in an impenetrable veil of sadness, grey on grey, which no golden ray of sunlight ever seems able to pierce, and which forms a fit setting for the white-faced, black-robed women who glide so sadly through the streets, some bearing their sorrow proudly as a crown to their lives, others bent and broken under a burden too heavy to be borne.
>
> But everywhere it will be the same; in Paris and London too everyone will be gazing at their Christmas trees with eyes dim with tears.
>
> We made some joint efforts to celebrate Christmas for others by preparing small gifts for the soldiers and for the poor. The shops made some rather futile attempts at Christmas sales, which were peremptorily forbidden, and the crowds which had collected from all parts of Berlin were dispersed without having made any purchases. No textile goods might be sold in special sales!
>
> ... the snow had been falling unceasingly, and as we all went off together to Midnight Mass at the Convent Hospital, the silent streets and houses lay shrouded with pure white snow. The church was crowded with wounded soldiers, nurses, nuns, and pale-faced, broken-hearted women.[1]

The impact of the war on the economy was severe, with many businesses losing access to valuable foreign markets and others being forced to close due to conscription of their workforce. It was estimated that families whose main breadwinner had been summoned to the ranks lost at least two thirds of their income despite welfare payments, and when combined with wartime inflation, this created increasing hardship throughout Germany.[2]

The Austro-Hungarian Empire had shown worrying signs of war-weariness in the first winter of the war, and discontent was far stronger by the end of 1915.

Unable to rely on nationalist sentiment as other Great Powers could do, the empire was strongly dependent upon the Catholic Church, particularly as the immediate enemies of Austria-Hungary were Orthodox Christians, and many priests took it upon themselves to portray the war as one to protect Catholicism from Orthodox dominance. This line naturally became harder to maintain once Italy entered the war on the side of the Entente, but the widespread hostility towards the 'treachery' of the Italians helped mitigate this. As with so many things, though, there were nuances to the religious exhortations to continue fighting. When speaking to his clergy in early 1915, the Polish Bishop Józef Sebastyan Pelczar of Przemyśl said that the war was about 'not only the integrity and honour of the Austro-Hungarian monarchy but also the future of Poland and Catholic interests, threatened by the Orthodox Church and Freemasonry.'[3]

The appalling casualties (after taking into account soldiers who recovered from their wounds and returned to service, over 37,000 officers and over two million men had been killed or disabled) had destroyed the peacetime army and its careful arrangement of regiments linked by ethnicity, in which most officers spoke the languages of their troops. Formations strong in Austrian or Hungarian personnel remained – to a point – reliable, but widespread reports of defections of entire companies and battalions of Slav troops, particularly from Czech and Ruthenian parts of the empire, continued to cause great concern. Whilst these reports appear to have overstated the problem, there is no question that many such desertions did in fact occur. Graffiti appeared in cities like Prague condemning the war, and recruits for two Prague regiments marched off to war in September 1915 carrying banners that proclaimed 'We are marching against the Russians and we do not know why.'[4] Attempts to deal with the issue by reviving laws that allowed the authorities to seize the property of deserters had little effect other than creating bitterness and alienation in Bohemia and other affected regions. Matters were made worse by the attitude of the army, which was a hotbed of suspicion about certain ethnicities. In many respects, this suspicion tended to establish a self-feeding cycle: the authorities became ever more repressive, feeding resentment and resistance, which in turn led to more suspicion and repression.

Although Falkenhayn wished the entry of German troops into Warsaw to be a low-key event so as not to jeopardise potential peace negotiations with Russia, there was widespread rejoicing across Poland. Many hoped that the Central Powers would use the opportunity to reunite Poland. This was not remotely on the agenda of either Germany or Austria-Hungary, and their rapid imposition of control on the areas of central and eastern Poland represented another potential missed opportunity. Although Polish troops continued to fight for the Central Powers, there was potential to have made more of Polish resentment of Russian occupation, but in Berlin thoughts were already turning to the possible future shape of Europe, and there was no place for an independent Poland in this vision.

Even between the Austrians and Hungarians, there were bitter arguments about their contribution to the war. The Hungarian prime minister, István Tisza, complained in September 1915 that Hungary formed slightly less than 41 per cent of the population of the empire, but it provided nearly 43.5 per cent of the army's manpower, and that Austria should therefore immediately increase its share of the burden. The response was that Austrian territory included parts of Galicia that had been occupied by the Russians and could therefore not contribute manpower, and further wrangling about what proportion of the dead had come from each country did little to improve relations.[5] Nor did the authorities attempt to engage the Czech population by giving them good motives to fight against Russia. This was certainly an option – most Poles rightly regarded Russia as the most repressive nation to have occupied Polish territory, and it might have been possible for Austro-Hungarian politicians to urge Czechs and other minorities to join a general war against an autocratic, despotic regime. Instead, the answer was merely an attempt to suppress all opposition.

As was the case in Germany, money was raised by selling war bonds, which were taken up with steadily diminishing enthusiasm as the war progressed. There were many approaches to raising money for war relief; a theme in both Germany and Austria-Hungary was the proliferation of 'iron men' as a symbol of support for the war. Wooden figures, posts, and other objects were erected in many cities, and civilians were invited to 'buy' a nail, which they then hammered into the timber structure. The proceeds were used for wartime charities, and in some cases people had the choice of buying iron, silver or even gold nails at different prices. The iron men were sometimes named after mythological heroes, or more recent figures such as Hindenburg; on other occasions, local symbols were used. In some parts of the Austro-Hungarian Empire, these local symbols merely accentuated the differences within the empire. For example, the monument in Krakow was named the 'Column of the Legions' and used to collect money for the families of men serving in the *k.u.k.* Army's Polish Legions.[6]

In common with every Great Power, conscription left the economy of the empire struggling to keep up civilian living standards. Some German observers, such as Hoffmann at *OHL*, felt that some of the problems of the Dual Monarchy were self-imposed:

[A colleague] gave a description of the mess in Austria. The situation there is perhaps somewhat worse than was previously thought. The worst is the old emperor with the old Habsburg hatred for the Hohenzollerns. Inflation is twice as bad as with us. The government doesn't intervene because the upper aristocracy – with Archduke Frederick in the first rank – are making a substantial profit.[7]

Whilst most of what Hoffmann describes may have been widely accepted in Germany, there is little foundation to the suggestion that Franz Joseph was in any way hostile to the German royal family during the war, or that Archduke Frederick was profiteering.

Because the war had been anticipated to be short, there were no exemptions at first for workers in 'key industries' and it took until the spring of 1915 for many of these men to be released. Despite the best efforts of those involved to raise money for war loans, these were not enough to bridge the gap between Austria-Hungary's war expenditure and the available funds. Substantial subsidies were needed from Germany, and attempts by Vienna to make ends meet simply by printing more money led to a steady fall in the value of the Austro-Hungarian Krone in the United States and Switzerland. Galicia had been a substantial net exporter of food to the rest of the empire before the war, and although the province was back in Austro-Hungarian hands, the devastation of so many campaigns and the absence of so many men – either serving in the army, or in many cases forcibly deported by the retreating Russians – left agriculture throughout Galicia unable to produce remotely as much as it had done in earlier years. Food rationing was steadily extended throughout the empire, though in a rather disorderly and sometimes arbitrary manner. This, too, became a source of bitter argument between Austria and Hungary, with the latter trying to retain as much of its agricultural produce as possible. The results were soaring prices and a thriving black market, and in an attempt to head off unrest within the army about the situation in the homeland, Conrad demanded that the army played a larger role in ensuring adequate food distribution in larger cities. There was no prospect of the civilian authorities agreeing to such a suggestion, particularly given the army's failure to excel in its own field.[8]

The people of Russia were no exception to the general experience of a wave of patriotism when war broke out, though divisions were close to the surface from the start. The left-wing elements of the Duma were broadly anti-war, and made little attempt to hide their views. At first, it was relatively straightforward for them to be sidelined, but growing discontent within Russia as setback followed setback gave the anti-war groups an increasingly receptive audience. Compared to Germany and the Austro-Hungarian Empire, Russia faced problems of literacy, relative lack of education, and sheer scale, and the approach of the authorities to enthuse the people for war was therefore somewhat different. There was a widespread network of publishing houses across European Russia, and these were rapidly pressed into service, producing propaganda material for the government. Russia had a tradition of cartoons or *Lubki*, usually produced by simple woodblock printing techniques, which had been used in earlier wars to depict Russian soldiers bravely defeating their foes. Large numbers of *Lubki* appeared shortly after the beginning of the war, ranging from crude if traditional representations of doughty Russian peasants fighting off marauding Germans to more sophisticated pictures of battles. The former were often intended to make their audience smile or laugh – one shows a Cossack downing a German Zeppelin with his lance, and his wife subsequently sewing him a pair of trousers from the salvaged envelope of the balloon – whereas the more realistic images followed a standard form, with terrain kept to a minimum and viewer's eye drawn to the conflict portrayed, usually involving Russians advancing from the right- hand side of the image against their foes. *Lubki* did more than depict caricatures of war; many showed the new technologies of fighting, on land, sea and in the air, while others showed other faces of war, such as nurses with the wounded, or allegories of war involving angels and knights who would come to Russia's aid.[9]

The era of *Lubki* was relatively short-lived, and few if any were produced after 1915. Another popular Russian medium, widespread in fairgrounds, was the use of material similar to *Lubki* in 'peep shows' with crude animation, known as *Raek*. These were frequently performed by invalided soldiers, adding to their impact. In the cities, there were numerous publications that carried similar messages to a more literate audience, and postcards were also widely used, with the additional impact of the message written on their reverse side, either by soldiers writing home or by their families trying to contact them. War posters also appeared in larger towns and cities, advertising events to raise money for the war effort. The imagery of all of these media gradually evolved from the jingoistic, bellicose pictures of 1914 to more sombre material as the war drew on. The reduction of Kaiser Wilhelm to a laughable caricature was a popular motif, but this approach readily lent itself to images that were critical of others. By mid-1915, images were appearing that portrayed some of Russia's aristocracy as avoiding military duty, and of industrialists who prospered while others died at the front.

A recurrent theme for the Russians through much of 1915 was the shortage of ammunition. To a large extent, this was the result of vastly optimistic estimates both of the monthly requirement in wartime and the duration of the war. Within weeks of the war's beginning, *Stavka* was estimating that 1.5 million shells were required per month, compared with a pre-war estimate of only 500,000. Even this figure proved to be too low, with the monthly requirement climbing to over 3 million shells by mid-1915. The retreat exacerbated matters further, particularly with the loss of so much *matériel* when the great fortresses were abandoned. At the start of the year, monthly production of shells in Russia was about 450,000, and this steadily increased until it passed one million in September. This was still far short of the requirement, and this led to a preoccupation with the ammunition shortage as being the most important factor in Russia's defeats. The reality was that whilst the Germans enjoyed a substantial artillery advantage on the Eastern Front, it was generally less than that enjoyed by Britain and France on the Western Front. By concentrating on the shortage of ammunition, the Russians failed to recognise that there were other means of countering the German advantage, such as better construction of field positions. To an extent, this was still a hangover from the pre-war emphasis on offensive operations at every opportunity, and a belief that allowing troops to dig in thoroughly would in some way reduce their willingness to press home attacks.

There were similar shortages of rifles, and both shortages were addressed in a variety of ways. Attempts to purchase supplies from the United States and Britain were of limited effectiveness for several reasons: some western businesses dealt with Russia unfairly, requiring higher payments than was the case with other customers; there were a few cases of plain fraud; and the ability of foreign suppliers to get their products to Russia was very limited. Turkey continued to control the gates to the Black Sea, leaving only the very limited routes via Archangel in the north or Vladivostok and the Trans-Siberian Railway. Ultimately, with the failure of foreign suppliers to satisfy Russia's needs, the government turned to domestic industry and began to develop and adapt it in the same manner that other nations had already done, realising belatedly that whilst buying overseas might seem like a faster way of procuring goods, it was better in the long term to build up domestic capacity. The earlier reluctance of the government to rely on domestic producers came from several sources. Much of what was needed was based upon pre-war specifications that emphasised very high quality – for example, artillery fuses incorporated safety devices that were almost unique and merely added to the complexity and cost of manufacture with little benefit – and there were long memories of failures of Russian factories to produce such items. In an attempt to help, the French dispatched a delegation in early 1915, but the team made little headway in their attempts to introduce simpler, cheaper fuses and other items, encountering obstructive bureaucracy and suspicion at every turn.[10]

A major problem faced by Russian industry was that in the years before the war, it had become heavily reliant upon Germany, partly because so much industry was controlled by foreign investors who preferred to source supplies from elsewhere. Over 50 per cent of Russia's machine tools and chemicals were imported from its western neighbour, even though in many cases it would have been perfectly possible for these to be produced locally. Although the military had been planning for a war with Germany for many years, the inevitable consequences for Russian industry had received almost no attention. Forced by isolation to turn inwards, Russian industry and science began a process of increasing self-reliance, often working more closely together than in the west, a trend that developed still further after the Russian Revolution. From a pre-war state of very little practical development of domestic scientific discovery, Russia moved swiftly to a level of integration that lasted nearly a century.[11]

By 1915, sporadic food shortages were becoming commonplace in Russia. This was often due to the dislocation of peacetime transport, with so much of Russia's railway rolling stock serving the needs of the war effort – either moving men and supplies, or towards the end of the year attempting to evacuate industrial equipment from threatened parts of the tsar's empire, particularly Riga, which was a notable industrial centre – and partly due to a shortage of men on the land for agricultural work. To an extent, this latter problem was alleviated by the use of the large numbers of Austro-Hungarian prisoners of war; in an identical manner, Russian prisoners of war were widely used by the Central Powers to release manpower from agriculture for front-line service. The price of sugar increased in a year by 50 per cent; other food shortages added to the general gloom, and combined with the constant bad news from the front, and the rising casualty count, this led to a growing feeling – particularly in Moscow and Petrograd – that Russia's war was being mismanaged at every level. George Buchanan, the British ambassador in Petrograd, described the general mood. His observations about Jews show the casual way in which they were treated with suspicion by almost everyone in Europe:

> The internal situation ... was going from bad to worse, and the general dissatisfaction with the conduct of the war was venting itself in attacks on the Emperor and Empress. The latter was always spoken of as 'The German', in spite of the fact that she had, as she told me herself, broken all the ties that connected her with Germany. Rasputin was at the same time accused of being in German pay – a charge that was, strictly speaking, not correct. He was not in immediate communication with Berlin, and he did not receive money directly from the

Germans; but he was largely financed by certain Jewish bankers, who were, to all intents and purposes, German agents. As he was in the habit of repeating to these Jewish friends of his all that he heard at Tsarskoe, and as the Empress consulted him on both military and political questions, much useful information reached the Germans through this indirect channel. Without being their regular agent, he was, moreover, rendering them yeoman service by discrediting the Imperial regime and by thus paving the way for the revolution.

The situation was one which the Germans were not slow to exploit. They had already started their peace propaganda among the troops at the front, and had their spies everywhere ... Petrograd was throughout the war infested with their secret agents and sympathisers. The atmosphere was generally regarded with pessimism, and exaggerated reports were constantly circulated respecting the hopelessness of the military outlook. At Moscow it was different. There the national spirit, instead of being cowed by the disheartening news from the front, was stirred to fresh efforts, and the anti-German feeling was so strong that in June all shops bearing German names or that were suspected of having any German connexions were raided.[12]

The Germans continued to make tentative approaches in hope of securing peace on the Eastern Front. In December 1915, August Graf zu Eulenberg, grand marshal of the kaiser's court in Berlin, wrote to his friend Vladimir Borisovich Frederichs, a minister in the Duma, urging him to try to persuade the tsar to commence negotiations. Frederichs read the letter to Nicholas, who at first drafted a response to the effect that he would only consider such a move if Germany were to approach all of the nations with which it was at war; the following day, he decided not to send any reply at all.[13]

The fighting had inflicted considerable damage upon the terrain that had been contested. The German press made much of the depredations of Russian forces in East Prussia prior to their expulsion in early 1915; several villages and small towns were razed, and it was estimated that the Russians had killed over 1,600 civilians, destroyed some 17,000 buildings, and killed or stolen over half a million horses, cows and pigs.[14] Whilst the Germans had devastated parts of Poland during their retreat in the autumn of 1914, the damage inflicted by the Russian Army was significantly greater, though almost negligible when compared with the horrors of the Second World War, and it still created headlines at the time. The Austro-Hungarian province of Galicia, which was recaptured during the year, also suffered badly. The Russians were accused of widespread destruction as they retreated, leaving vast swathes of agricultural land fallow, and thousands of Jews had been persecuted, robbed, beaten, or simply executed. Again, the newspapers of the Central Powers that reported these 'atrocities' were silent on the scorched earth policy adopted by German and Austro-Hungarian troops the previous year, which had left much of western Poland devastated and facing winter without food or shelter. It is perhaps characteristic of the Russian 'scorched earth' policy in Galicia that they failed to destroy the oil extraction facilities in the province. At the time, Galicia was the single largest source of oil for the Central Powers, and although many facilities were damaged, this was done in a haphazard manner, and most were back in production by the end of 1915. Had they been permanently disabled, it is unlikely that Germany's U-boats would have been able to conduct their Atlantic operations as easily as they did.

The year saw further heavy casualties on all sides, and it was inevitable that this would have an impact upon their armies. The German Army entered the year in the best shape, and although it could look back on the campaigns of 1915 with considerable satisfaction, the losses suffered had a considerable impact on the nature of the army. The old pool of pre-war officers had been drawn largely from the aristocracy, not least because of the high educational requirements for selection, but the high loss rate amongst low- to middle-rank officers depleted this pool badly. Their replacements tended to be men who had joined since the beginning of the war, and whilst they were more representative of German society, particularly the middle classes, this actually resulted in a widening gulf between officers and men. The traditional 'Prussian' officers might have been from a completely different social setting than their soldiers, but they were strongly inculcated with traditional notions of service, duty and a sense of *noblesse oblige*; from the moment they joined the army, they were taught to concern themselves with the well-being of their men, and they generally led by example in almost every respect. Their replacements often showed a less instinctive feel for man-management, leading many war-weary soldiers to draw attention to almost every distinction between officers and men. This extended beyond the usual military grumbles about rations and clothing. In an attempt to reduce the incidence of sexually transmitted diseases – and perhaps to lessen the risk of soldiers raping women in occupied territories – the German Army established a system of brothels, supervised and regularly inspected by medical personnel. Separate brothels were created for officers, as it was felt that it would be bad for discipline if soldiers and officers shared the same brothels, but this inevitably led to allegations that all the best-looking prostitutes were reserved for officers.

Despite its successes, the German Army suffered substantial losses during 1915, and the pool of experienced and highly trained NCOs and officers

The Eastern Front, late 1915

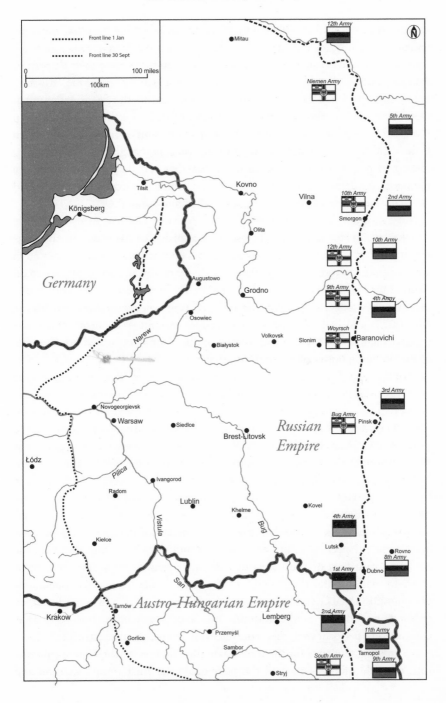

continued to diminish. Nevertheless, there could be no question that the army remained the most formidable of the three forces on the Eastern Front. At every level, its men and formations continued to perform better than their Russian or Austro-Hungarian counterparts, and it is noteworthy that the Russians consistently preferred to attack parts of the line held by the *k.u.k.* Army rather than those held by the Germans. Every senior German officer on the Eastern Front could look back on the year with satisfaction at his own performance, even if those in *Ober Ost* continued to complain that they might have achieved far more had they been given the priority that they felt they deserved. For the moment, it seemed that Falkenhayn's undoubtedly successful strategy had allowed him to prevail over his critics, but the feud was not over.

Like most armies in wars throughout history, the German Army constantly felt that it did not have enough resources available to carry out all the tasks required of it – there weren't enough men, enough heavy guns, or enough ammunition. Nevertheless, compared with other Great Powers the German Army improved in many respects during 1915. By the end of the year, it was numerically stronger than before, despite suffering over one million casualties in all theatres, and had more heavy artillery and machine-guns than before. The bigger issue was that the demands placed on the army were greater, not least due to the declining power of Austria-Hungary.

Strategically, Falkenhayn's repeated intention of switching attention to the west was a mixed success. On the one hand, the end of the year saw the Russian Army reduced in strength to a mere shadow of what it had been, allowing for forces to be dispatched both to the west and to Serbia. On the other hand, there were more German divisions on the Eastern Front at the end of the year than at the beginning. The front was also far longer than before – the advance into Lithuania and Latvia in particular added substantially to the length of the front line, and although large sectors in the north were covered by relatively modest cavalry formations, this still placed a growing demand on very limited resources.

The armies of the Austro-Hungarian Empire started the year in a poor state, and in most respects were in even worse condition by the end of the year. The appalling casualties of the Carpathian fighting caused irreparable damage to many formations, and the inability of the army to mount effective operations without substantial German assistance was once more underlined in the disastrous fighting in Volhynia in the autumn. Just as German officers at every level continued to perform well, their equivalents in the *k.u.k.* Army struggled. There was a growing tendency for them to blame their failures on their subordinates – thus the field officers lamented the poor quality of their troops, division and corps commanders complained that their juniors lacked determination and drive, and at the very top of the hierarchy Conrad continued to show an extraordinary mixture of unfounded confidence and bitter disappointment. Despite numerous failures, he continued to behave as if all his formations were highly capable and at full strength, and remained in Teschen or Vienna for almost the entire year; by contrast, Falkenhayn repeatedly visited his army commanders to get a personal feel for what was happening, and in a similar manner his army commanders frequently visited their subordinate corps commanders.

Conrad also interfered repeatedly in matters that were technically beyond his remit. At a time when all his attention should have been on improving the performance of his armies, he bombarded the foreign minister in Vienna with memoranda about how Serbia should be treated after it had been occupied. Nor did he show any awareness of the importance of sustaining public support for the war; one of his contemporaries observed that he appeared completely indifferent to public opinion.[15] Even more than in 1914, he was a distant, isolated figure, sometimes appearing to be more concerned with his new wife than with his duties. His insistence on preparing for an invasion of Montenegro in early 1916 was contrary to the wishes of Falkenhayn, and led to an almost complete breakdown of relations between *AOK* and *OHL*, with almost no communication between the two headquarters towards the end of the year.

Whilst the *k.u.k.* Army suffered badly during 1915, at least it could hold onto the consolation that it had taken part in several successful campaigns, albeit as a junior partner of an increasingly assertive German partner. The Russian Army had no such consolations. Its only significant successes in 1915 occurred in Volhynia towards the end of the year, inflicting major losses on predominantly Austro-Hungarian forces. The victories came too late to have a major outcome on the year's campaigning, and there was widespread concern that on every occasion that the Russians came up against the Germans, they seemed to come off the worse. A closer look at events shows that this was not entirely true; prior to the great retreat across Poland, Russian forces in the centre of the long front repeatedly stopped German attacks, and after the fall of Lemberg even Mackensen's armies struggled to make the sort of progress that they had sustained earlier in the year.

Nevertheless, the tsar's armies finished the war in bad shape. The number of experienced and well-trained personnel had plummeted alarmingly, and the inadequacies of the training regimes of replacement drafts were cruelly exposed as the troops were fed into the front line. At the higher levels, there were several changes, but the upper echelons looked remarkably similar at the end of the year.

Ruzsky in particular resurfaced in another role, despite not having achieved anything of note to date, largely because there were so few alternatives – during the year's fighting, practically no division or corps commanders distinguished themselves sufficiently to be considered for promotion. Brusilov enjoyed mixed fortunes, and at least succeeded in preventing his army from being badly defeated during its retreat; his front commander, Ivanov, must have come close to dismissal in the first half of the year, but at least redeemed himself by badly mauling the Austro-Hungarian forces – and the German South Army – in Volhynia at the end of the year.

The greatest change, of course, was the dismissal of Grand Duke Nikolai and his replacement by the tsar himself. It was a singularly inauspicious moment for the tsar to take command, and in the circumstances even the most gifted of generals would have struggled to make a good impression in just a few months. It seems that Tsar Nicholas did no more than confirm in the eyes of senior commanders that he was singularly unsuited to the role.

Danilov, who started the war as quartermaster-general, was moved as part of the rearrangements that followed Grand Duke Nikolai's departure. He was dispatched to take command of XXV Corps in the northern part of the front line. He left behind him a mixed reputation. Most accounts of the First World War have been kind to him during his tenure as quartermaster-general, but to an extent this is because of the detailed account that he left of his time in office. Like all such memoirs, this is as self-serving a document as the recollections of Falkenhayn, Ludendorff, Hindenburg and Hoffmann; whilst it is full of criticisms – most of them well-argued – of other senior figures, at no stage does Danilov accept any fault on his own part. His contemporaries were less kind in their opinions. Brusilov (whose own memoirs are subject to the same caveats) held Danilov and Sukhomlinov jointly responsible for overstating the abilities of the Russian Army on the basis of unrealistic wargames conducted before the war, and criticised Danilov for being 'narrow and obstinate'.[16] Georgi Ivanovich Shavelsky, head of the army's chaplains' department, acknowledged Danilov's diligence and industry, but added that he lacked imagination and 'the spark that marks those specially selected by God'.[17] Petr Konstantinovich Konderovsky, a senior staff officer at *Stavka*, was more critical, accusing Danilov of self-aggrandisement and trying to portray himself as a great commander and military genius.[18]

The summary of the overall situation offered by Danilov is a reasonable one:

> Thus towards the end of 1915 there was little favourable about the military situation
> of the Entente Powers. Having endured all the heavy blows of the Central Powers'

summer offensive campaigns, Russia found herself considerably weakened and her army was obliged to make a considerable retreat. On the Western Front, the offensive plans, so long and well prepared by our allies, had not succeeded. The entry of Italy into the war did not achieve what was expected and brought almost no respite. On the Balkan front, Serbia was temporarily *hors de combat*, and the situation in Montenegro was becoming desperate. The Dardanelles expedition had completely failed; the situation of the Salonika group, reduced to passive defence, was very uncertain. Germany, the heart of the enemy alliance, seemed to be at the height of her military successes. But this was no more than a first impression. Her plan of decisive blows had not succeeded in the west or in the east. The titanic struggle took on a prolonged and exhausting character and it seemed impossible to predict the final result with clarity.

... in 1914, Russia entered the war in very advantageous strategic and political circumstances. She began by taking the initiative with resolve and invaded a substantial portion of enemy territory, something that promised brilliant results; during the following year she abandoned all the conquered regions, lost a considerable amount of her own territory, and her army was forced to adopt a passive stance, entrenched behind coils of barbed wire.[19]

The question for all parties inevitably was, what to do next? For the Germans as well as their enemies, it was clear that quick, decisive victories were simply not possible, though Conrad continued to dream in Teschen of grandiose, war-winning encirclements and the officers of *Ober Ost* lamented how a great opportunity to destroy the Russian Army had been missed. Instead, thoughts turned to the new nature of war and how it might prove possible to defeat a nation in this era of artillery and machine-guns. On the Western Front, General Philippe Pétain commented as early as June 1915:

Success will come eventually to the side that has the last man. The only objective we should seek is to kill as many Germans as we can while suffering a minimum of losses.[20]

In December 1915, this became the official policy of the Entente Powers after a conference in Chantilly. All of the participants agreed to grind down the Central Powers in a series of battles of attrition, launching coordinated offensives to prevent the Germans from shuffling troops from one front to another. By this means, victory would be achieved by the end of the coming year.

Falkenhayn, too, had come to the same conclusion as Pétain. Whilst Russia remained in the war, its armies were now sufficiently weakened to allow Germany to concentrate in the west, where the chief of the German general staff had already decided the war would have to be won. Judging that Britain's overseas empire and navy made it almost impregnable, he concluded that Germany would have to force the French out of the war. To this end, he drew up a memorandum in December – broadly at the same time that the Entente Powers were resolving to grind the Central Powers to defeat – that he sent to Kaiser Wilhelm, describing the situation:

> … The strain on France has almost reached breaking point – though it is certainly borne with the most remarkable devotion. If we succeeded in opening the eyes of her people to the fact that in a military sense they have nothing more to hope for, that breaking point would be reached and England's best sword knocked out of her hand. To achieve that object the uncertain method of a mass breakthrough, in any case beyond our means, is unnecessary. We can probably do enough for our purposes with limited resources. Within our reach behind the French sector of the Western Front there are objectives for the retention of which the French General Staff would be compelled to throw in every man they have. If they do so the forces of France will bleed to death – as there can be no question of a voluntary withdrawal – whether we reach our goal or not. If they do not do so, and we reach our objectives, the morale effect on France will be enormous.
>
> … The objectives of which I am speaking now are Belfort and Verdun.
>
> The considerations above apply to both, yet the preference must be given to Verdun.[21]

In other words, the French Army would be drawn into a bloody and prolonged defence of an exposed salient, where its formations would be bled white.

Meanwhile, in Teschen, Conrad continued to make his own plans. He blamed the setbacks in Volhynia on poor leadership, and saw the success of the Serbian invasion as evidence that his armies were quite capable of mounting successful operations, ignoring the reality that the Serbian invasion had been carried out with substantial German forces and help from Bulgaria, under overall German command. Ever since he had held a command in Trieste, which was at that time part of the Austro-Hungarian Empire, Conrad had disliked the Italians. When they entered the war on the side of the Entente, this grew to intense hatred of the state that he regarded as traitorous, and he repeatedly called for a joint offensive by the German and *k.u.k.* Armies against Italy. Falkenhayn consistently vetoed such proposals, but with Serbia defeated and Russia forced into a passive stance, Conrad saw an opportunity. Initially, he asked Falkenhayn to assign nine German divisions to Galicia, in order to release Austro-Hungarian formations for use against Italy. Once a decisive blow had been struck here – characteristically, his operation would be a sweeping advance that would pin the Italian Army against the coast and would force Italy from the war in one battle – the *k.u.k.* Army would be able to dispatch hundreds of thousands of men to the Western Front.

Falkenhayn continued to be sceptical. Even if the nine German divisions were sent to the Alps, he felt that the likelihood of a decisive blow being struck against Italy was too small – if they were threatened, the Italians would simply withdraw faster than they could be outflanked. However, Germany was technically not at war with Italy, and Falkenhayn had no intention of committing forces to Conrad's venture. He sent a lengthy telegram to Teschen in mid-December:

> ... Your Excellency is planning a thrust from the region of Trent on a front of about 30 miles ... for which purpose eight or nine Austro-Hungarian divisions, to be relieved by German troops, are to be brought from the Galician front.
>
> There is no doubt that if such an operation were successful it would have a very great effect. Yet all my ripe experience goes to show that 25 divisions will be needed for its execution, which can be neither a strategic or tactical surprise, since the deployment is limited to a single railway ... I do not know whether it may be possible to get up the heavy artillery which will be required – we put this at not less than a battery for every 160 yards of front on the sector to be attacked – as well as the copious supplies of ammunition it needs.[22]

If the Germans wouldn't help him, Conrad decided that he would plan an operation against Italy using troops that he intended to extract from the Eastern Front. The fact that his armies had failed to win even modest victories played no part in his calculations. Nor did he assign any significance to the failure of his troops to fight their way through the Carpathians in early 1915. Thus, at a time when their enemies were agreeing to coordinate their efforts, the Central Powers chose to make their plans without consultation with each other.

The stage was set for another year of fighting. It remained to be seen whether it would bring the war any closer to conclusion.

NOTES

INTRODUCTION

1. See, for example, Kluck, A. von, *Die Marsch auf Paris und die Marneschlacht* (1920, republished 2013 by Salzwasser, Paderborn); Herwig, H., *The Marne 1914: The Opening of World War I and the Battle That Changed the World* (Random House, New York, 2009)

2   Zuber, T., *Inventing the Schlieffen Plan: German War Planning 1871–1914* (Oxford University Press, Oxford, 2002); Schlieffen, A. von, *Cannae* (Mittler, Berlin, 1925)

3   Danilov, Y., *La Russie Dans La Guerre Mondiale* (Payot, Paris, 1927), p. 190

4   For a comprehensive examination of the development of offensive doctrine in Europe in the years preceding the First World War, see Snyder, J., *The Ideology Of The Offensive* (Cornell University Press, Ithaca, 1984)

5   Brauner, J., Czegka, E., Diaków, J., Franek, F., Kiszling, R., Steinitz, E., and Wisshaupt, E., *Österreich-Ungarns Letzter Krieg 1914–1918*, vol. 2, 1915 (Verlag der Militärwissenschaftlichen Mitteilungen, Vienna, 1930), part I, table 3

6   See, for example, Csicserics, M., *Die Schlacht: Studie Auf Grund Des Krieges in Ostasien 1904–1905*, (Siedel, Vienna, 1908)

7   Knox, A., *With the Russian Army 1914–1917* (Hutchinson, London, 1921), p. 221

8   Danilov (1927), p. 336

9   Brauner et al (1930), vol. 2, part I, p. 19

10 ibid., p. 11

11 Molisch, P., *Vom Kampf der Tschechen um Ihren Staat* (Braumüller, Vienna, 1929), p. 33

12 Williamson, D., *Walther Rathenau and the KRA August 1914 – March 1915* in *Zeitschrift für Unternehmensgeschichte* 11 (1978), pp. 118–36

13 Knox (1921), p. 193

CHAPTER 1

1   Barsukov, E., *Podgotovka Rossii k Mirovoj Vojne v Artillerijskom Otnosenii* (Gosvoenizdat, Moscow, 1926), pp. 56–57, 70

2   Stone, N., *The Eastern Front 1914–1917* (Penguin, London, 1975), p. 48

3   Knox (1921), pp. 229–30

4   Danilov (1927), p. 352

5   ibid., pp. 352–53

6   ibid., p. 355

7   ibid., pp. 357–58

8   Brauner et al (1930), vol. 2, part I, p. 9

9   ibid., p. 10

10 Conrad von Hötzendorf, F., *Die Gefechtsausbildung der Infanterie* (Seidel, Vienna, 1900)

11 Stone, J. and Schmidl, E., *The Boer War and Military* Reforms (University Press of America, Lanham, Maryland, 1988), p. 263

12 See, for example, Horvat, J., *Politička povijest Hrvatske* (Binoza, Zagreb, 1938), vol. 1, p. 344

13 See, for example, Asprey, R., *The German High Command at War: Hindenburg and Ludendorff Conduct World War I* (William Morrow, New York, 1991)

14 Hindenburg, P. von, trans. F. Holt, *Out of my Life* (Cassell, London, 1920), pp. 84–86

15 Roos, H., *A History of Modern Poland, From the Foundation of the State in the First World War to the Present Day* (Knopf, New York, 1966), p. 16

16 Buttar, P., *Collision of Empires* (Osprey, Oxford, 2014), pp. 27–40

17 Ludendorff, E., *Meine Kriegserinnerungen 1914–1918* (Mittler, Berlin, 1919), p. 77

18 Mackensen, A. von, *Briefe und Auszeichnungen des Generalfeldmarschalls aus Krieg und Frieden* (Bibliographisches Institut, Leipzig, 1938), p. 123

19 Sondhaus, L., *Franz Conrad von Hötzendorf: Architect of the Apocalypse* (Humanities Press, Boston, Maryland, 2000), p. 169

20 Cramon, A. von, *Unser Österreichisch-Ungarisher Bundesgenosse im Weltkriege* (Mittler, Berlin, 1922), p. 5

21 Falkenhayn, E. von, *General Headquarters 1914–1916, and its Critical Decisions* (Hutchinson, London, 1919), pp. 6–7

22 Falkenhayn (1919), pp. 19–20, 56

23 Hindenburg (1920), p. 132

24 Ludendorff (1919), pp. 88–89

25 Brauner et al (1930), vol. 2, pp. 55–57

26 ibid., p. 94

27 Ludendorff (1919), p. 89

28 Freytag-Loringhoven, A. Freiherr von, *Menschen und Dinge Wie Ich Sie In Meinem Leben Sah* (Mittler, Berlin, 1923), p. 259

29 Bundesarchiv-Militärarchiv Freiburg, WA 10/50656 Tagebuch von Plessen, 15/1/15

30 Zechlin, E., *Ludendorff im Jahre 1915* (Cotte, Munich, 1970), pp. 323, 346

CHAPTER 2

1   Brusilov, A., *Moi Vospominaniia* (Voenizdat, Moscow, 1967), p. 31

2   Brauner et al (1930), vol. 2, p. 73

3   For a detailed account of the fortress and its siege, see Forster, F., *Przemyśl: Österreich-Hungarns Bedeutendste Festung* (Österreichischer Bundesverlag, Vienna, 1987)

4   Palmer, S. and Wallis, S., *A War in Words* (Simon & Schuster, London, 2003), pp. 78–79

5   Kriegsarchiv Vienna, 523: B/1137

6   Brauner et al (1930), p. 11

7   Brauner et al (1930), vol. 2, p. 103

8   Nesnamov, A., *Strategicheskiye Issledovaniya* (Gosvoenizdat, Moscow, 1922), vol. 3, p. 23

9   Ludendorff (1919), pp. 90–91

10 Quoted in Simonds, F., *History of the Great War 1914–1918* (Collier, New York, 1920), vol. 4, pp. 94–95

11 Ratzenhofer, E., *Truppentransporte beim Winterfeldzug in den Karpathen* (Wissen und Wehr, Vienna, 1929), vol. 8, p. 30

12 Brauner et al (1930), vol. 2, p. 110

13 Brusilov (1967), p. 40

14 ibid., p. 42

15 Kriegsarchiv Vienna, B/509

16 Much of the narrative that follows draws upon Brauner et al (1930), pp. 129–47

17 Weith, G., *Werdegang und Schicksal der österreichisch-ungarischen Armee im Weltkriege* (1922), manuscript in Kriegsarchiv, Vienna, p. 108

18 Simonds (1920), p. 96

19 Kriegsarchiv Vienna, NFA 1929 5/1

20 Joseph Ferdinand, *A világháború amilyennek én láttam: 1914 július 31. - 1915 május 25* (M.Tud. Akademie, Budapest, 1924) quoted in Tunstall, G., *Blood on the Snow* (University of Kansas Press, Lawrence, Ka., 2010), p. 83

21 Weith (1922), p. 119

22 Kriegsarchiv Vienna, NFA 42 3070/11

23   Kriegsarchiv Vienna, NFA V Corps Tagebuch
24   Kriegsarchiv Vienna, NFA 346/1 K1802
25   Tunstall (2010), p. 82
26   Kriegsarchiv Vienna, B/1450: 357

CHAPTER 3

1   Ludendorff (1919), p. 91
2   Litzmann, K., *Lebenserinnerungen* (Eisenschmidt, Berlin, 1927), vol. 1, pp. 312–13
3   ibid., p. 315
4   Ludendorff (1919), pp. 91–92
5   Knox (1921), p. 236
6   ibid., p. 235
7   Kolenkovsky, A., *Russkaya Armiya v Velikoy Voyne: Zimnyaya Operatsiya v Vostochnoy Prussii v 1915* (Voenizdat, Moscow, 1927), pp. 18–19
8   ibid., p. 39
9   ibid., p. 45
10   Danilov (1927), p. 366
11   Kolenkovsky (1927), p. 30
12   Gurko, V., *War and Revolution in Russia* (Macmillan, New York, 1919), pp. 107–08
13   Mackensen (1938), p. 126
14   Letter from Zabudsky to Secretary of General Staff, 29 January 1915, in Voyenno-Istoricheskiy Archiv, Moscow: hereafter cited as VIA, 507-3-19,2 pp. 1–2
15   Ipatieff, V., *The Life of a Chemist: Memoirs of Vladimir N Ipatieff* (Stanford University Press, Stanford, 1946), pp.218–35; Kojevnikov, A., *Stalin's Great Science: The Times and Adventures of Soviet Physicists* (World Scientific Publishing Company, Singapore, 2004), pp. 10–11
16   Quoted in Osburg, W-R, *Hineingeworfen: Der Erste Weltkrieg in den Erinnerungen seiner Teilnehmer* (Aufbau, Berlin, 2014), p. 297
17   Quoted in ibid., pp. 297–98
18   ibid., pp. 308–10
19   Hoffmann, M., *War Diaries and Other Papers* (Secker, London, 1929), vol. 1, p. 60
20   Litzmann (1927), p. 321
21   Ludendorff (1919), p. 96
22   Quoted in Kolenkovsky (1927), p. 63
23   Osburg (2014), pp. 306–07
24   Litzmann (1927), pp. 326–27
25   ibid., pp. 331–32
26   Kolenkovsky (1927), pp. 73–74

27   ibid., pp. 75–76
28   ibid., pp. 92–93
29   ibid., p. 81
30   Danilov (1927), p. 368
31   Kolenkovsky (1927), p. 95
32   Litzmann (1927), p. 339
33   Morgen, C. von, *Meiner Truppen Heldenkämpfe* (Mittler, Berlin, 1920), p. 57
34   Litzmann (1927), pp. 339–42
35   ibid., p. 343
36   Kolenkovsky (1927), p. 101
37   Belolipetsky, V., *Zimniye deystviya pekhotnogo polka v Avgustovskikh lesakh. 1915* (Voyenno-Istoricheskaya Biblioteka, Moscow, 1940), pp. 61–62
38   Kolenkovsky (1927), p. 109
39   ibid., p. 117
40   ibid., p. 118
41   Litzmann (1927), p. 347
42   Belolipetsky (1940), p. 65
43   ibid., pp. 8–11
44   ibid., pp. 18–19
45   ibid., p. 32
46   ibid., p. 38
47   ibid., pp. 79–80; Kolenkovsky (1927), pp. 135–37
48   Belolipetsky (1940), pp. 87–99
49   Redern, H. von, *Die Winterschlacht in Masuren* (Stalling, Oldenburg, 1918), p. 50
50   Morgen (1920), p. 60
51   ibid., p. 62
52   Litzmann (1927), p. 354
53   Kolenkovsky (1927), p. 139
54   Danilov (1927), pp. 369–70
55   ibid., pp. 373–74
56   Ludendorff (1919), p. 105
57   Kolenkovsky (1927), p. 150

CHAPTER 4

1   Falkenhayn (1919), pp. 62–63
2   Danilov (1927), p. 384
3   Bonch-Bruyevich, M., *Poterya Nami Galitsii* (Voenizdat, Moscow, 1921), vol. 1, p. 51

4 Brauner et al (1930), vol. 2, p. 162
5 Telegram from Yanushkevich to Northwest Front, 1 March 1915, quoted in Bonch-Bruyevich (1921), vol. 1, p. 60
6 Danilov (1927), p. 375
7 Bonch-Bruyevich (1921), vol. 1, p. 78
8 Danilov (1927), pp. 376–77
9 Bonch-Bruyevich (1921), vol. 1, p. 72
10 ibid., p. 56
11 Zalesskiy K., *Kto Hyl Kto v Pervoy Mirovoy Voyne* (Astrel, Moscow, 2003), p. 386
12 Paléologue, M., trans. F. Holt, An Ambassador's Memoirs (Doran, New York, 1923), vol. 1, p. 161
13 Brauner et al (1930), vol. 2, p. 167
14 ibid., p. 171
15 ibid., p. 174
16 Weith, G., *Werdegang und Schicksal der österreichisch-ungarischen Armee im Weltkriege* (1922), manuscript in Kriegsarchiv, Vienna, pp. 140–41
17 Kriegsarchiv Vienna, KFA/42
18 Kriegsarchiv Vienna, NFA/95
19 Brusilov (1967), p. 42
20 Kriegsarchiv Vienna, B600/Lehar
21 Richert, D., *The Kaiser's Reluctant Conscript* (Pen and Sword, Barnsley, 2012), pp. 55–57
22 Brauner et al (1930), vol. 2, p. 194
23 Kriegsarchiv Vienna, NFA 2 Army/58
24 Weith (1922), p. 151
25 Brauner et al (1930), vol. 2, p. 208
26 Palmer and Wallis (2003), pp. 80–81
27 ibid., p. 81
28 Brauner et al (1930), vol. 2, pp. 208–09
29 Sondhaus (2000), pp. 170–72
30 Quoted in Brauner et al (1930), vol. 2, p. 213
31 Quoted in ibid., pp. 213–14
32 ibid., p. 214
33 Rothenburg, G., *The Army of Francis Joseph* (Purdue University Press, West Lafayette, 1976), p. 185
34 Palmer and Wallis (2003), p. 82
35 ibid., p. 86
36 ibid., pp. 87–88

37 Washburn, S., *The Russian Campaign April to August 1915* (Melrose, London, 1922), pp. 3–4

38 Danilov (1927), p. 390

39 Cramon (1922), p. 8

40 Telegram 4568 from Ivanov to *Stavka* quoted in Bonch-Bruyevich (1921), vol. 1, p. 88

41 Telegram 9495 from Yanushkevich to Ivanov, quoted in Bonch-Bruyevich (1921), vol. 1, p. 90

42 Bonch-Bruyevich (1921), vol. 1, p. 98

43 Quoted in Brauner et al (1930), vol. 2, p. 248

44 Kriegsarchiv Vienna, AOK/501

45 Bundesarchiv-Militärarchiv Freiburg, W10/51388

46 Telegram 5333 from Ivanov to *Stavka* quoted in Bonch-Bruyevich (1921), vol. 2, p. 23

47 Kriegsarchiv Vienna, MKSM 1915 52-4/16

48 Kriegsarchiv Vienna, MKSM 69-8/9, *Betrachtungen über die Verlusten im jetzigen Kriege*

49 Brusilov (1967), pp. 41–42

50 Danilov (1927), p. 389

CHAPTER 5

1 Falkenhayn (1919), p. 76

2 See, for example, Danilov (1927), p. 396

3 Danilov (1927), pp. 399–400

4 Brauner et al (1930), vol. 2, p. 297

5 Cramon (1922), p. 11

6 Falkenhayn (1919), pp. 80–81

7 Bundesarchiv-Militärarchiv Freiburg, W10/51388

8 Bundesarchiv-Militärarchiv Freiburg, N46/41

9 Quoted in François, H. von, *Gorlice 1915, Der Karpathendurchbruch und die Befreiung von Galizien* (Koehler, Leipzig, 1922), p. 10

10 Bundesarchiv-Militärarchiv Freiburg, W10/51388

11 Quoted in Falkenhayn (1919), pp. 81–82

12 Quoted in ibid., p. 82

13 Mackensen (1938), p. 129

14 Quoted in ibid., p. 134

15 ibid., p. 137

16 ibid, p. 138

17   Cramon (1922), pp. 14–15

18   See, for example, Preussisches Kriegsministerium, *Felddienst-Ordnung* (Berlin, 1908), p. 10

19   François (1922), p. 14

20   ibid., p. 20

21   Quoted in Osburg (2014), p. 400

22   For a detailed discussion of this subject, see Watson, A., *Ring of Steel: Germany and Austria-Hungary at War, 1914–1918* (Allen Lane, London, 2014), pp. 210–25

23   Redlich, J., *Schicksalsjahre Österreichs 1908–1919* (Graz, 1953), vol. 1, p. 265

24   Watson (2014), p. 225

25   François (1922), p. 22

26   Sabsay, N., *A Moment in History: A Russian Soldier in the First World War* (Caxton, Caldwell, 1960), p. 14

27   ibid., p. 18

28   François (1922), pp. 25–26

29   Bose, T. von, *Das Kaiser Alexander Garde-Grenadier Regiment Nr. 1 im Weltkriege 1914–1918* (Sporn, Zeulenroda, 1932), p. 162

30   Mackensen (1938), p. 144

31   ibid., p. 146

32   Ludendorff (1919), p. 104

33   Brauner et al (1930), vol. 2, p. 315

34   Croddy, E., *Chemical and Biological Warfare: a Comprehensive Guide for the Concerned Citizen* (Copernicus, Göttingen, 2002), pp. 143–44

35   Brusilov (1967), p. 42

36   Danilov (1927), p. 391

37   ibid., p. 392

38   Bonch-Bruyevich (1921), vol. 2, pp. 48–50

39   Danilov (1927), p. 394

40   François (1922), p. 46

41   Stone (1975), p. 136

42   Rerberg, F., *Memoirs* (1922–1925) in Hoover Institution Archives, Stanford, XX576, p. 200

43   Brusilov (1967), p. 42

44   François (1922), p. 27

45   ibid., p. 29

46   Quoted in ibid., pp. 34–35

47   ibid., p. 42

48   ibid., pp. 47–48

49   Stengel, F. Freiherr von, *Das K.B. 3 Infanterie-Regiment Prinz Karl von Bayern*

(Verlag Bayerisches Kriegsarchiv, Munich, 1922), p. 15

50   François (1922), p. 53

51   ibid., pp. 49–50, 57

52   Arz, A., *Kampf und Sturz der Kaiserreiche* (Günther, Vienna, 1935), p. 60

53   Bundesarchiv-Militärarchiv Freiburg, W 10/51393

54   Rosenberg-Lipinsky, H.-O. von, *Das Königin-Elizabeth Garde-Grenadier Regiment Nr. 3 im Weltkrieg 1914–1918* (Sporn, Zeulenroda, 1935), p. 150; Bose (1932), pp. 165–67

55   François (1922), p. 63

56   Mackensen (1938), p. 148

57   ibid., p. 148; François (1922), p. 64

58   Bonch-Bruyevich (1921), vol. 2, p. 70

59   Quoted in François (1922), p. 67

60   François (1922), pp. 64–65

61   ibid., pp. 70–71

62   Telegram 1191 from Dimitriev to Ivanov, quoted in Bonch-Bruyevich (1921), vol. 2, pp. 72–73

63   François (1922), pp. 76–77

64   ibid., p. 79

65   Brauner et al (1930), vol. 2, p. 328

66   François (1922), pp. 80–83; Mackensen (1938), pp. 152–54

67   Stone (1975), p. 136

68   Knox (1921), pp. 254–55

69   For a comprehensive account of the functioning of the Russian railways during the war, see Ronzhin, S., *Zhelieznyia Dorogi v Voennoe Vremia* (1925) in Hoover Institution Archives, Stanford, XX450; see also Chaadaeva, D., *Armiya Nakanune Fevral'skoi Revolyutsii* (Gosudarstvennoi Sotsialisticheско-Ekonomicheskoe Izdatel'stvo, Moscow, 1935), p. 19

70   Knox (1921), p. 247

71   ibid., p. 249

72   Stone (1975), p. 137

73   Brusilov (1967), p. 45

74   Danilov (1927), p. 411

75   ibid., p. 190

CHAPTER 6

1   Brauner et al (1930), vol. 2, p. 332

2   *Regiments-Geschichte des Infanterie-Regiment 14: Ein Buch der Erinnerung an Grossen Seiten 1914–1918* (Hessen, Linz, 1919), p. 38

3   Brauner et al (1930), vol. 2, p. 334
4   Mackensen (1938), pp. 153–54
5   Brauner et al (1930), vol. 2, p. 337
6   François (1922), p. 88
7   ibid., pp. 90–91
8   Samuels, M., *Command or Control? Command, Training and Tactics in the British and German Armies 1888–1918* (Psychology, Hove, 1995), pp. 168–71
9   Quoted in Mackensen (1938), p. 157
10   Brauner et al (1930), vol. 2, p. 353
11   François (1922), p. 99
12   Bonch-Bruyevich (1921), vol. 2, p. 110
13   Telegram 169 Danilov to Dragomirov, quoted in Bonch-Bruyevich (1921), vol. 2, pp. 121–22
14   Gurko (1919), p. 136
15   Telegram 155973 Dragomirov to Yanushkevich, quoted in Bonch-Bruyevich (1921), vol. 2, pp. 124–25
16   Bonch-Bruyevich (1921), vol. 2, p. 127
17   Danilov (1927), pp. 416–18
18   François (1922), p. 109
19   Brauner et al (1930), vol. 2, p. 389
20   ibid, p. 376
21   François (1922), p. 114
22   Stone (1975), p. 140
23   Quoted in Bonch-Bruyevich (1921), vol. 2, pp. 145–46
24   François (1922), p. 121
25   Nesnamov, A., *Strategicheskiye Issledovaniya* (Gosvoenizdat, Moscow, 1922), vol. 4, p. 44
26   Mackensen (1938), p. 160
27   Brauner et al (1930), vol. 2, p. 397
28   Bonch-Bruyevich (1921), vol. 2, p. 170
29   Danilov (1927), p. 426
30   Brauner et al (1930), vol. 2, p. 418
31   Brusilov (1967), p. 47
32   François (1922), p. 141
33   ibid., p. 142
34   Horne, C. (ed.), *The Great Events of the Great War* (National Alumni, New York, 1920), vol. 3, p. 216
35   ibid., vol. 3, p. 217
36   Brusilov (1967), p. 46

37   Brauner et al (1930), vol. 2, p. 419

38   Zayontchovsky, A., *Perveya Mirovaya Voyna* (Polygon, Moscow, 2002), p. 302

39   François (1922), p. 161; Brauner et al (1930), vol. 2, pp. 426–29

40   Mackensen (1938), p. 164

41   Brauner et al (1930), vol. 2, p. 431

42   ibid., pp. 420–21

43   François (1922), pp. 158–59

44   ibid., pp. 155–73, Brusilov (1967), pp. 46–47

45   Mackensen (1938), p. 167

46   François (1922), p. 174

47   Watson (2014), p. 195

48   Prusin, A., *Nationalising a Borderland: War, Ethnicity and Anti-Jewish Violence in East Galicia 1914–1920* (University of Alabama Press, Tuscaloosa, 2005), pp. 48–54

49   Quoted in François (1922), pp. 176–77

50   Richert (2012), pp. 65–66

51   Pflanzer-Baltin, K., Nachlass B/50 *Tagebuch Jan-Jun 1915* in Kriegsarchiv Vienna

52   Richert (2012), p. 69

53   Parsky, D., *Operatsiya chastey XXX armeyskogo korpusa na prute i v predgoriyakh Karpat mezhdu Delyatin - Kolomyya 19-24 maya (1-6 iyunya) 1915 goda (Prutskaya operatsiya)* in *Voyenno-Istorichesky Sbornik*, vol. 3 (1920), pp. 42–63

54   Richert (2012), p. 77

55   ibid., p. 78

CHAPTER 7

1   See for example Bonch-Bruyevich (1921), vol. 2, pp. 171–72

2   Order 2504 3 June 1915, quoted in Bonch-Bruyevich (1921), vol. 2, pp. 180–81

3   Bonch-Bruyevich (1921), vol. 2, p. 179

4   Brusilov (1967), p. 47

5   Brauner et al (1930), vol. 2, p. 451

6   Müller-Brandenburg, H., *Die Schlacht Bei Grodek-Lemberg* (Stalling, Oldenburg, 1918), pp. 18–19

7   Brusilov (1967), p. 47

8   Bonch-Bruyevich (1921), vol. 2, p. 259

9   Czernin von und zu Chudenitz, O. Graf, *In the World War* (Harper & Collins, New York, 1920), p. 102

10   ibid., p. 110

11   Danilov (1937), p. 429

12   Müller-Brandenburg (1918), p. 21 footnote

13   Falkenhayn (1919), pp. 101–02

14   Brauner et al (1930); p. 450; Burián von Rajecz, S., *Austria in Dissolution: Being the Personal Recollections of Stephan, Count Burián* (Benn, London, 1925), pp. 62–63

15   Mackensen (1938), p. 172

16   François (1922), pp. 200–01

17   ibid., pp. 179–80

18   Kriegsarchiv Vienna, R512; François (1922), pp. 189–90; see also DiNardo, R., Breakthrough: the Gorlice-Tarnow Campaign 1915 (Praeger, Santa Barbara, 2010), pp. 87–88; *Österreichisches Bibliographisches Lexikon 1815–1950* (Österreichische Akademie der Wissenschaften, Vienna, 1969), vol. 4, p. 278

19   François (1922), pp. 201–04

20   ibid., p. 200

21   For an account of the fighting in Bukovina at this time, see Brauner et al (1930), vol. 2, pp. 456–69

22   Zeynek, T. Ritter von, *Ein Offizier im Generalstabskorps Erinnert Sich* (Böhlau, Vienna, 2009) p. 230

23   ibid., p. 235

24   Mackensen (1938), p. 173

25   François (1922), pp. 204–05

26   Reichsarchiv, *Der Weltkrieg 1914–1918* (Mittler, Berlin, 1925–30), vol. 8, p. 223

27   François (1922), p. 207

28   ibid., p. 209

29   Brauner et al (1930), vol. 2, pp. 472–73

30   Müller-Brandenburg (1918), p. 31

31   François (1922), p. 216

32   Brauner et al (1930), vol. 2, pp. 496–97

33   Brusilov (1967), p. 48

34   Knox (1921), p. 288

35   Brauner et al (1930), vol. 2, p. 480

36   ibid., p. 491

37   François (1922), pp. 224–25

38   ibid., pp. 226–27

39   Mackensen (1938), p. 177

40   François (1922), pp. 228–29

41   Zayontchovsky (2002), p. 308

42   François (1922), pp. 233–34

43   Hagen, M. von, *War in a European Borderland: Occupations and Occupation Plans in Galicia* (University of Washington Press, Seattle, 2007), p. 19

44 Bociurkiw, B., *Sheptytsky and the Ukrainian Greek Catholic Church under the Soviet Occupation of 1939–1941*, p. 101, in Magocsi, P. (ed.), *Morality and Reality: The Life and Times of Andrei Sheptytskyi* (Canadian Institute of Ukrainian Studies, Alberta, 1989)

45 Knox (1921), p. 290

46 Ansky, S., *Enemy at his Pleasure: A Journey Through the Jewish Pale of Settlement in World War I* (Metropolitan, New York, this edition 2003), pp. 122–23

47 Levine, M., *The Crisis of Genocide. Devastation: The European Rimlands 1912– 1938* (Oxford University Press, Oxford, 2013), p. 60

48 Hindenburg (1920), p. 140

49 Mackensen (1938), p. 178

50 Ludwigstorff, G., *Die Feldmarschälle der k.u.k. Armee* (Universitätsverlag, Vienna, 1989), pp. 66, 68–70

51 François (1922), p. 241

CHAPTER 8

1   Quoted in Mackensen (1938), p. 185

2   Conrad von Hötzendorf, F., *Aus Meiner Dienstzeit* (Rikola, Vienna, 1921), vol. 4, p. 774

3   Morgen (1920), p. 70

4   Knox (1921), p. 231

5   Hoffmann, M., trans. A. Charnot, *The War of Lost Opportunities* (Paul, French, Trubner & Co, London, 1924), p. 101

6   Ludendorff (1919), p. 114

7   Falkenhayn (1919), p. 108

8   Hoffmann (1929), p. 72

9   See, for example, Stone (1975), pp. 176–77

10 Serbian General Staff, *Veliki Rat Serbije Za Oslobodelje i Ujedljelje Serba, Hrvata i Slovenaca* (Štamlarska Padionica Milistarstva i Mornarice, Belgrade, 1925), vol. 8, pp. 121–39

11 Knox (1921), p. 293

12 Korolkov, G., *Nesbyvshiyesya Kanny: Neudavshiysya Razgrom Russkikh Letom 1915 g: Strategicheskiy Etyud* (Gosvoenizdat, Moscow, 1926), p. 14

13 Danilov (1927), pp. 432–33

14 Quoted in ibid., p. 435

15 Danilov (1927), pp. 436–37

16 Paléologue (1923), vol. 1, p. 83

17 Doumbadze, V., *Russia's War Minister* (Simpkin & Co, London, 1915), p. 18

18   Sidorov, A., *Ekonomichesko Polozhenie* (IAN-SSSR, Moscow, 1967), vol. 1, p. 36

19   Zalesski, S., *Mobilizatsia Gornozavodskoy Promyshlennosti Na Urale* in *Istoreshskiye Zapiski* (IAN-SSSR, Moscow, 1959), vol. 65, p. 95

20   Pares, B., *The Fall of the Russian Monarchy* (Phoenix, London, 2001), pp. 120–21

21   Buttar (2014), pp. 79–82; for a full account of the Redl Affair, see Markus, G., *Der Fall Redl* (Amalthea, Vienna, 1984)

22   Shatsillo, K., *Delo Polkovnika Myasoyedova in Vaprosi Istorii* (Flag Rossii RAN, Moscow, 1967), 1967/4

23   Fuller, W., *The Foe Within: Fantasies of Treason and the End of Imperial Russia* (Cornell, Ithaca, 2006), p. 224; Interrogation of Anna and Nikolai Goshkevich, Rossiiskii Gosudarstvennyi Voyenno-Istoricheskiy Archiv, 962/2/134/34 and 962/2/135/56

24   Richert (2012), pp. 89–91

25   Zeynek (2009), pp. 235–36

26   Kriegsarchiv Vienna, R512

27   Zayontchovsky (2002), p. 325

28   Danilov (1927), p. 443

29   Brauner et al (1930), vol. 2, p. 607

30   Stone (1975), p. 175

31   Danilov (1927), p. 442

32   Bundesarchiv-Militärarchiv Freiburg, W10/50661

CHAPTER 9

1   Brauner et al (1930), vol. 2, p. 616

2   DiNardo (2010), p. 121

3   Mönckeberg, K., *Bei Süd- und Bug-Armee* (Deutsche Verlags-Anstalt, Berlin, 1917), p. 47

4   Brauner et al (1930), vol. 2, p. 625

5   Bundesarchiv-Militärarchiv Freiburg W10/50656

6   Clemenz, B., *Generalfeldmarschall von Woyrsch und seine Schlesier* (Flemming, Berlin, 1919), pp. 148–52

7   Hoffmann (1929), p. 75

8   Stone (1975), p. 184

9   Mönckeberg (1917), p. 60

10   Hoffmann (1929), p. 76

11   Brauner et al (1930), vol. 2, pp. 634–35

12   Mackensen (1938), p. 193

13   Knox (1921), p. 303

14 Mackensen (1938), p. 193

15 Ludendorff (1919), pp. 117–18

16 Clemenz (1919), p. 154

17 Mönckeberg (1917), p. 50

18 Quoted in Osburg (2014), p. 377

19 Quoted in ibid., p. 207

20 Kriegsarchiv Vienna, R512

21 Sondhaus, L., *World War One: The Global Revolution* (Cambridge University Press, Cambridge, 2011), p. 144

22 Thompson, W., *In the Eye of the Storm: Kurt Riezler and the Crises of Modern Germany* (University of Iowa Press, 1980), pp. 88–89

23 Stevenson, D., *Cataclysm: The First World War as Political Tragedy* (Basic Books, New York, 2005), p. 107

24 Litzmann (1927), vol. 2, pp. 1–7

25 Russian Army Bulletin 5 May 1915, quoted in Stein, L., trans. J. Goldstein, *The Exile of the Lithuanian Jews in the Conflagration of the First World War*, (Lite, Kaunas, 1941), p. 95

26 Stein (1941), pp. 96–97

27 Litzmann (1927), vol. 2, p. 21

28 ibid., p. 24

29 For a German account of the capture of Kovno, see Litzmann (1927), vol. 2, pp. 1–29

30 ibid., pp. 29–30

31 Knox (1921), pp. 327–28

32 DiNardo (2010), p. 129

33 For an account of the siege of Novogeorgievsk, see Kihntopf, M., *The Fall of Novogeorgievsk: the End of Russian Dominance in Poland* in *Strategy and Tactics* (Bakersfield, 2005), vol. 231, pp. 33–35; Bettag, F., *Die Eroberung von Nowo Georgiewsk* (Stalling, Berlin, 1926)

34 For a Russian account of the gas attack and its aftermath, see Khmelkov, S., *Borba za Osovets* (Gosudarstvennoye Voyennoye Izdatelstvo Narkomata Oborony Soyuza SSR, Moscow, 1939)

35 Brauner et al (1930), vol. 2, pp. 667–68

36 Mackensen (1938), p. 198

37 Nesnamov (1922), vol. 4, p. 84

38 Danilov (1927), p. 453

39 Mackensen (1938), p. 203

40 Stone (1975), p. 183

41 Ludendorff (1919), p. 129

42 Danilov (1927), p. 471

43 ibid., pp. 171–72

44 Bourne, J., *Who's Who in World War I* (Routledge, New York, 2002), p. 236

45 Danilov (1927), p. 473

46 Stone (1975), p. 187

47 Danilov (1927), p. 475

48 Pares (2001), p. 225

49 ibid., p. 270

50 Buchanan, G., *My Mission to Russia and Other Diplomatic Memories* (Cassell, London, 1923), pp. 243–44

51 Hagberg Wright, C. (ed.), *The Letters of the Tsar to the Tsaritsa, 1914–1917* (Bodley Head, London, 1976), p. 87

52 Brusilov (1967), p. 51

53 ibid., p. 51

CHAPTER 10

1   Brusilov (1967), p. 49

2   Brauner et al (1930), vol. 3, p. 52

3   ibid., p. 61

4   ibid., p. 62

5   Kriegsarchiv Vienna, Nachlass B/509 vol. 2 Tagebuch Scheller 3/9/15

6   Brauner et al (1930), vol. 3, p. 81

7   Zayontchovsky (2002), p. 371

8   Brauner et al (1930), vol. 3, p. 98

9   ibid., p. 113

10 ibid., p. 105

11 Falkenhayn (1919), p. 151

12 Quoted in Brauner et al (1930), vol. 3, p. 120

13 Nesnamov (1922), vol. 4, p. 127

14 Brauner et al (1930), vol. 3, p. 127

15 ibid., pp. 128–29

16 ibid., p. 132

17 Nesnamov (1922), vol. 4, p. 127

18 Brusilov (1967), p. 52

19 Brauner et al (1930), vol. 3, pp. 140–41

20 Brusilov (1967), p. 53

21 For his own version of the incident, see Denikin, A., *The Career of a Tsarist Officer: Memoirs, 1872–1916* (Minnesota University Press, 1975), pp. 264–65

22 Brusilov (1967), p. 53

23   Rauchensteiner, M., *Der Tod des Doppeladlers* (Styria Premium, Vienna, 1994), p. 290

24   Kriegsarchiv Vienna, Nachlass B/509 vol. 2, Tagebuch Scheller, 2/10/15

25   Bundesarchiv-Militärarchiv Freiburg, Nachlass Moltke N79 vol. 35, see also Bayerisches Hauptstaatsarchiv Munich, MA3079

26   Cramon (1922), pp. 65–66

27   Mönckeberg (1917), pp. 77–79

28   Quoted in Foerster, W., *Graf Schlieffen und der Weltkrieg* (Mittler, Berlin, 1925), vol. 2, p. 139

29   Falkenhayn (1919), pp. 126–27

30   ibid., pp. 127–28

31   ibid., p. 144

32   ibid., p. 145

33   ibid., pp. 146–48

34   Hindenburg (1920), pp. 143–44

35   Brauner et al (1930), Annex IV, table 1

CHAPTER 11

1   Reed, J., quoted in Mitrović, A., *Serbia's Great War 1914–1918* (Hurst, London, 2007), p. 102

2   Scianna, B., *Reporting Atrocities: Archibald Reiss in Serbia 1914–1918* in *Journal of Slavic Military Studies* 25(4) (London: Routledge, London, 2012), pp. 597–607

3   Staatsarchiv Vienna, PA I, K789

4   Auswärtiges Amt, Bonn, Oxford cat. pp. 1029–30

5   Stanković, Dj., *Nikola Pašić, Saveznici I Stvaranje Jugoslavije* (Nolit, Belgrade, 1984), pp. 74–76

6   Crampton, R., *A Concise History of Bulgaria* (Cambridge University Press, Cambridge, 2005), p. 137

7   Ilchev, I., *Bŭlgariya i Antantata Prez Pŭrvata Svetovna Voĭna* (Nauka i Izkustvo, Sofia, 1990), p. 210

8   Shanafeld, G., *The Secret Enemy: Austria-Hungary and the German Alliance* (Columbia University Press, New York, 1985), pp. 744–46

9   ibid., p. 69

10   Rothenberg (1976), p. 190

11   Paléologue (1923), vol. 2, p. 44

12   Aronson, T., *Crowns in Conflict: The Triumph and the Tragedy of European Monarchy 1910–1918* (John Murray, London, 1986), p. 86

13   Hoffmann (1929), p. 86

14 Mackensen (1938), p. 212

15 Brauner et al (1930), vol. 3, p. 190

16 Krauss, A., *Die Ursachen Unserer Niederlage* (Lehmann, Munich, 1921), p. 165

17 Brauner et al (1930), vol. 3, pp. 196–97

18 Mackensen (1938), pp. 217–18

19 Brauner et al (1930), vol. 3, pp. 194–95

20 Nédeff, N. and Goetzmann, E., *Les Opérations en Macédoine. L'épopée de Doiran 1915–1918* (Armeyski Voenno-Ozdat, Sofia, 1927), p. 10

21 Roberts, K., *Politicians, Diplomacy and War in Modern British History* (Continuum International, London, 1994), p. 237

22 Wulff, O., *Österreich-Ungarns Donauflotille in den Kriegsjahren 1914–1916* (Siedel, Vienna, 1918), p. 117

23 Joachim, T., *Der Feldzug in Serbien* in Schwarte, M., *Der Weltkampf um Ehre und Recht* (Barth, Leipzig, 1919), pp. 336–37

24 Brauner et al (1930), vol. 3, pp. 207–08

25 Skoko, S., *Vojvoda Radomir Putnik* (BIGZ, Belgrade, 1985), vol. 2, p. 80

26 Serbian General Staff, *Veliki Rat Serbije Oslobodelje i Ujedljelje Serba, Hrvata i Slovenaca* (Štamlarska Padionica Milistarstva i Mornarice, Belgrade, 1925), vol. 9, p. 66

27 Wulff (1918), p. 103

28 Mackensen (1938), pp. 223–24

29 Joachim, in Schwarte (1919), pp. 340–41

30 Serbian General Staff (1925), vol. 9, p. 149

31 Mackensen (1938), pp. 224–25

32 Ward Price, G., *The Story of the Salonica Army* (Clode, New York, 1918), available at www.gwpda.org/memoir/salonica, chapter 3

33 ibid., chapter 3

34 Mackensen (1938), pp. 231–32

35 Serbian General Staff (1925), vol. 13, p. 75

36 ibid., p. 116, 136

37 Mackensen (1938), p. 242

38 Balakov, G., *Istoriya na Bŭlgarite: Voenna Istoriya na Bŭlgarite ot Drevnostta do Nashi Dni* (Izdat, Sofia, 2007), p. 463

39 Mackensen (1938), p. 242; Tucker, S., *World War I Encyclopaedia* (ABC, Santa Barbara, 2005), p. 1077

40 Quoted in Englund, P., *Schönheit und Schrecken* (Rowohlt, Berlin, 2011), pp. 191–92

41 Staatsarchiv Vienna, PA1 K497

CHAPTER 12

1   Blücher, E., *An English Wife in Berlin* (Constable & Co, London, 1921), pp. 100–02

2   Daniel, U., trans. M. Ries, *The War from Within: German Working-Class Women in the First World War* (Berg, Oxford, 1997), p. 26

3   Quoted in Watson (2014), p. 243

4   Zeman, Z., *The Break-Up of the Austro-Hungarian Empire* (Oxford University Press, Oxford, 1961), pp. 51–52

5   Galantai, J., trans. E. Grusz and J. Pokoly, *Hungary in the First World War* (Akadémiai Kiadó, Budapest, 1990), p. 135

6   Watson (2014), pp. 218–20

7   Hoffmann (1929), p. 99

8   Herwig, H., *The First World War: Germany and Austria-Hungary 1914–1918* (Arnold, London, 1997), p. 233

9   For a detailed discussion of *Lubki*, see Jahn, H., *Patriotic Culture in Russia During World War I* (Cornell, Ithaca, 1995), pp. 12–29

10 Stone (1975), pp. 144–63

11 For a detailed discussion of this subject, see Kojevnikov, A., *The Great War, the Russian Civil War, and the Invention of Big Science in Science in Context* (Cambridge University Press, Cambridge, 2002), 15(2), pp. 239–75

12 Buchanan (1923), pp. 245–46

13 ibid., pp. 251–52

14 Reichsarchiv, *Der Weltkrieg*, vol. 2, pp. 325–30

15 Redlich (1953), vol. 1, p. 271

16 Brusilov (1967), p. 89 and footnote

17 Shavelsky, G., *Velikoy, Svitloy Pamyati Pochivshikh Vozhdey Dobrovol'cheskoy Armíi Generalov: Alekseva, Kornilova, Markova, Drozdovskago, polk. Míochinskago, Donskogo Atamana Generaloy Kaledina* (unknown publisher, Rostov, 1919), p. 91

18 Konderovsky, P., *V Stavke Verkhovnogo. Vospominaniya Dezhurnogo Generala pri Verkhovnom Glavnokomanduyushchem* (Voyennaya Byl', Paris, 1967), p. 88

19 Danilov (1927), p. 484

20 Quoted in Doughty, R., *Pyrrhic Victory: French Strategy and Operations in the Great War* (Harvard University Press, Cambridge, Mass., 2008), p. 172

21 Falkenhayn (1919), pp. 217–18

22 ibid., pp. 197–98

BIBLIOGRAPHY

RESEARCH INSTITUTES

Auswärtiges Amt, Bonn
Bundesarchiv-Militärarchiv, Freiburg
Voyenno-Istoricheskiy Archiv, Moscow
Bayerisches Hauptstaatsarchiv, Munich
Hoover Institution Archives, Stanford
Kriegsarchiv/Staatsarchiv, Vienna

JOURNALS

Zeitschrift für Unternehmensgeschichte, Beck, Munich
Strategy and Tactics, Bakersfield
Science in Context, Cambridge University Press
Voyenno-Istorichesky Sbornik, Sofia

SECONDARY SOURCES

Ansky, S., *Enemy at his Pleasure: A Journey Through the Jewish Pale of Settlement in World War I* (Metropolitan, New York, this edition 2003)

Aronson, T., *Crowns in Conflict: The Triumph and the Tragedy of European Monarchy 1910–1918* (John Murray, London, 1986)

Arz, A., *Kampf und Sturz der Kaiserreiche* (Günther, Vienna, 1935)

Asprey, R., *The German High Command at War: Hindenburg and Ludendorff Conduct World War I* (William Morrow, New York, 1991)

Balakov, G., *Istoriya na Bŭlgarite: Voenna Istoriya na Bŭlgarite ot Drevnostta do Nashi Dni* (Izdat, Sofia, 2007)

Barsukov, E., *Podgotovka Rossii k Mirovoj Vojne v Artillerijskom Otnosenii* (Gosvoenizdat, Moscow, 1926)

Belolipetsky, V., *Zimniye deystviya pekhotnogo polka v Avgustovskikh lesakh. 1915* (Voyenno-Istoricheskaya Biblioteka, Moscow, 1940)

Bettag, F., *Die Eroberung von Nowo Georgiewsk* (Stalling, Berlin, 1926)

Blücher, E., *An English Wife in Berlin* (Constable & Co, London, 1921)

Bonch-Bruyevich, M., *Poterya Nami Galitsii* (Voenizdat, Moscow, 1921)

Bose, T. von, *Das Kaiser Alexander Garde-Grenadier Regiment Nr. 1 im Weltkriege 1914–1918* (Sporn, Zeulenroda, 1932)

Bourne, J., *Who's Who in World War I* (Routledge, New York, 2002)

Brauner, J., Czegka, E., Diaków, J., Franek, F., Kiszling, R., Steinitz, E. and Wisshaupt, E., *Österreich-Ungarns Letzter Krieg 1914–1918*, vols. 2 and 3 (Verlag der Militärwissenschaftlichen Mitteilungen, Vienna, 1930)

Brusilov, A., *Moi Vospominaniia* (Voenizdat, Moscow, 1967)

Buchanan, G., *My Mission to Russia and Other Diplomatic Memories* (Cassell, London, 1923)

Burián von Rajecz, S., *Austria in Dissolution: Being the Personal Recollections of Stephan, Count Burián* (Benn, London, 1925)

Buttar, P., *Collision of Empires* (Osprey, Oxford, 2014)

Chaadaeva, D., *Armiya Nakanune Fevral'skoi Revolyutsii* (Gosudarstvennoi Sotsialistichesko-Ekonomicheskoe Izdatel'stvo, Moscow, 1935)

Clemenz, B., *Generalfeldmarschall von Woyrsch und seine Schlesier* (Flemming, Berlin, 1919)

Conrad von Hötzendorf, F., *Die Gefechtsausbildung der Infanterie* (Seidel, Vienna, 1900)

Conrad von Hötzendorf, F., *Aus Meiner Dienstzeit* (Rikola, Vienna, 1921)

Cramon, A. von, *Unser Österreichisch-Ungarisher Bundesgenosse im Weltkriege* (Mittler, Berlin, 1922)

Crampton, R., *A Concise History of Bulgaria* (Cambridge University Press, Cambridge, 2005)

Croddy, E., *Chemical and Biological Warfare: a Comprehensive Guide for the Concerned Citizen* (Copernicus, Göttingen, 2002)

Czernin von und zu Chudenitz, O. Graf, *In the World War* (Harper & Collins, New York, 1920)

Czicserics, M., *Die Schlacht: Studie Auf Grund Des Krieges in Ostasien 1904–1905* (Seidel, Vienna, 1908)

Daniel, U., trans. M. Ries, *The War from Within: German Working-Class Women in the First World War* (Berg, Oxford, 1997)

Danilov, Y., *La Russie Dans La Guerre Mondiale* (Payot, Paris, 1927)

Denikin, A., *The Career of a Tsarist Officer: Memoirs, 1872–1916* (Minnesota University Press, 1975)

DiNardo, R., *Breakthrough: the Gorlice-Tarnów Campaign 1915* (Praeger, Santa Barbara, 2010)

Doughty, R., *Pyrrhic Victory: French Strategy and Operations in the Great War* (Harvard University Press, Cambridge, Mass., 2008)

Doumbadze, V., *Russia's War Minister* (Simpkin & Co, London, 1915)

Englund, P., *Schönheit und Schrecken* (Rowohlt, Berlin, 2011)

Falkenhayn, E. von, *General Headquarters 1914–1916, and its Critical Decisions* (Hutchinson, London, 1919)

Foerster, W., *Graf Schlieffen und der Weltkrieg* (Mittler, Berlin, 1925)

Forster, F., *Przemyśl: Österreich-Hungarns Bedeutendste Festung* (Österreichischer Bundesverlag, Vienna, 1987)

François, H. von, *Gorlice 1915, Der Karpathendurchbruch und die Befreiung von Galizien* (Koehler, Leipzig, 1922)

Freytag-Loringhoven, A. Freiherr von, *Menschen und Dinge Wie Ich Sie In Meinem Leben Sah* (Mittler, Berlin, 1923)

Fuller, W., *The Foe Within: Fantasies of Treason and the End of Imperial Russia* (Cornell, Ithaca, 2006)

Galantai, J., trans. E. Grusz and J. Pokoly, *Hungary in the First World War* (Akadémiai Kiadó, Budapest, 1990)

Gurko, V., *War and Revolution in Russia* (Macmillan, New York, 1919)

Hagberg Wright, C. (ed.), *The Letters of the Tsar to the Tsaritsa, 1914–1917* (Bodley Head, London, 1976)

Hagen, M. von, *War in a European Borderland: Occupations and Occupation Plans in Galicia* (University of Washington Press, Seattle, 2007)

Herwig, H., *The First World War: Germany and Austria-Hungary 1914–1918* (Arnold, London, 1997)

Herwig, H., *The Marne 1914: The Opening of World War I and the Battle That Changed the World* (Random House, New York, 2009)

Hindenburg, P. von, trans. F. Holt, *Out of my Life* (Cassell, London, 1920)

Hoffmann, M., trans. A. Charnot, *The War of Lost Opportunities* (Paul, French, Trubner & Co, London, 1924)

Hoffmann, M., *War Diaries and Other Papers* (Secker, London, 1929)

Horne, C. (ed.), *The Great Events of the Great War* (National Alumni, New York, 1920)

Horvat, J., *Politička povijest Hrvatske* (Binoza, Zagreb, 1938)

Ilchev, I., *Bŭlgariya i Antantata Prez Pŭrvata Svetovna Voĭna* (Nauka i Izkustvo, Sofia, 1990)

Ipatieff, V., *The Life of a Chemist: Memoirs of Vladimir N Ipatieff* (Stanford University Press, Stanford, 1946)

Jahn, H., *Patriotic Culture in Russia During World War I* (Cornell, Ithaca, 1995)

Khmelkov, S., *Borba za Osovets* (Gosudarstvennoye Voyennoye Izdatelstvo Narkomata Oborony Soyuza SSR, Moscow, 1939)

Kluck, A. von, *Die Marsch auf Paris und die Marneschlacht* (1920, republished by

Salzwasser, Paderborn, 2013)

Knox, A., *With the Russian Army 1914–1917* (Hutchinson, London, 1921)

Kojevnikov, A., *The Great War, the Russian Civil War, and the Invention of Big Science* in *Science in Context* (Cambridge University Press, Cambridge, 2002)

Kojevnikov, A., *Stalin's Great Science: The Times and Adventures of Soviet Physicists* (World Scientific

Publishing Company, Singapore, 2004)

Kolenkovsky, A., *Russkaya Armiya v Velikoy Voyne: Zimnyaya Operatsiya v Vostochnoy Prussii v 1915* (Voenizdat, Moscow, 1927)

Konderovsky, P., *V Stavke Verkhovnogo. Vospominaniya Dezhurnogo Generala pri Verkhovnom Glavnokomanduyushchem* (Voyennaya Byl', Paris, 1967)

Korolkov, G., *Nesbyvshiyesya Kanny: Neudavshiysya Razgrom Russkikh Letom 1915 g: Strategicheskiy Etyud* (Gosvoenizdat, Moscow, 1926)

Krauss, A., *Die Ursachen Unserer Niederlage* (Lehmann, Munich, 1921)

Levine, M., *The Crisis of Genocide. Devastation: The European Rimlands 1912–1938* (Oxford University Press, Oxford, 2013)

Litzmann, K., *Lebenserinnerungen* (Eisenschmidt, Berlin, 1927)

Ludendorff, E., *Meine Kriegserinnerungen 1914–1918* (Mittler, Berlin, 1919)

Ludwigstorff, G., *Die Feldmarschälle der k.u.k. Armee* (Universitätsverlag, Vienna, 1989)

Lutz, R., *Fall of the German Empire 1914–1918* (Stanford University Press, Stanford, 1932)

Mackensen, A. von, *Briefe und Auszeichnungen des Generalfeldmarschalls aus Krieg und Frieden* (Bibliographisches Institut, Leipzig, 1938)

Magocsi, P. (ed.), *Morality and Reality: The Life and Times of Andrei Sheptytskyi* (Canadian Institute of Ukrainian Studies, Alberta, 1989)

Markus, G., *Der Fall Redl* (Amalthea, Vienna, 1984)

Mitrović, A., *Serbia's Great War 1914–1918* (Hurst, London, 2007)

Molisch, P., *Vom Kampf der Tschechen um Ihren Staat* (Braumüller, Vienna, 1929)

Mönckeberg, K., *Bei Süd- und Bug-Armee* (Deutsche Verlags-Anstalt, Berlin, 1917)

Morgen, C. von, *Meiner Truppen Heldenkämpfe* (Mittler, Berlin, 1920)

Müller-Brandenburg, H., *Die Schlacht Bei Grodek-Lemberg* (Stalling, Oldenburg, 1918)

Nédeff, N. and E. Goetzmann, *Les Opérations en Macédoine. L'épopée de Doiran 1915–1918* (Armeyski Voenno-Ozdat, Sofia, 1927)

Nesnamov, A., *Strategicheskiye Issledovaniya* (Gosvoenizdat, Moscow, 1922)

Osburg, W-R, *Hineingeworfen: Der Erste Weltkrieg in den Erinnerungen seiner Teilnehmer* (Aufbau, Berlin, 2014)

Österreichisches Bibliographisches Lexikon 1815–1950 (Österreichische Akademie der Wissenschaften, Vienna, 1969)

Paléologue, M., trans. F. Holt, *An Ambassador's Memoirs* (Doran, New York, 1923)

Palmer, S. and Wallis, S., *A War in Words* (Simon & Schuster, London, 2003)

Pares, B., *The Fall of the Russian Monarchy* (Phoenix, London, 2001)

Preussisches Kriegsministerium, *Felddienst-Ordnung* (Berlin, 1908)

Prusin, A., *Nationalising a Borderland: War, Ethnicity and Anti-Jewish Violence in East Galicia 1914–1920* (University of Alabama Press, Tuscaloosa, 2005)

Ratzenhofer, E., *Truppentransporte beim Winterfeldzug in den Karpathen*, (Wissen und Wehr, Vienna, 1929)

Rauchensteiner, M., *Der Tod des Doppeladlers* (Styria Premium, Vienna, 1994)

Redern, H. von, *Die Winterschlacht in Masuren* (Stalling, Oldenburg, 1918)

Redlich, J., *Schicksalsjahre Österreichs 1908–1919* (Graz, 1953)

Regiments-Geschichte des Infanterie-Regiment 14: Ein Buch der Erinnerung an Grossen Seiten 1914–1918 (Hessen, Linz, 1919)

Reichsarchiv, *Der Weltkrieg 1914–1918* (Mittler, Berlin, 1925–30)

Richert, D., *The Kaiser's Reluctant Conscript* (Pen and Sword, Barnsley, 2012)

Roberts, K., *Politicians, Diplomacy and War in Modern British History* (Continuum International, London, 1994)

Roos, H., *A History of Modern Poland, From the Foundation of the State in the First World War to the Present Day* (Knopf, New York, 1966)

Rosenberg-Lipinsky, H.-O. von, *Das Königin-Elizabeth Garde-Grenadier Regiment Nr. 3 im Weltkrieg 1914–1918* (Sporn, Zeulenroda, 1935)

Rothenburg, G., *The Army of Francis Joseph* (Purdue University Press, West Lafayette, 1976)

Sabsay, N., *A Moment in History: A Russian Soldier in the First World War* (Caxton, Caldwell, 1960)

Samuels, M., *Command or Control? Command, Training and Tactics in the British and German Armies 1888–1918* (Psychology, Hove, 1995)

Schlieffen, A. von, *Cannae* (Mittler, Berlin, 1925)

Schwarte, M., *Der Weltkampf um Ehre und Recht* (Barth, Leipzig, 1919)

Serbian General Staff, *Veliki Rat Serbije Za Oslobodelje i Ujedljelje Serba, Hrvata i Slovenaca* (Štamlarska Padionica Militarstva i Mornarice, Belgrade, 1925)

Shanafeld, G., *The Secret Enemy: Austria-Hungary and the German Alliance* (Columbia University Press, New York, 1985)

Shatsillo, K., *Delo Polkovnika Myasoyedova* in *Vaprosi Istorii* (Flag Rossii RAN, Moscow, 1967)

Shavelsky, G., *Velikoy, Svitloy Pamyati Pochivshikh Vozhdey Dobrovol'cheskoy Armii Generalov: Alekseva, Kornilova, Markova, Drozdovskago, polk. Miochinskago, Donskogo Atamana Generaloy Kaledina* (unknown publisher, Rostov, 1919)

Sidorov, A., *Ekonomichesko Polozhenie* (IAN-SSSR, Moscow, 1967)

Simonds, F., *History of the Great War 1914–1918* (Collier, New York, 1920)

Skoko, S., *Vojvoda Radomir Putnik* (BIGZ, Belgrade, 1985)

Snyder, J., *The Ideology Of The Offensive* (Cornell University Press, Ithaca, 1984)

Sondhaus, L., *Franz Conrad von Hötzendorf: Architect of the Apocalypse* (Humanities Press, Boston, Maryland, 2000)

Sondhaus, L., *World War One: The Global Revolution* (Cambridge University Press, Cambridge, 2011)

Stanković, Dj., *Nikola Pašić, Saveznici I Stvaranje Jugoslavije* (Nolit, Belgrade, 1984)

Stein, L., trans. J. Goldstein, *The Exile of the Lithuanian Jews in the Conflagration of the First World War*, Lite, Kaunas, 1941)

Stengel, F. Freiherr von, *Das K.B. 3 Infanterie-Regiment Prinz Karl von Bayern* (Verlag Bayerisches Kriegsarchiv, Munich, 1922)

Stevenson, D., *Cataclysm: The First World War as Political Tragedy* (Basic Books, New York, 2005)

Stone, J. and Schmidl, E., *The Boer War and Military Reforms* (University Press of America, Lanham, Maryland, 1988)

Stone, N., *The Eastern Front 1914–1917* (Penguin, London, 1975)

Thompson, W., *In the Eye of the Storm: Kurt Riezler and the Crises of Modern Germany* (University of Iowa Press, 1980)

Tucker, S., *World War I Encyclopaedia* (ABC, Santa Barbara, 2005)

Tunstall, G., *Blood on the Snow* (University of Kansas Press, Lawrence, Ka., 2010)

Weith, G., *Werdegang und Schicksal der österreichisch-ungarischen Armee im Weltkriege* (1922), manuscript in Kriegsarchiv, Vienna

Ward Price, G., *The Story of the Salonica Army* (Clode, New York, 1918)

Washburn, S., *The Russian Campaign April to August 1915* (Melrose, London, 1922)

Watson, A., *Ring of Steel: Germany and Austria-Hungary at War, 1914–1918* (Allen Lane, London, 2014)

Wulff, O., *Österreich-Ungarns Donauflotille in den Kriegsjahren 1914–1916* (Siedel, Vienna, 1918)

Zalesski, S., *Mobilizatsia Gornozavodskoy Promyshlennosti Na Urale* in *Istoreshskiye Zapiski* (IAN-SSSR, Moscow, 1959)

Zalesskiy K., *Kto Hyl Kto v Pervoy Mirovoy Voyne* (Astrel, Moscow, 2003)

Zayontchovsky, A., *Perveya Mirovaya Voyna* (Polygon, Moscow, 2002)

Zechlin, E., *Ludendorff im Jahre 1915* (Cotte, Munich, 1970)

Zeman, Z., *The Break-Up of the Austro-Hungarian Empire* (Oxford University Press, Oxford, 1961)

Zeynek, T. Ritter von, *Ein Offizier im Generalstabskorps Erinnert Sich* (Böhlau, Vienna, 2009)

Zuber, T., *Inventing the Schlieffen Plan: German War Planning 1871–1914* (Oxford University Press, Oxford, 2002)

INDEX

Figures in **bold** refer to maps.